SAM AND TWITCH

ORIGINS HARDCOVER

BOOK 1

MANAGING EDITORS
BEN TIMMRECK, JEN CASSIDY

ART DIRECTOR
BEN TIMMRECK

ART DIRECTOR (ORIGINAL SERIES)
BRENT ASHE

PUBLISHER FOR IMAGE COMICS
ERIC STEPHENSON

SAM & TWITCH CREATED
BY TODD McFARLANE

image

TODD McFARLANE
PRODUCTIONS

SPAWN.COM

SAM AND TWITCH: ORIGINS HARDCOVER BOOK 1. June 2024. First Printing. Published by Image Comics, Inc. Office of publication: PO BOX 14457, Portland, OR 97293 USA. Originally published in single issue format as Sam and Twitch issues #1-13. Spawn, its logo and its symbol are registered trademarks © 2024 Todd McFarlane Productions, Inc. All other related characters are TM and © 2024 Todd McFarlane Productions, Inc. All rights reserved. The characters, events and stories in this publication are entirely fictional. "Image" and the Image Comics logos are registered trademarks of Image Comics, Inc. No part of this publication may be reproduced or transmitted, in any form or by any means (except for short excerpts for journalistic or review purposes), without the express written permission of Todd McFarlane Productions, Inc., or Image Comics, Inc. PRINTED IN CANADA. ISBN: 978-1-5343-2766-5.

STORY **BRIAN MICHAEL BENDIS**

PENCILS (ISSUES 1-8) **ANGEL MEDINA**

PENCILS (ISSUE 9) **JAMIE TOLAGSON**

PENCILS (ISSUES 10-13) **ALBERTO PONTICELLI**

INKS **JONATHAN GLAPION**

LETTERING **RICHARD STARKINGS/ COMICRAFT**

COLOR **TODD BROEKER**
JAY FOTOS
DREW HUTCHINSON

COVERS (SERIES AND BOOK) **ASHLEY WOOD**

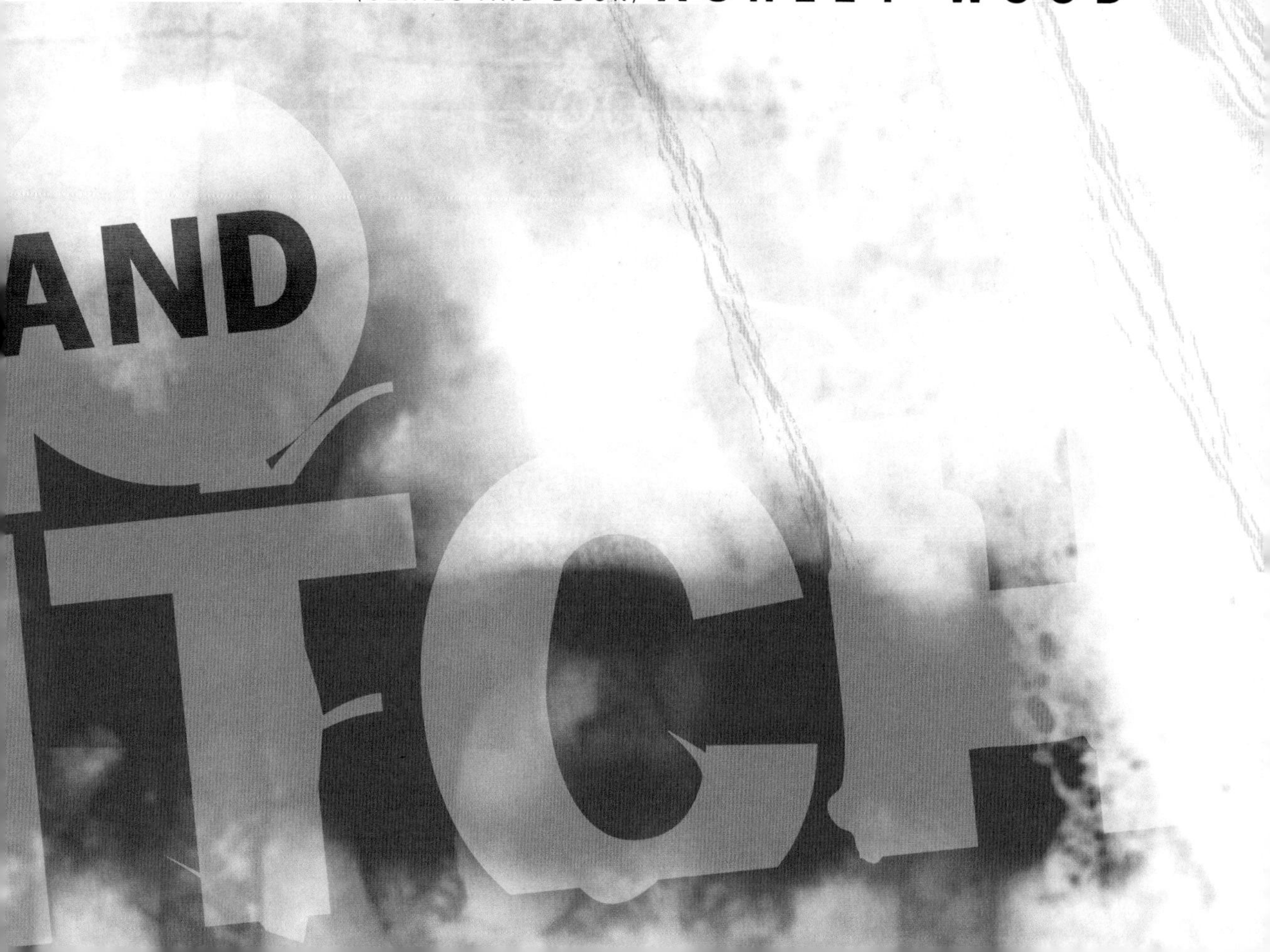
AND

INTRODUCTION

The characters of Sam and Twitch were born in June 1992 in the very first issue of *Spawn*, published by Image. So, they have been in front of the fans eyes for as long as that title's hero. The reason for having a pair of detectives introduced right at the onset of the book was to help bring a sense of reality to what could otherwise have been just another superhero title. Having just finished a long run drawing (and later writing) *Spider-man*, I was ready to creatively try my hand at doing more "real life" situations in the *Spawn* comic. Now, obviously, that may sound rather silly given that the hero is in a costume and he fought other costumed villains from time to time. Yet knowing that those elements were also going to be there, I was hoping to make some of the other parts of the Spawn mythology grounded in as much reality as I could.

Hence, Sam and Twitch. The characters are fully formed in my mind and I have a very clear pattern of both of their behaviors. Unfortunately, this clarity is at times lost on the readers (and sometimes the writers of these two characters) simply because of their physical looks. There is an easy tendency to fall into the Laurel and Hardy or Abbott and Costello routine. This is absolutely not how they work. To me, Twitch is the best marksmen on any police force. He also has a very keen intellect and is a stickler for details, as well as wanting to have evidence in front of him before jumping to any damning conclusions. Sam, on the other hand, is the prototypical cop who has devoted his entire adult life to his job. He has been on the force for so long that sending things about people and evidence is a lot more intuitive to him than it is to Twitch. So, at their very core, both of these detectives are the ones you would want first on the scene to solve your case.

Does their physical appearance say otherwise? Yes. But that was the fun I was looking for with these two. Having a couple of great detectives who don't look the part would, in my mind, make them more realistic. They're not just a couple of good-looking Hollywood actors. Yes, they joke around a bit, but if you re-read the stories I have written, you will see that their repartee with each other was only done when no one else was around. Basically, they can kid each other, but as soon as they walk out the door to a case, and are in front of other people, they are all business. Sarcasm is still a part of Sam's character, but he doesn't joke with Twitch while others are in earshot.

So, what does all of this have to do with Brian Michael Bendis, the writer of a good chunk of the *Sam and Twitch* comic series? Well, everything.

I first came upon Brian's writing when Image Comics was publishing his run on a black and white mini-series titled *Torso*. He was not only writing the book (along with his friend Marc Andreyko) but was also doing the artwork on that title as well. I was completely blown away by the book and immediately called him to see if he was interested in doing some other writing work. He graciously said "Yes." He also showed me another book he had worked on called *Jinx*. Again, I was thoroughly impressed. The things he was doing in both of these titles was creating a real world with real people. *Torso* was based on actual events, so that made it even more interesting to me. *Jinx*, on the other hand, was simply Brian cranking out some gritty, urban tales of a female bounty hunter. All of what I was reading made him the perfect candidate for writing a new title called Sam and Twitch. It was a book that I wanted to put together that would take a giant leap away from mainstream superhero comics. Brian enthusiastically jumped on board. His sense of people from the New York streets and his pacing were terrific right out of the box. And, since he was also doing little thumbnails for the artists he was working with, the book instantly headed in the direction I wanted. As each story arc concluded, the stories Brian wrote became even more realistic, so that by the end of his run on the book, he (and artist Alex Maleev) were turning out the best non-superhero comic on the stands, in my opinion.

In this collection you'll see Brian's first issues (he has since gone on to become a renowned writer at Marvel Comics). None of the stuff he was writing early in his career ever read like he was still learning. It always had a sophistication and tempo that few writers have been able to capture on a regular basis. Now that I had someone that could bring the detectives into a credible world we also needed our initial artist. This became Angel Medina, who was just finishing a long run on the *KISS Psycho Circus* comic we were putting out. Angel, guided by Brian, turned in a great salvo to kickstart this series. Later he would move on to the *Spawn* comic for 50 issues. So, my sentiments for his work are obvious in the fact that he worked on our flagship title for so long.

I hope you enjoy reading this offering as much as I enjoyed putting it together years ago.

Regards,

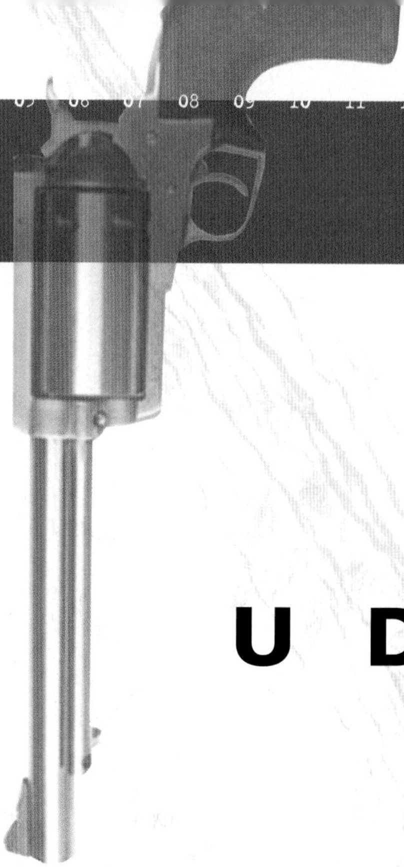

U D A K U

P A R T 1

SAM AND TWITCH

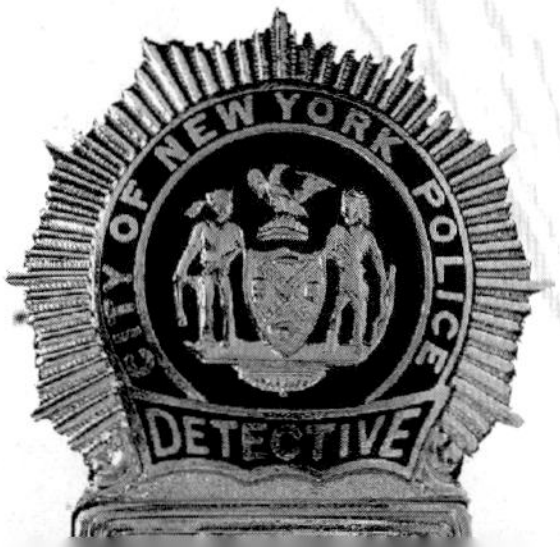
CITY OF NEW YORK POLICE
DETECTIVE

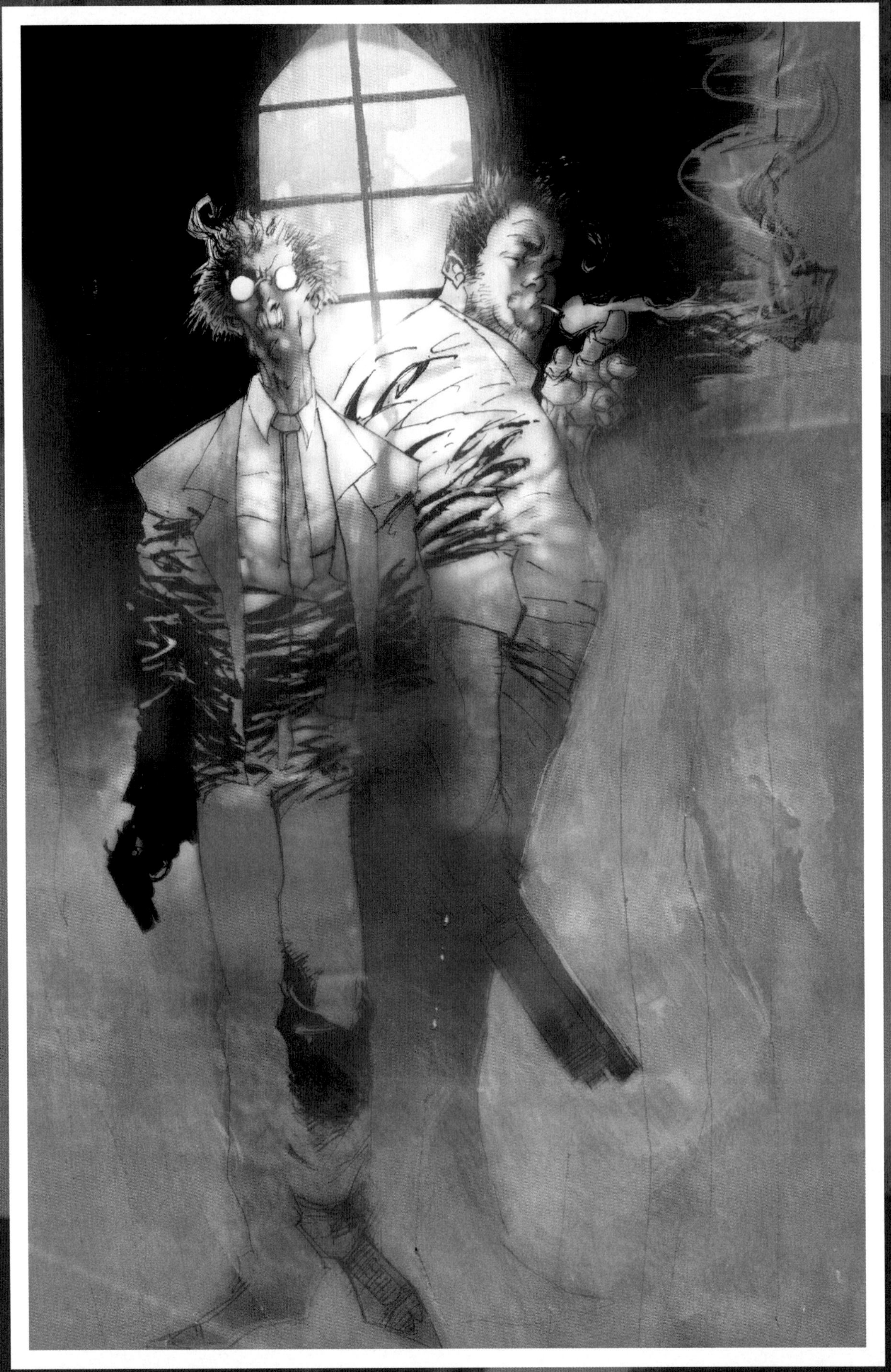

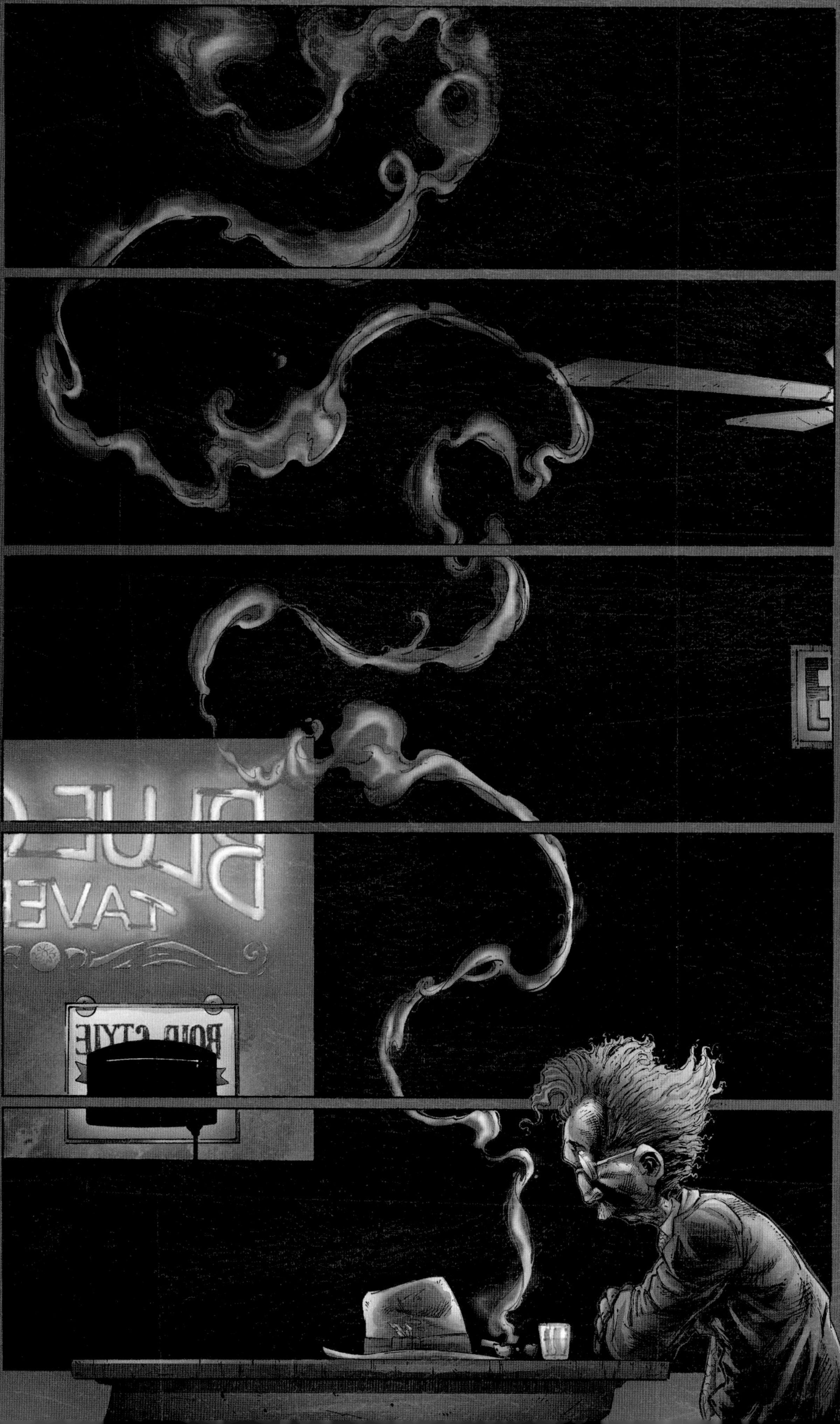

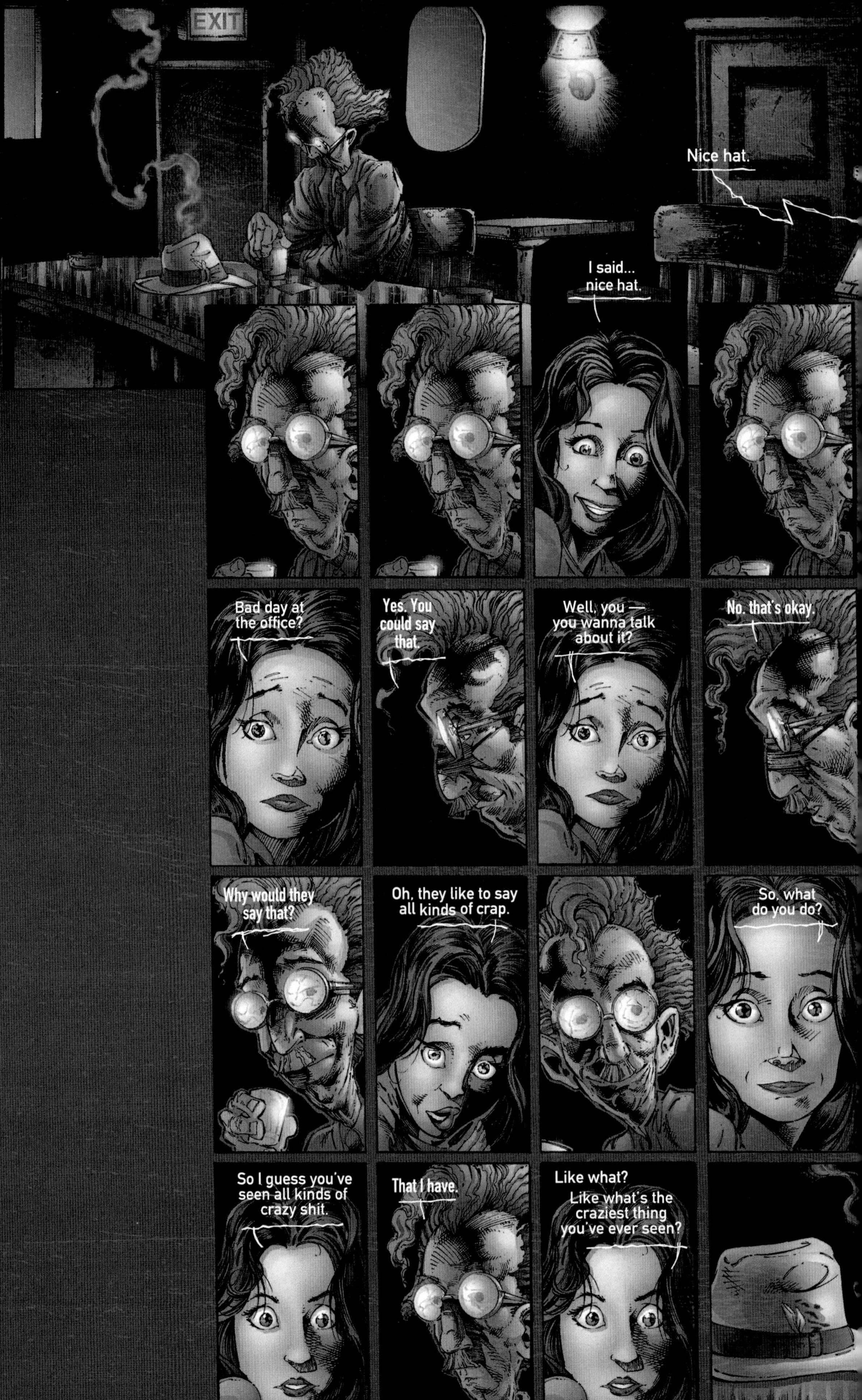
EXIT
Nice hat.
I said...
nice hat.
Bad day at
the office?
Yes. You
could say
that.
Well, you —
you wanna talk
about it?
No, that's okay.
Why would they
say that?
Oh, they like to say
all kinds of crap.
So, what
do you do?
So I guess you've
seen all kinds of
crazy shit.
That I have.
Like what?
Like what's the
craziest thing
you've ever seen?

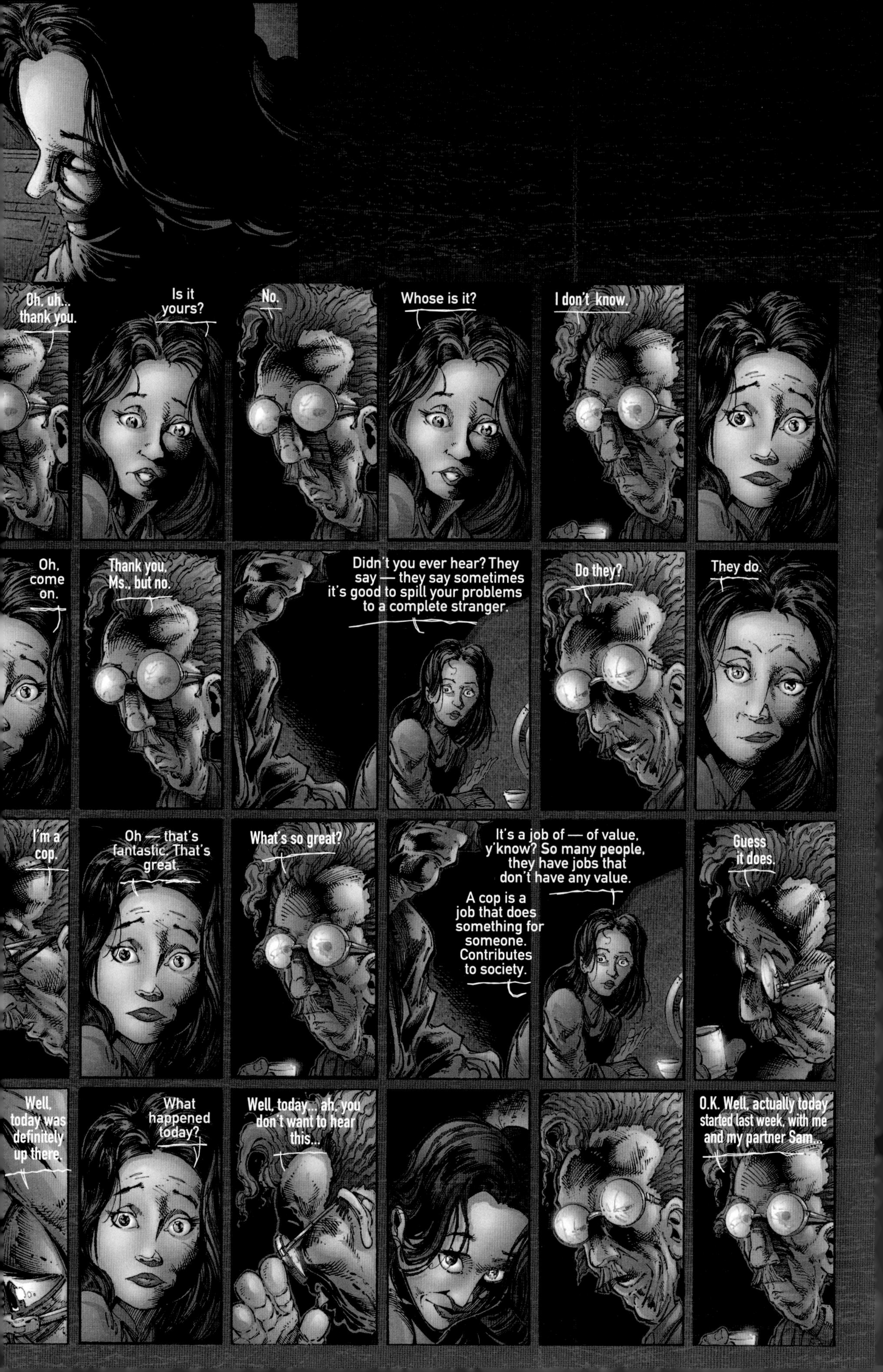
Oh, uh... thank you.
Is it yours?
No.
Whose is it?
I don't know.
Oh, come on.
Thank you, Ms., but no.
Didn't you ever hear? They say — they say sometimes it's good to spill your problems to a complete stranger.
Do they?
They do.
I'm a cop.
Oh — that's fantastic. That's great.
What's so great?
It's a job of — of value, y'know? So many people, they have jobs that don't have any value.
A cop is a job that does something for someone. Contributes to society.
Guess it does.
Well, today was definitely up there.
What happened today?
Well, today... ah, you don't want to hear this...
O.K. Well, actually today started last week, with me and my partner Sam...

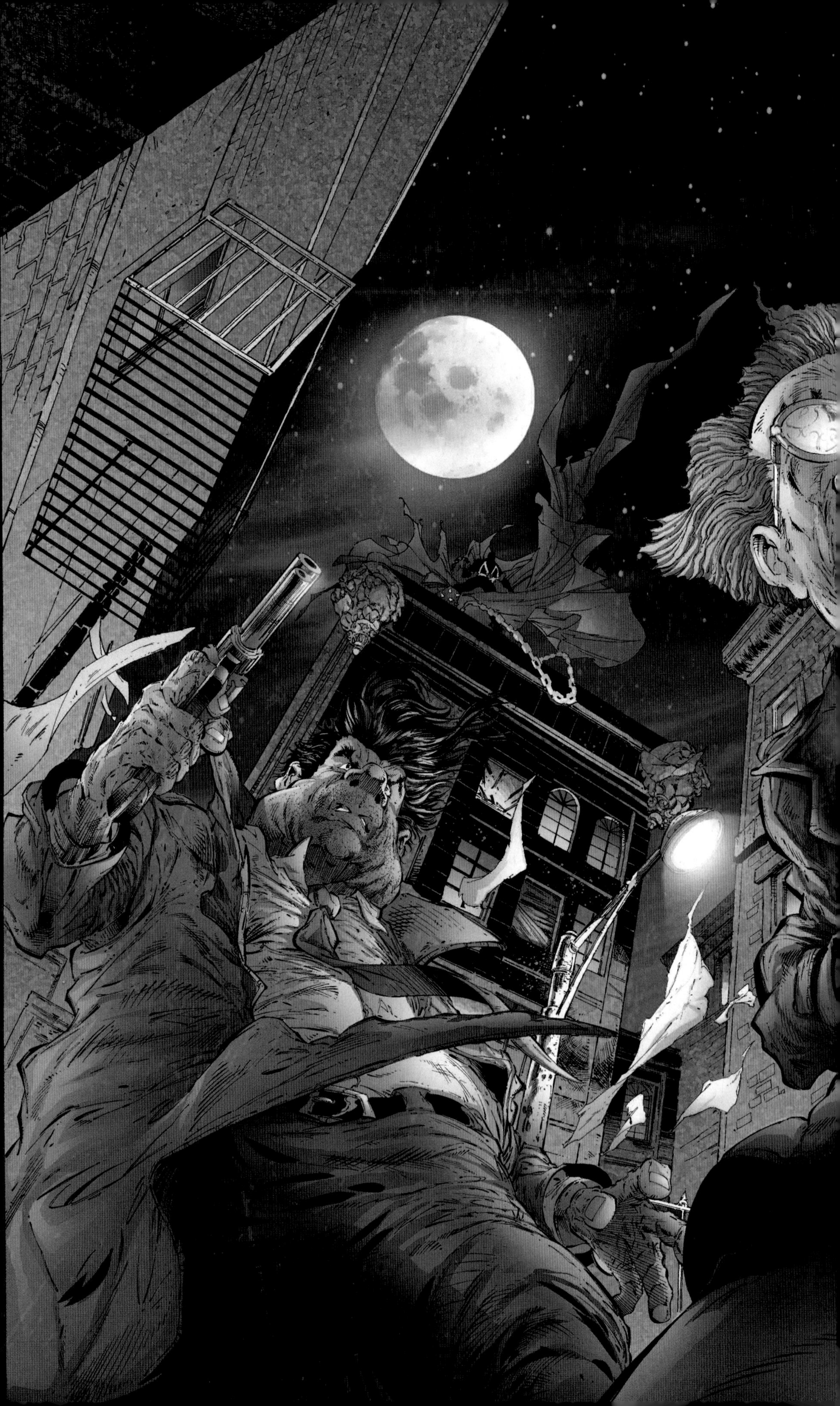

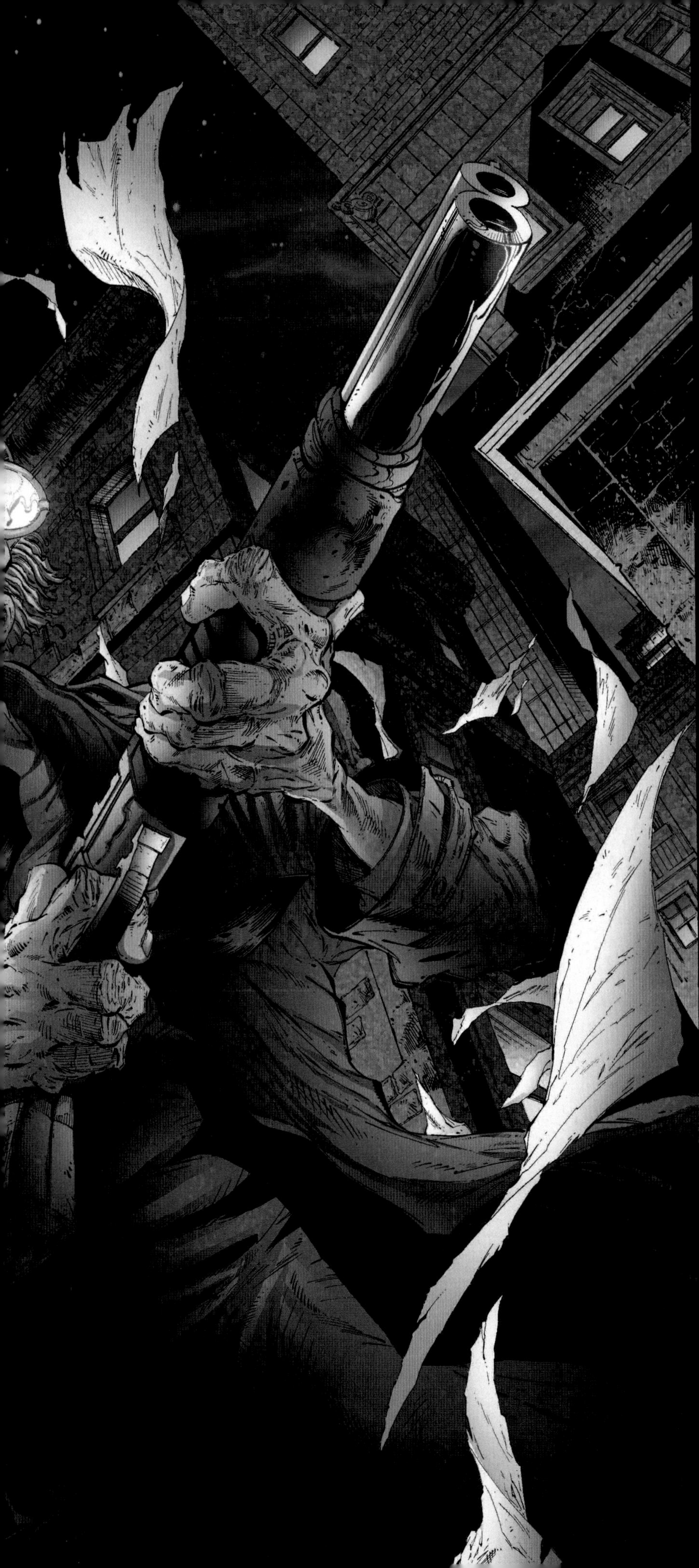

My partner.
His name's Sam. He's
loud, verbose, mule headed.
Frighteningly overweight.

He habitually smells
like whatever he had for
lunch the day before.

He has the worst
case of low blood sugar
I have ever, EVER
been witness to.

But there is no man —
no man on this earth
that I value more. The
day we were partnered
together, that was a —
that was a good day.

That's so great.

We've seen everything
together.

Well, we've —
we've seen it all.
And — and well,
we got sick of it all.
We got sick of the
cop rat-race.
The finger-pointing.
The politics. The
in-house corruption.

We'd had it up to here
and then some…

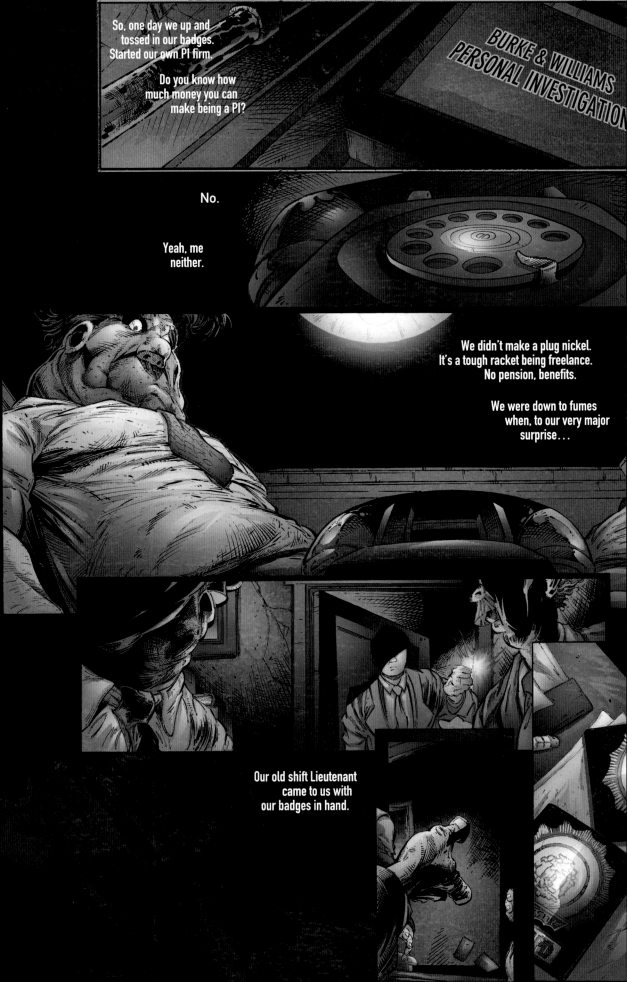

So, one day we up and tossed in our badges. Started our own PI firm.

Do you know how much money you can make being a PI?

BURKE & WILLIAMS PERSONAL INVESTIGATION

No.

Yeah, me neither.

We didn't make a plug nickel. It's a tough racket being freelance. No pension, benefits.

We were down to fumes when, to our very major surprise...

Our old shift Lieutenant came to us with our badges in hand.

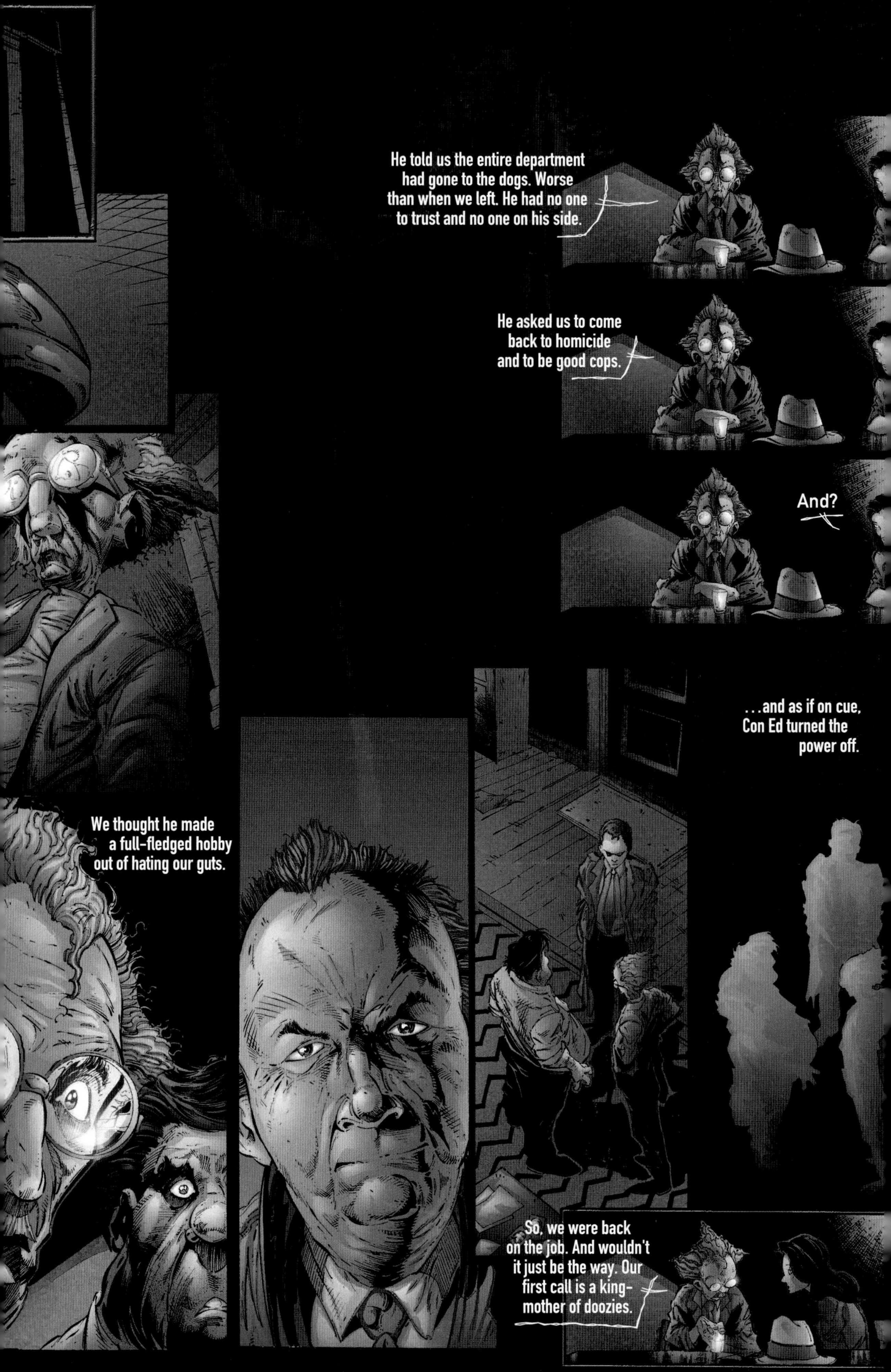
He told us the entire department had gone to the dogs. Worse than when we left. He had no one to trust and no one on his side.
He asked us to come back to homicide and to be good cops.
And?
We thought he made a full-fledged hobby out of hating our guts.
...and as if on cue, Con Ed turned the power off.
So, we were back on the job. And wouldn't it just be the way. Our first call is a king-mother of doozies.

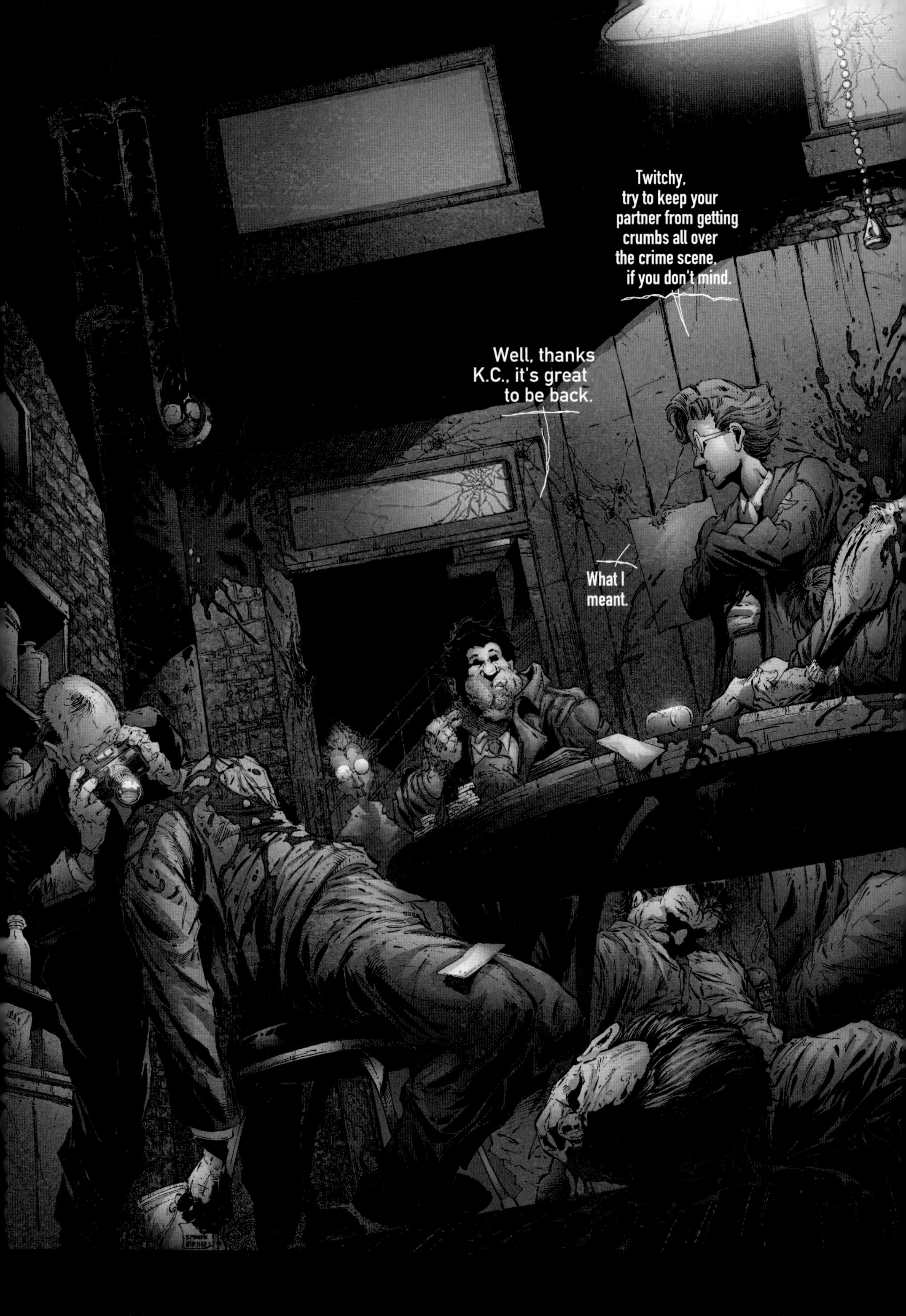
Twitchy, try to keep your partner from getting crumbs all over the crime scene, if you don't mind.
Well, thanks K.C., it's great to be back.
What I meant.

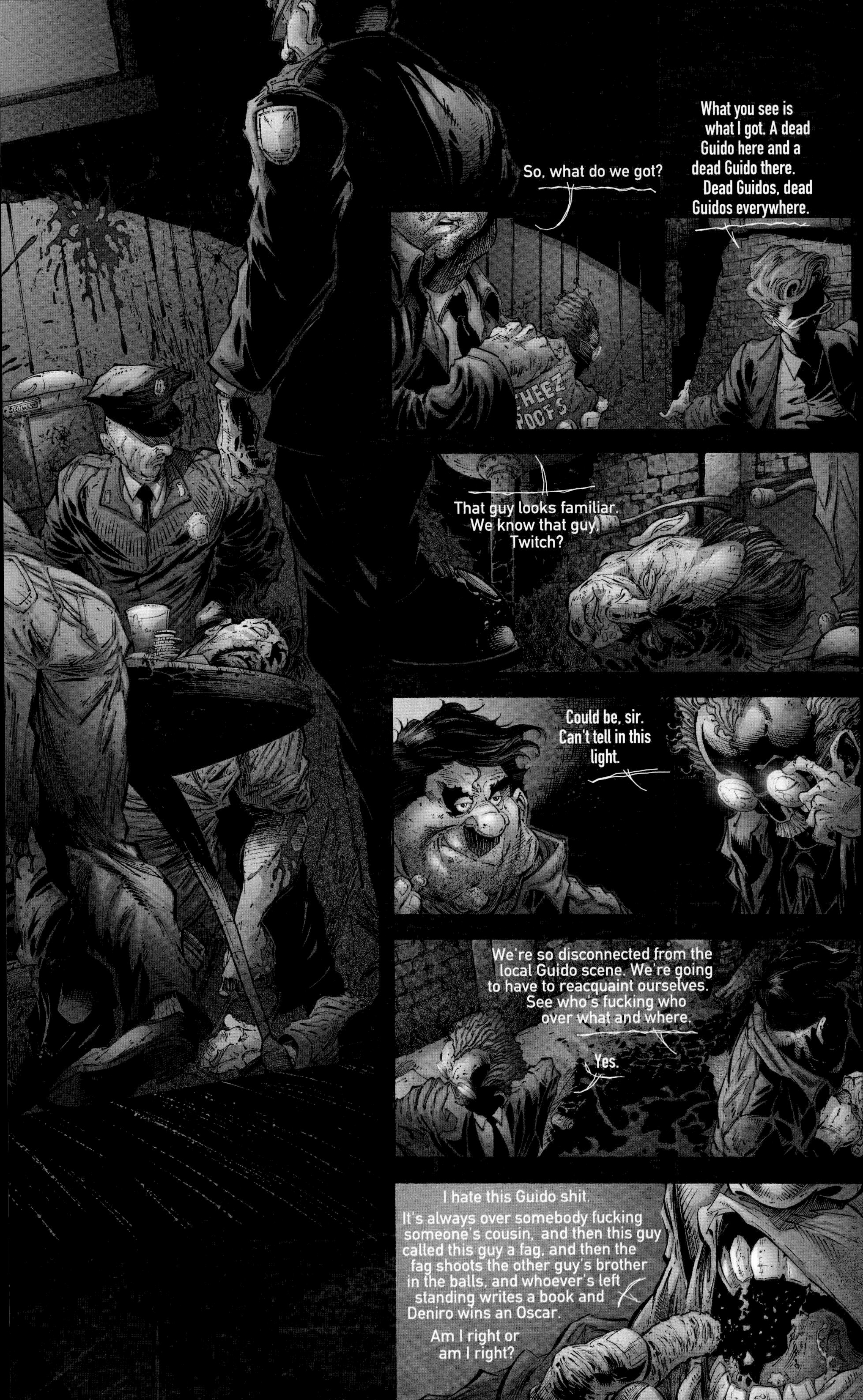

So, what do we got?
What you see is what I got. A dead Guido here and a dead Guido there. Dead Guidos, dead Guidos everywhere.
That guy looks familiar. We know that guy. Twitch?
Could be, sir. Can't tell in this light.
We're so disconnected from the local Guido scene. We're going to have to reacquaint ourselves. See who's fucking who over what and where.
Yes.
I hate this Guido shit.
It's always over somebody fucking someone's cousin, and then this guy called this guy a fag, and then the fag shoots the other guy's brother in the balls, and whoever's left standing writes a book and Deniro wins an Oscar.
Am I right or am I right?
CHEEZ POOFS

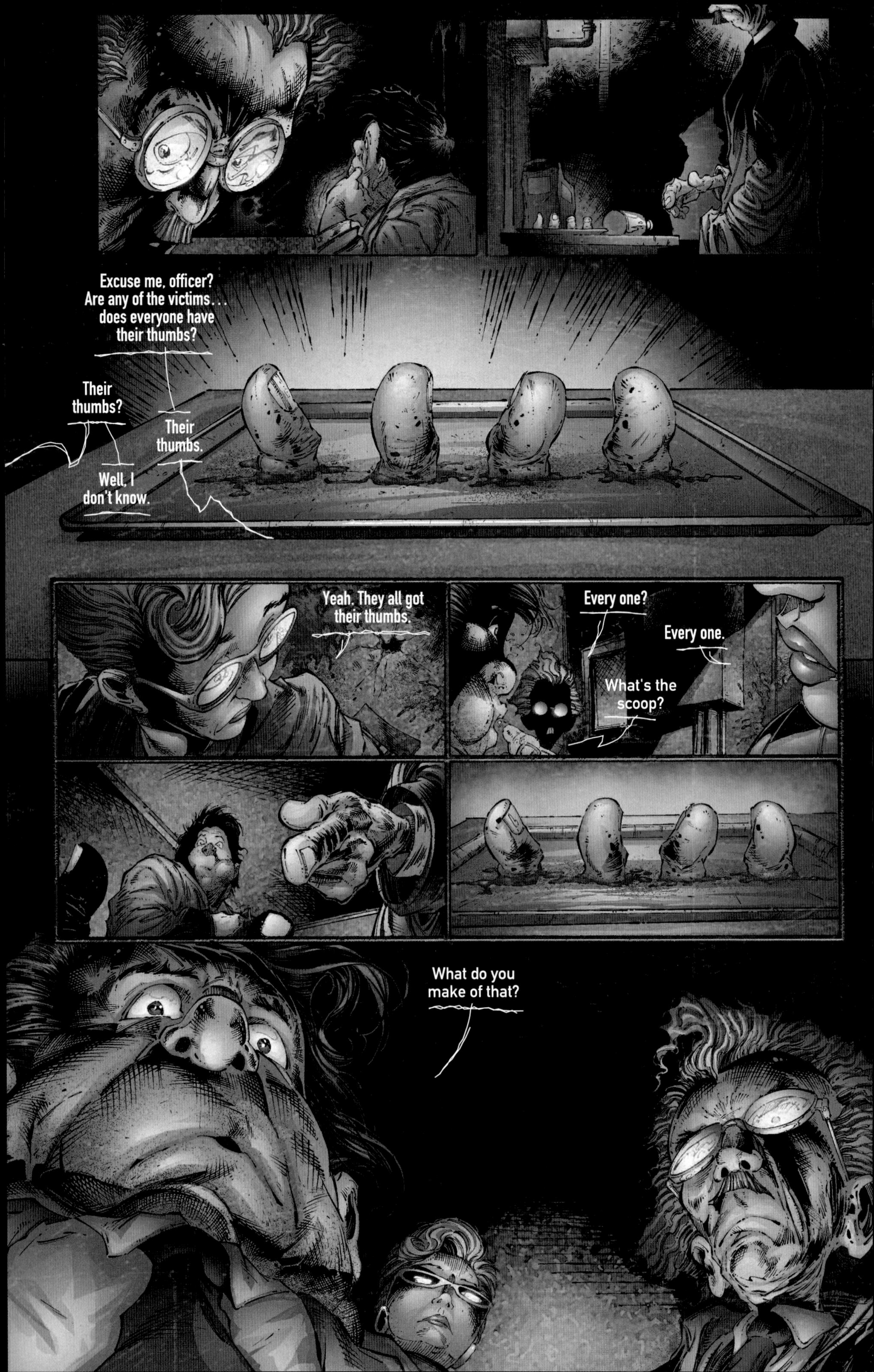
Excuse me, officer? Are any of the victims... does everyone have their thumbs?
Their thumbs?
Their thumbs.
Well, I don't know.
Yeah. They all got their thumbs.
Every one?
Every one.
What's the scoop?
What do you make of that?

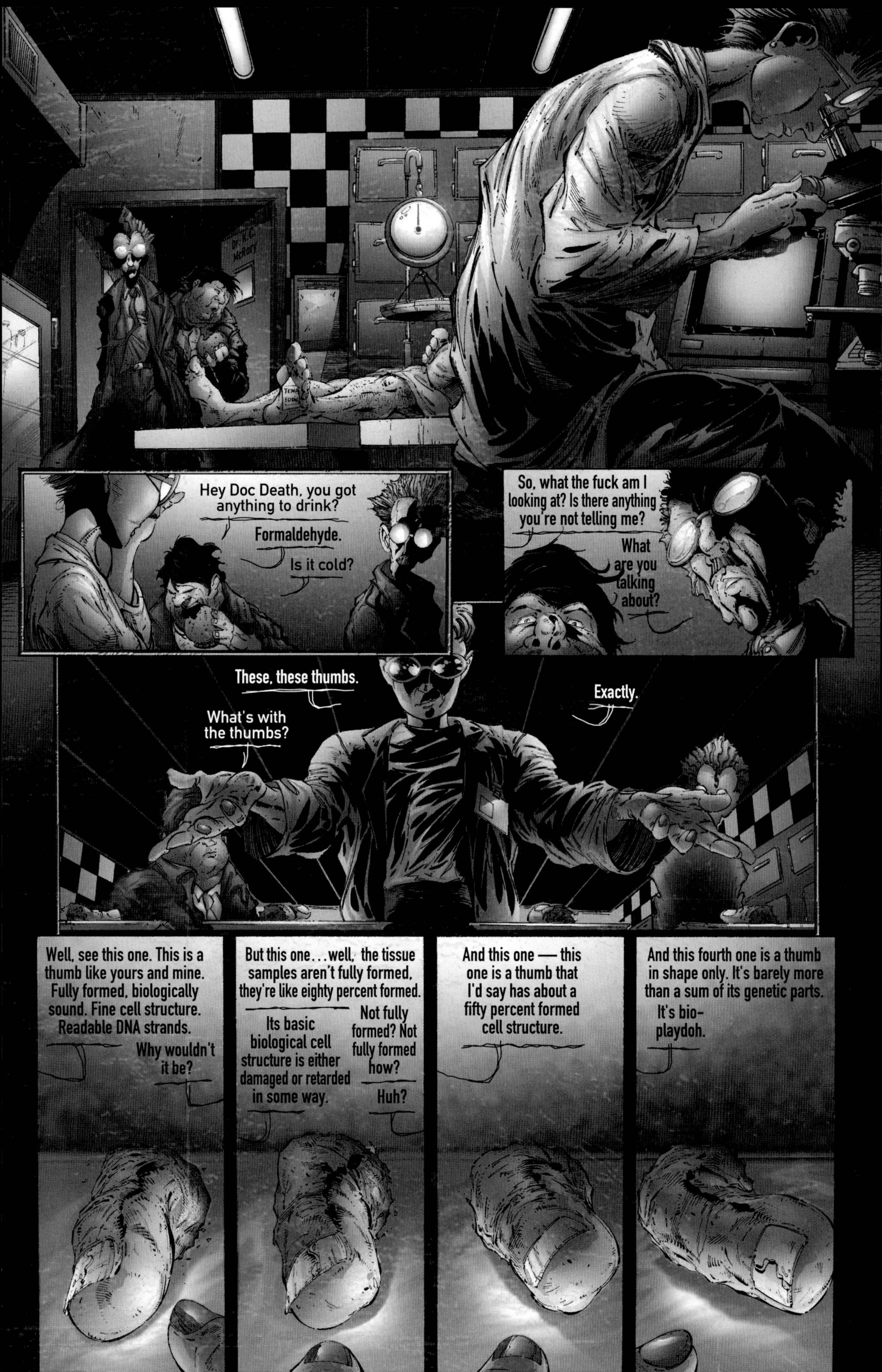
Hey Doc Death, you got anything to drink?
Formaldehyde.
Is it cold?
So, what the fuck am I looking at? Is there anything you're not telling me?
What are you talking about?
These, these thumbs.
What's with the thumbs?
Exactly.
Well, see this one. This is a thumb like yours and mine. Fully formed, biologically sound. Fine cell structure. Readable DNA strands.
Why wouldn't it be?
But this one...well, the tissue samples aren't fully formed, they're like eighty percent formed.
Its basic biological cell structure is either damaged or retarded in some way.
Not fully formed? Not fully formed how?
Huh?
And this one — this one is a thumb that I'd say has about a fifty percent formed cell structure.
And this fourth one is a thumb in shape only. It's barely more than a sum of its genetic parts.
It's bio-playdoh.

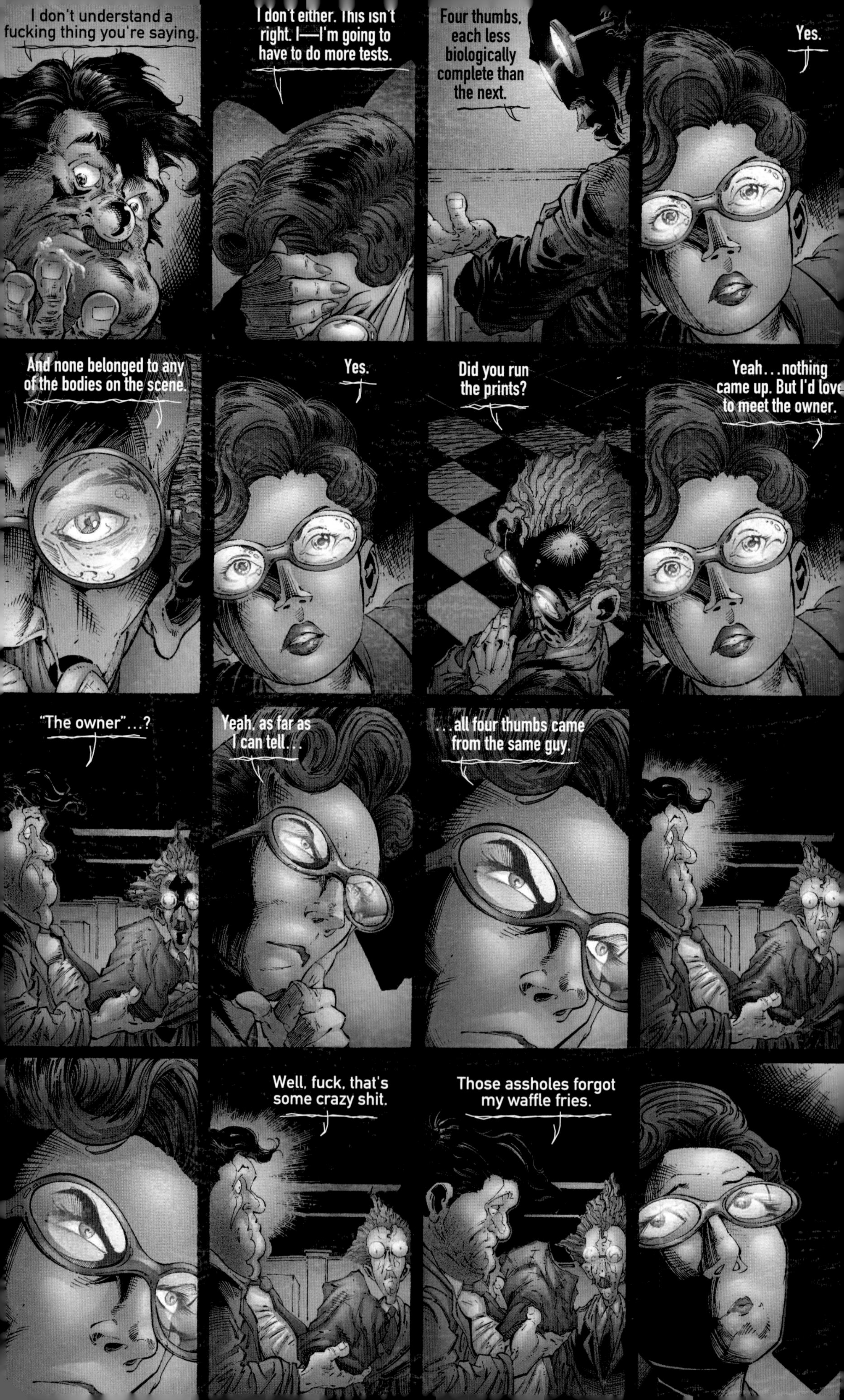
I don't understand a fucking thing you're saying.
I don't either. This isn't right. I—I'm going to have to do more tests.
Four thumbs, each less biologically complete than the next.
Yes.
And none belonged to any of the bodies on the scene.
Yes.
Did you run the prints?
Yeah. . .nothing came up. But I'd love to meet the owner.
"The owner". . .?
Yeah, as far as I can tell. . .
. . .all four thumbs came from the same guy.
Well, fuck, that's some crazy shit.
Those assholes forgot my waffle fries.

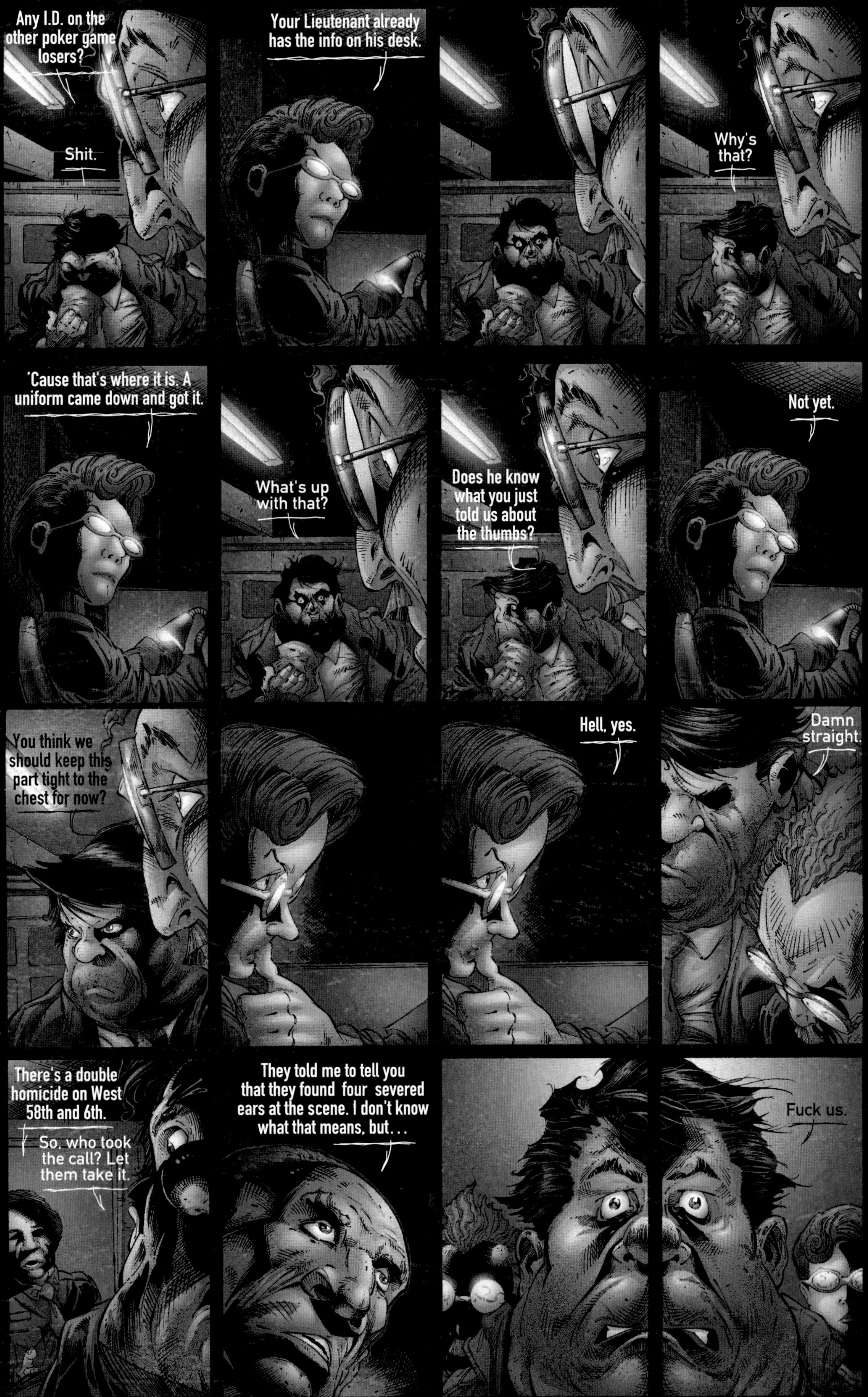
Any I.D. on the other poker game losers?
Shit.
Your Lieutenant already has the info on his desk.
Why's that?
'Cause that's where it is. A uniform came down and got it.
What's up with that?
Does he know what you just told us about the thumbs?
Not yet.
You think we should keep this part tight to the chest for now?
Hell, yes.
Damn straight.
There's a double homicide on West 58th and 6th.
So, who took the call? Let them take it.
They told me to tell you that they found four severed ears at the scene. I don't know what that means, but...
Fuck us.

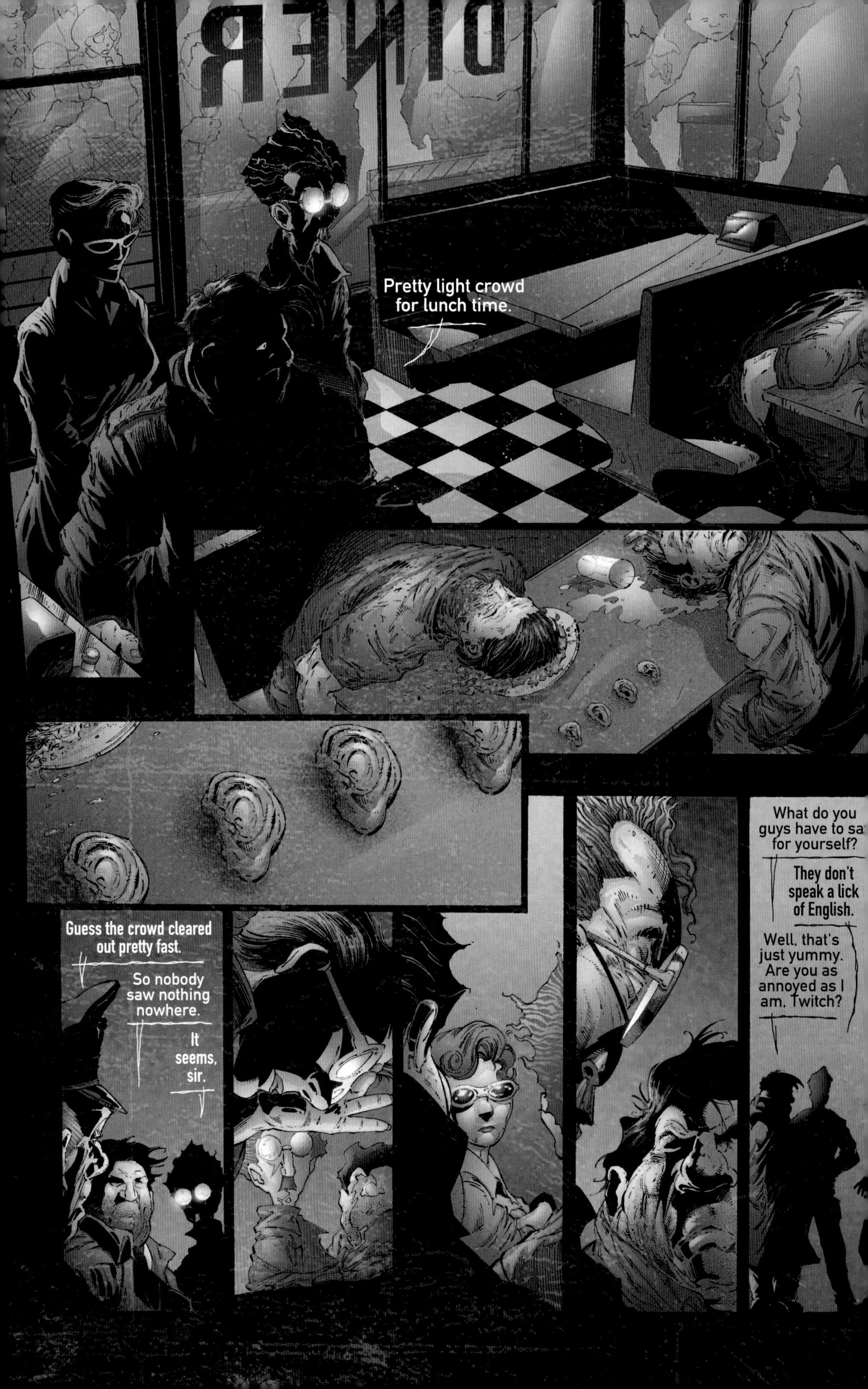
DINER
Pretty light crowd for lunch time.
Guess the crowd cleared out pretty fast.
So nobody saw nothing nowhere.
It seems, sir.
What do you guys have to sa for yourself?
They don't speak a lick of English.
Well, that's just yummy. Are you as annoyed as I am, Twitch?

You always have a head start on me, sir.

Could you get a couple of shots of the crowd? Thanks.

Done.

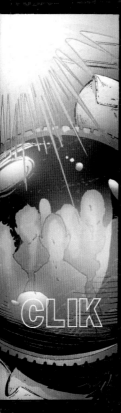
CLIK

Take them to the station and find a fuckin' interpreter.

Right.

Wait!

How much is your cheesesteak?

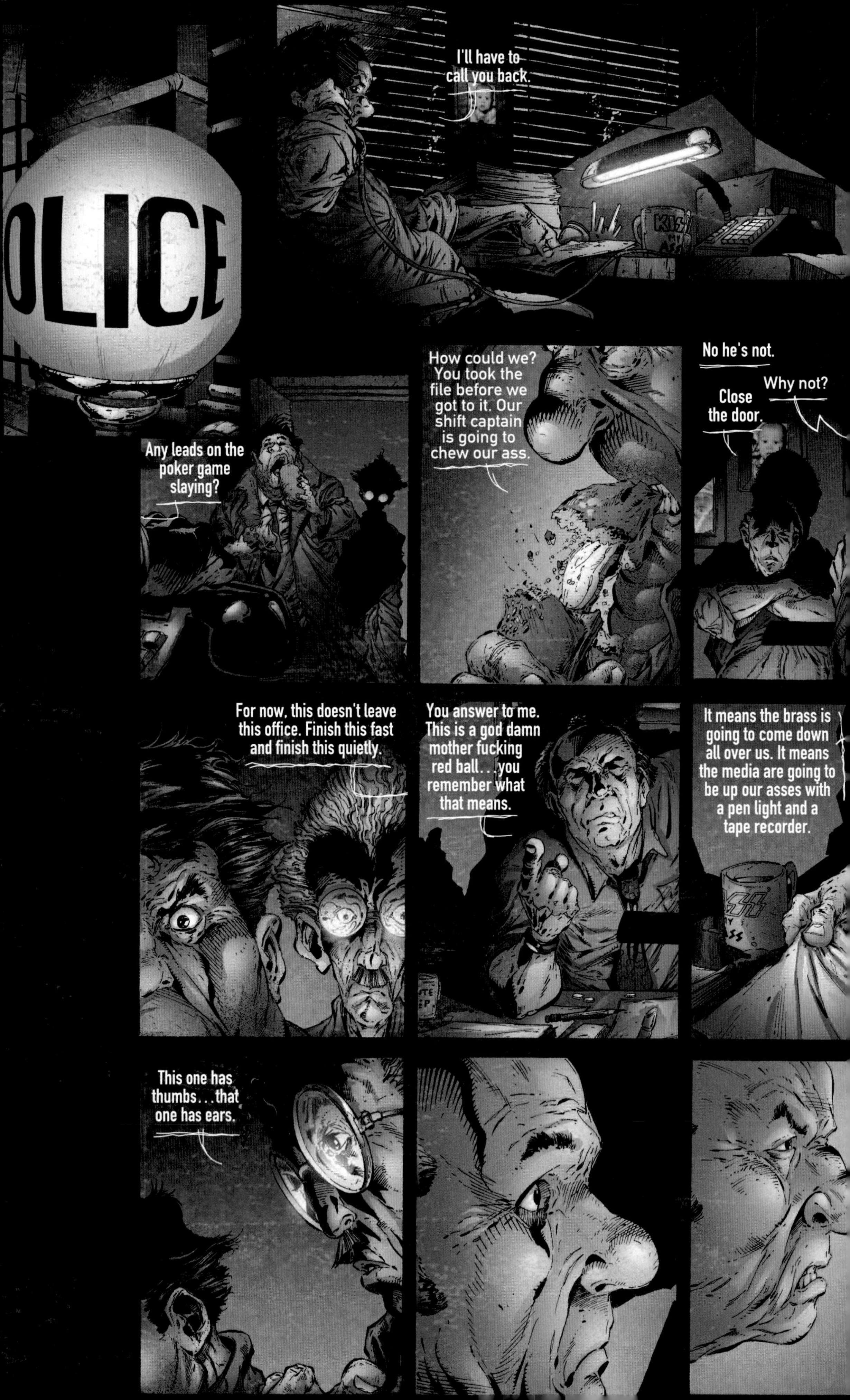
OLICE
I'll have to call you back.
Any leads on the poker game slaying?
How could we? You took the file before we got to it. Our shift captain is going to chew our ass.
No he's not.
Why not?
Close the door.
For now, this doesn't leave this office. Finish this fast and finish this quietly.
You answer to me. This is a god damn mother fucking red ball...you remember what that means.
It means the brass is going to come down all over us. It means the media are going to be up our asses with a pen light and a tape recorder.
This one has thumbs...that one has ears.

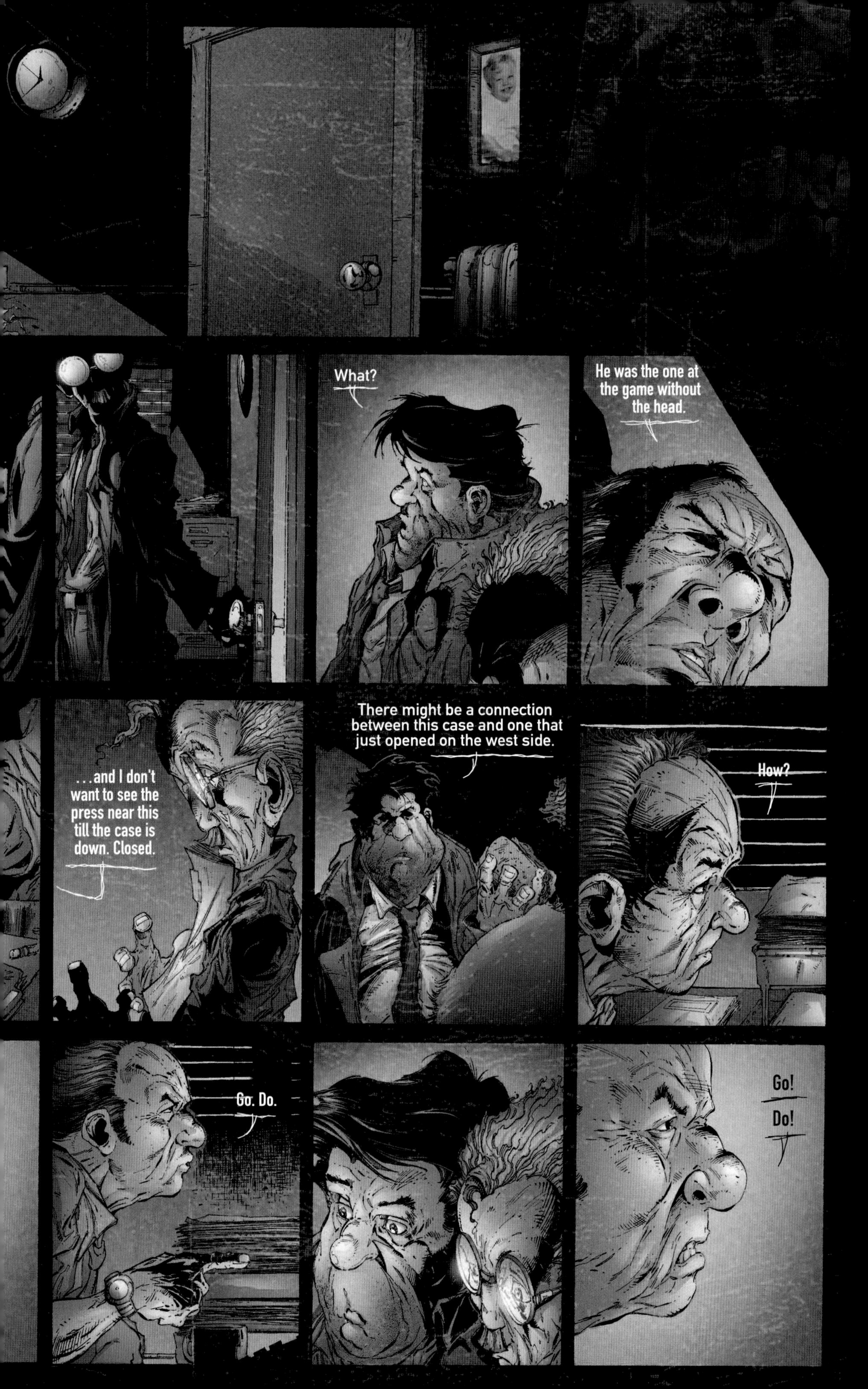
What?
He was the one at the game without the head.
. . .and I don't want to see the press near this till the case is down. Closed.
There might be a connection between this case and one that just opened on the west side.
How?
Go. Do.
Go!
Do!

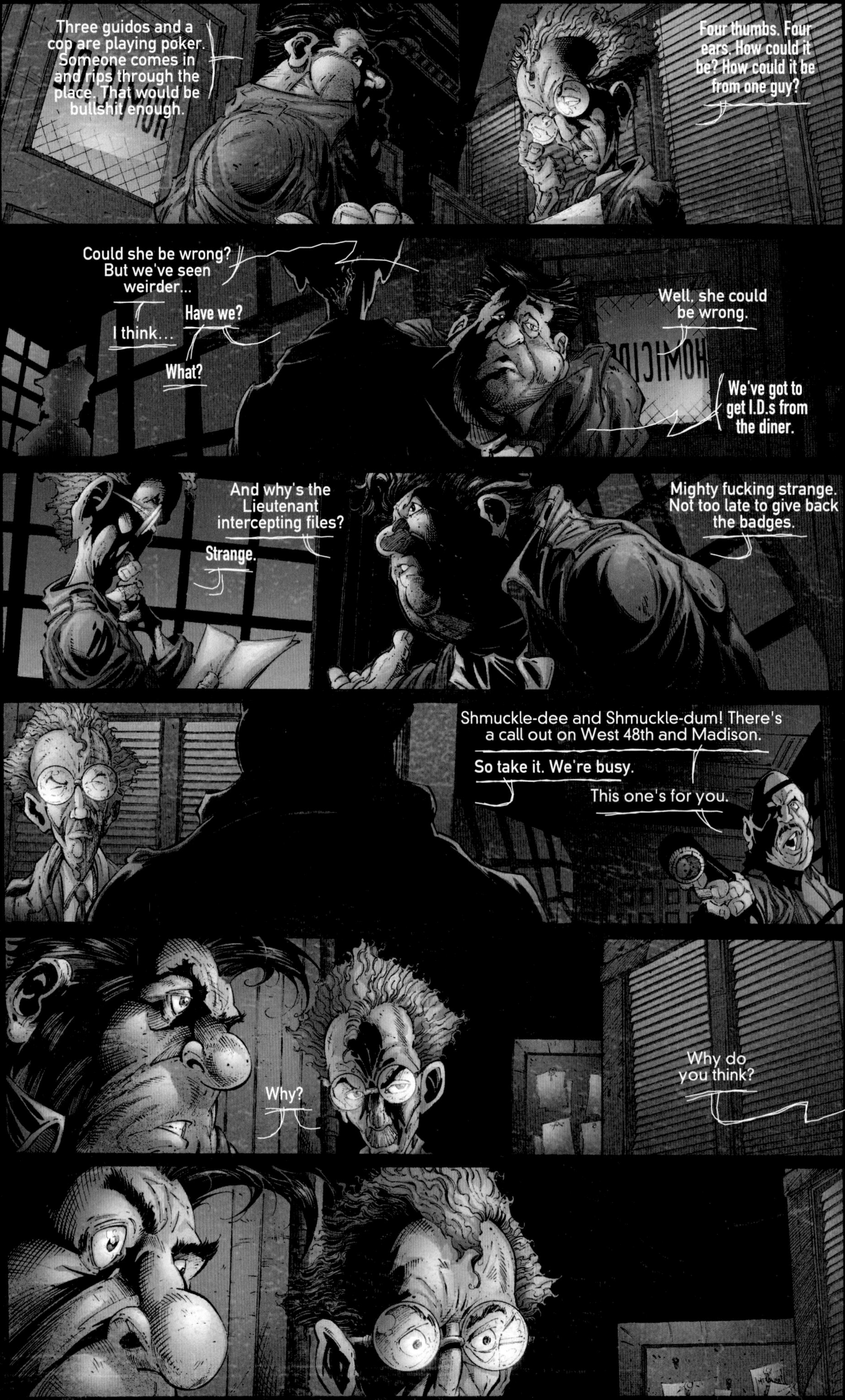
Three guidos and a cop are playing poker. Someone comes in and rips through the place. That would be bullshit enough.
Four thumbs. Four ears. How could it be? How could it be from one guy?
Could she be wrong? But we've seen weirder...
Have we?
I think...
What?
Well, she could be wrong.
We've got to get I.D.s from the diner.
And why's the Lieutenant intercepting files?
Strange.
Mighty fucking strange. Not too late to give back the badges.
Shmuckle-dee and Shmuckle-dum! There's a call out on West 48th and Madison.
So take it. We're busy.
This one's for you.
Why?
Why do you think?

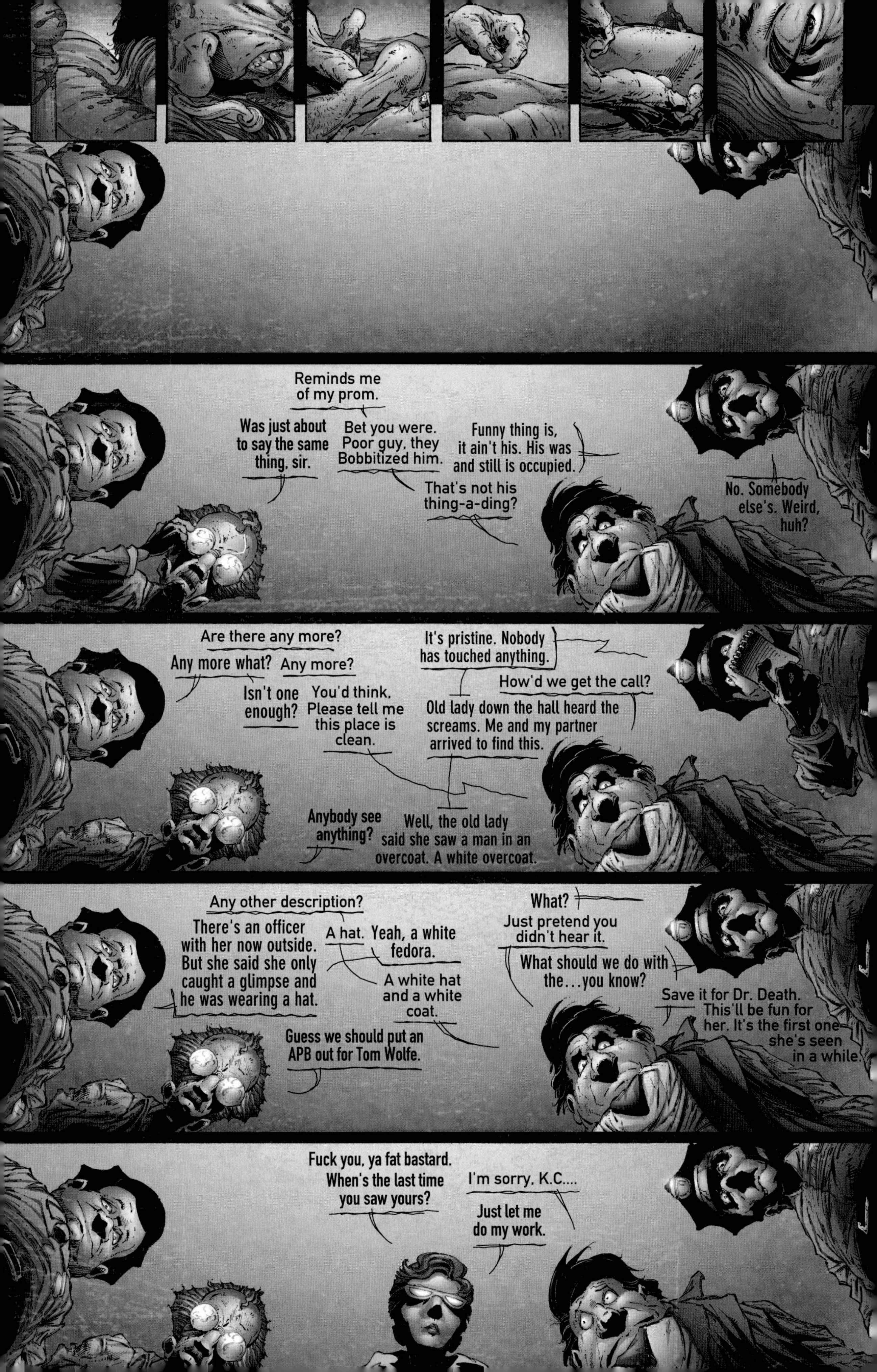

Reminds me of my prom.
Was just about to say the same thing, sir.
Bet you were. Poor guy, they Bobbitized him.
Funny thing is, it ain't his. His was and still is occupied.
That's not his thing-a-ding?
No. Somebody else's. Weird, huh?
Are there any more?
Any more what?
Any more?
Isn't one enough?
You'd think. Please tell me this place is clean.
It's pristine. Nobody has touched anything.
How'd we get the call?
Old lady down the hall heard the screams. Me and my partner arrived to find this.
Anybody see anything?
Well, the old lady said she saw a man in an overcoat. A white overcoat.
Any other description?
There's an officer with her now outside. But she said she only caught a glimpse and he was wearing a hat.
A hat.
Yeah, a white fedora.
A white hat and a white coat.
Guess we should put an APB out for Tom Wolfe.
What?
Just pretend you didn't hear it.
What should we do with the...you know?
Save it for Dr. Death. This'll be fun for her. It's the first one she's seen in a while.
Fuck you, ya fat bastard. When's the last time you saw yours?
I'm sorry, K.C....
Just let me do my work.

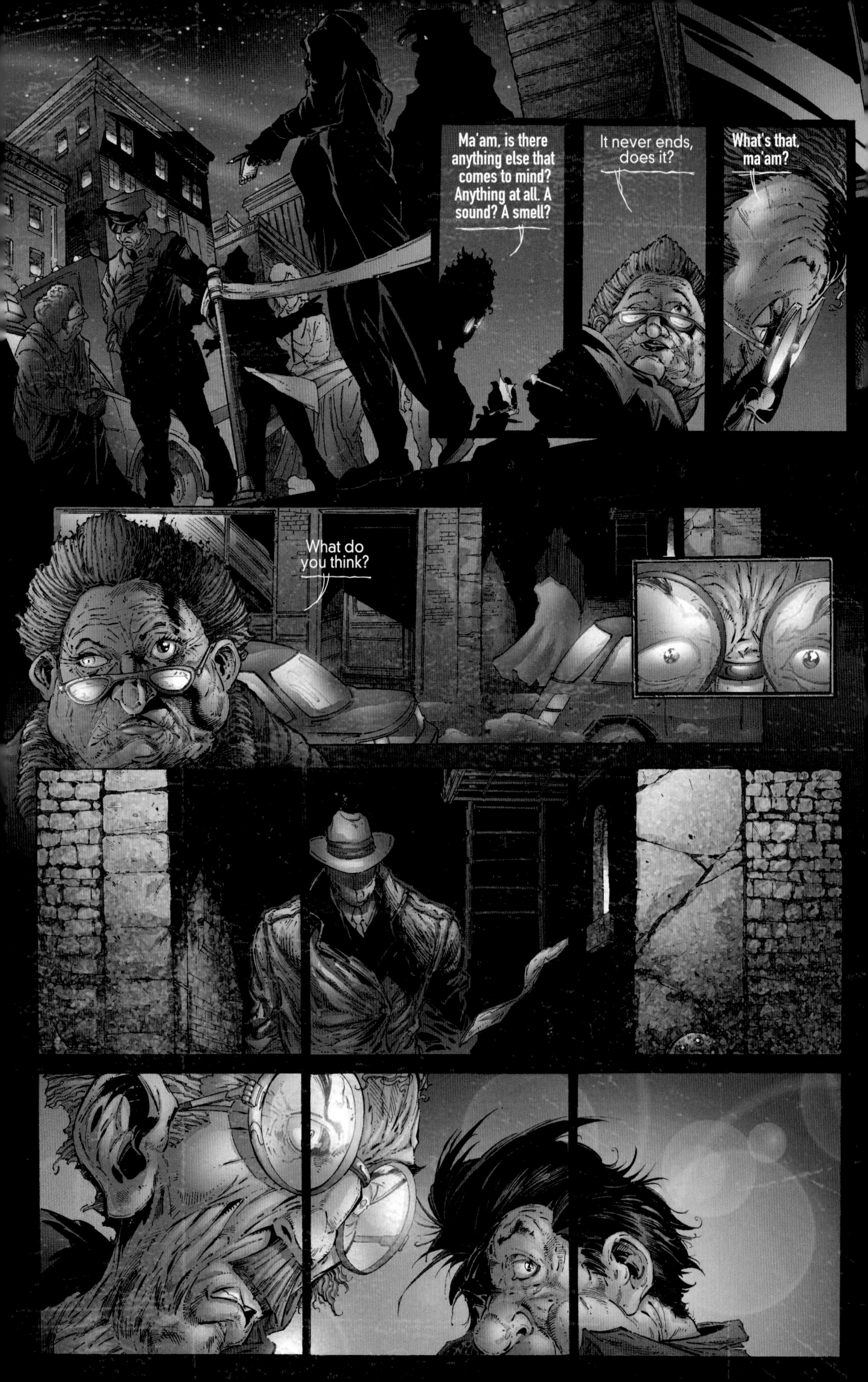
Ma'am, is there anything else that comes to mind? Anything at all. A sound? A smell?
It never ends, does it?
What's that, ma'am?
What do you think?

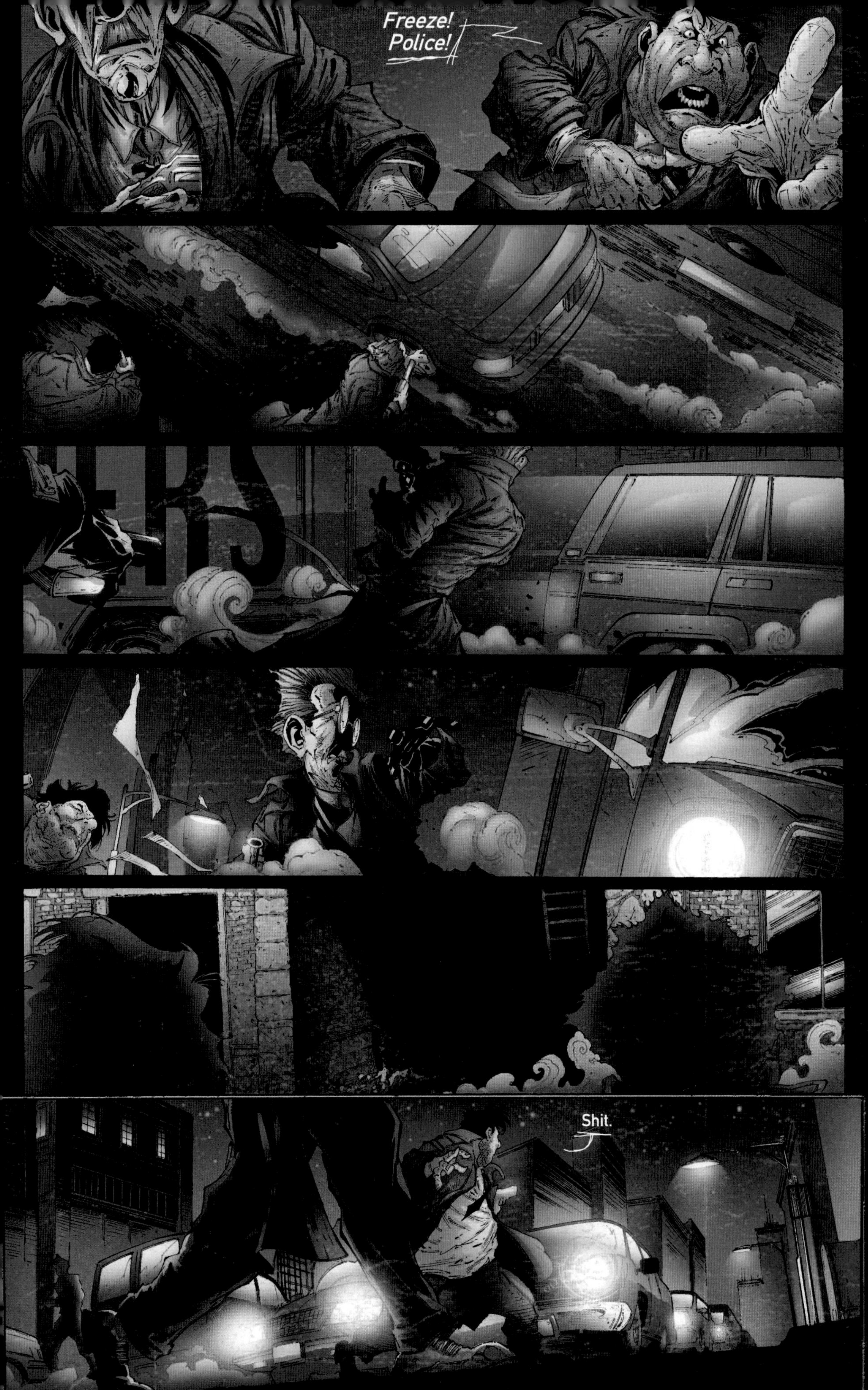
Freeze! Police!
Shit.

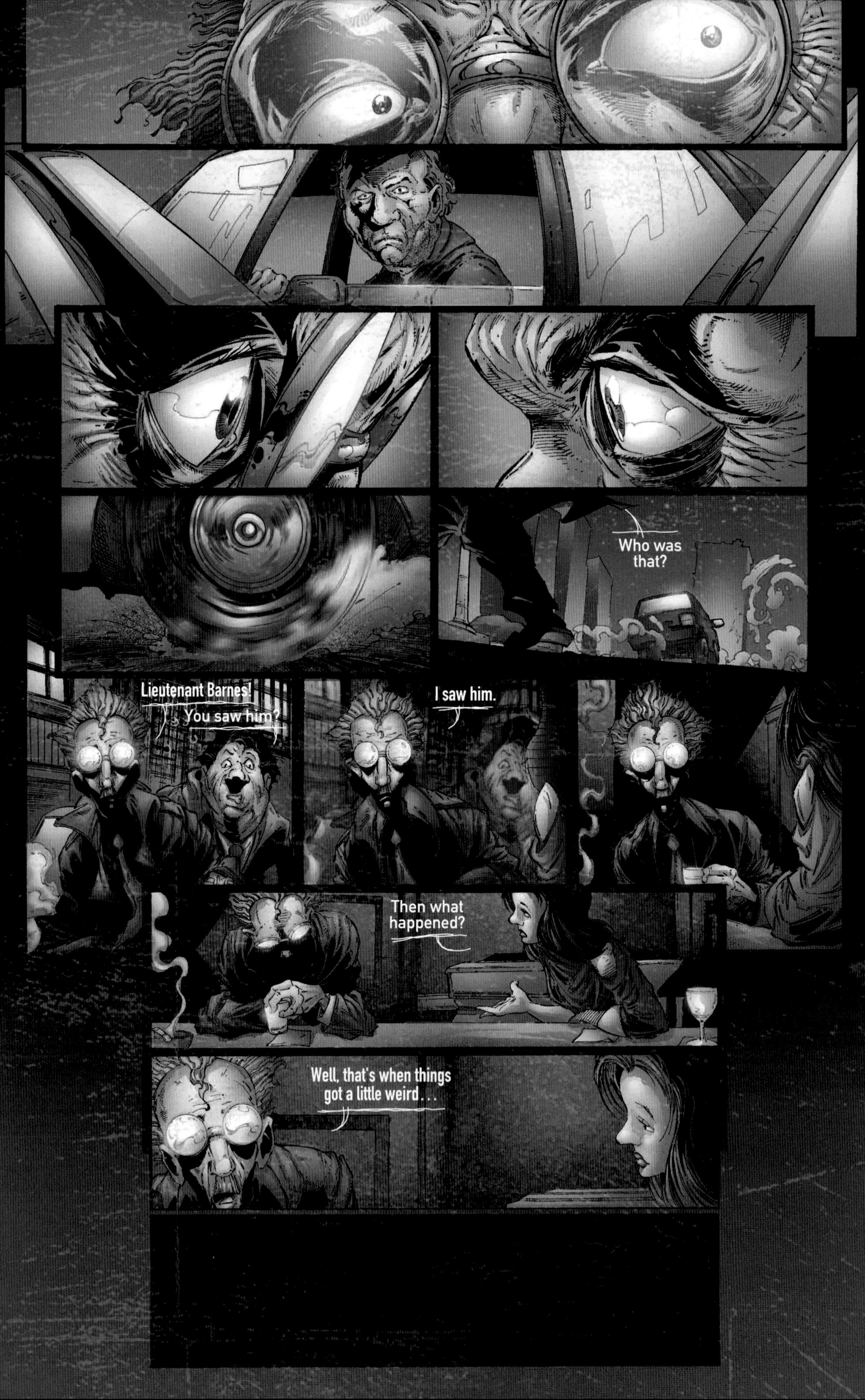
Who was that?
Lieutenant Barnes!
You saw him?
I saw him.
Then what happened?
Well, that's when things got a little weird...

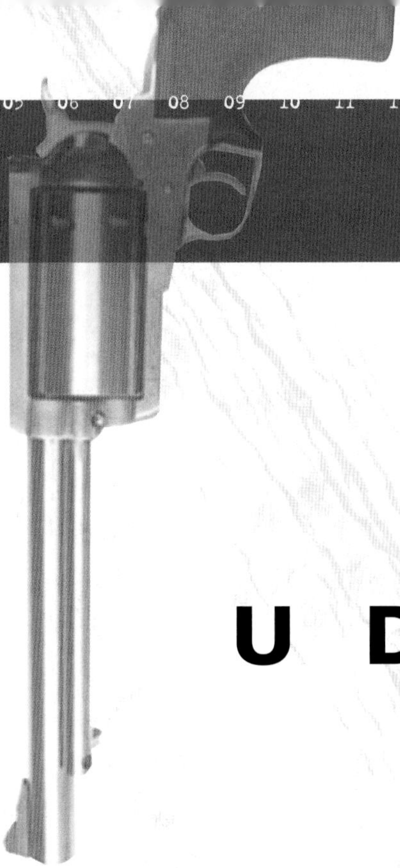

UDAKU

PART 2

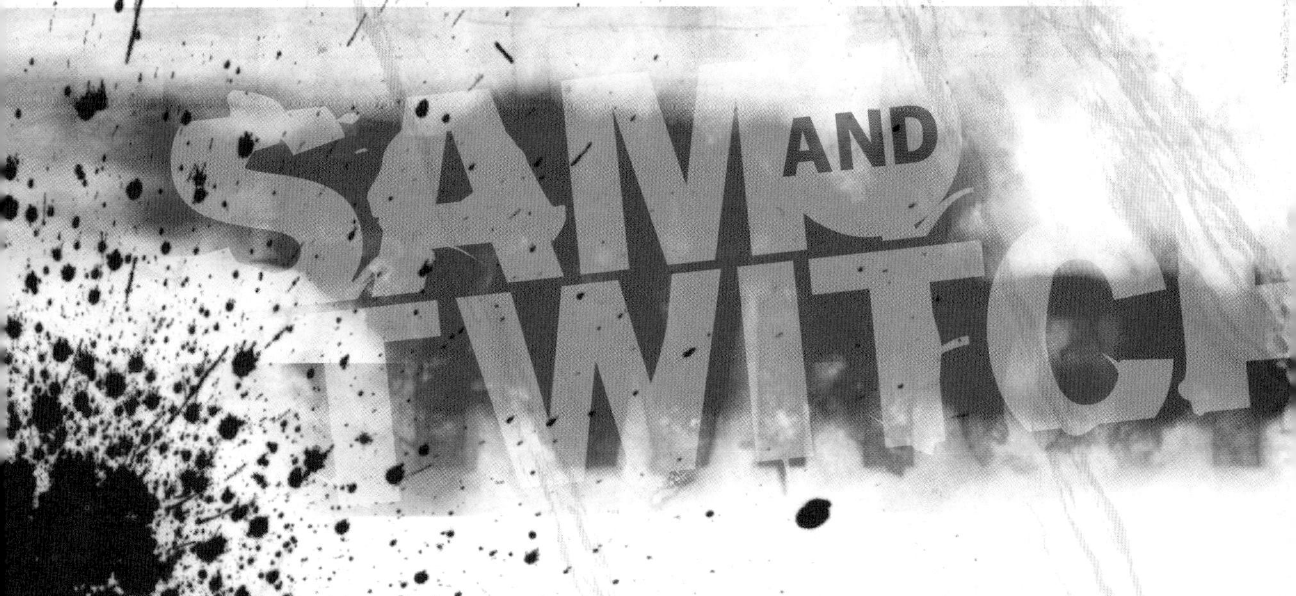
SAM AND TWITCH

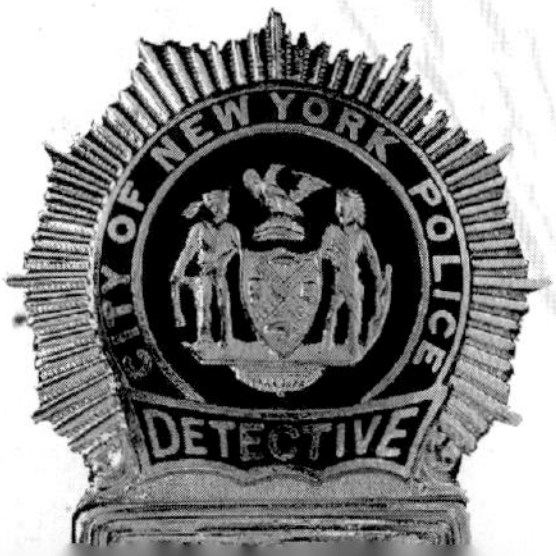
CITY OF NEW YORK POLICE
DETECTIVE

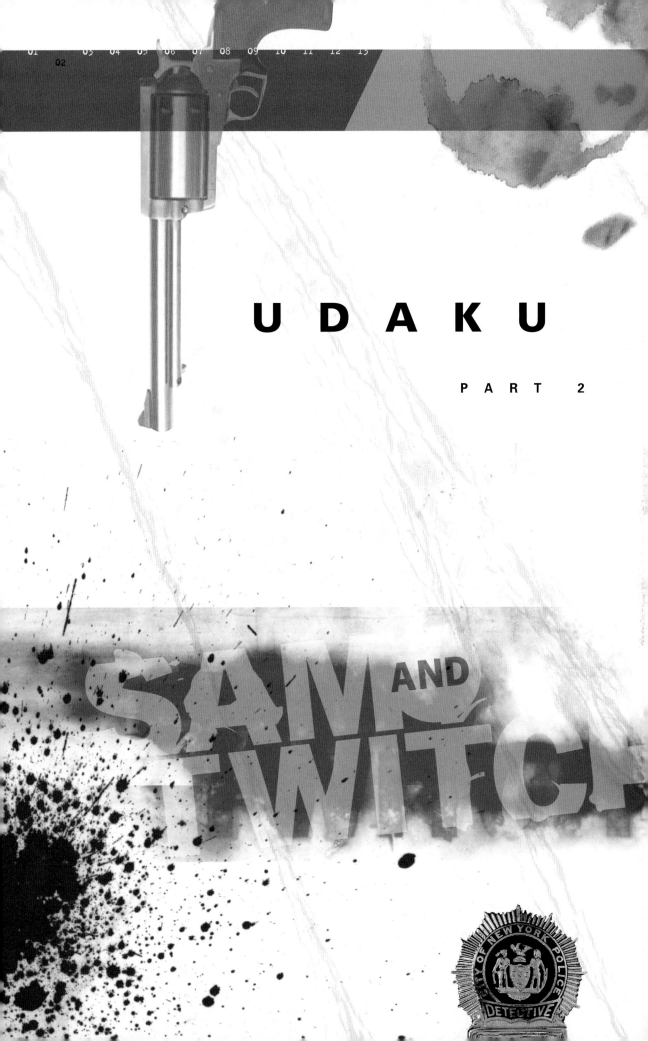

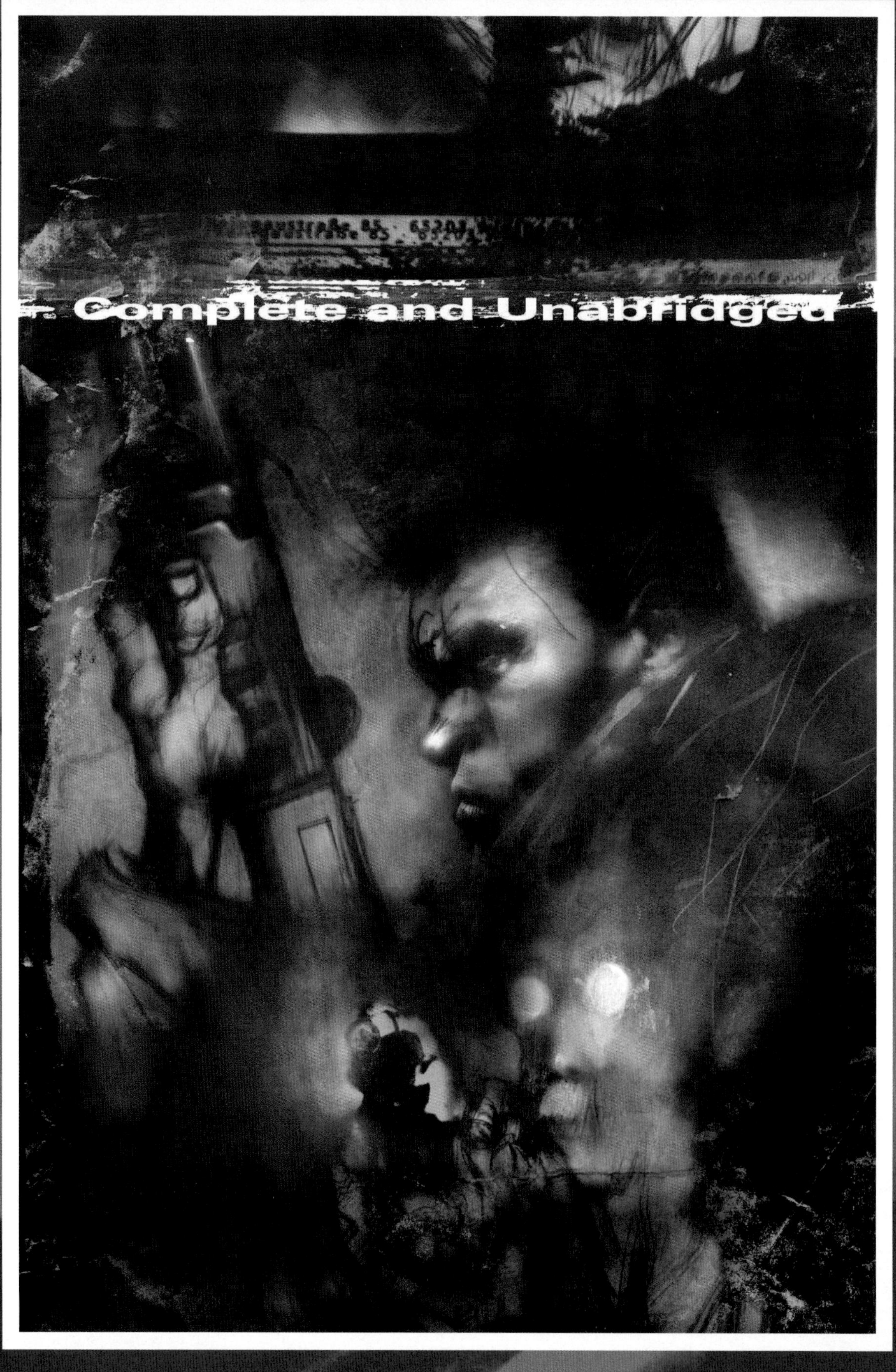
Complete and Unabridged

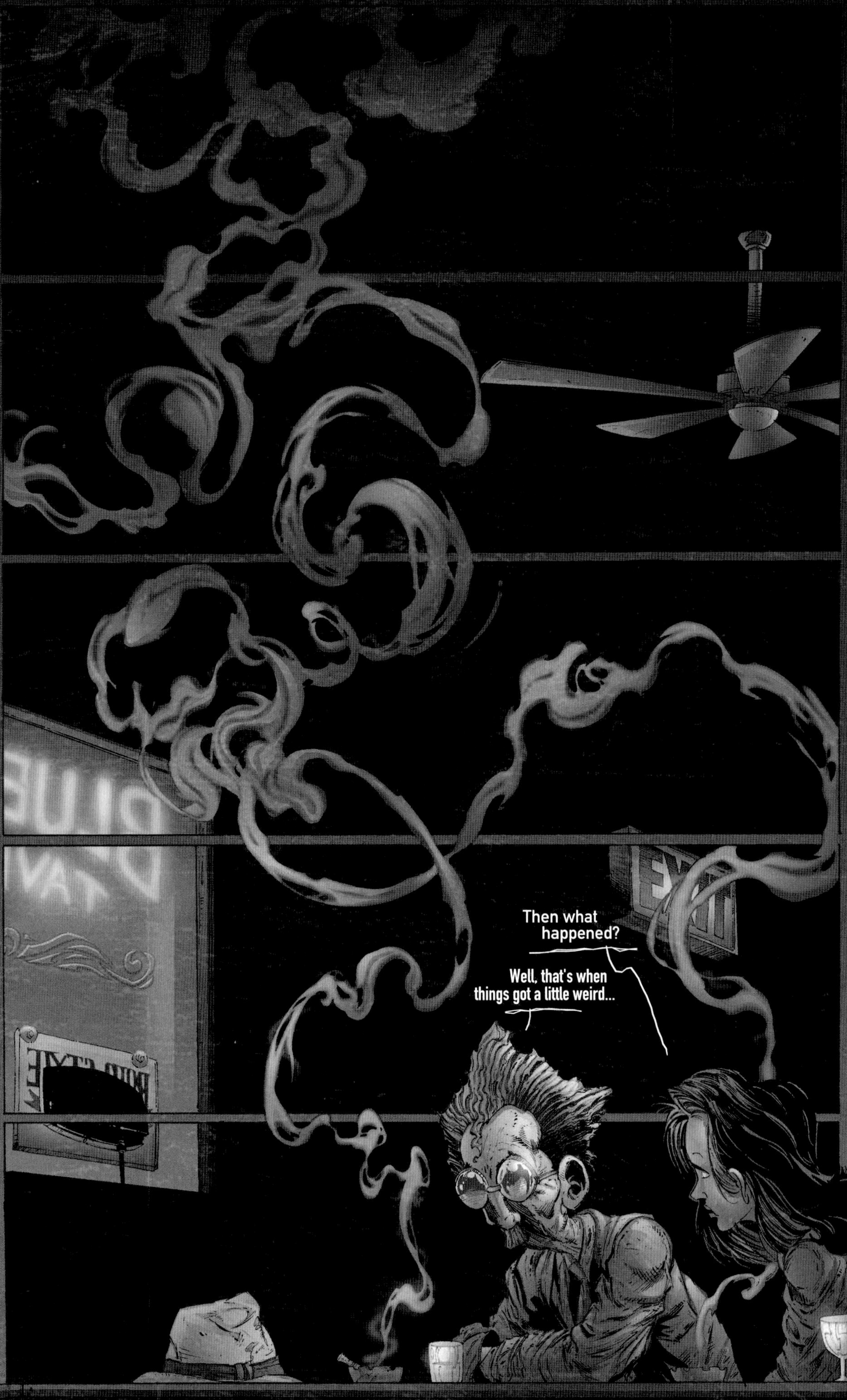
EXIT
Then what happened?
Well, that's when things got a little weird...

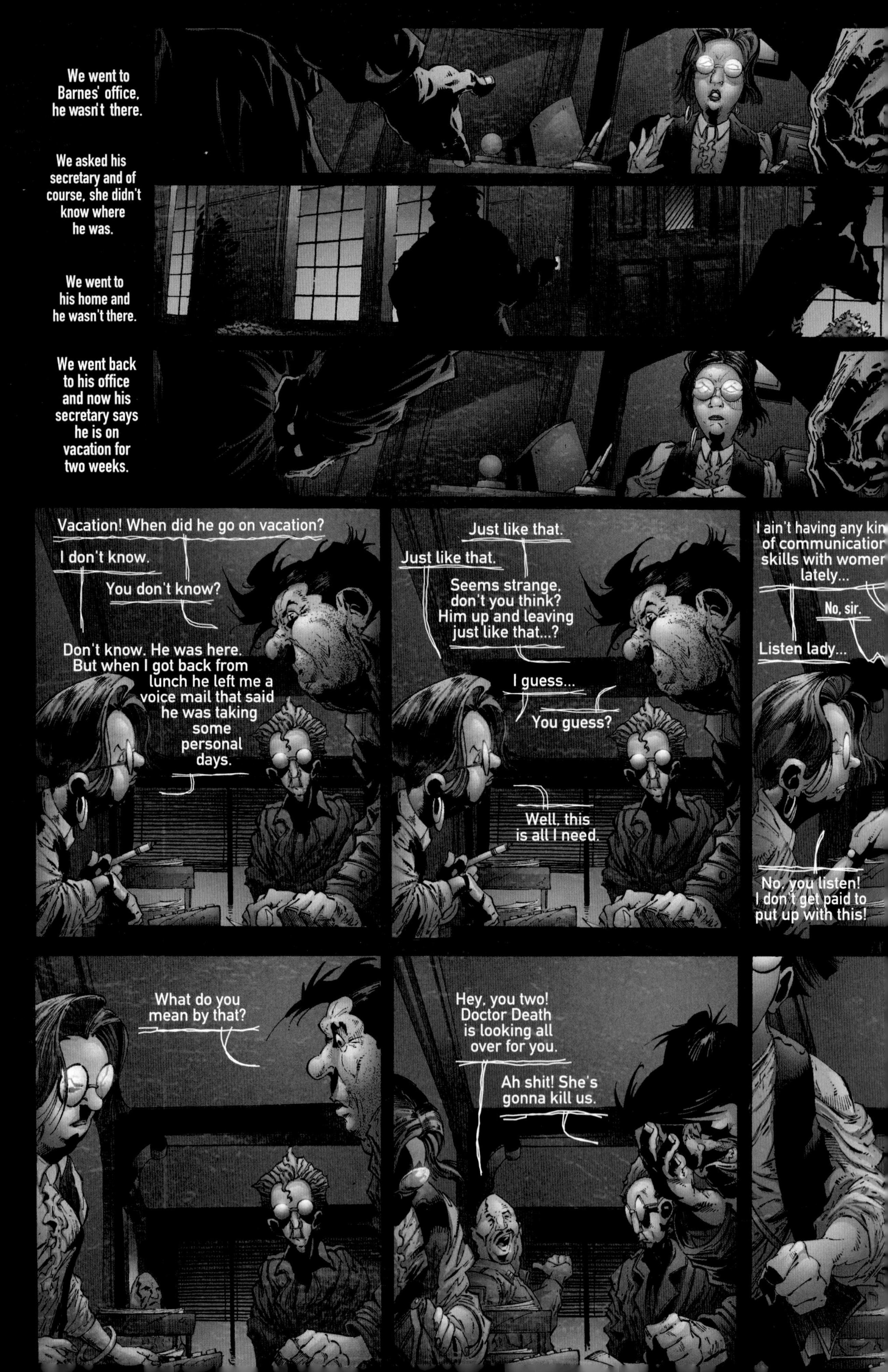

We went to Barnes' office, he wasn't there.
We asked his secretary and of course, she didn't know where he was.
We went to his home and he wasn't there.
We went back to his office and now his secretary says he is on vacation for two weeks.
Vacation! When did he go on vacation?
I don't know.
You don't know?
Don't know. He was here. But when I got back from lunch he left me a voice mail that said he was taking some personal days.
Just like that.
Just like that.
Seems strange, don't you think? Him up and leaving just like that...?
I guess...
You guess?
Well, this is all I need.
I ain't having any kin of communicatior skills with womer lately...
No, sir.
Listen lady...
No, you listen! I don't get paid to put up with this!
What do you mean by that?
Hey, you two! Doctor Death is looking all over for you.
Ah shit! She's gonna kill us.

With what?
You busting my hump! I'm just a goddamn assistant and I don't know shit about ...
Then why are you wigging out? We asked you a simple question.
Because you're yelling at me and questioning me and as far as I can tell I'm the only one in the whole goddamn building you shouldn't be questioning!
Lady....
Forget how to be real cops?
Fuck on outta here, AFFLEK!

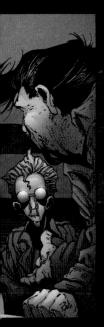

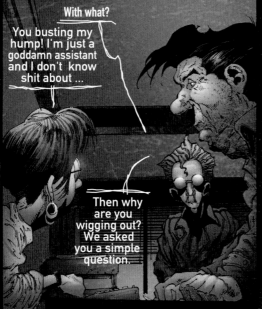

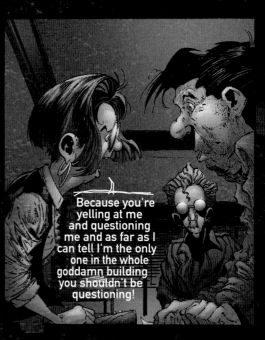

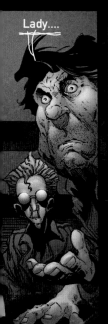

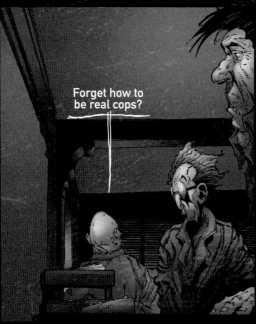

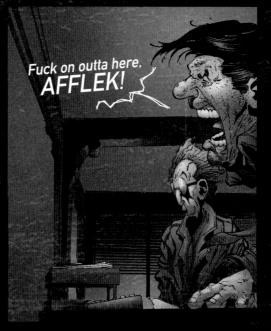

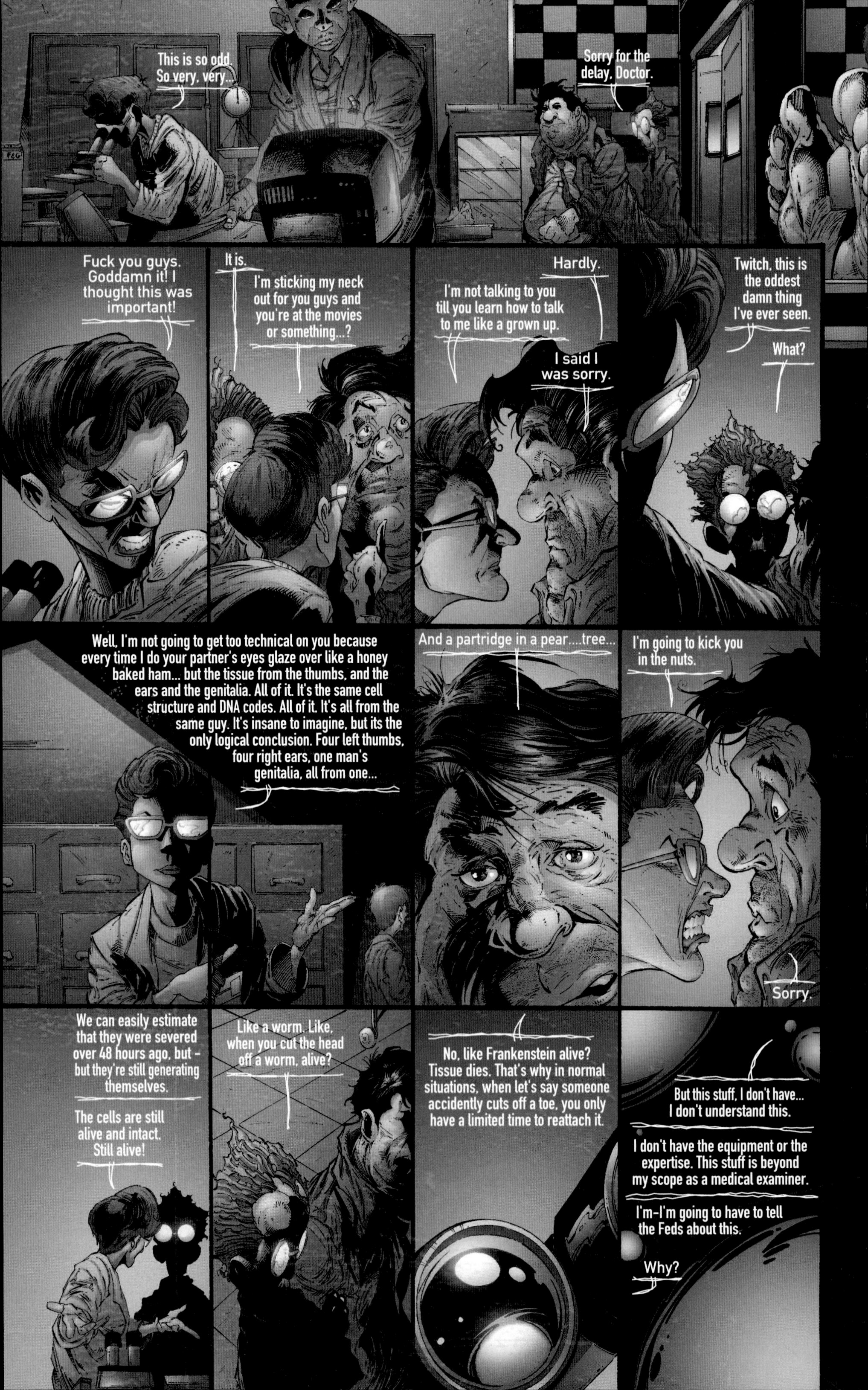
This is so odd. So very, very...
Sorry for the delay, Doctor.
Fuck you guys. Goddamn it! I thought this was important!
It is.
I'm sticking my neck out for you guys and you're at the movies or something...?
Hardly.
I'm not talking to you till you learn how to talk to me like a grown up.
I said I was sorry.
Twitch, this is the oddest damn thing I've ever seen.
What?
Well, I'm not going to get too technical on you because every time I do your partner's eyes glaze over like a honey baked ham... but the tissue from the thumbs, and the ears and the genitalia. All of it. It's the same cell structure and DNA codes. All of it. It's all from the same guy. It's insane to imagine, but its the only logical conclusion. Four left thumbs, four right ears, one man's genitalia, all from one...
And a partridge in a pear....tree...
I'm going to kick you in the nuts.
Sorry.
We can easily estimate that they were severed over 48 hours ago, but - but they're still generating themselves.
The cells are still alive and intact. Still alive!
Like a worm. Like, when you cut the head off a worm, alive?
No, like Frankenstein alive? Tissue dies. That's why in normal situations, when let's say someone accidently cuts off a toe, you only have a limited time to reattach it.
But this stuff, I don't have... I don't understand this.
I don't have the equipment or the expertise. This stuff is beyond my scope as a medical examiner.
I'm-I'm going to have to tell the Feds about this.
Why?

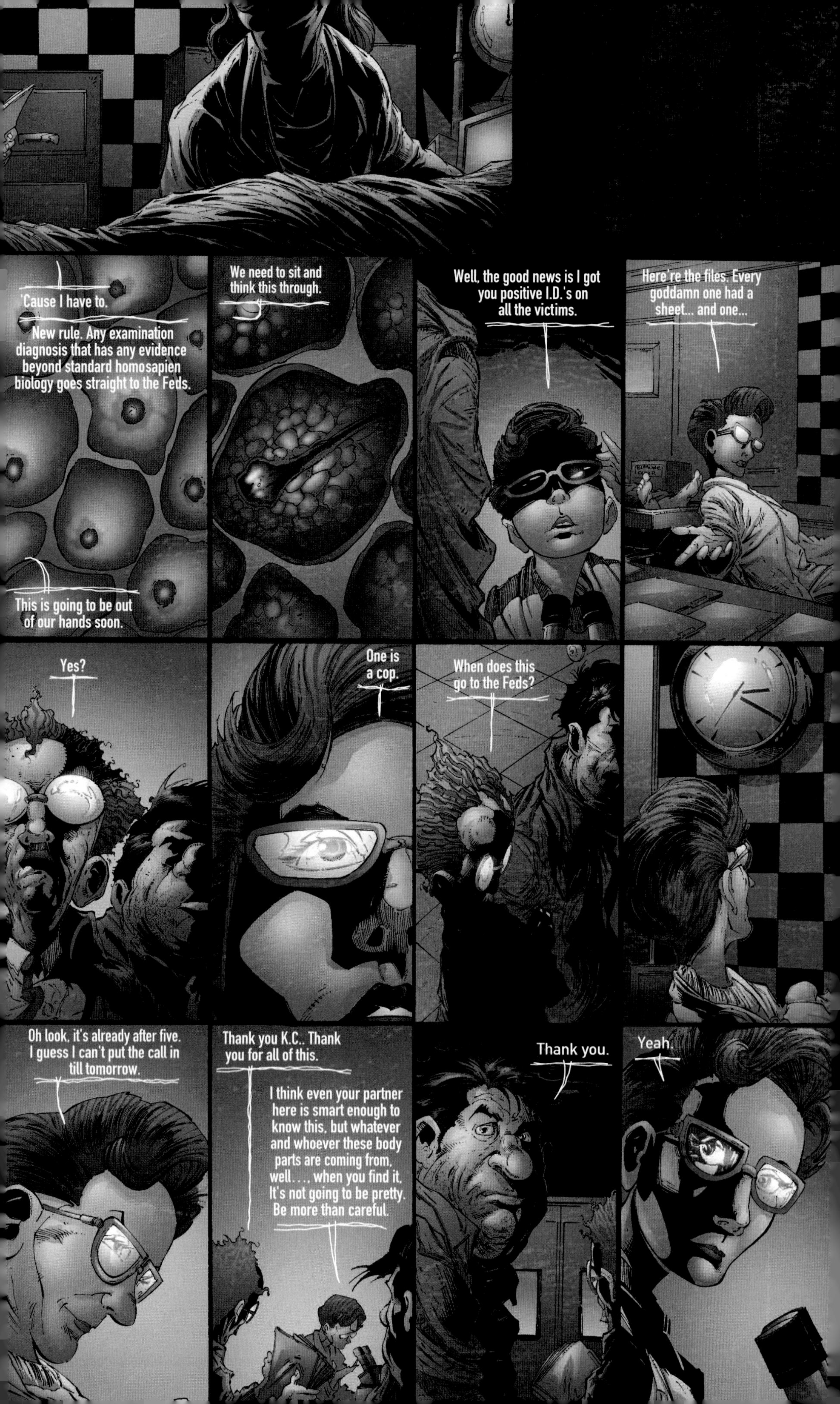

'Cause I have to.
New rule. Any examination diagnosis that has any evidence beyond standard homosapien biology goes straight to the Feds.
This is going to be out of our hands soon.
We need to sit and think this through.
Well, the good news is I got you positive I.D.'s on all the victims.
Here're the files. Every goddamn one had a sheet... and one...
Yes?
One is a cop.
When does this go to the Feds?
Oh look, it's already after five. I guess I can't put the call in till tomorrow.
Thank you K.C.. Thank you for all of this.
I think even your partner here is smart enough to know this, but whatever and whoever these body parts are coming from, well..., when you find it, It's not going to be pretty. Be more than careful.
Thank you.
Yeah.

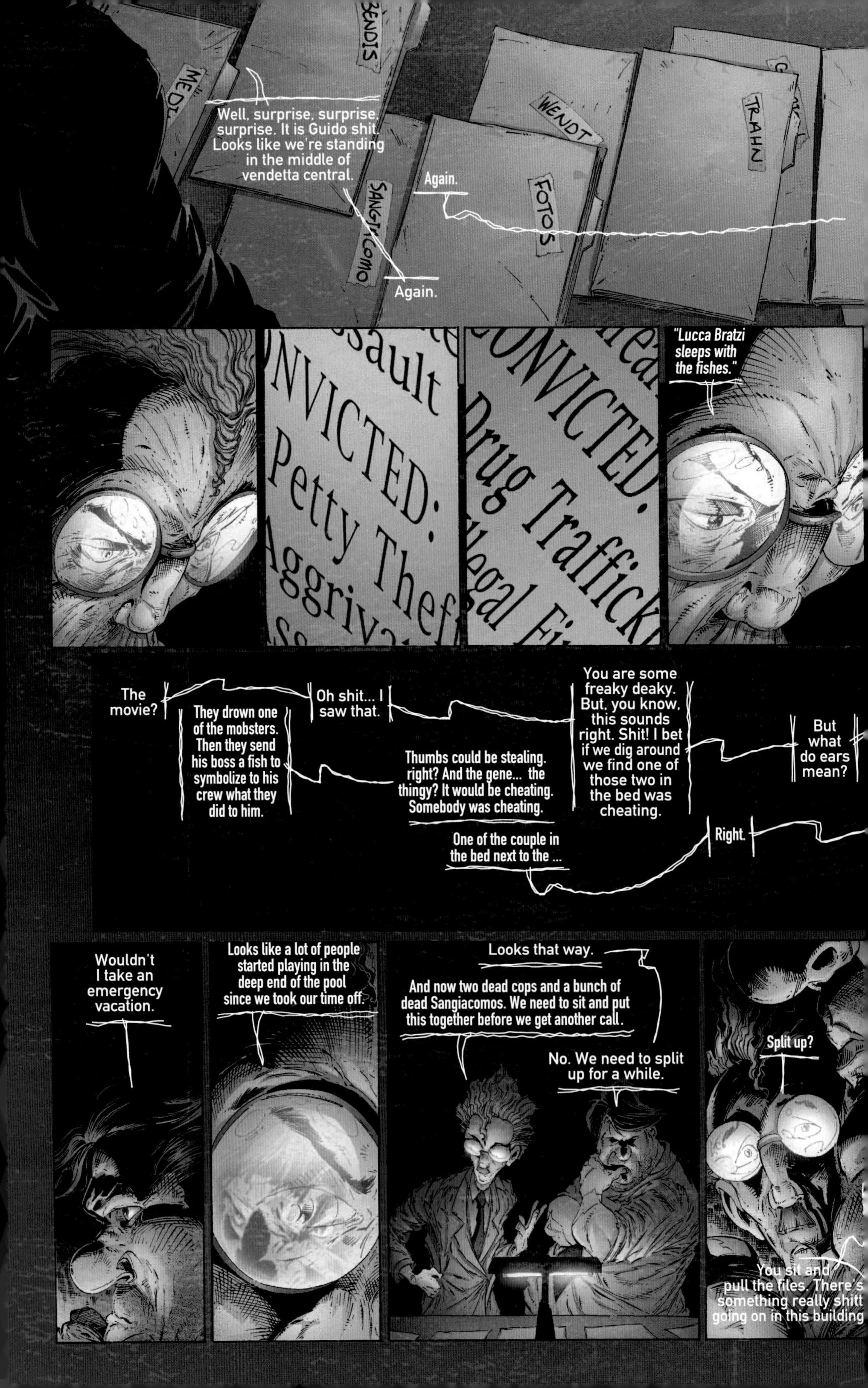

BENDIS
MEDI
WENDT
TRAHN
FOTOS
SANGIACOMO
Well, surprise, surprise, surprise. It is Guido shit. Looks like we're standing in the middle of vendetta central.
Again.
Again.
ssault
NVICTED:
Petty Thef
Aggrivat
ONVICTED:
Drug Traffick
"Lucca Bratzi sleeps with the fishes."
The movie?
They drown one of the mobsters. Then they send his boss a fish to symbolize to his crew what they did to him.
Oh shit... I saw that.
Thumbs could be stealing, right? And the gene... the thingy? It would be cheating. Somebody was cheating.
One of the couple in the bed next to the ...
You are some freaky deaky. But, you know, this sounds right. Shit! I bet if we dig around we find one of those two in the bed was cheating.
Right.
But what do ears mean?
Wouldn't I take an emergency vacation.
Looks like a lot of people started playing in the deep end of the pool since we took our time off.
Looks that way.
And now two dead cops and a bunch of dead Sangiacomos. We need to sit and put this together before we get another call.
No. We need to split up for a while.
Split up?
You sit and pull the files. There's something really shitt going on in this building

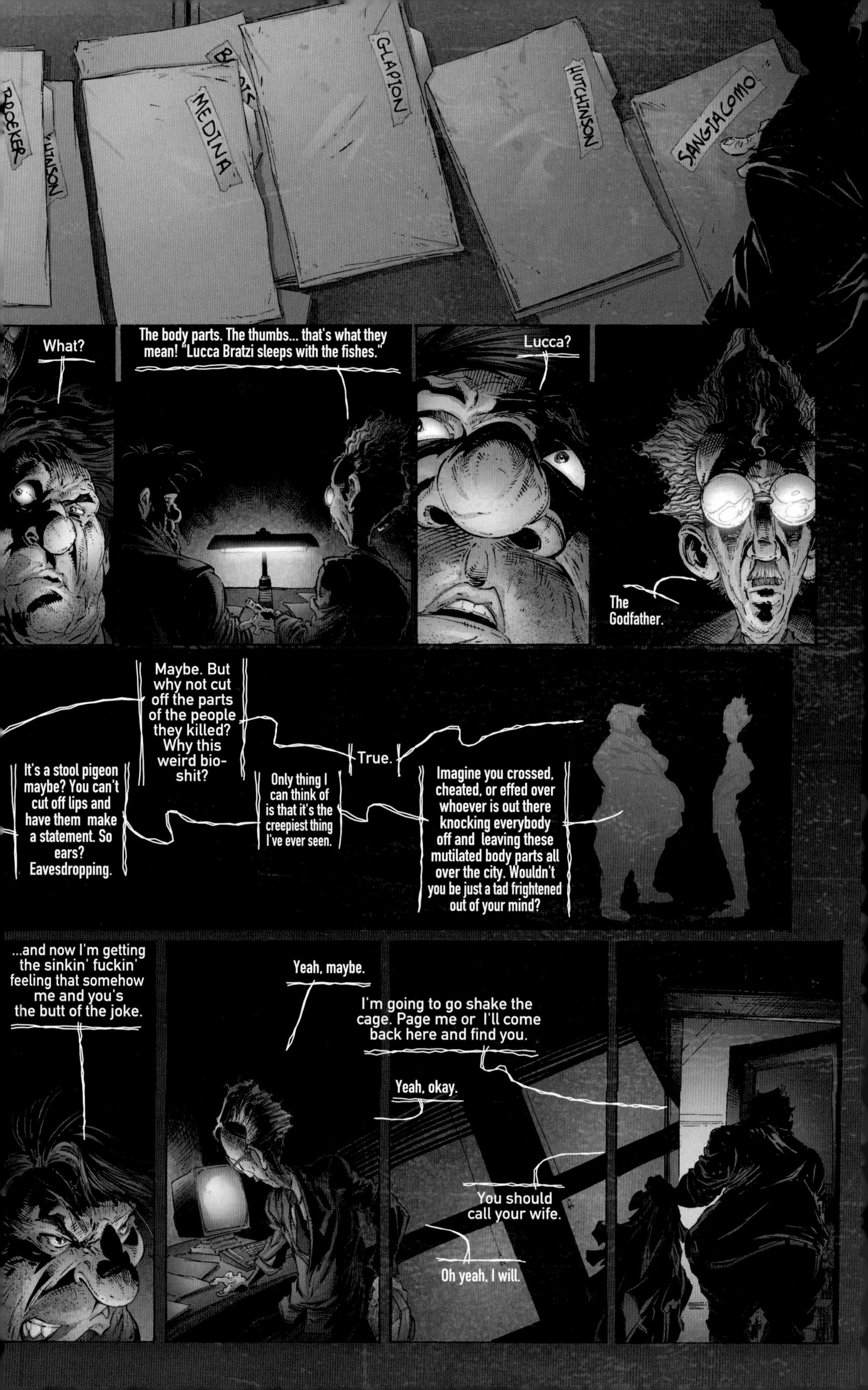
BROEKER
HUTCHINSON
MEDINA
GLAPION
HUTCHINSON
SANGIACOMO
What?
The body parts. The thumbs... that's what they mean! "Lucca Bratzi sleeps with the fishes."
Lucca?
The Godfather.
Maybe. But why not cut off the parts of the people they killed? Why this weird bio-shit?
True.
It's a stool pigeon maybe? You can't cut off lips and have them make a statement. So ears? Eavesdropping.
Only thing I can think of is that it's the creepiest thing I've ever seen.
Imagine you crossed, cheated, or effed over whoever is out there knocking everybody off and leaving these mutilated body parts all over the city. Wouldn't you be just a tad frightened out of your mind?
...and now I'm getting the sinkin' fuckin' feeling that somehow me and you's the butt of the joke.
Yeah, maybe.
I'm going to go shake the cage. Page me or I'll come back here and find you.
Yeah, okay.
You should call your wife.
Oh yeah, I will.

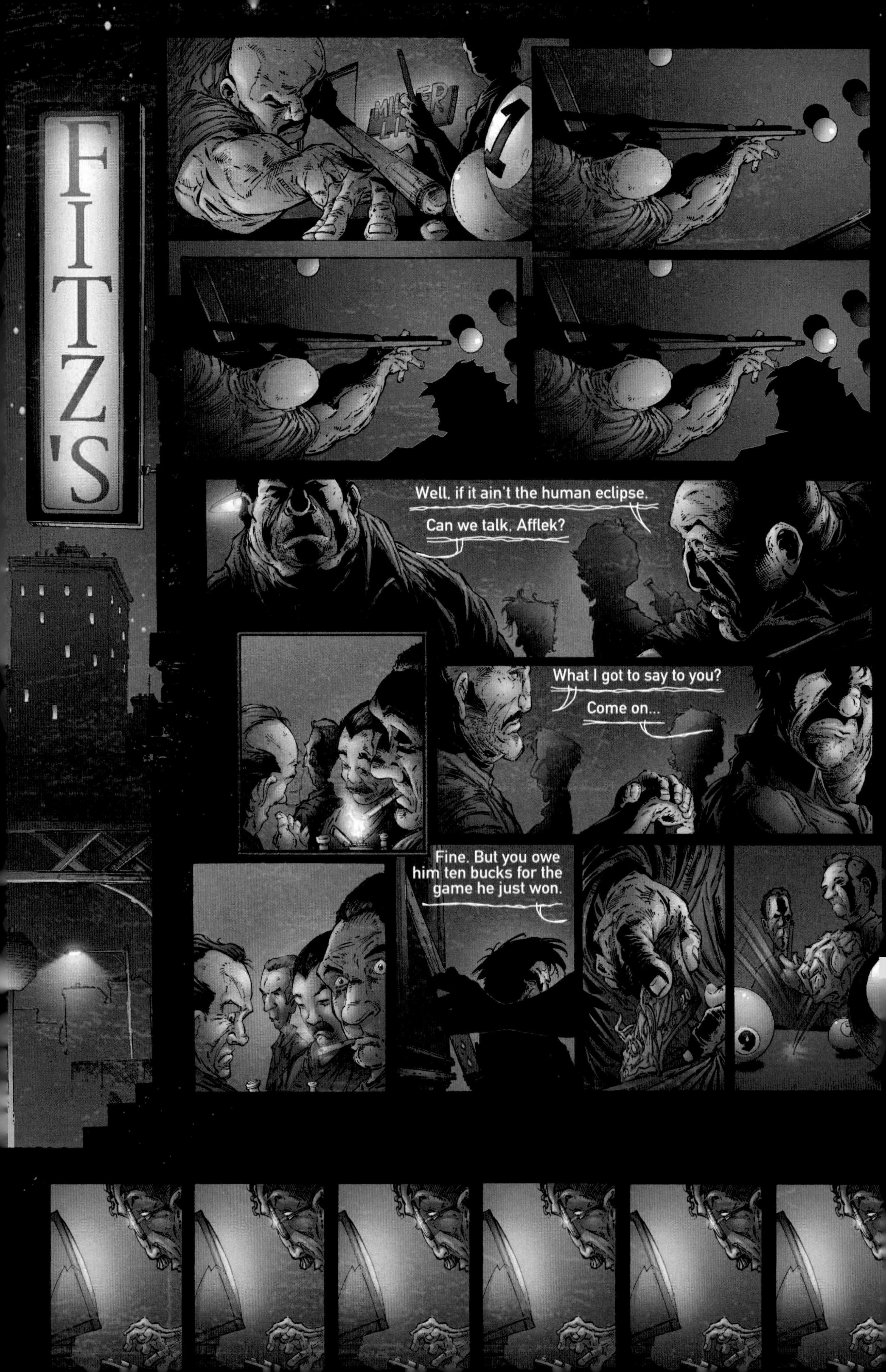

FITZ'S
MILLER LITE
Well, if it ain't the human eclipse.
Can we talk, Afflek?
What I got to say to you?
Come on...
Fine. But you owe him ten bucks for the game he just won.

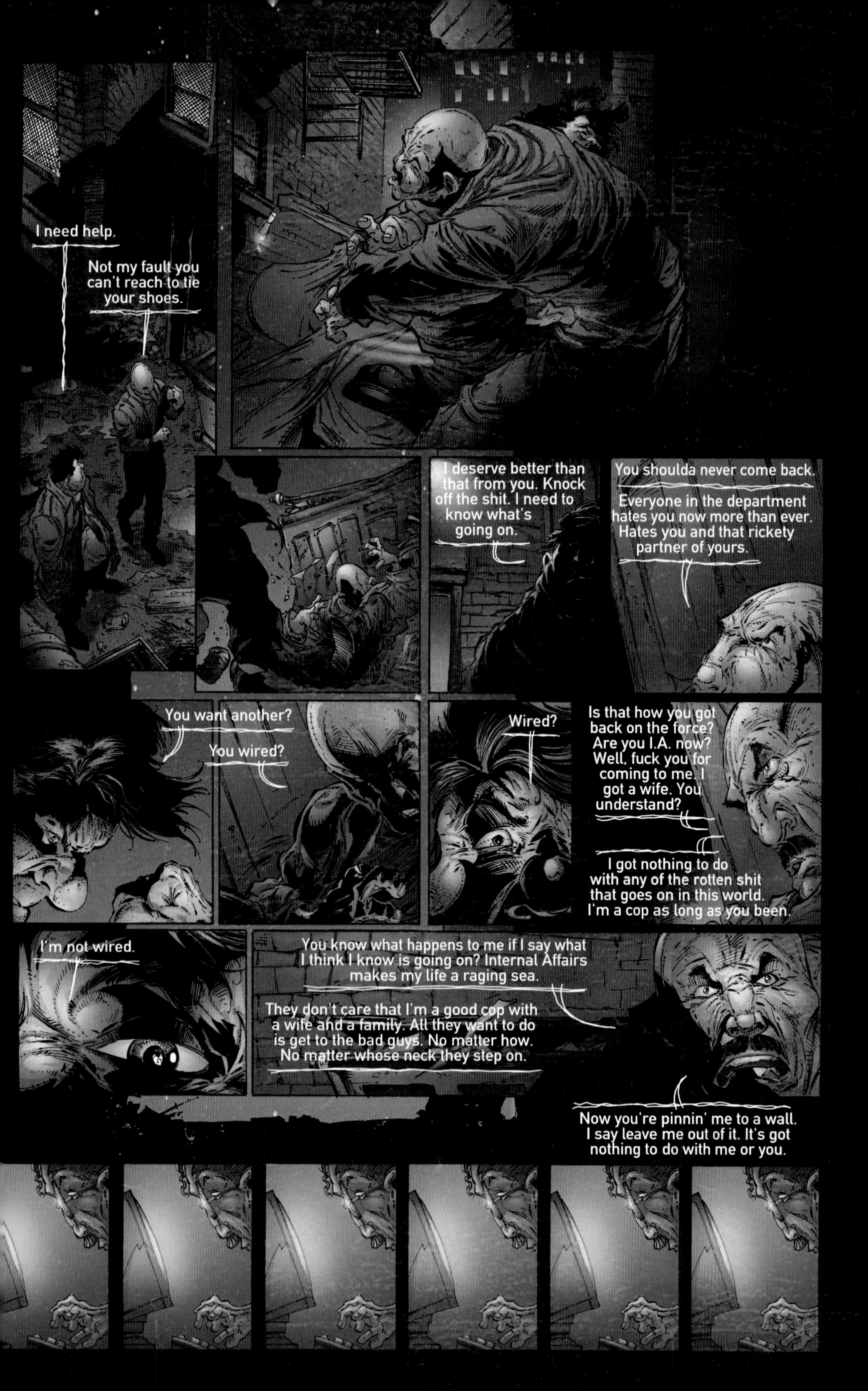

I need help.
Not my fault you can't reach to tie your shoes.
I deserve better than that from you. Knock off the shit. I need to know what's going on.
You shoulda never come back.
Everyone in the department hates you now more than ever. Hates you and that rickety partner of yours.
You want another?
You wired?
Wired?
Is that how you got back on the force? Are you I.A. now? Well, fuck you for coming to me. I got a wife. You understand?
I got nothing to do with any of the rotten shit that goes on in this world. I'm a cop as long as you been.
I'm not wired.
You know what happens to me if I say what I think I know is going on? Internal Affairs makes my life a raging sea.
They don't care that I'm a good cop with a wife and a family. All they want to do is get to the bad guys. No matter how. No matter whose neck they step on.
Now you're pinnin' me to a wall. I say leave me out of it. It's got nothing to do with me or you.

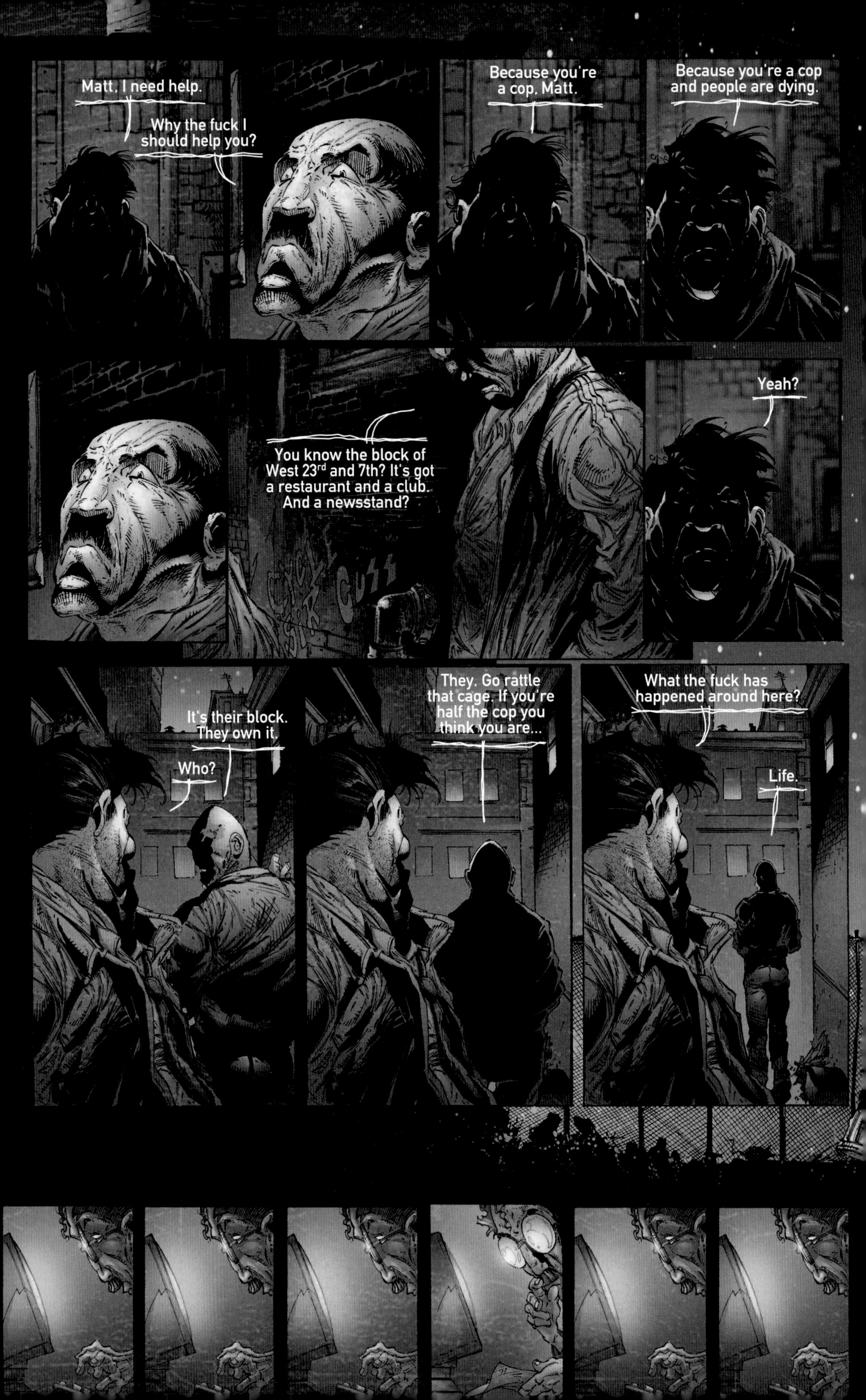

Matt, I need help.
Why the fuck I should help you?
Because you're a cop, Matt.
Because you're a cop and people are dying.
Yeah?
You know the block of West 23rd and 7th? It's got a restaurant and a club. And a newsstand?
It's their block. They own it.
Who?
They. Go rattle that cage. If you're half the cop you think you are...
What the fuck has happened around here?
Life.

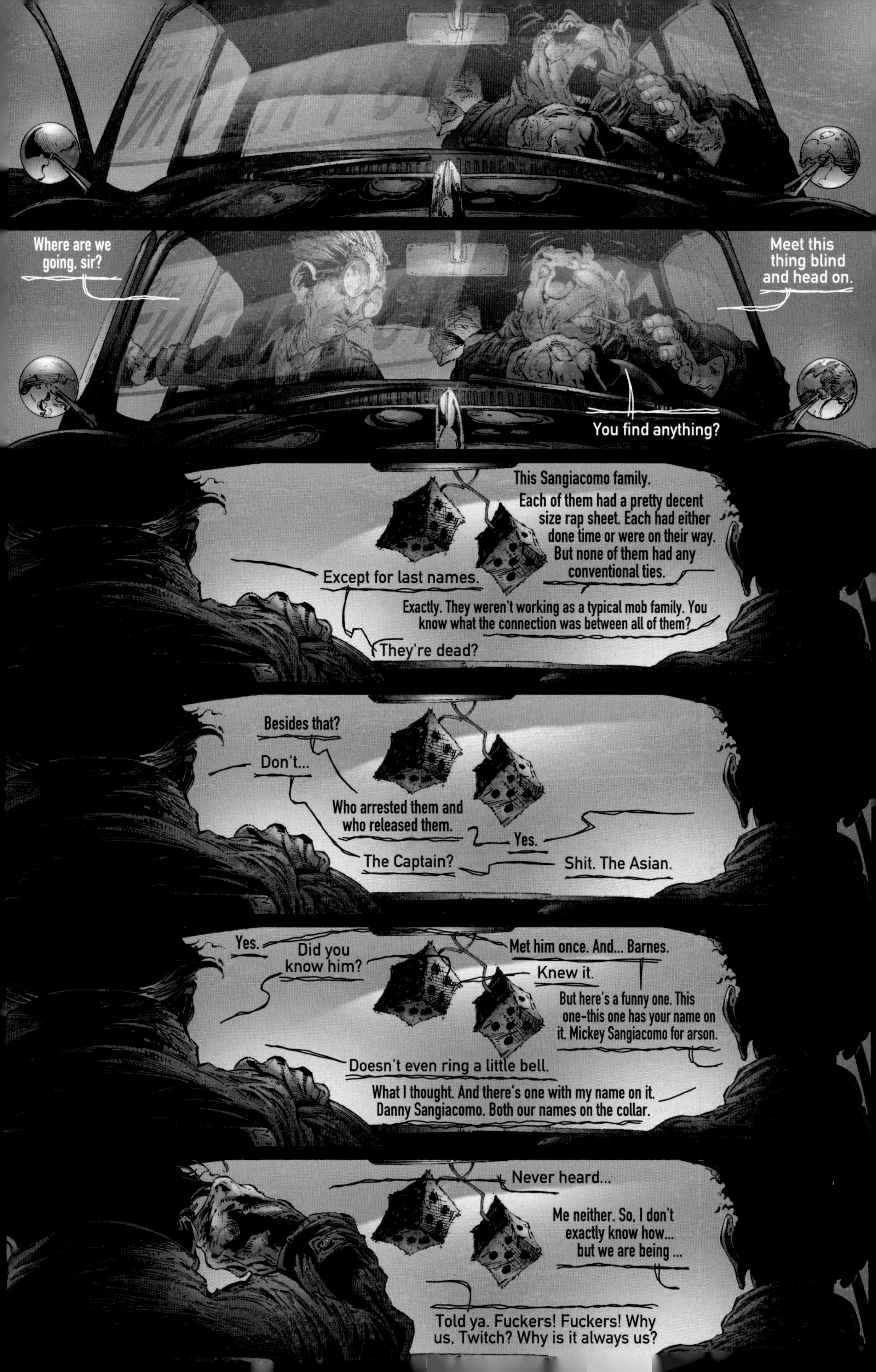
Where are we going, sir?
Meet this thing blind and head on.
You find anything?
This Sangiacomo family.
Each of them had a pretty decent size rap sheet. Each had either done time or were on their way. But none of them had any conventional ties.
Except for last names.
Exactly. They weren't working as a typical mob family. You know what the connection was between all of them?
They're dead?
Besides that?
Don't...
Who arrested them and who released them.
Yes.
The Captain?
Shit. The Asian.
Yes.
Did you know him?
Met him once. And... Barnes.
Knew it.
But here's a funny one. This one–this one has your name on it. Mickey Sangiacomo for arson.
Doesn't even ring a little bell.
What I thought. And there's one with my name on it. Danny Sangiacomo. Both our names on the collar.
Never heard...
Me neither. So, I don't exactly know how... but we are being ...
Told ya. Fuckers! Fuckers! Why us, Twitch? Why is it always us?

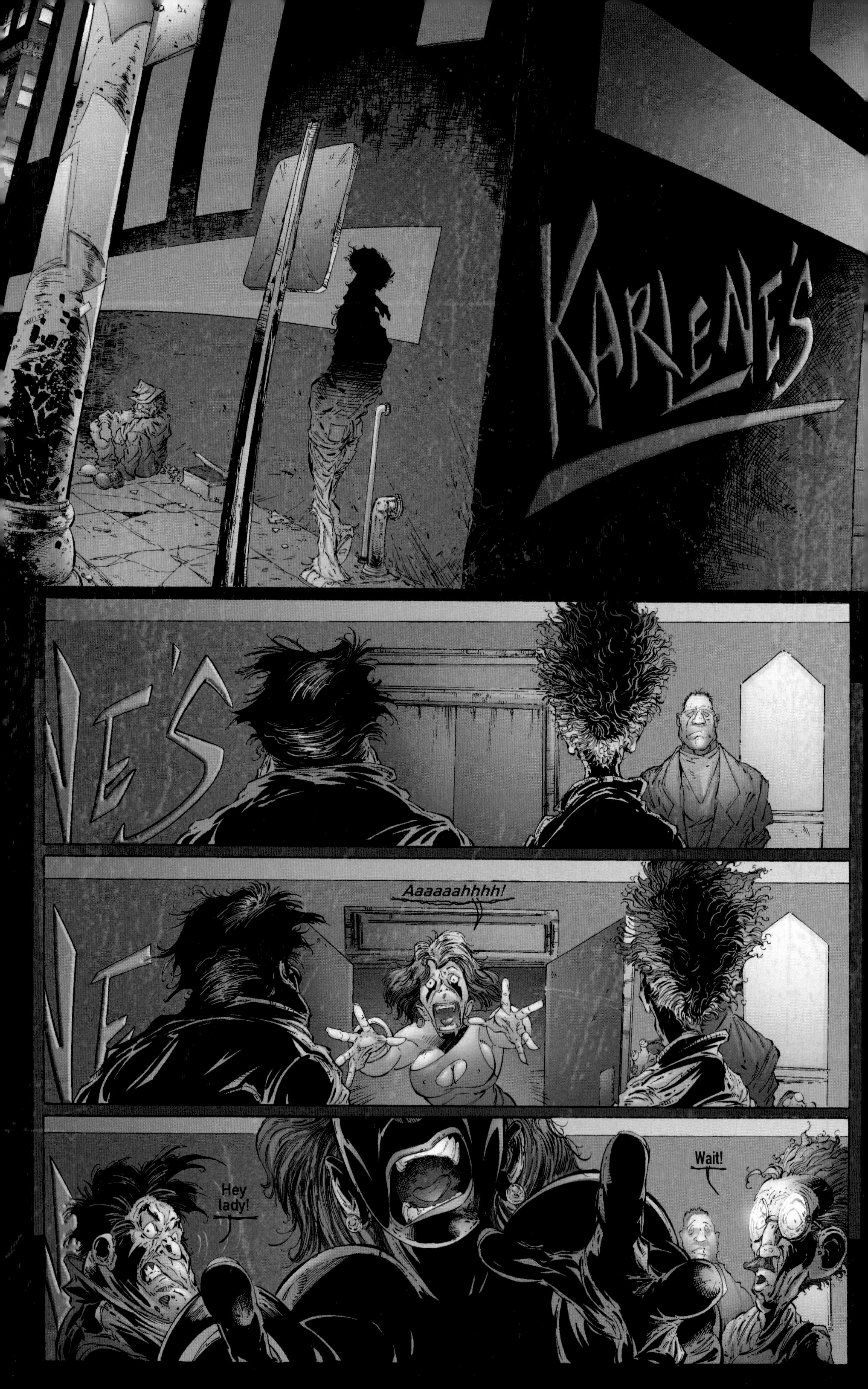
KARLENE'S
Aaaaaahhhh!
Hey lady!
Wait!

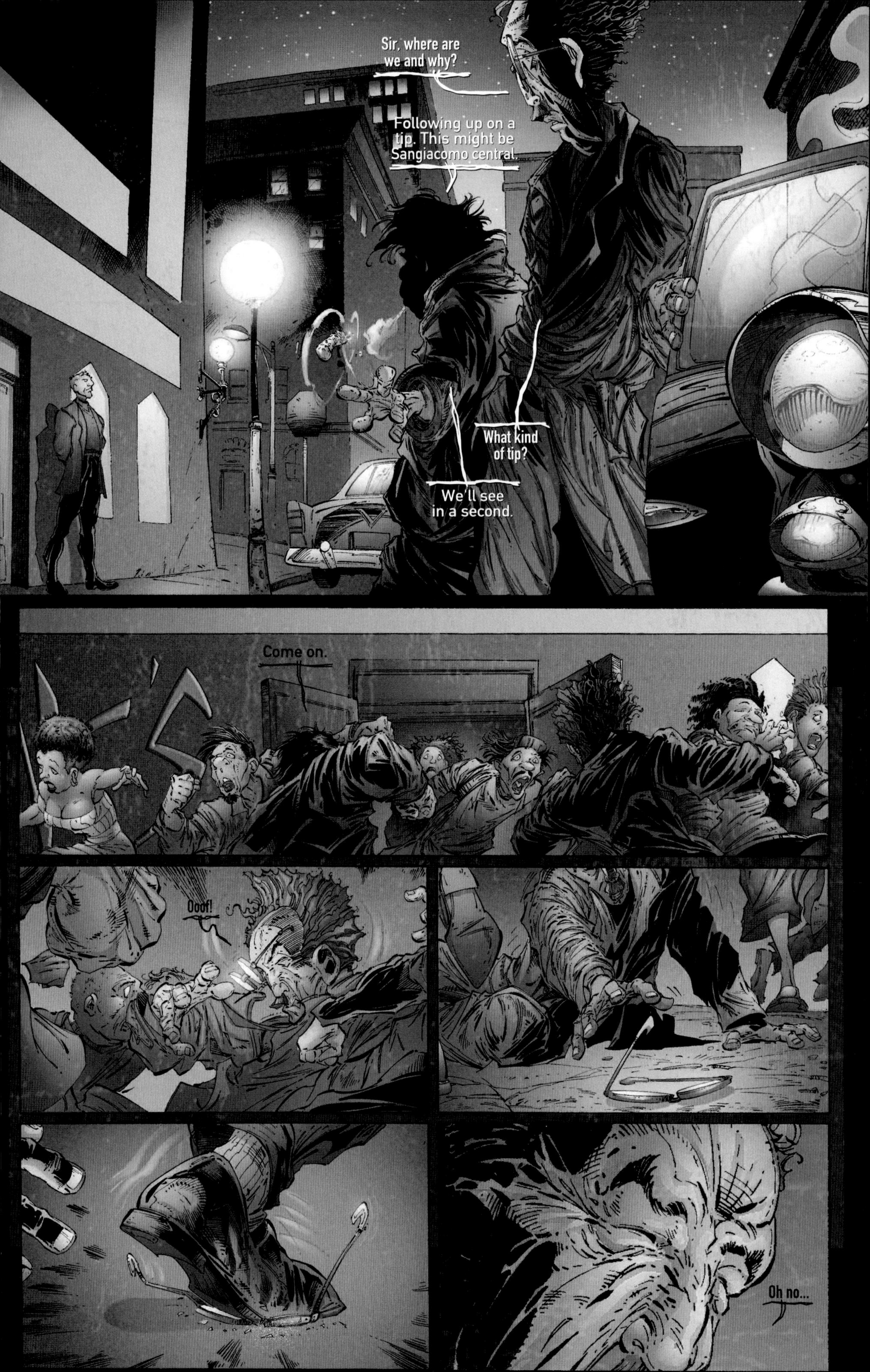
Sir, where are we and why?
Following up on a tip. This might be Sangiacomo central.
What kind of tip?
We'll see in a second.
Come on.
Ooof!
Oh no...

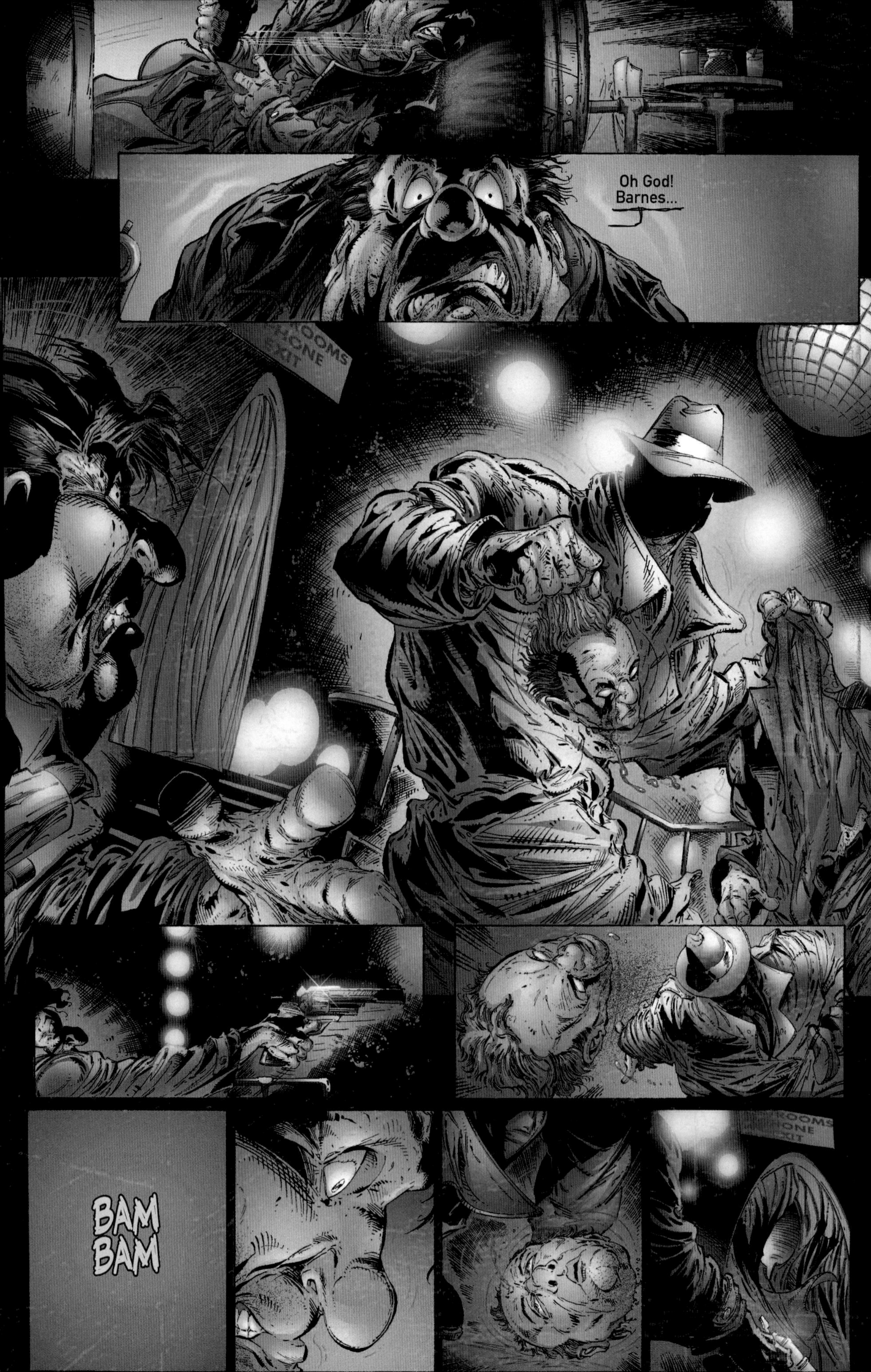
Oh God!
Barnes...
BAM
BAM

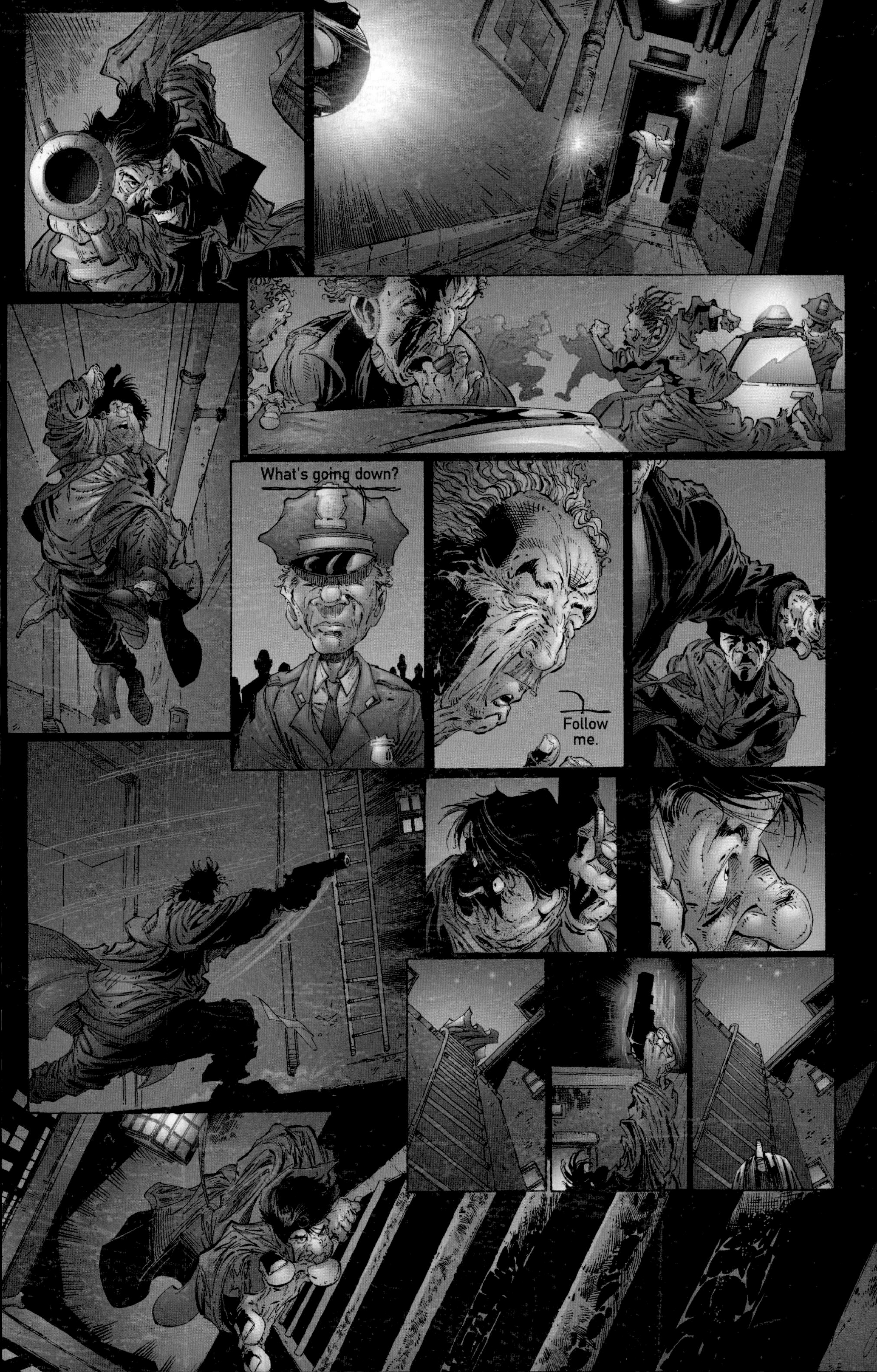
What's going down?
Follow me.

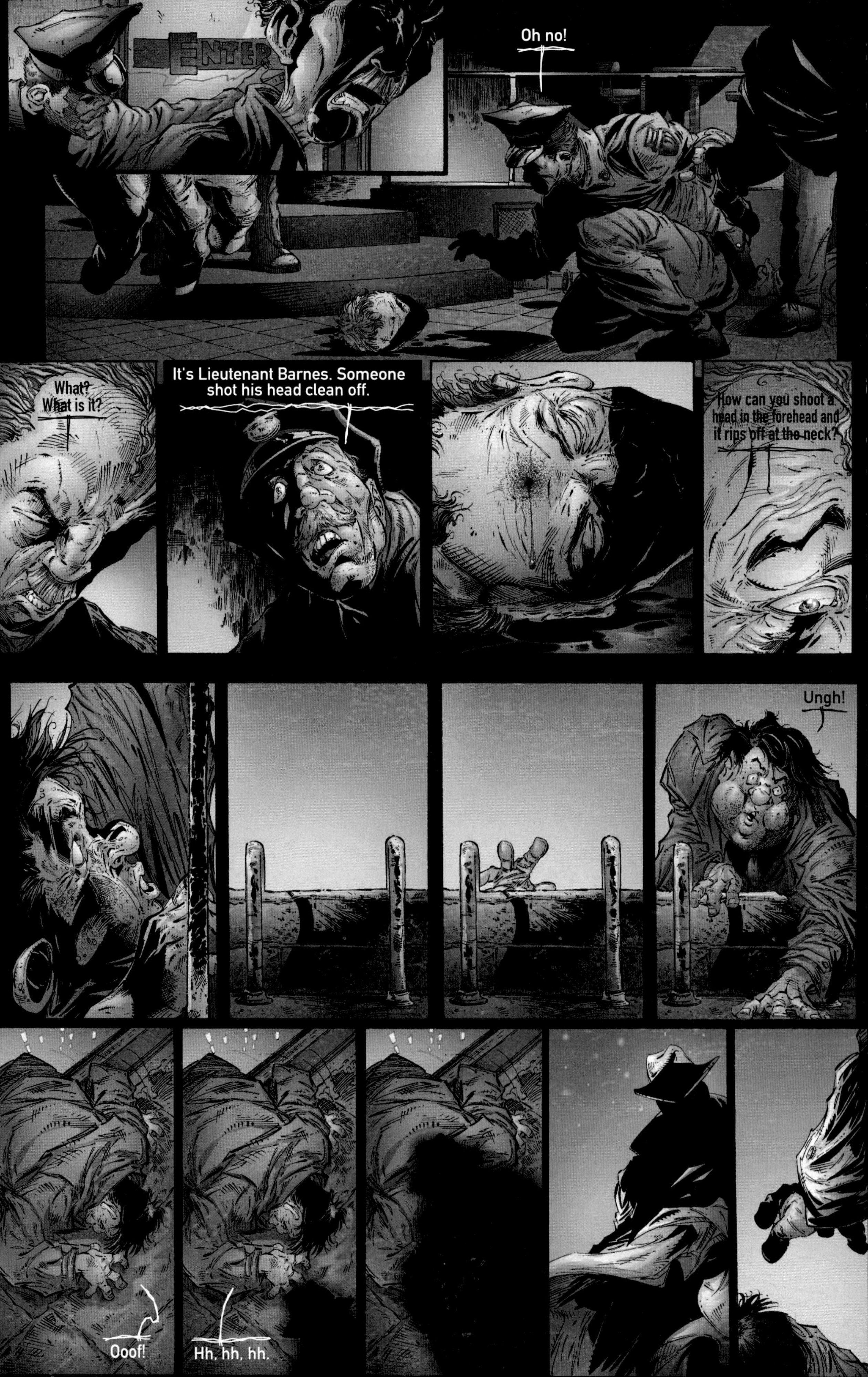

ENTER
Oh no!
What? What is it?
It's Lieutenant Barnes. Someone shot his head clean off.
How can you shoot a head in the forehead and it rips off at the neck?
Ungh!
Ooof!
Hh, hh, hh.

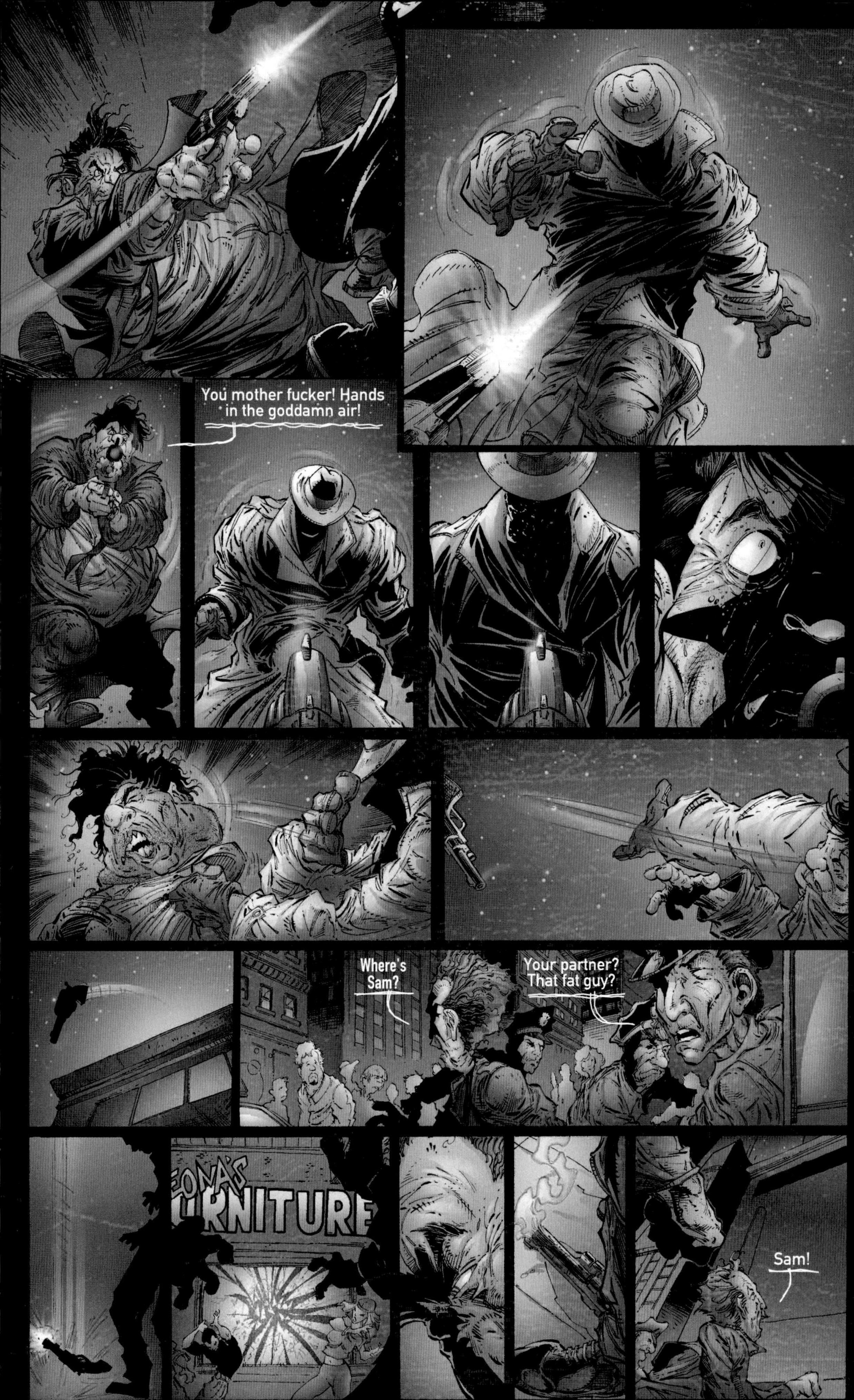
You mother fucker! Hands in the goddamn air!
Where's Sam?
Your partner? That fat guy?
ONA'S
RNITURE
Sam!

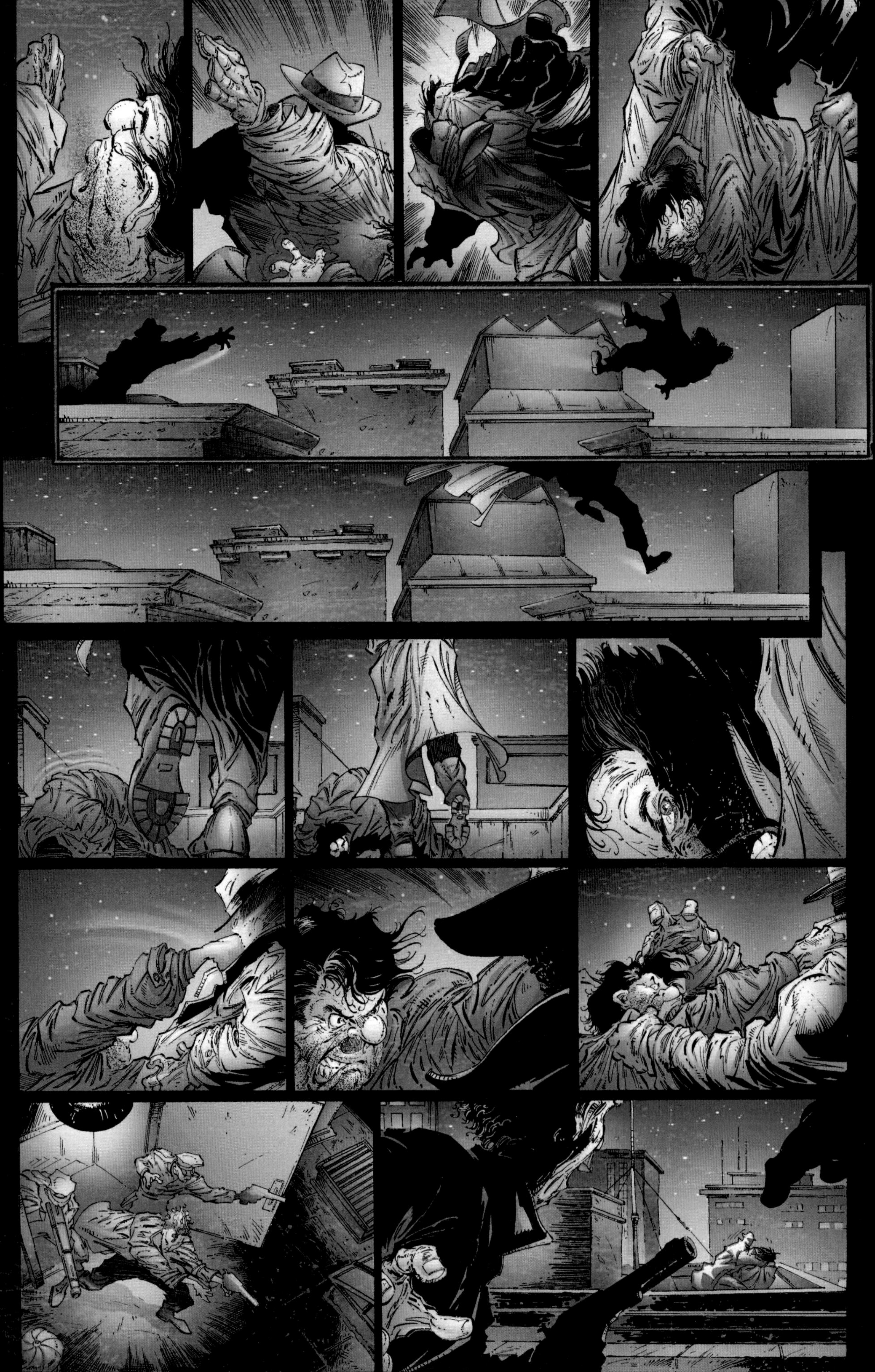

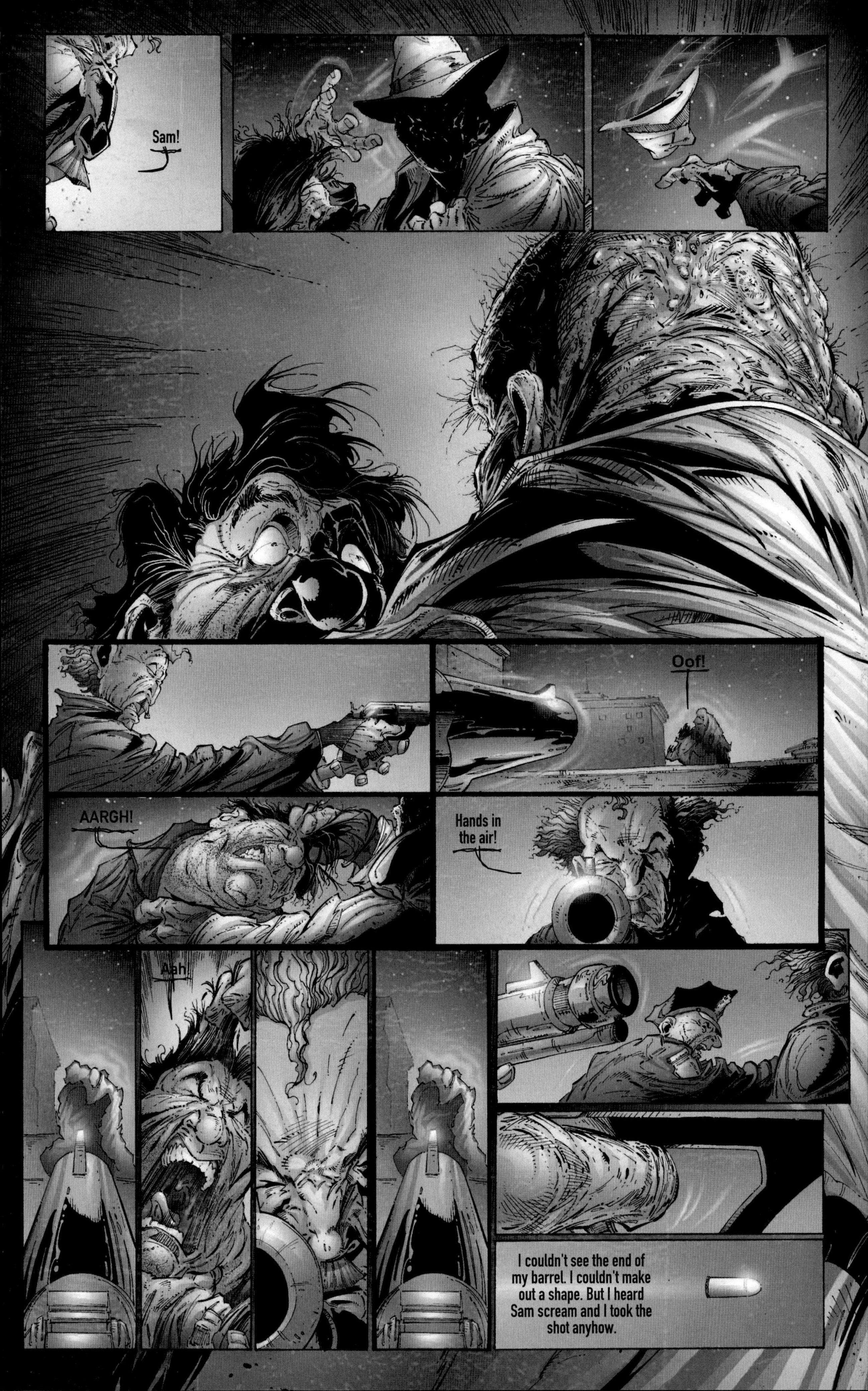
Sam!
Oof!
AARGH!
Hands in the air!
Aah!
I couldn't see the end of my barrel. I couldn't make out a shape. But I heard Sam scream and I took the shot anyhow.

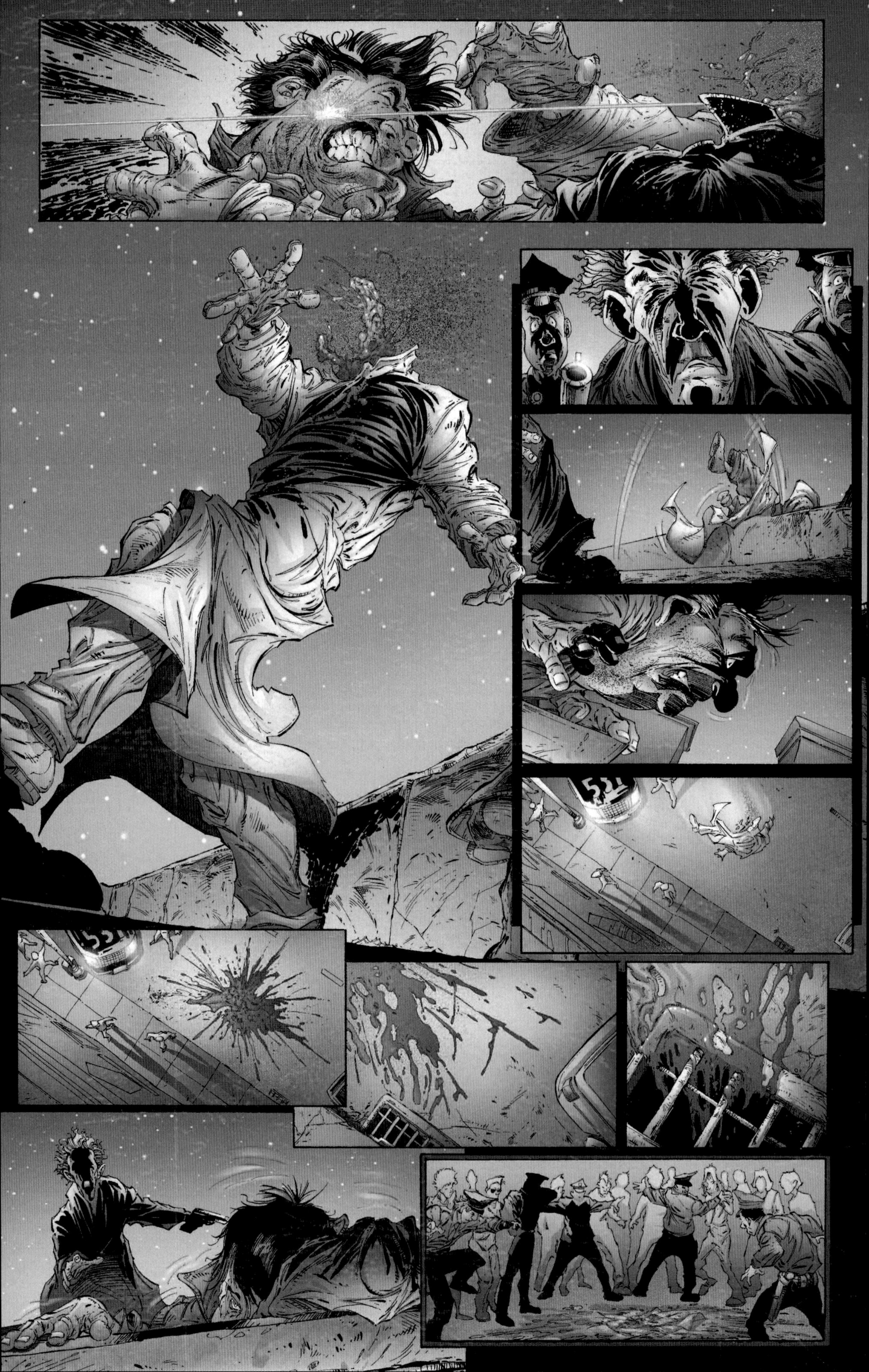

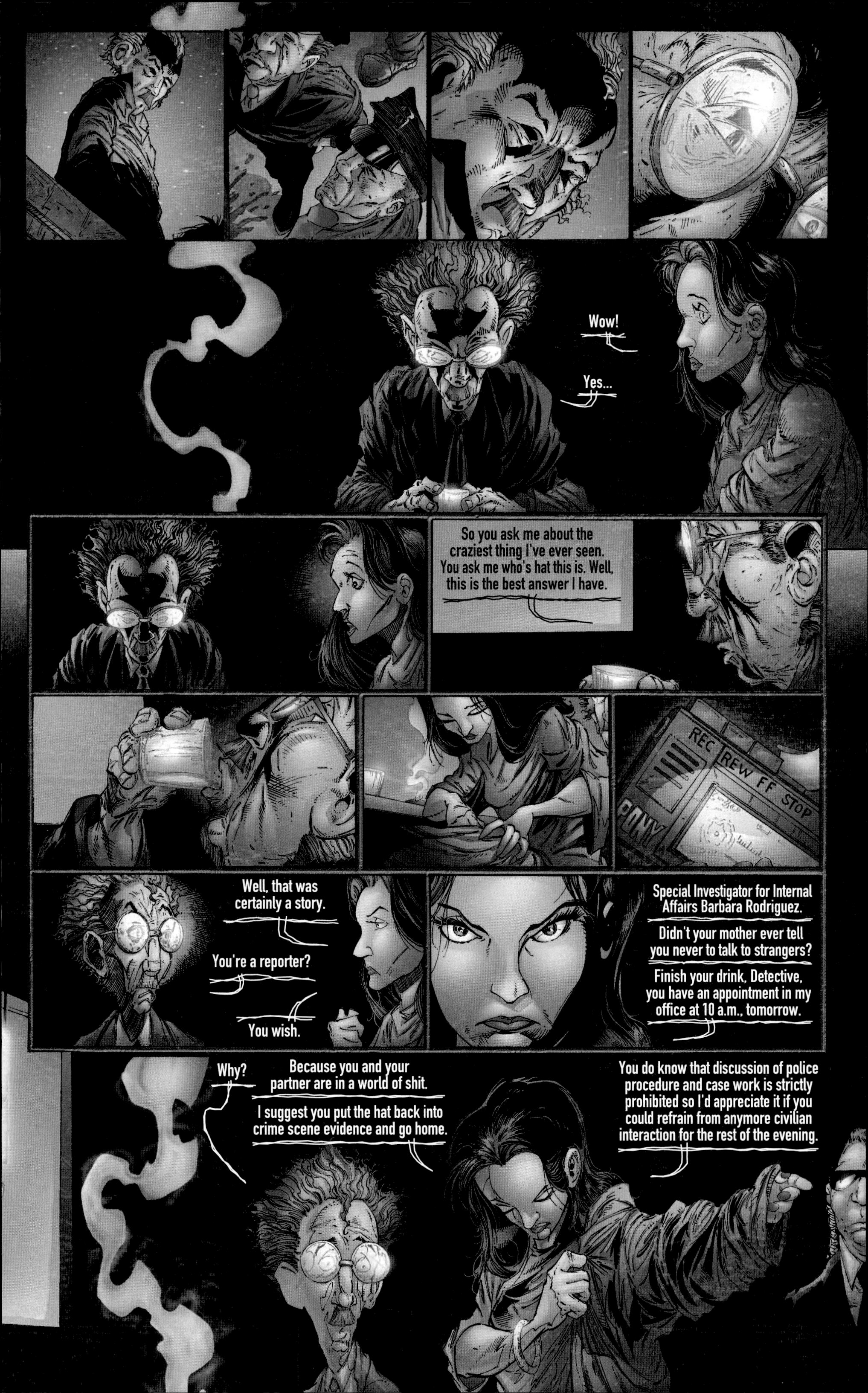

Wow!
Yes...
So you ask me about the craziest thing I've ever seen. You ask me who's hat this is. Well, this is the best answer I have.
REC REW FF STOP
Well, that was certainly a story.
You're a reporter?
You wish.
Special Investigator for Internal Affairs Barbara Rodriguez.
Didn't your mother ever tell you never to talk to strangers?
Finish your drink, Detective, you have an appointment in my office at 10 a.m., tomorrow.
Why?
Because you and your partner are in a world of shit.
I suggest you put the hat back into crime scene evidence and go home.
You do know that discussion of police procedure and case work is strictly prohibited so I'd appreciate it if you could refrain from anymore civilian interaction for the rest of the evening.

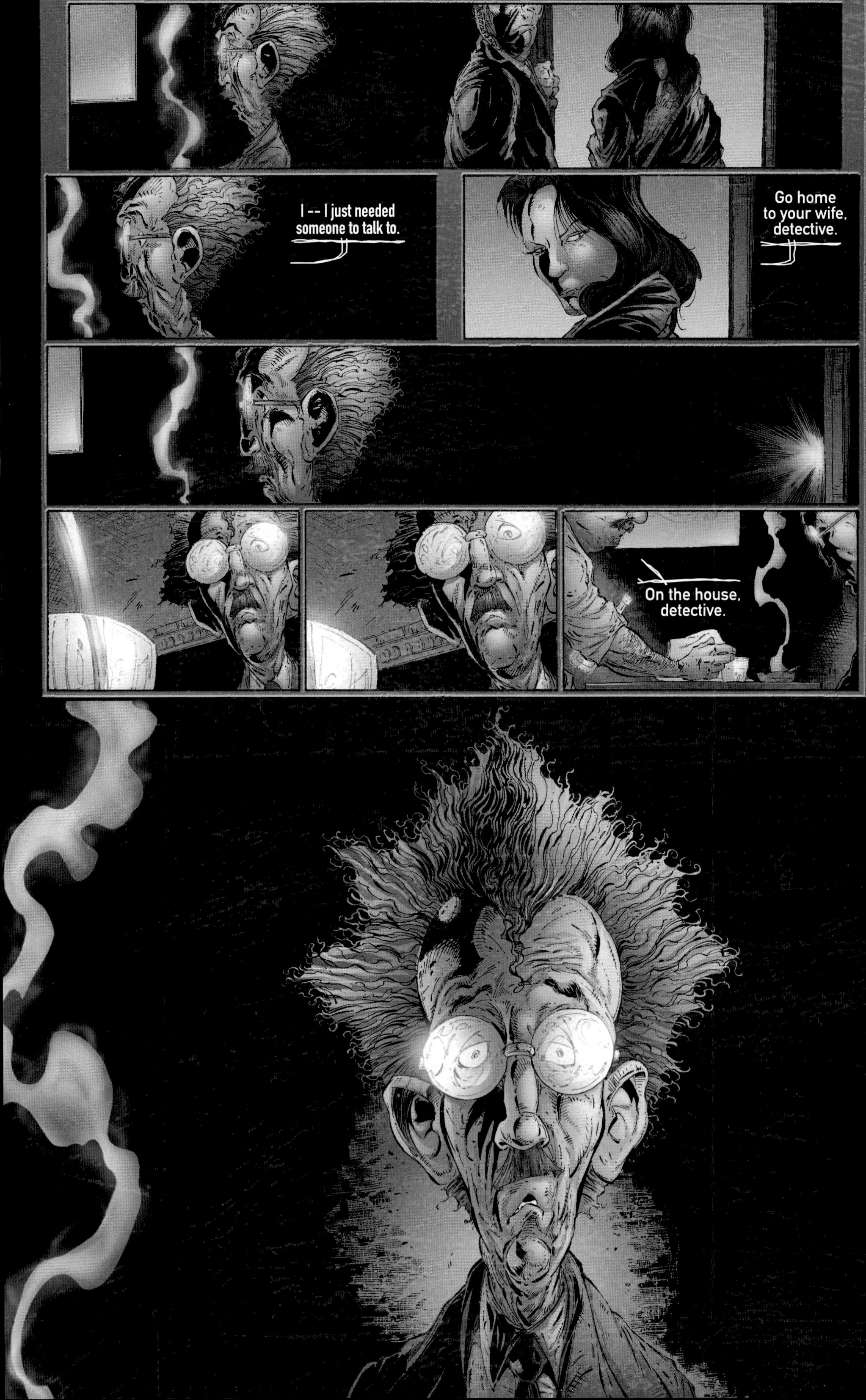

I -- I just needed someone to talk to.
Go home to your wife, detective.
On the house, detective.

01 02 03 04 05 06 07 08 09 10 11 12 13

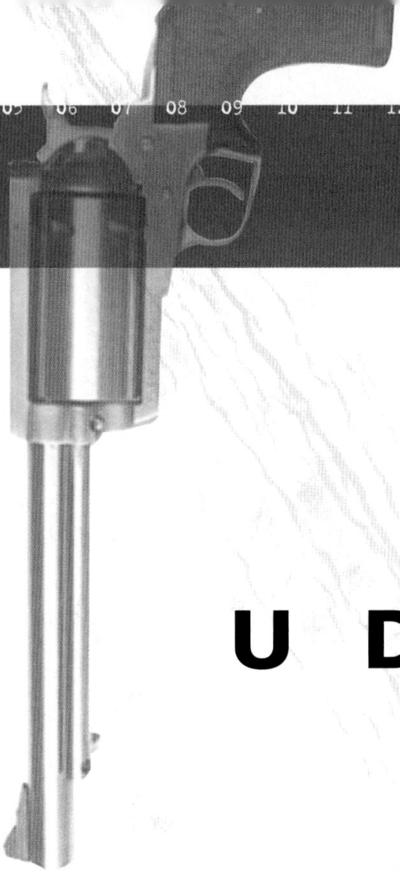

U D A K U

P A R T 3

SAM AND TWITCH

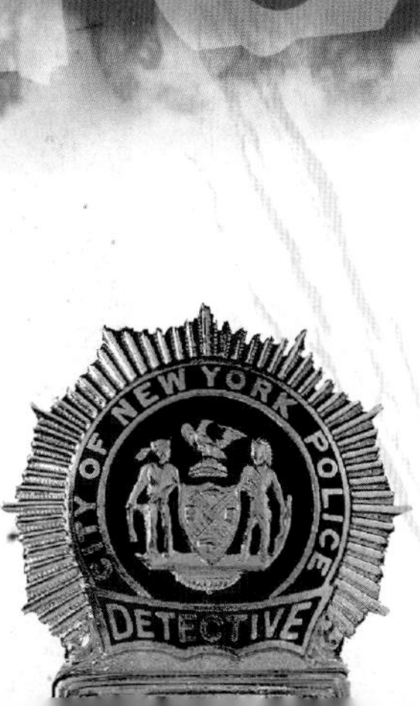
CITY OF NEW YORK POLICE
DETECTIVE

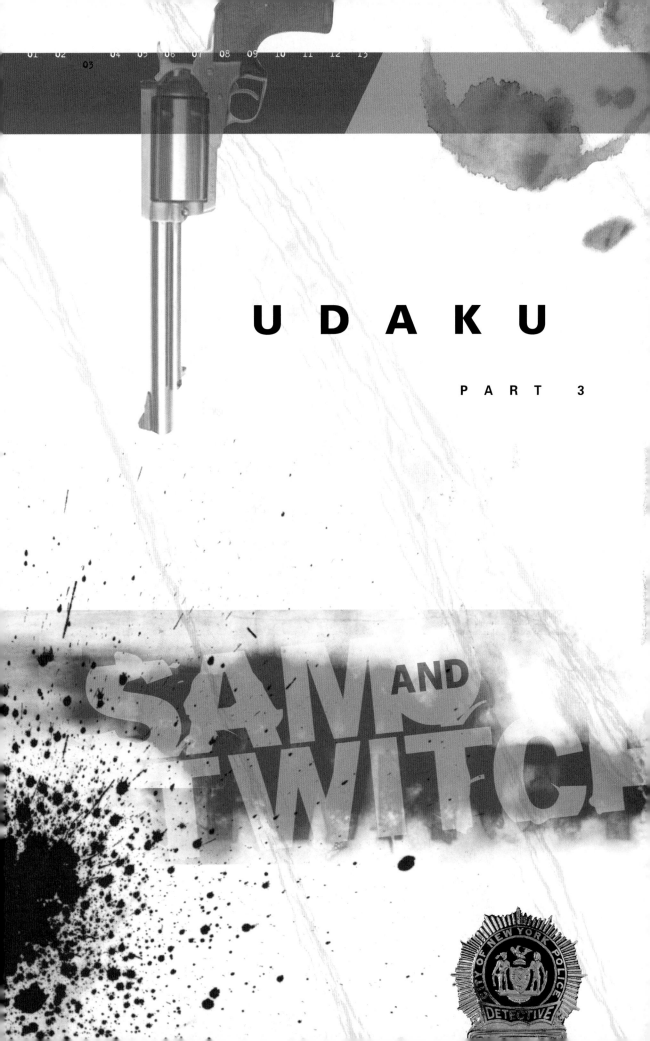

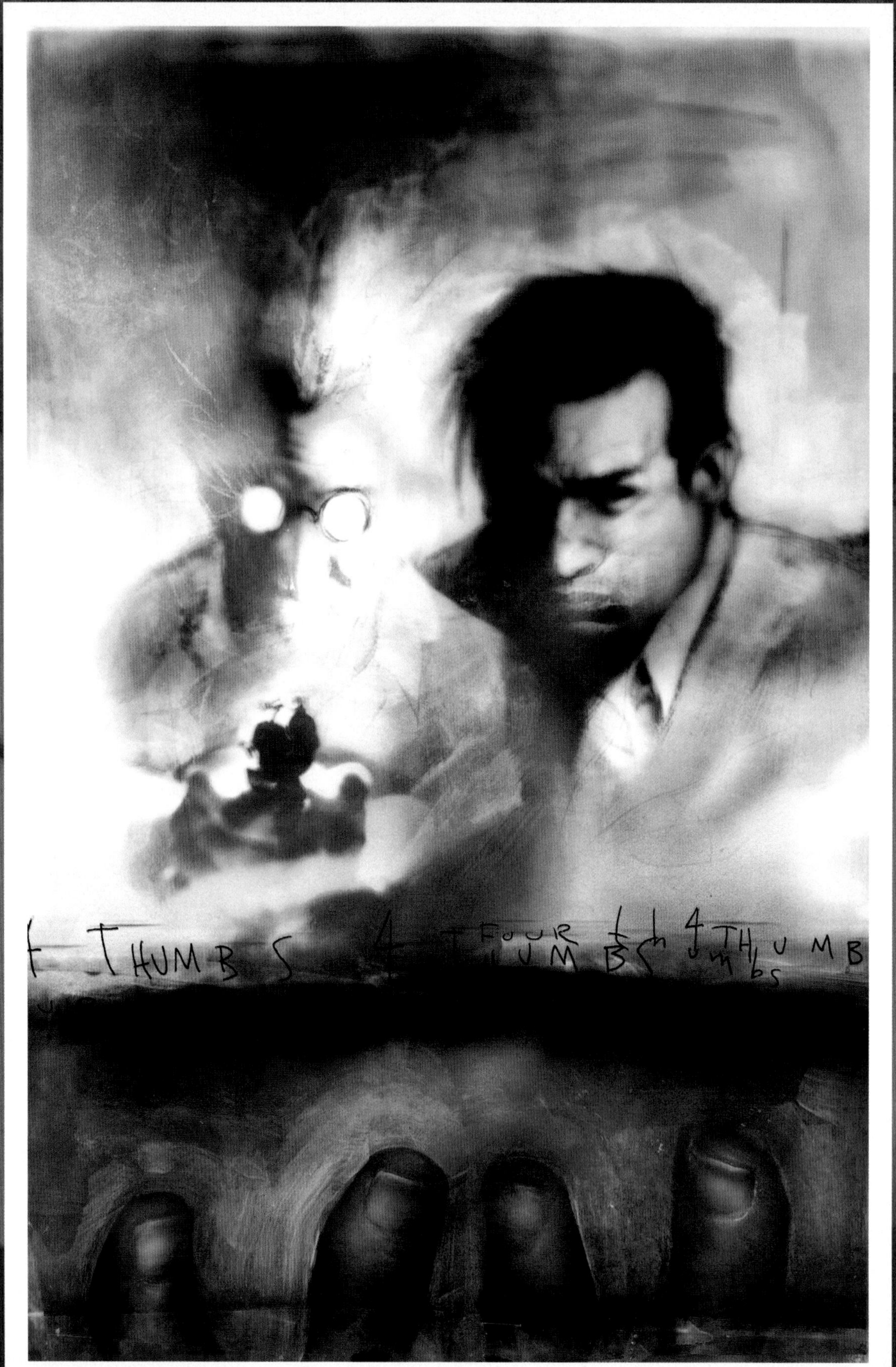
THUMBS 4 FOUR 4 THUMB

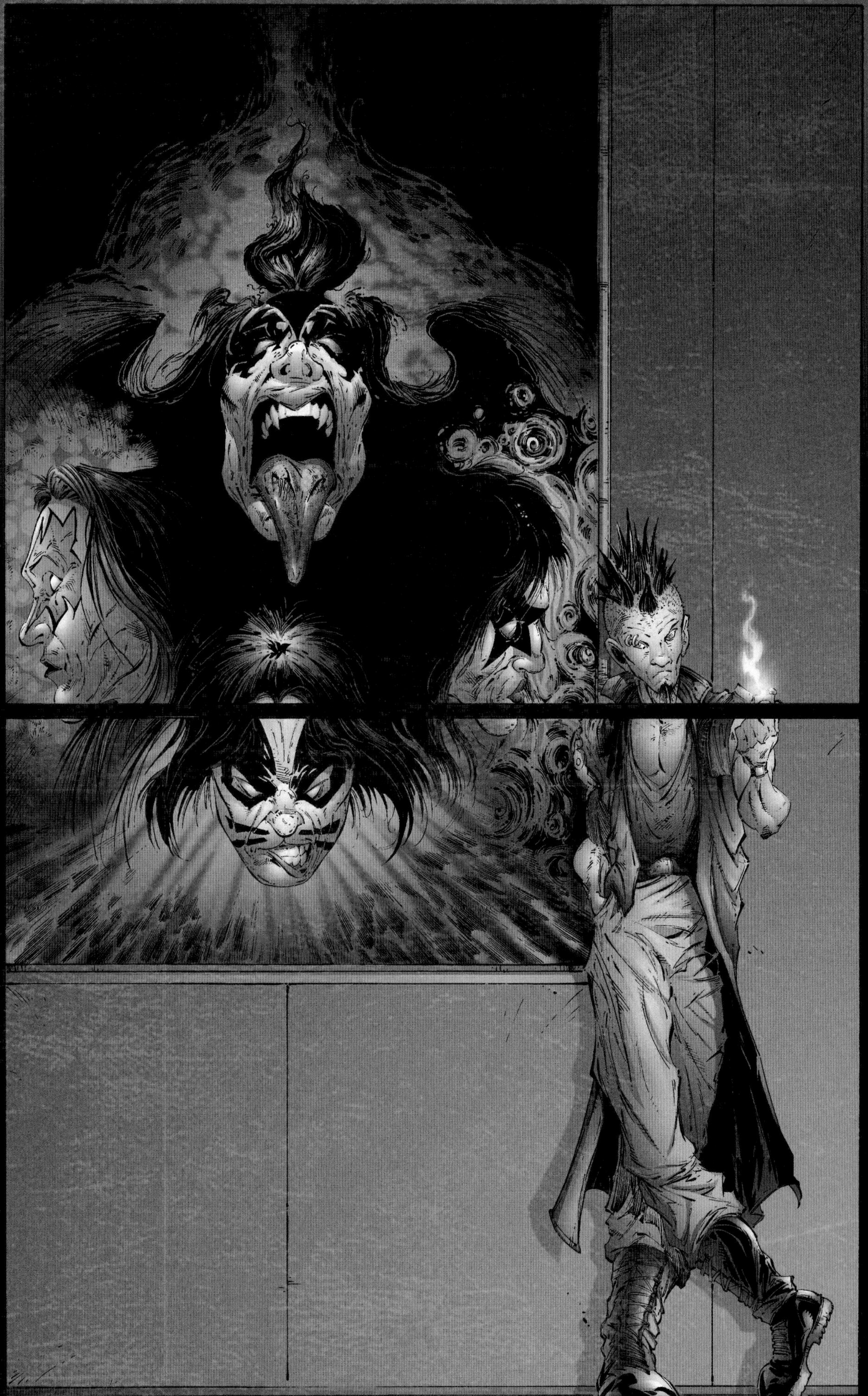

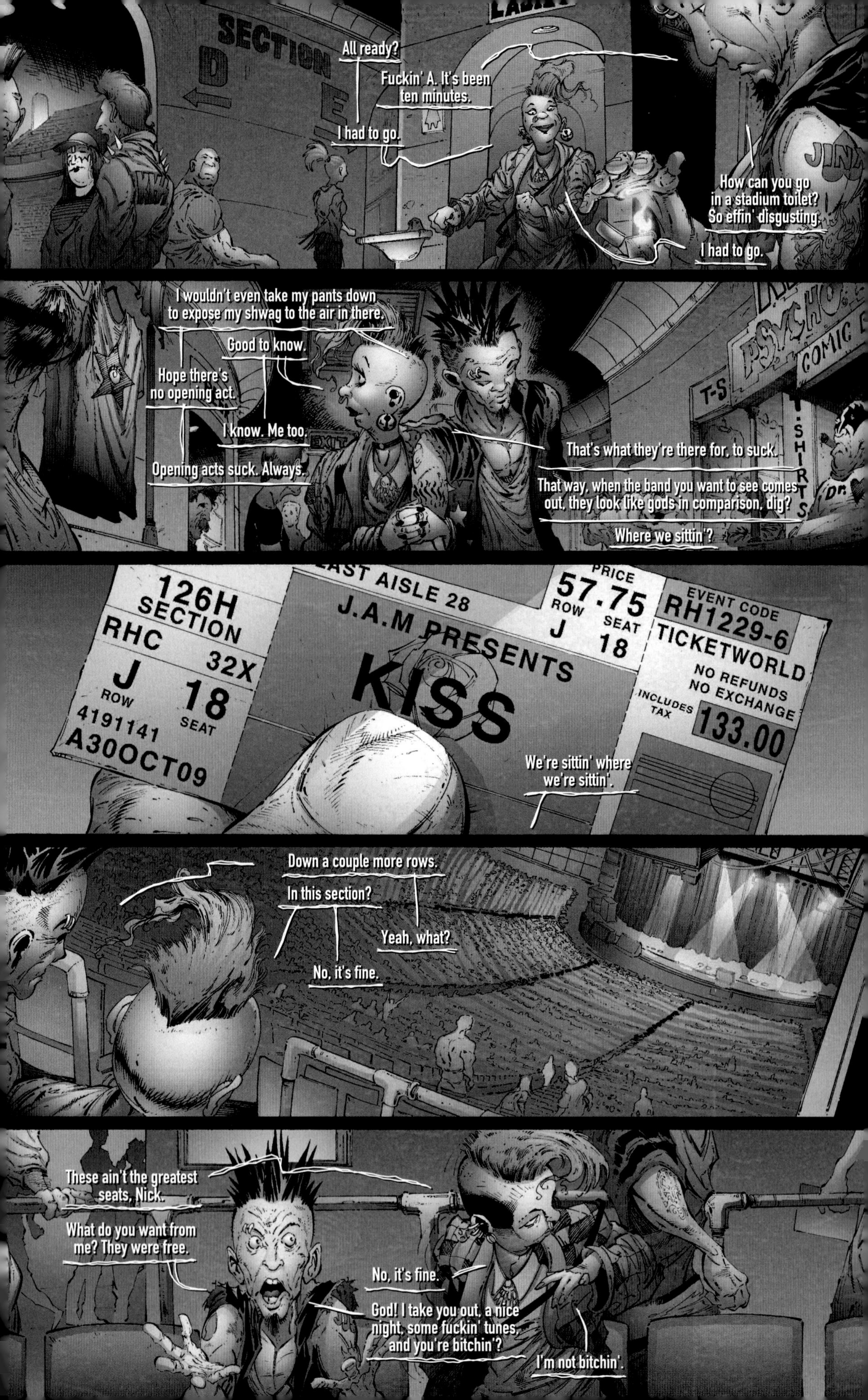
SECTION
D
E
All ready?
Fuckin' A. It's been ten minutes.
I had to go.
How can you go in a stadium toilet? So effin' disgusting.
I had to go.
I wouldn't even take my pants down to expose my shwag to the air in there.
Good to know.
Hope there's no opening act.
I know. Me too.
Opening acts suck. Always.
That's what they're there for, to suck.
That way, when the band you want to see comes out, they look like gods in comparison, dig?
Where we sittin'?
126H SECTION
RHC 32X
J ROW 18 SEAT
4191141
A30OCT09
EAST AISLE 28
J.A.M PRESENTS
KISS
PRICE 57.75
ROW J SEAT 18
EVENT CODE RH1229-6
TICKETWORLD
NO REFUNDS NO EXCHANGE
INCLUDES TAX 133.00
We're sittin' where we're sittin'.
Down a couple more rows.
In this section?
Yeah, what?
No, it's fine.
These ain't the greatest seats, Nick.
What do you want from me? They were free.
No, it's fine.
God! I take you out, a nice night, some fuckin' tunes, and you're bitchin'?
I'm not bitchin'.

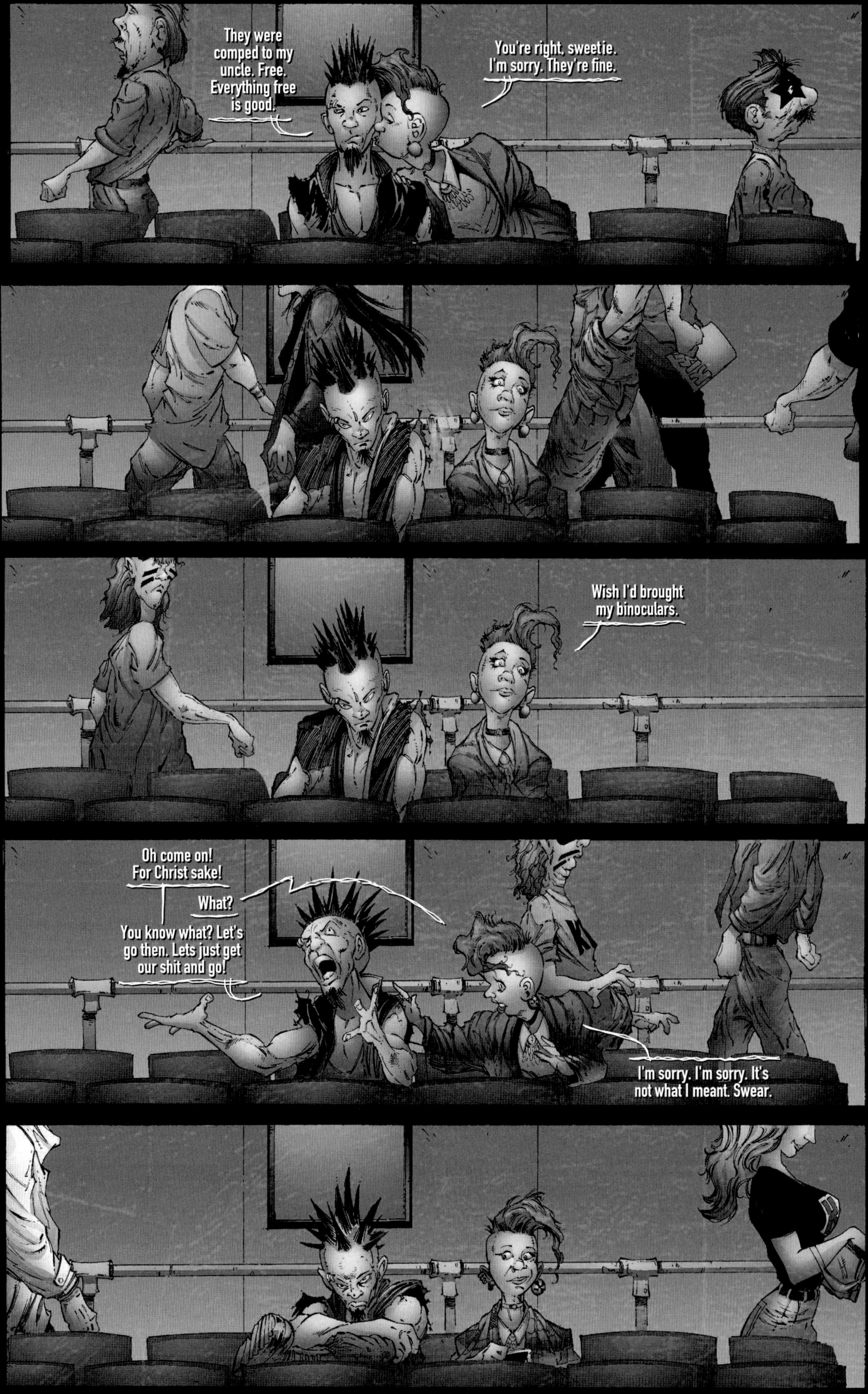
They were comped to my uncle. Free. Everything free is good.
You're right, sweetie. I'm sorry. They're fine.
Wish I'd brought my binoculars.
Oh come on! For Christ sake!
What?
You know what? Let's go then. Lets just get our shit and go!
I'm sorry, I'm sorry. It's not what I meant. Swear.

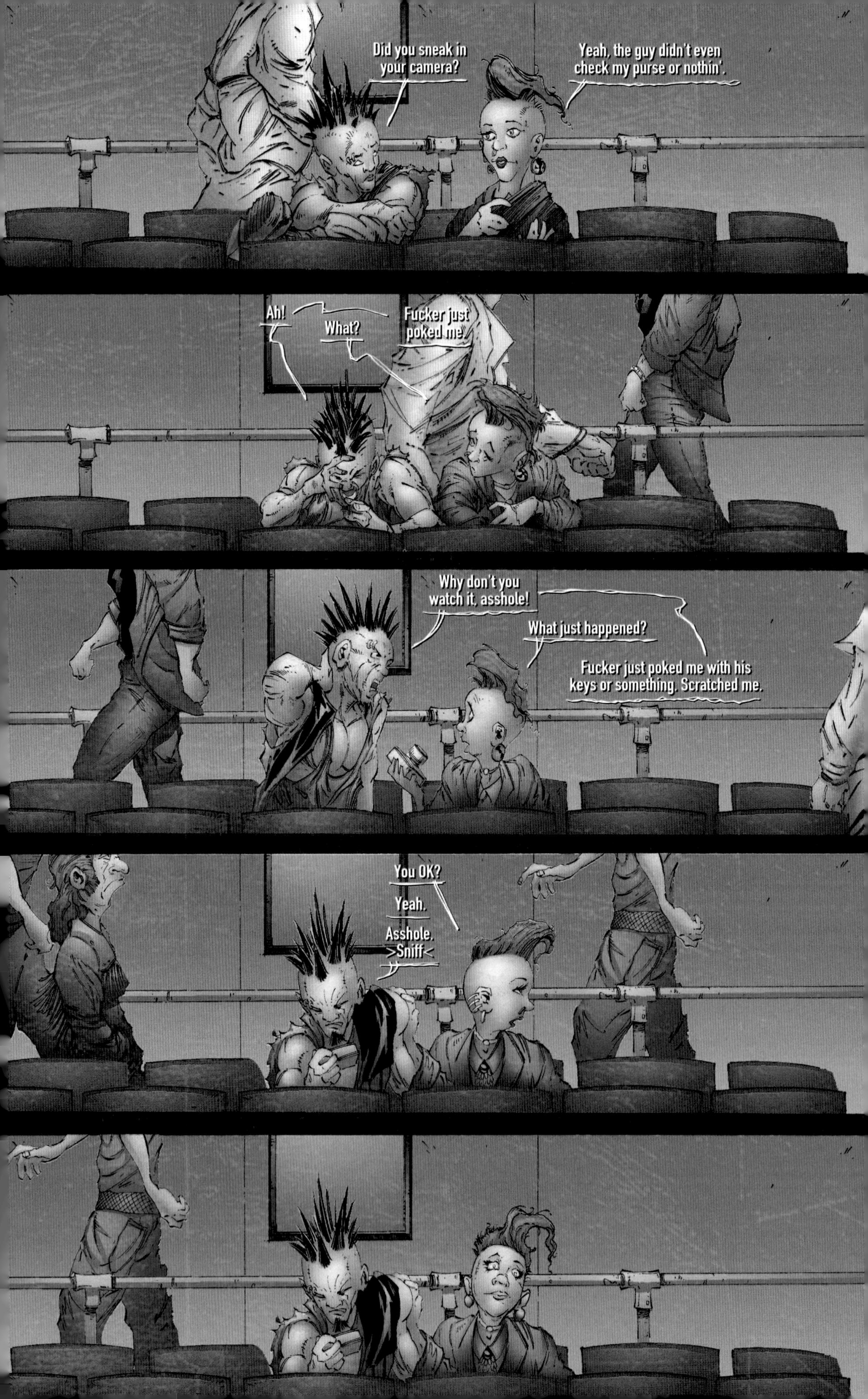
Did you sneak in your camera?
Yeah, the guy didn't even check my purse or nothin'.
Ah!
What?
Fucker just poked me.
Why don't you watch it, asshole!
What just happened?
Fucker just poked me with his keys or something. Scratched me.
You OK?
Yeah.
Asshole. >Sniff<

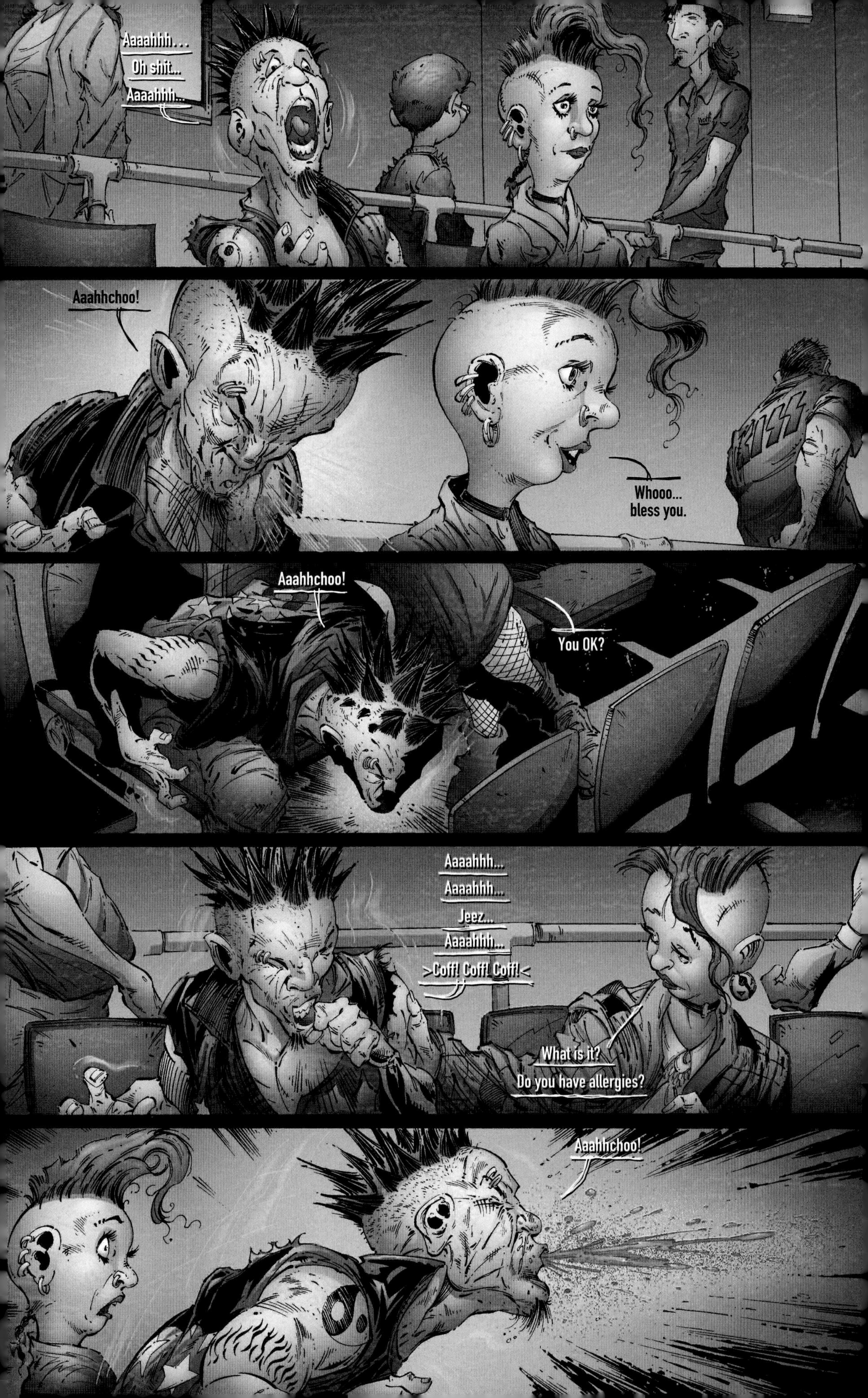
Aaaahhh...
Oh shit...
Aaaahhh...
Aaahhchoo!
Whooo... bless you.
Aaahhchoo!
You OK?
Aaaahhh...
Aaaahhh...
Jeez...
Aaaahhh...
>Coff! Coff! Coff!<
What is it?
Do you have allergies?
Aaahhchoo!

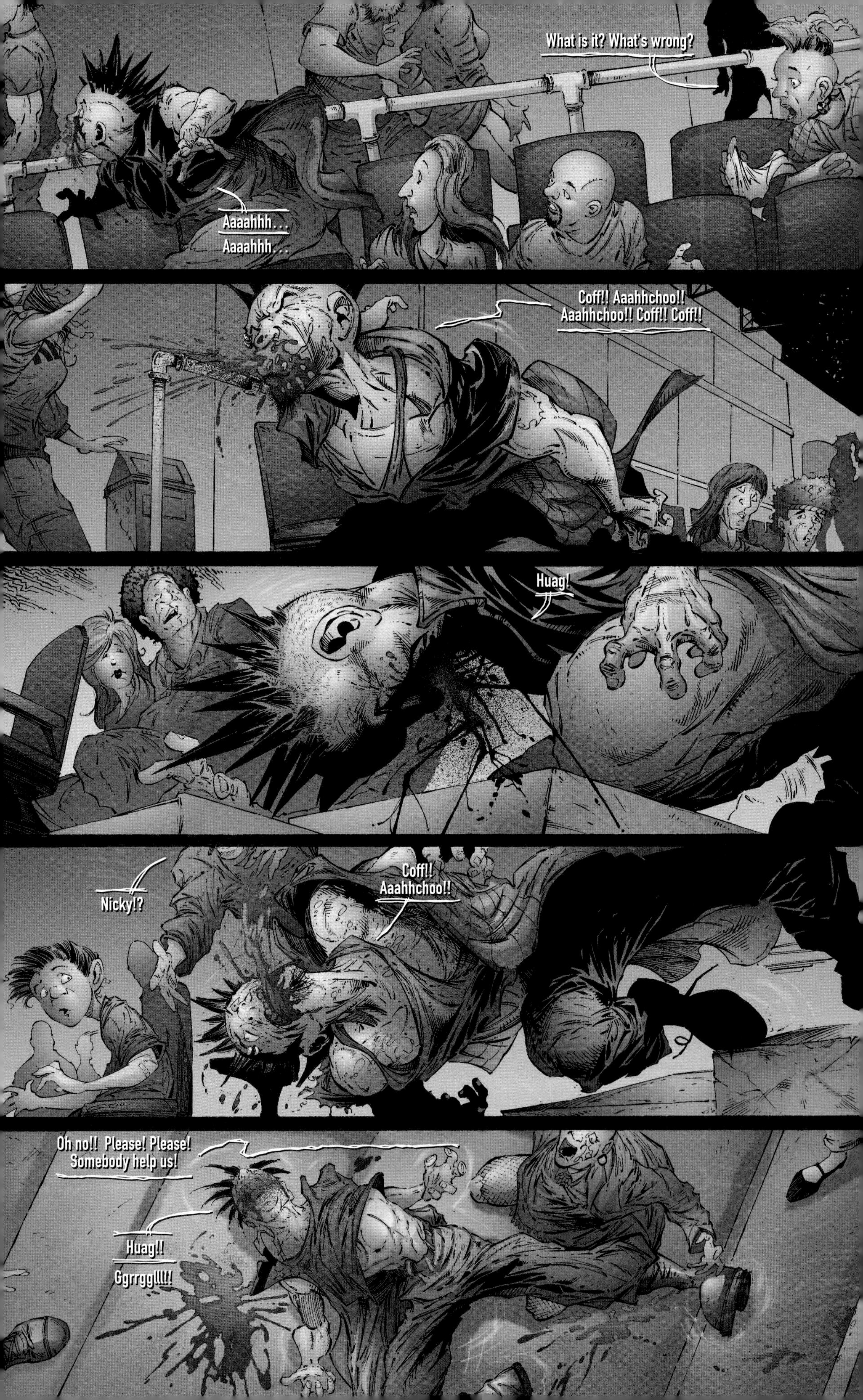
What is it? What's wrong?
Aaaahhh...
Aaaahhh...
Coff!! Aaahhchoo!! Aaahhchoo!! Coff!! Coff!!
Huag!
Nicky!?
Coff!! Aaahhchoo!!
Oh no!! Please! Please! Somebody help us!
Huag!!
Ggrrrggl!!!!

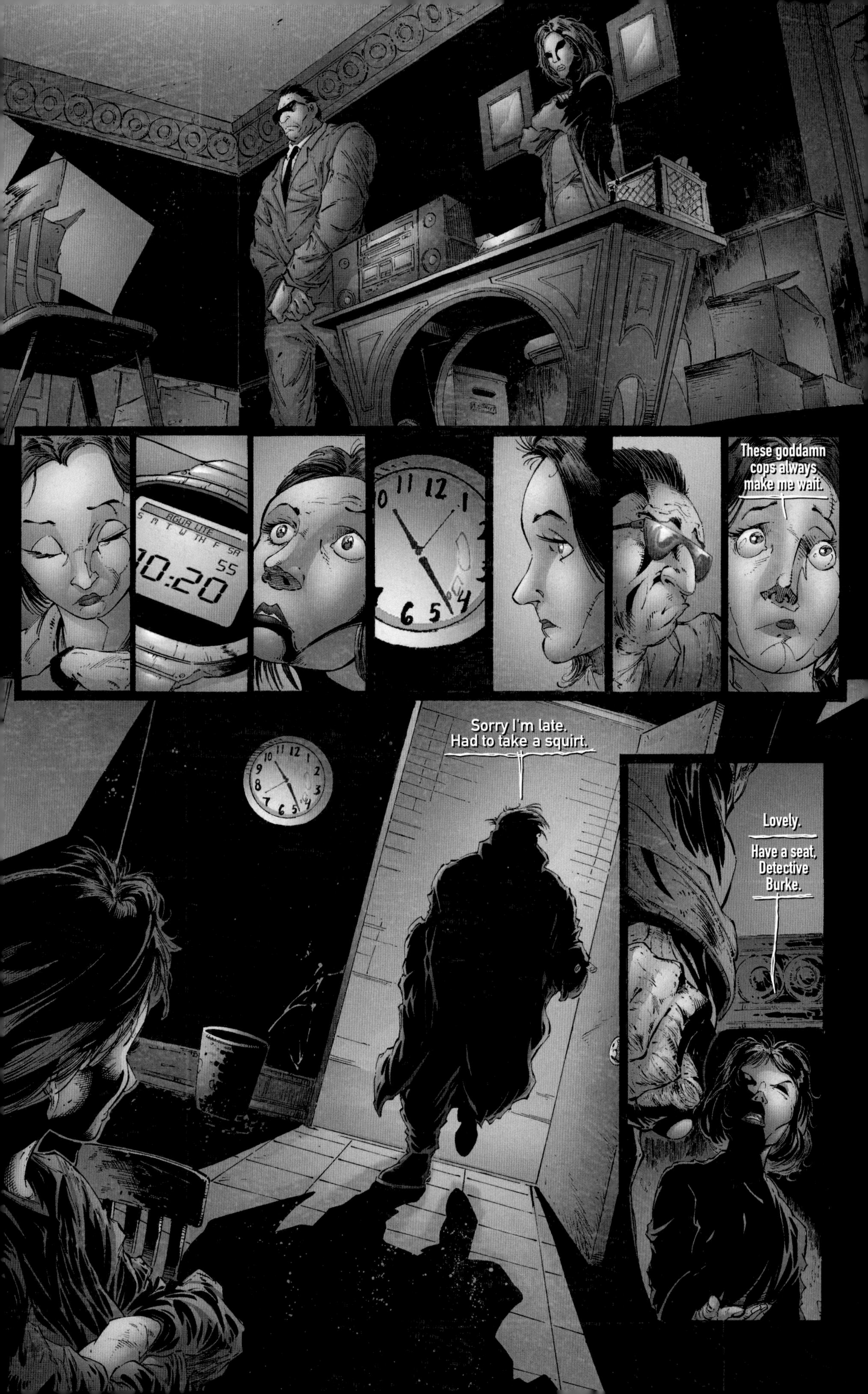
These goddamn cops always make me wait.
Sorry I'm late. Had to take a squirt.
Lovely.
Have a seat, Detective Burke.

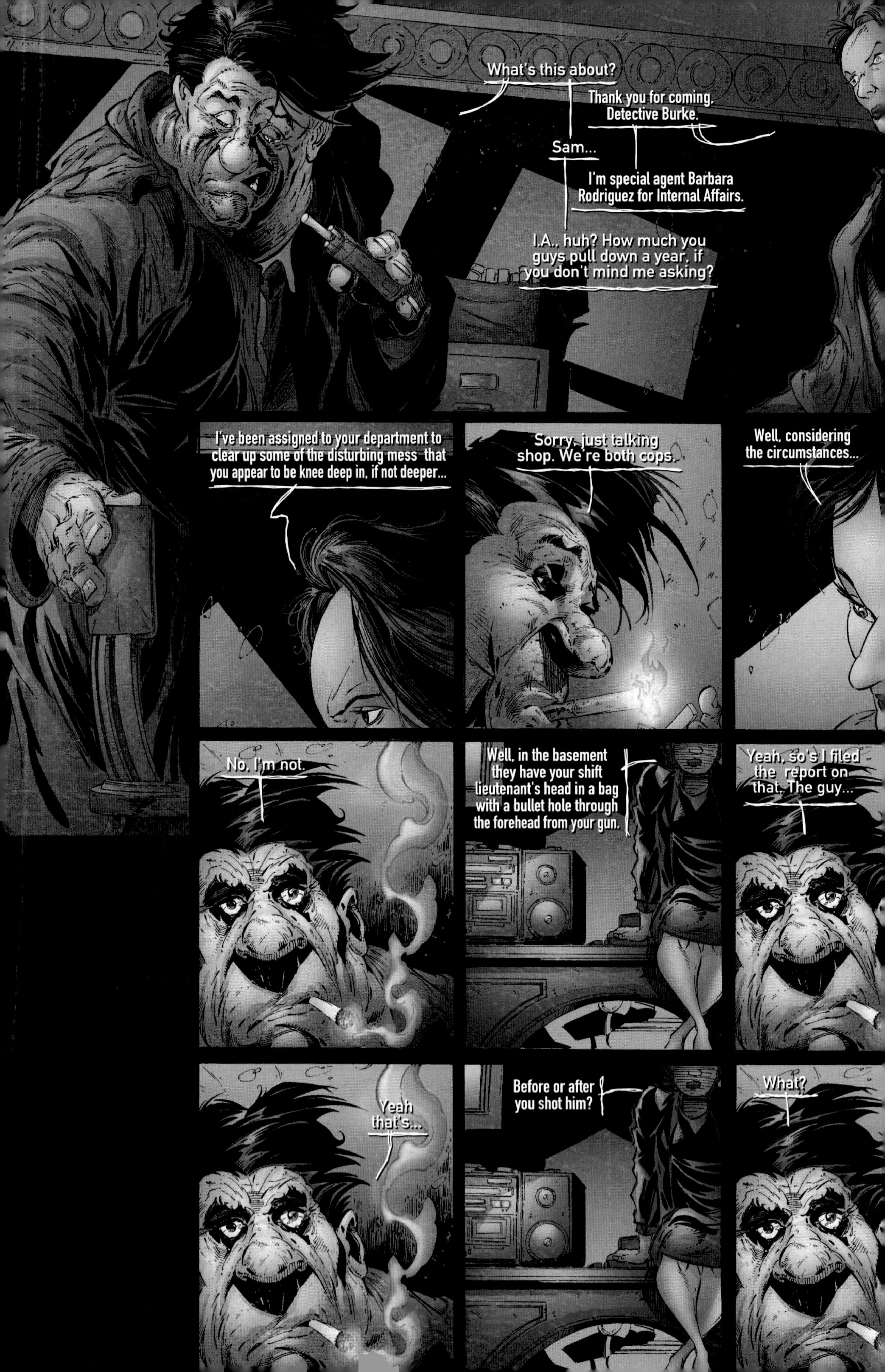

What's this about?
Thank you for coming. Detective Burke.
Sam...
I'm special agent Barbara Rodriguez for Internal Affairs.
I.A., huh? How much you guys pull down a year, if you don't mind me asking?
I've been assigned to your department to clear up some of the disturbing mess that you appear to be knee deep in, if not deeper...
Sorry, just talking shop. We're both cops.
Well, considering the circumstances...
No, I'm not.
Well, in the basement they have your shift lieutenant's head in a bag with a bullet hole through the forehead from your gun.
Yeah, so's I filed the report on that. The guy...
Yeah that's...
Before or after you shot him?
What?

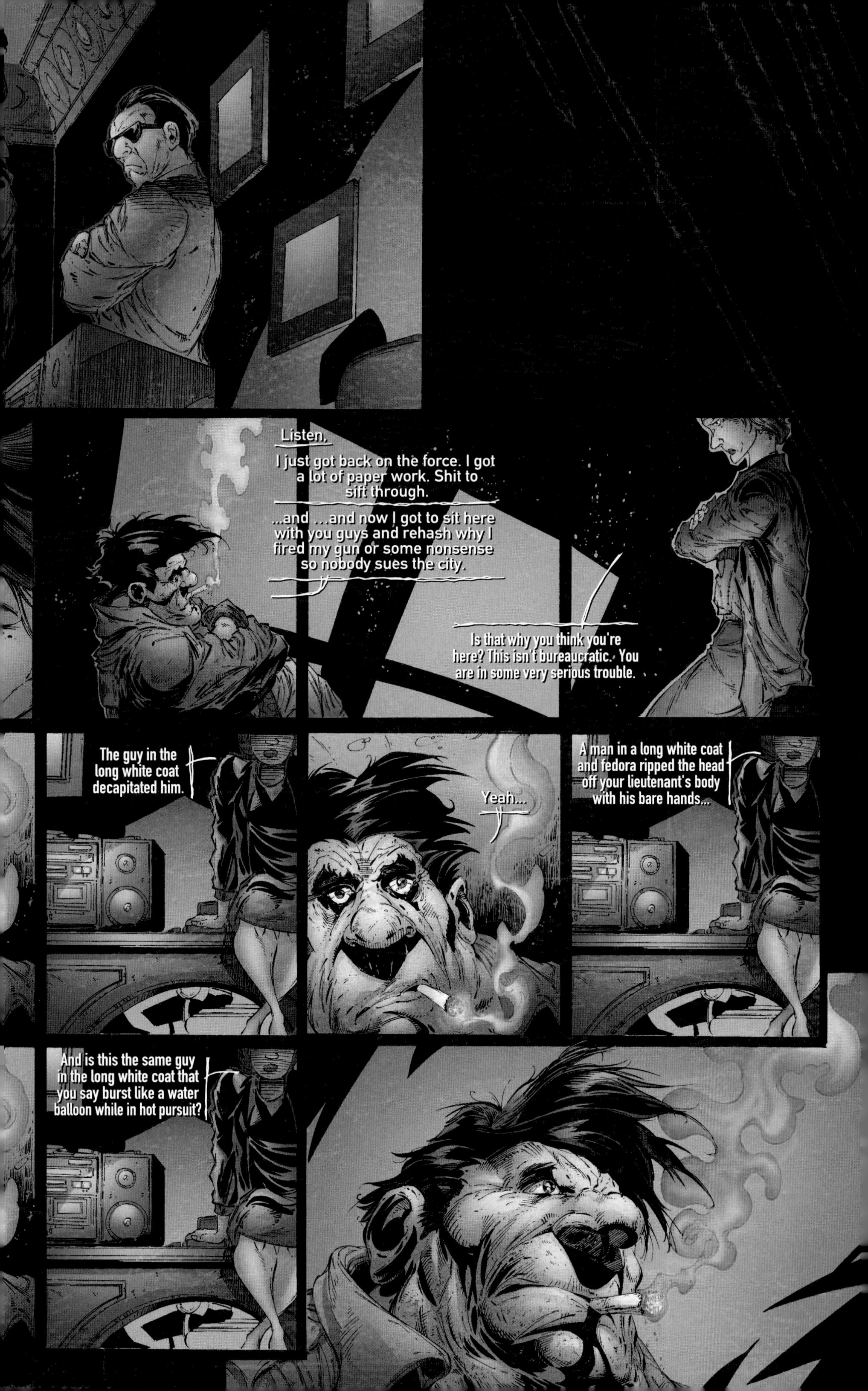
Listen.
I just got back on the force. I got a lot of paper work. Shit to sift through.
...and ...and now I got to sit here with you guys and rehash why I fired my gun or some nonsense so nobody sues the city.
Is that why you think you're here? This isn't bureaucratic. You are in some very serious trouble.
The guy in the long white coat decapitated him.
Yeah...
A man in a long white coat and fedora ripped the head off your lieutenant's body with his bare hands...
And is this the same guy in the long white coat that you say burst like a water balloon while in hot pursuit?

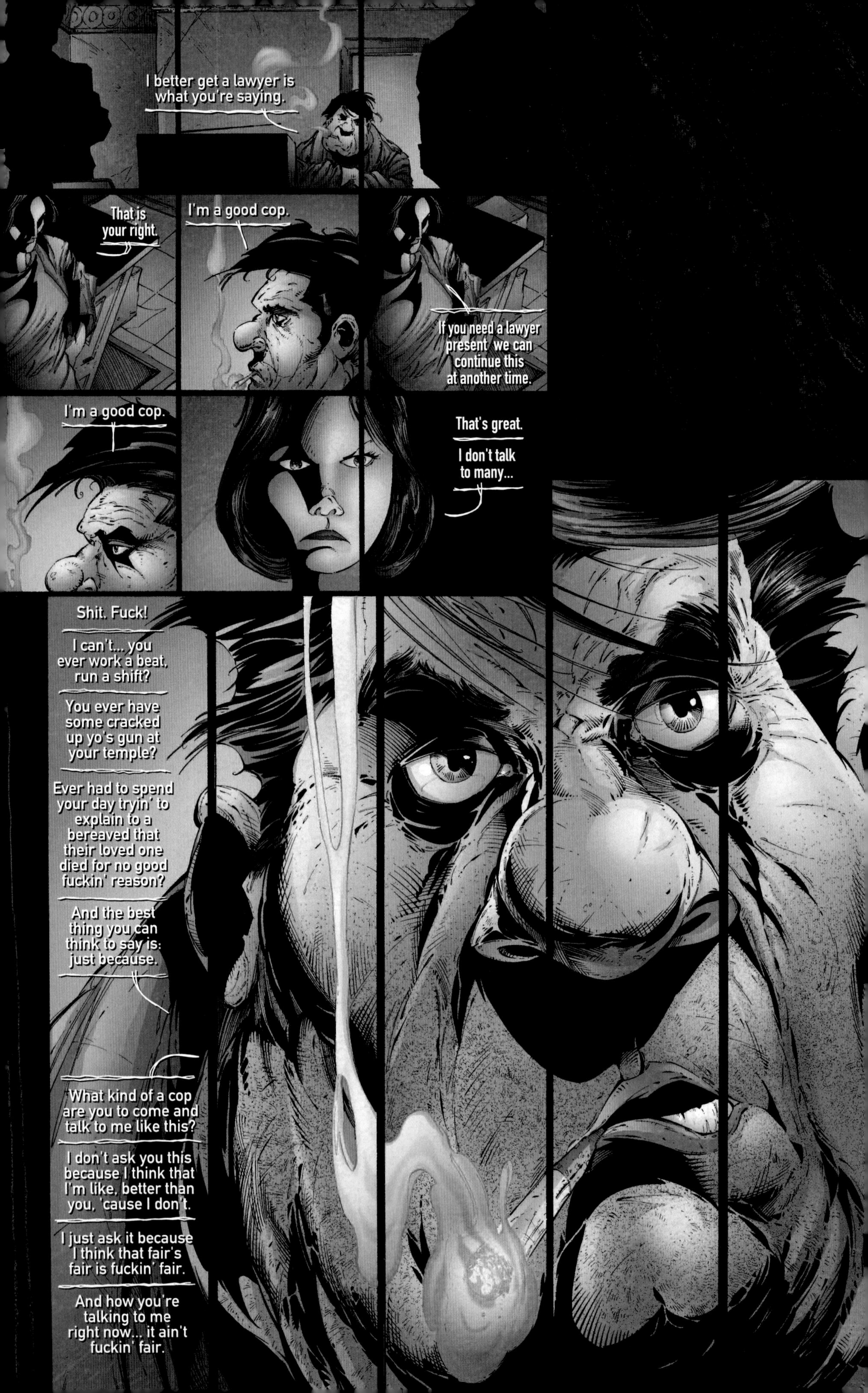
I better get a lawyer is what you're saying.
That is your right.
I'm a good cop.
If you need a lawyer present we can continue this at another time.
I'm a good cop.
That's great.
I don't talk to many...
Shit. Fuck!
I can't... you ever work a beat, run a shift?
You ever have some cracked up yo's gun at your temple?
Ever had to spend your day tryin' to explain to a bereaved that their loved one died for no good fuckin' reason?
And the best thing you can think to say is: just because.
What kind of a cop are you to come and talk to me like this?
I don't ask you this because I think that I'm like, better than you, 'cause I don't.
I just ask it because I think that fair's fair is fuckin' fair.
And how you're talking to me right now... it ain't fuckin' fair.

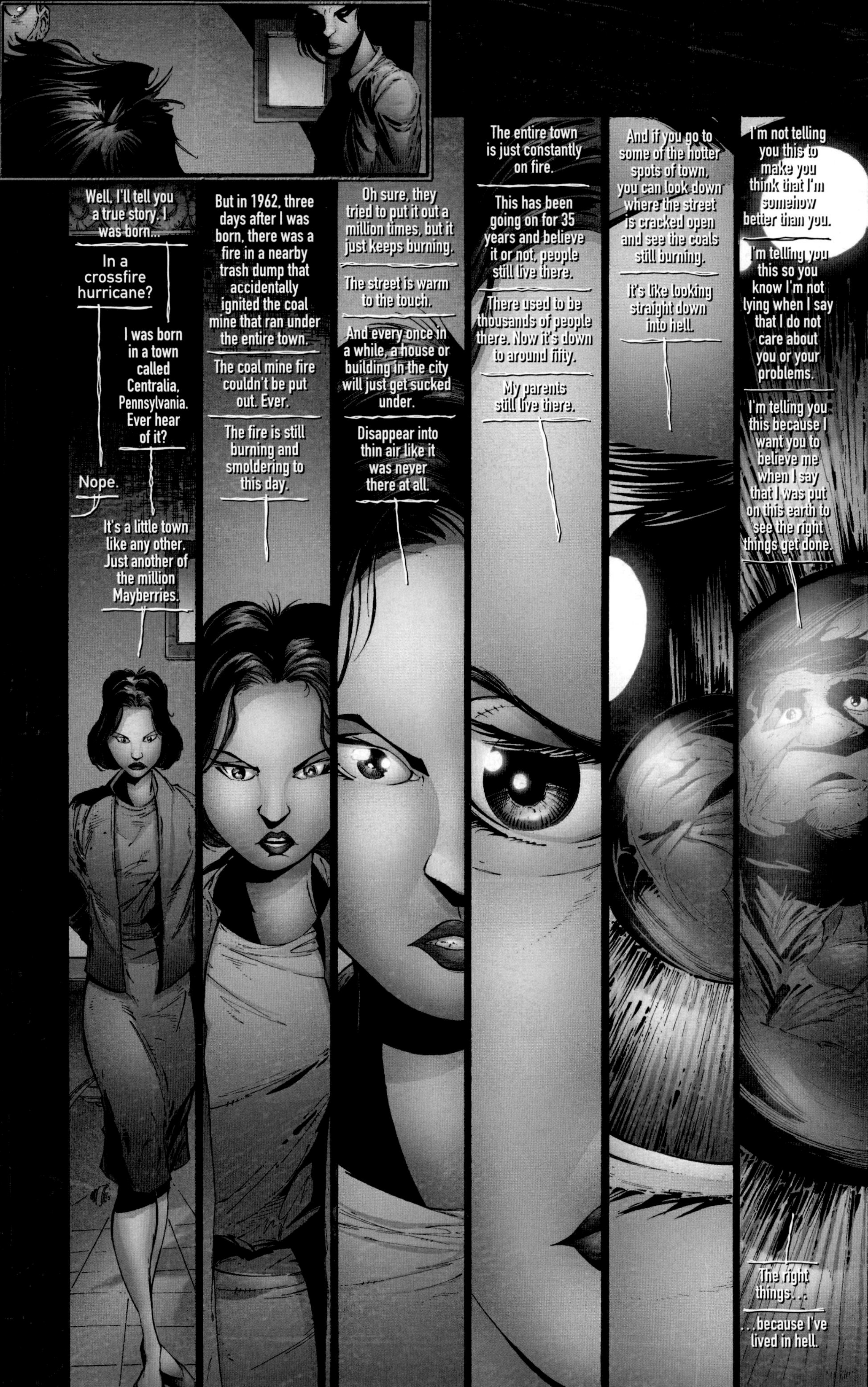

Well, I'll tell you a true story. I was born...
In a crossfire hurricane?
I was born in a town called Centralia, Pennsylvania. Ever hear of it?
Nope.
It's a little town like any other. Just another of the million Mayberries.
But in 1962, three days after I was born, there was a fire in a nearby trash dump that accidentally ignited the coal mine that ran under the entire town.
The coal mine fire couldn't be put out. Ever.
The fire is still burning and smoldering to this day.
Oh sure, they tried to put it out a million times, but it just keeps burning.
The street is warm to the touch.
And every once in a while, a house or building in the city will just get sucked under.
Disappear into thin air like it was never there at all.
The entire town is just constantly on fire.
This has been going on for 35 years and believe it or not, people still live there.
There used to be thousands of people there. Now it's down to around fifty.
My parents still live there.
And if you go to some of the hotter spots of town, you can look down where the street is cracked open and see the coals still burning.
It's like looking straight down into hell.
I'm not telling you this to make you think that I'm somehow better than you.
I'm telling you this so you know I'm not lying when I say that I do not care about you or your problems.
I'm telling you this because I want you to believe me when I say that I was put on this earth to see the right things get done.
The right things...
...because I've lived in hell.

Miss, can I help you?

Anyone know anything about that girl out there?

She came with that drop off. It's not a homicide. The guy just keeled over.

Man, I don't even get to sit down.

Could someone go out there and get that poor girl a blanket and some tea or something?

MEDICAL EXAMINER
IDENTIFICATION TAG
NAME SANGIACOMO, NICKY
(Last, First)
Address 54 E. AVE. A
City/State NEW YORK, NY
D.O.B. 5.8.74 Sex M   M W

Sangiacomo?

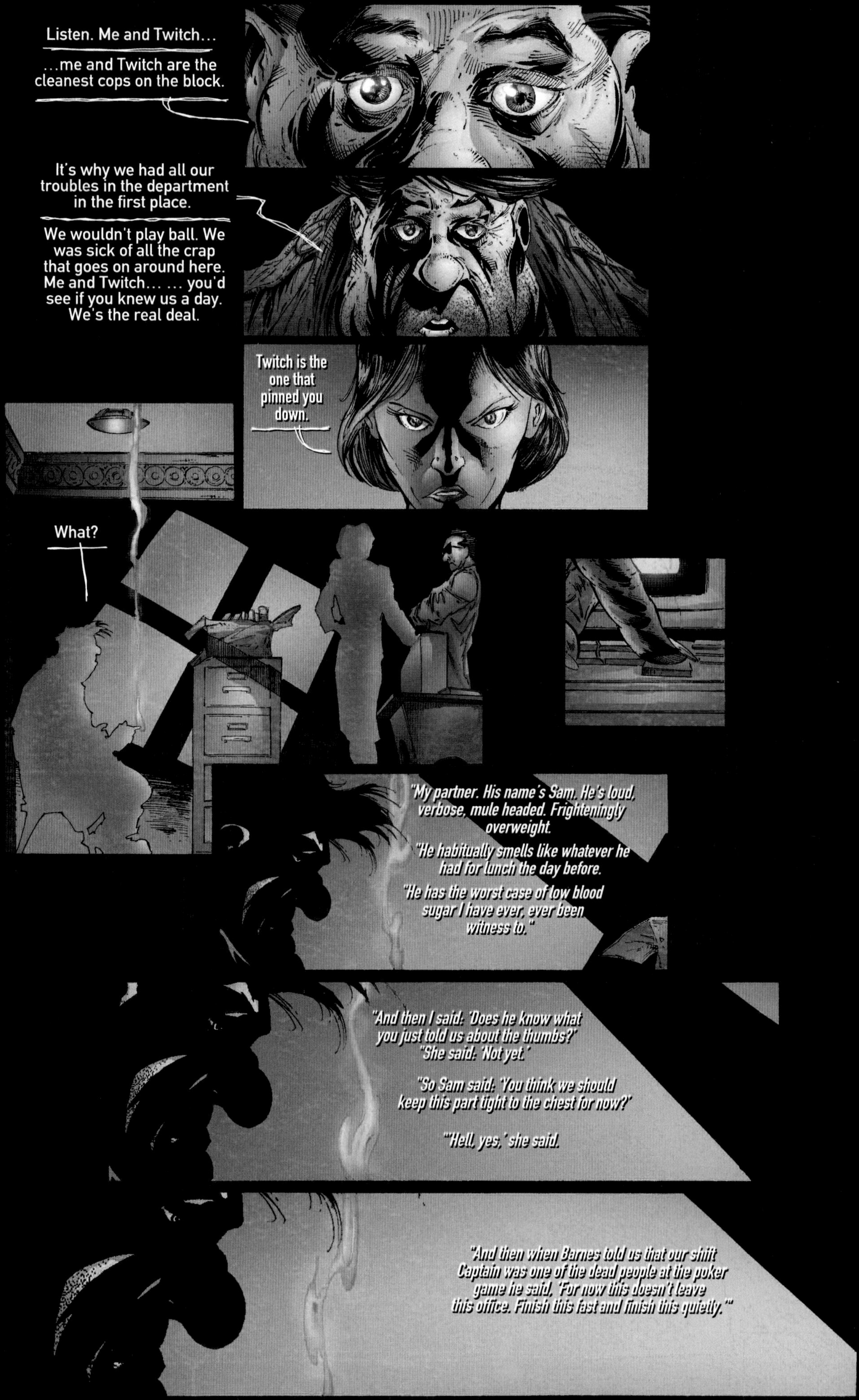

Listen. Me and Twitch...
...me and Twitch are the cleanest cops on the block.
It's why we had all our troubles in the department in the first place.
We wouldn't play ball. We was sick of all the crap that goes on around here. Me and Twitch... ... you'd see if you knew us a day. We's the real deal.
Twitch is the one that pinned you down.
What?
"My partner. His name's Sam. He's loud, verbose, mule headed. Frighteningly overweight.
"He habitually smells like whatever he had for lunch the day before.
"He has the worst case of low blood sugar I have ever, ever been witness to."
"And then I said: 'Does he know what you just told us about the thumbs?' "She said: 'Not yet.'
"So Sam said: 'You think we should keep this part tight to the chest for now?'
"'Hell, yes,' she said.
"And then when Barnes told us that our shift Captain was one of the dead people at the poker game he said, 'For now this doesn't leave this office. Finish this fast and finish this quietly.'"

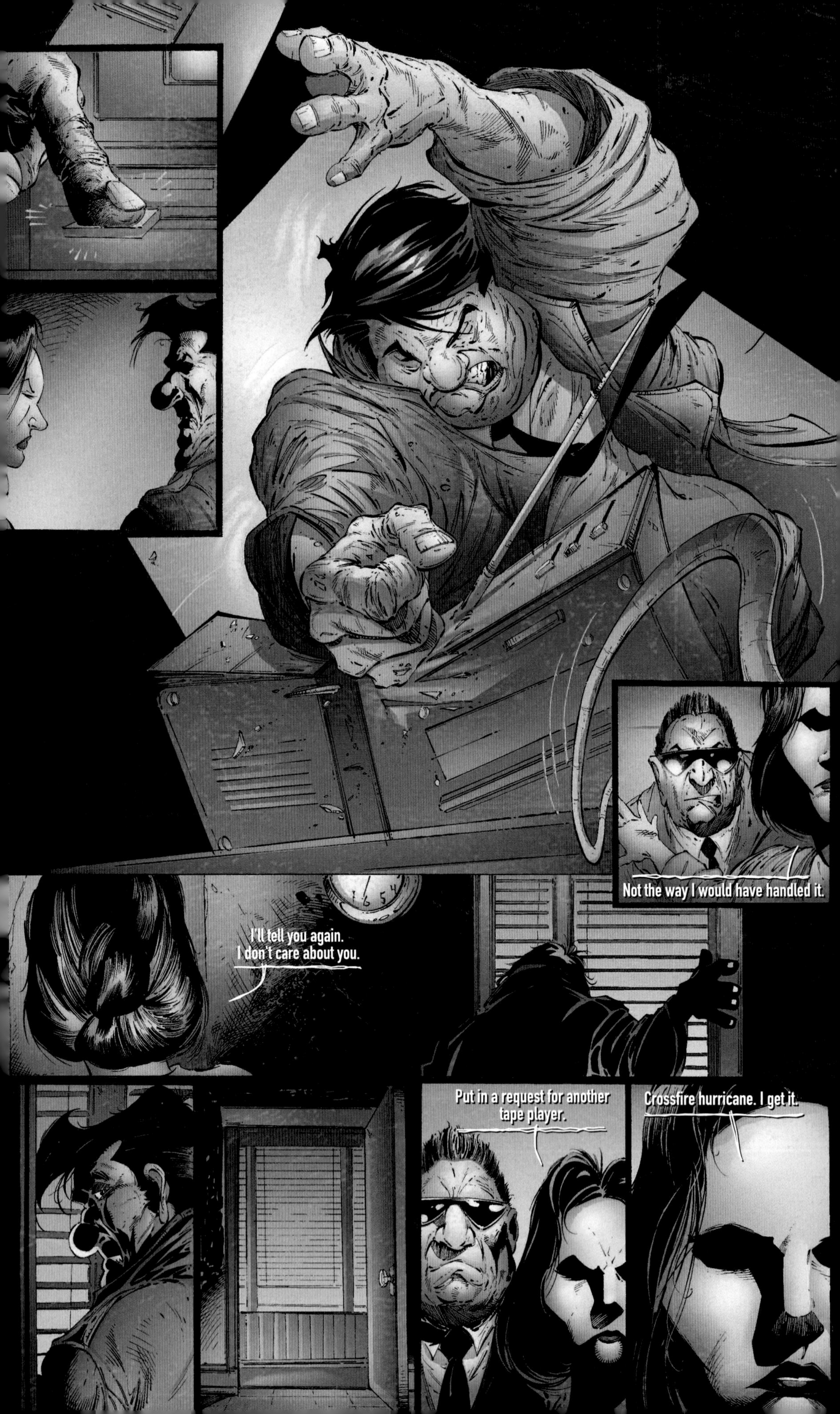
Not the way I would have handled it.
I'll tell you again. I don't care about you.
Put in a request for another tape player.
Crossfire hurricane. I get it.

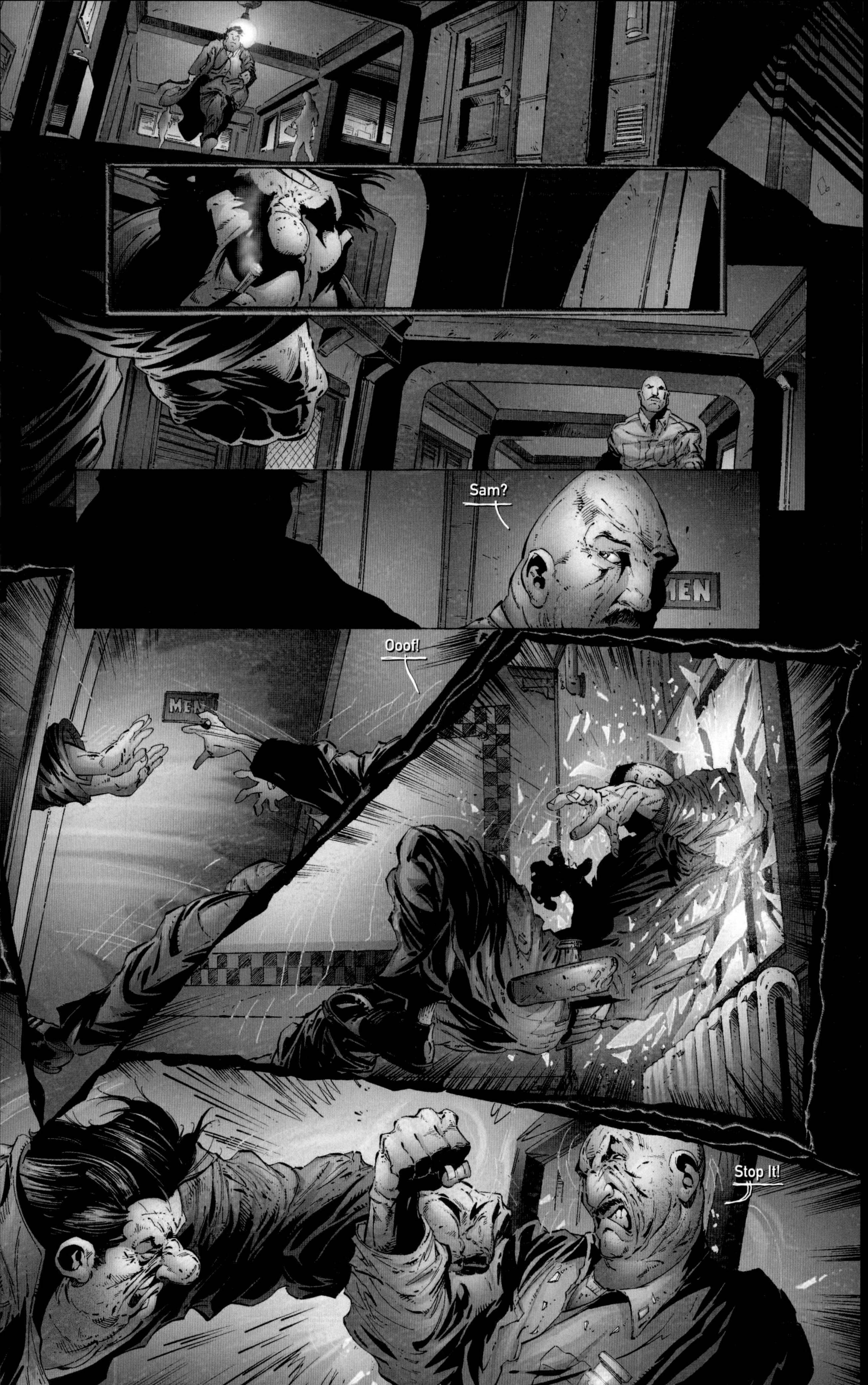
Sam?
MEN
Ooof!
MEN
Stop It!

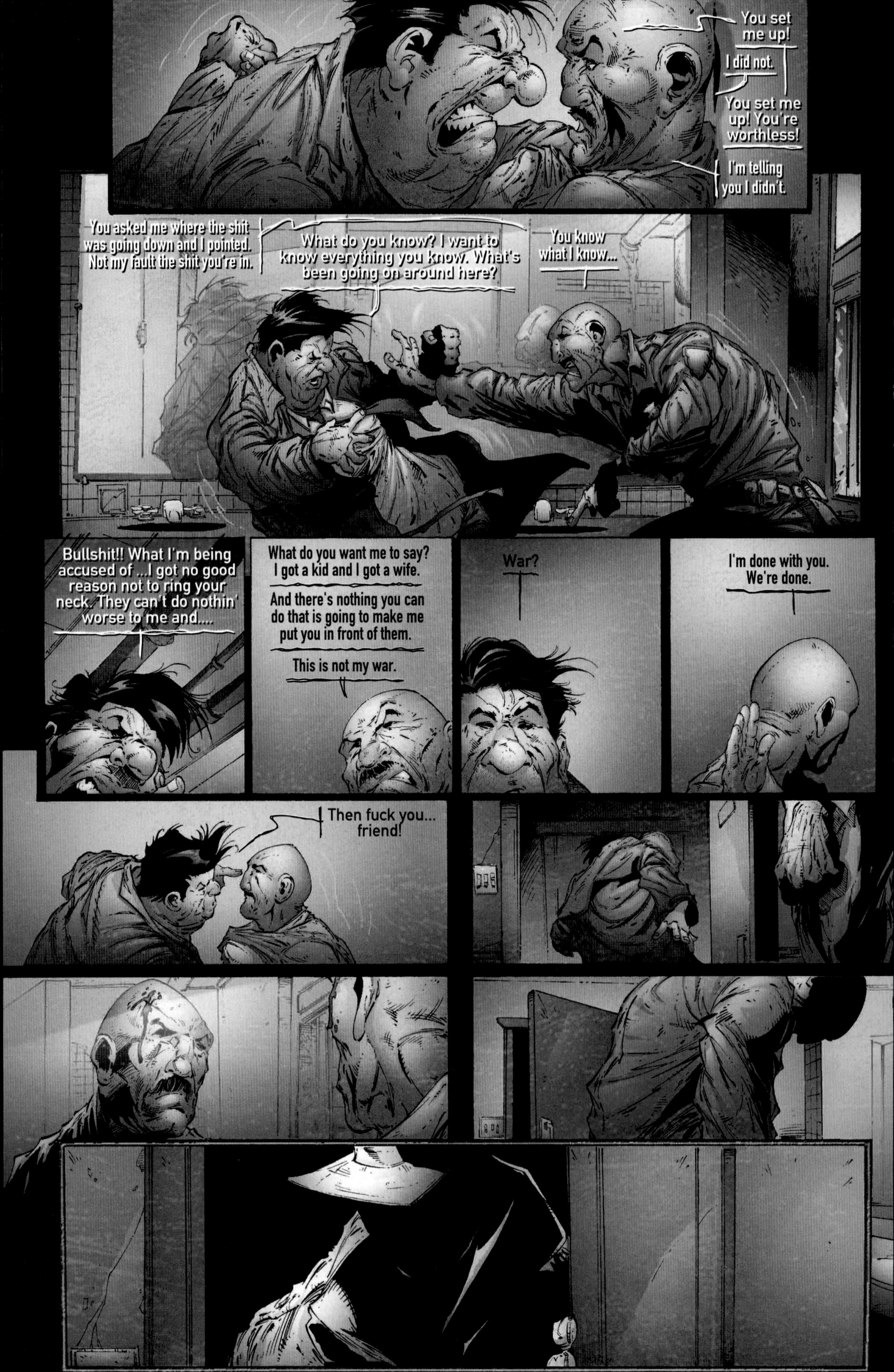
You set me up!
I did not.
You set me up! You're worthless!
I'm telling you I didn't.
You asked me where the shit was going down and I pointed. Not my fault the shit you're in.
What do you know? I want to know everything you know. What's been going on around here?
You know what I know...
Bullshit!! What I'm being accused of ...I got no good reason not to ring your neck. They can't do nothin' worse to me and....
What do you want me to say? I got a kid and I got a wife.
And there's nothing you can do that is going to make me put you in front of them.
This is not my war.
War?
I'm done with you. We're done.
Then fuck you... friend!

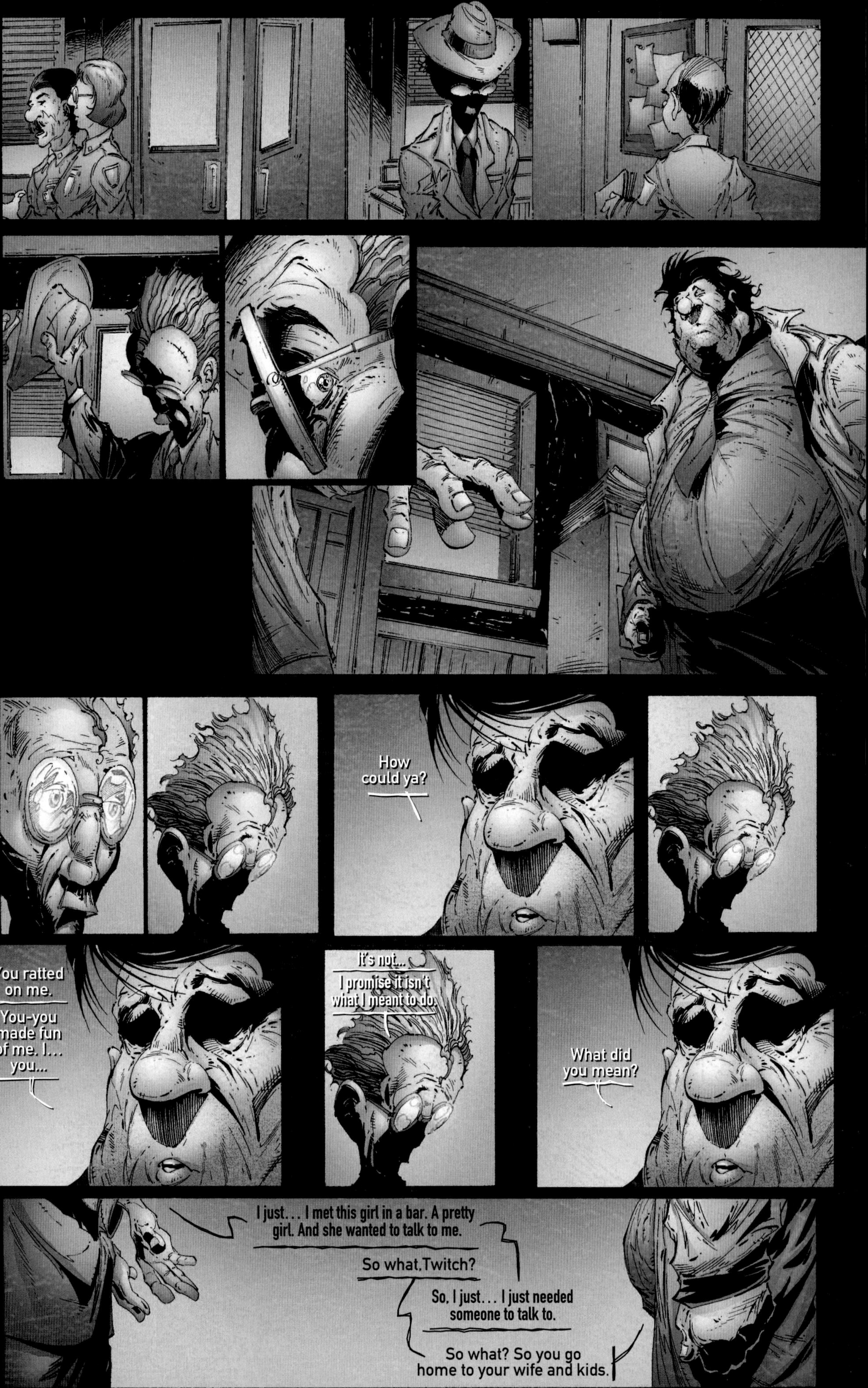

How could ya?
You ratted on me.
You-you made fun of me. I... you...
It's not... I promise it isn't what I meant to do.
What did you mean?
I just... I met this girl in a bar. A pretty girl. And she wanted to talk to me.
So what, Twitch?
So, I just... I just needed someone to talk to.
So what? So you go home to your wife and kids.

I can't. My wife kicked me out of the house two months ago.

What?!

She told me that if I continued chasing around the city with you and didn't get my ass back on the force, and start providing decently for our family...

Then in her eyes I had somehow chosen between the two of you. So, she kicked me out.

Twitch, I didn't know that.

I know.

Why wouldn't you tell me that?

Why would I? What purpose would it have served? It was my decision. It was my decision.

But Twitch...?

Guys. Guys. Guys. Guys. Guys.

You are never going to believe what I have in my basement.

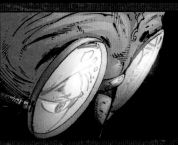

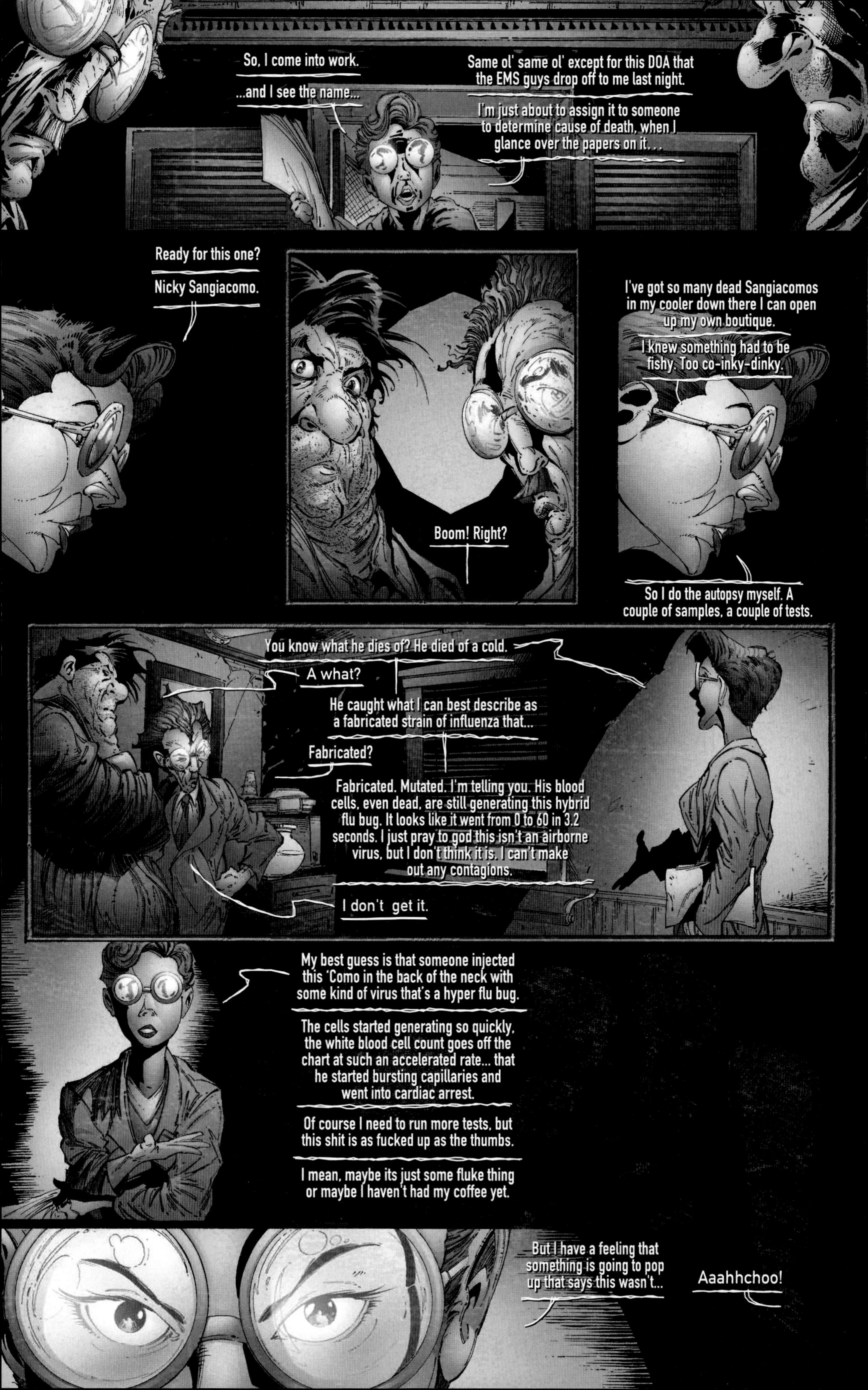

So, I come into work.
...and I see the name...
Same ol' same ol' except for this DOA that the EMS guys drop off to me last night.
I'm just about to assign it to someone to determine cause of death, when I glance over the papers on it...
Ready for this one?
Nicky Sangiacomo.
Boom! Right?
I've got so many dead Sangiacomos in my cooler down there I can open up my own boutique.
I knew something had to be fishy. Too co-inky-dinky.
So I do the autopsy myself. A couple of samples, a couple of tests.
You know what he dies of? He died of a cold.
A what?
He caught what I can best describe as a fabricated strain of influenza that...
Fabricated?
Fabricated. Mutated. I'm telling you. His blood cells, even dead, are still generating this hybrid flu bug. It looks like it went from 0 to 60 in 3.2 seconds. I just pray to god this isn't an airborne virus, but I don't think it is. I can't make out any contagions.
I don't get it.
My best guess is that someone injected this 'Como in the back of the neck with some kind of virus that's a hyper flu bug.
The cells started generating so quickly, the white blood cell count goes off the chart at such an accelerated rate... that he started bursting capillaries and went into cardiac arrest.
Of course I need to run more tests, but this shit is as fucked up as the thumbs.
I mean, maybe its just some fluke thing or maybe I haven't had my coffee yet.
But I have a feeling that something is going to pop up that says this wasn't...
Aaahhchoo!

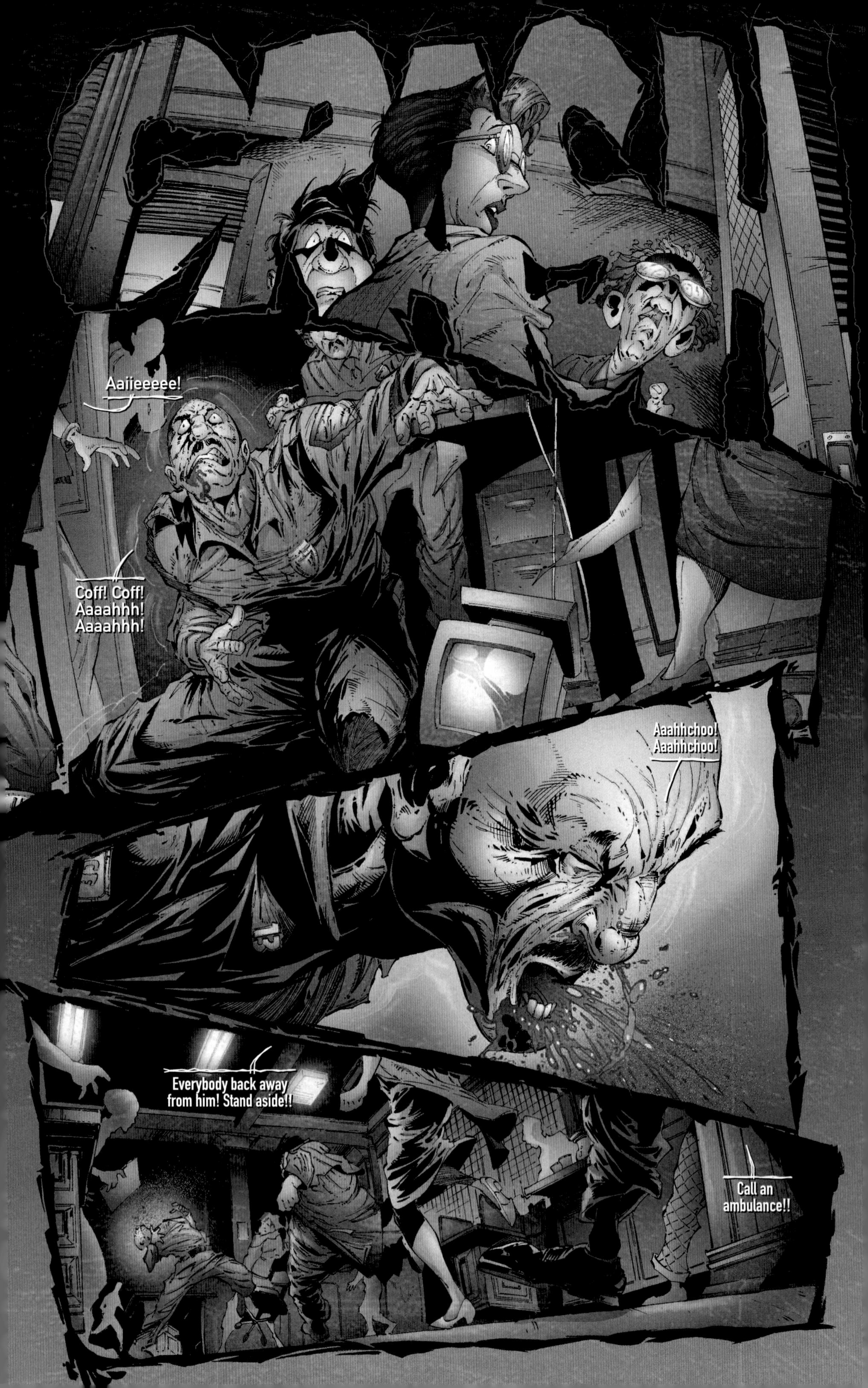
Aaiieeeee!
Coff! Coff! Aaaahhh! Aaaahhh!
Aaahhchoo! Aaahhchoo!
Everybody back away from him! Stand aside!!
Call an ambulance!!

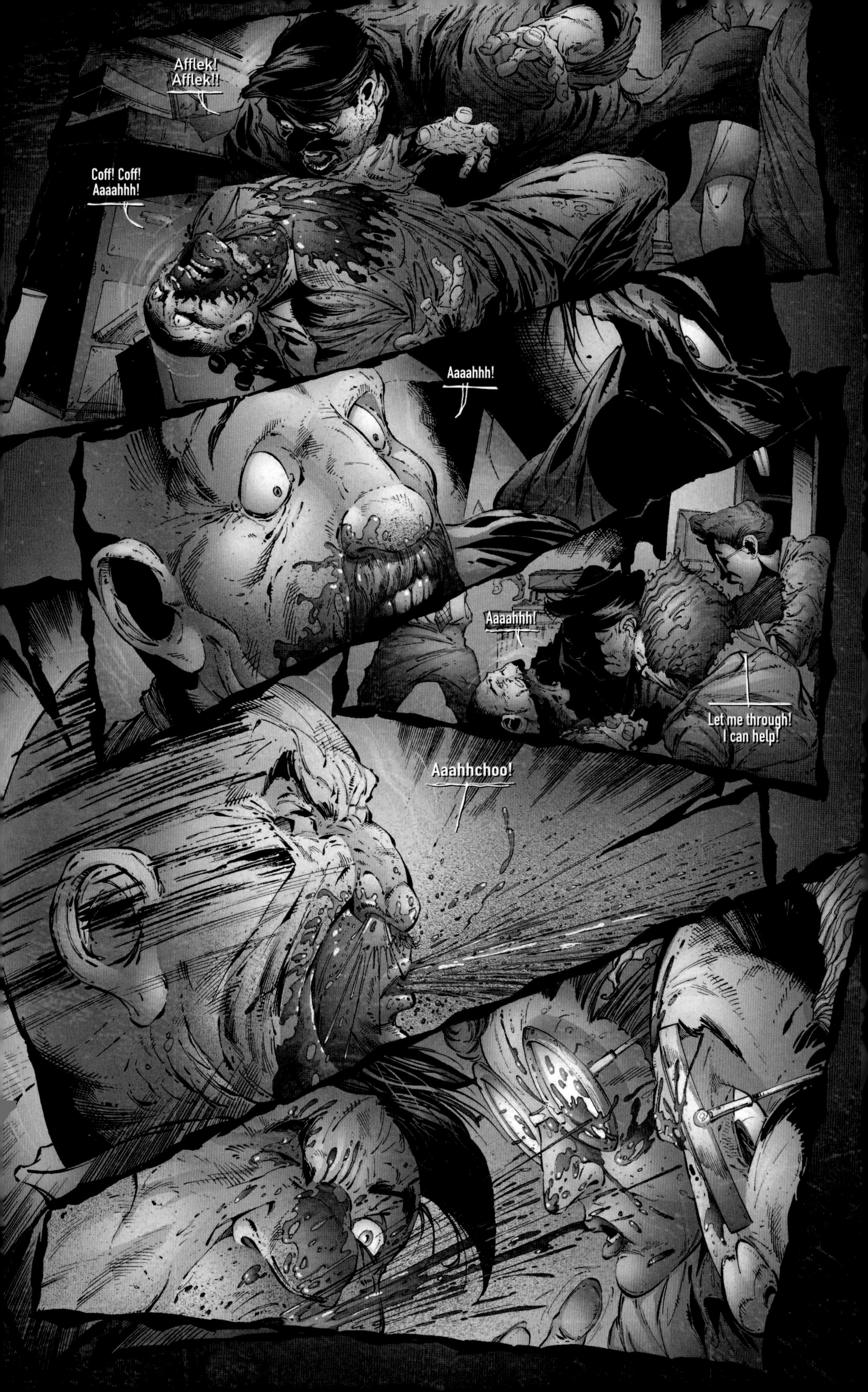
Afflek!
Afflek!!
Coff! Coff!
Aaaahhh!
Aaaahhh!
Aaaahhh!
Let me through!
I can help!
Aaahhchoo!

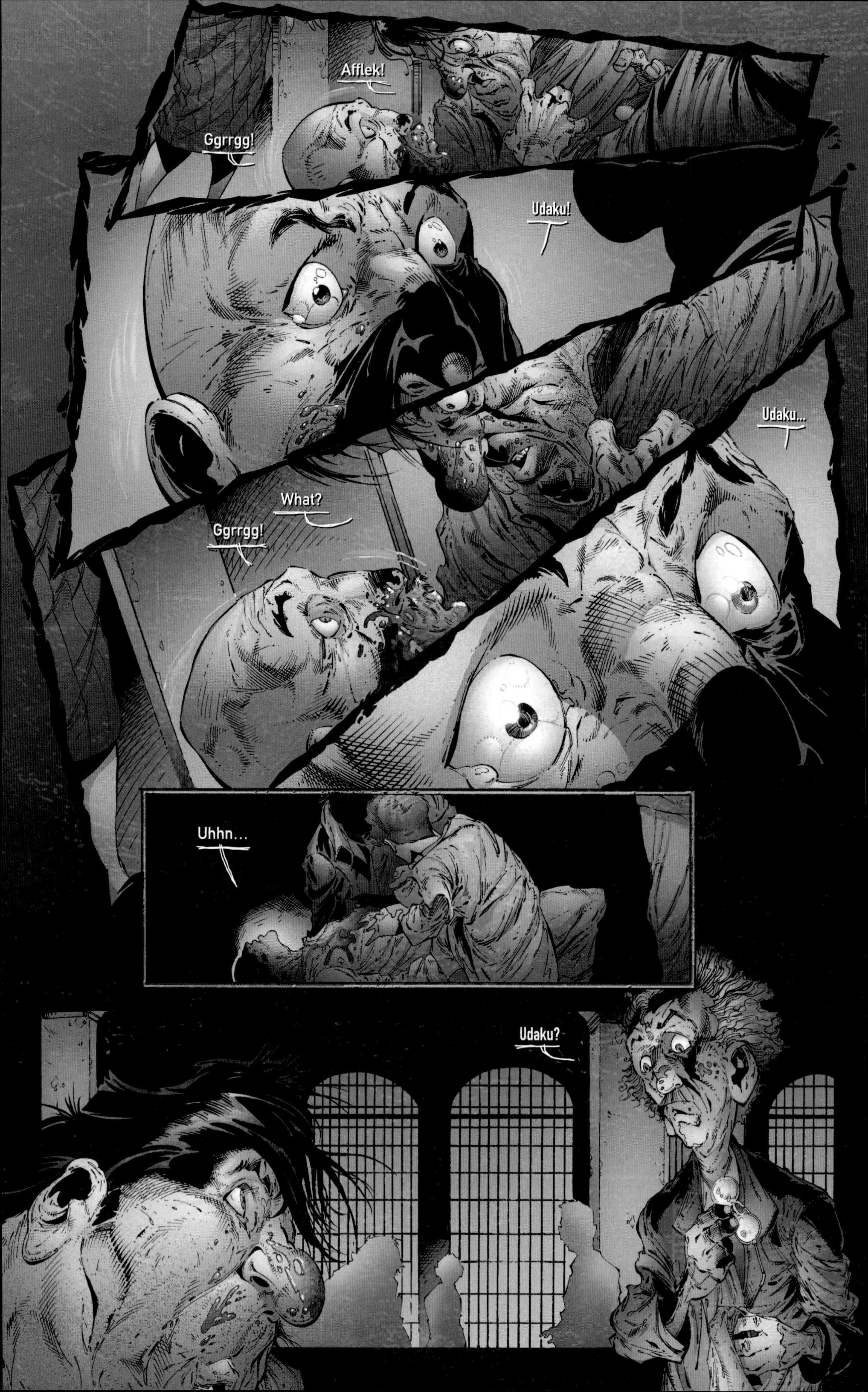
Afflek!
Ggrrgg!
Udaku!
Udaku...
What?
Ggrrgg!
Uhhn...
Udaku?

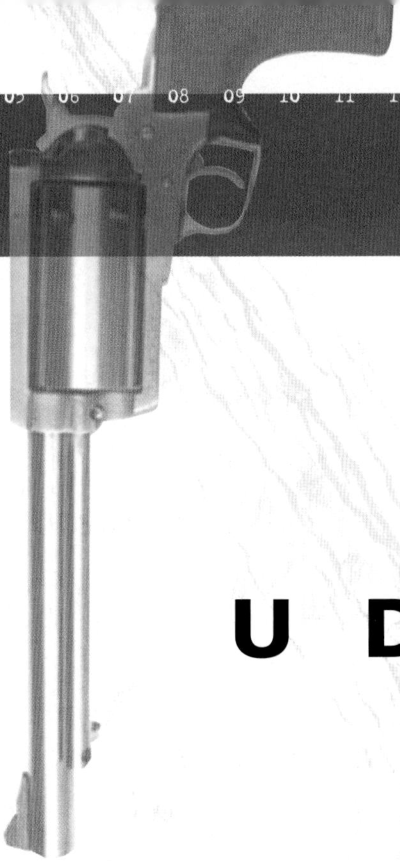

UDAKU

PART 4

SAM AND TWITCH

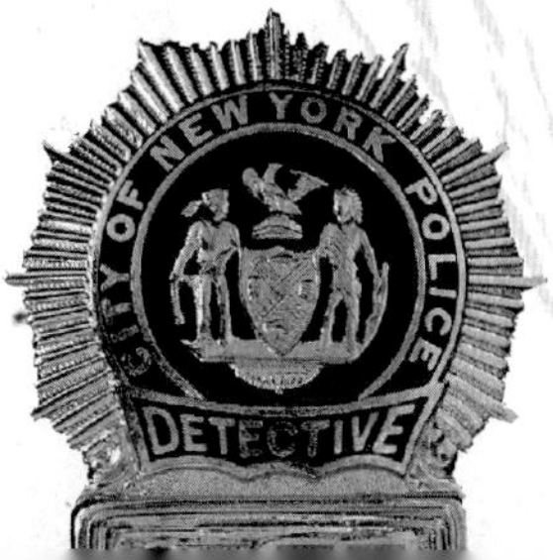
CITY OF NEW YORK POLICE
DETECTIVE

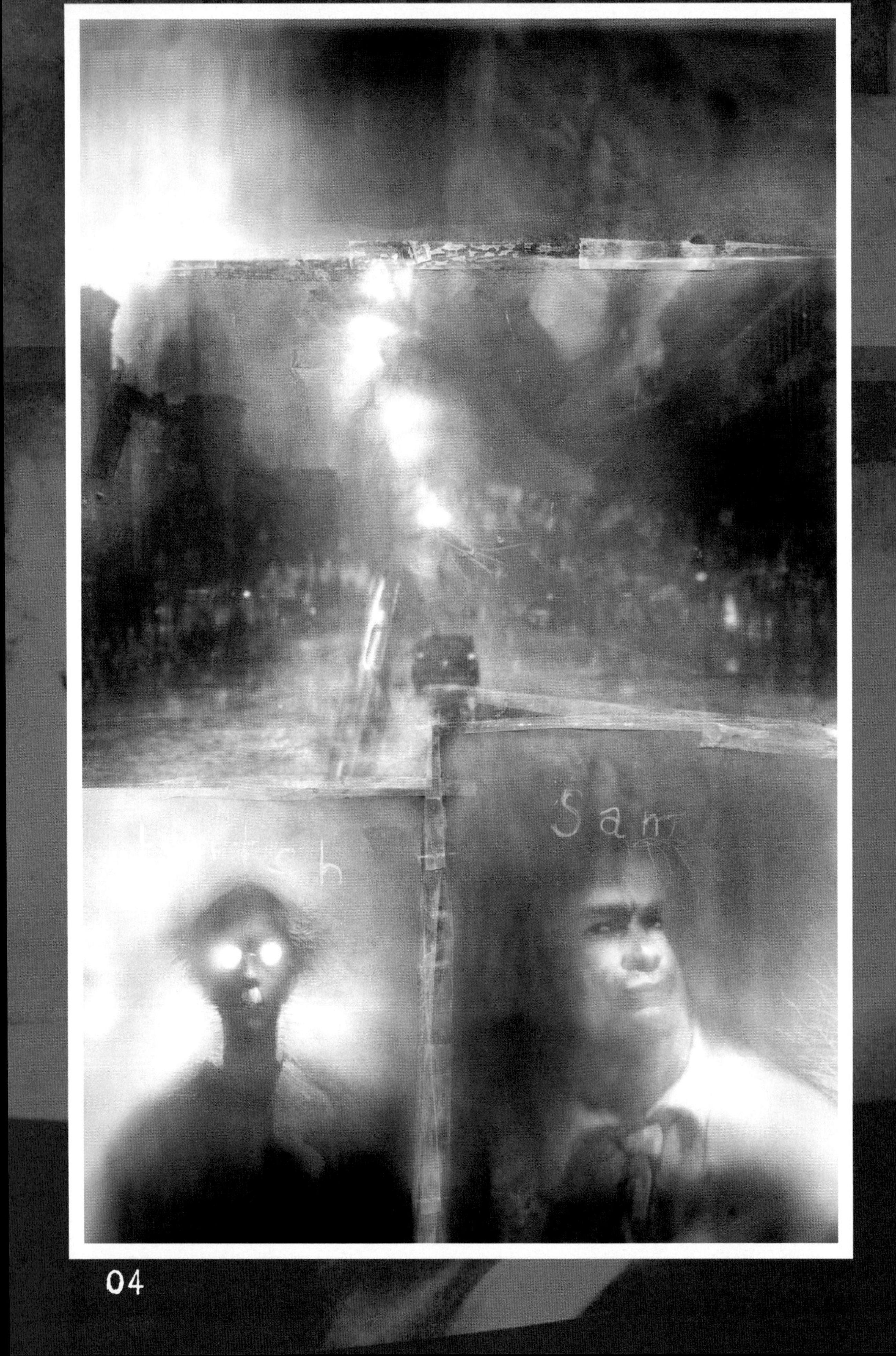
Sam

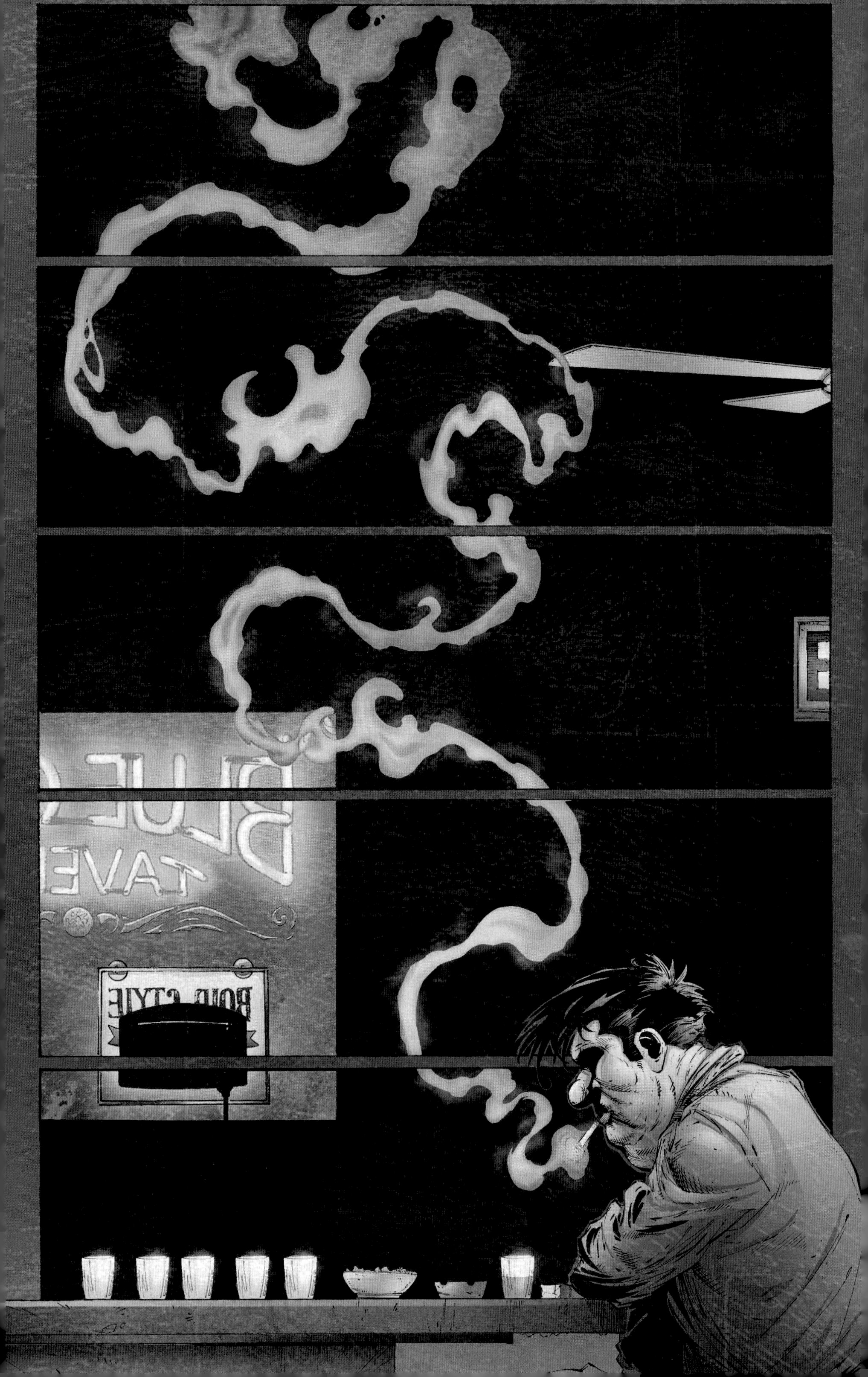

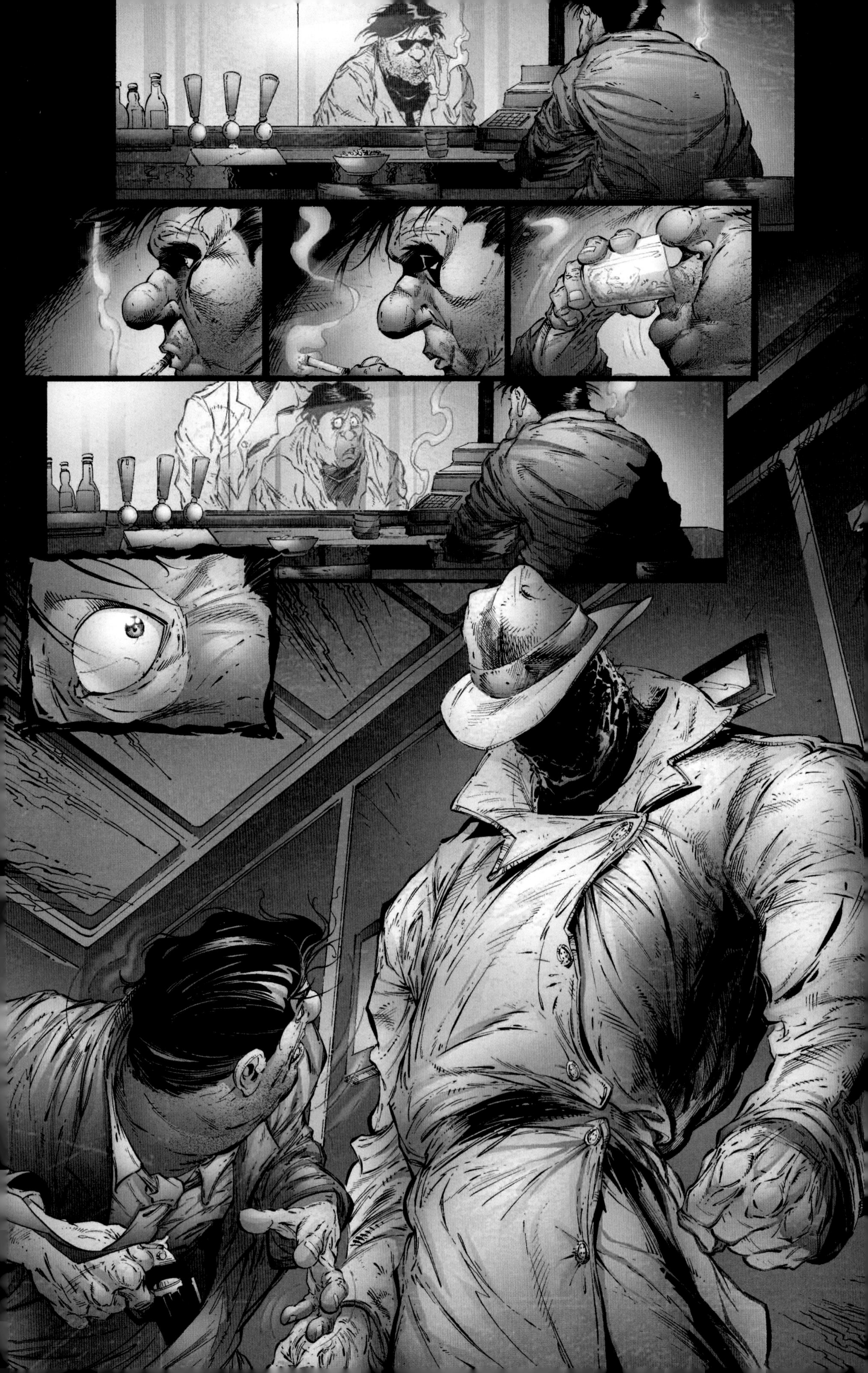

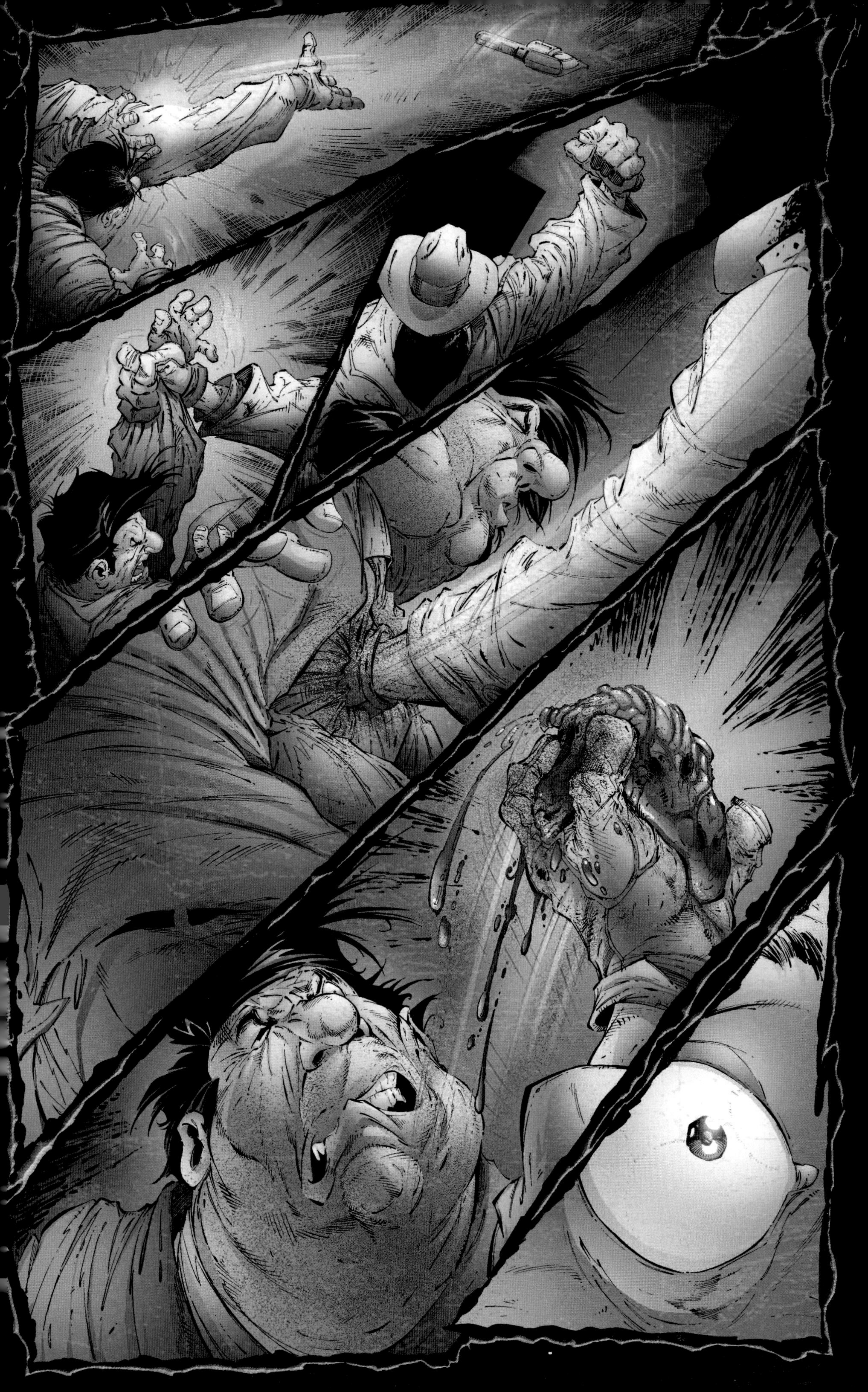

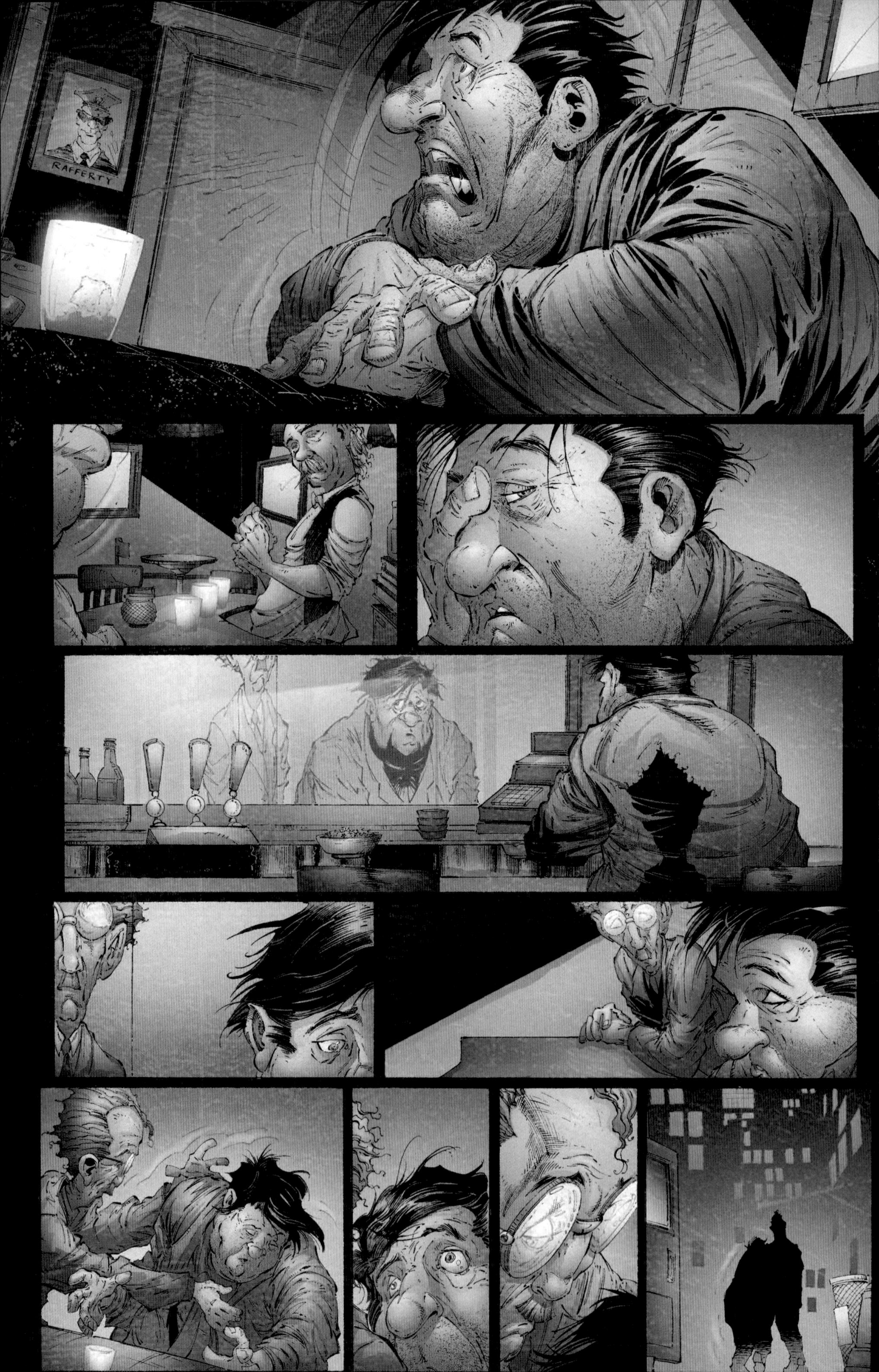
RAFFERTY

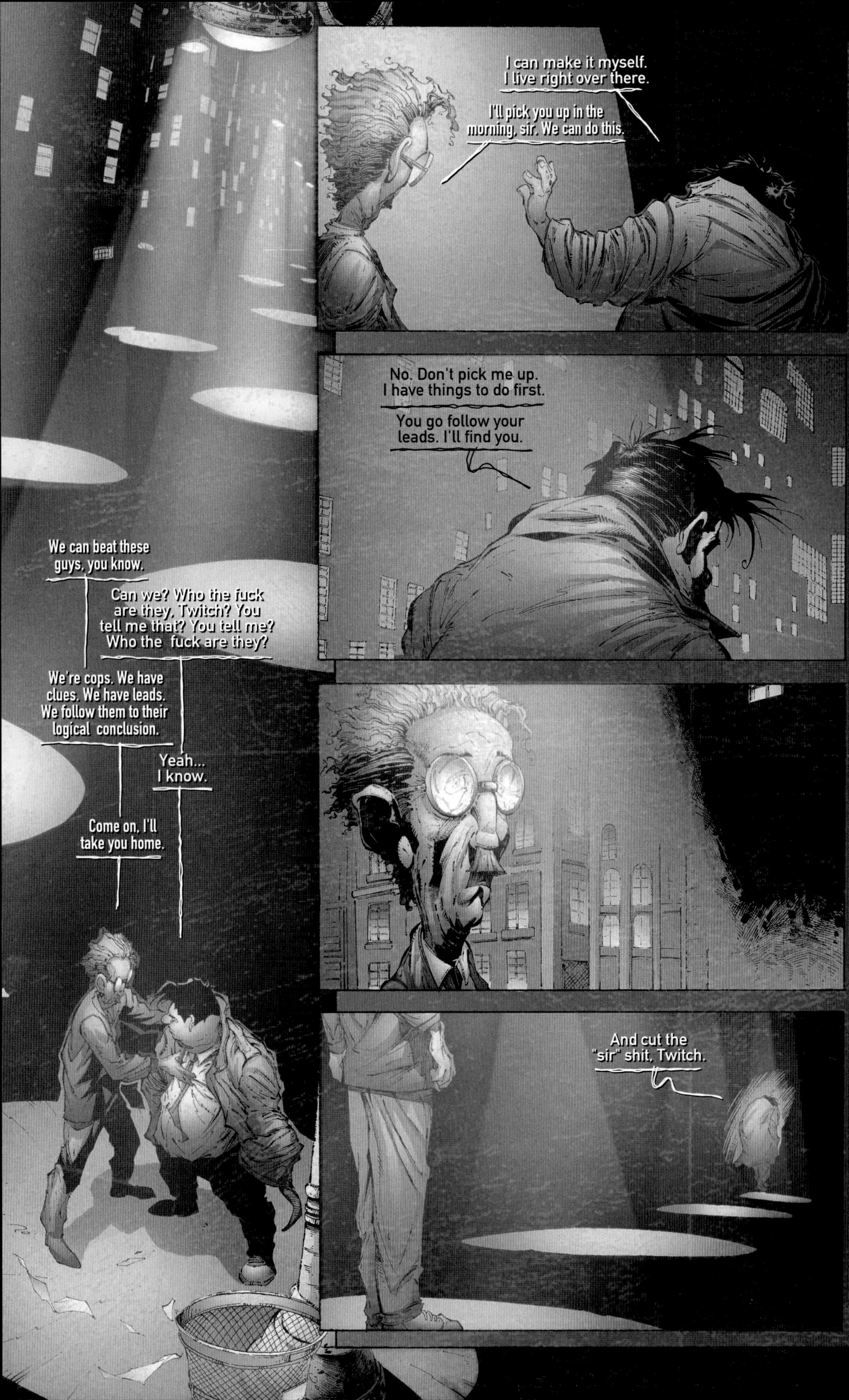
We can beat these guys, you know.
Can we? Who the fuck are they, Twitch? You tell me that? You tell me? Who the fuck are they?
We're cops. We have clues. We have leads. We follow them to their logical conclusion.
Yeah... I know.
Come on, I'll take you home.
I can make it myself. I live right over there.
I'll pick you up in the morning, sir. We can do this.
No. Don't pick me up. I have things to do first.
You go follow your leads. I'll find you.
And cut the "sir" shit, Twitch.

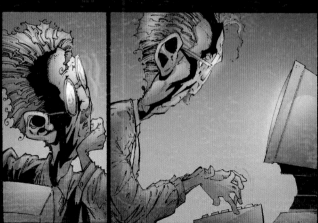POLICE
WEB
SEARCH
ENGINEUDA

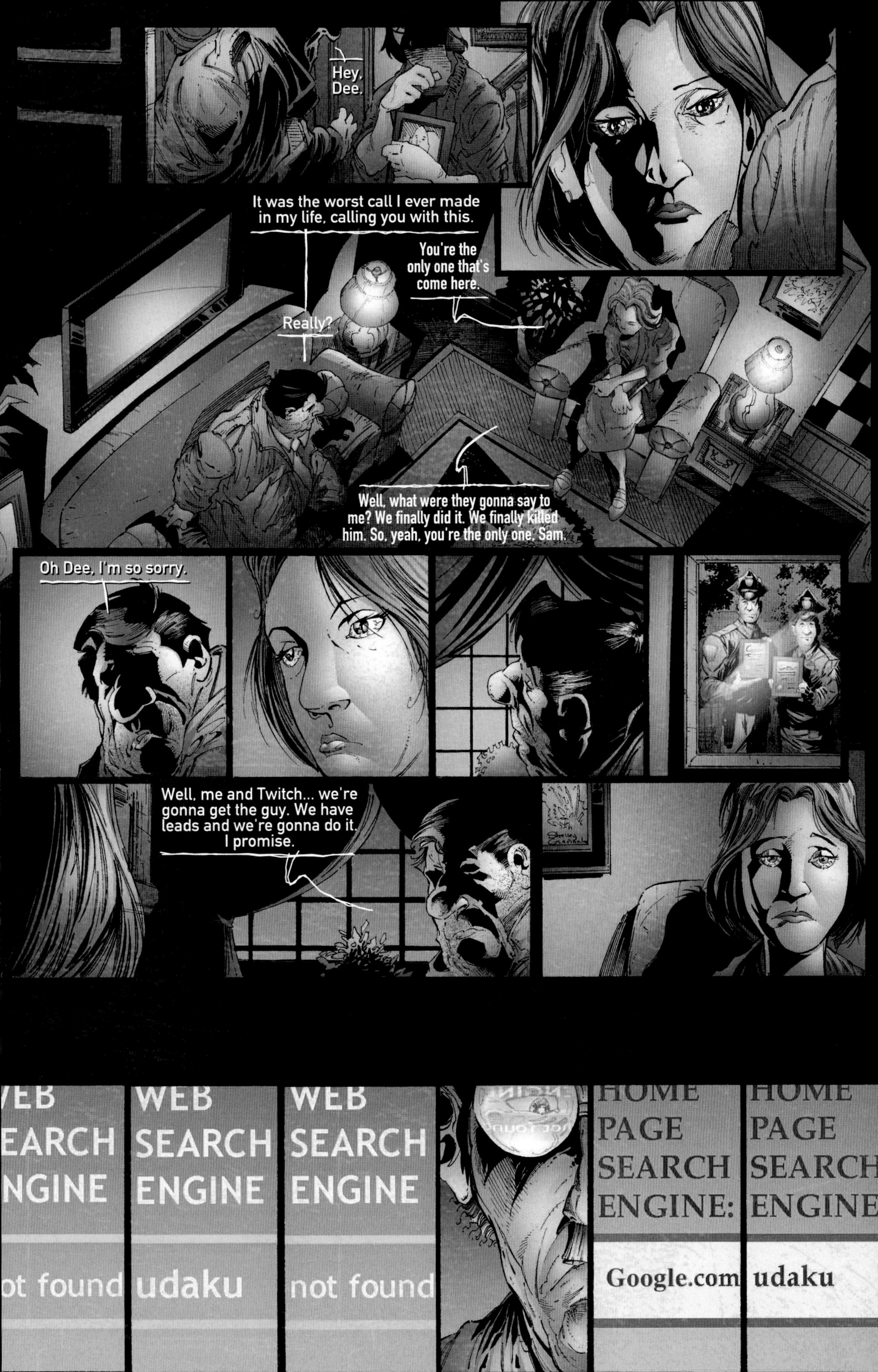
Hey, Dee.
It was the worst call I ever made in my life, calling you with this.
You're the only one that's come here.
Really?
Well, what were they gonna say to me? We finally did it. We finally killed him. So, yeah, you're the only one, Sam.
Oh Dee, I'm so sorry.
Well, me and Twitch... we're gonna get the guy. We have leads and we're gonna do it. I promise.
WEB SEARCH ENGINE
not found
WEB SEARCH ENGINE
udaku
WEB SEARCH ENGINE
not found
HOME PAGE SEARCH ENGINE:
Google.com
HOME PAGE SEARCH ENGINE
udaku

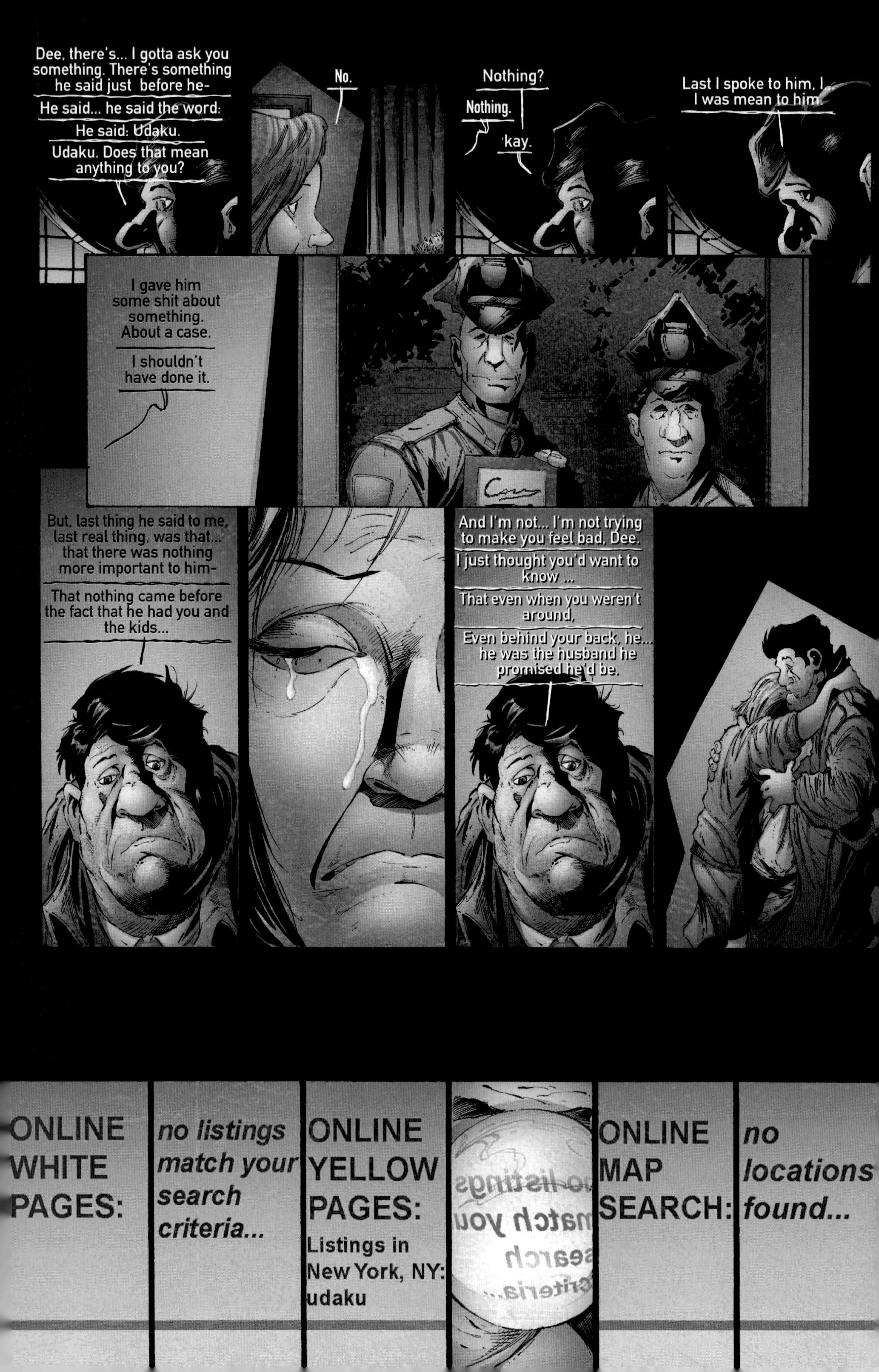
Dee, there's... I gotta ask you something. There's something he said just before he-
He said... he said the word:
He said: Udaku.
Udaku. Does that mean anything to you?
No.
Nothing?
Nothing.
'kay.
Last I spoke to him, I... I was mean to him.
I gave him some shit about something. About a case.
I shouldn't have done it.
But, last thing he said to me, last real thing, was that... that there was nothing more important to him-
That nothing came before the fact that he had you and the kids...
And I'm not... I'm not trying to make you feel bad, Dee.
I just thought you'd want to know ...
That even when you weren't around,
Even behind your back, he... he was the husband he promised he'd be.
ONLINE WHITE PAGES:
no listings match your search criteria...
ONLINE YELLOW PAGES:
Listings in New York, NY: udaku
no listings match your search criteria...
ONLINE MAP SEARCH:
no locations found...

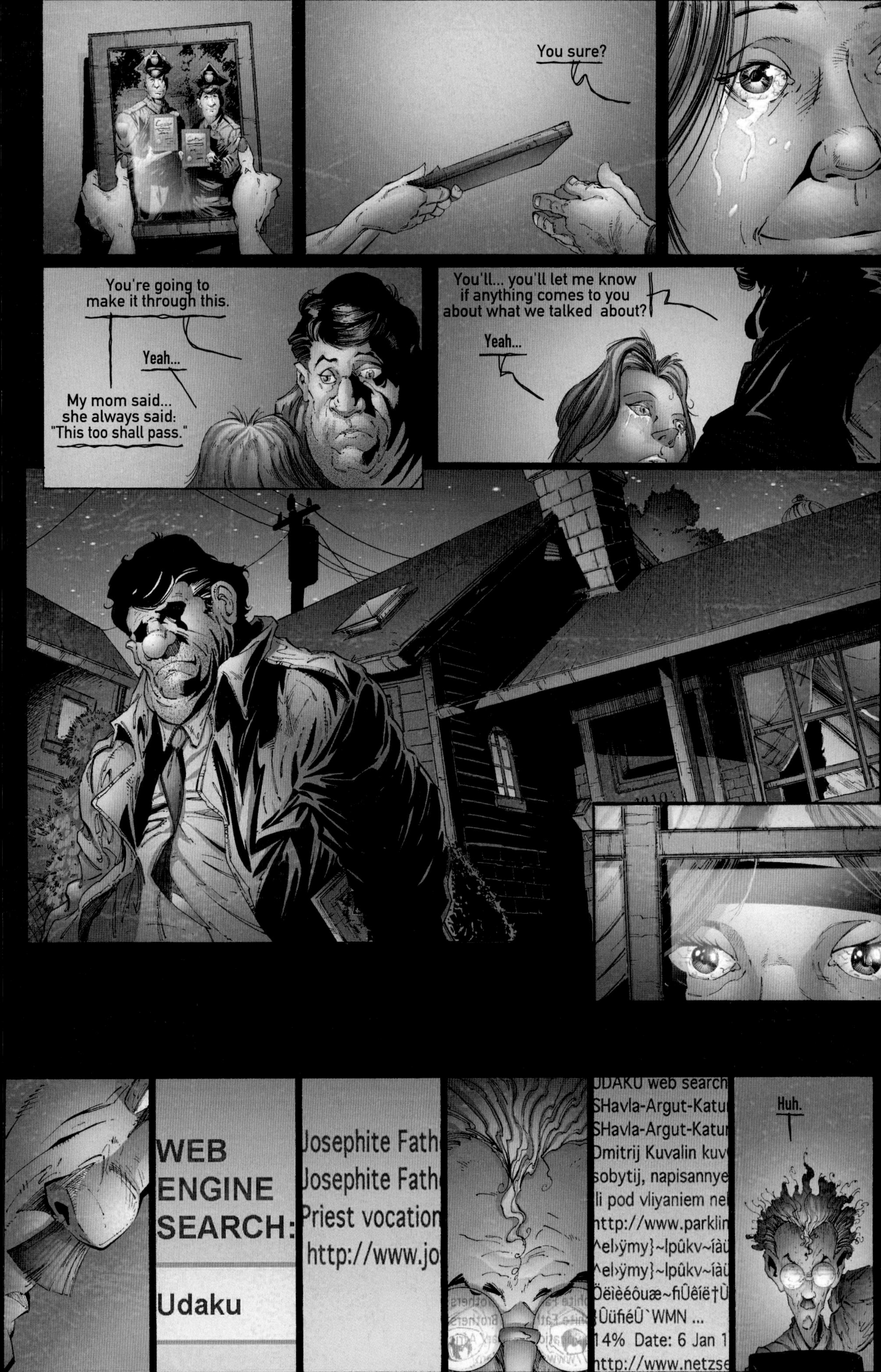
You sure?
You're going to make it through this.
Yeah...
My mom said... she always said: "This too shall pass."
You'll... you'll let me know if anything comes to you about what we talked about?
Yeah...
WEB ENGINE SEARCH:
Udaku
Josephite Fath
Josephite Fath
Priest vocation
http://www.jo
UDAKU web search
SHavla-Argut-Katu
SHavla-Argut-Katu
Dmitrij Kuvalin kuv
sobytij, napisannye
li pod vliyaniem ne
http://www.parklin
14% Date: 6 Jan 1
http://www.netzse
Huh.

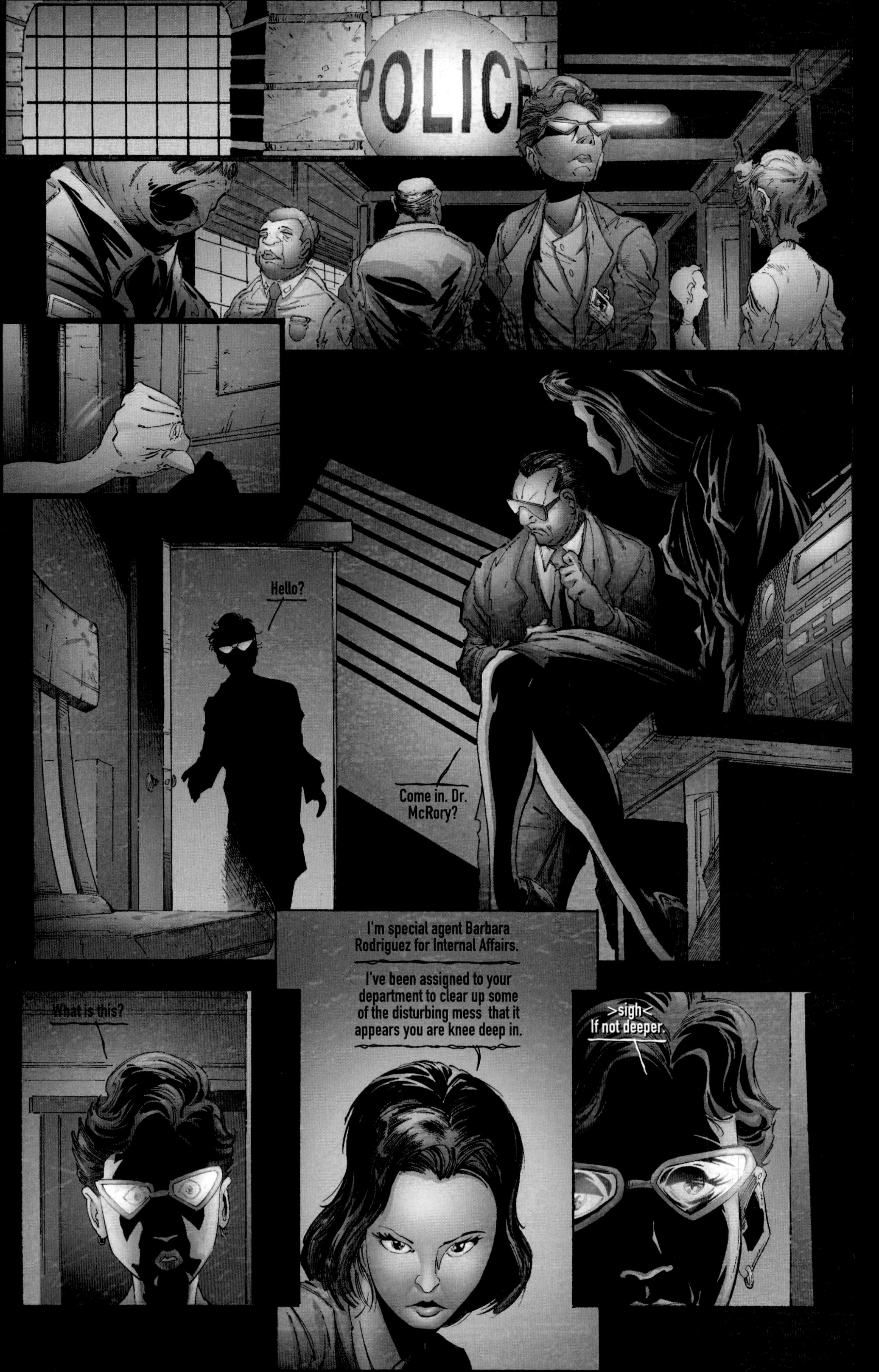
POLICE
Hello?
Come in. Dr. McRory?
What is this?
I'm special agent Barbara Rodriguez for Internal Affairs.
I've been assigned to your department to clear up some of the disturbing mess that it appears you are knee deep in.
>sigh<
If not deeper.

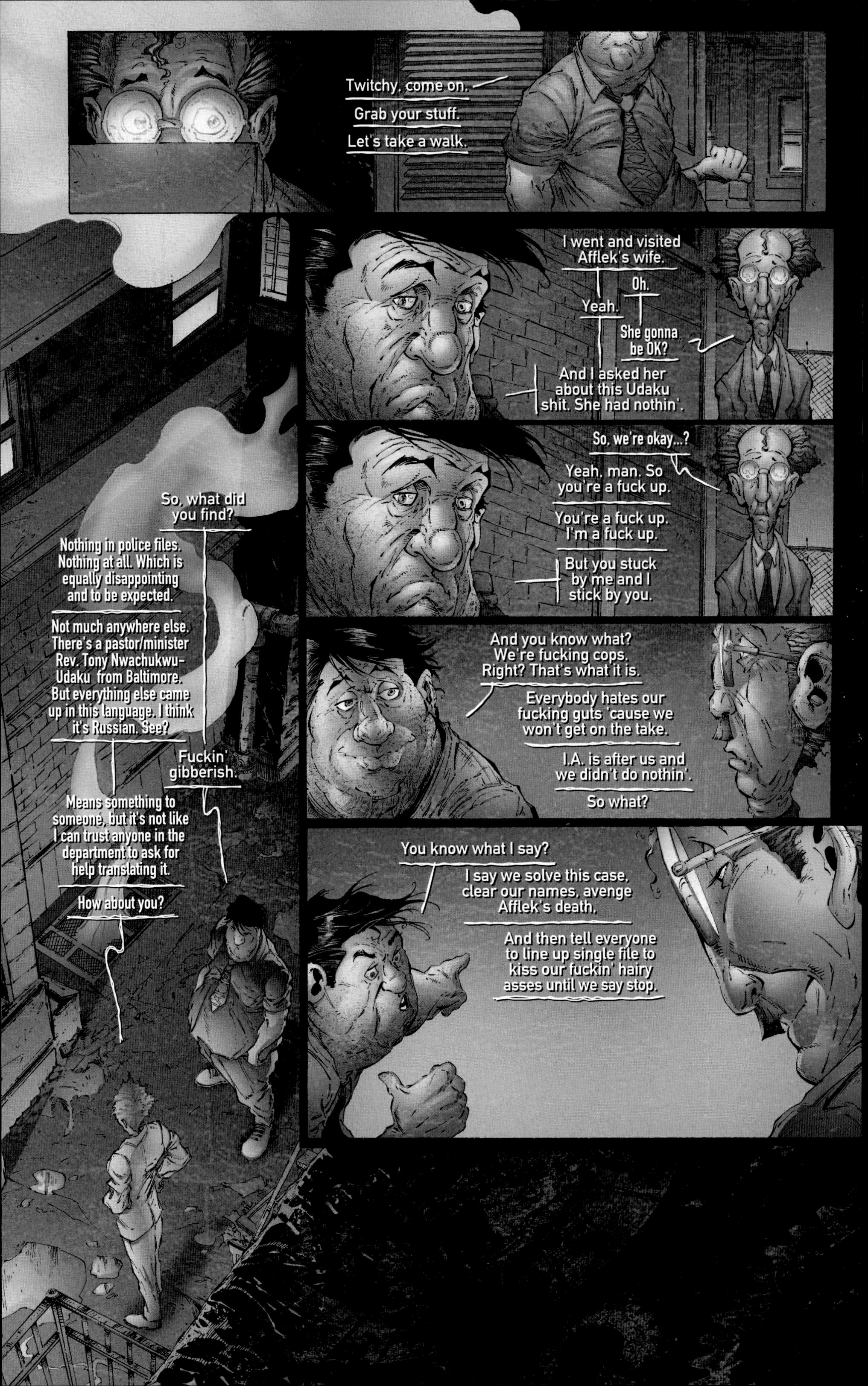

Twitchy, come on.
Grab your stuff.
Let's take a walk.
So, what did you find?
Nothing in police files. Nothing at all. Which is equally disappointing and to be expected.
Not much anywhere else. There's a pastor/minister Rev. Tony Nwachukwu-Udaku from Baltimore. But everything else came up in this language. I think it's Russian. See?
Fuckin' gibberish.
Means something to someone, but it's not like I can trust anyone in the department to ask for help translating it.
How about you?
I went and visited Afflek's wife.
Oh.
Yeah.
She gonna be OK?
And I asked her about this Udaku shit. She had nothin'.
So, we're okay...?
Yeah, man. So you're a fuck up.
You're a fuck up. I'm a fuck up.
But you stuck by me and I stick by you.
And you know what? We're fucking cops. Right? That's what it is.
Everybody hates our fucking guts 'cause we won't get on the take.
I.A. is after us and we didn't do nothin'.
So what?
You know what I say?
I say we solve this case, clear our names, avenge Afflek's death.
And then tell everyone to line up single file to kiss our fuckin' hairy asses until we say stop.

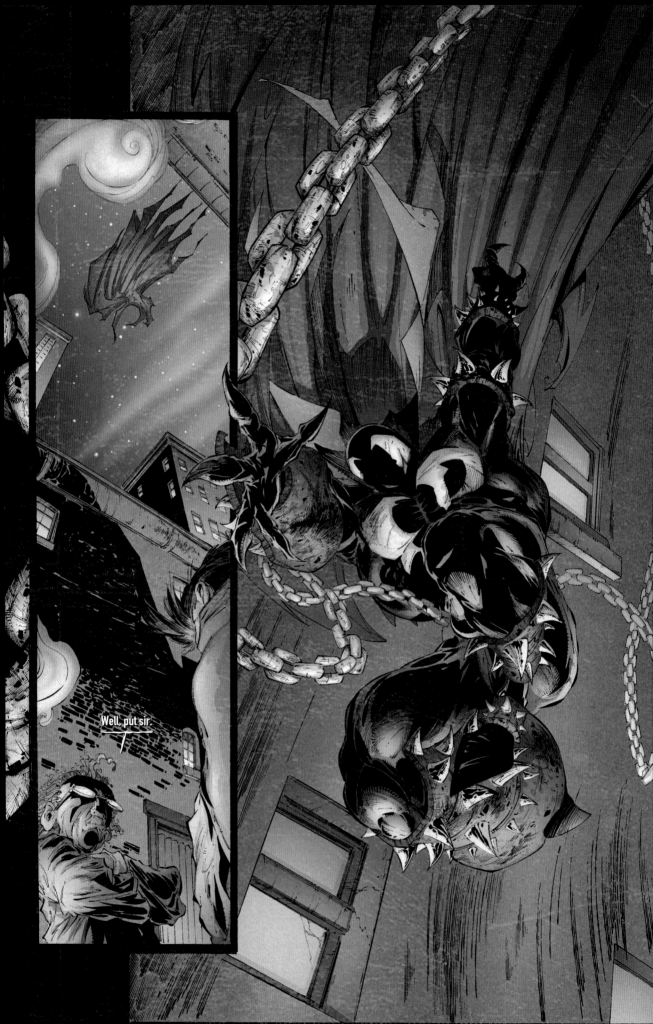

Well, put sir.

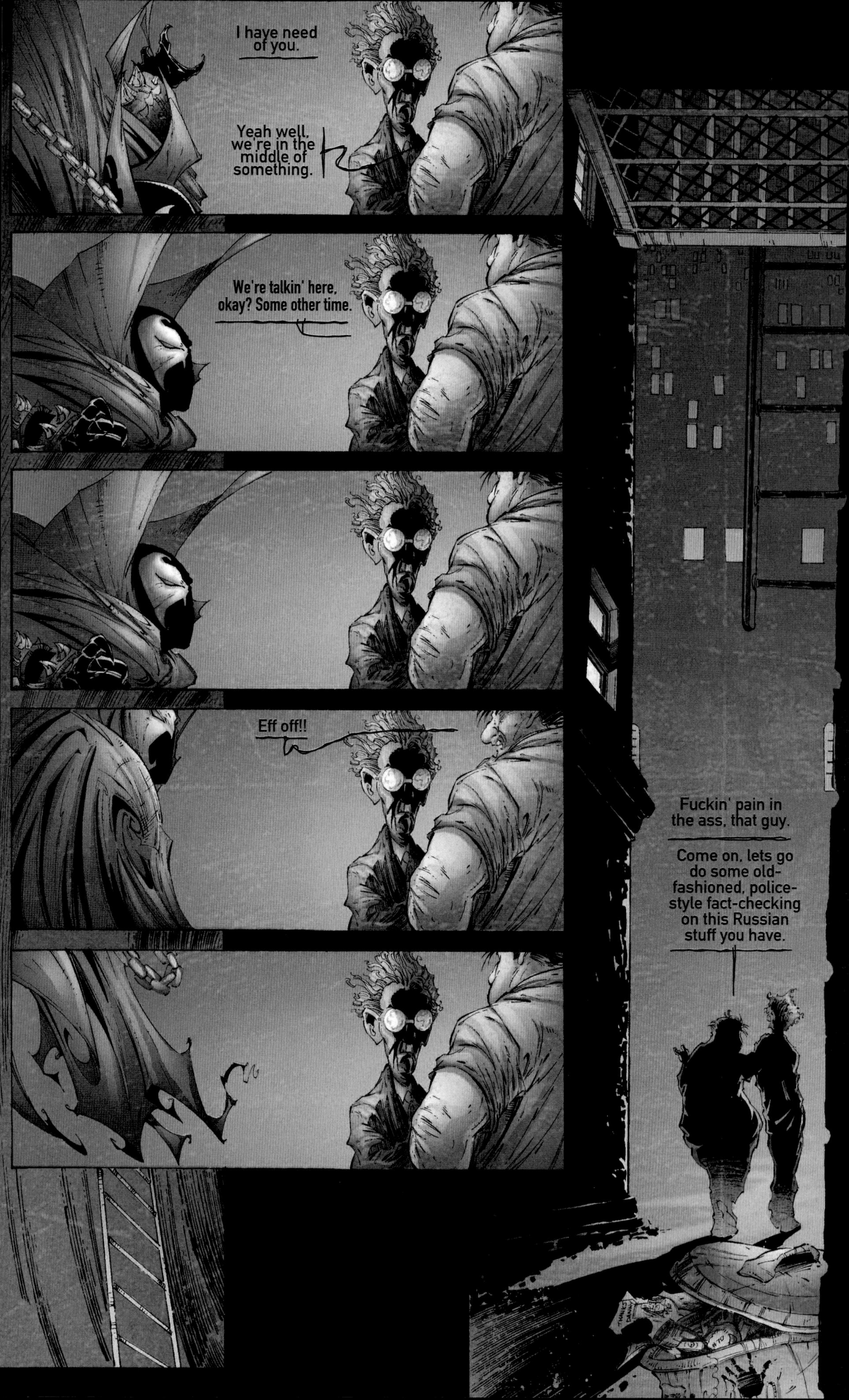

I haye need of you.
Yeah well, we're in the middle of something.
We're talkin' here, okay? Some other time.
Eff off!!
Fuckin' pain in the ass, that guy.
Come on, lets go do some old-fashioned, police-style fact-checking on this Russian stuff you have.

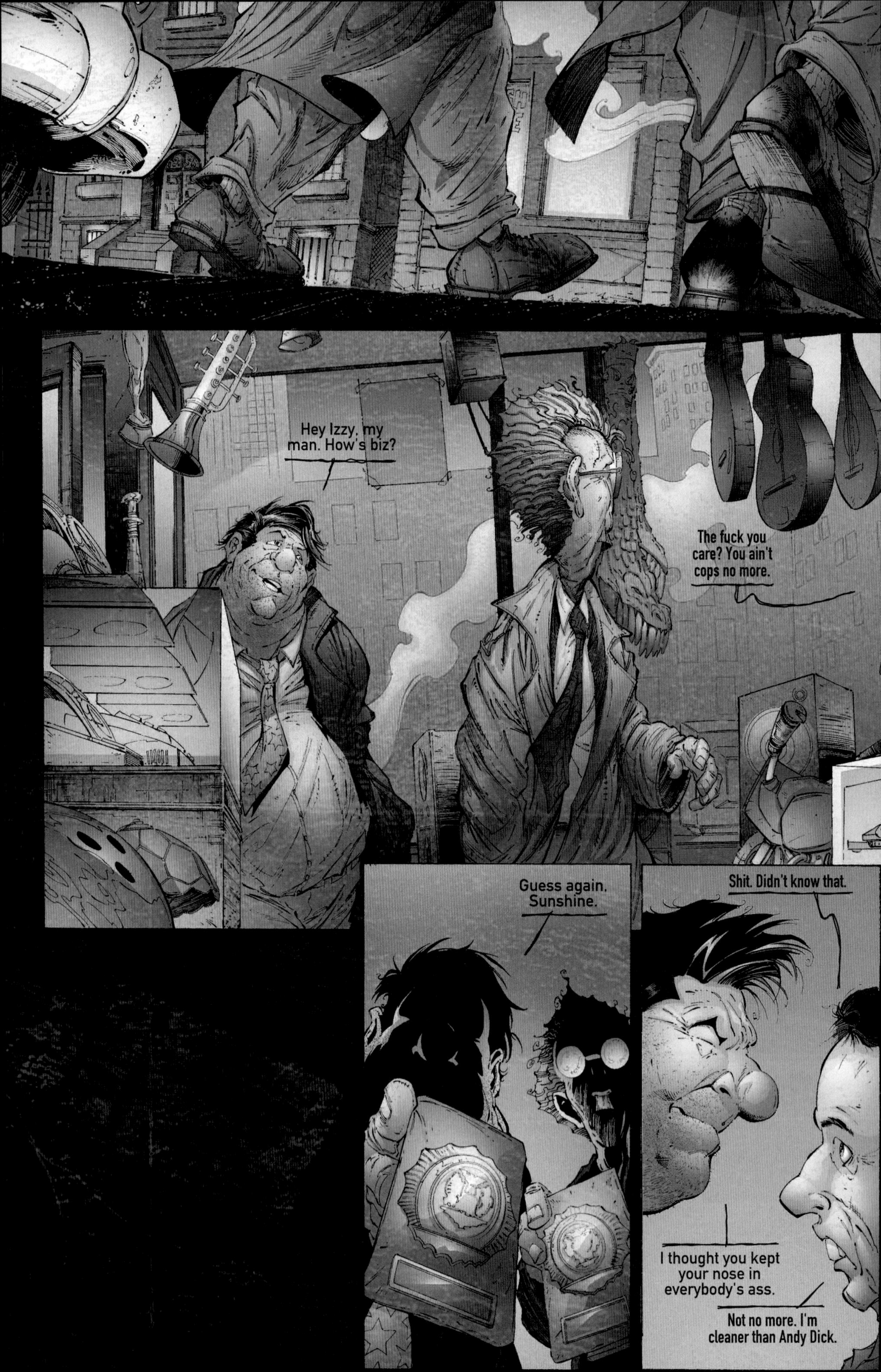
Hey Izzy, my man. How's biz?
The fuck you care? You ain't cops no more.
Guess again, Sunshine.
Shit. Didn't know that.
I thought you kept your nose in everybody's ass.
Not no more. I'm cleaner than Andy Dick.

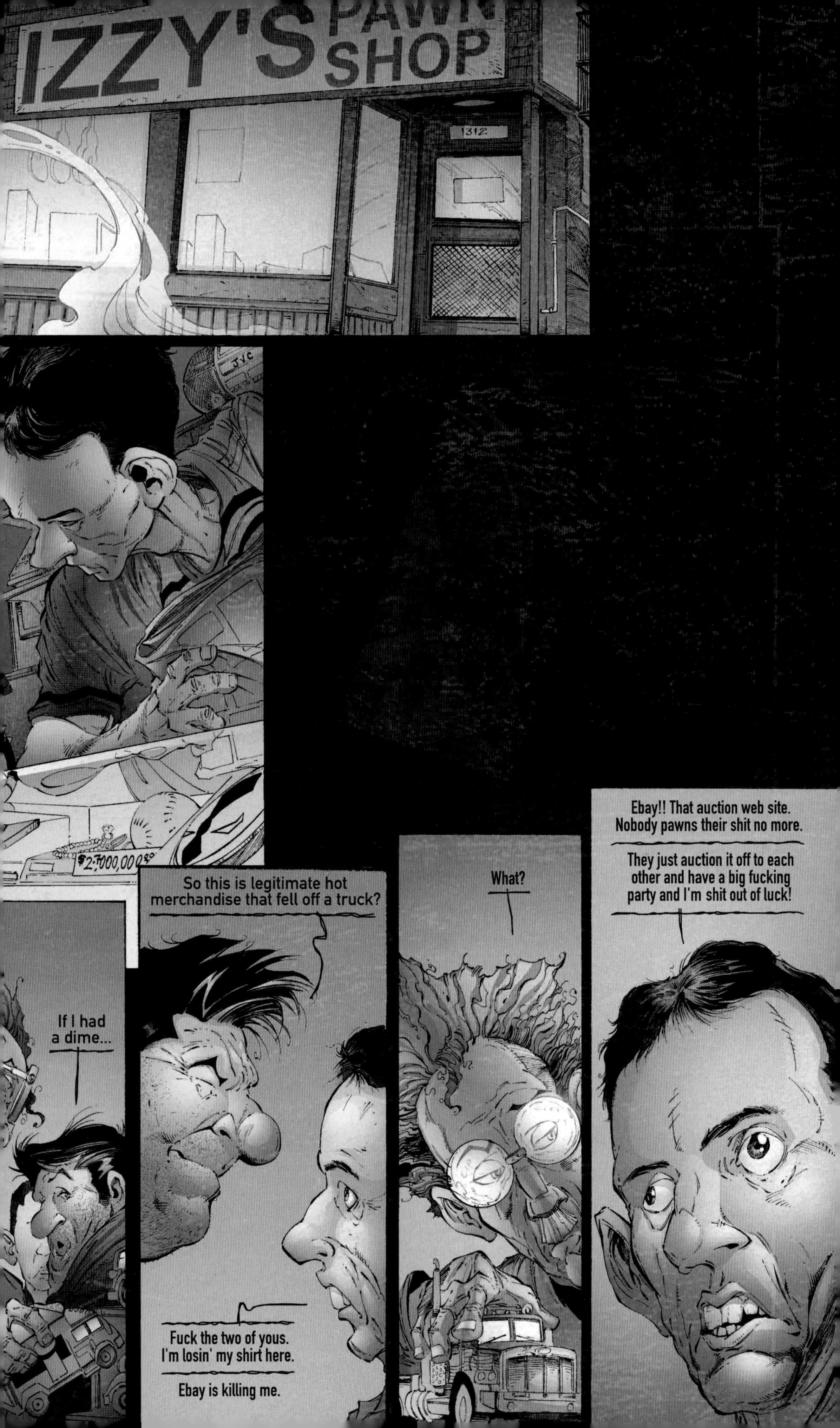
IZZY'S PAWN SHOP
1312
$2,000,000
If I had a dime...
So this is legitimate hot merchandise that fell off a truck?
Fuck the two of yous. I'm losin' my shirt here.
Ebay is killing me.
What?
Ebay!! That auction web site. Nobody pawns their shit no more.
They just auction it off to each other and have a big fucking party and I'm shit out of luck!

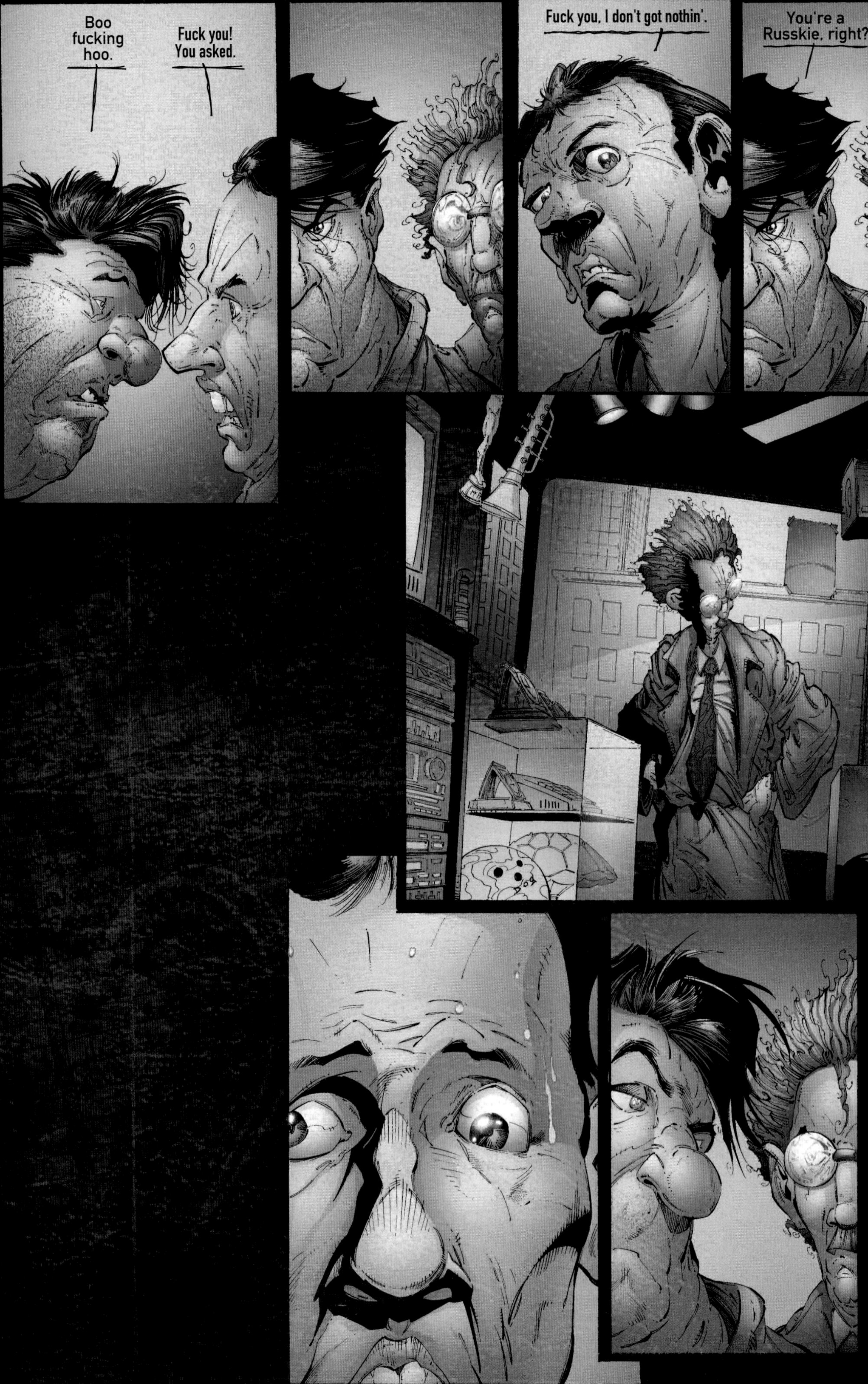
Boo fucking hoo.
Fuck you! You asked.
Fuck you, I don't got nothin'.
You're a Russkie, right?

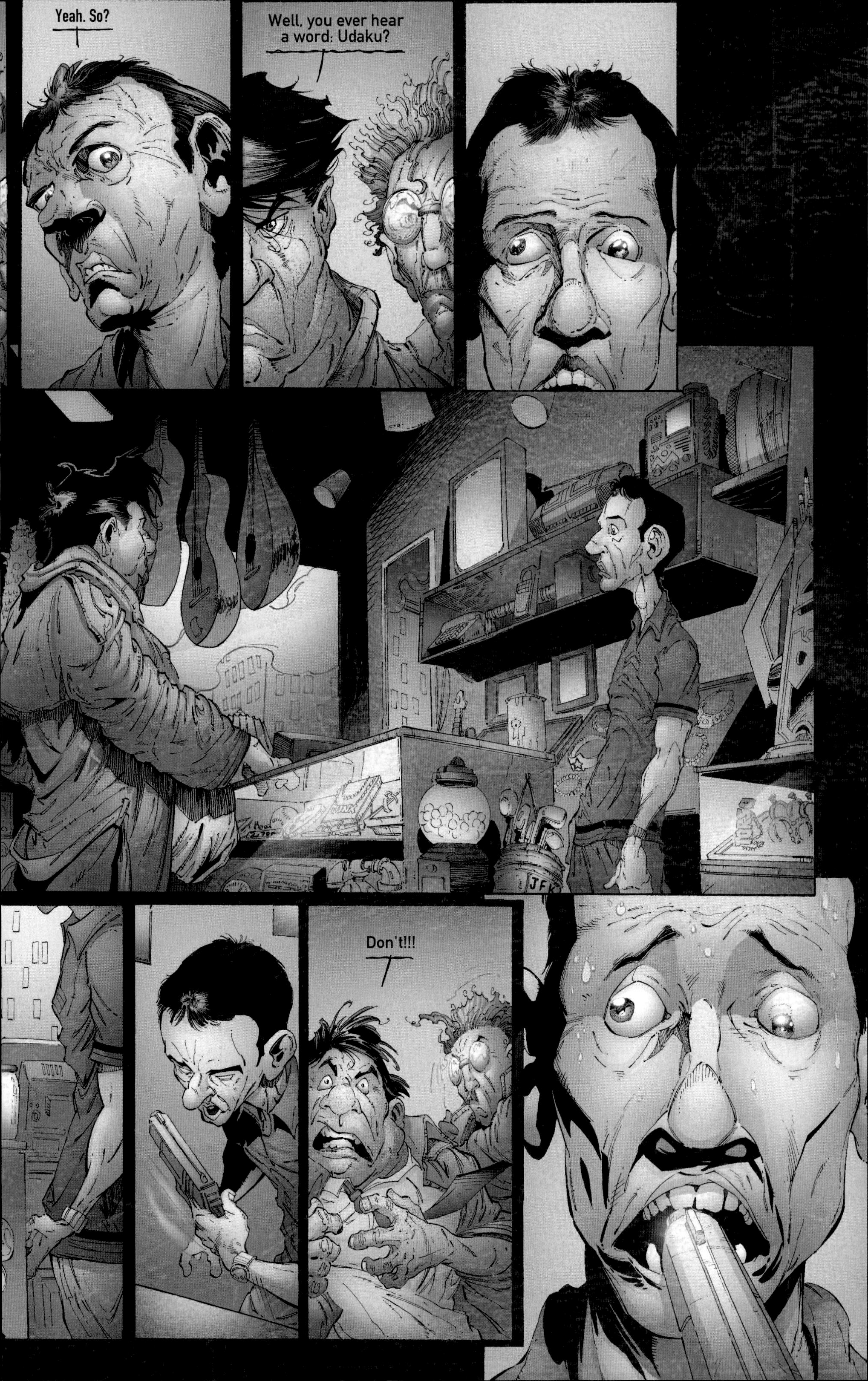
Yeah. So?
Well, you ever hear a word: Udaku?
Don't!!!

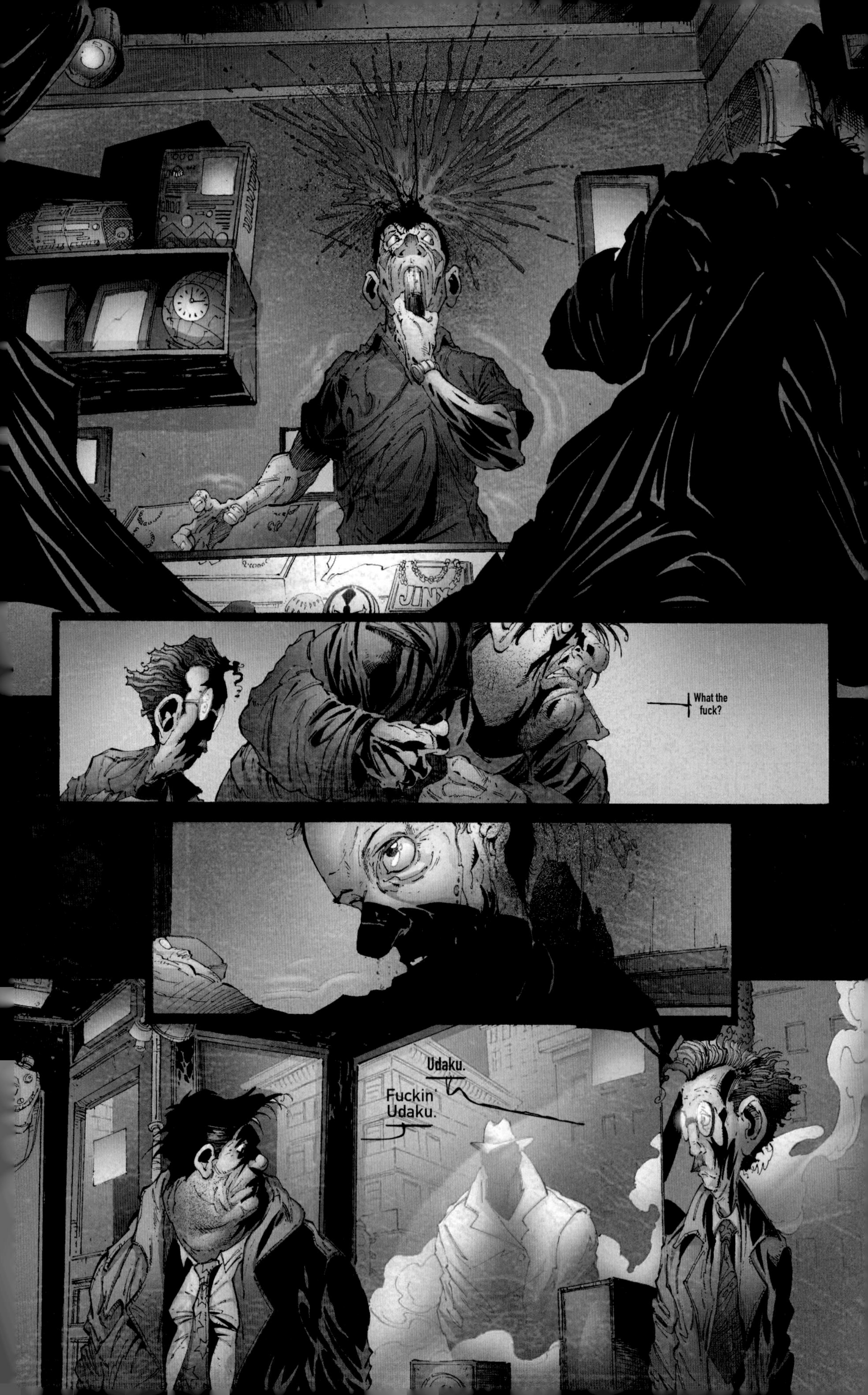
What the fuck?
Udaku.
Fuckin' Udaku.

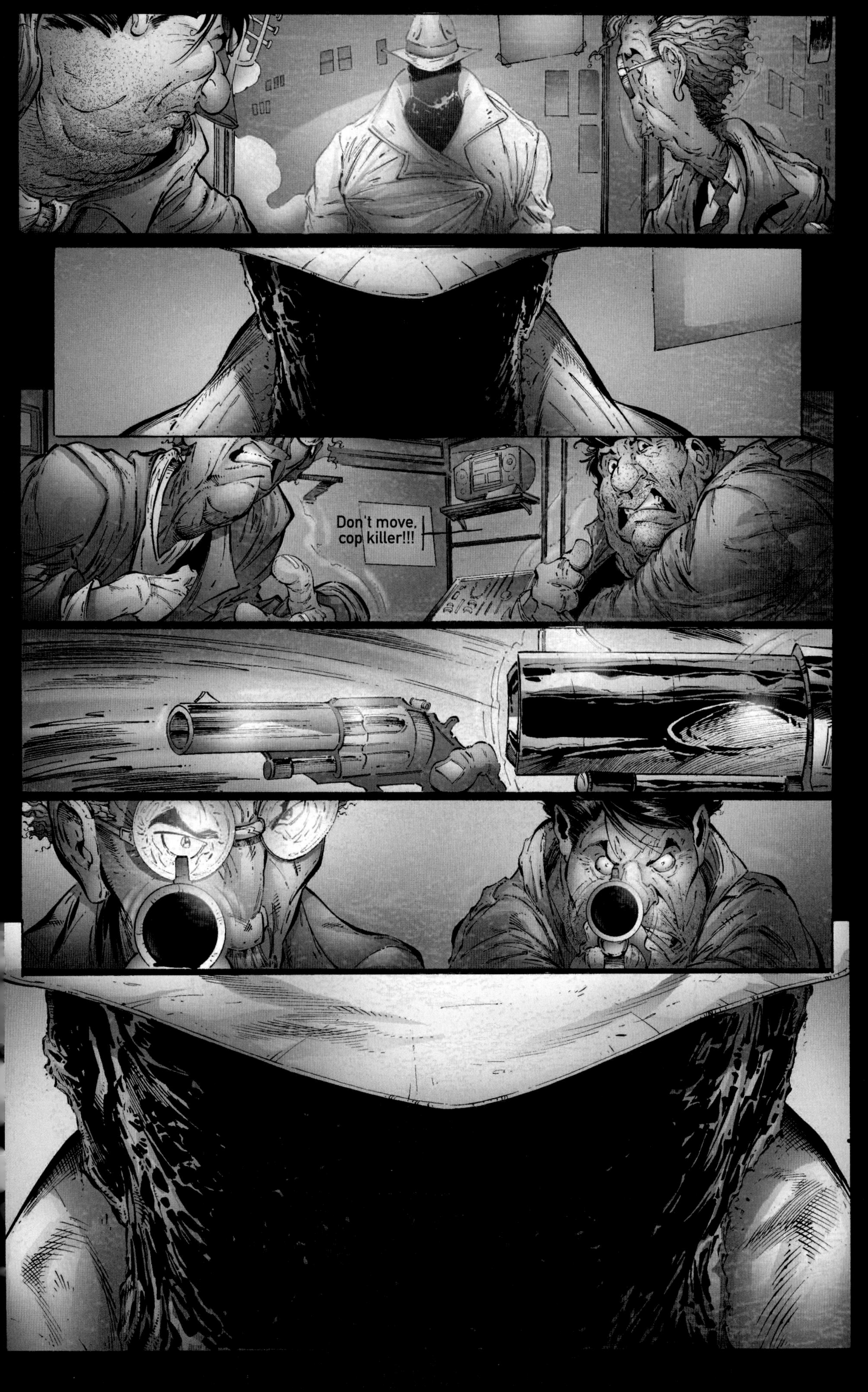
Don't move, cop killer!!!

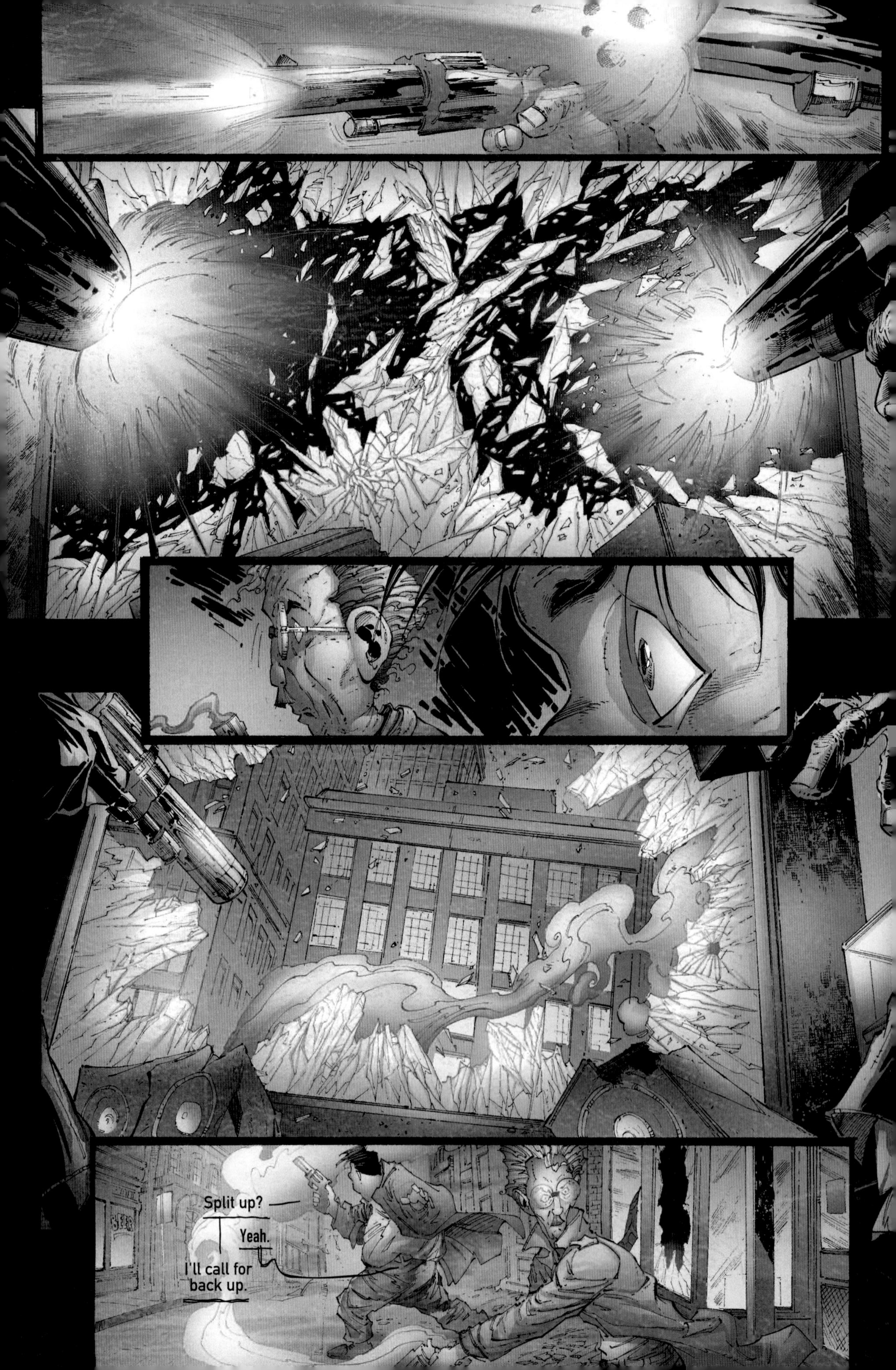

Split up?
Yeah.
I'll call for back up.

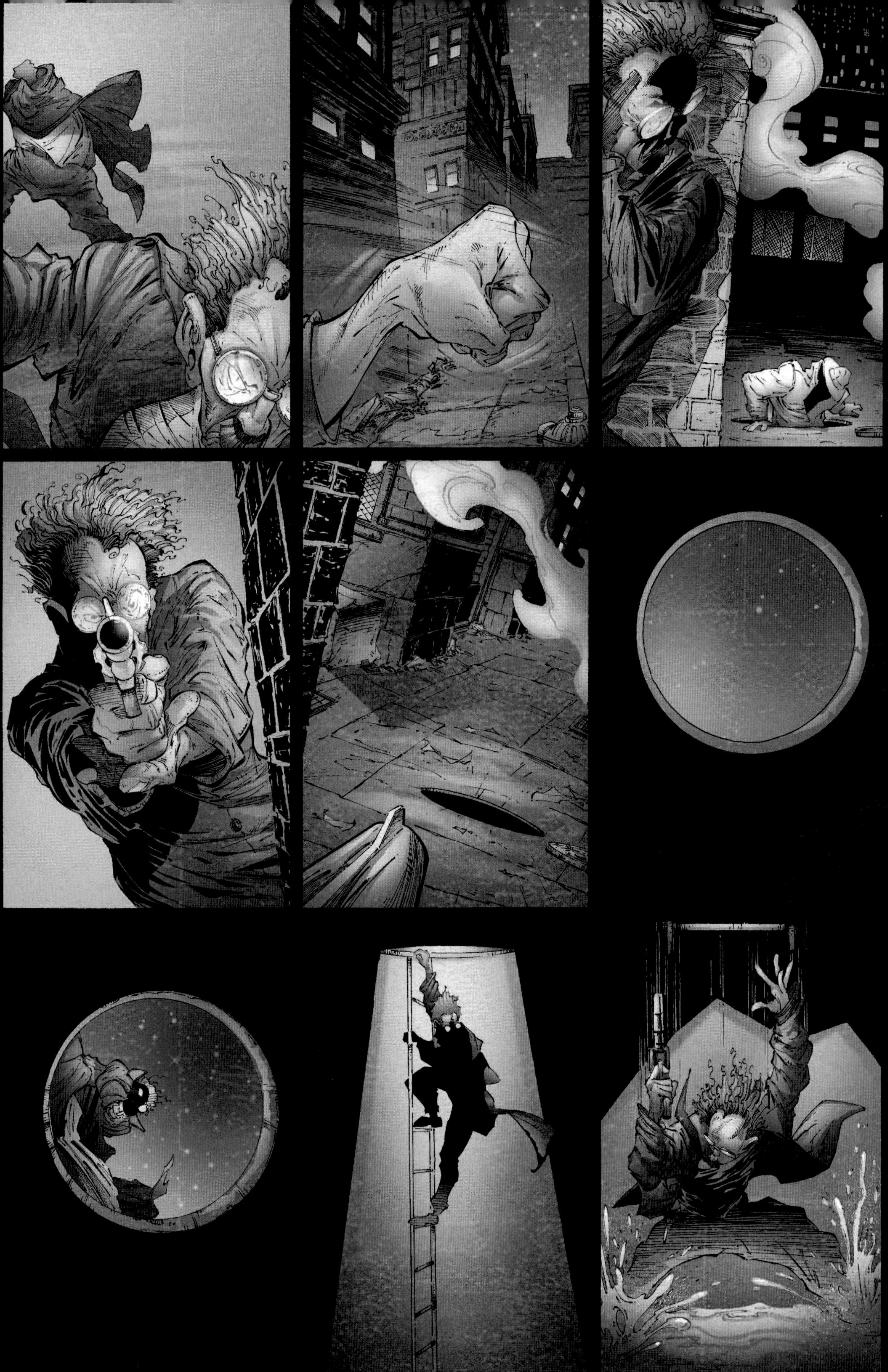

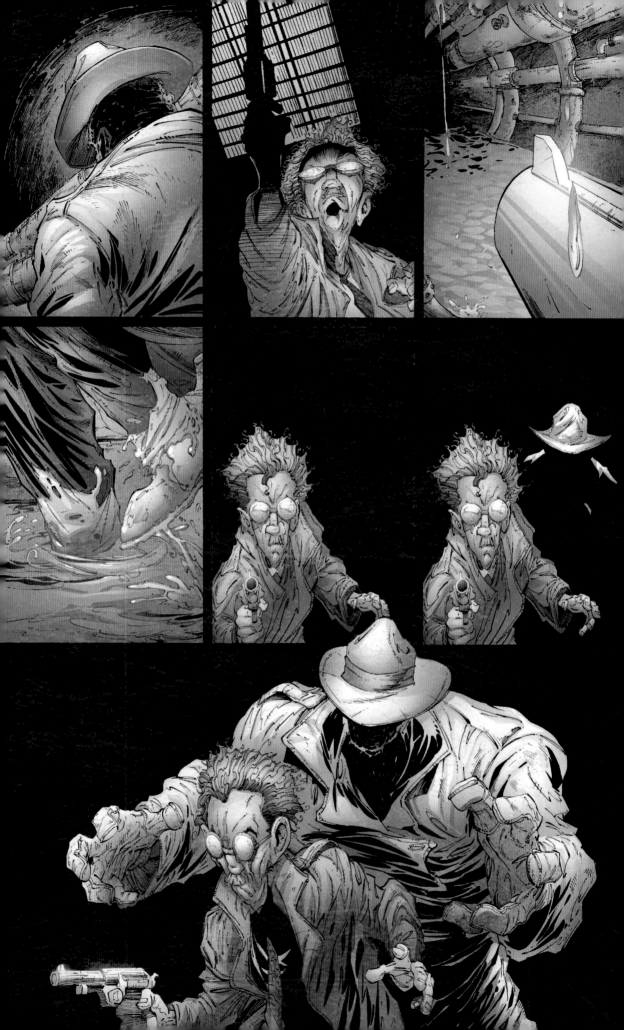

UDAKU

PART 5

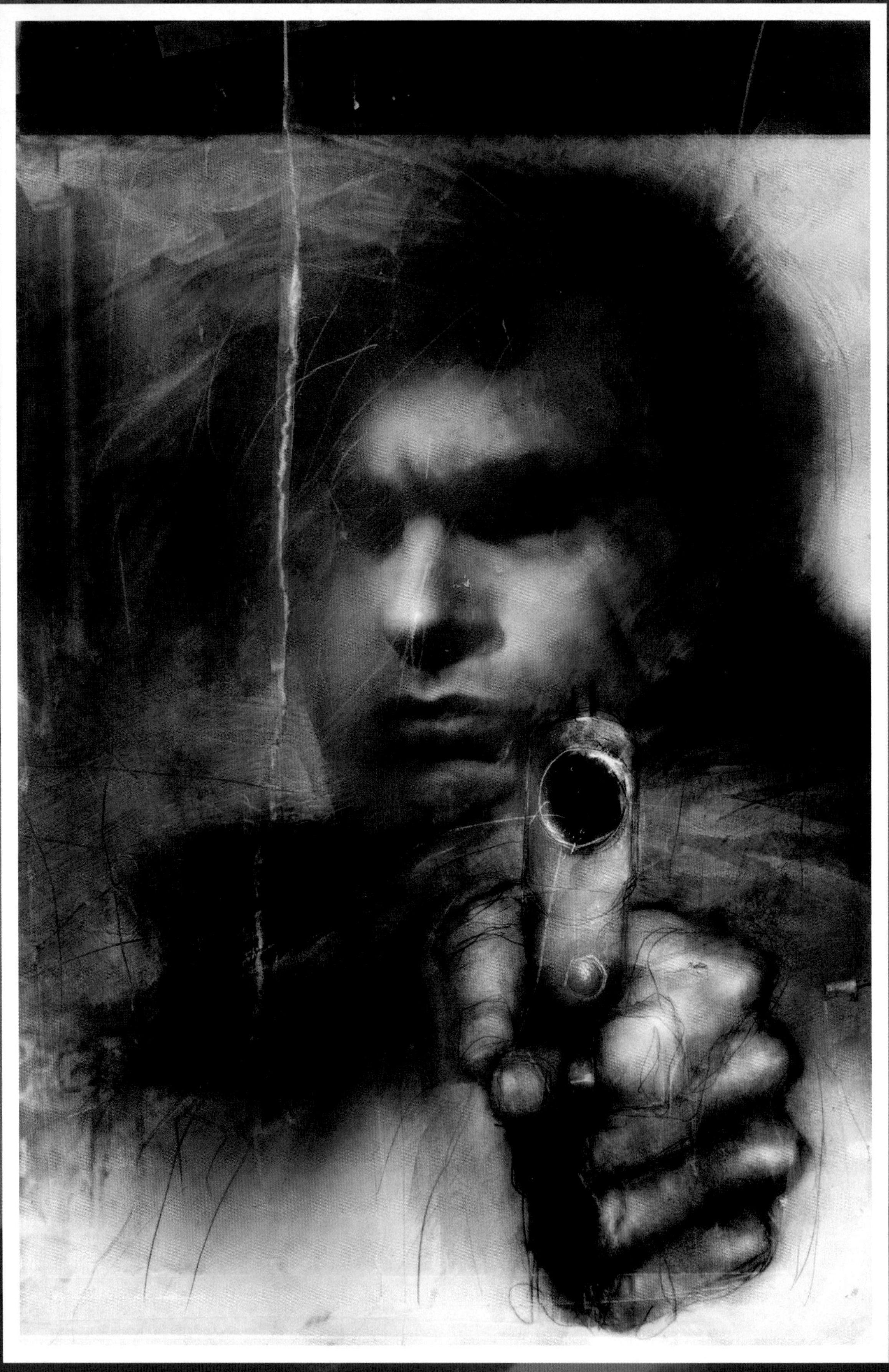

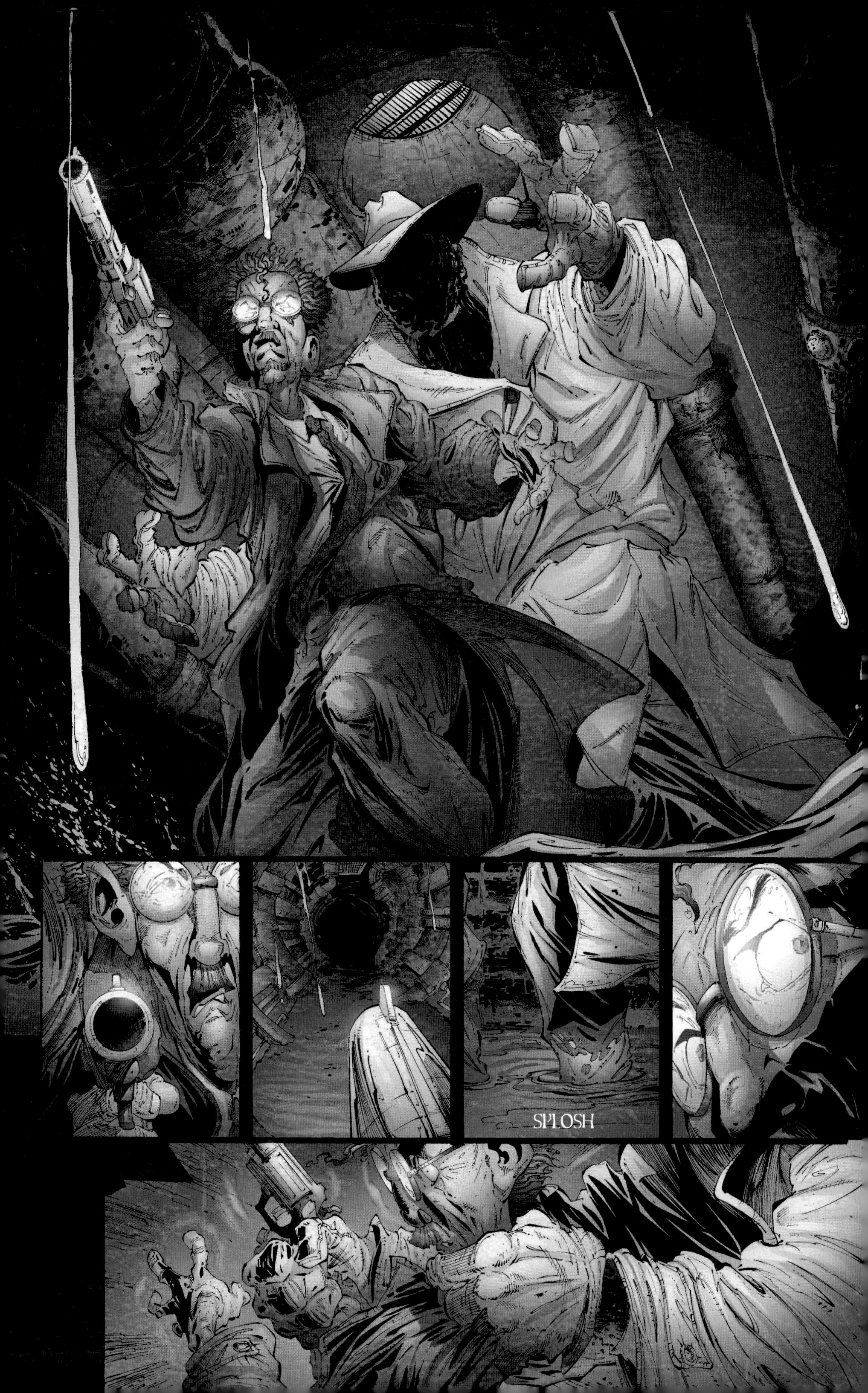
SPLOSH

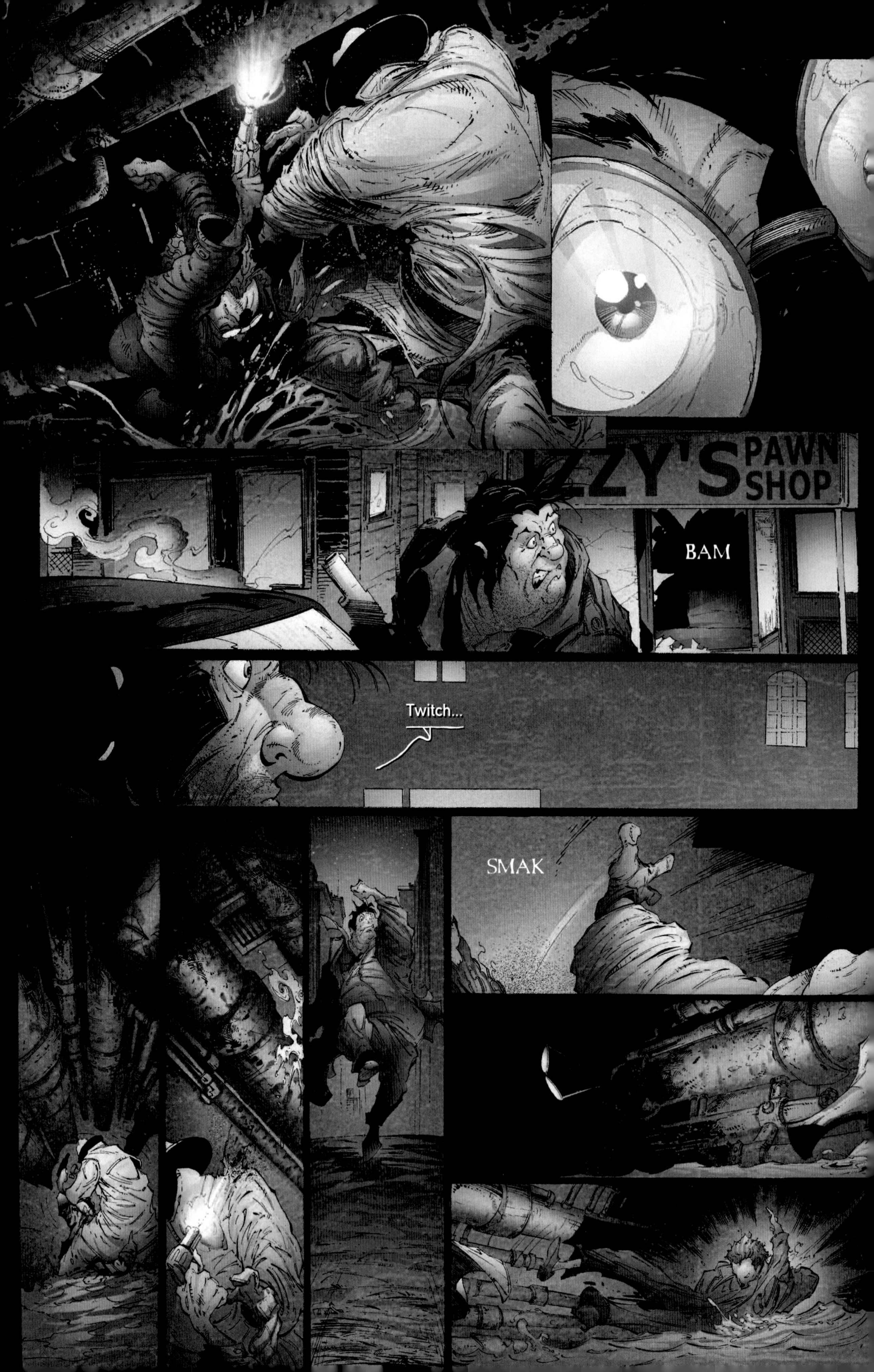

IZZY'S PAWN SHOP
BAM
Twitch...
SMAK

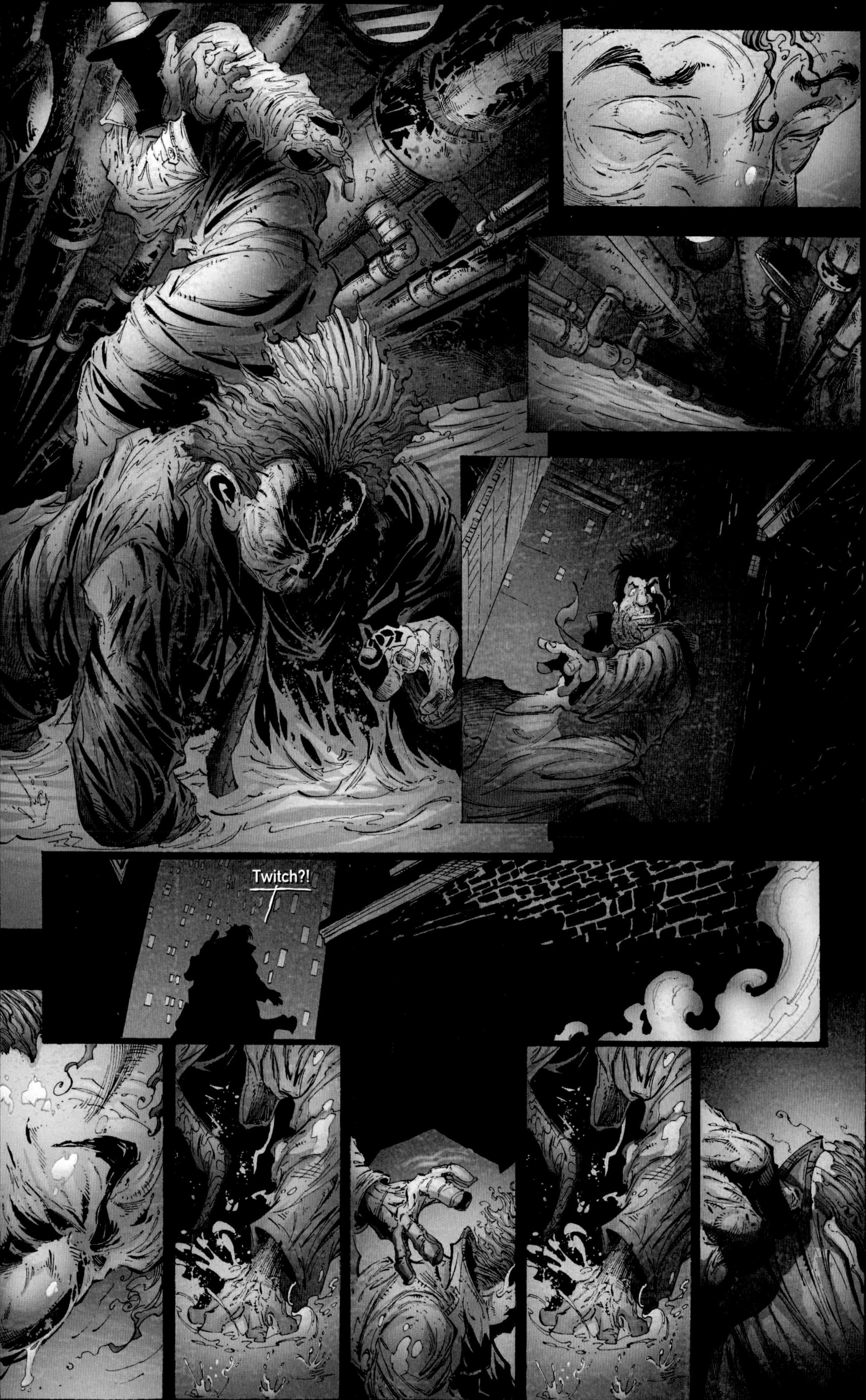
Twitch?!

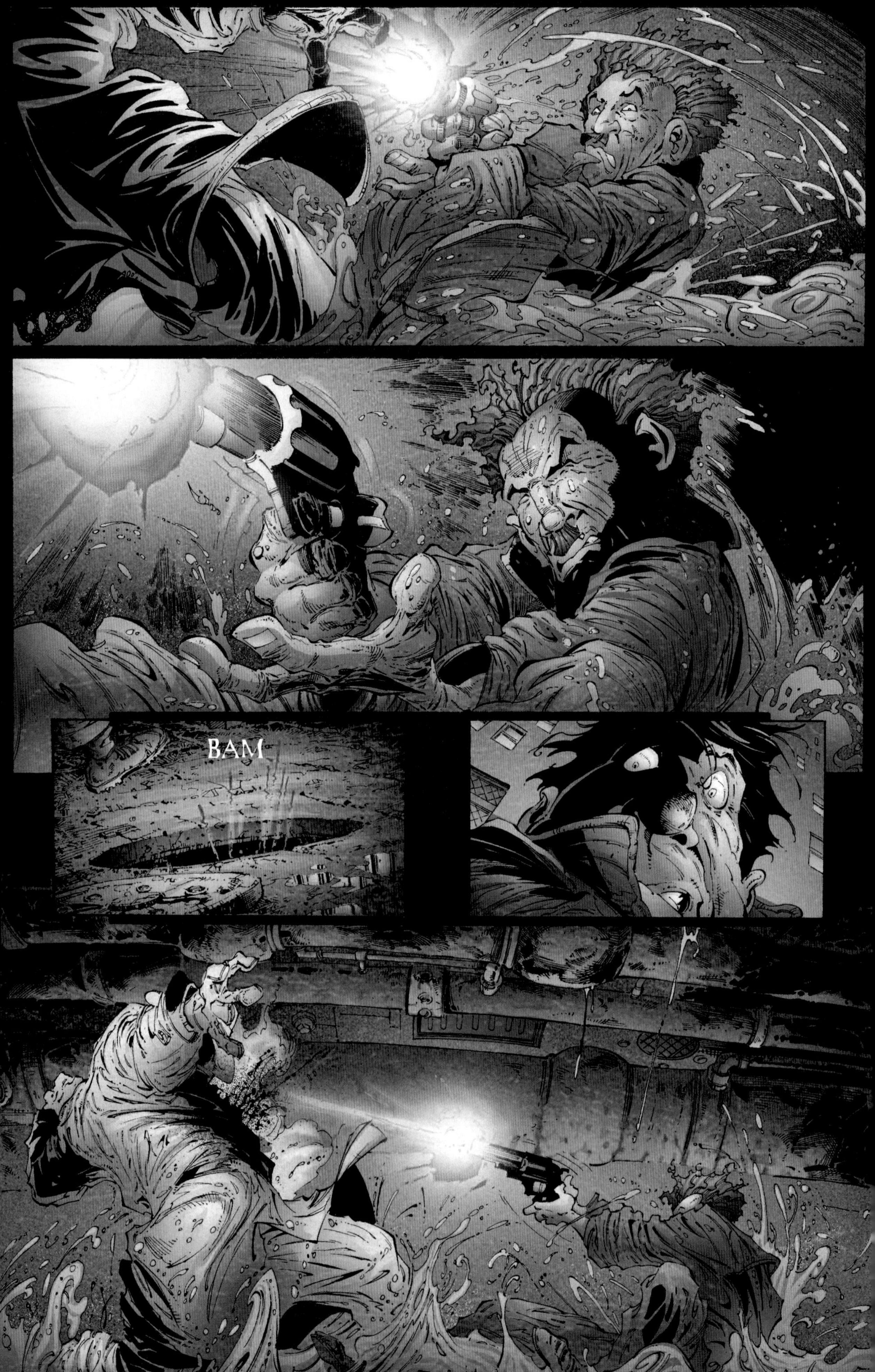
BAM

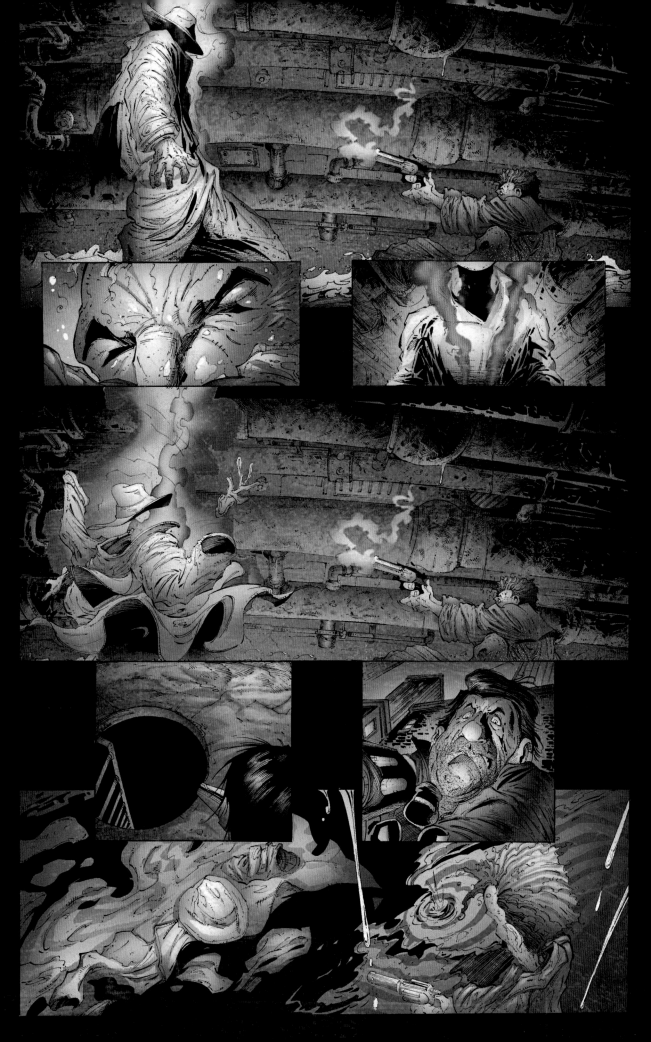

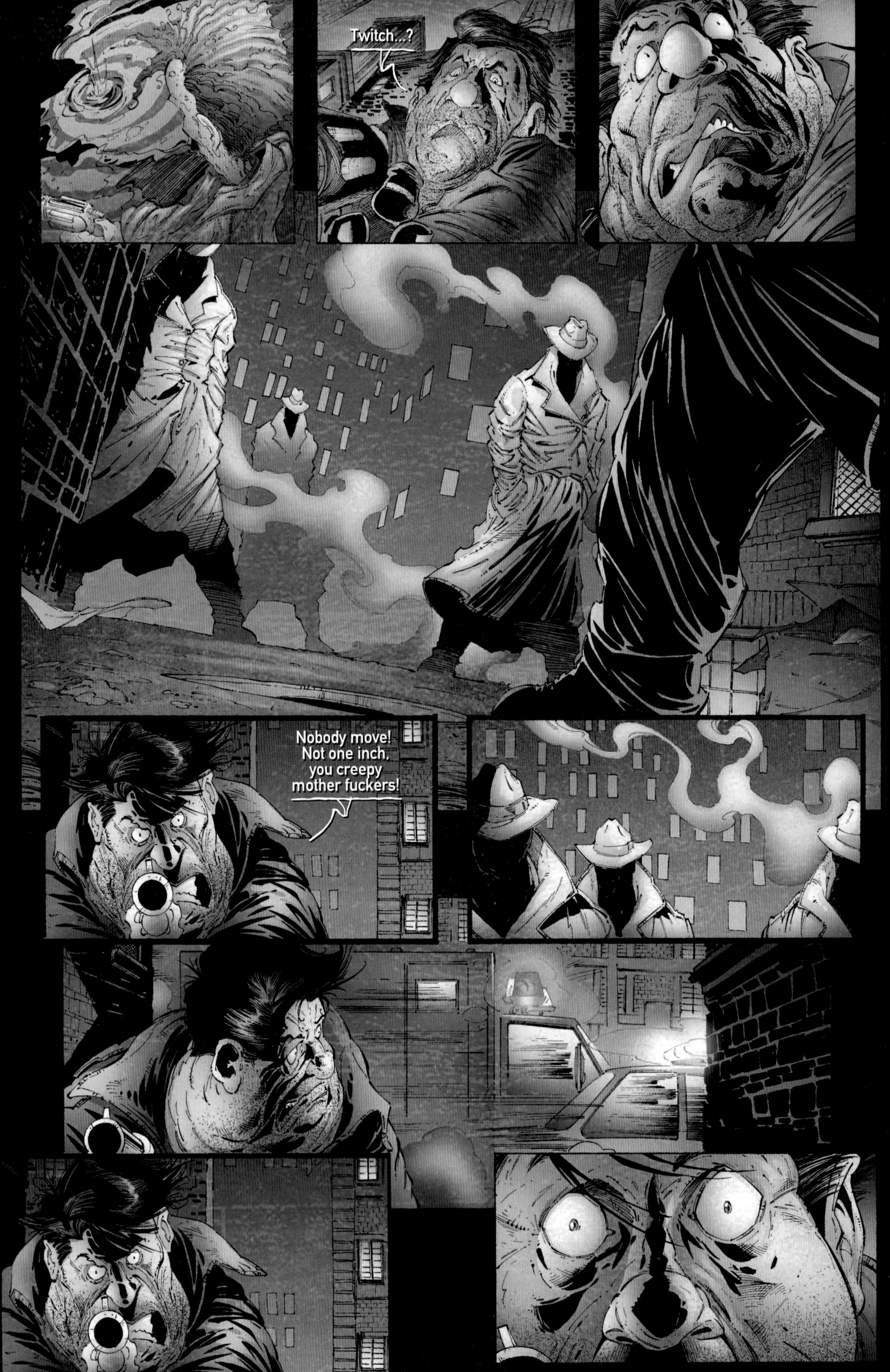
Twitch...?
Nobody move! Not one inch, you creepy mother fuckers!

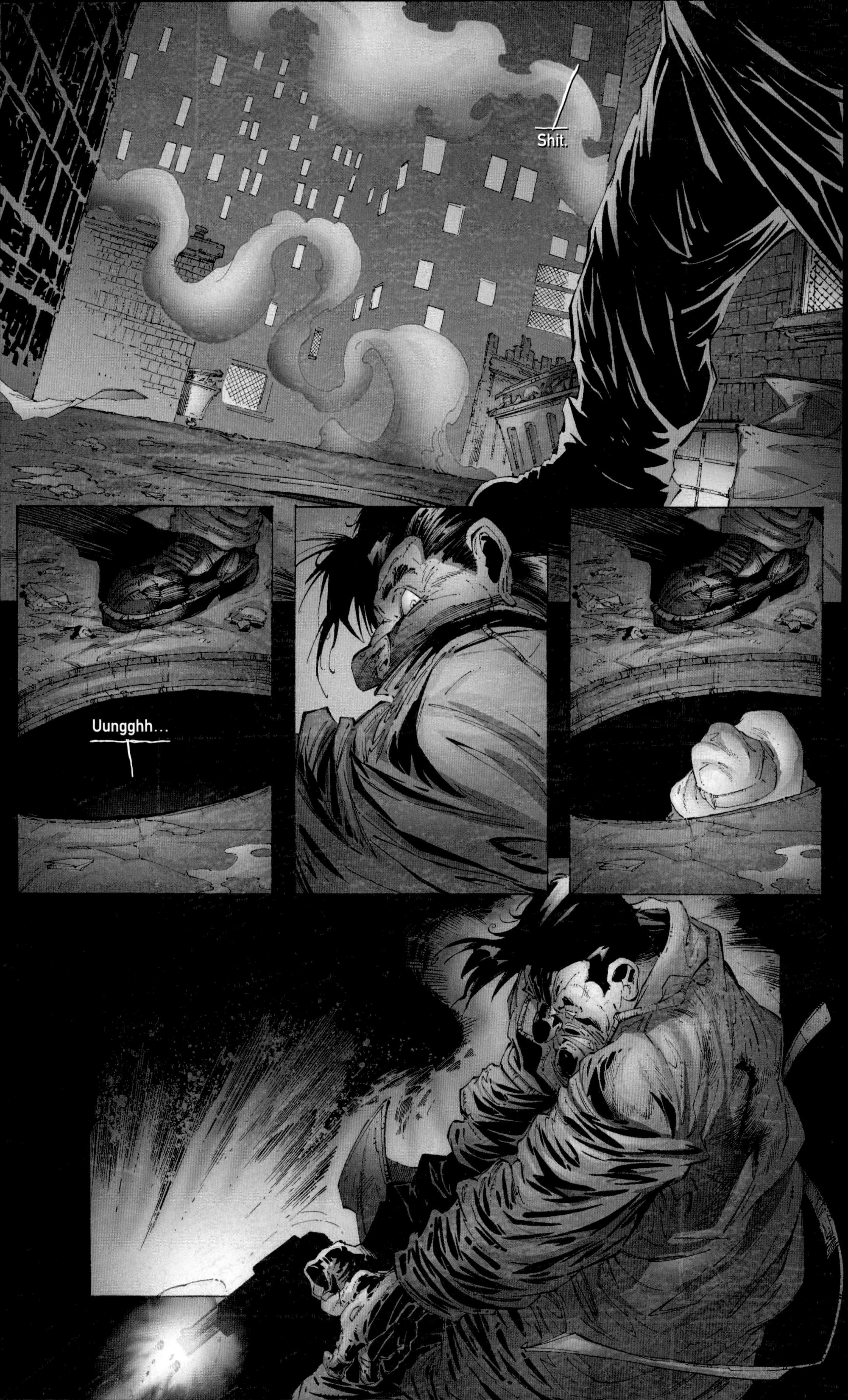
Shit.
Uungghh...

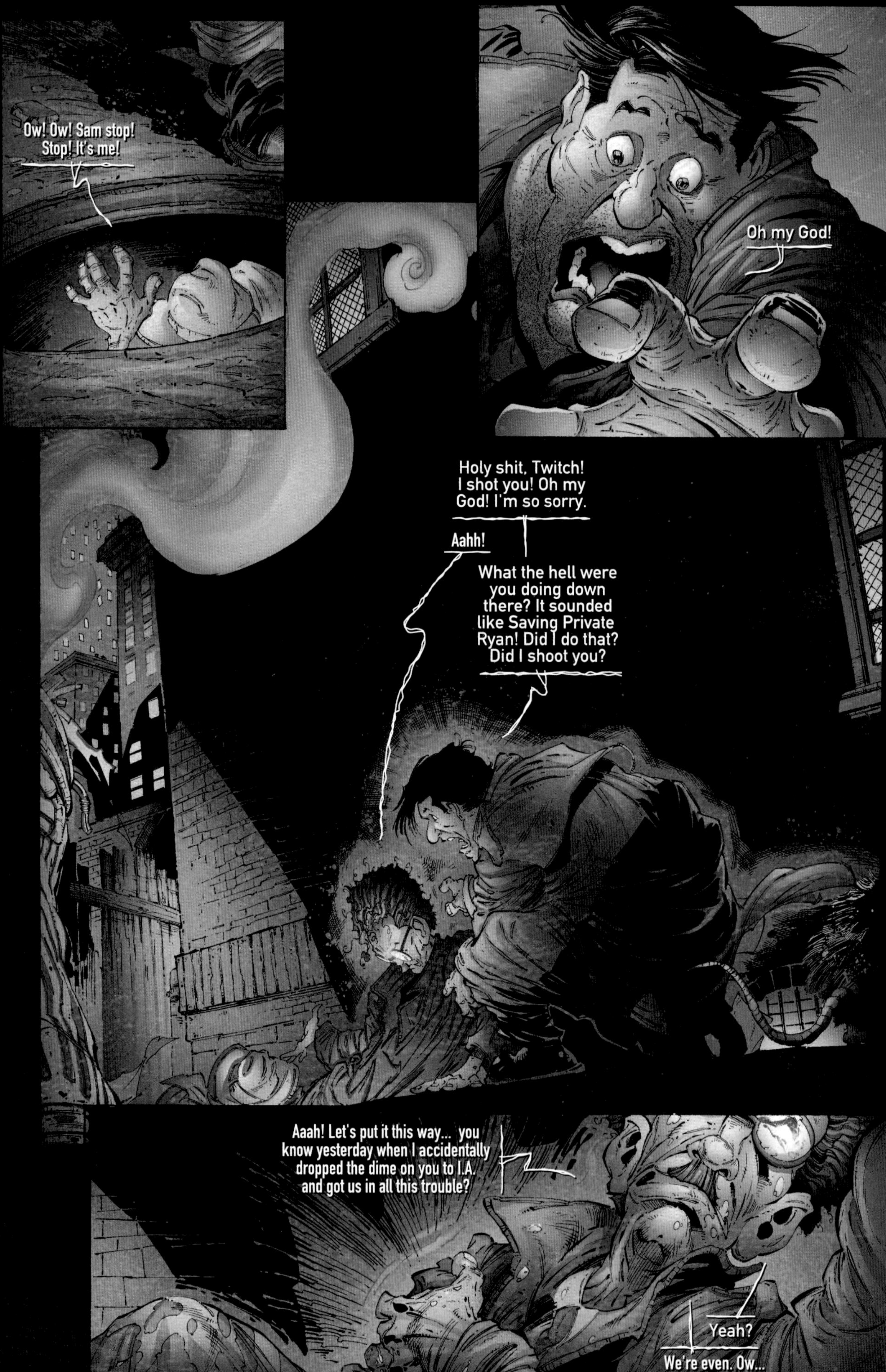
Ow! Ow! Sam stop! Stop! It's me!
Oh my God!
Holy shit, Twitch! I shot you! Oh my God! I'm so sorry.
Aahh!
What the hell were you doing down there? It sounded like Saving Private Ryan! Did I do that? Did I shoot you?
Aaah! Let's put it this way... you know yesterday when I accidentally dropped the dime on you to I.A. and got us in all this trouble?
Yeah?
We're even. Ow...

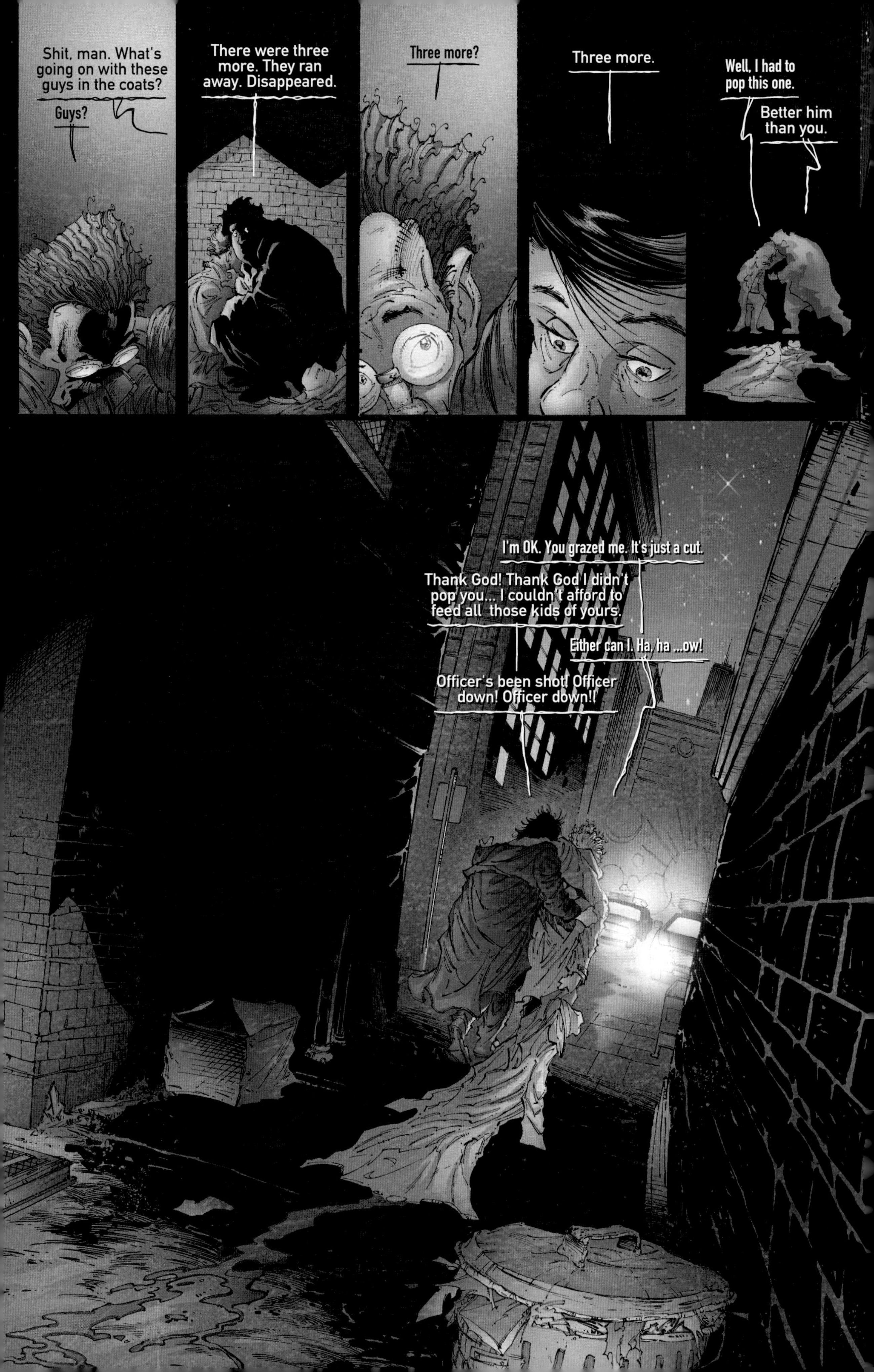
Shit, man. What's going on with these guys in the coats?
Guys?
There were three more. They ran away. Disappeared.
Three more?
Three more.
Well, I had to pop this one.
Better him than you.
I'm OK. You grazed me. It's just a cut.
Thank God! Thank God I didn't pop you... I couldn't afford to feed all those kids of yours.
Either can I. Ha, ha ...ow!
Officer's been shot! Officer down! Officer down!!

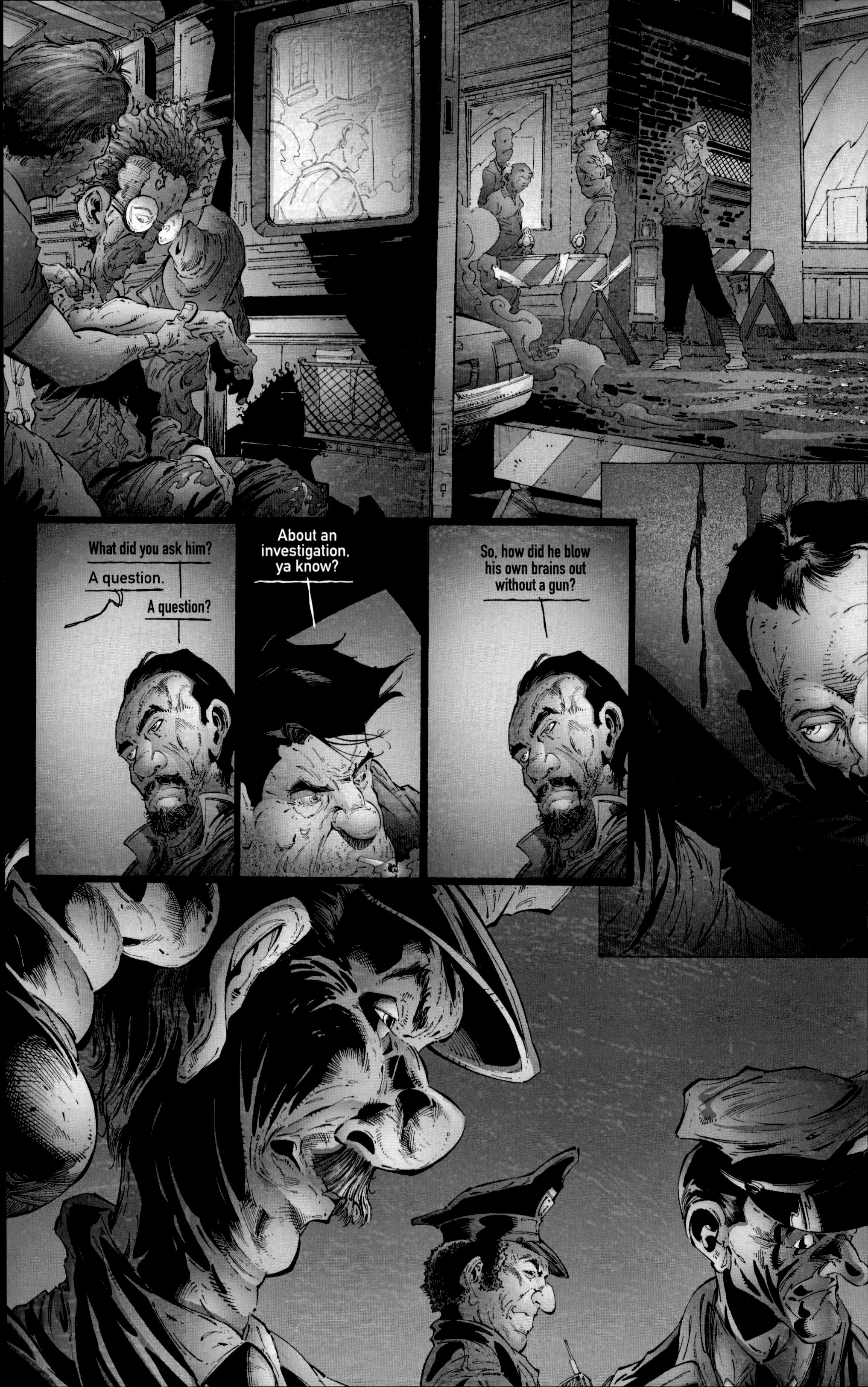
What did you ask him?
A question.
A question?
About an investigation, ya know?
So, how did he blow his own brains out without a gun?

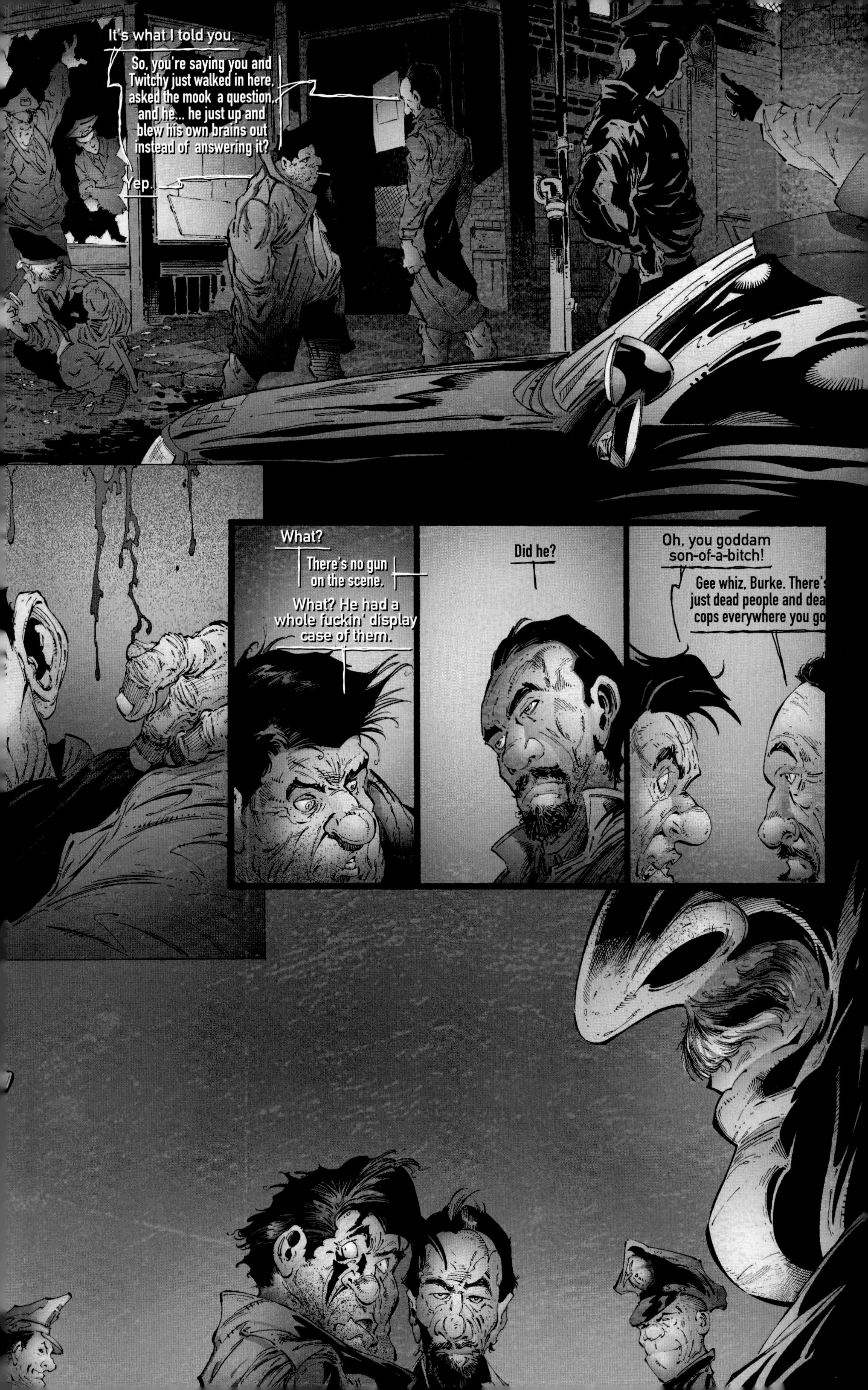
It's what I told you.
So, you're saying you and Twitchy just walked in here, asked the mook a question, and he... he just up and blew his own brains out instead of answering it?
Yep.
What?
There's no gun on the scene.
What? He had a whole fuckin' display case of them.
Did he?
Oh, you goddam son-of-a-bitch!
Gee whiz, Burke. There's just dead people and dea cops everywhere you go

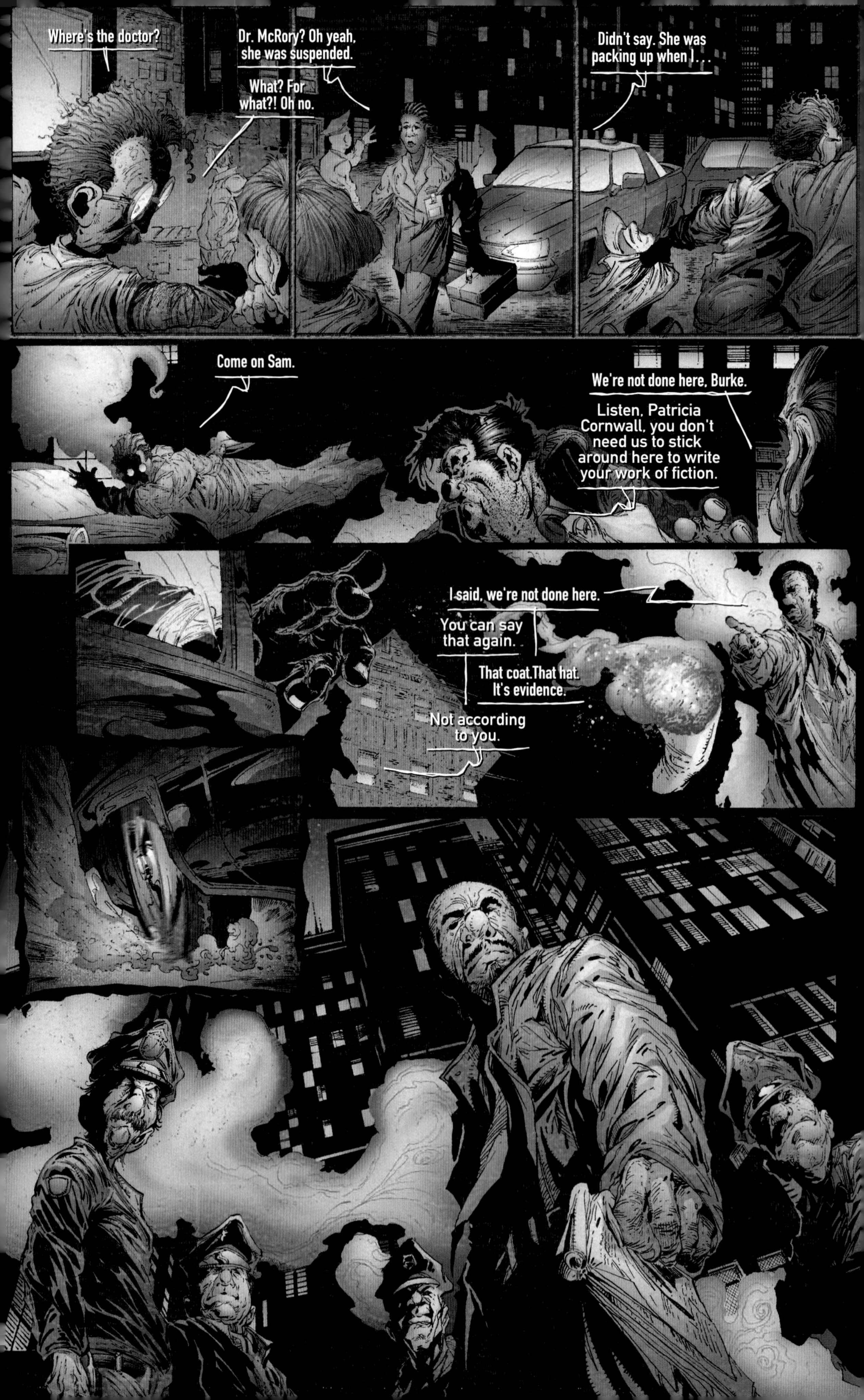

Where's the doctor?
Dr. McRory? Oh yeah, she was suspended.
What? For what?! Oh no.
Didn't say. She was packing up when I. . .
Come on Sam.
We're not done here, Burke.
Listen, Patricia Cornwall, you don't need us to stick around here to write your work of fiction.
I said, we're not done here.
You can say that again.
That coat. That hat. It's evidence.
Not according to you.

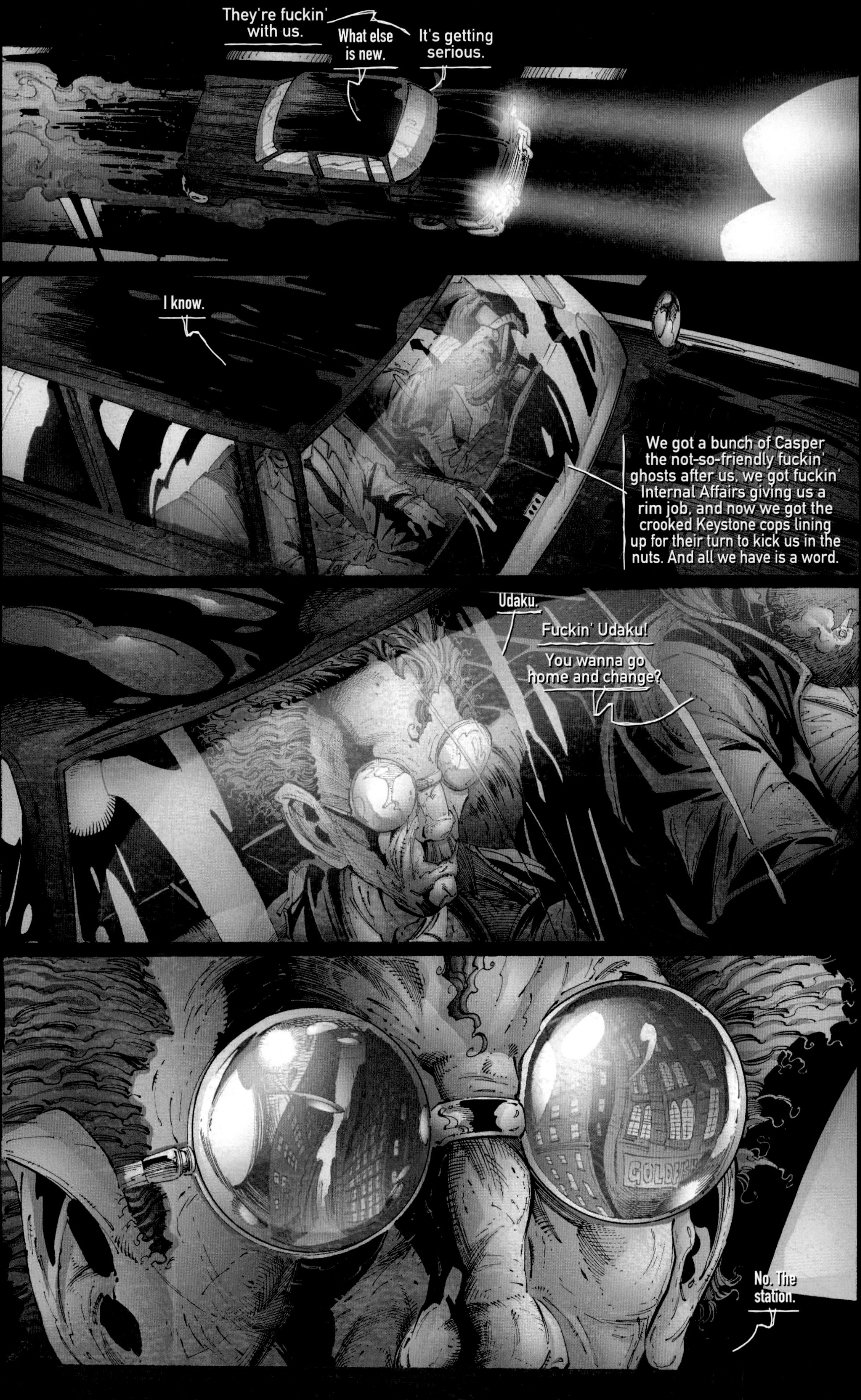
They're fuckin' with us.
What else is new.
It's getting serious.
I know.
We got a bunch of Casper the not-so-friendly fuckin' ghosts after us, we got fuckin' Internal Affairs giving us a rim job, and now we got the crooked Keystone cops lining up for their turn to kick us in the nuts. And all we have is a word.
Udaku.
Fuckin' Udaku!
You wanna go home and change?
No. The station.

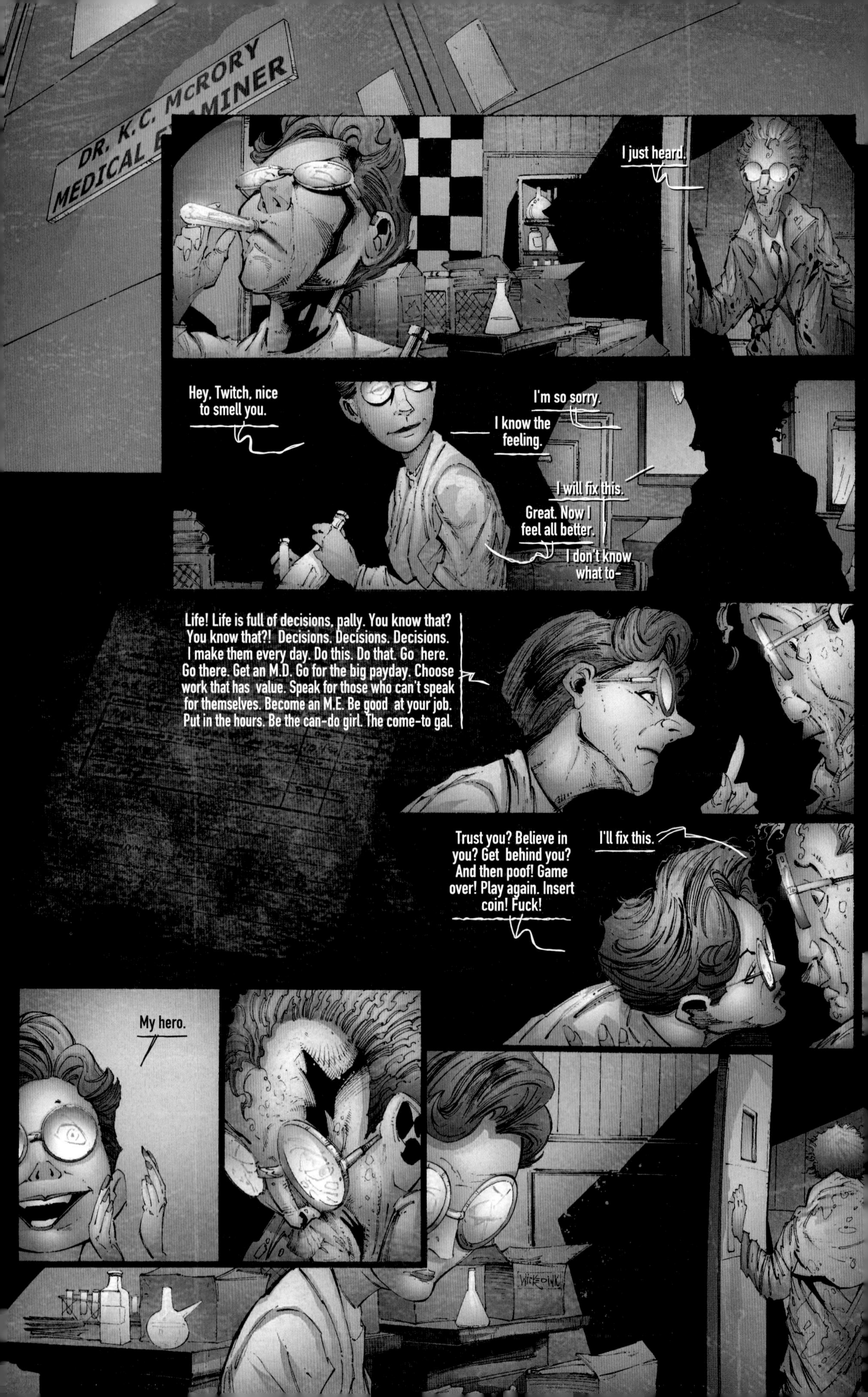
DR. K.C. McRORY
MEDICAL EXAMINER
I just heard.
Hey, Twitch, nice to smell you.
I'm so sorry.
I know the feeling.
I will fix this.
Great. Now I feel all better.
I don't know what to-
Life! Life is full of decisions, pally. You know that? You know that?! Decisions. Decisions. Decisions. I make them every day. Do this. Do that. Go here. Go there. Get an M.D. Go for the big payday. Choose work that has value. Speak for those who can't speak for themselves. Become an M.E. Be good at your job. Put in the hours. Be the can-do girl. The come-to gal.
Trust you? Believe in you? Get behind you? And then poof! Game over! Play again. Insert coin! Fuck!
I'll fix this.
My hero.

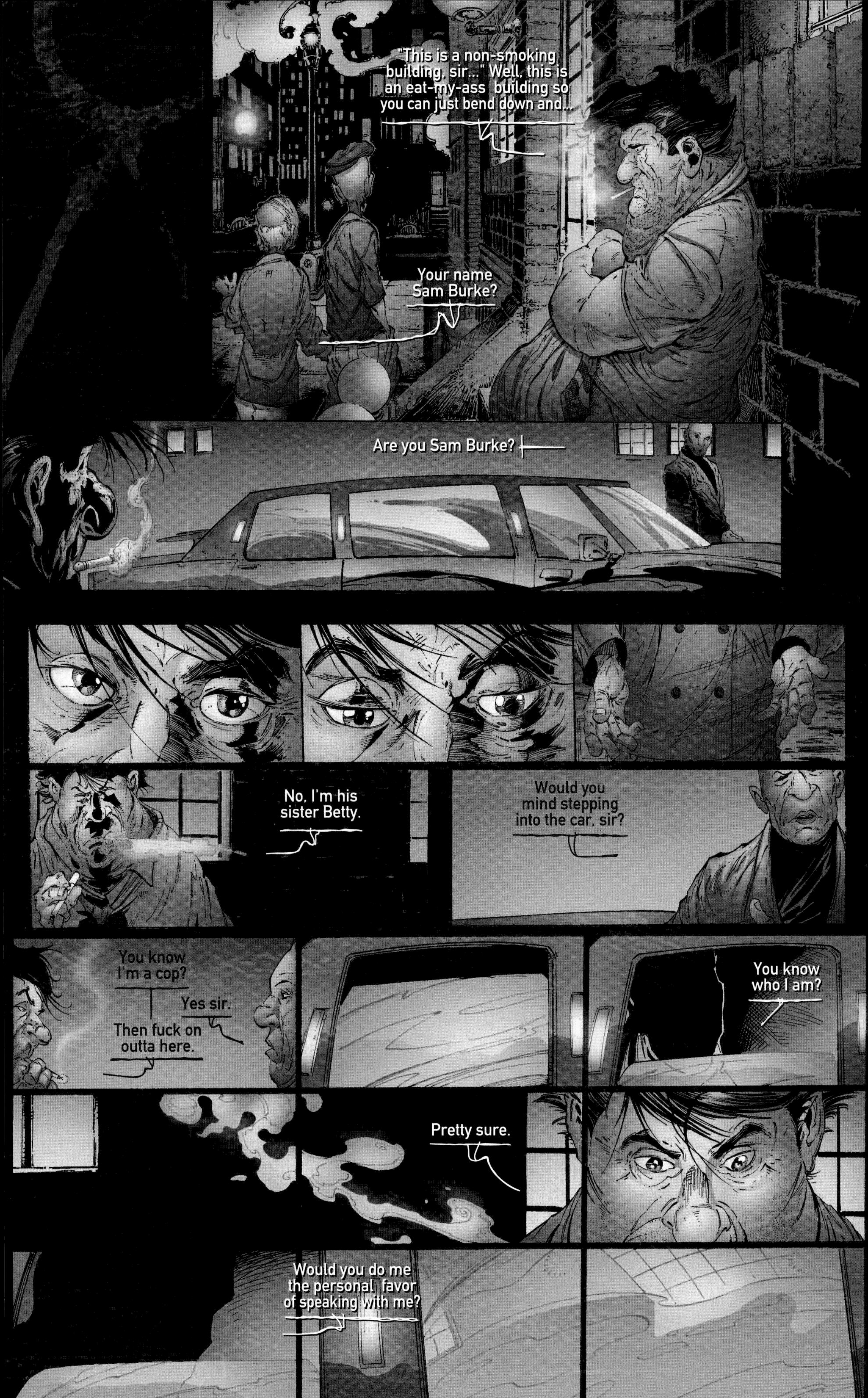
"This is a non-smoking building, sir..." Well, this is an eat-my-ass building so you can just bend down and...
Your name Sam Burke?
Are you Sam Burke?
No, I'm his sister Betty.
Would you mind stepping into the car, sir?
You know I'm a cop?
Yes sir.
Then fuck on outta here.
You know who I am?
Pretty sure.
Would you do me the personal favor of speaking with me?

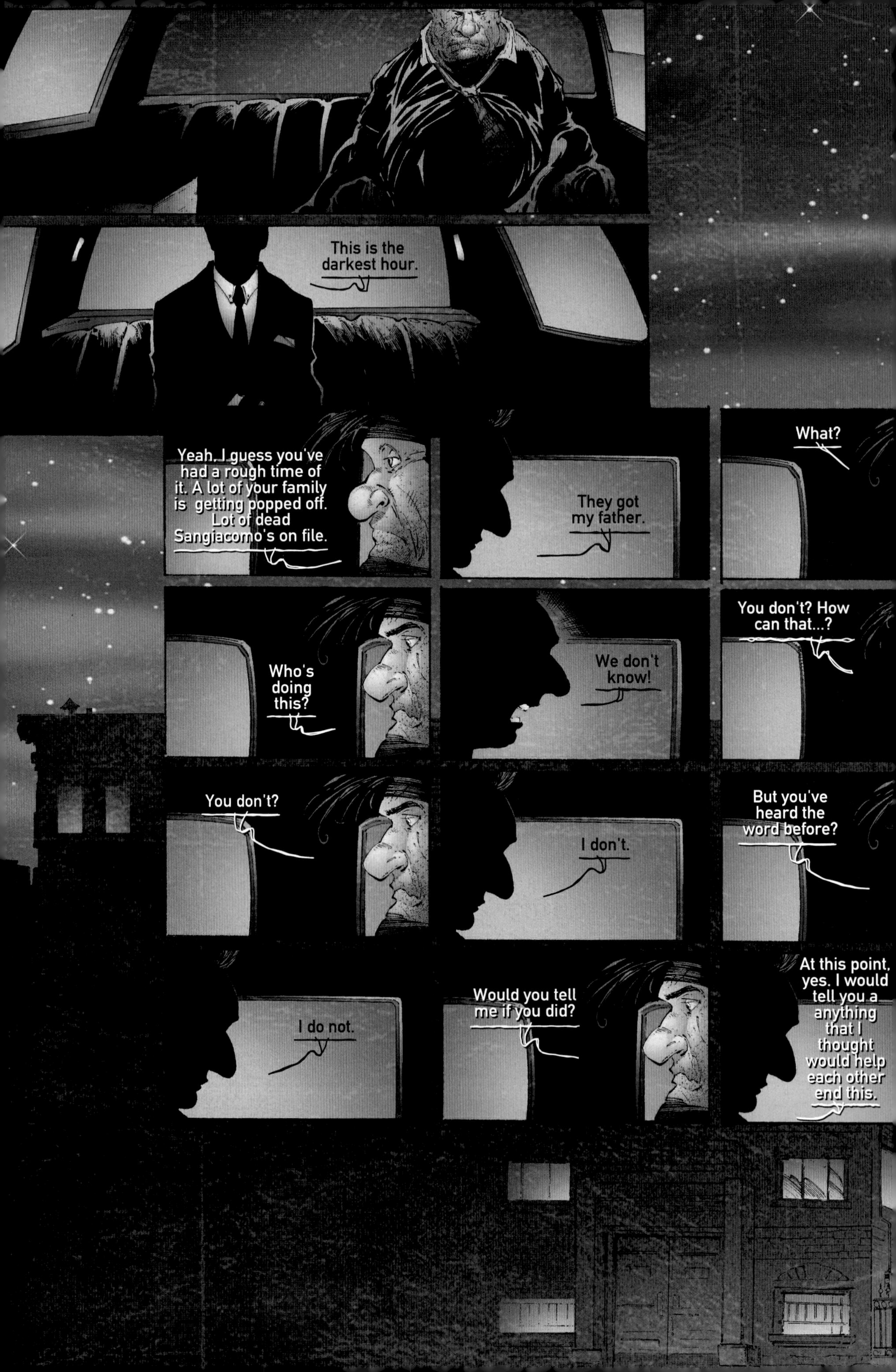
This is the darkest hour.
Yeah. I guess you've had a rough time of it. A lot of your family is getting popped off. Lot of dead Sangiacomo's on file.
They got my father.
What?
Who's doing this?
We don't know!
You don't? How can that...?
You don't?
I don't.
But you've heard the word before?
I do not.
Would you tell me if you did?
At this point, yes. I would tell you a anything that I thought would help each other end this.

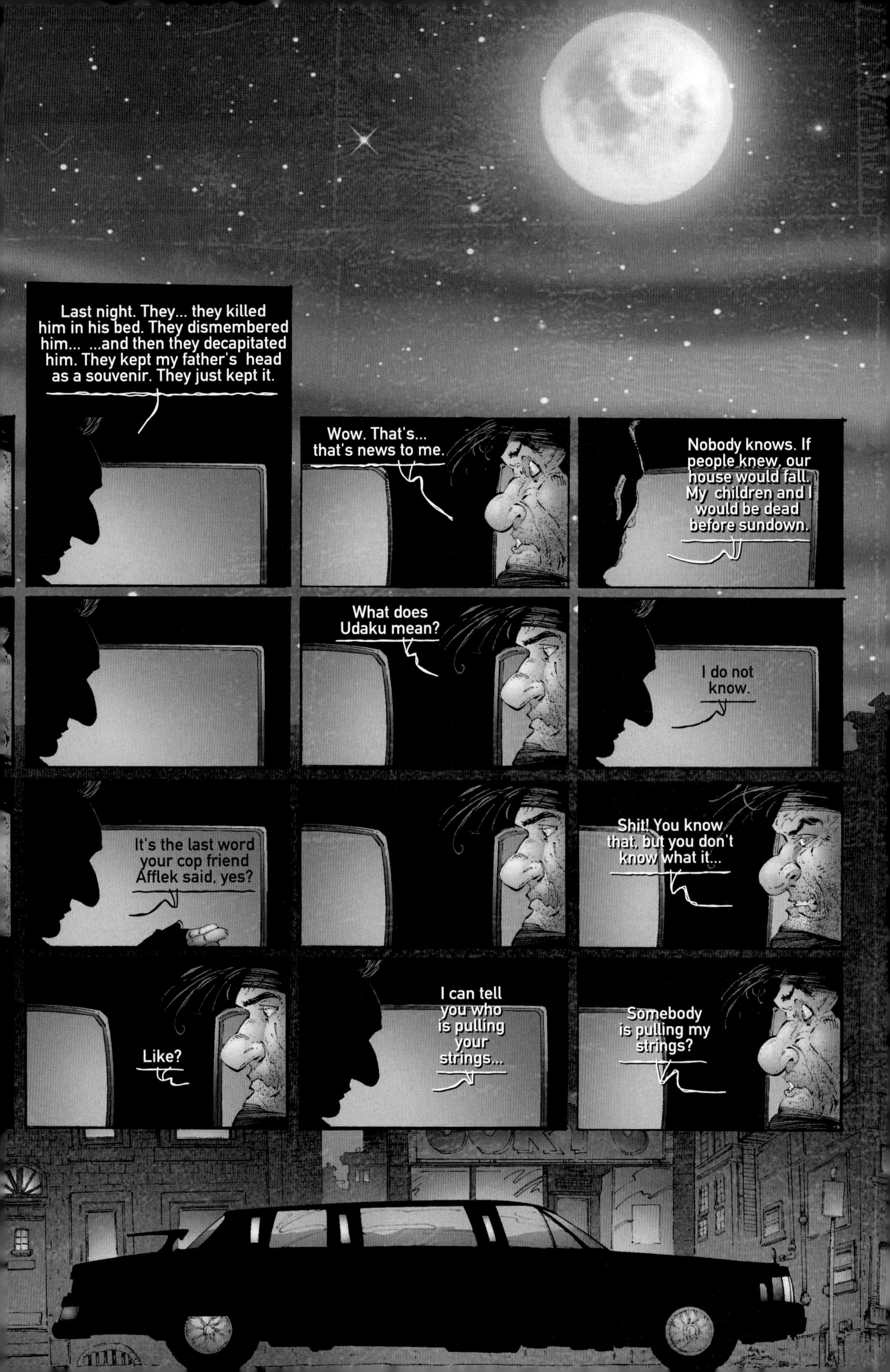
Last night. They... they killed him in his bed. They dismembered him... ...and then they decapitated him. They kept my father's head as a souvenir. They just kept it.
Wow. That's... that's news to me.
Nobody knows. If people knew, our house would fall. My children and I would be dead before sundown.
What does Udaku mean?
I do not know.
It's the last word your cop friend Afflek said, yes?
Shit! You know that, but you don't know what it...
Like?
I can tell you who is pulling your strings...
Somebody is pulling my strings?

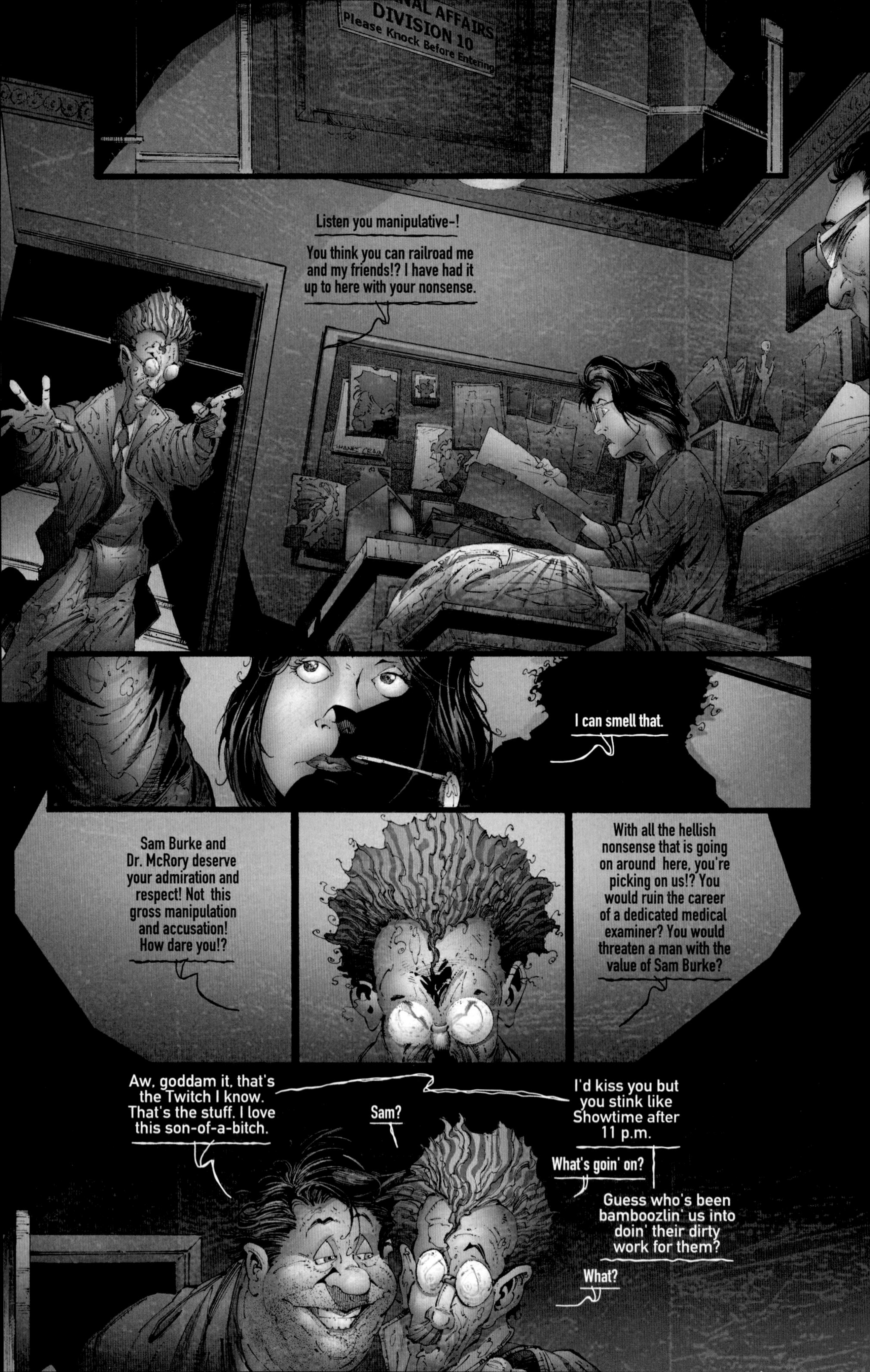

DIVISION 10
Please Knock Before Entering
Listen you manipulative-!
You think you can railroad me and my friends!? I have had it up to here with your nonsense.
I can smell that.
Sam Burke and Dr. McRory deserve your admiration and respect! Not this gross manipulation and accusation! How dare you!?
With all the hellish nonsense that is going on around here, you're picking on us!? You would ruin the career of a dedicated medical examiner? You would threaten a man with the value of Sam Burke?
Aw, goddam it, that's the Twitch I know. That's the stuff. I love this son-of-a-bitch.
I'd kiss you but you stink like Showtime after 11 p.m.
Sam?
What's goin' on?
Guess who's been bamboozlin' us into doin' their dirty work for them?
What?

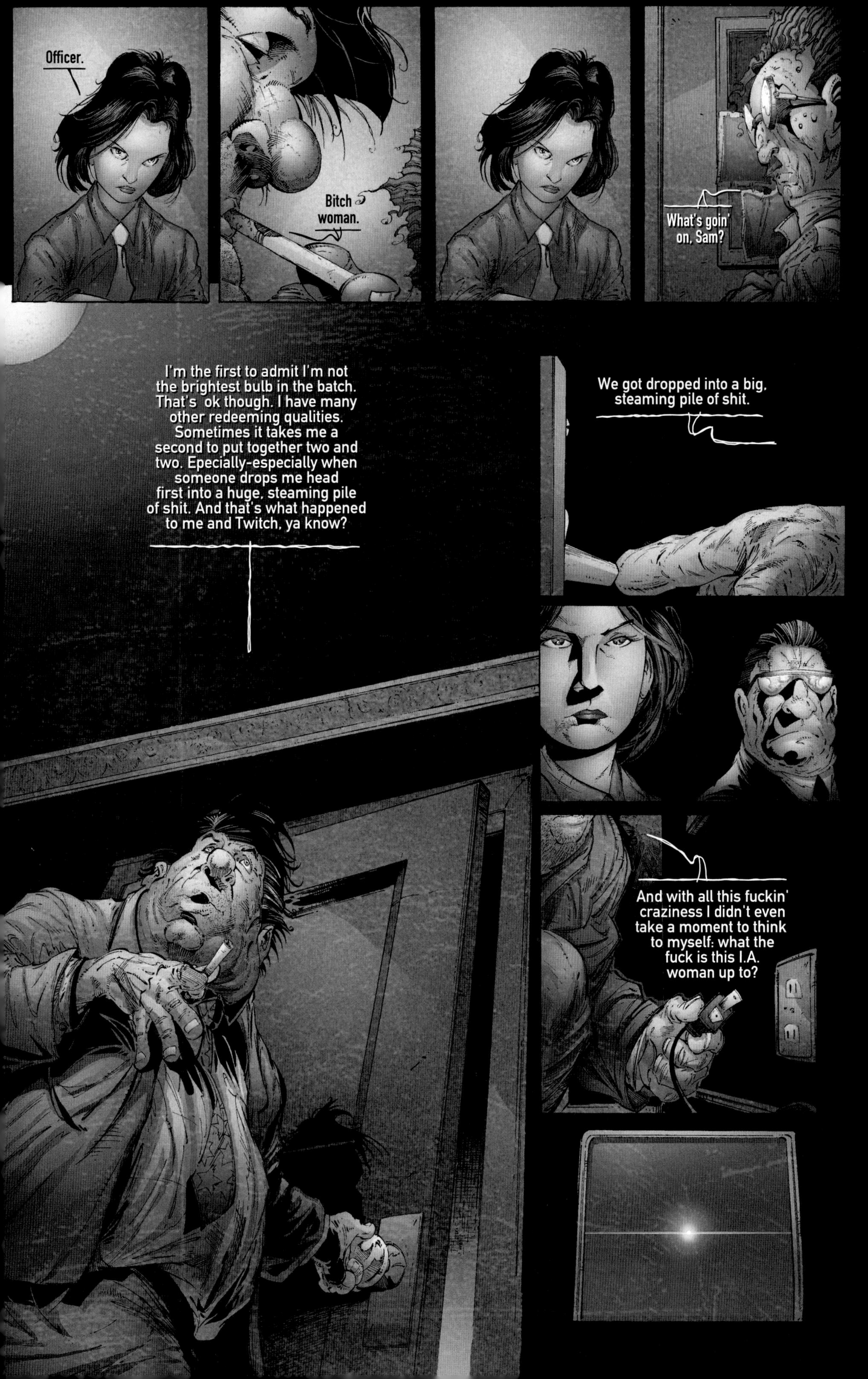
Officer.
Bitch woman.
What's goin' on, Sam?
I'm the first to admit I'm not the brightest bulb in the batch. That's ok though. I have many other redeeming qualities. Sometimes it takes me a second to put together two and two. Epecially-especially when someone drops me head first into a huge, steaming pile of shit. And that's what happened to me and Twitch, ya know?
We got dropped into a big, steaming pile of shit.
And with all this fuckin' craziness I didn't even take a moment to think to myself: what the fuck is this I.A. woman up to?

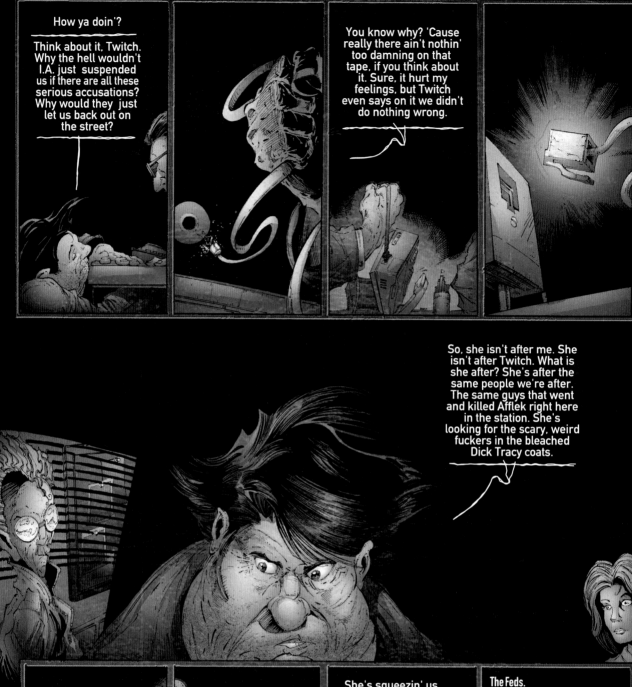

How ya doin'?

Think about it, Twitch. Why the hell wouldn't I.A. just suspended us if there are all these serious accusations? Why would they just let us back out on the street?

You know why? 'Cause really there ain't nothin' too damning on that tape, if you think about it. Sure, it hurt my feelings, but Twitch even says on it we didn't do nothing wrong.

So, she isn't after me. She isn't after Twitch. What is she after? She's after the same people we're after. The same guys that went and killed Afflek right here in the station. She's looking for the scary, weird fuckers in the bleached Dick Tracy coats.

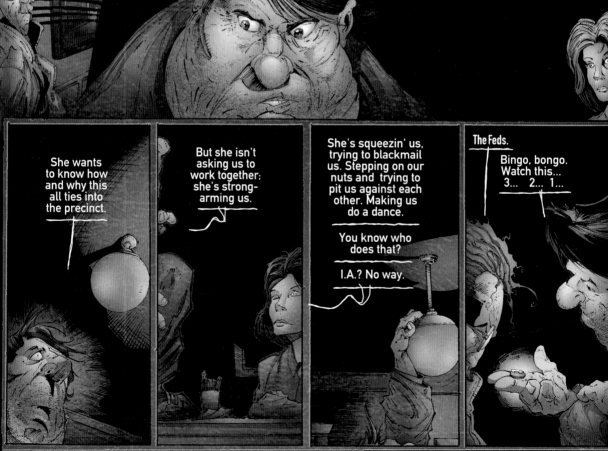

She wants to know how and why this all ties into the precinct.

But she isn't asking us to work together: she's strong-arming us.

She's squeezin' us, trying to blackmail us. Stepping on our nuts and trying to pit us against each other. Making us do a dance.

You know who does that?

I.A.? No way.

The Feds.

Bingo, bongo. Watch this... 3... 2... 1...

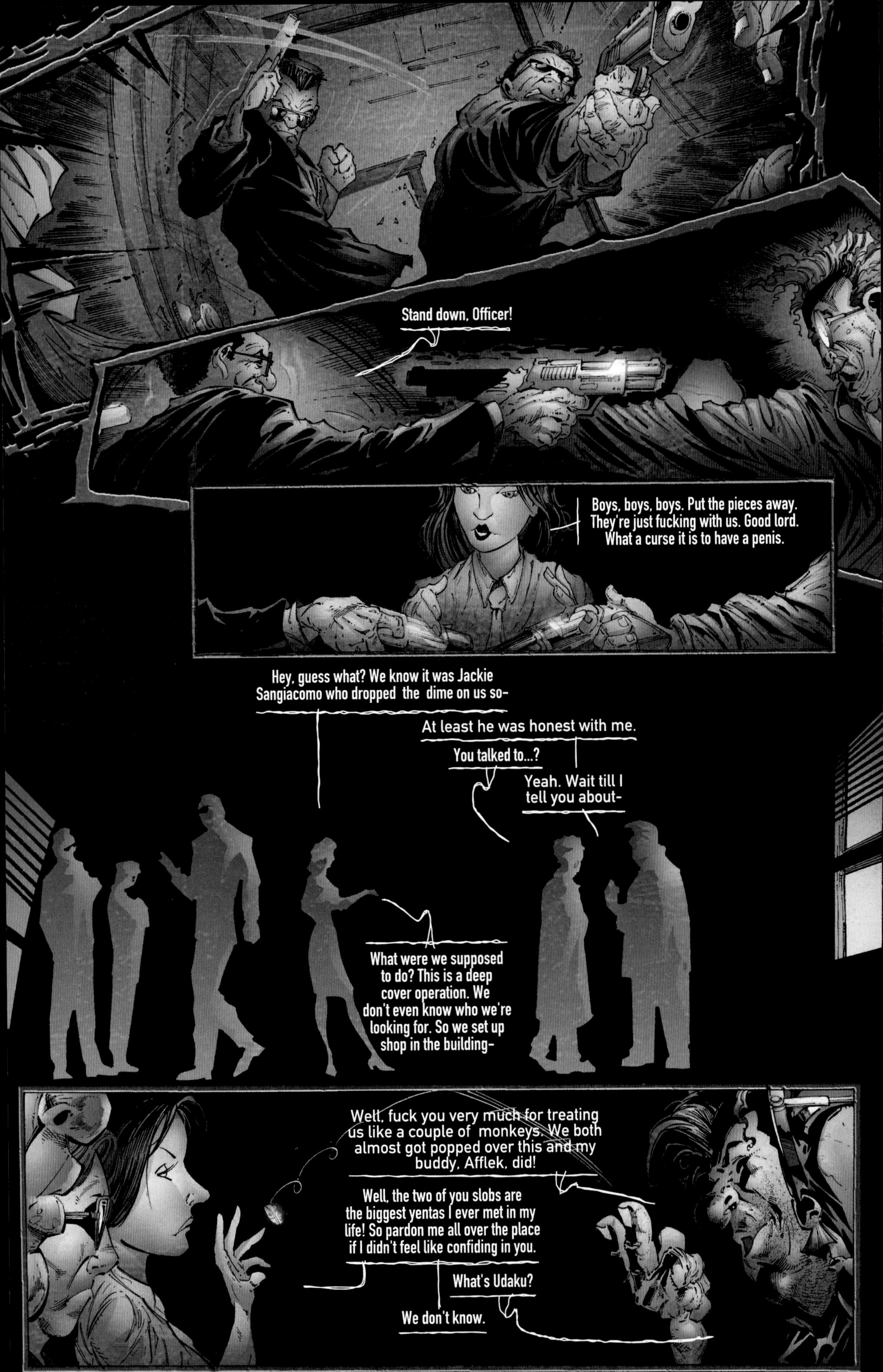
Stand down, Officer!
Boys, boys, boys. Put the pieces away. They're just fucking with us. Good lord. What a curse it is to have a penis.
Hey, guess what? We know it was Jackie Sangiacomo who dropped the dime on us so-
At least he was honest with me.
You talked to...?
Yeah. Wait till I tell you about-
What were we supposed to do? This is a deep cover operation. We don't even know who we're looking for. So we set up shop in the building-
Well, fuck you very much for treating us like a couple of monkeys. We both almost got popped over this and my buddy, Afflek, did!
Well, the two of you slobs are the biggest yentas I ever met in my life! So pardon me all over the place if I didn't feel like confiding in you.
What's Udaku?
We don't know.

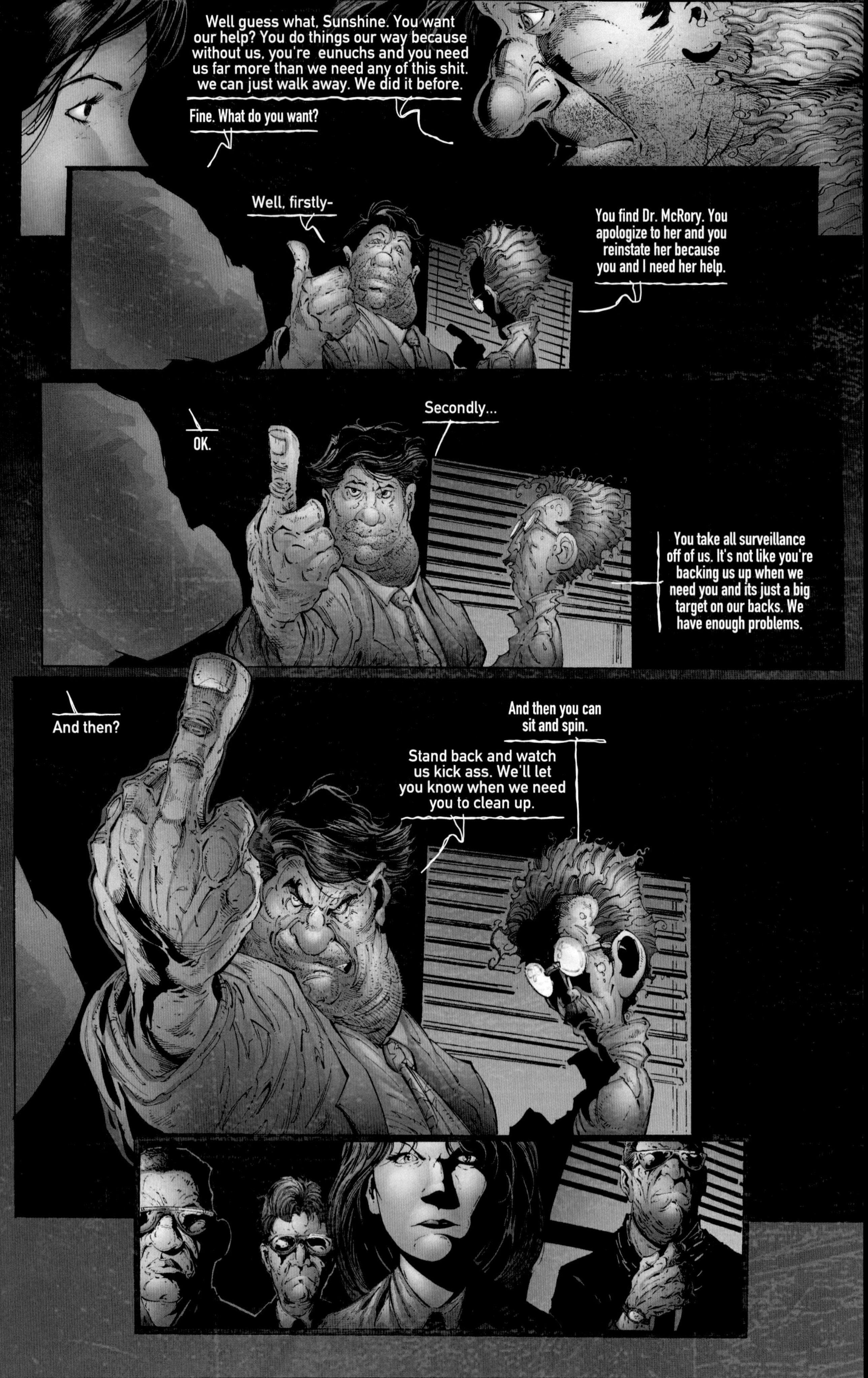
Well guess what, Sunshine. You want our help? You do things our way because without us, you're eunuchs and you need us far more than we need any of this shit. we can just walk away. We did it before.
Fine. What do you want?
Well, firstly-
You find Dr. McRory. You apologize to her and you reinstate her because you and I need her help.
OK.
Secondly...
You take all surveillance off of us. It's not like you're backing us up when we need you and its just a big target on our backs. We have enough problems.
And then?
And then you can sit and spin.
Stand back and watch us kick ass. We'll let you know when we need you to clean up.

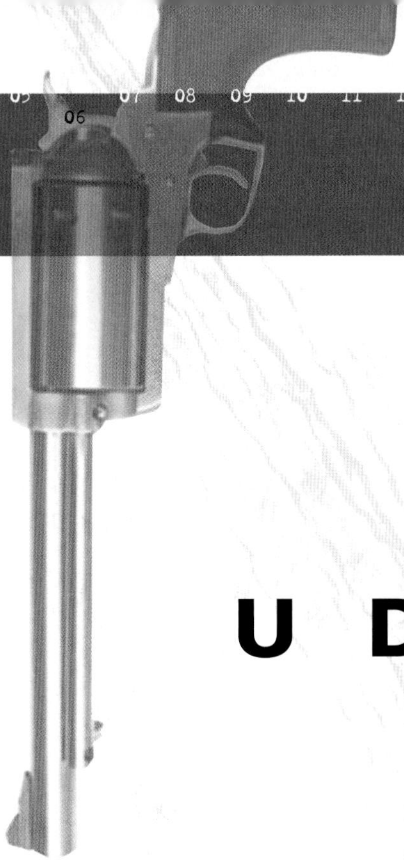

UDAKU

PART 6

SAM AND TWITCH

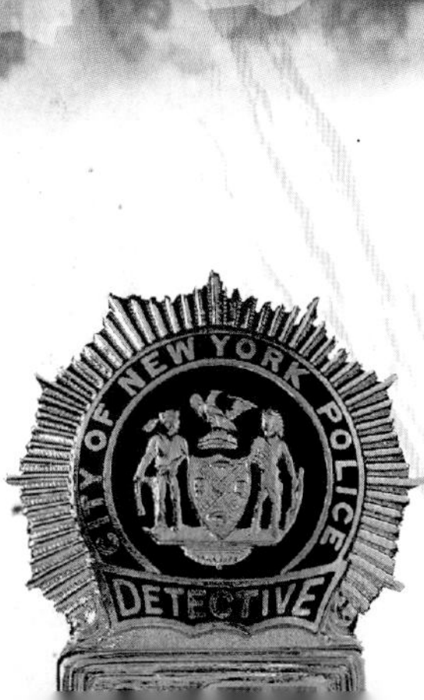
CITY OF NEW YORK POLICE
DETECTIVE

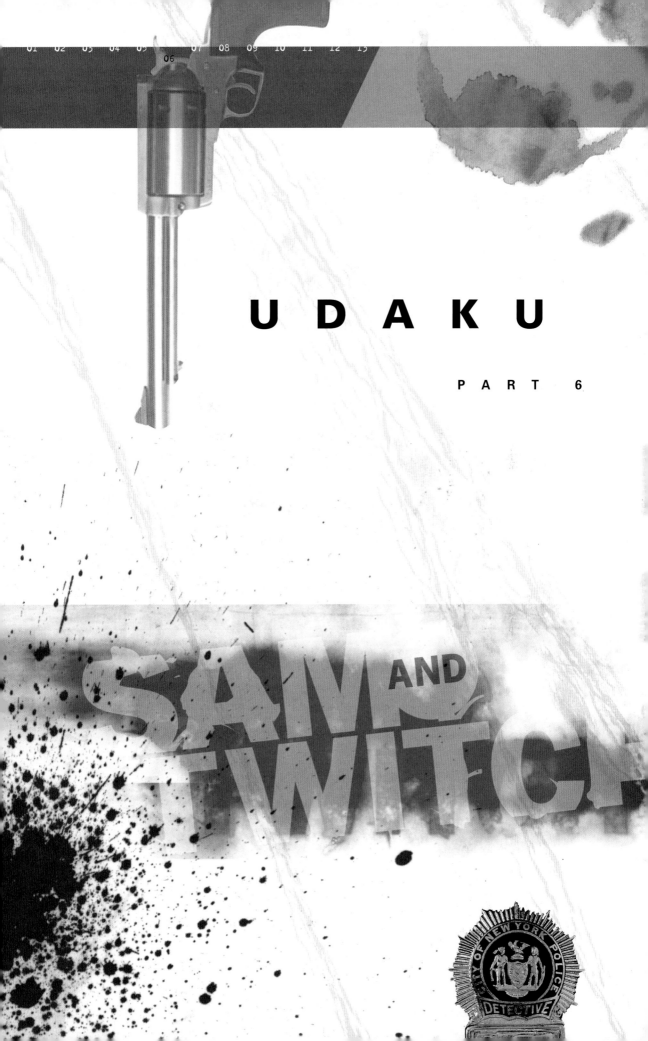

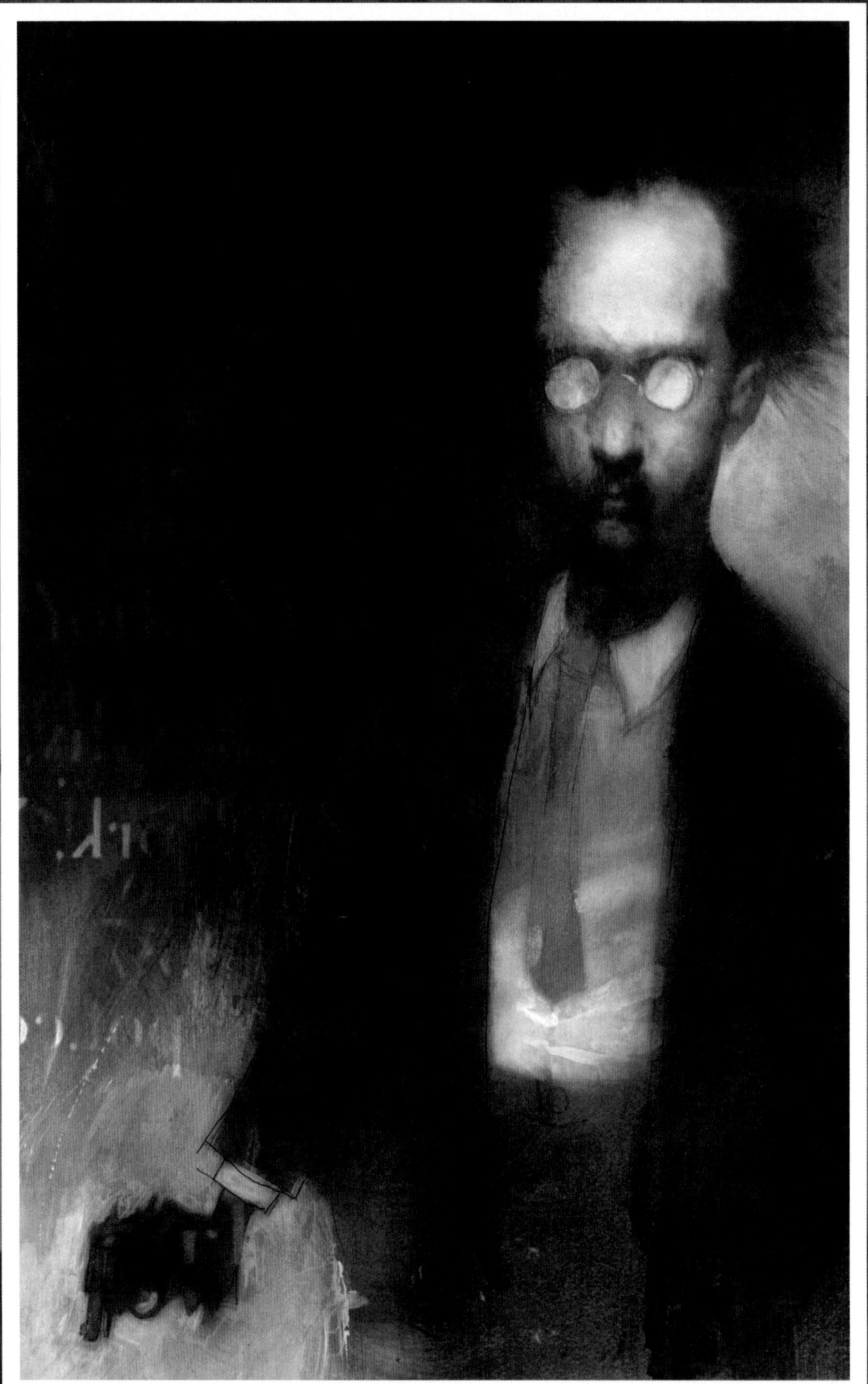

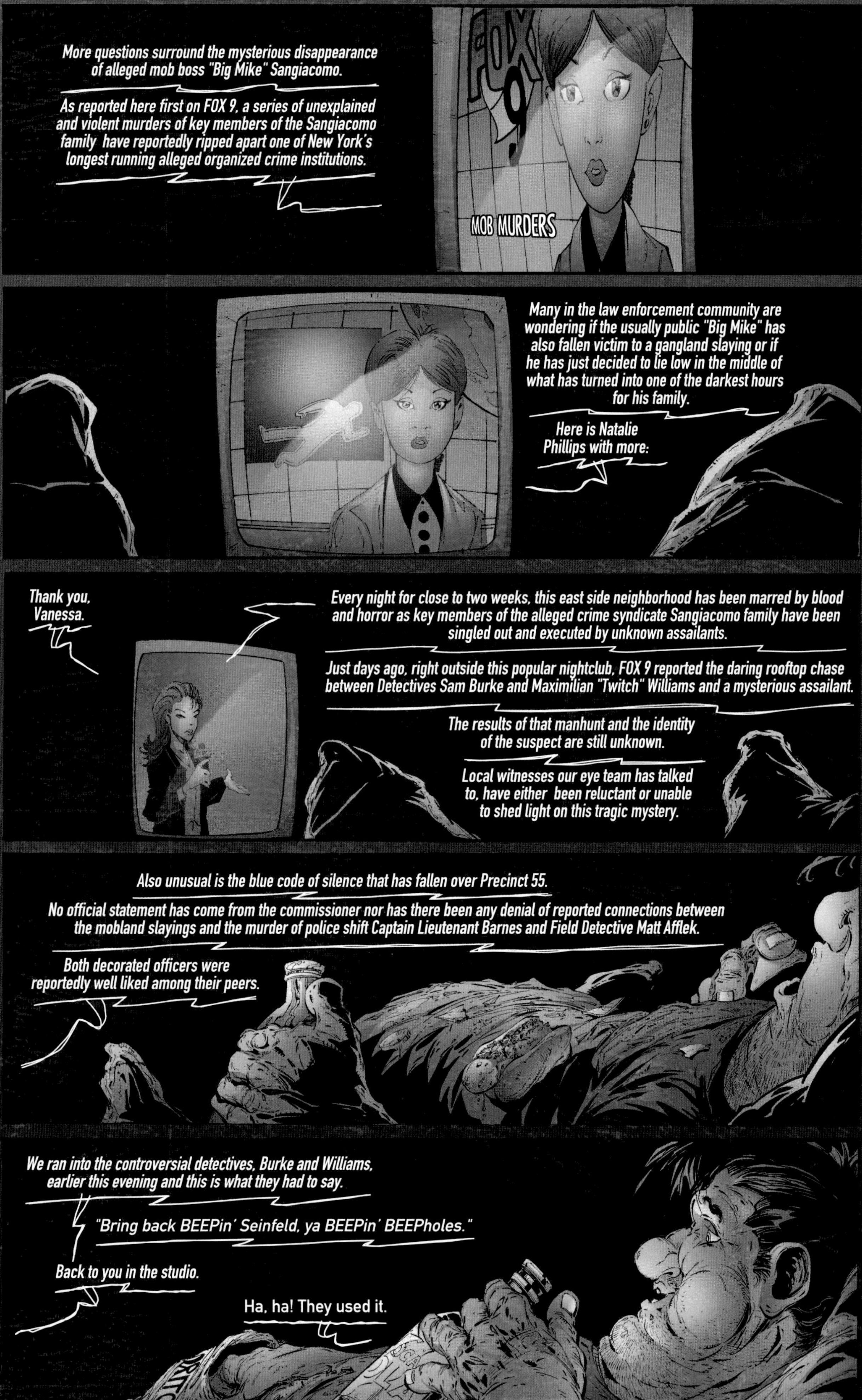

More questions surround the mysterious disappearance of alleged mob boss "Big Mike" Sangiacomo.

As reported here first on FOX 9, a series of unexplained and violent murders of key members of the Sangiacomo family have reportedly ripped apart one of New York's longest running alleged organized crime institutions.

MOB MURDERS

Many in the law enforcement community are wondering if the usually public "Big Mike" has also fallen victim to a gangland slaying or if he has just decided to lie low in the middle of what has turned into one of the darkest hours for his family.

Here is Natalie Phillips with more:

Thank you, Vanessa.

Every night for close to two weeks, this east side neighborhood has been marred by blood and horror as key members of the alleged crime syndicate Sangiacomo family have been singled out and executed by unknown assailants.

Just days ago, right outside this popular nightclub, FOX 9 reported the daring rooftop chase between Detectives Sam Burke and Maximilian "Twitch" Williams and a mysterious assailant.

The results of that manhunt and the identity of the suspect are still unknown.

Local witnesses our eye team has talked to, have either been reluctant or unable to shed light on this tragic mystery.

Also unusual is the blue code of silence that has fallen over Precinct 55.

No official statement has come from the commissioner nor has there been any denial of reported connections between the mobland slayings and the murder of police shift Captain Lieutenant Barnes and Field Detective Matt Afflek.

Both decorated officers were reportedly well liked among their peers.

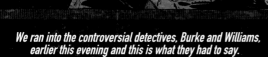

We ran into the controversial detectives, Burke and Williams, earlier this evening and this is what they had to say.

"Bring back BEEPin' Seinfeld, ya BEEPin' BEEPholes."

Back to you in the studio.

Ha, ha! They used it.

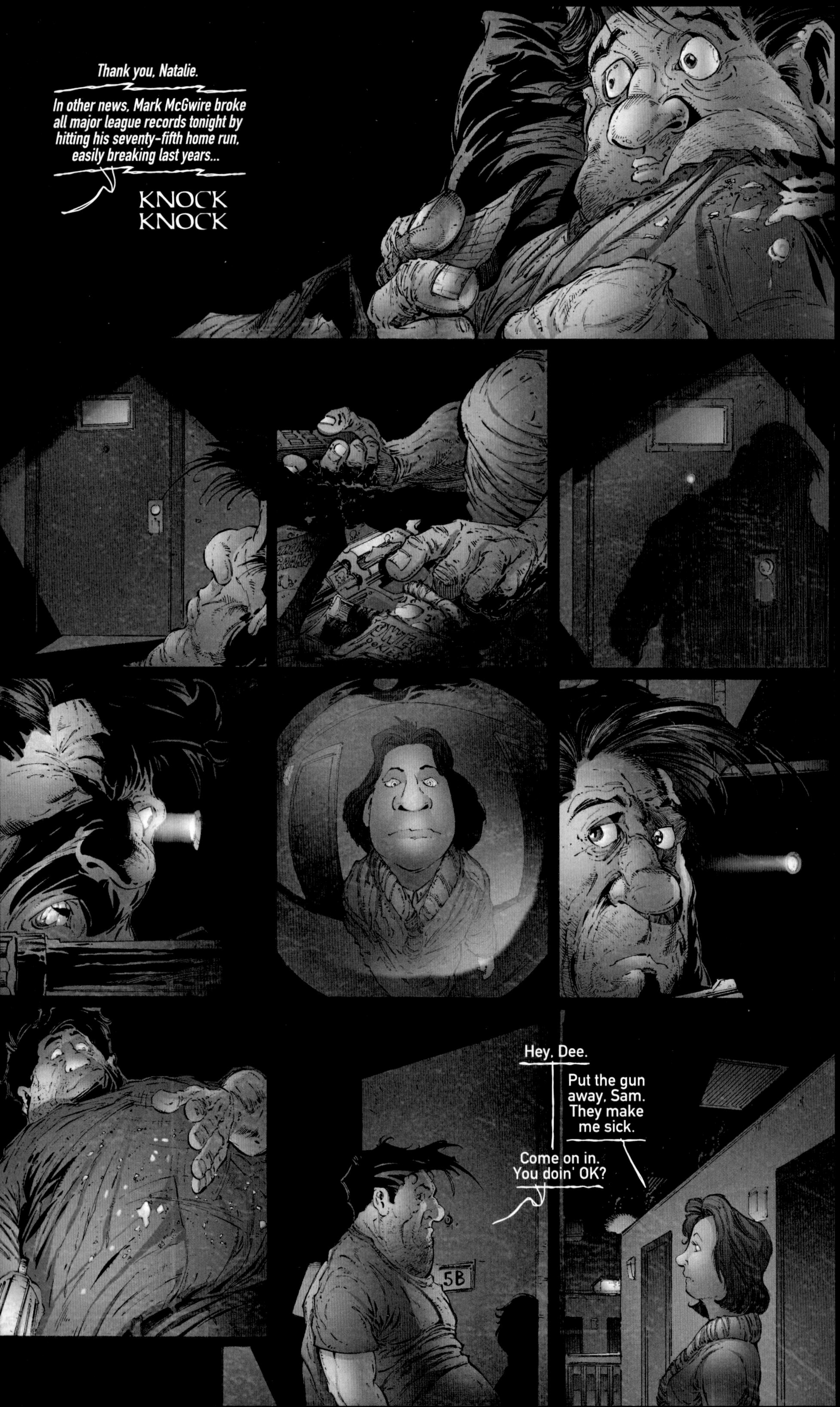
Thank you, Natalie.
In other news, Mark McGwire broke all major league records tonight by hitting his seventy-fifth home run, easily breaking last years...
KNOCK KNOCK
Hey, Dee.
Put the gun away, Sam. They make me sick.
Come on in. You doin' OK?

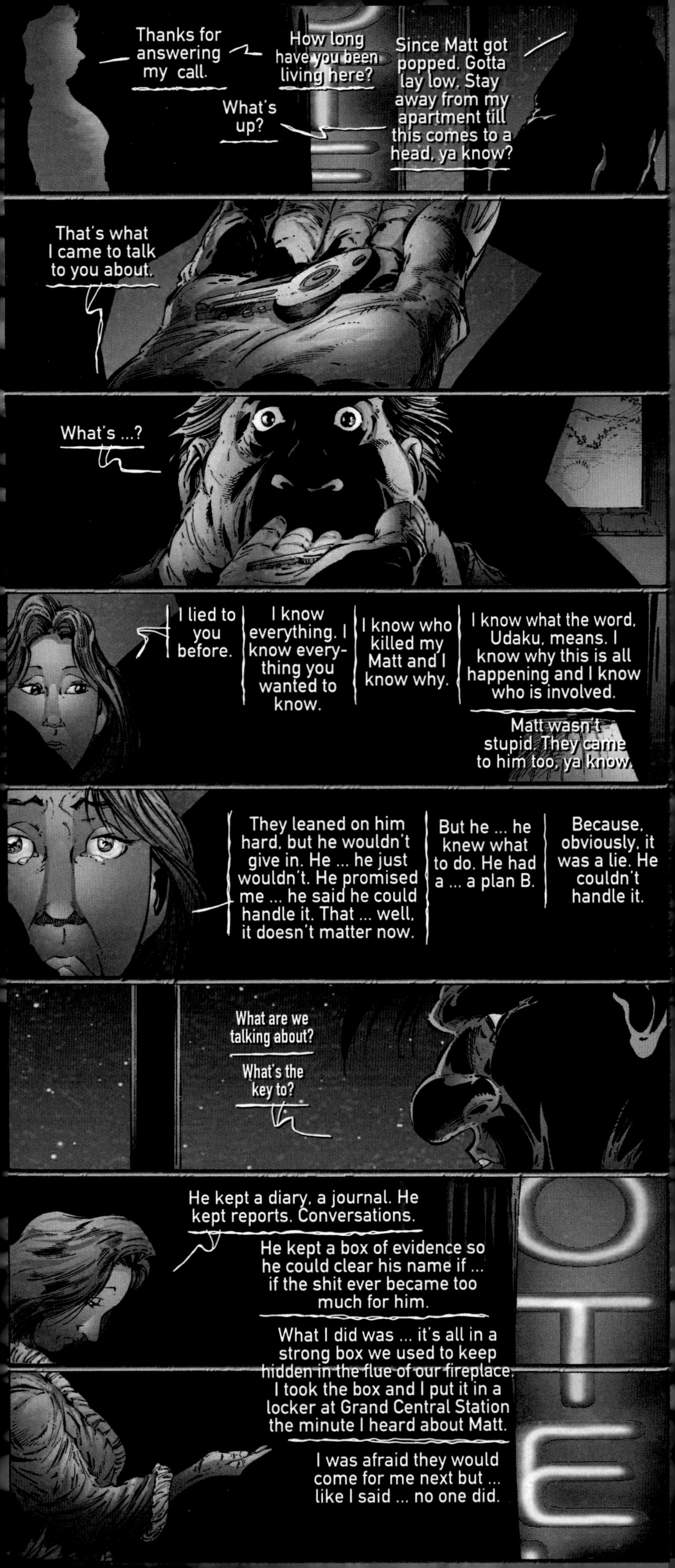

Thanks for answering my call.
What's up?
How long have you been living here?
Since Matt got popped. Gotta lay low. Stay away from my apartment till this comes to a head, ya know?
That's what I came to talk to you about.
What's ...?
I lied to you before.
I know everything. I know every-thing you wanted to know.
I know who killed my Matt and I know why.
I know what the word, Udaku, means. I know why this is all happening and I know who is involved.
Matt wasn't stupid. They came to him too, ya know.
They leaned on him hard, but he wouldn't give in. He ... he just wouldn't. He promised me ... he said he could handle it. That ... well, it doesn't matter now.
But he ... he knew what to do. He had a ... a plan B.
Because, obviously, it was a lie. He couldn't handle it.
What are we talking about?
What's the key to?
He kept a diary, a journal. He kept reports. Conversations.
He kept a box of evidence so he could clear his name if ... if the shit ever became too much for him.
What I did was ... it's all in a strong box we used to keep hidden in the flue of our fireplace. I took the box and I put it in a locker at Grand Central Station the minute I heard about Matt.
I was afraid they would come for me next but ... like I said ... no one did.

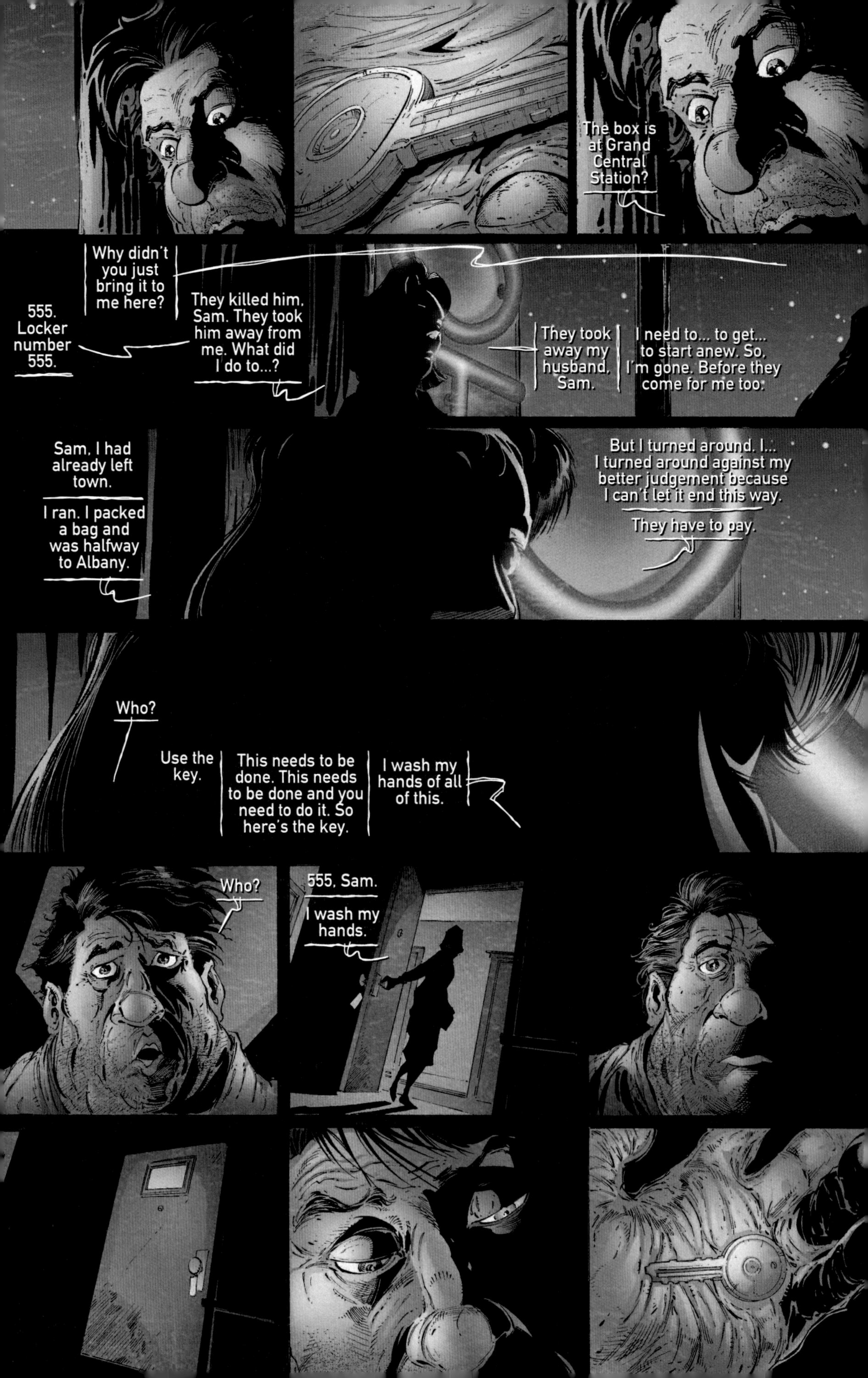
The box is at Grand Central Station?
Why didn't you just bring it to me here?
555. Locker number 555.
They killed him, Sam. They took him away from me. What did I do to...?
They took away my husband, Sam.
I need to... to get... to start anew. So, I'm gone. Before they come for me too.
Sam, I had already left town.
I ran. I packed a bag and was halfway to Albany.
But I turned around. I... I turned around against my better judgement because I can't let it end this way.
They have to pay.
Who?
Use the key.
This needs to be done. This needs to be done and you need to do it. So here's the key.
I wash my hands of all of this.
Who?
555, Sam.
I wash my hands.

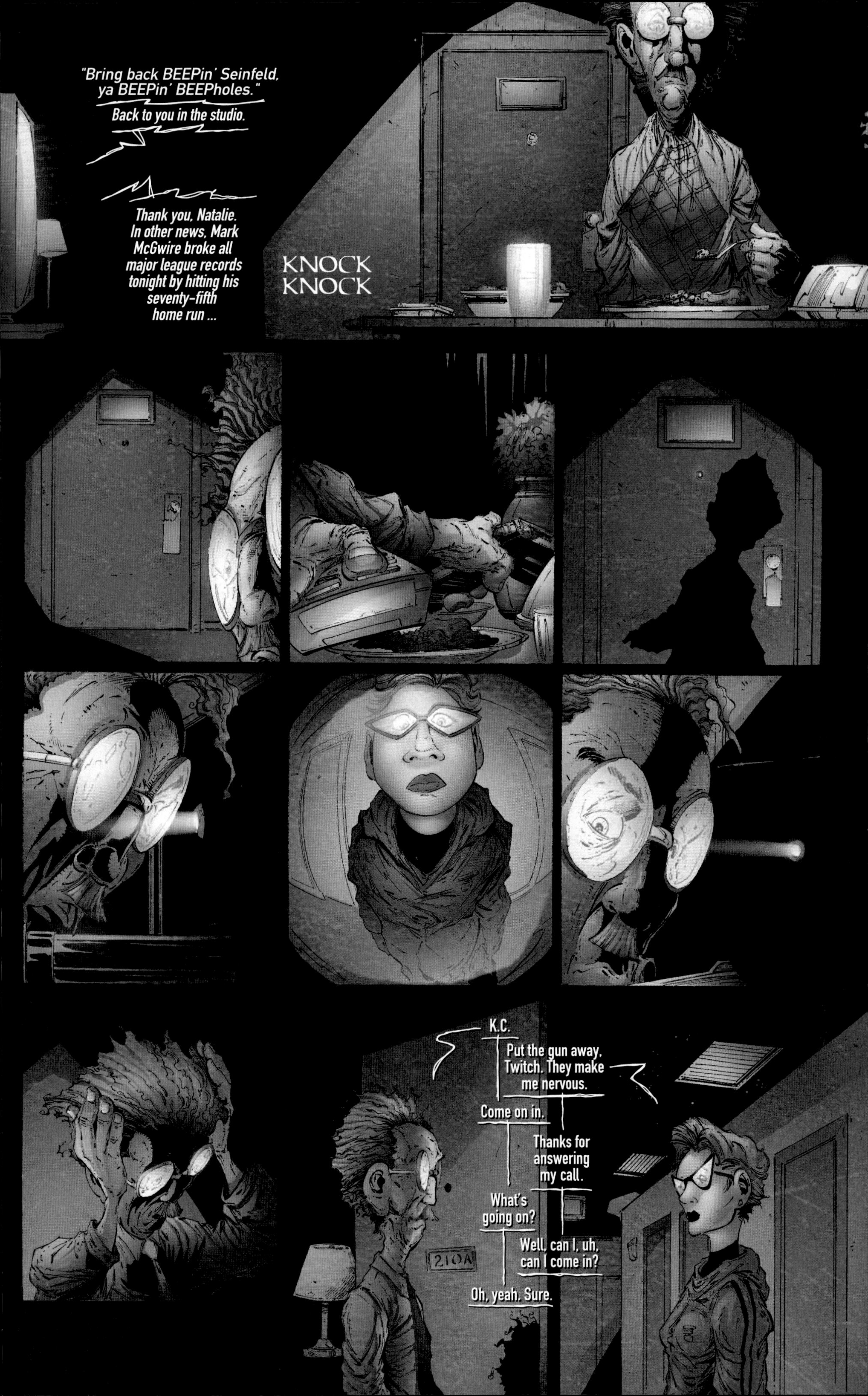
"Bring back BEEPin' Seinfeld, ya BEEPin' BEEPholes."
Back to you in the studio.
Thank you, Natalie. In other news, Mark McGwire broke all major league records tonight by hitting his seventy-fifth home run ...
KNOCK KNOCK
K.C.
Put the gun away, Twitch. They make me nervous.
Come on in.
Thanks for answering my call.
What's going on?
Well, can I, uh, can I come in?
Oh, yeah. Sure.
210A

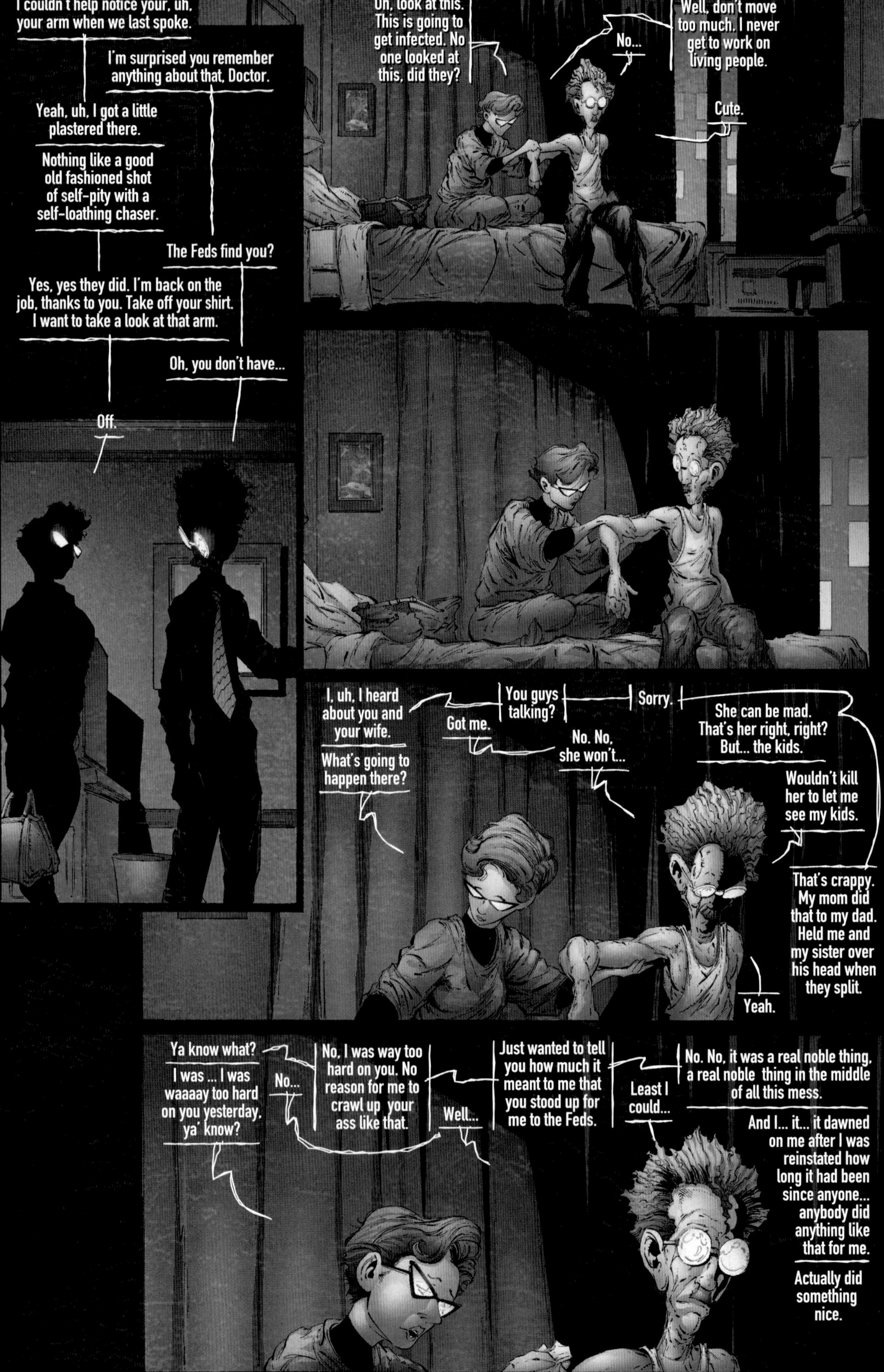

I couldn't help notice your, uh, your arm when we last spoke.
I'm surprised you remember anything about that, Doctor.
Yeah, uh, I got a little plastered there.
Nothing like a good old fashioned shot of self-pity with a self-loathing chaser.
The Feds find you?
Yes, yes they did. I'm back on the job, thanks to you. Take off your shirt. I want to take a look at that arm.
Oh, you don't have...
Off.
Oh, look at this. This is going to get infected. No one looked at this, did they?
No...
Well, don't move too much. I never get to work on living people.
Cute.
I, uh, I heard about you and your wife.
Got me.
You guys talking?
Sorry.
No. No, she won't...
What's going to happen there?
She can be mad. That's her right, right? But... the kids.
Wouldn't kill her to let me see my kids.
That's crappy. My mom did that to my dad. Held me and my sister over his head when they split.
Yeah.
Ya know what?
I was ... I was waaaay too hard on you yesterday, ya' know?
No...
No, I was way too hard on you. No reason for me to crawl up your ass like that.
Well...
Just wanted to tell you how much it meant to me that you stood up for me to the Feds.
Least I could...
No. No, it was a real noble thing, a real noble thing in the middle of all this mess.
And I... it... it dawned on me after I was reinstated how long it had been since anyone... anybody did anything like that for me.
Actually did something nice.

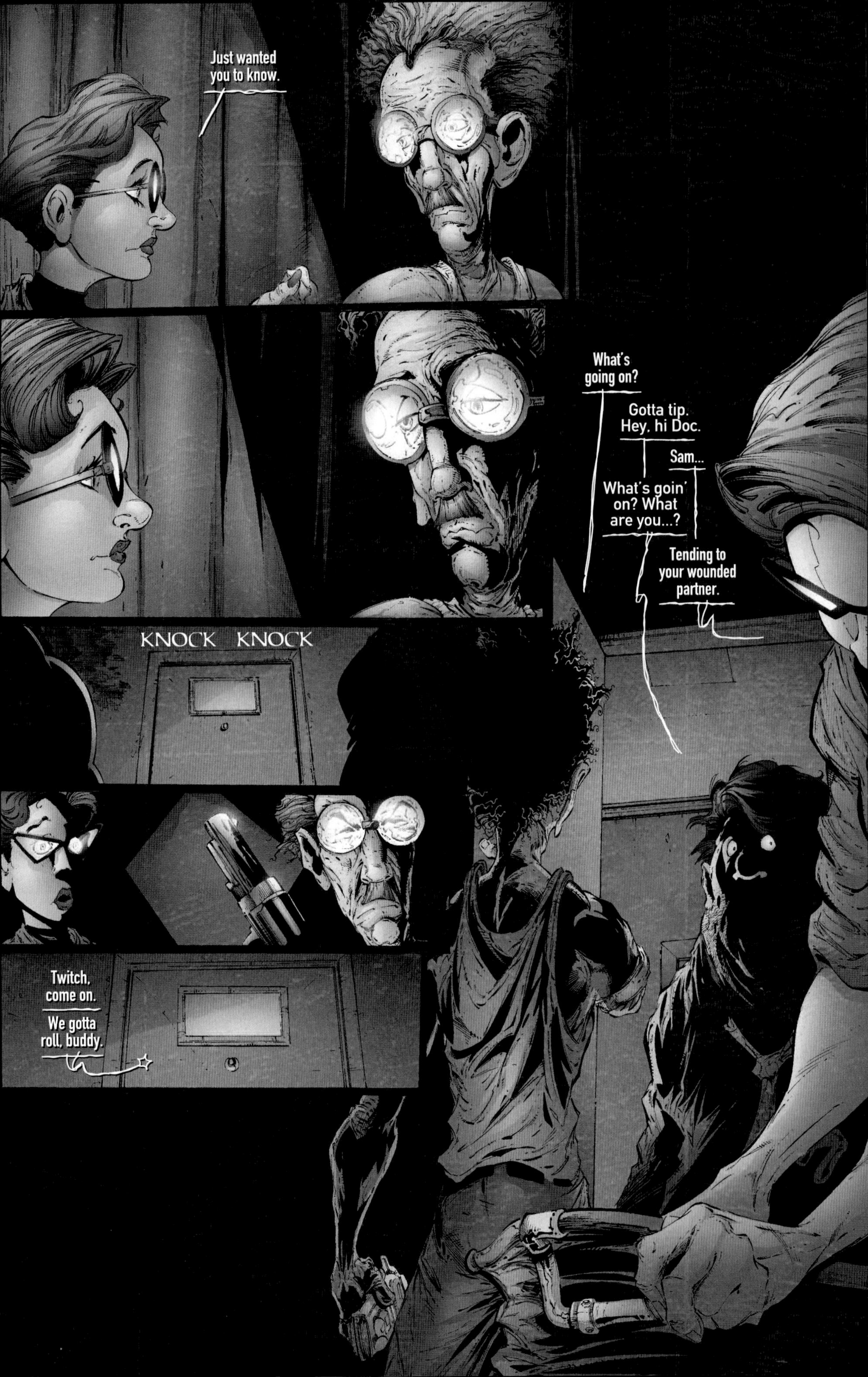
Just wanted you to know.
What's going on?
Gotta tip. Hey, hi Doc.
Sam...
What's goin' on? What are you...?
Tending to your wounded partner.
KNOCK KNOCK
Twitch, come on.
We gotta roll, buddy.

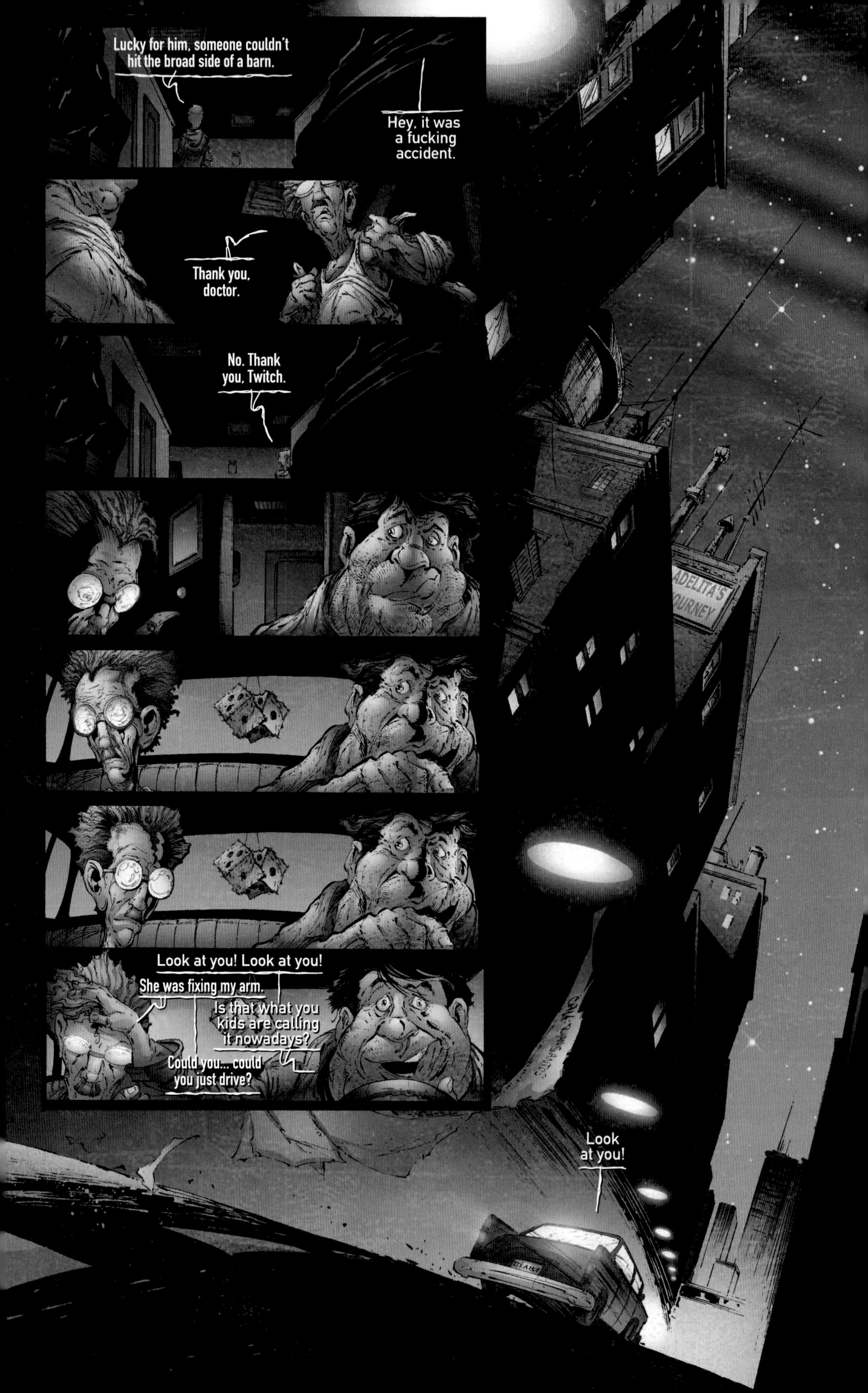

Lucky for him, someone couldn't hit the broad side of a barn.
Hey, it was a fucking accident.
Thank you, doctor.
No. Thank you, Twitch.
ADELITA'S JOURNEY
Look at you! Look at you!
She was fixing my arm.
Is that what you kids are calling it nowadays?
Could you... could you just drive?
Look at you!

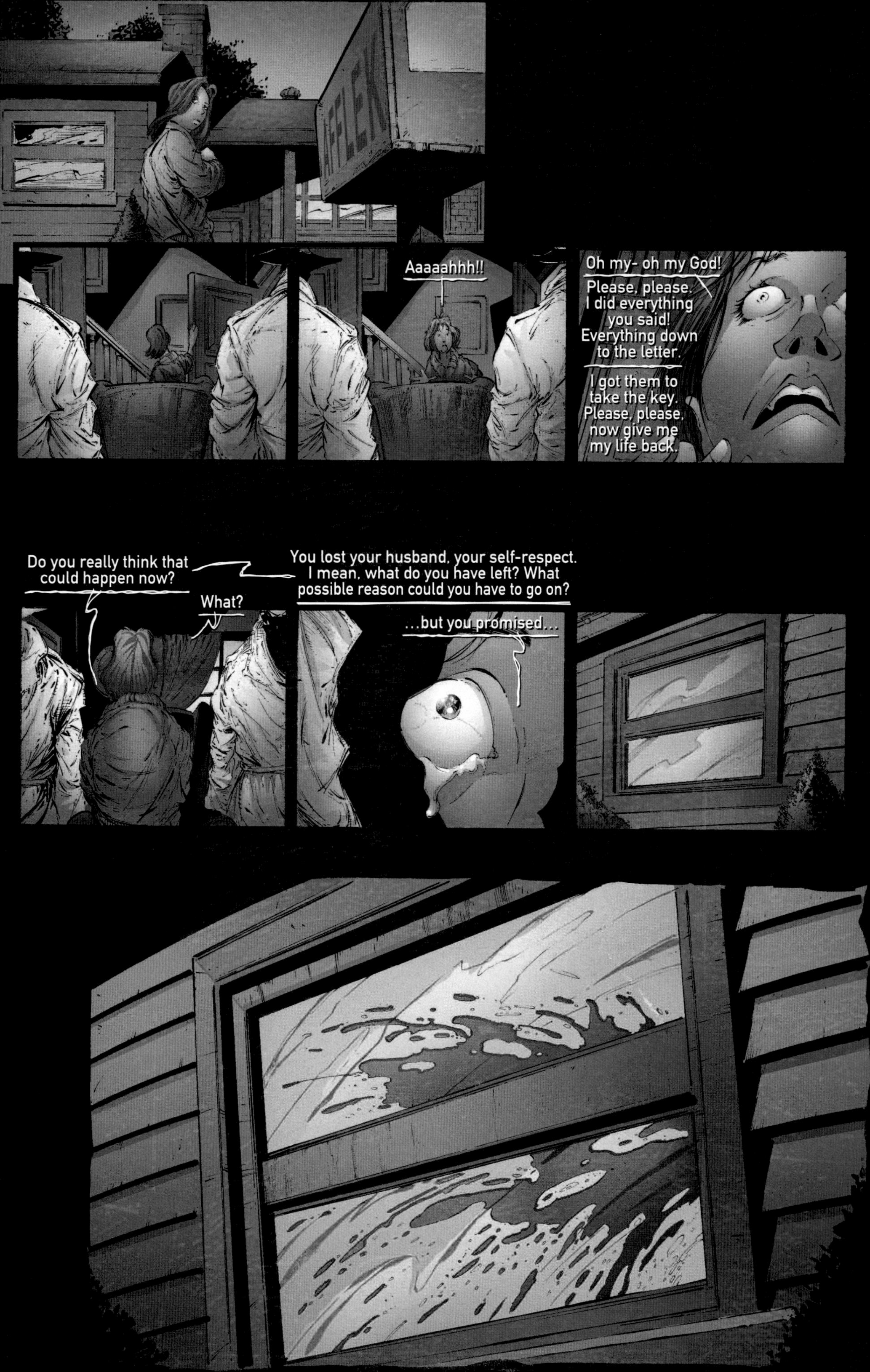
AFFLEK
Aaaaahhh!!
Oh my- oh my God!
Please, please. I did everything you said! Everything down to the letter.
I got them to take the key. Please, please, now give me my life back.
Do you really think that could happen now?
What?
You lost your husband, your self-respect. I mean, what do you have left? What possible reason could you have to go on?
...but you promised...

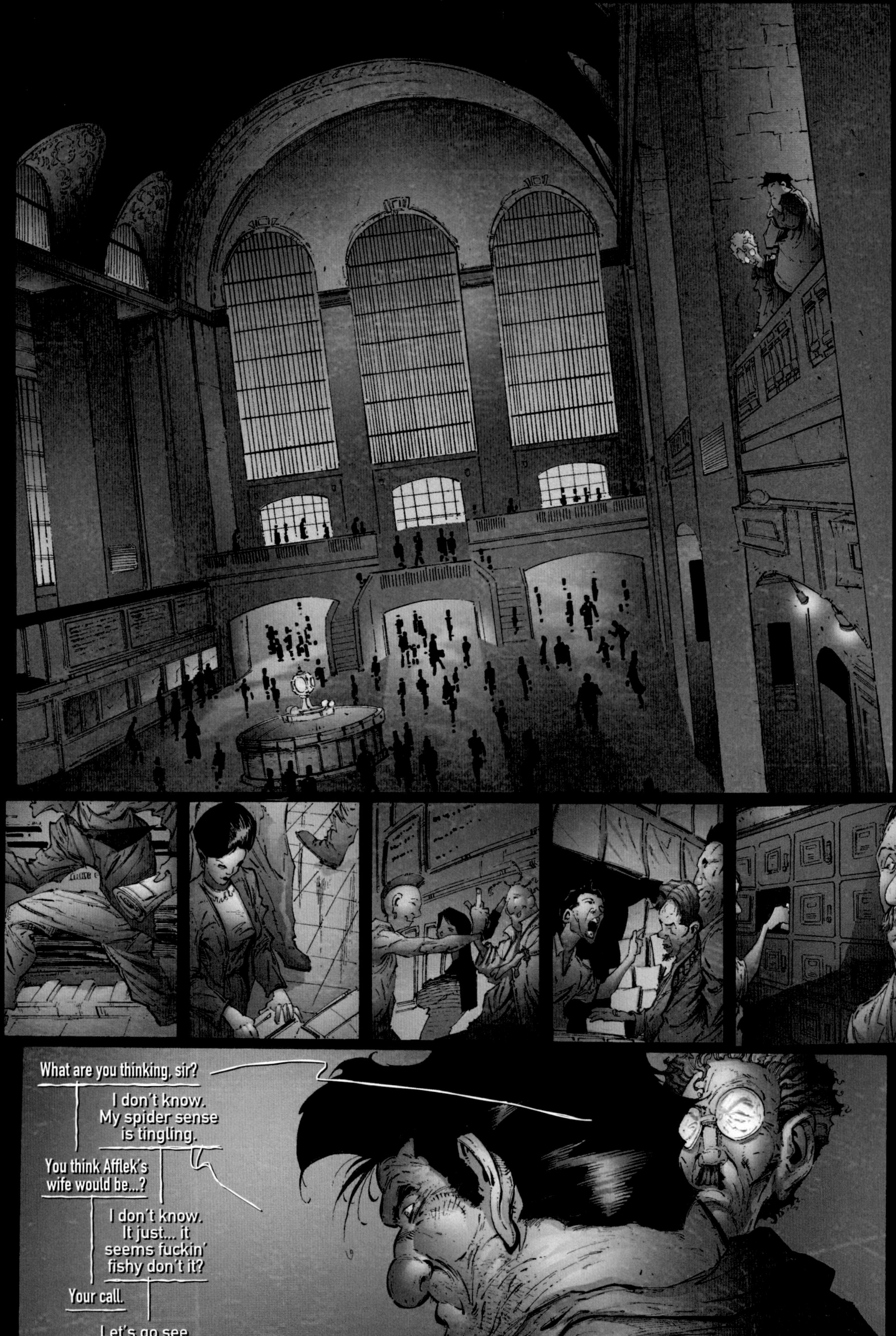
What are you thinking, sir?
I don't know. My spider sense is tingling.
You think Afflek's wife would be...?
I don't know. It just... it seems fuckin' fishy don't it?
Your call.
Let's go see what we see.

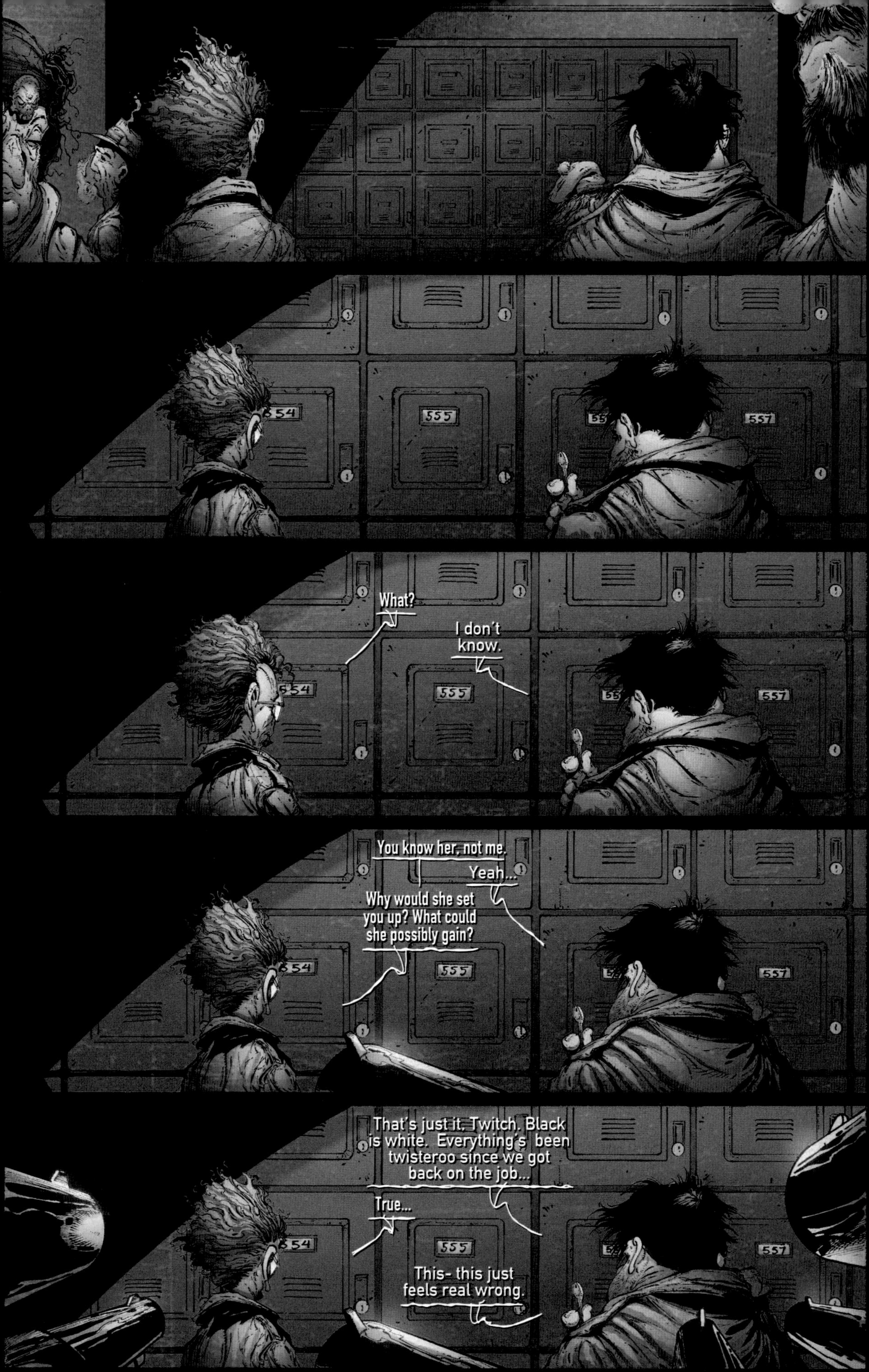

554
555
557
What?
I don't know.
You know her, not me.
Yeah...
Why would she set you up? What could she possibly gain?
That's just it, Twitch. Black is white. Everything's been twisteroo since we got back on the job...
True...
This- this just feels real wrong.

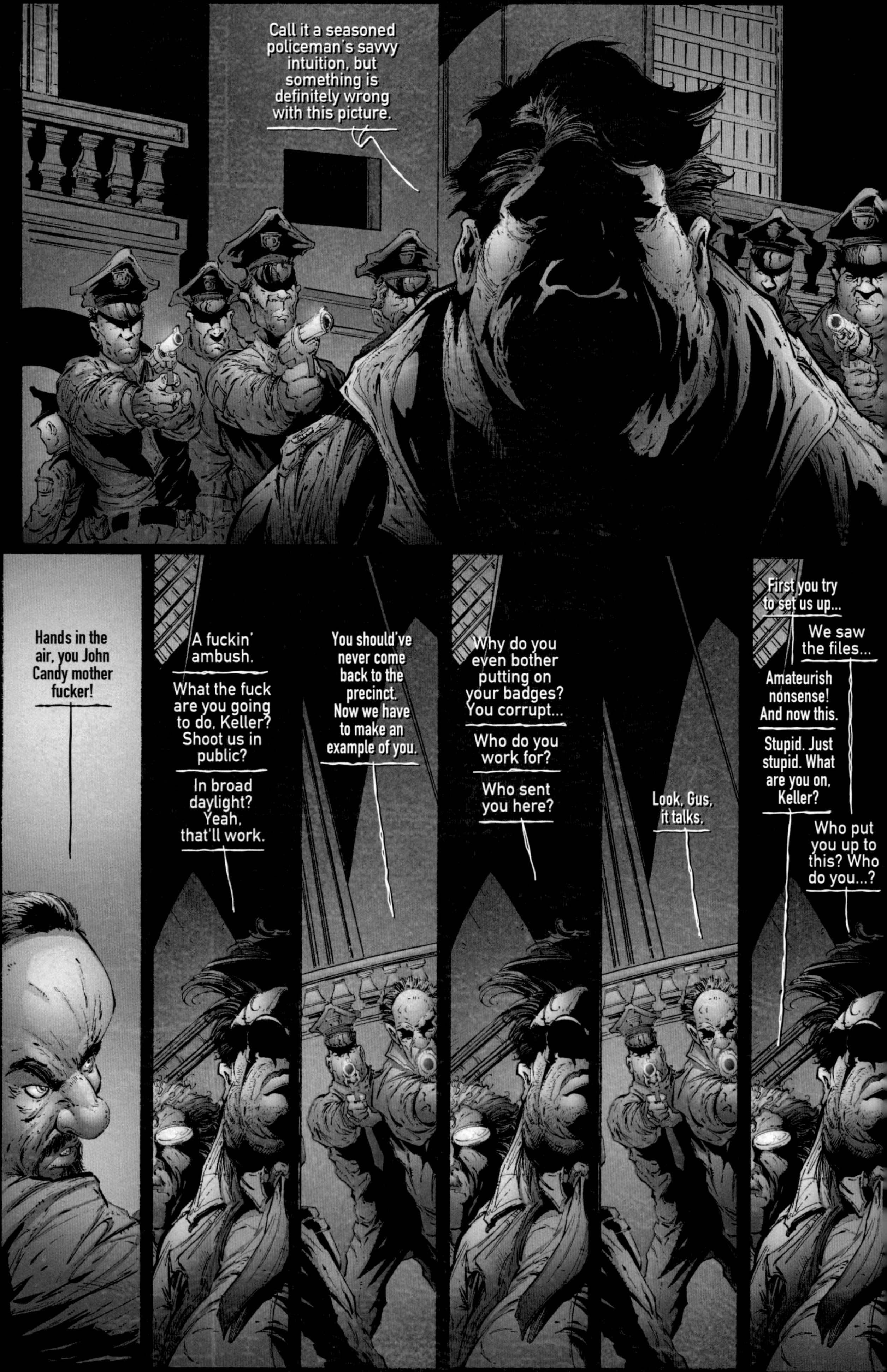
Call it a seasoned policeman's savvy intuition, but something is definitely wrong with this picture.
Hands in the air, you John Candy mother fucker!
A fuckin' ambush.
What the fuck are you going to do, Keller? Shoot us in public?
In broad daylight? Yeah, that'll work.
You should've never come back to the precinct. Now we have to make an example of you.
Why do you even bother putting on your badges? You corrupt...
Who do you work for?
Who sent you here?
Look, Gus, it talks.
First you try to set us up...
We saw the files...
Amateurish nonsense! And now this.
Stupid. Just stupid. What are you on, Keller?
Who put you up to this? Who do you...?

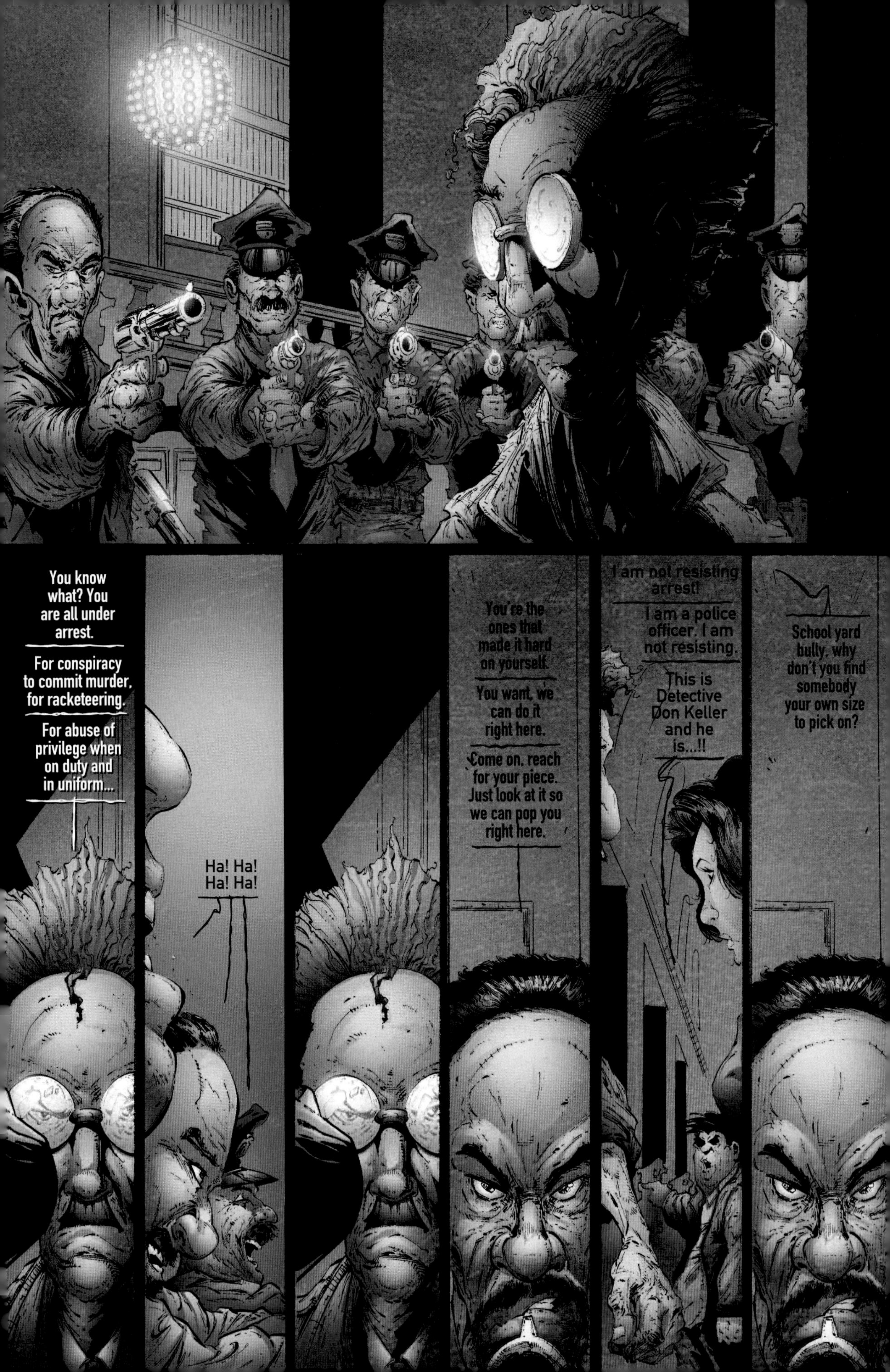
You know what? You are all under arrest.
For conspiracy to commit murder, for racketeering.
For abuse of privilege when on duty and in uniform...
Ha! Ha! Ha! Ha!
You're the ones that made it hard on yourself.
You want, we can do it right here.
Come on, reach for your piece. Just look at it so we can pop you right here.
I am not resisting arrest!
I am a police officer. I am not resisting.
This is Detective Don Keller and he is...!!
School yard bully, why don't you find somebody your own size to pick on?

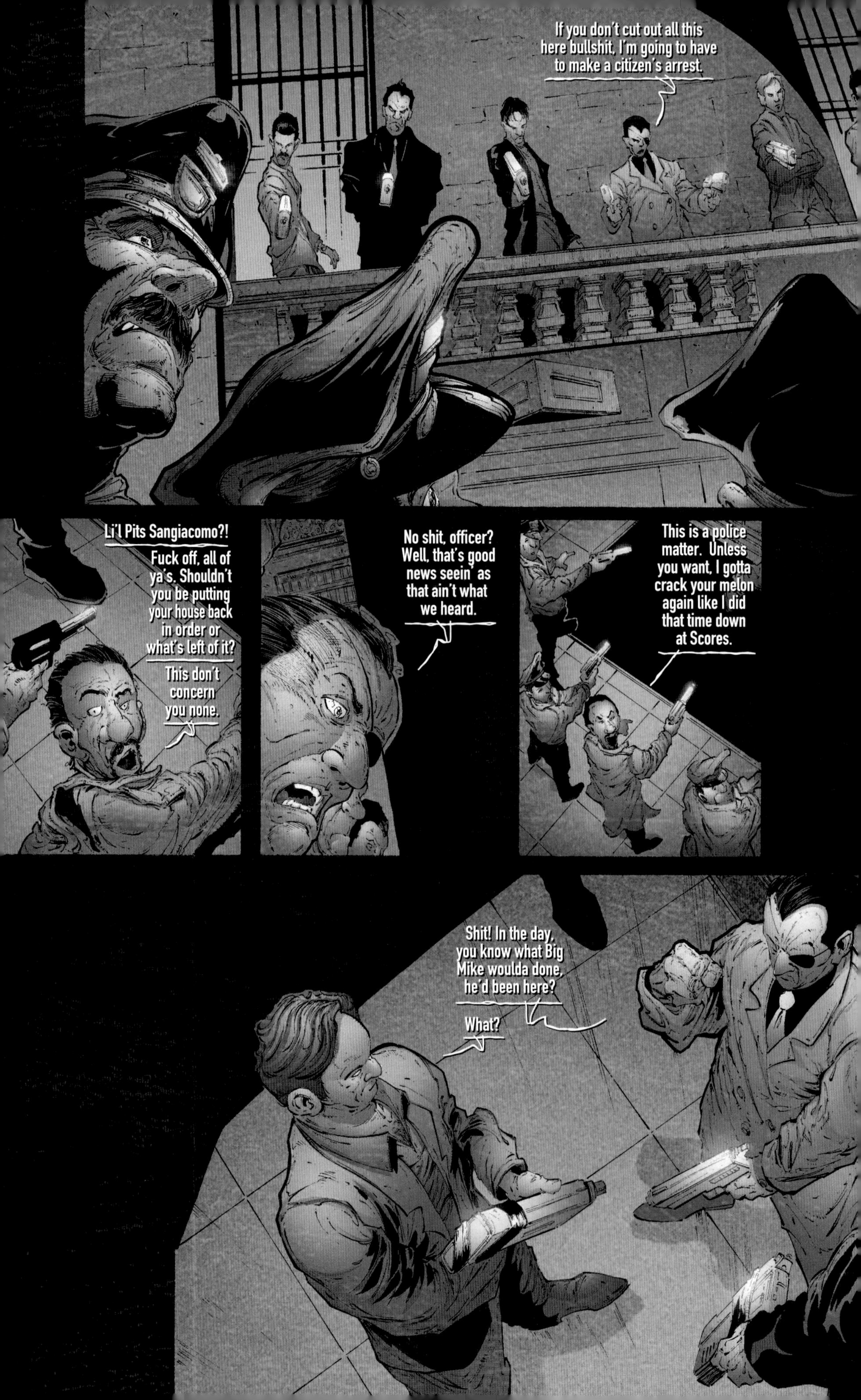
If you don't cut out all this here bullshit, I'm going to have to make a citizen's arrest.
Li'l Pits Sangiacomo?!
Fuck off, all of ya's. Shouldn't you be putting your house back in order or what's left of it?
This don't concern you none.
No shit, officer? Well, that's good news seein' as that ain't what we heard.
This is a police matter. Unless you want, I gotta crack your melon again like I did that time down at Scores.
Shit! In the day, you know what Big Mike woulda done, he'd been here?
What?

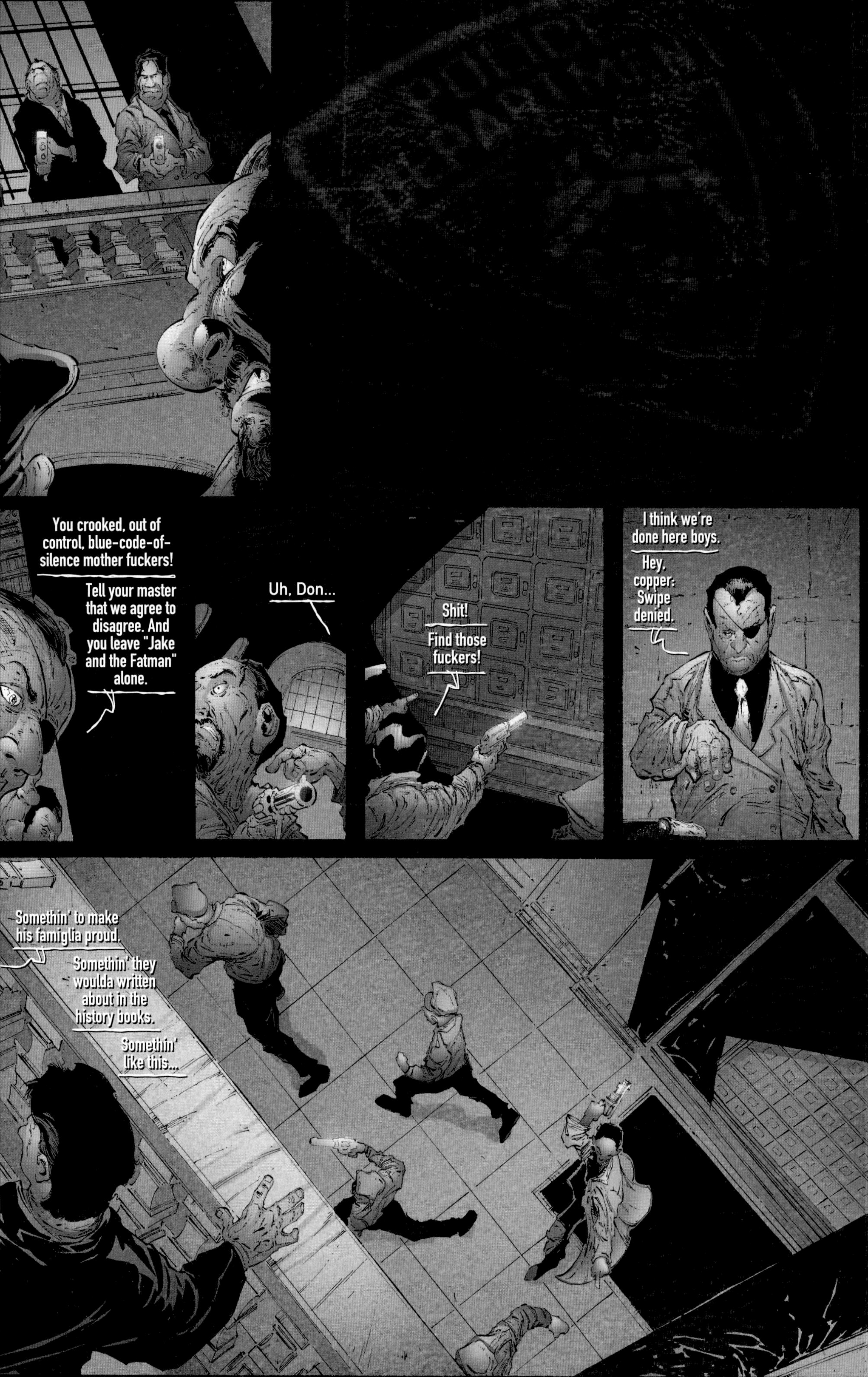
You crooked, out of control, blue-code-of-silence mother fuckers!
Tell your master that we agree to disagree. And you leave "Jake and the Fatman" alone.
Uh, Don...
Shit!
Find those fuckers!
I think we're done here boys.
Hey, copper: Swipe denied.
Somethin' to make his famiglia proud.
Somethin' they woulda written about in the history books.
Somethin' like this...

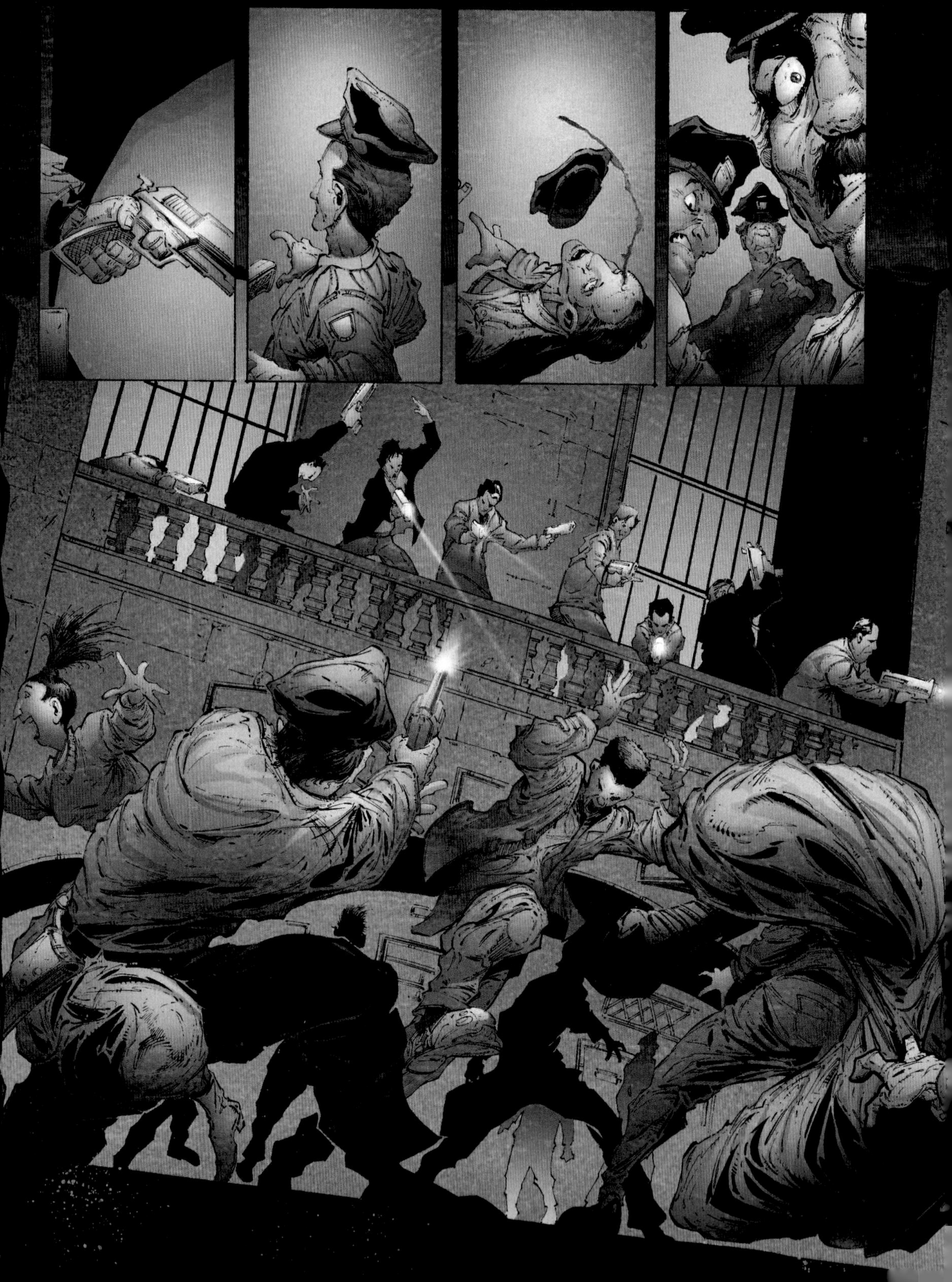

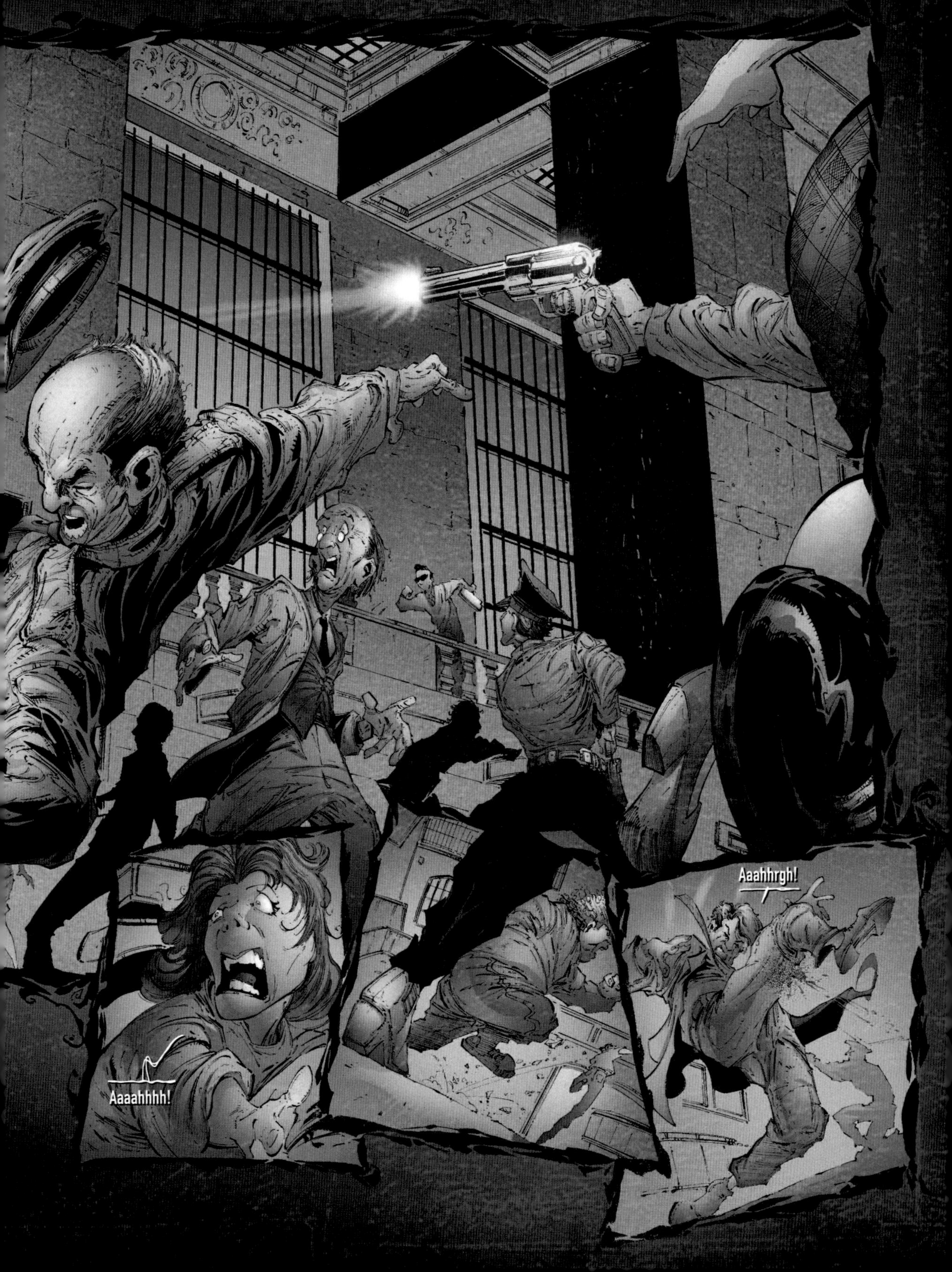
Aaaahhhh!
Aaahhrgh!

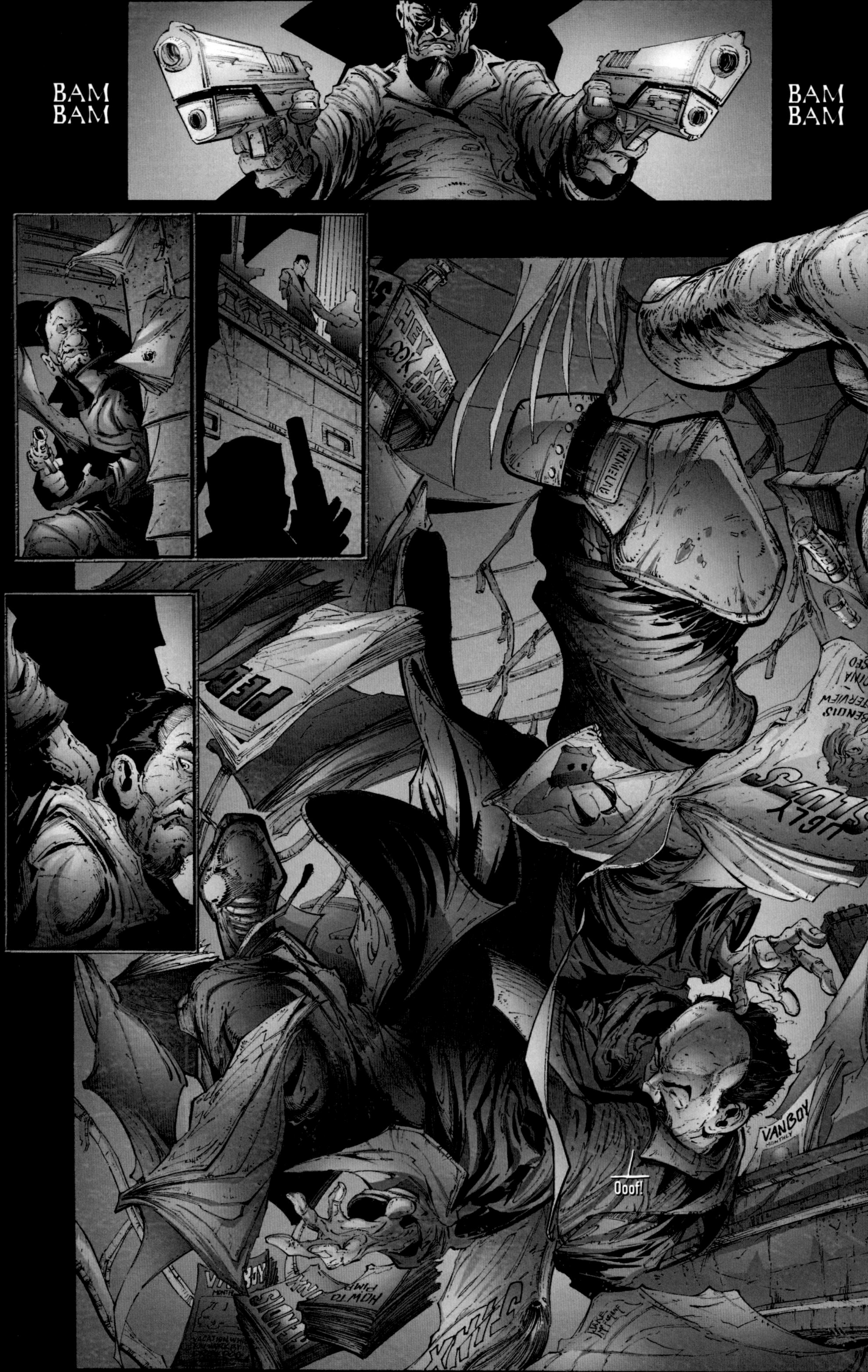

BAM
BAM
BAM
BAM
Ooof!

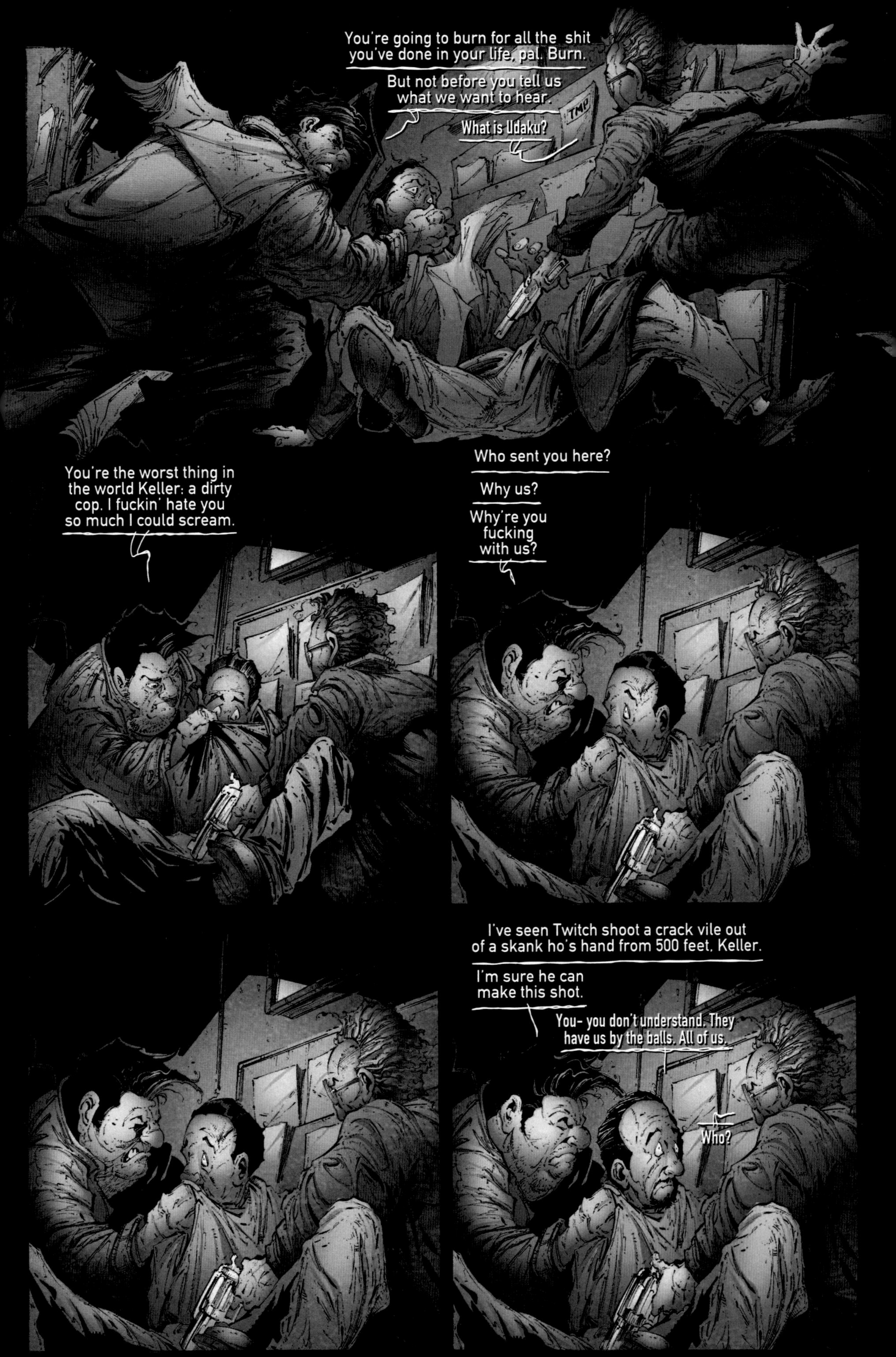
You're going to burn for all the shit you've done in your life, pal. Burn.
But not before you tell us what we want to hear.
What is Udaku?
You're the worst thing in the world Keller: a dirty cop. I fuckin' hate you so much I could scream.
Who sent you here?
Why us?
Why're you fucking with us?
I've seen Twitch shoot a crack vile out of a skank ho's hand from 500 feet. Keller.
I'm sure he can make this shot.
You- you don't understand. They have us by the balls. All of us.
Who?

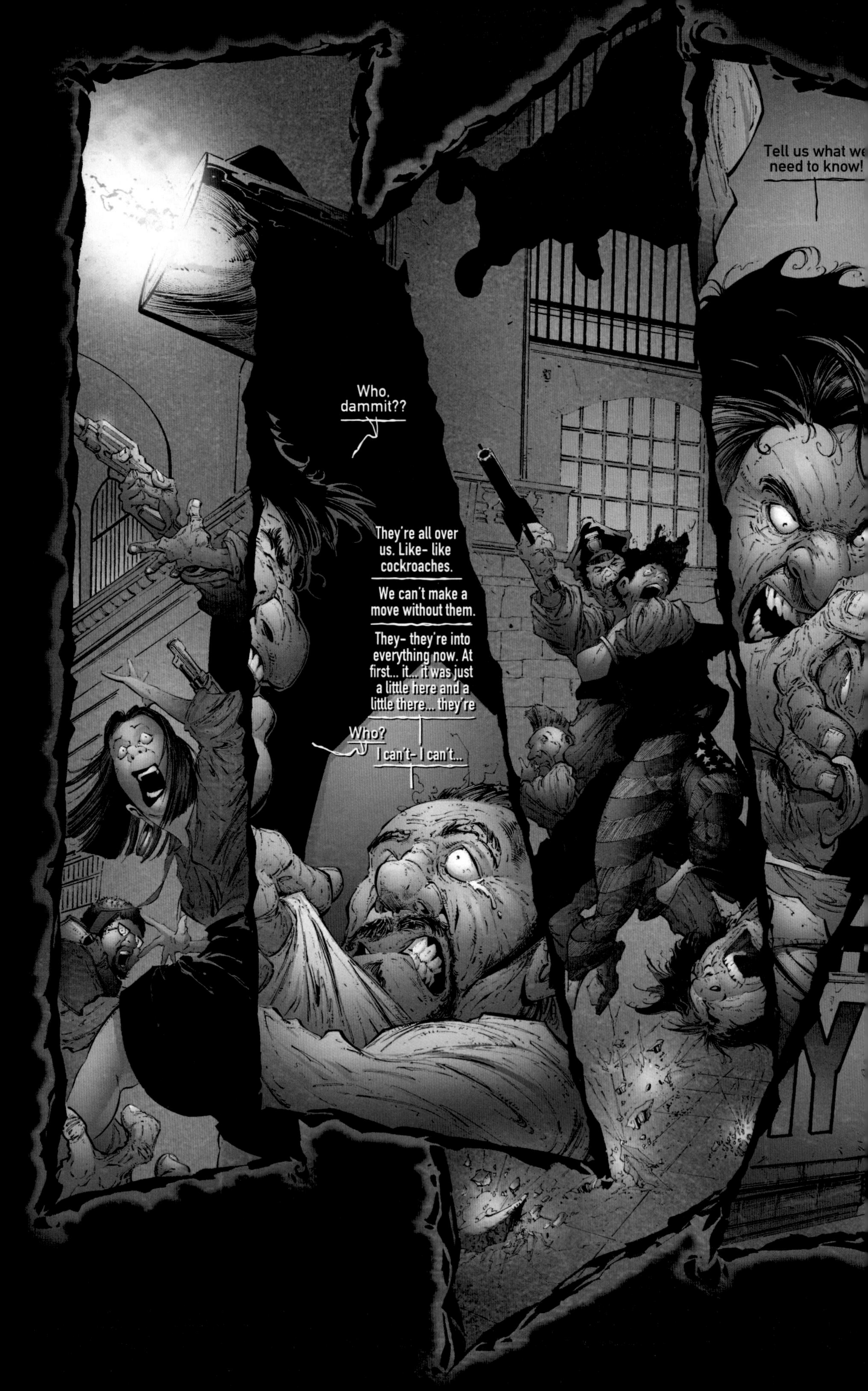
Tell us what we
need to know!
Who,
dammit??
They're all over
us. Like- like
cockroaches.
We can't make a
move without them.
They- they're into
everything now. At
first... it... it was just
a little here and a
little there... they're
Who?
I can't- I can't...

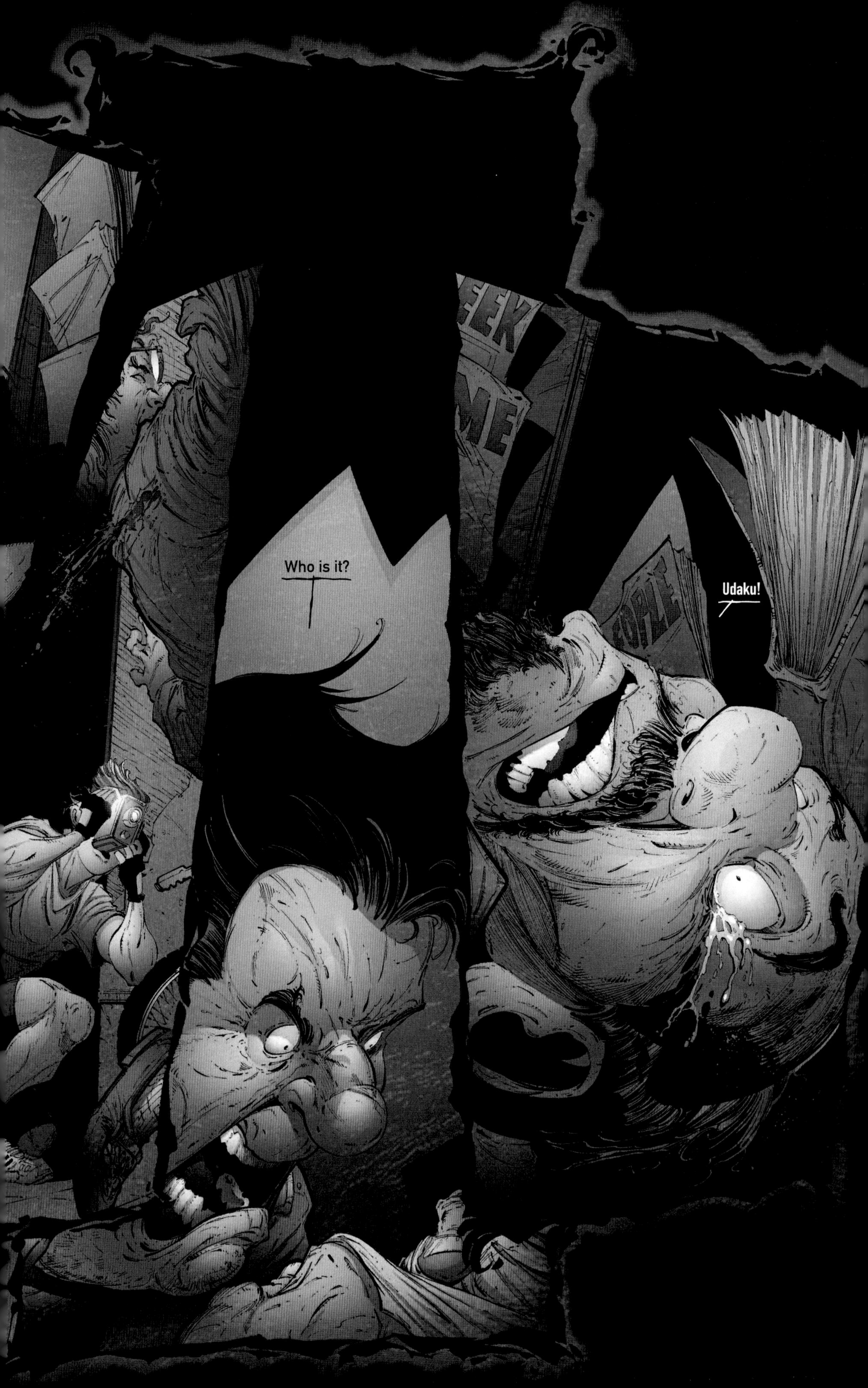
Who is it?
Udaku!

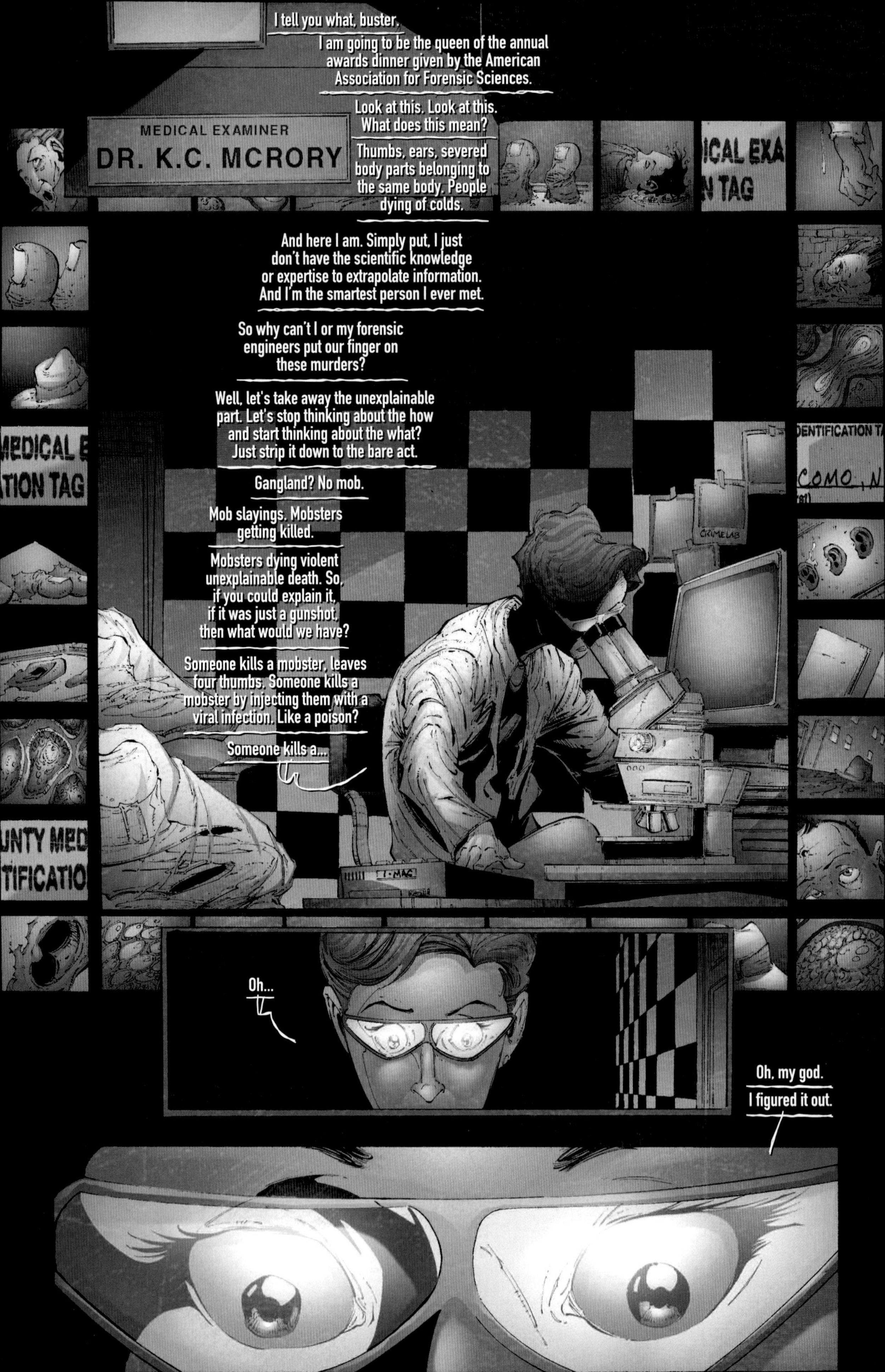
I tell you what, buster.
I am going to be the queen of the annual awards dinner given by the American Association for Forensic Sciences.
MEDICAL EXAMINER
DR. K.C. MCRORY
Look at this. Look at this. What does this mean?
Thumbs, ears, severed body parts belonging to the same body. People dying of colds.
And here I am. Simply put, I just don't have the scientific knowledge or expertise to extrapolate information. And I'm the smartest person I ever met.
So why can't I or my forensic engineers put our finger on these murders?
Well, let's take away the unexplainable part. Let's stop thinking about the how and start thinking about the what? Just strip it down to the bare act.
Gangland? No mob.
Mob slayings. Mobsters getting killed.
Mobsters dying violent unexplainable death. So, if you could explain it, if it was just a gunshot, then what would we have?
Someone kills a mobster, leaves four thumbs. Someone kills a mobster by injecting them with a viral infection. Like a poison?
Someone kills a...
Oh...
Oh, my god.
I figured it out.

01 02 03 04 05 06 07 08 09 10 11 12 13

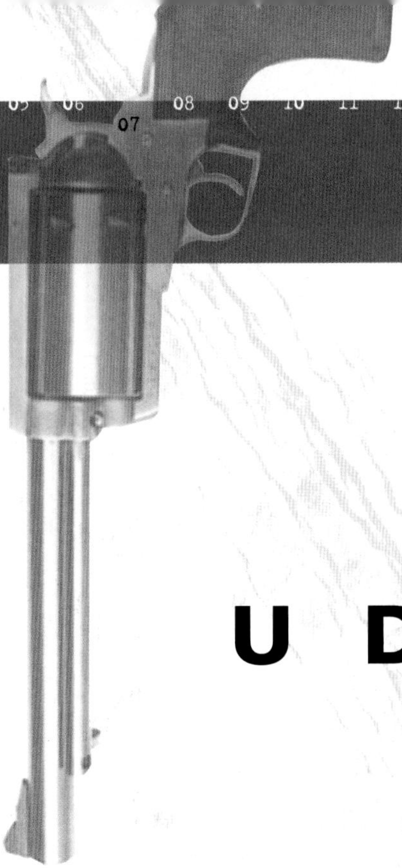

U D A K U

P A R T 7

SAM AND TWITCH

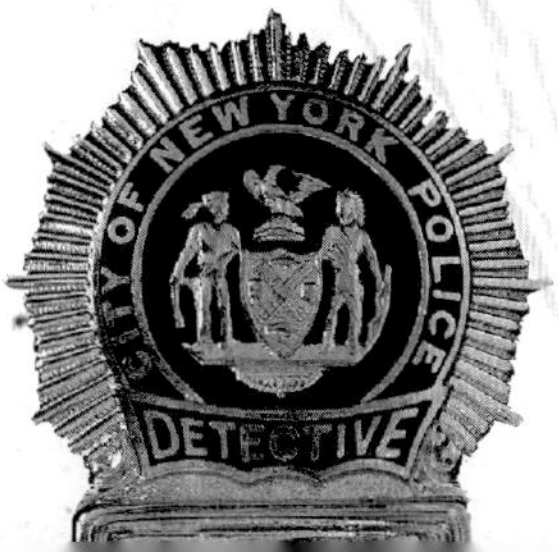
CITY OF NEW YORK POLICE
DETECTIVE

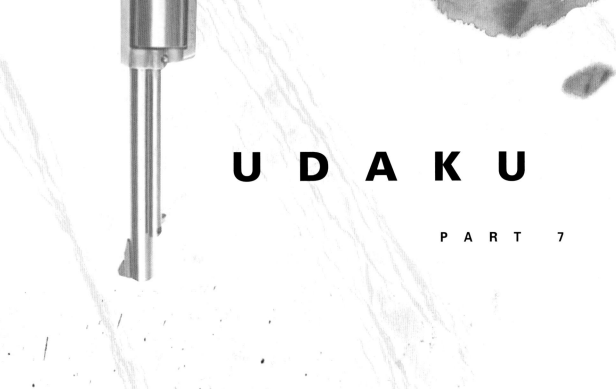

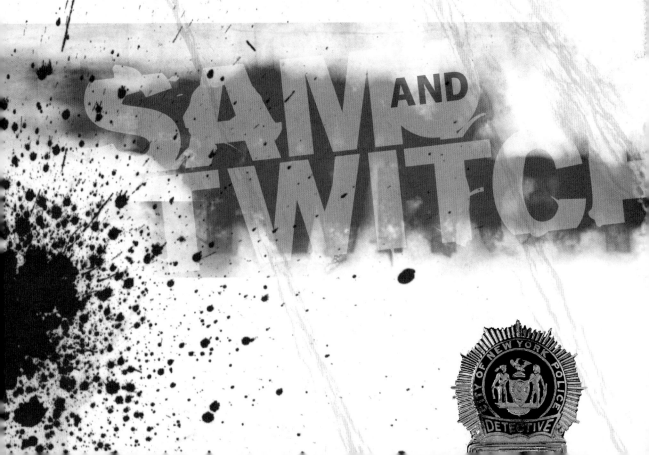

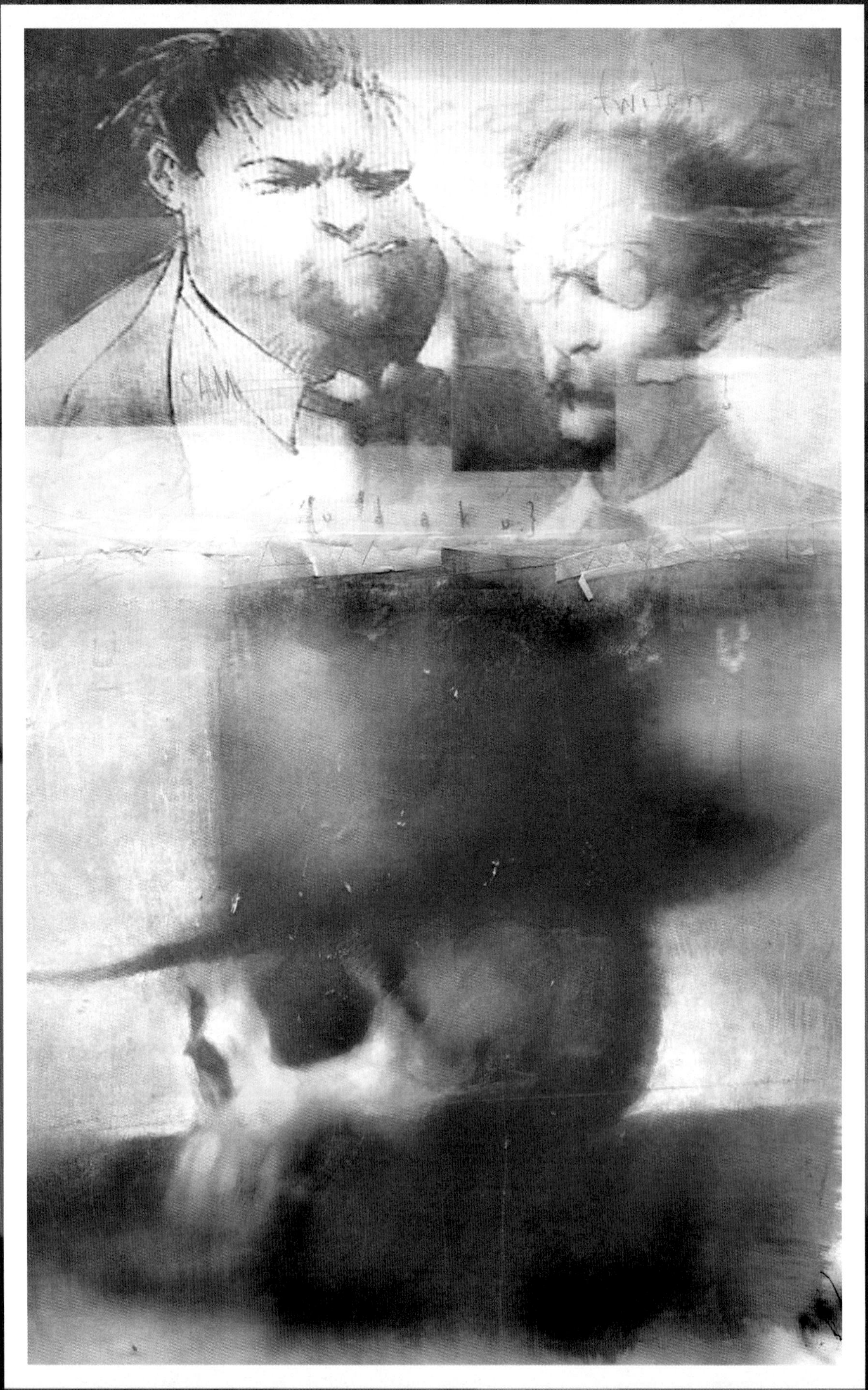
SAM

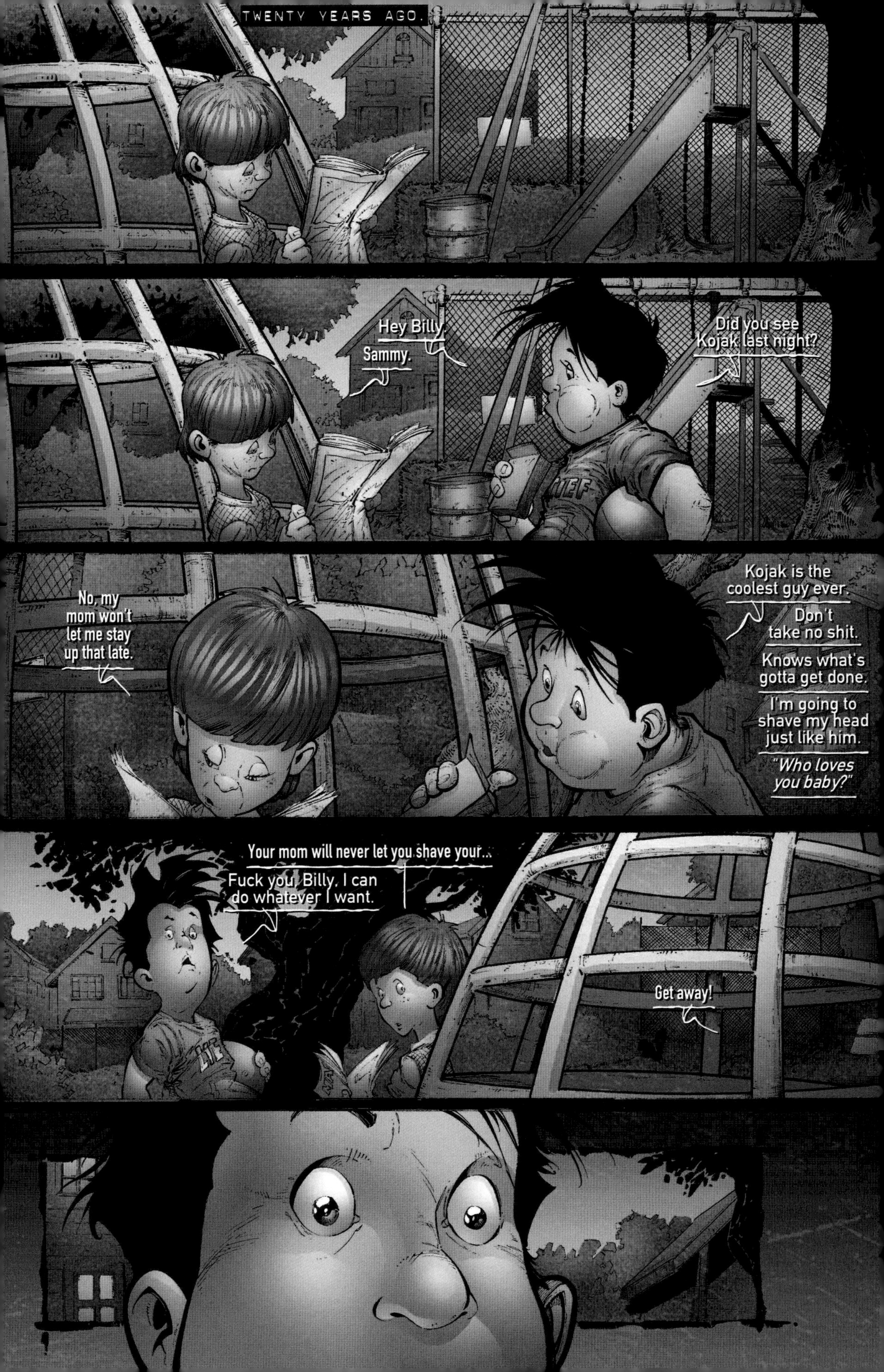
TWENTY YEARS AGO.
Hey Billy.
Sammy.
Did you see Kojak last night?
No, my mom won't let me stay up that late.
Kojak is the coolest guy ever.
Don't take no shit.
Knows what's gotta get done.
I'm going to shave my head just like him.
"Who loves you baby?"
Your mom will never let you shave your...
Fuck you, Billy. I can do whatever I want.
Get away!

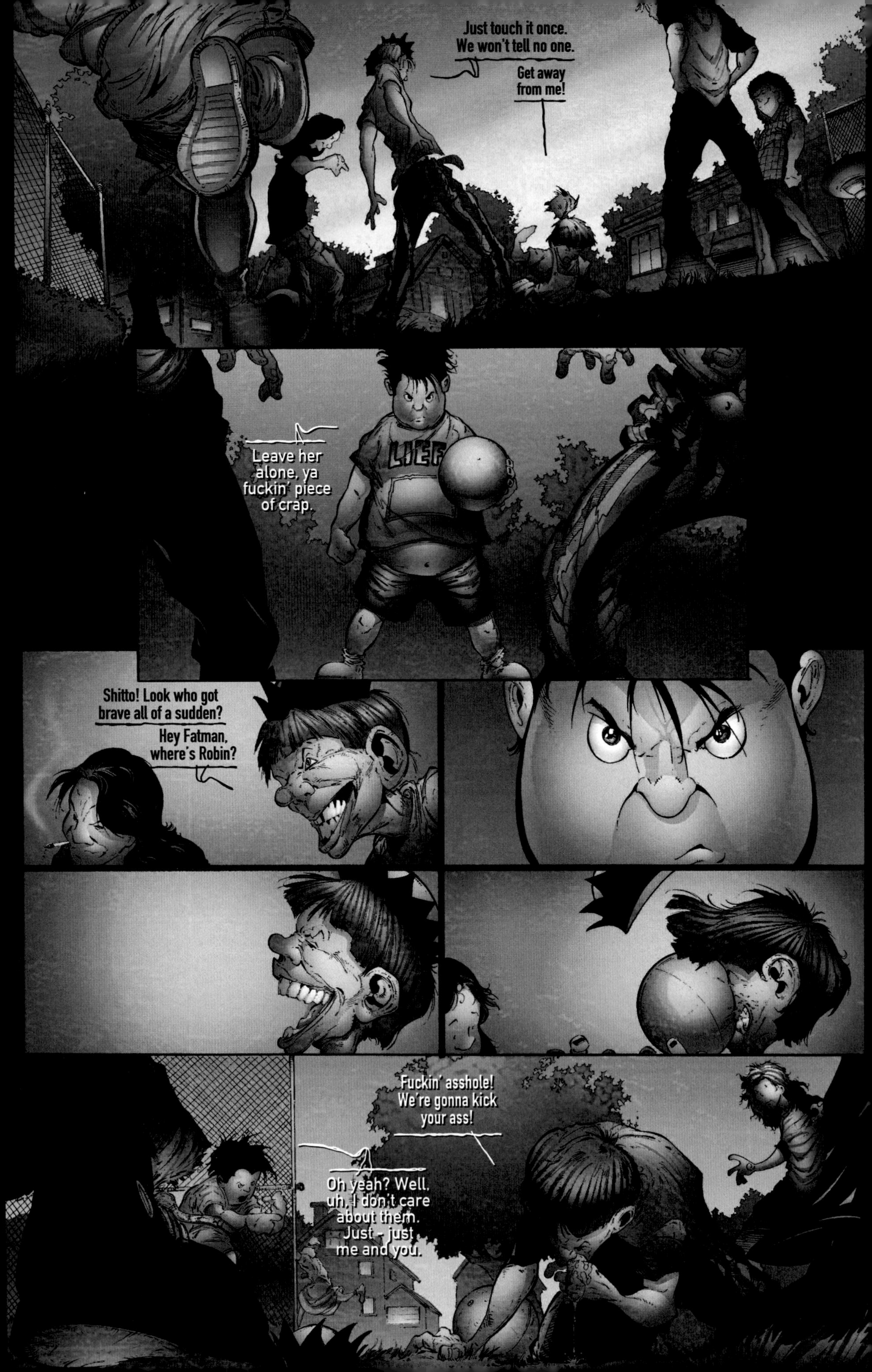
Just touch it once. We won't tell no one.
Get away from me!
Leave her alone, ya fuckin' piece of crap.
Shitto! Look who got brave all of a sudden?
Hey Fatman, where's Robin?
Fuckin' asshole! We're gonna kick your ass!
Oh yeah? Well, uh, I don't care about them. Just - just me and you.

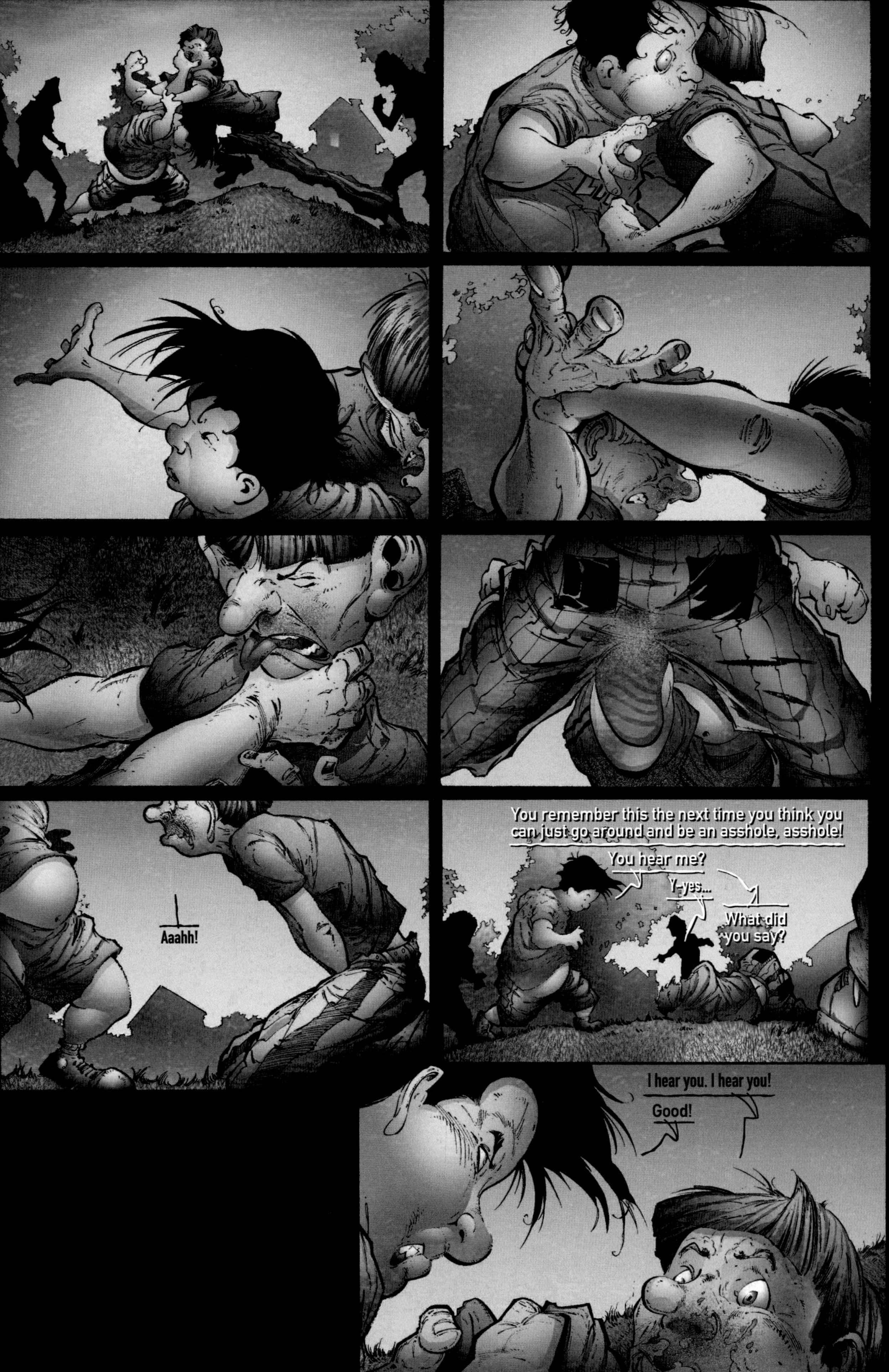
Aaahh!
You remember this the next time you think you can just go around and be an asshole, asshole!
You hear me?
Y-yes...
What did you say?
I hear you. I hear you!
Good!

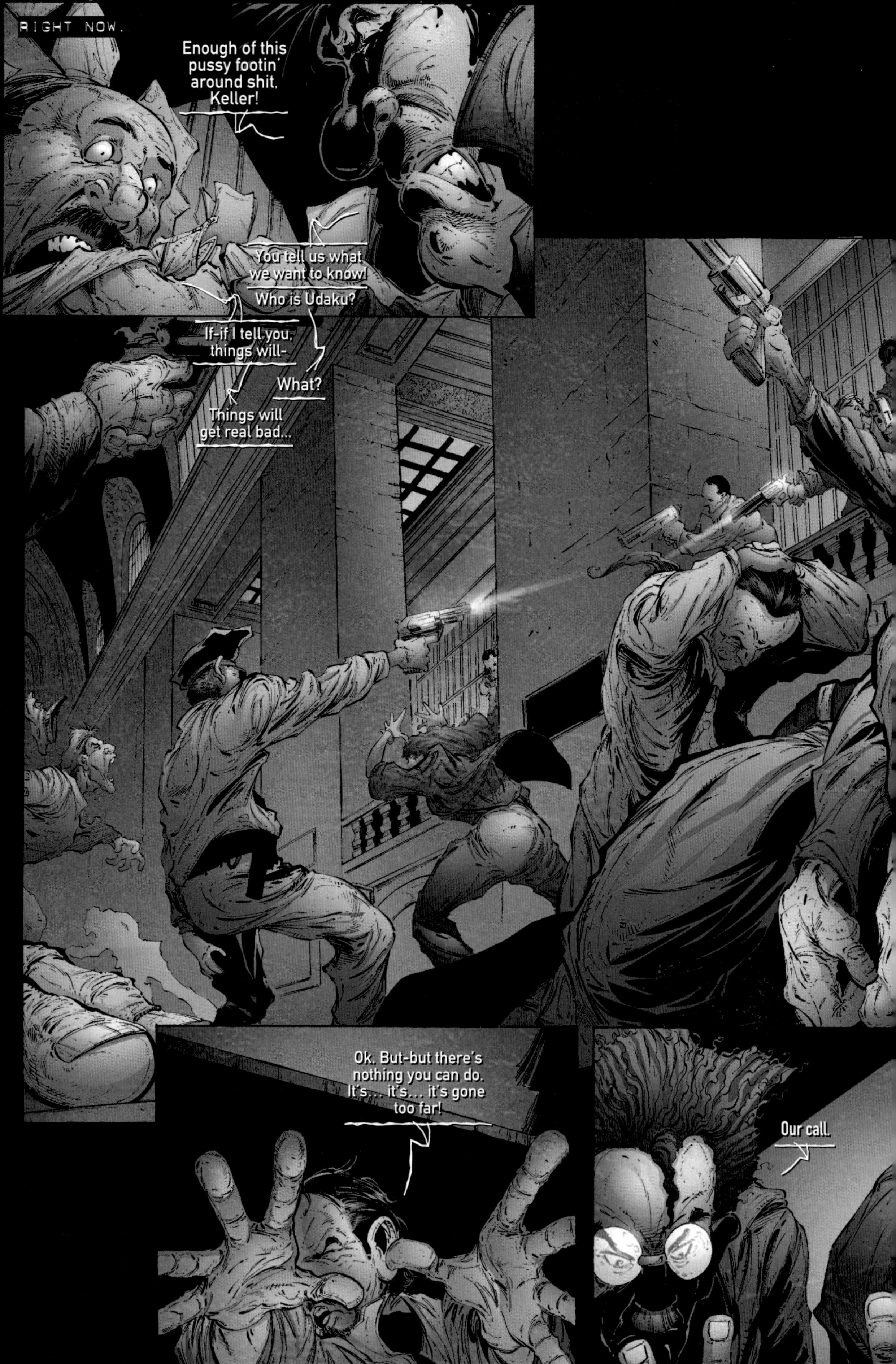
RIGHT NOW.
Enough of this pussy footin' around shit, Keller!
You tell us what we want to know!
Who is Udaku?
If-if I tell you, things will-
What?
Things will get real bad...
Ok. But-but there's nothing you can do. It's... it's... it's gone too far!
Our call.

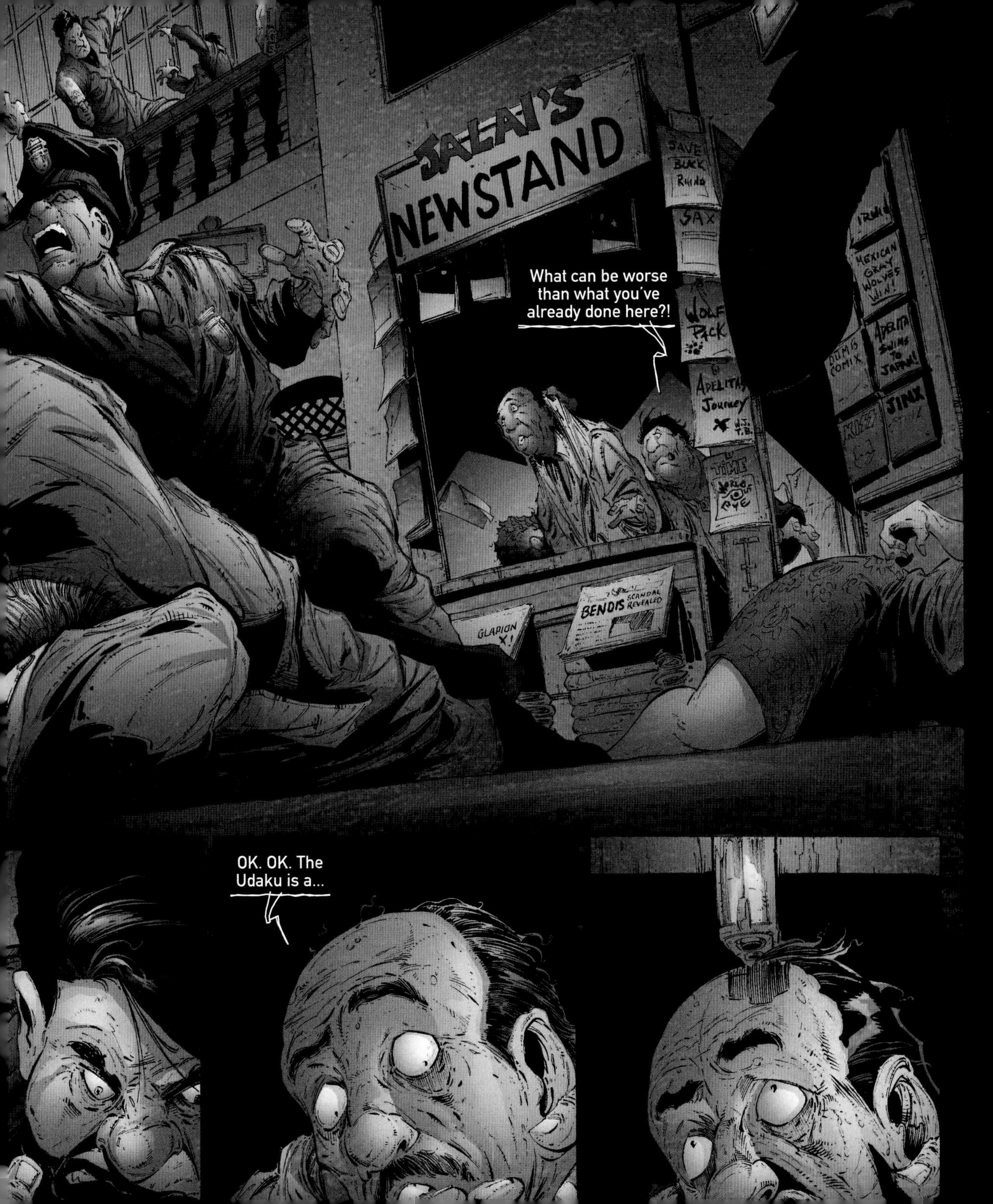
NEWSTAND
What can be worse than what you've already done here?!
BENDIS SCANDAL REVEALED
OK. OK. The Udaku is a...

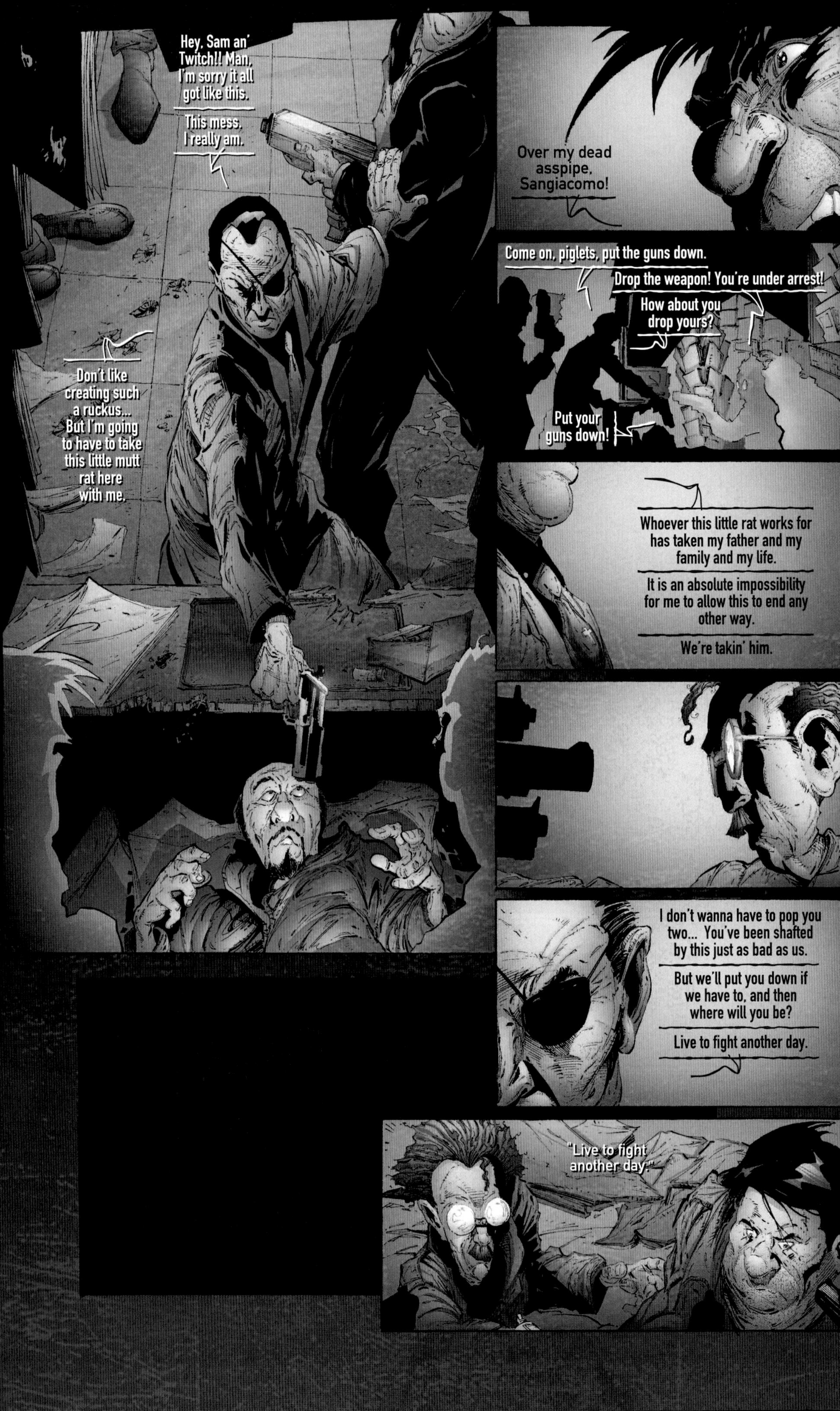

Hey, Sam an' Twitch!! Man, I'm sorry it all got like this.
This mess. I really am.
Don't like creating such a ruckus... But I'm going to have to take this little mutt rat here with me.
Over my dead asspipe, Sangiacomo!
Come on, piglets, put the guns down.
Drop the weapon! You're under arrest!
How about you drop yours?
Put your guns down!
Whoever this little rat works for has taken my father and my family and my life.
It is an absolute impossibility for me to allow this to end any other way.
We're takin' him.
I don't wanna have to pop you two... You've been shafted by this just as bad as us.
But we'll put you down if we have to, and then where will you be?
Live to fight another day.
"Live to fight another day."

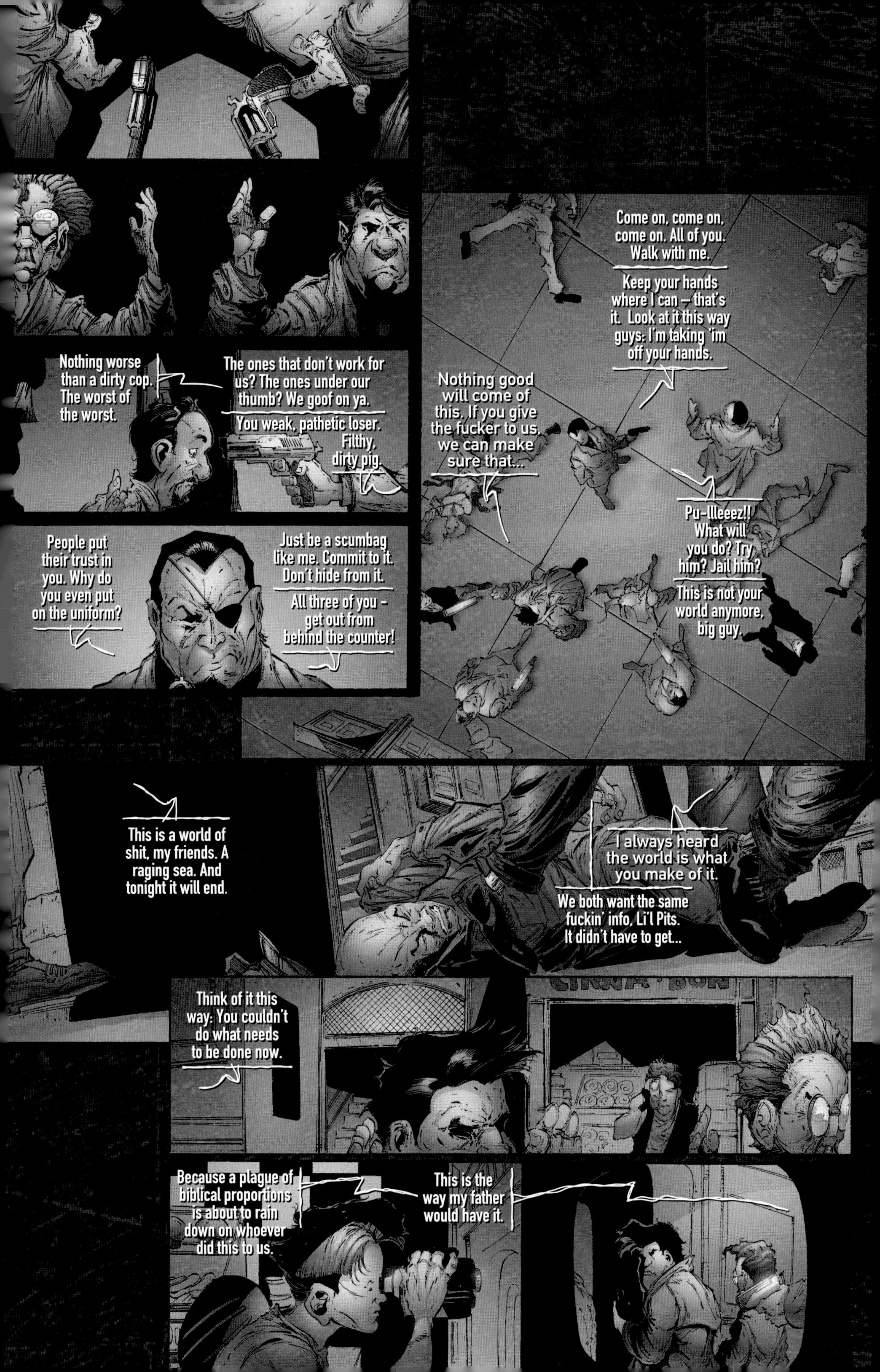

Nothing worse than a dirty cop. The worst of the worst.
The ones that don't work for us? The ones under our thumb? We goof on ya.
You weak, pathetic loser.
Filthy, dirty pig.
People put their trust in you. Why do you even put on the uniform?
Just be a scumbag like me. Commit to it. Don't hide from it.
All three of you - get out from behind the counter!
Come on, come on, come on. All of you. Walk with me.
Keep your hands where I can – that's it. Look at it this way guys: I'm taking 'im off your hands.
Nothing good will come of this. If you give the fucker to us, we can make sure that...
Pu-llleeez!! What will you do? Try him? Jail him?
This is not your world anymore, big guy.
This is a world of shit, my friends. A raging sea. And tonight it will end.
I always heard the world is what you make of it.
We both want the same fuckin' info, Li'l Pits. It didn't have to get...
Think of it this way: You couldn't do what needs to be done now.
Because a plague of biblical proportions is about to rain down on whoever did this to us.
This is the way my father would have it.

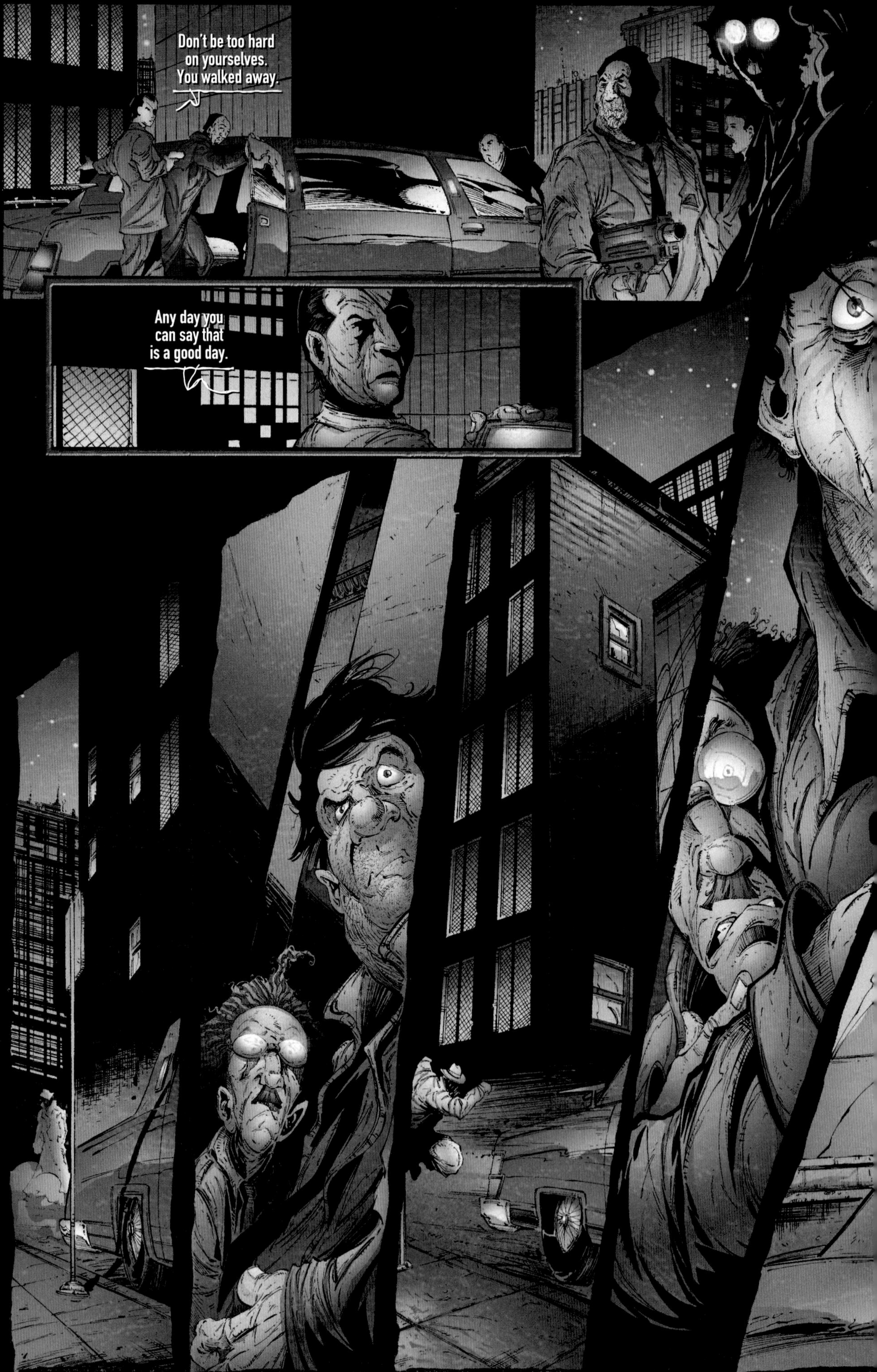
Don't be too hard on yourselves. You walked away.
Any day you can say that is a good day.

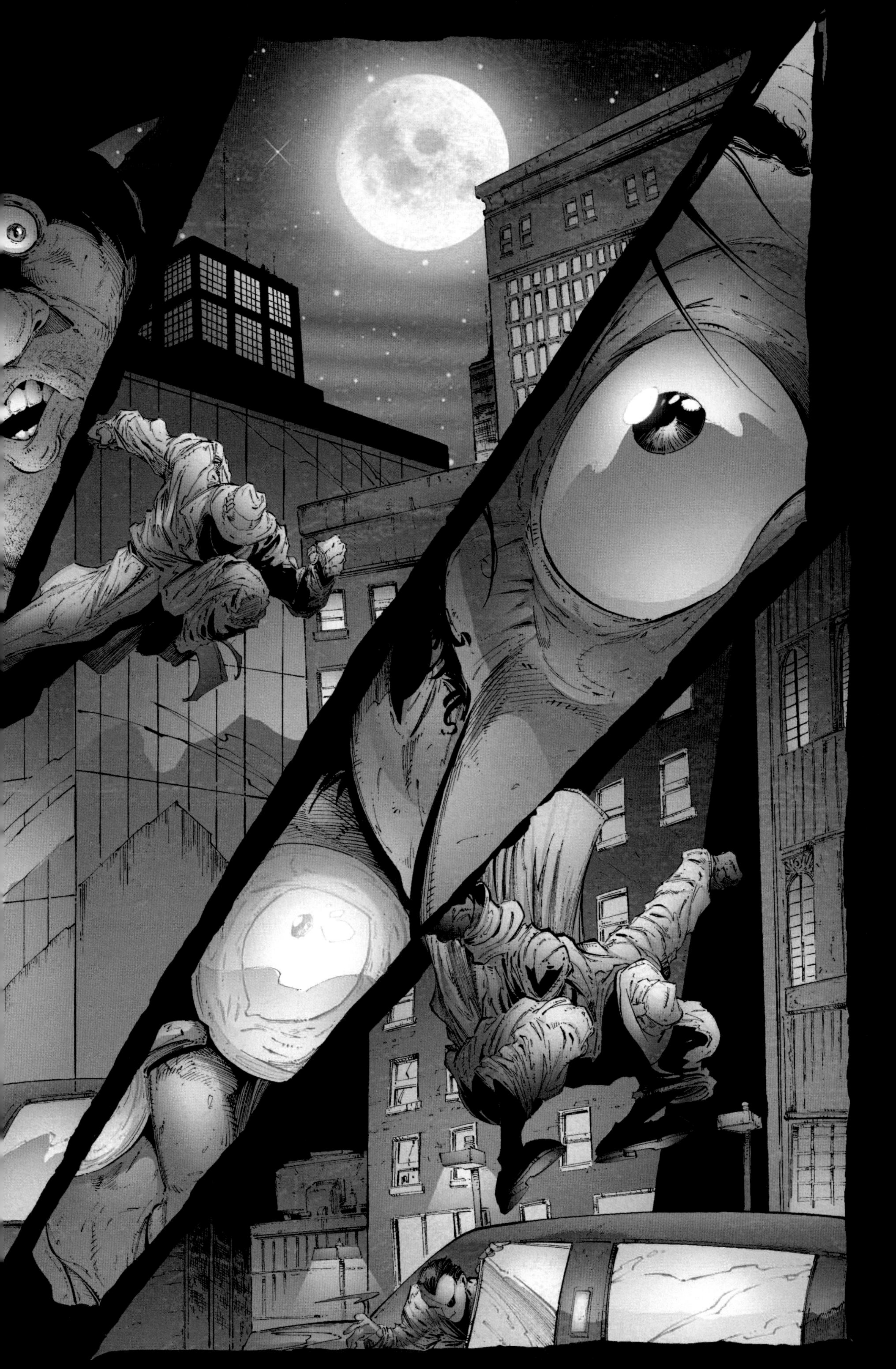

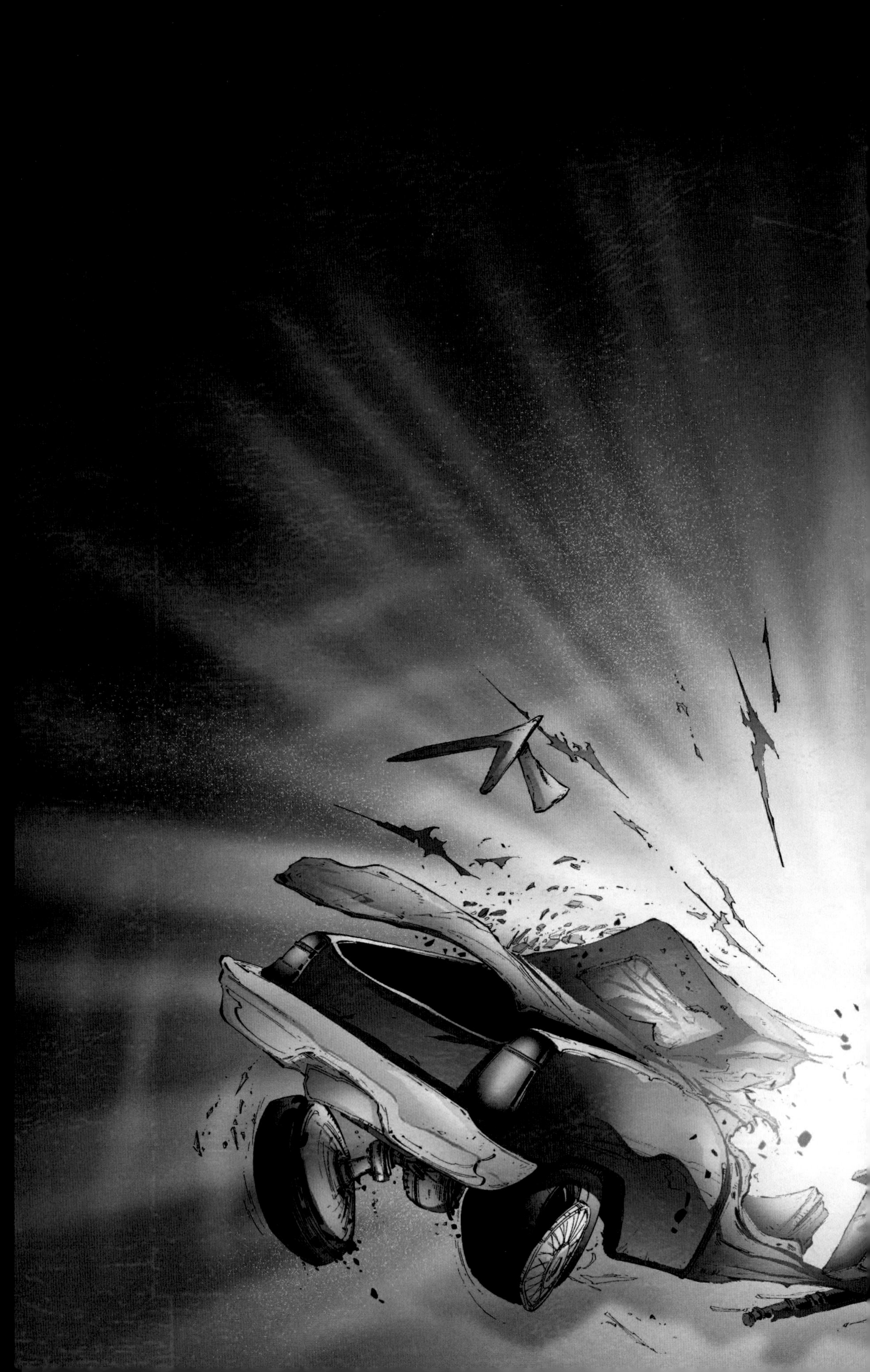

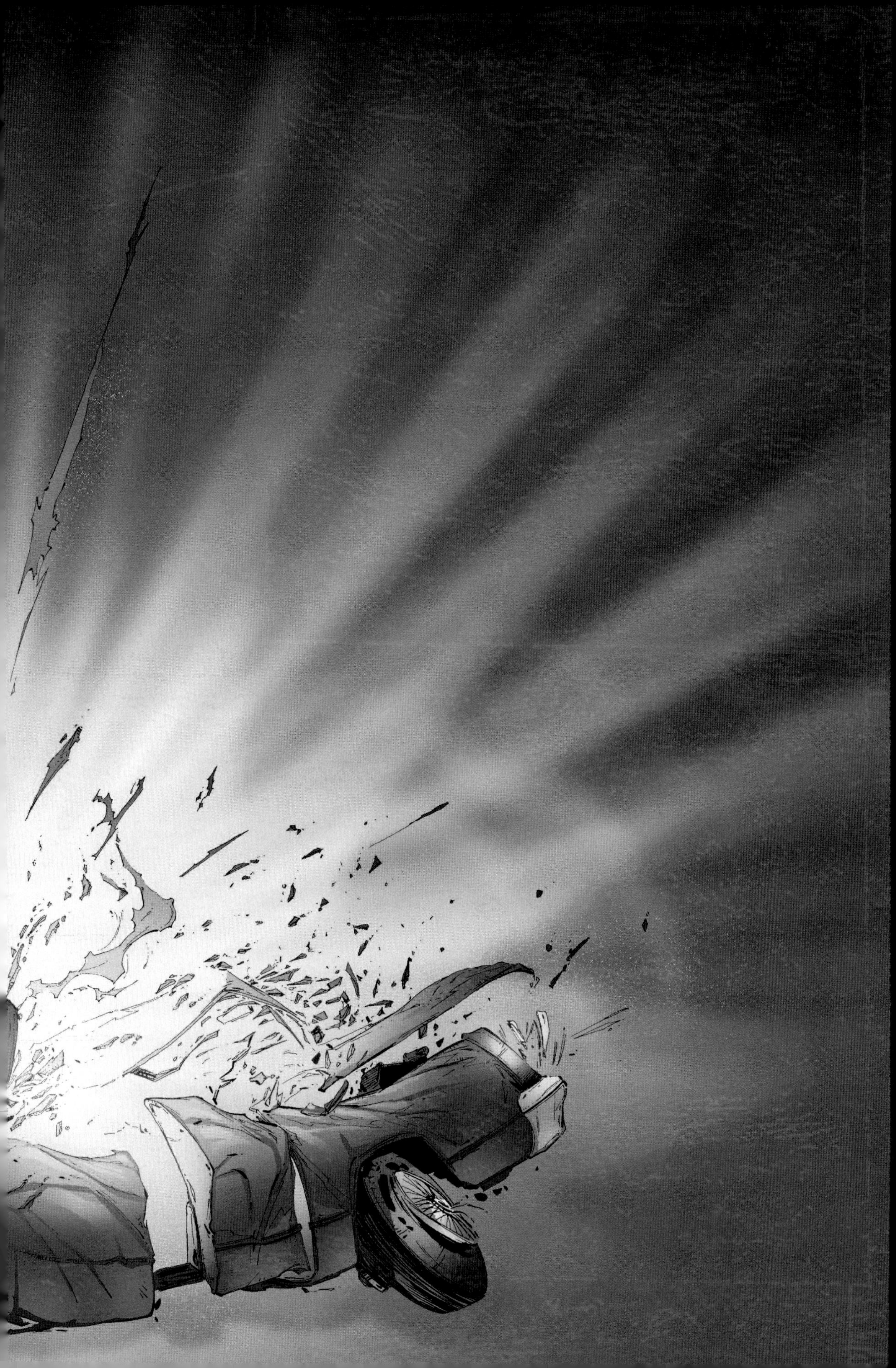

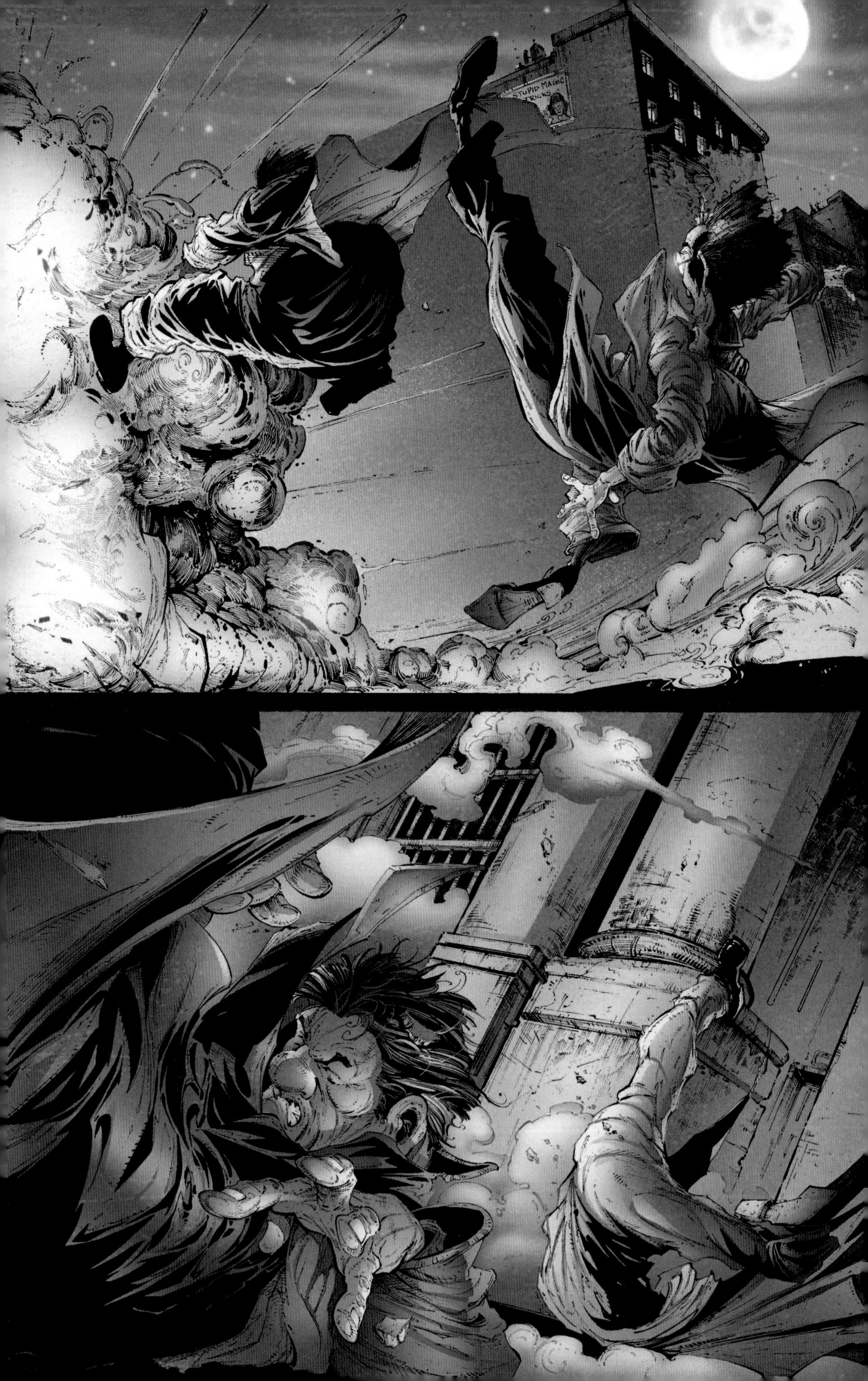
STUPID MAGIC TRICKS

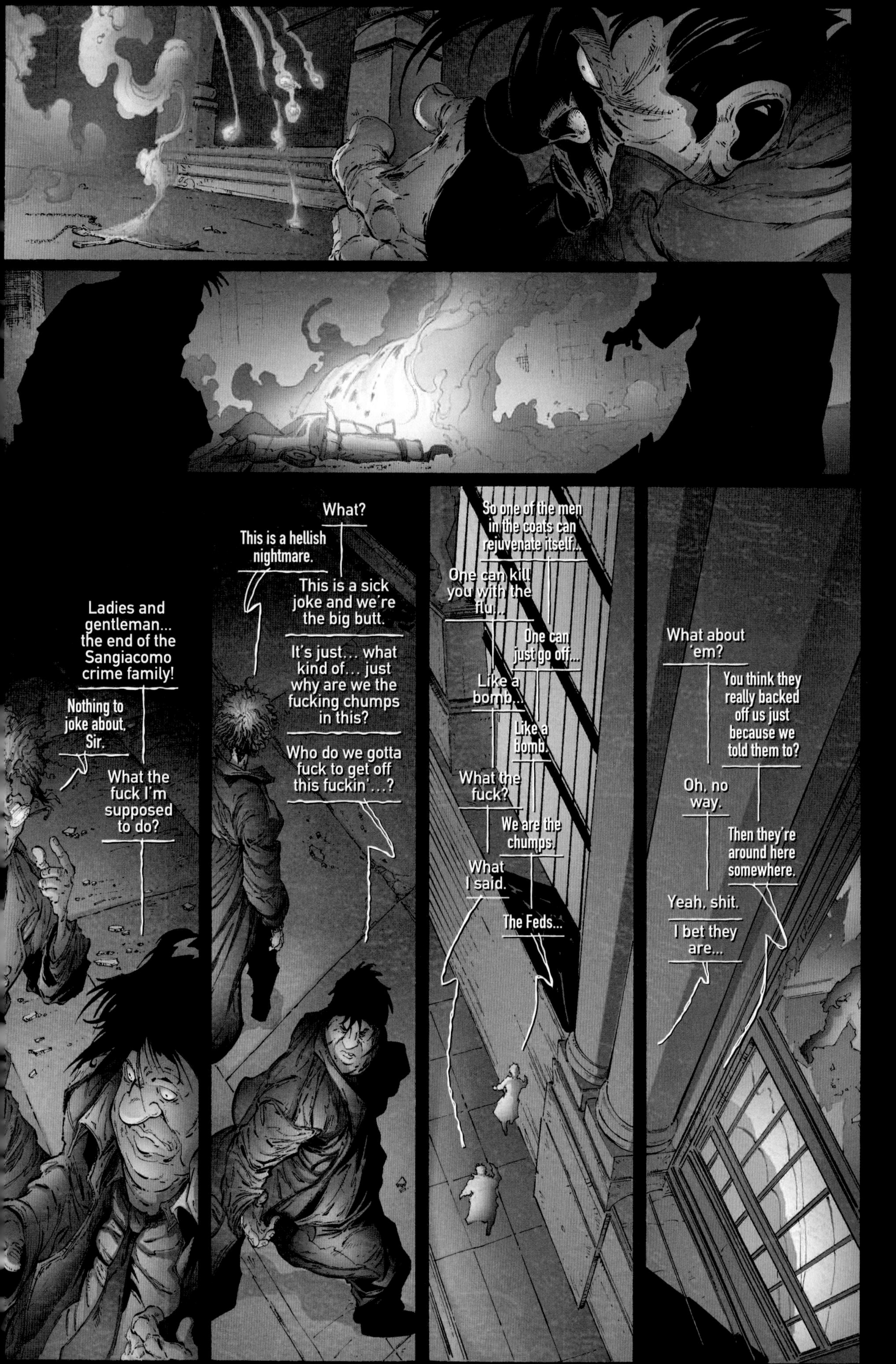

Ladies and gentleman... the end of the Sangiacomo crime family!
Nothing to joke about, Sir.
What the fuck I'm supposed to do?
What?
This is a hellish nightmare.
This is a sick joke and we're the big butt.
It's just... what kind of... just why are we the fucking chumps in this?
Who do we gotta fuck to get off this fuckin'...?
So one of the men in the coats can rejuvenate itself...
One can kill you with the flu...
One can just go off...
Like a bomb...
Like a bomb.
What the fuck?
We are the chumps.
What I said.
The Feds...
What about 'em?
You think they really backed off us just because we told them to?
Oh, no way.
Then they're around here somewhere.
Yeah, shit.
I bet they are...

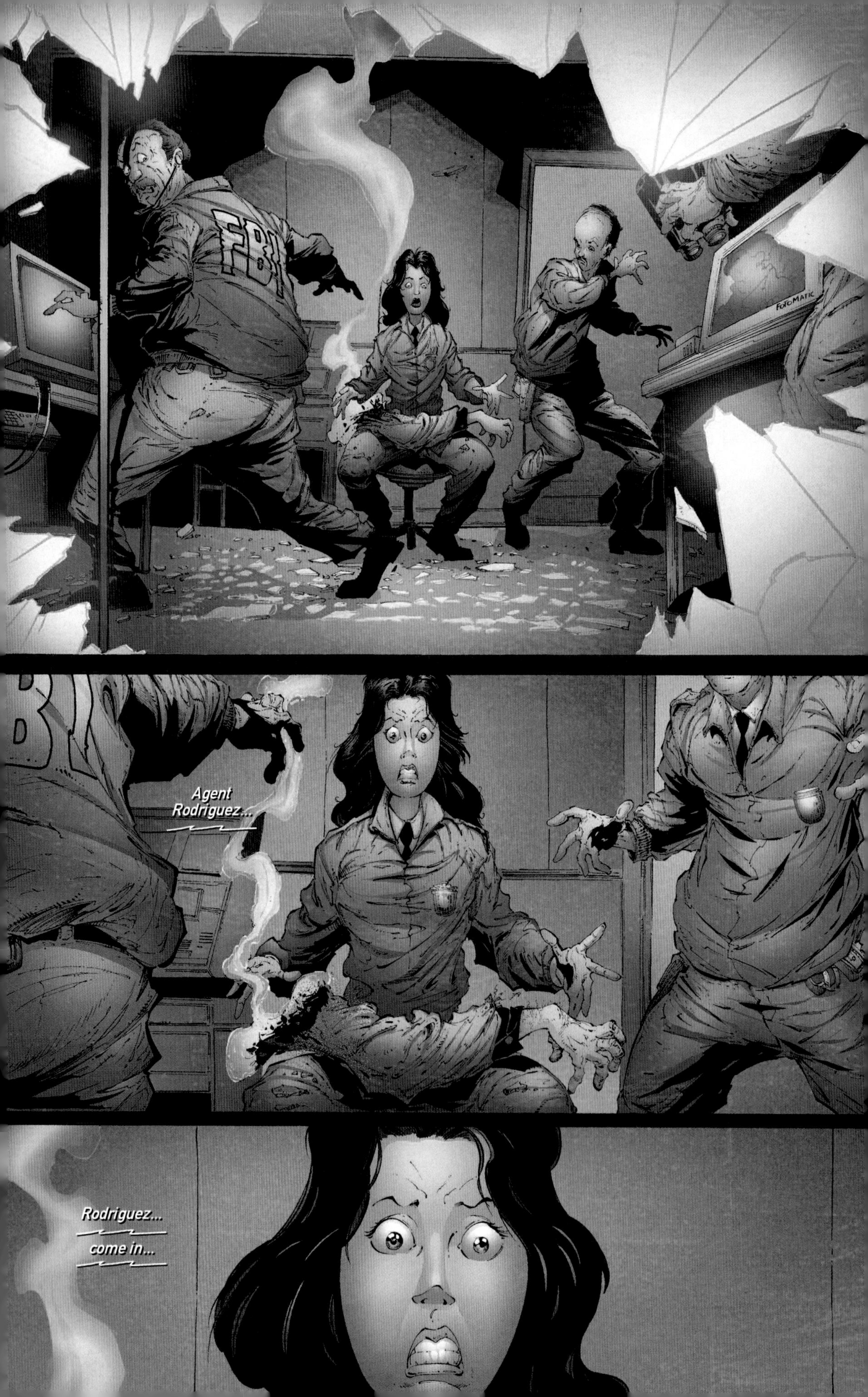
FBI
FOTOMATIC
Agent Rodriguez...
Rodriguez...
come in...

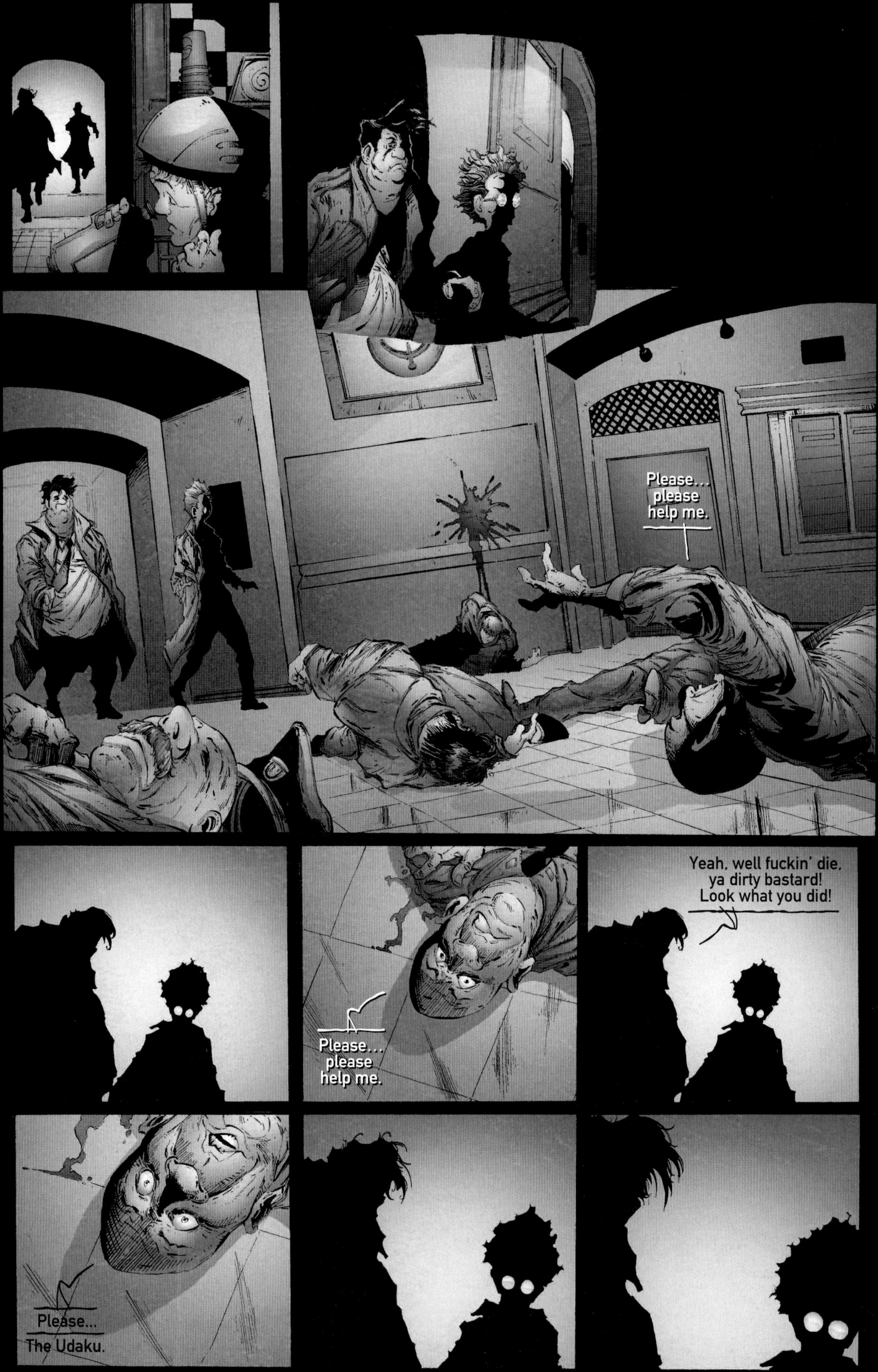
Please... please help me.
Please... please help me.
Yeah, well fuckin' die, ya dirty bastard! Look what you did!
Please...
The Udaku.

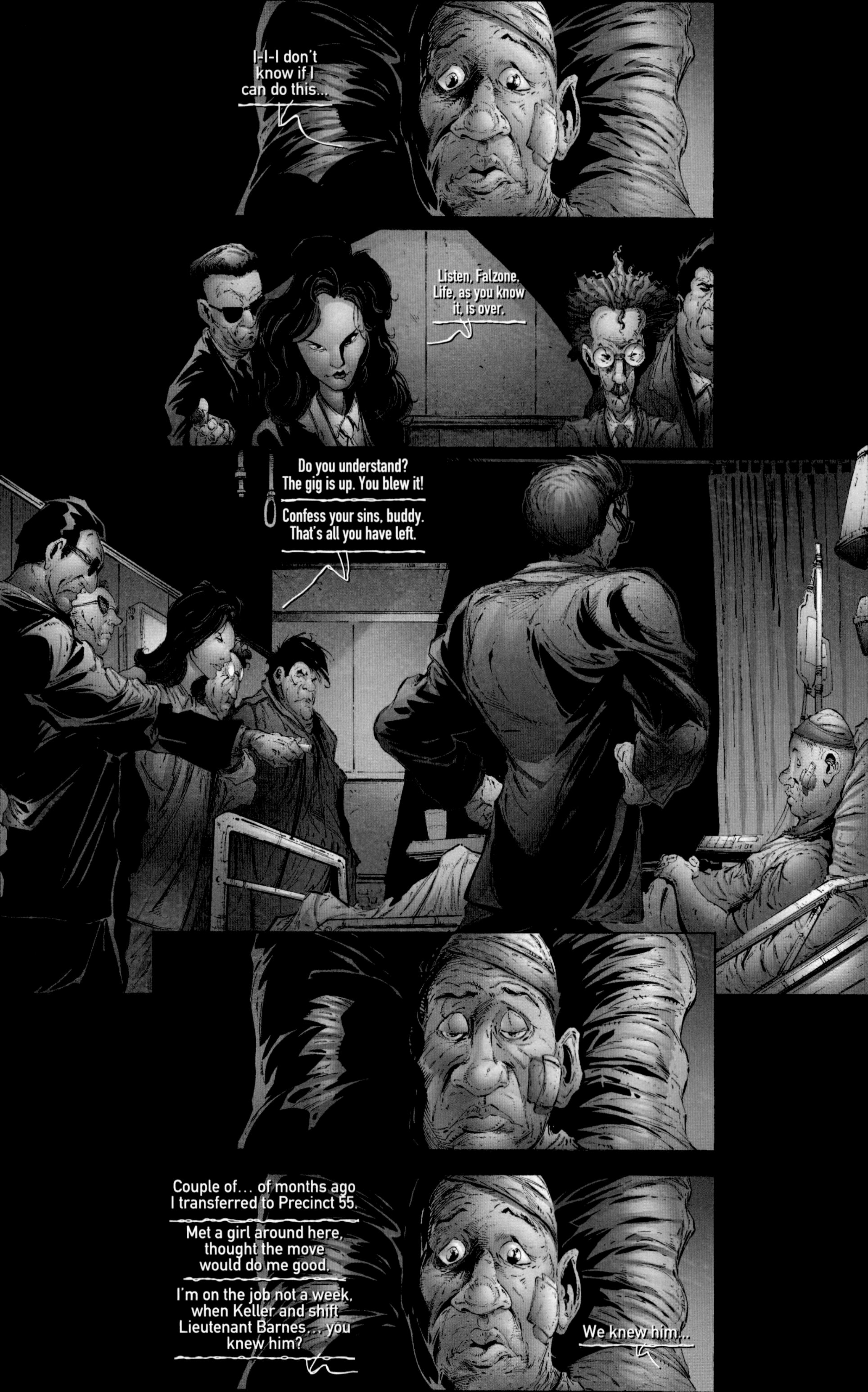

I-I-I don't know if I can do this...
Listen, Falzone. Life, as you know it, is over.
Do you understand? The gig is up. You blew it!
Confess your sins, buddy. That's all you have left.
Couple of... of months ago I transferred to Precinct 55.
Met a girl around here, thought the move would do me good.
I'm on the job not a week, when Keller and shift Lieutenant Barnes... you knew him?
We knew him...

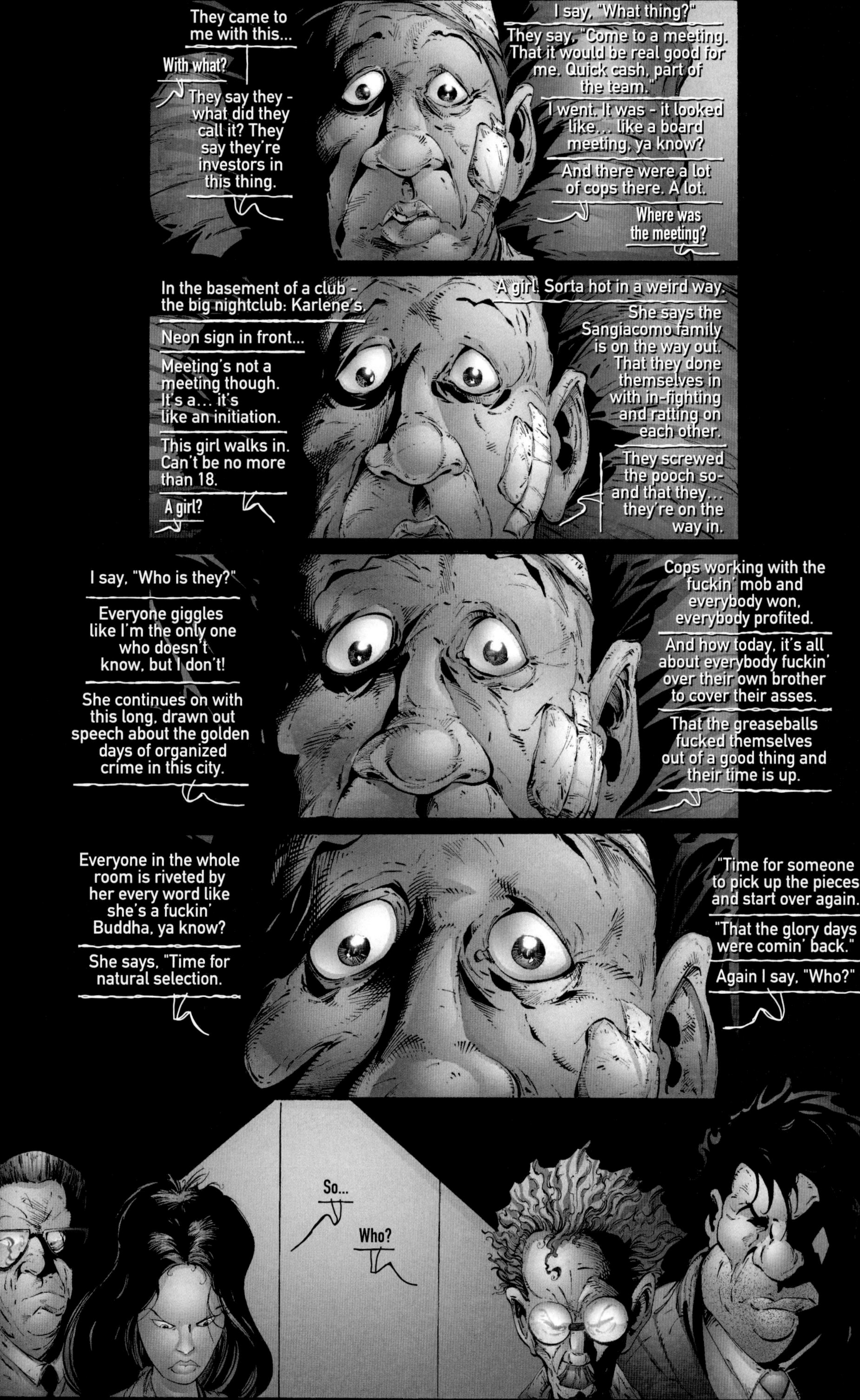
They came to me with this...
With what?
They say they - what did they call it? They say they're investors in this thing.
I say, "What thing?"
They say, "Come to a meeting. That it would be real good for me. Quick cash, part of the team."
I went. It was - it looked like... like a board meeting, ya know?
And there were a lot of cops there. A lot.
Where was the meeting?
In the basement of a club - the big nightclub: Karlene's.
Neon sign in front...
Meeting's not a meeting though. It's a... it's like an initiation.
This girl walks in. Can't be no more than 18.
A girl?
A girl. Sorta hot in a weird way.
She says the Sangiacomo family is on the way out. That they done themselves in with in-fighting and ratting on each other.
They screwed the pooch so- and that they... they're on the way in.
I say, "Who is they?"
Everyone giggles like I'm the only one who doesn't know, but I don't!
She continues on with this long, drawn out speech about the golden days of organized crime in this city.
Cops working with the fuckin' mob and everybody won, everybody profited.
And how today, it's all about everybody fuckin' over their own brother to cover their asses.
That the greaseballs fucked themselves out of a good thing and their time is up.
Everyone in the whole room is riveted by her every word like she's a fuckin' Buddha, ya know?
She says, "Time for natural selection.
"Time for someone to pick up the pieces and start over again.
"That the glory days were comin' back."
Again I say, "Who?"
So...
Who?

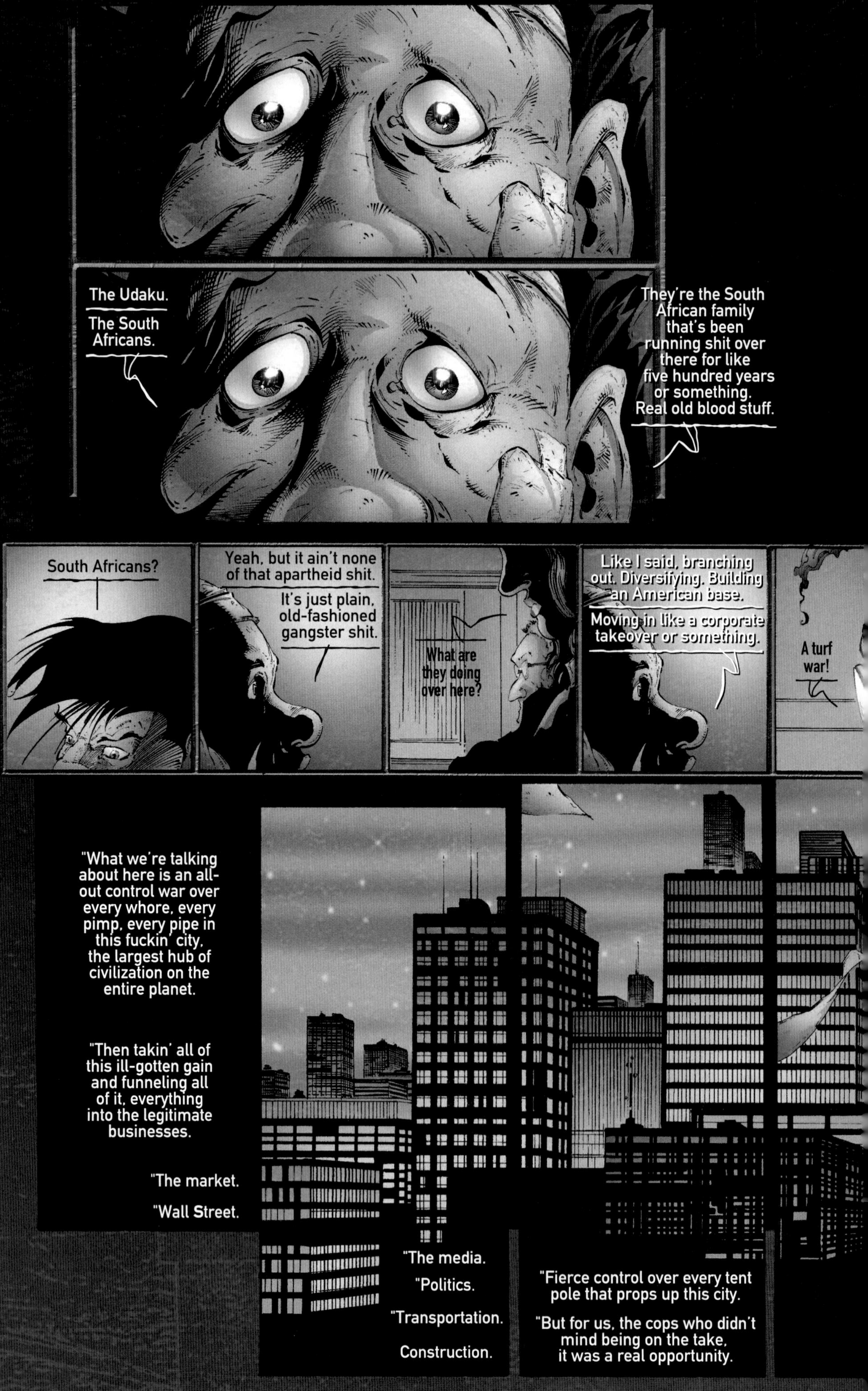

The Udaku.
The South Africans.
They're the South African family that's been running shit over there for like five hundred years or something. Real old blood stuff.
South Africans?
Yeah, but it ain't none of that apartheid shit.
It's just plain, old-fashioned gangster shit.
What are they doing over here?
Like I said, branching out. Diversifying. Building an American base.
Moving in like a corporate takeover or something.
A turf war!
"What we're talking about here is an all-out control war over every whore, every pimp, every pipe in this fuckin' city, the largest hub of civilization on the entire planet.
"Then takin' all of this ill-gotten gain and funneling all of it, everything into the legitimate businesses.
"The market.
"Wall Street.
"The media.
"Politics.
"Transportation.
Construction.
"Fierce control over every tent pole that props up this city.
"But for us, the cops who didn't mind being on the take, it was a real opportunity.

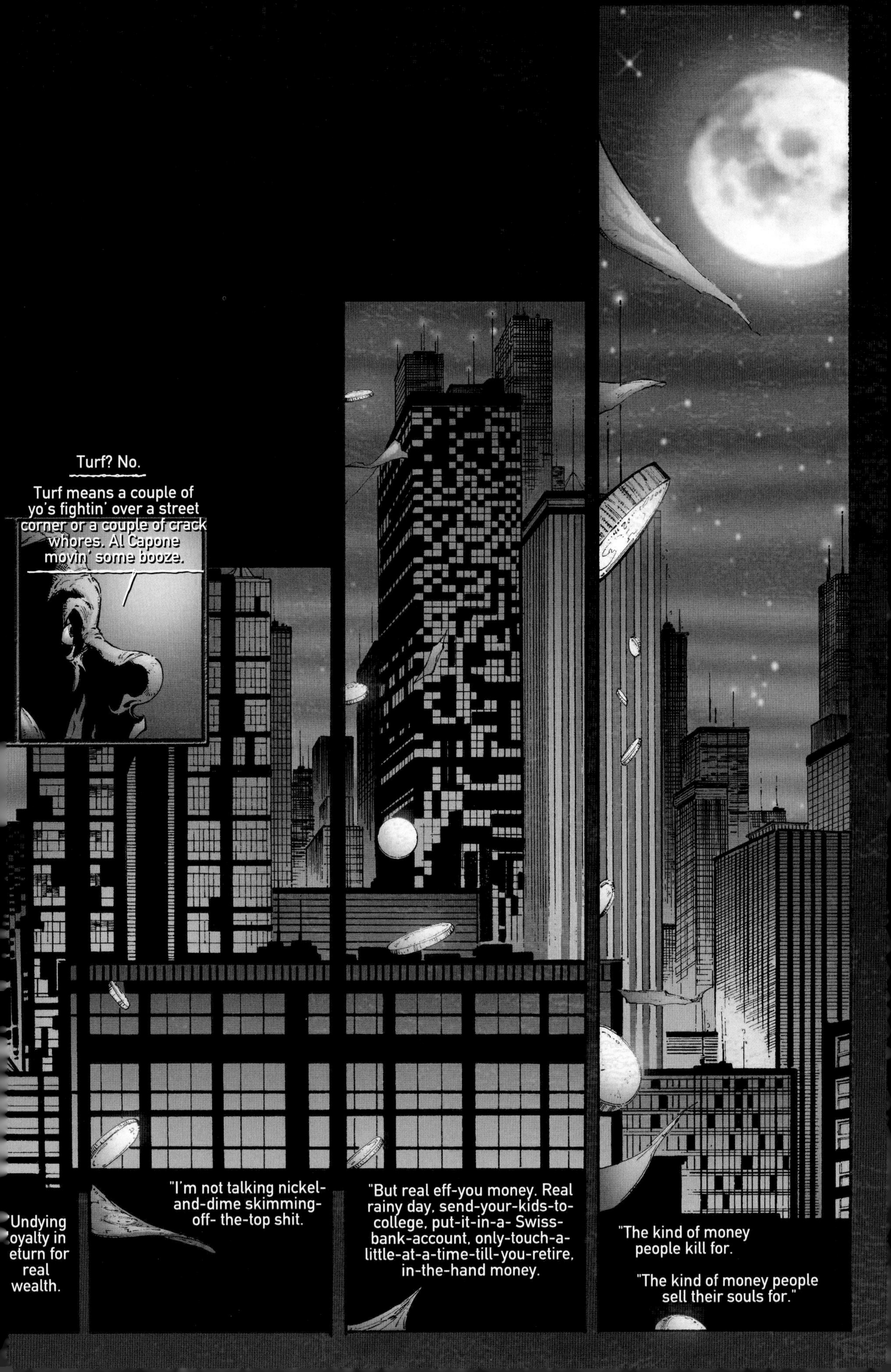
Turf? No.
Turf means a couple of yo's fightin' over a street corner or a couple of crack whores. Al Capone movin' some booze.
'Undying oyalty in eturn for real wealth.
"I'm not talking nickel-and-dime skimming-off- the-top shit.
"But real eff-you money. Real rainy day, send-your-kids-to-college, put-it-in-a- Swiss-bank-account, only-touch-a-little-at-a-time-till-you-retire, in-the-hand money.
"The kind of money people kill for.
"The kind of money people sell their souls for."

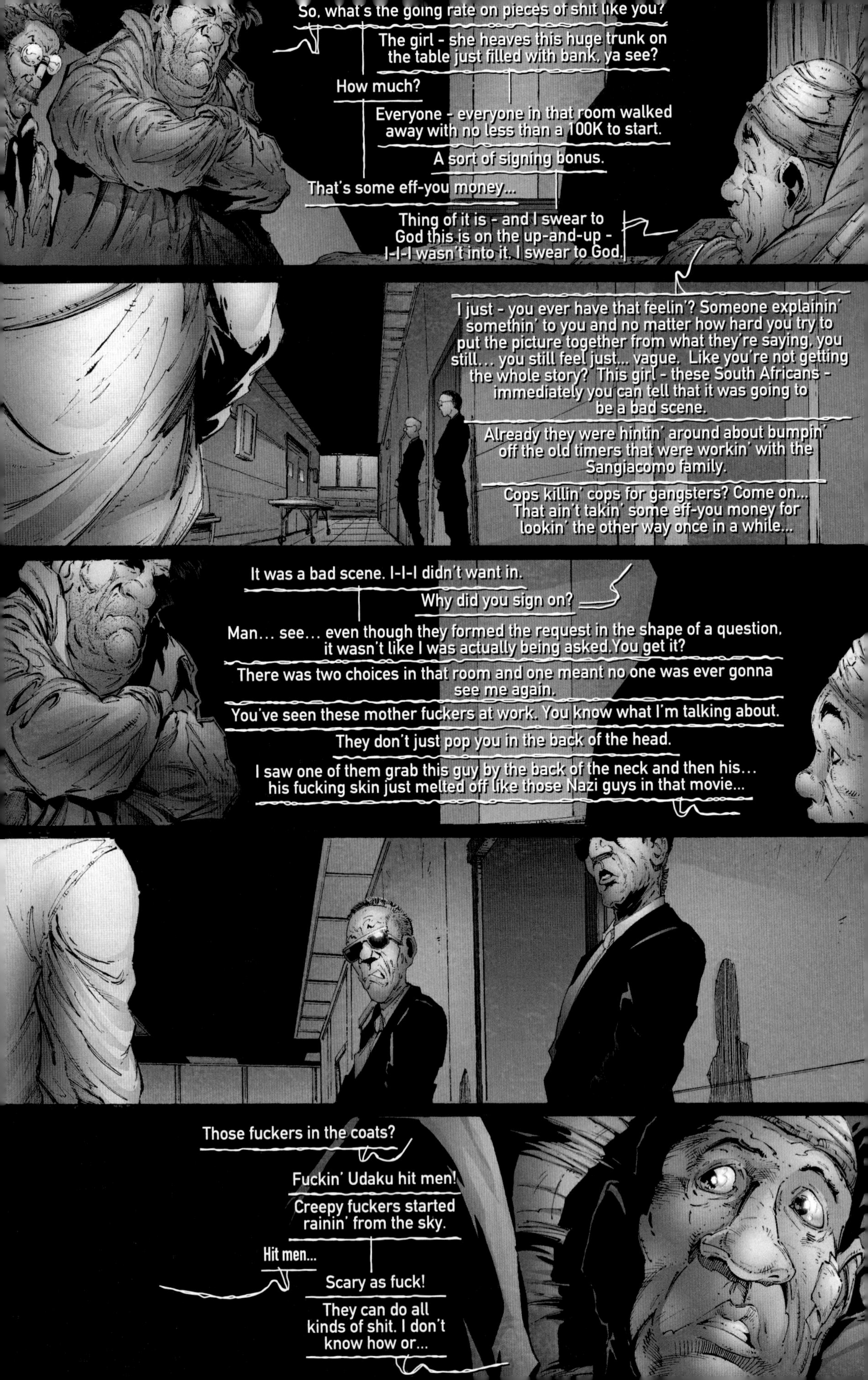
So, what's the going rate on pieces of shit like you?
The girl - she heaves this huge trunk on the table just filled with bank, ya see?
How much?
Everyone - everyone in that room walked away with no less than a 100K to start.
A sort of signing bonus.
That's some eff-you money...
Thing of it is - and I swear to God this is on the up-and-up - I-I-I wasn't into it. I swear to God.
I just - you ever have that feelin'? Someone explainin' somethin' to you and no matter how hard you try to put the picture together from what they're saying, you still... you still feel just... vague. Like you're not getting the whole story? This girl - these South Africans - immediately you can tell that it was going to be a bad scene.
Already they were hintin' around about bumpin' off the old timers that were workin' with the Sangiacomo family.
Cops killin' cops for gangsters? Come on... That ain't takin' some eff-you money for lookin' the other way once in a while...
It was a bad scene. I-I-I didn't want in.
Why did you sign on?
Man... see... even though they formed the request in the shape of a question, it wasn't like I was actually being asked.You get it?
There was two choices in that room and one meant no one was ever gonna see me again.
You've seen these mother fuckers at work. You know what I'm talking about.
They don't just pop you in the back of the head.
I saw one of them grab this guy by the back of the neck and then his... his fucking skin just melted off like those Nazi guys in that movie...
Those fuckers in the coats?
Fuckin' Udaku hit men!
Creepy fuckers started rainin' from the sky.
Hit men...
Scary as fuck!
They can do all kinds of shit. I don't know how or...

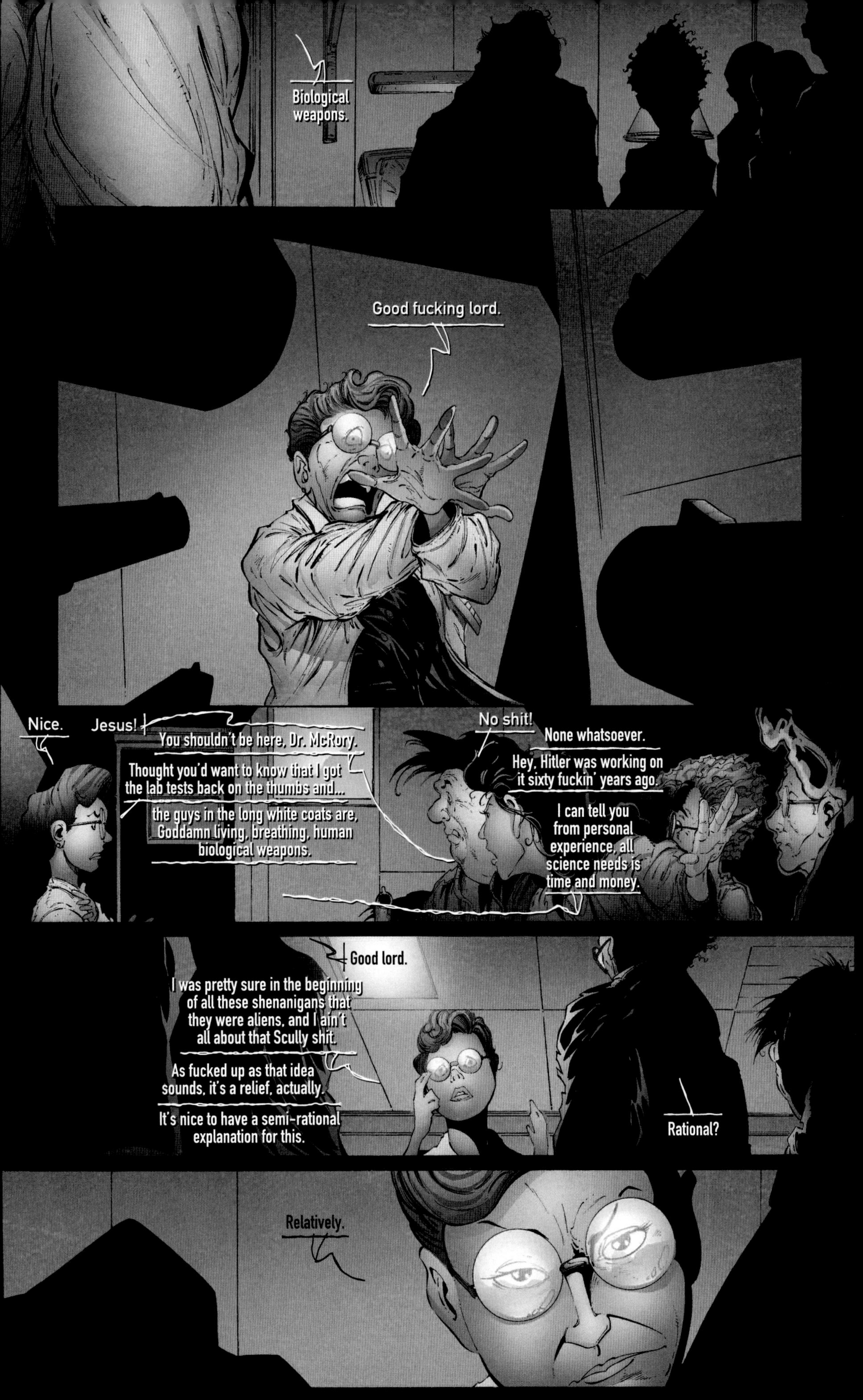
Biological weapons.
Good fucking lord.
Nice.
Jesus!
You shouldn't be here, Dr. McRory.
Thought you'd want to know that I got the lab tests back on the thumbs and...
the guys in the long white coats are, Goddamn living, breathing, human biological weapons.
No shit!
None whatsoever.
Hey, Hitler was working on it sixty fuckin' years ago.
I can tell you from personal experience, all science needs is time and money.
Good lord.
I was pretty sure in the beginning of all these shenanigans that they were aliens, and I ain't all about that Scully shit.
As fucked up as that idea sounds, it's a relief, actually.
It's nice to have a semi-rational explanation for this.
Rational?
Relatively.

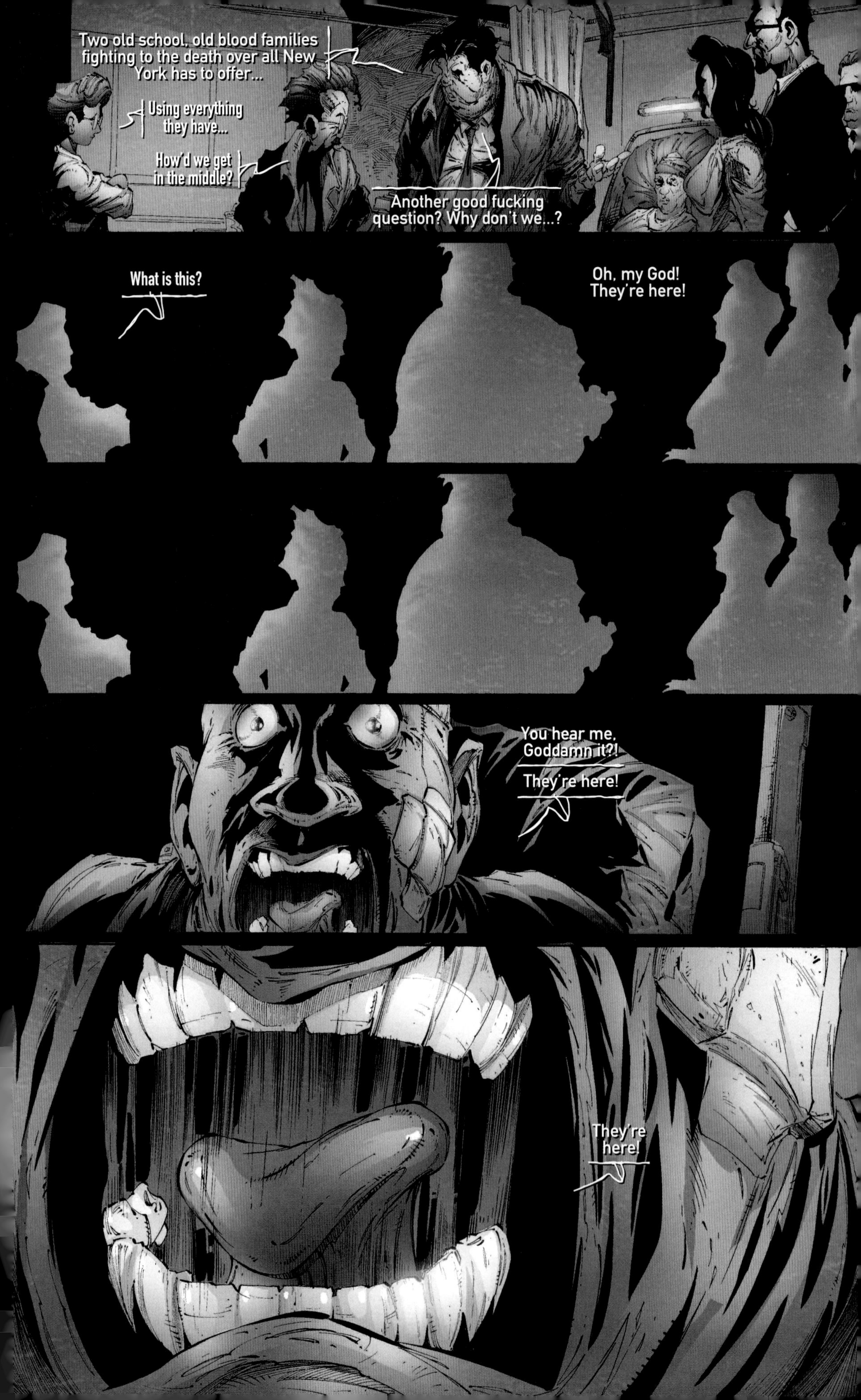
Two old school, old blood families fighting to the death over all New York has to offer...
Using everything they have...
How'd we get in the middle?
Another good fucking question? Why don't we...?
What is this?
Oh, my God! They're here!
You hear me, Goddamn it?!
They're here!
They're here!

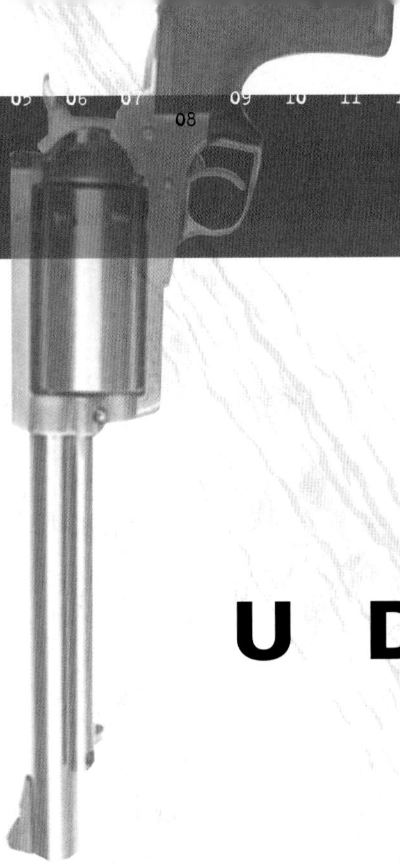

UDAKU

PART 8

SAM AND TWITCH

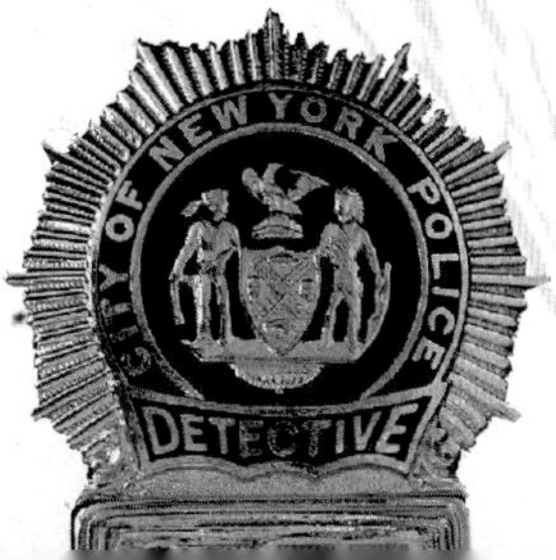
CITY OF NEW YORK POLICE
DETECTIVE

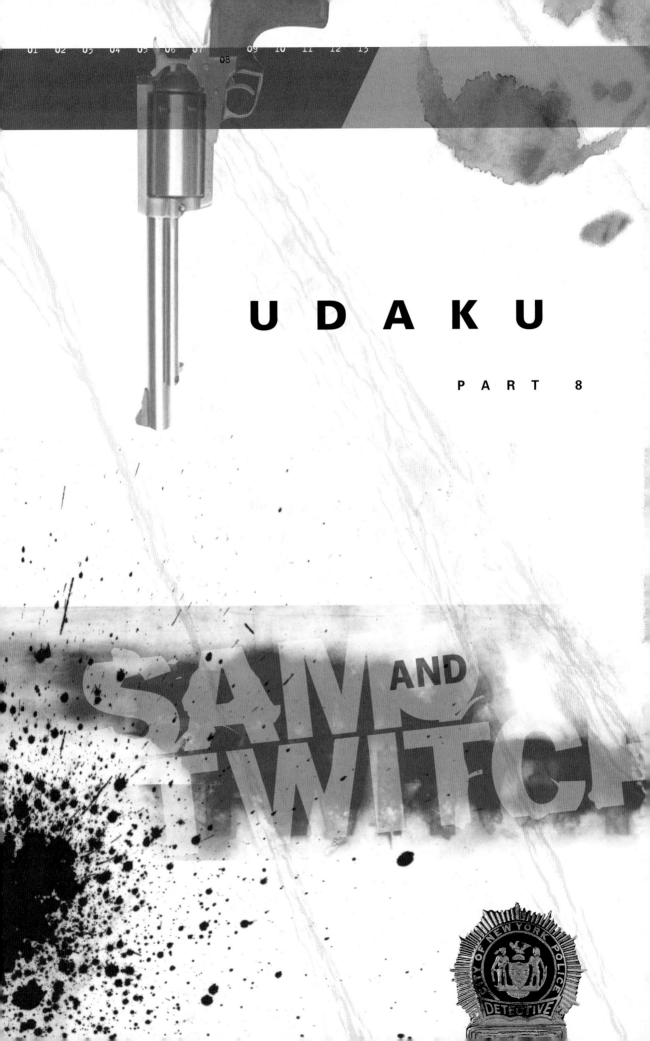

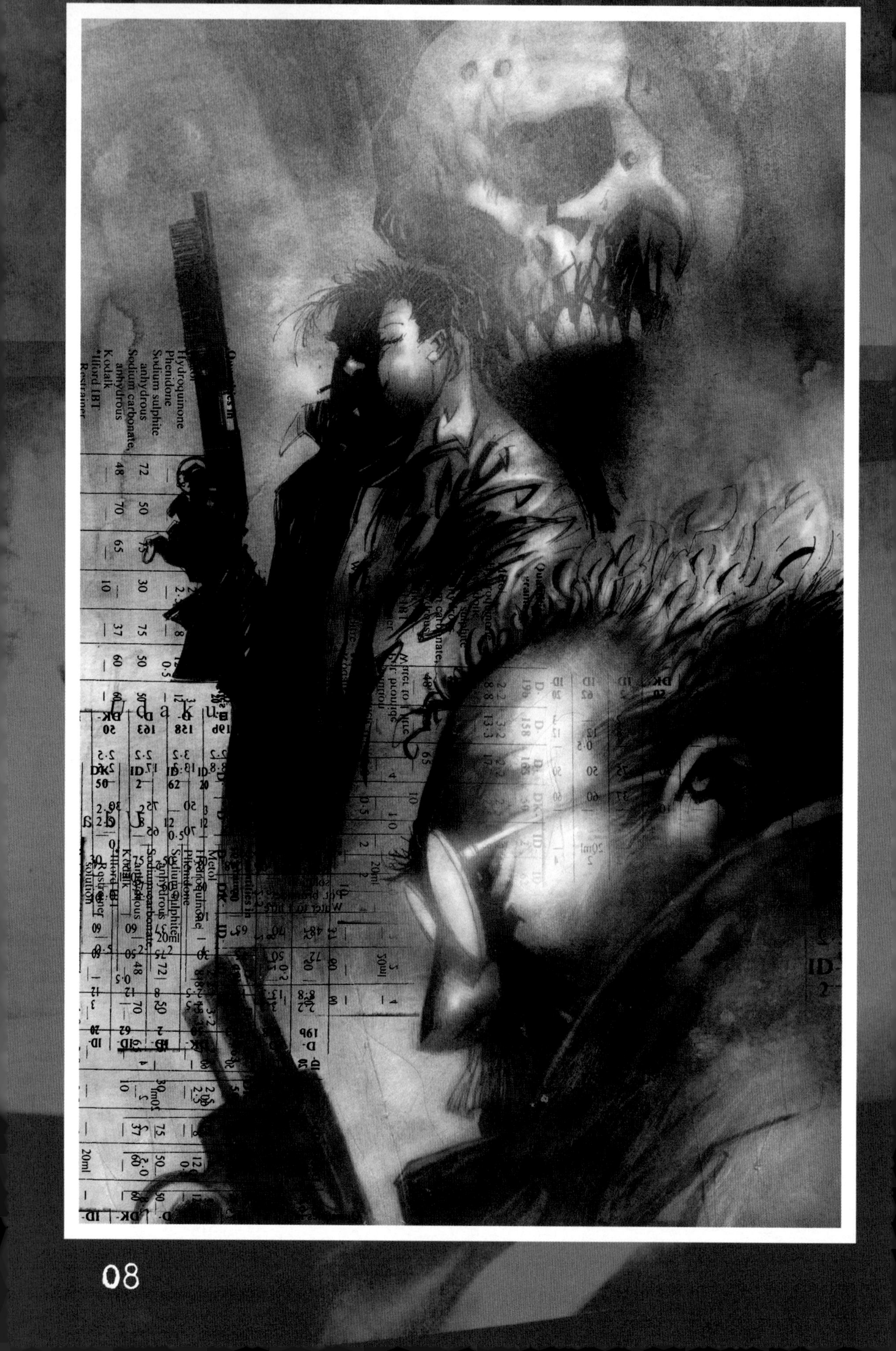

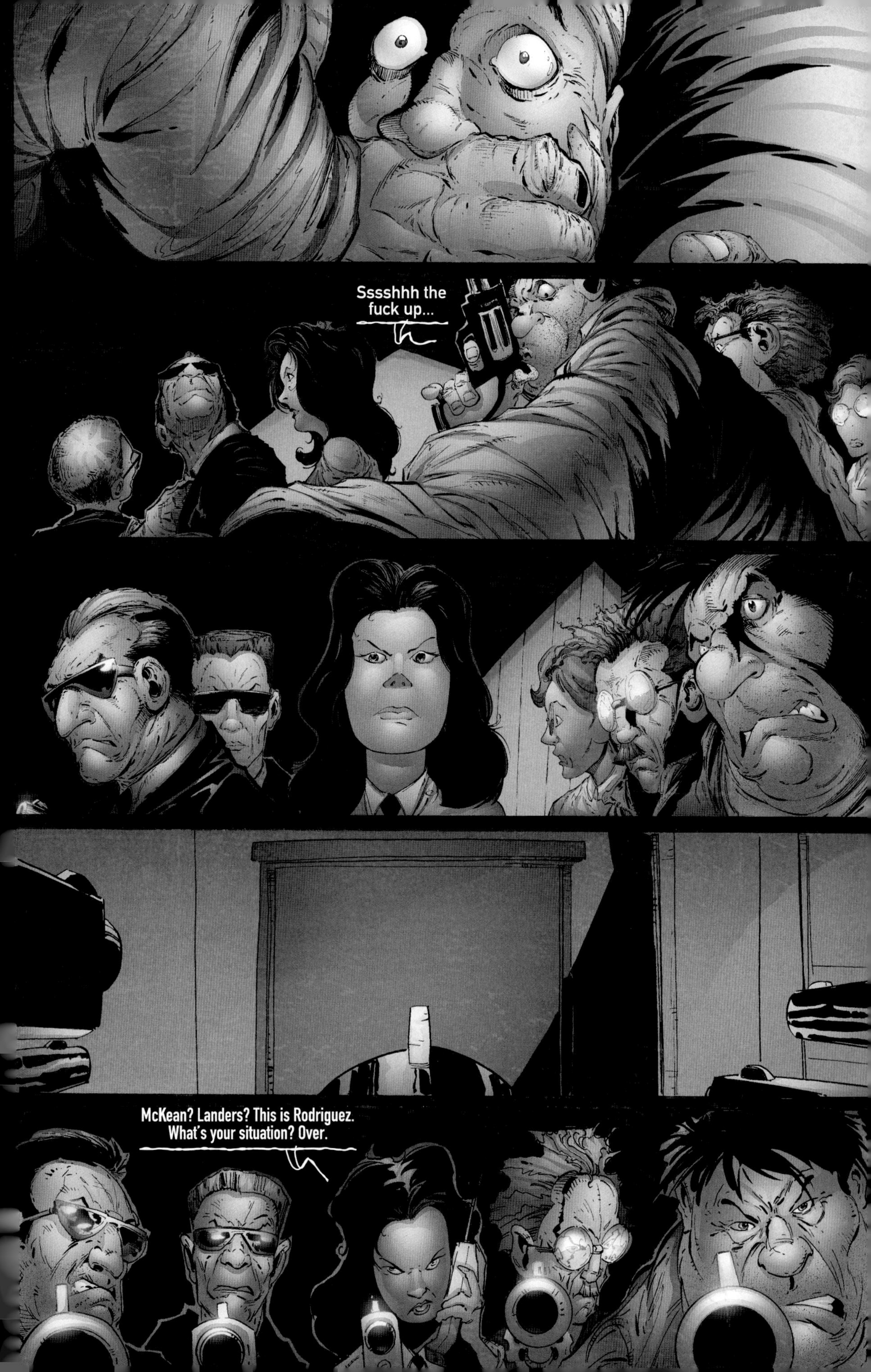
Sssshhh the fuck up...
McKean? Landers? This is Rodriguez. What's your situation? Over.

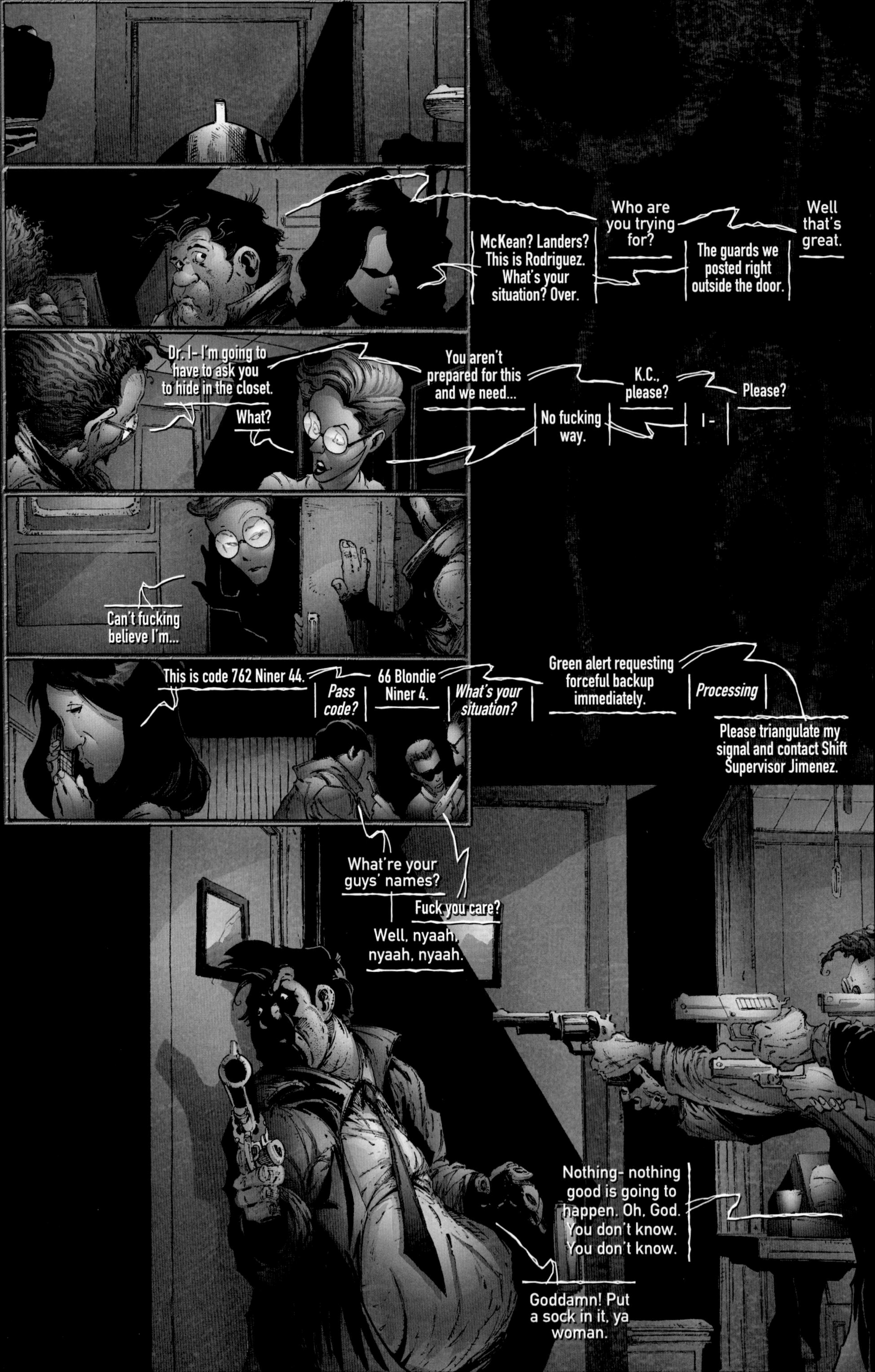
McKean? Landers? This is Rodriguez. What's your situation? Over.
Who are you trying for?
The guards we posted right outside the door.
Well that's great.
Dr. I- I'm going to have to ask you to hide in the closet.
What?
You aren't prepared for this and we need...
No fucking way.
K.C., please?
I -
Please?
Can't fucking believe I'm...
This is code 762 Niner 44.
Pass code?
66 Blondie Niner 4.
What's your situation?
Green alert requesting forceful backup immediately.
Processing
Please triangulate my signal and contact Shift Supervisor Jimenez.
What're your guys' names?
Fuck you care?
Well, nyaah, nyaah, nyaah.
Nothing- nothing good is going to happen. Oh, God. You don't know. You don't know.
Goddamn! Put a sock in it, ya woman.

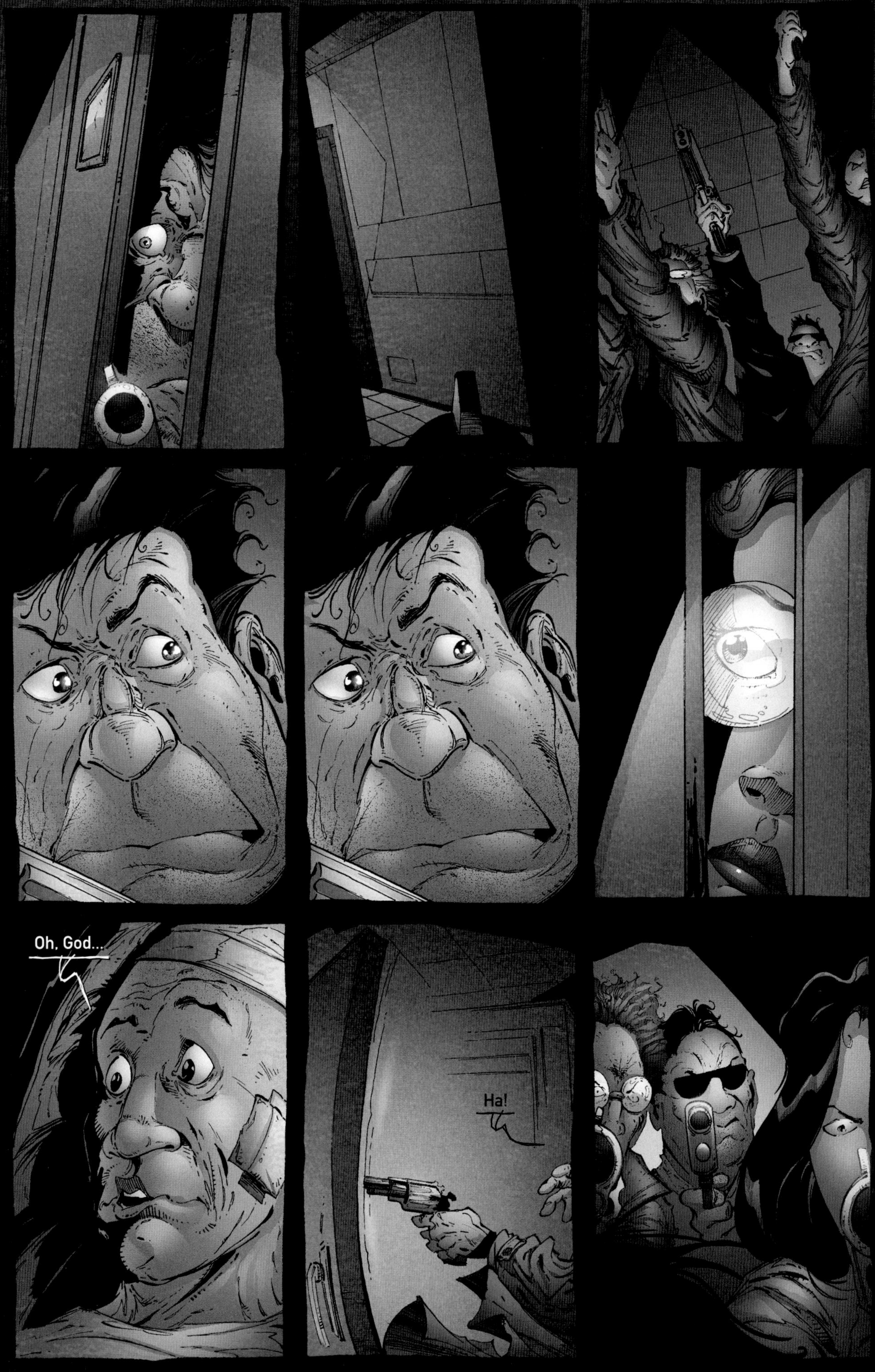
Oh, God...
Ha!

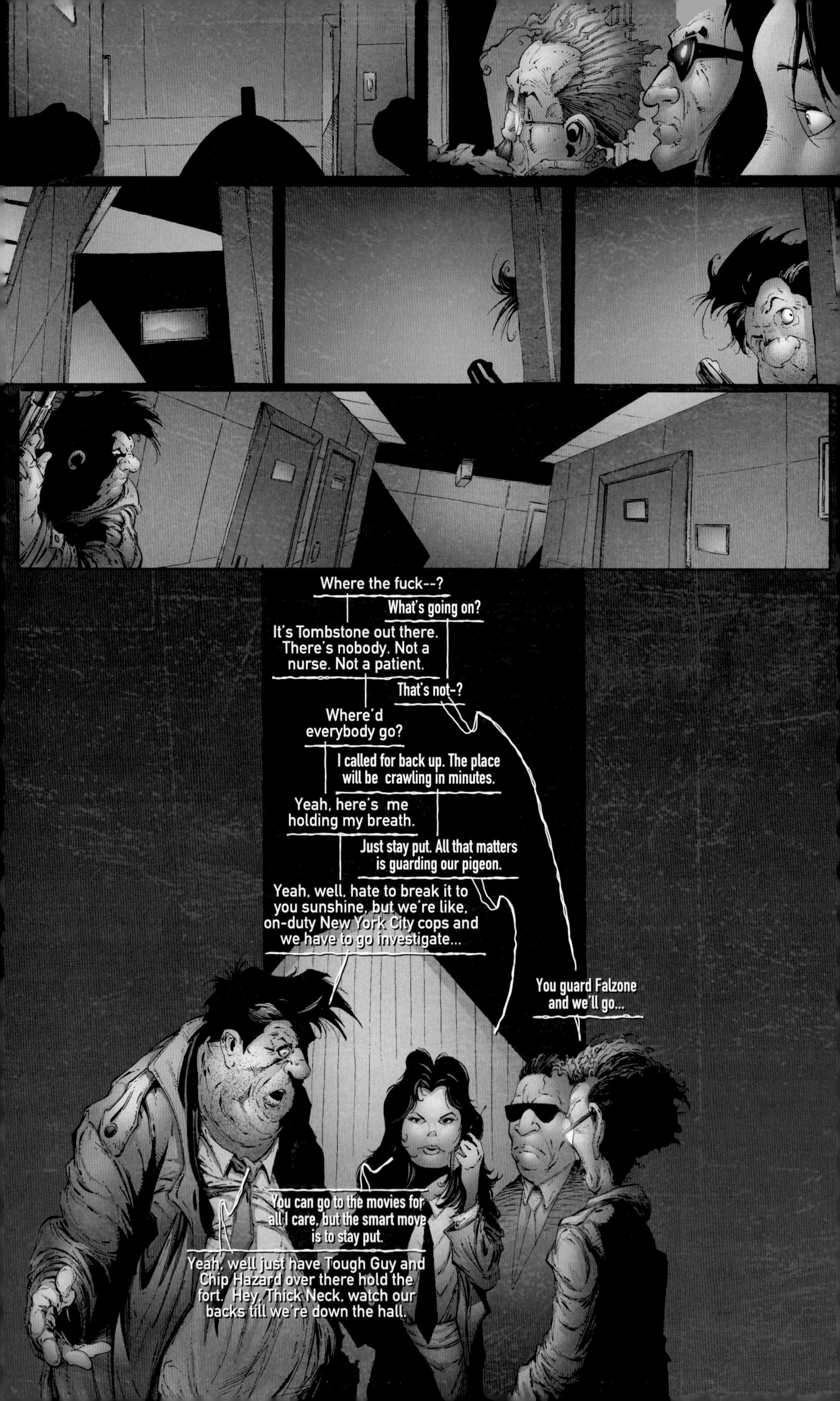

Where the fuck--?
What's going on?
It's Tombstone out there. There's nobody. Not a nurse. Not a patient.
That's not-?
Where'd everybody go?
I called for back up. The place will be crawling in minutes.
Yeah, here's me holding my breath.
Just stay put. All that matters is guarding our pigeon.
Yeah, well, hate to break it to you sunshine, but we're like, on-duty New York City cops and we have to go investigate...
You guard Falzone and we'll go...
You can go to the movies for all I care, but the smart move is to stay put.
Yeah, well just have Tough Guy and Chip Hazard over there hold the fort. Hey, Thick Neck, watch our backs till we're down the hall.

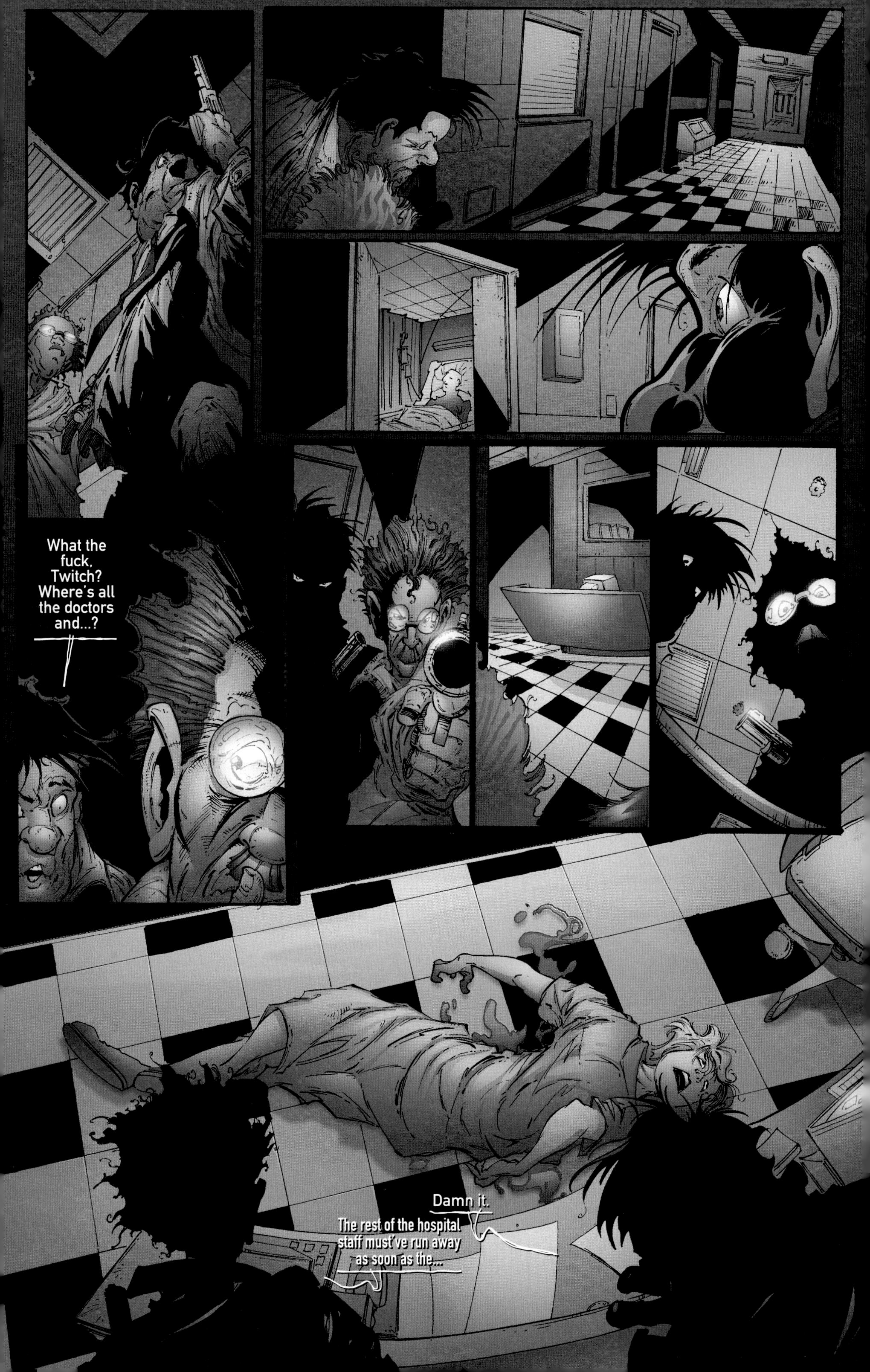
What the fuck, Twitch? Where's all the doctors and...?
Damn it.
The rest of the hospital staff must've run away as soon as the...

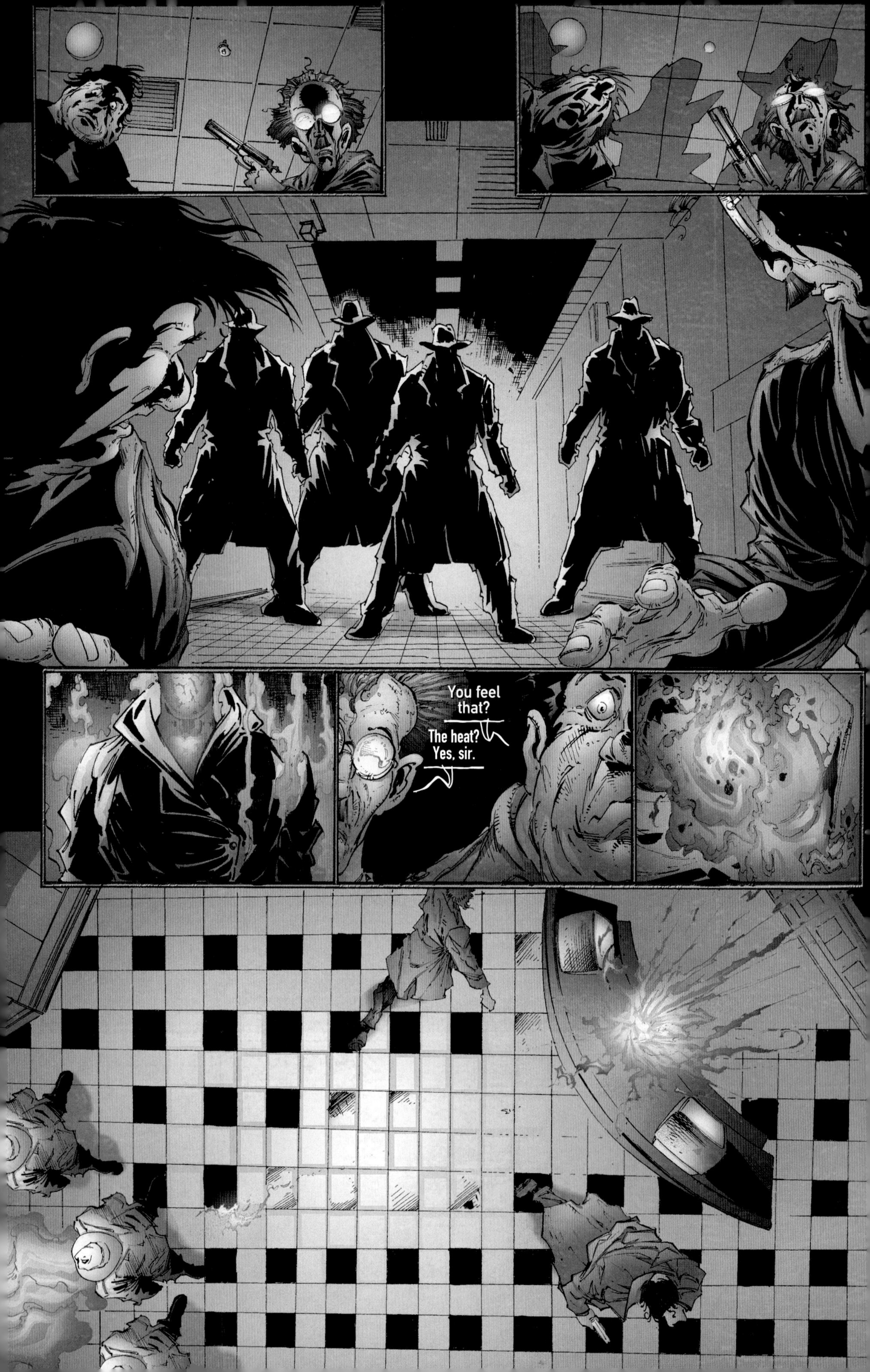
You feel that?
The heat? Yes, sir.

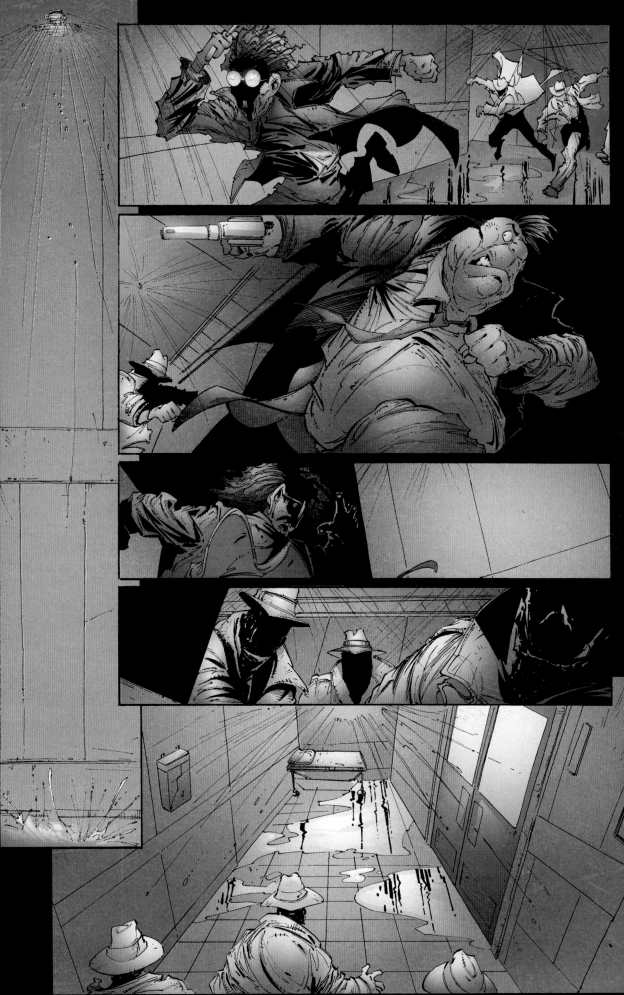

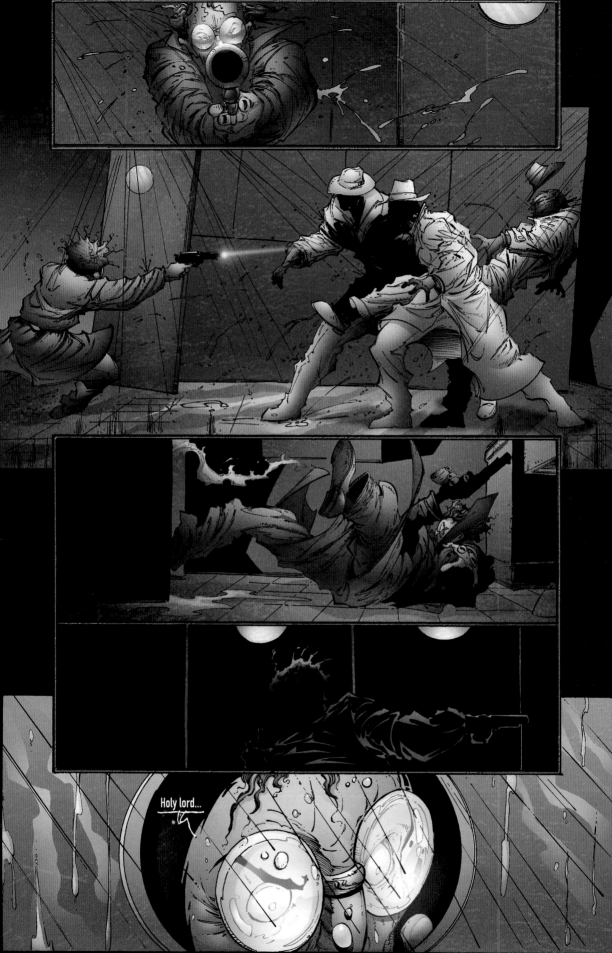

Holy lord...

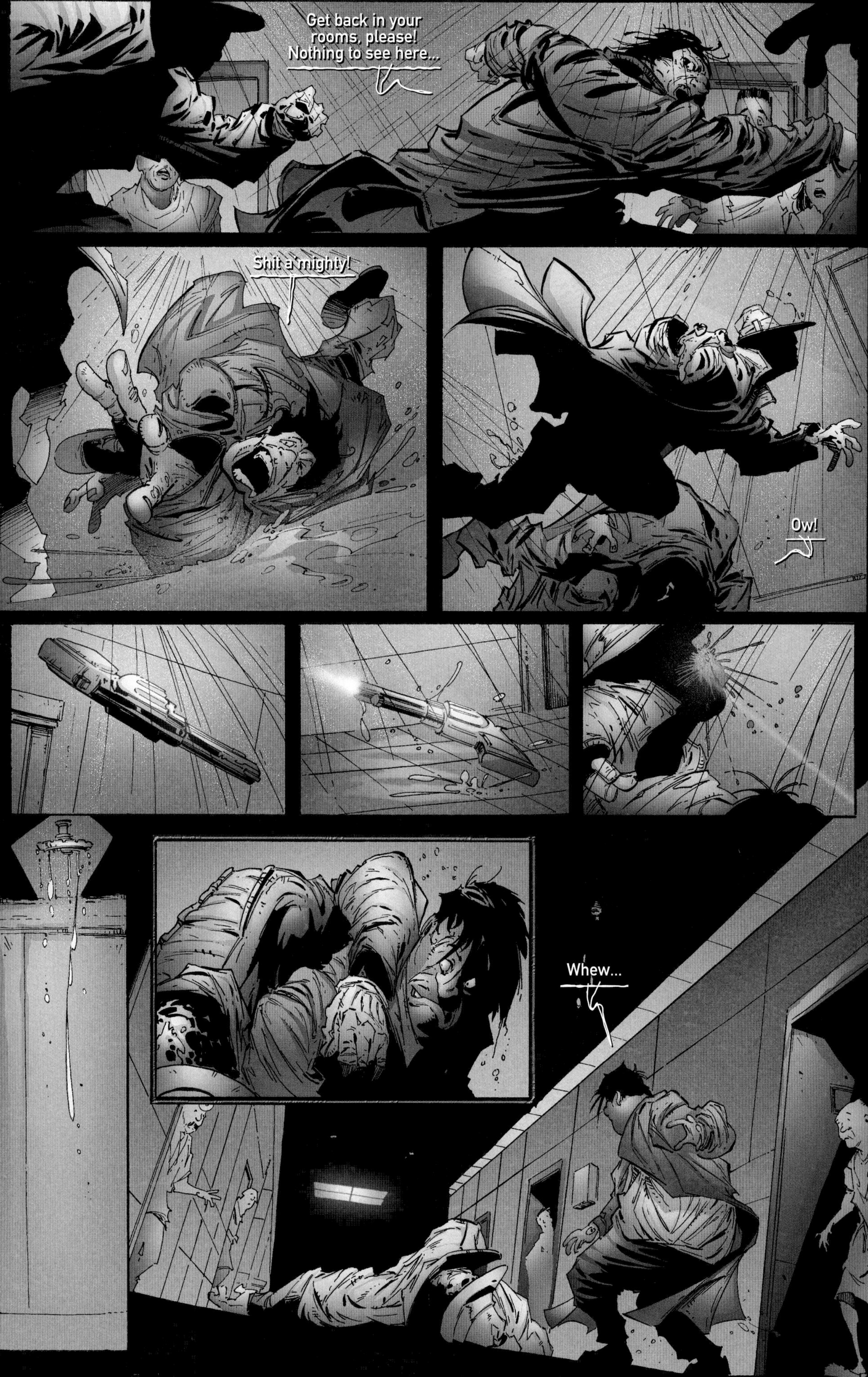
Get back in your rooms, please! Nothing to see here...
Shit a mighty!
Ow!
Whew...

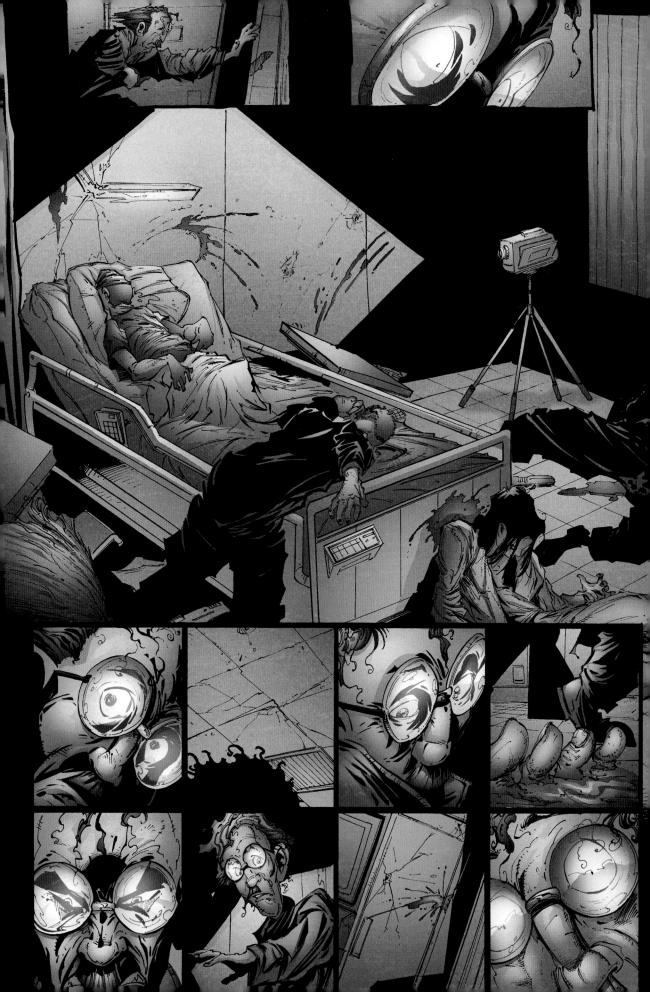

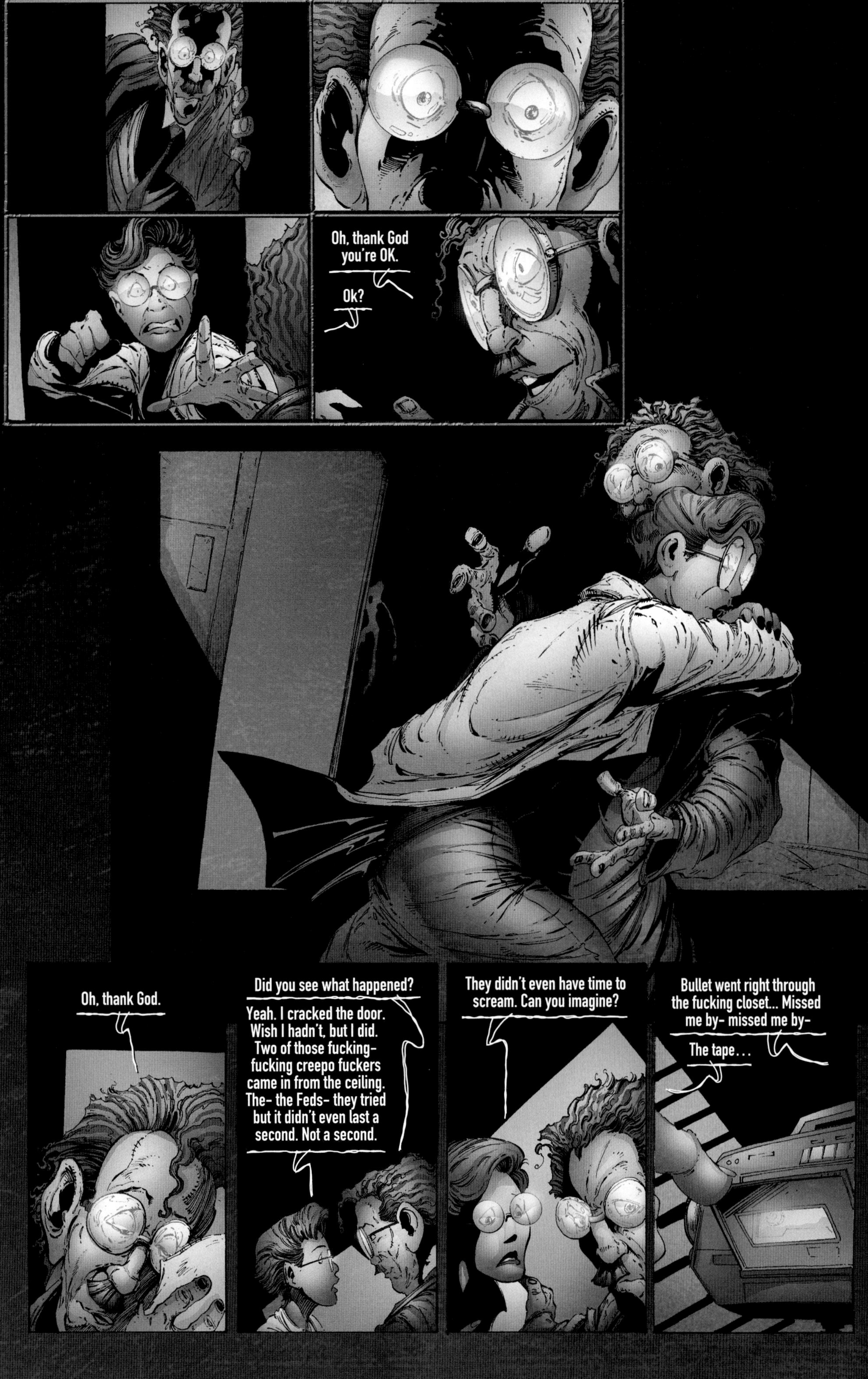
Oh, thank God you're OK.
Ok?
Oh, thank God.
Did you see what happened?
Yeah. I cracked the door. Wish I hadn't, but I did. Two of those fucking-fucking creepo fuckers came in from the ceiling. The- the Feds- they tried but it didn't even last a second. Not a second.
They didn't even have time to scream. Can you imagine?
Bullet went right through the fucking closet... Missed me by- missed me by-
The tape...

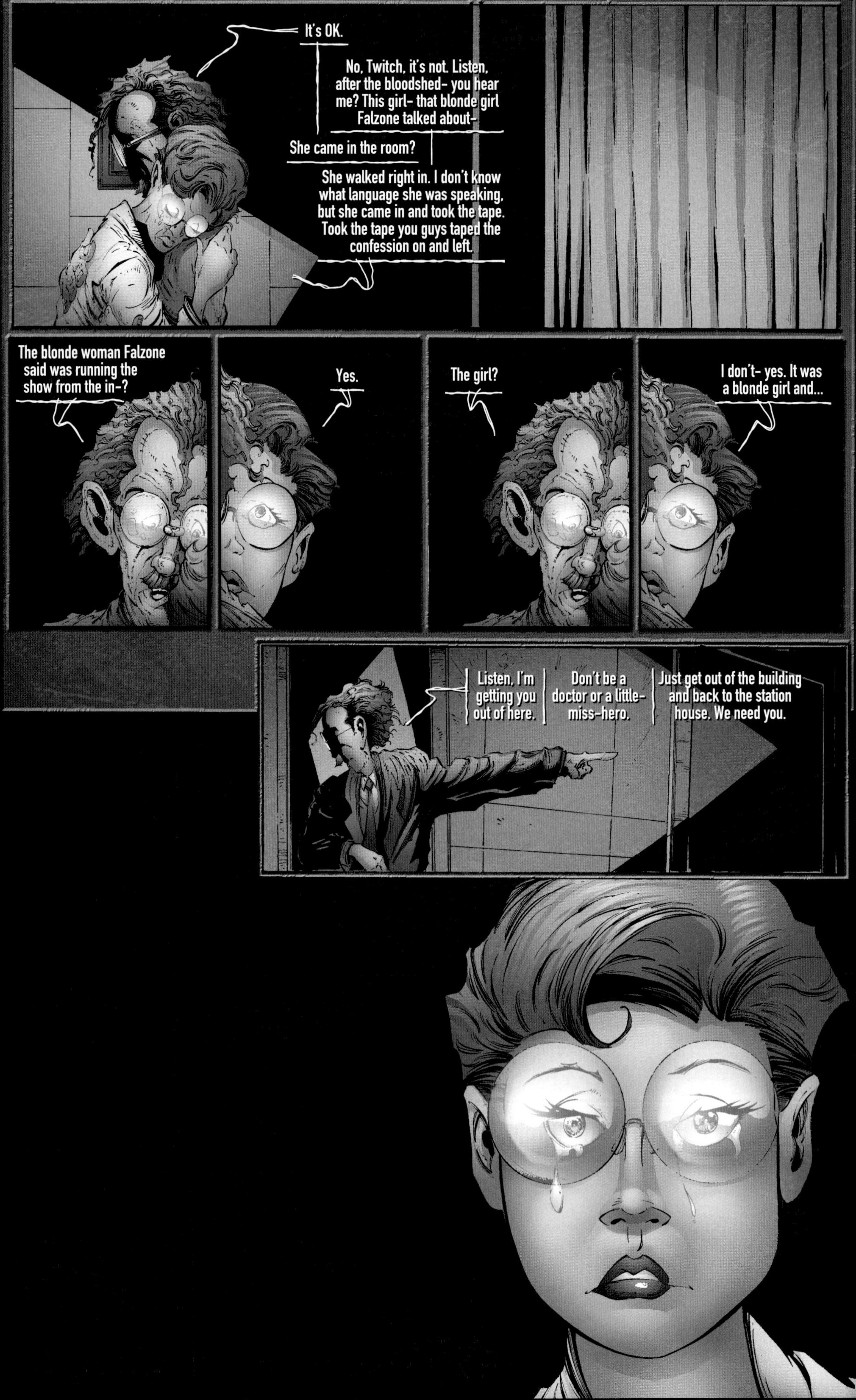

It's OK.
No, Twitch, it's not. Listen, after the bloodshed- you hear me? This girl- that blonde girl Falzone talked about-
She came in the room?
She walked right in. I don't know what language she was speaking, but she came in and took the tape. Took the tape you guys taped the confession on and left.
The blonde woman Falzone said was running the show from the in-?
Yes.
The girl?
I don't- yes. It was a blonde girl and...
Listen, I'm getting you out of here.
Don't be a doctor or a little-miss-hero.
Just get out of the building and back to the station house. We need you.

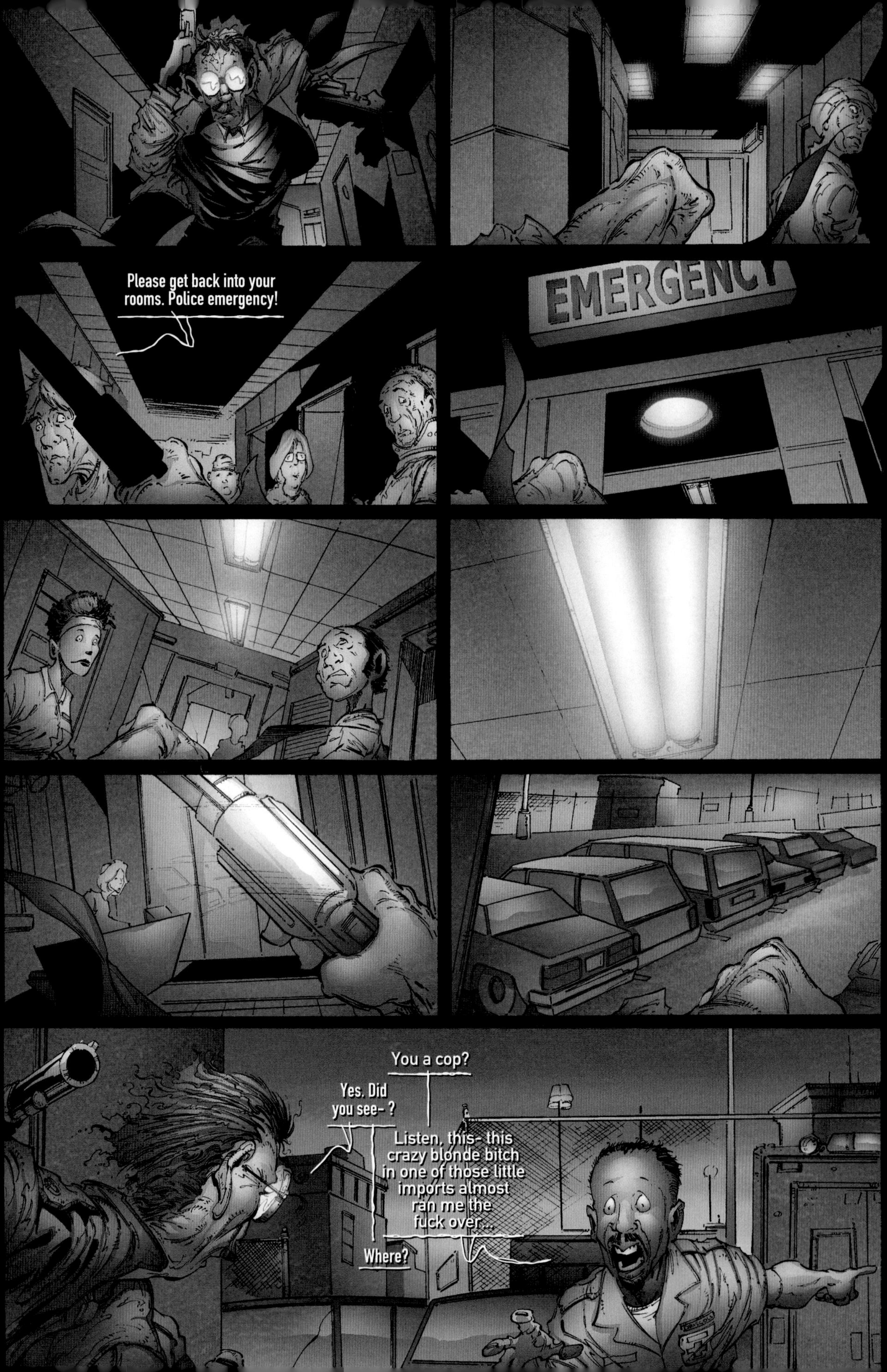
Please get back into your rooms. Police emergency!
EMERGENCY
You a cop?
Yes. Did you see- ?
Listen, this- this crazy blonde bitch in one of those little imports almost ran me the fuck over...
Where?

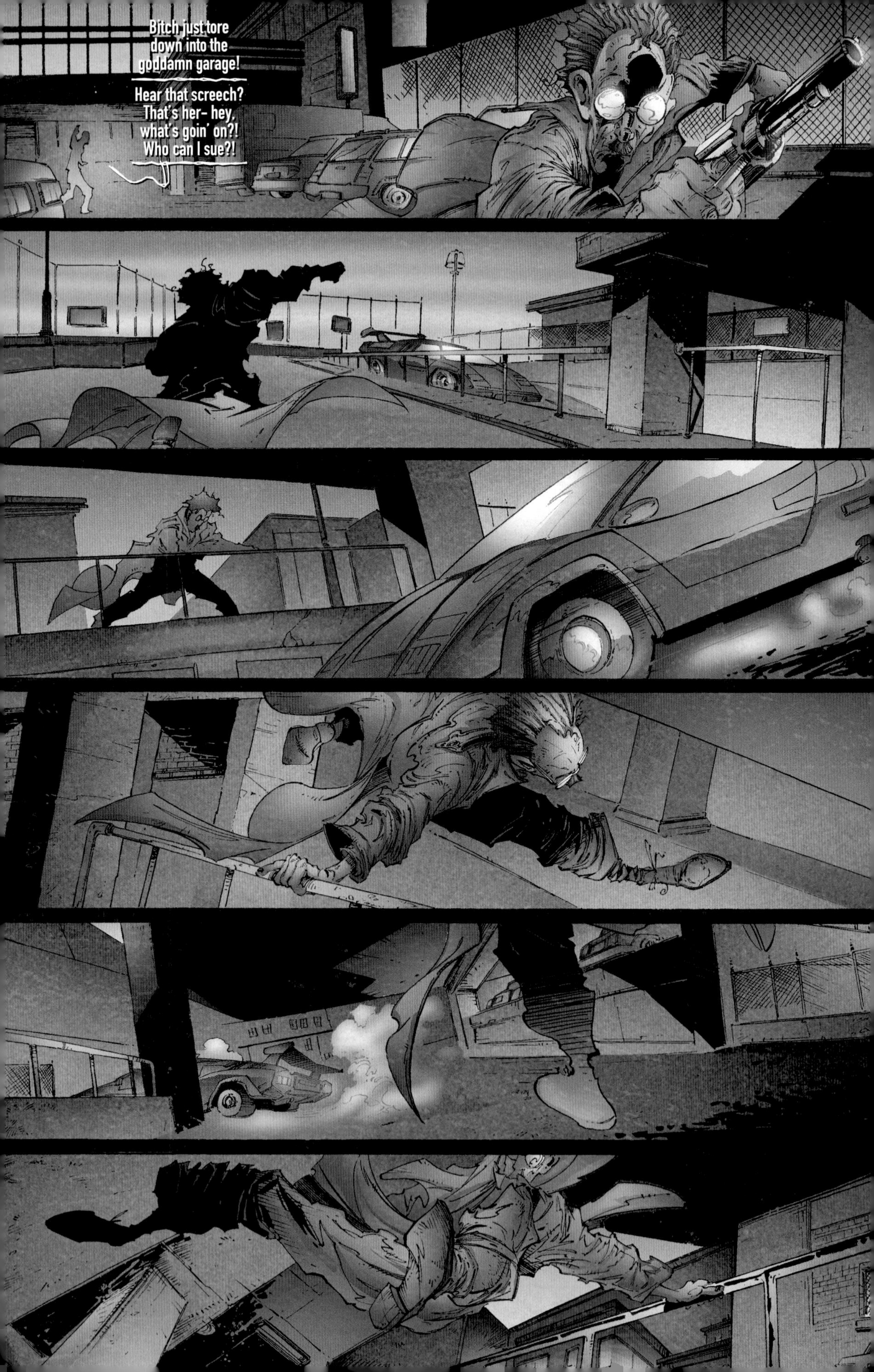
Bitch just tore down into the goddamn garage!
Hear that screech? That's her- hey, what's goin' on?! Who can I sue?!

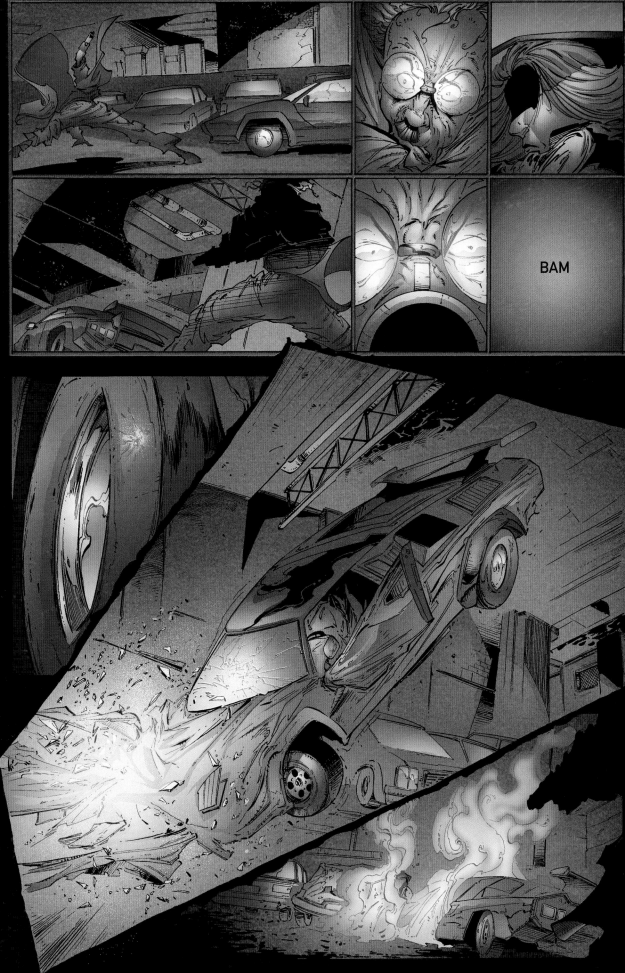

BAM

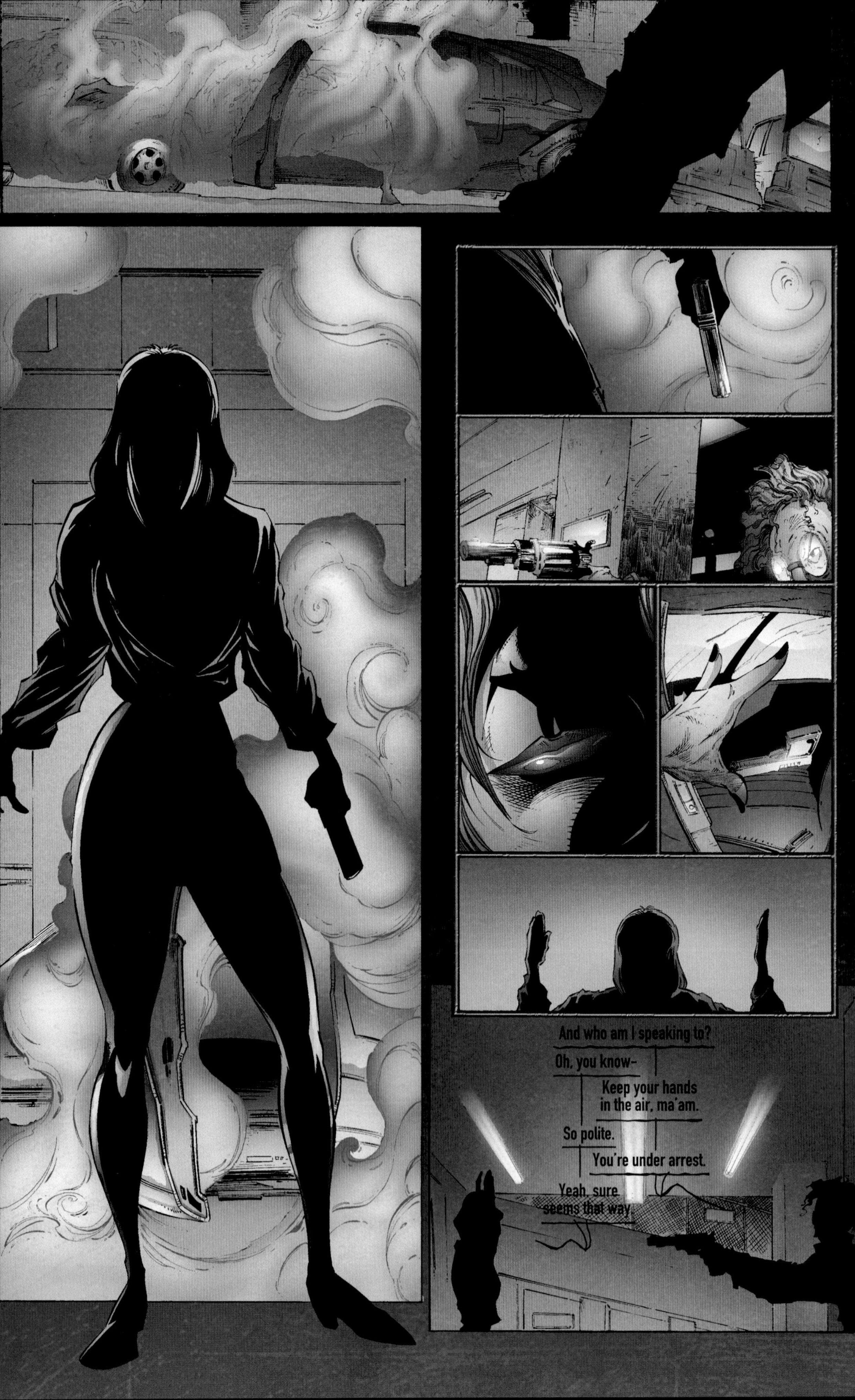
And who am I speaking to?
Oh, you know-
Keep your hands in the air, ma'am.
So polite.
You're under arrest.
Yeah, sure seems that way.

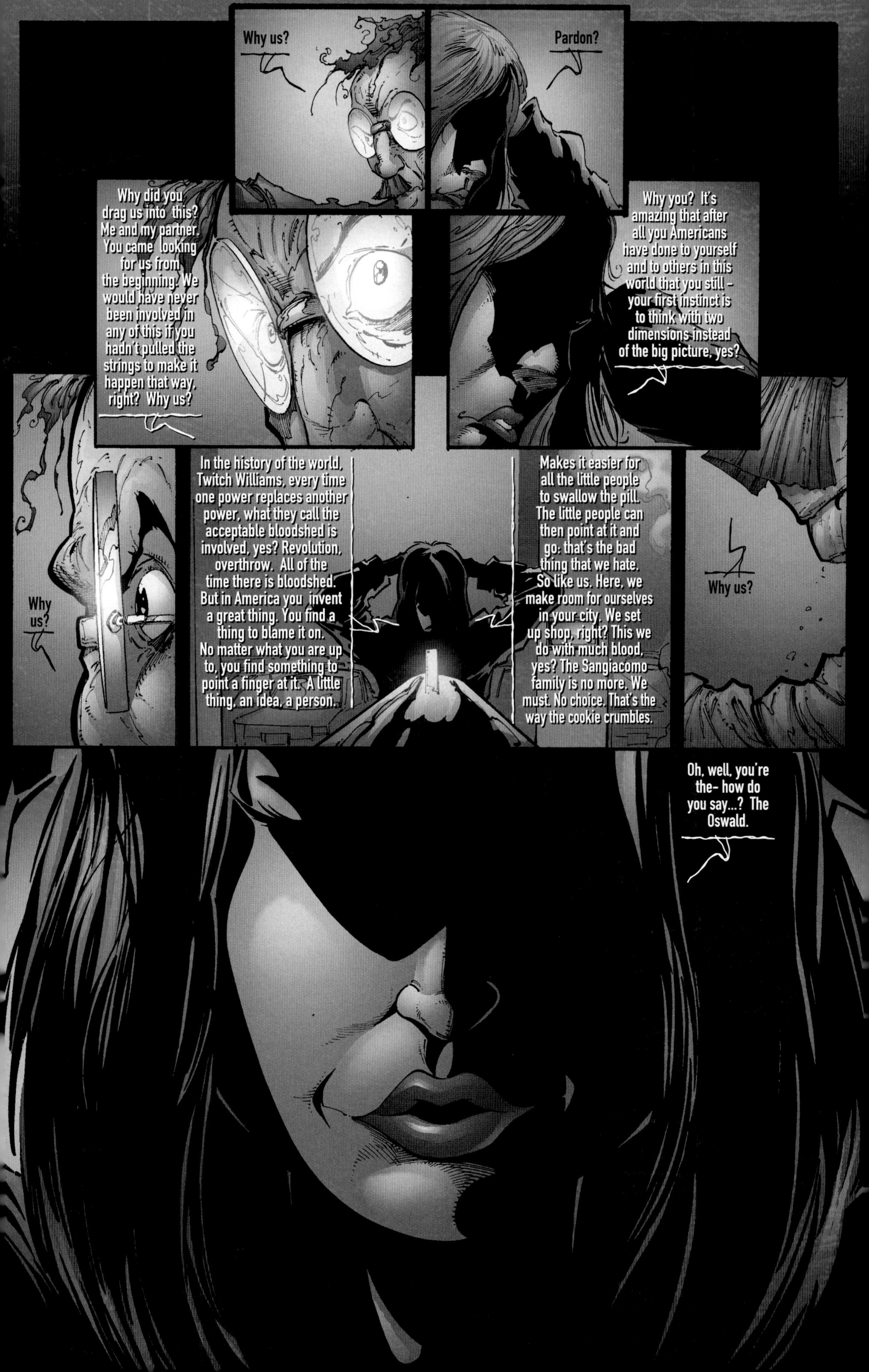

Why us?
Pardon?
Why did you drag us into this? Me and my partner. You came looking for us from the beginning. We would have never been involved in any of this if you hadn't pulled the strings to make it happen that way, right? Why us?
Why you? It's amazing that after all you Americans have done to yourself and to others in this world that you still – your first instinct is to think with two dimensions instead of the big picture, yes?
Why us?
In the history of the world, Twitch Williams, every time one power replaces another power, what they call the acceptable bloodshed is involved, yes? Revolution, overthrow. All of the time there is bloodshed. But in America you invent a great thing. You find a thing to blame it on. No matter what you are up to, you find something to point a finger at it. A little thing, an idea, a person.
Makes it easier for all the little people to swallow the pill. The little people can then point at it and go: that's the bad thing that we hate. So like us. Here, we make room for ourselves in your city. We set up shop, right? This we do with much blood, yes? The Sangiacomo family is no more. We must. No choice. That's the way the cookie crumbles.
Why us?
Oh, well, you're the- how do you say...? The Oswald.

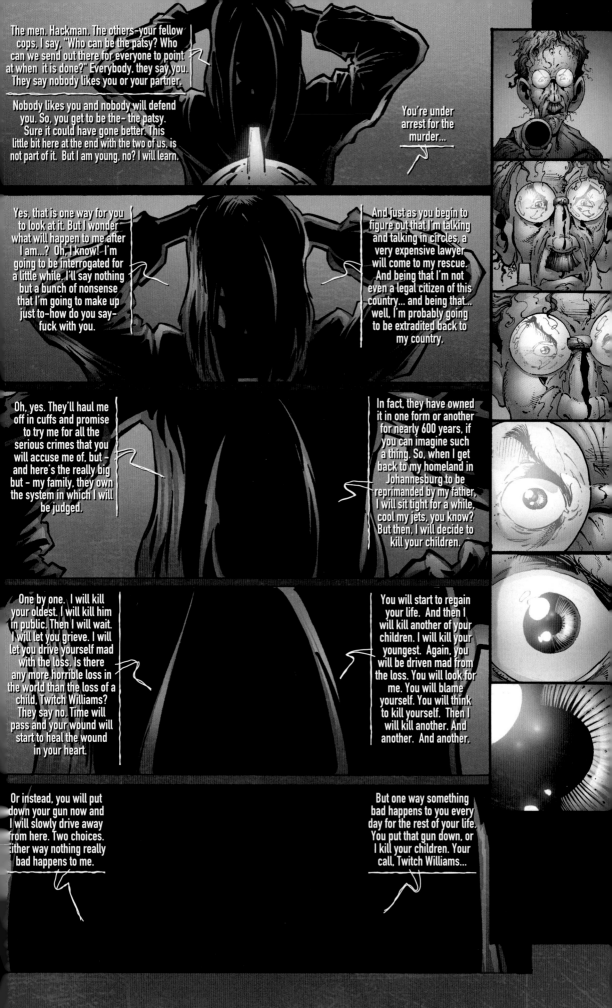

The men. Hackman. The others-your fellow cops, I say, "Who can be the patsy? Who can we send out there for everyone to point at when it is done?" Everybody, they say you. They say nobody likes you or your partner.

Nobody likes you and nobody will defend you. So, you get to be the- the patsy. Sure it could have gone better. This little bit here at the end with the two of us, is not part of it. But I am young, no? I will learn.

You're under arrest for the murder...

Yes, that is one way for you to look at it. But I wonder what will happen to me after I am...? Oh, I know! I'm going to be interrogated for a little while. I'll say nothing but a bunch of nonsense that I'm going to make up just to-how do you say- fuck with you.

And just as you begin to figure out that I'm talking and talking in circles, a very expensive lawyer will come to my rescue. And being that I'm not even a legal citizen of this country... and being that... well, I'm probably going to be extradited back to my country.

Oh, yes. They'll haul me off in cuffs and promise to try me for all the serious crimes that you will accuse me of, but - and here's the really big but - my family, they own the system in which I will be judged.

In fact, they have owned it in one form or another for nearly 600 years, if you can imagine such a thing. So, when I get back to my homeland in Johannesburg to be reprimanded by my father, I will sit tight for a while, cool my jets, you know? But then, I will decide to kill your children.

One by one. I will kill your oldest. I will kill him in public. Then I will wait. I will let you grieve. I will let you drive yourself mad with the loss. Is there any more horrible loss in the world than the loss of a child, Twitch Williams? They say no. Time will pass and your wound will start to heal the wound in your heart.

You will start to regain your life. And then I will kill another of your children. I will kill your youngest. Again, you will be driven mad from the loss. You will look for me. You will blame yourself. You will think to kill yourself. Then I will kill another. And another. And another.

Or instead, you will put down your gun now and I will slowly drive away from here. Two choices. Either way nothing really bad happens to me.

But one way something bad happens to you every day for the rest of your life. You put that gun down, or I kill your children. Your call, Twitch Williams...

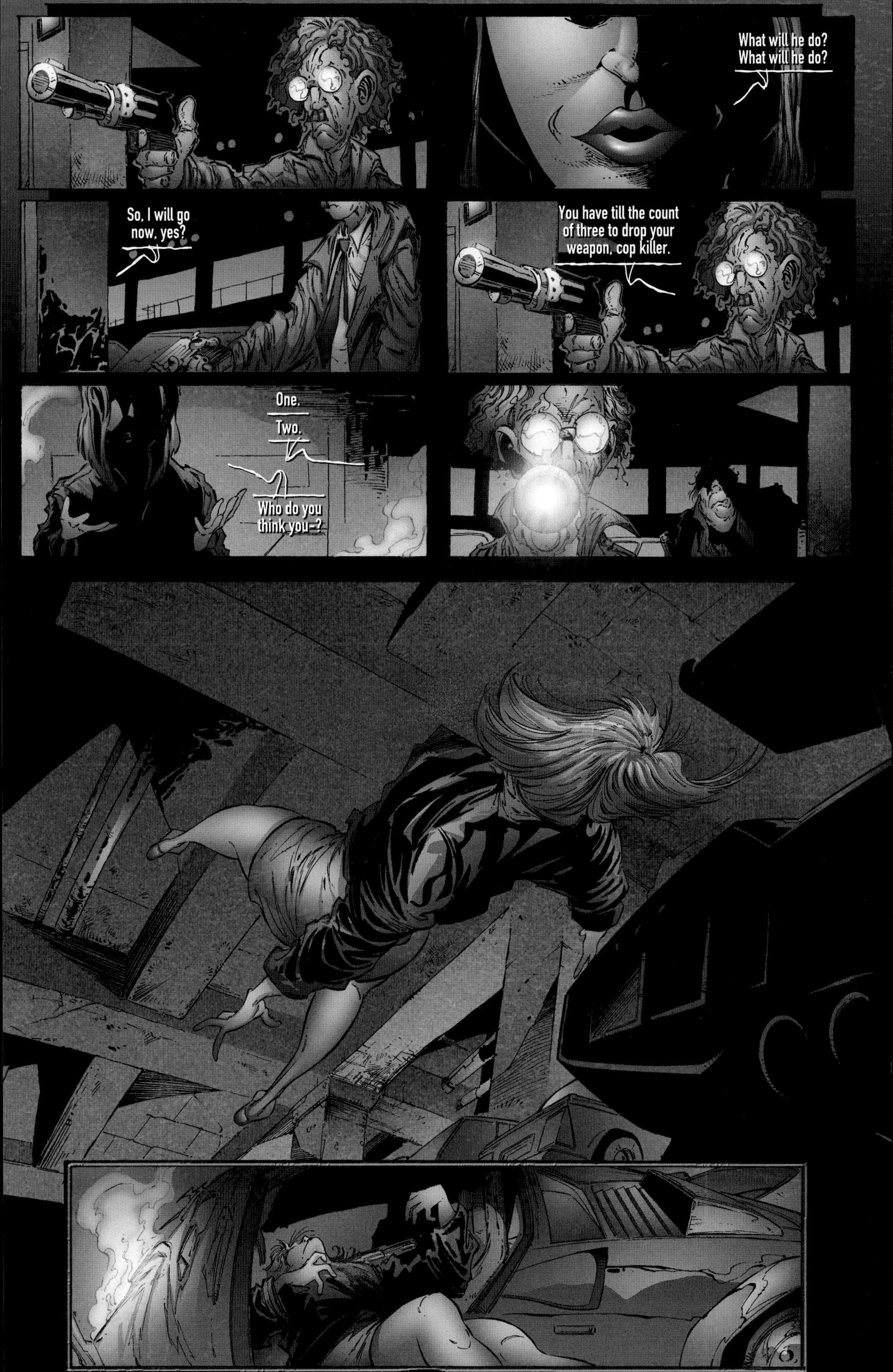
What will he do?
What will he do?
So, I will go now, yes?
You have till the count of three to drop your weapon, cop killer.
One.
Two.
Who do you think you-?

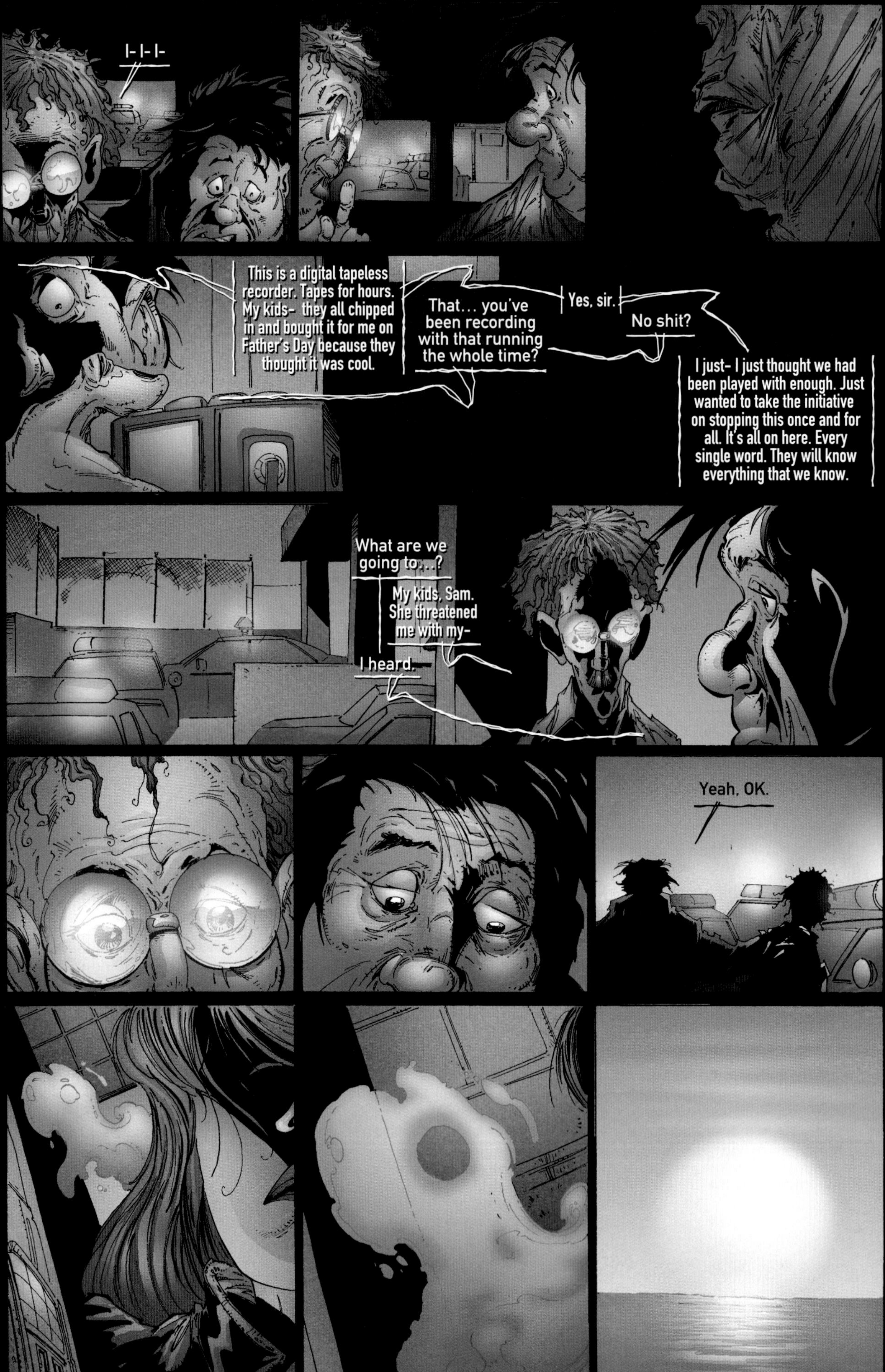

I- I- I-
This is a digital tapeless recorder. Tapes for hours. My kids- they all chipped in and bought it for me on Father's Day because they thought it was cool.
That… you've been recording with that running the whole time?
Yes, sir.
No shit?
I just- I just thought we had been played with enough. Just wanted to take the initiative on stopping this once and for all. It's all on here. Every single word. They will know everything that we know.
What are we going to…?
My kids, Sam. She threatened me with my-
I heard.
Yeah, OK.

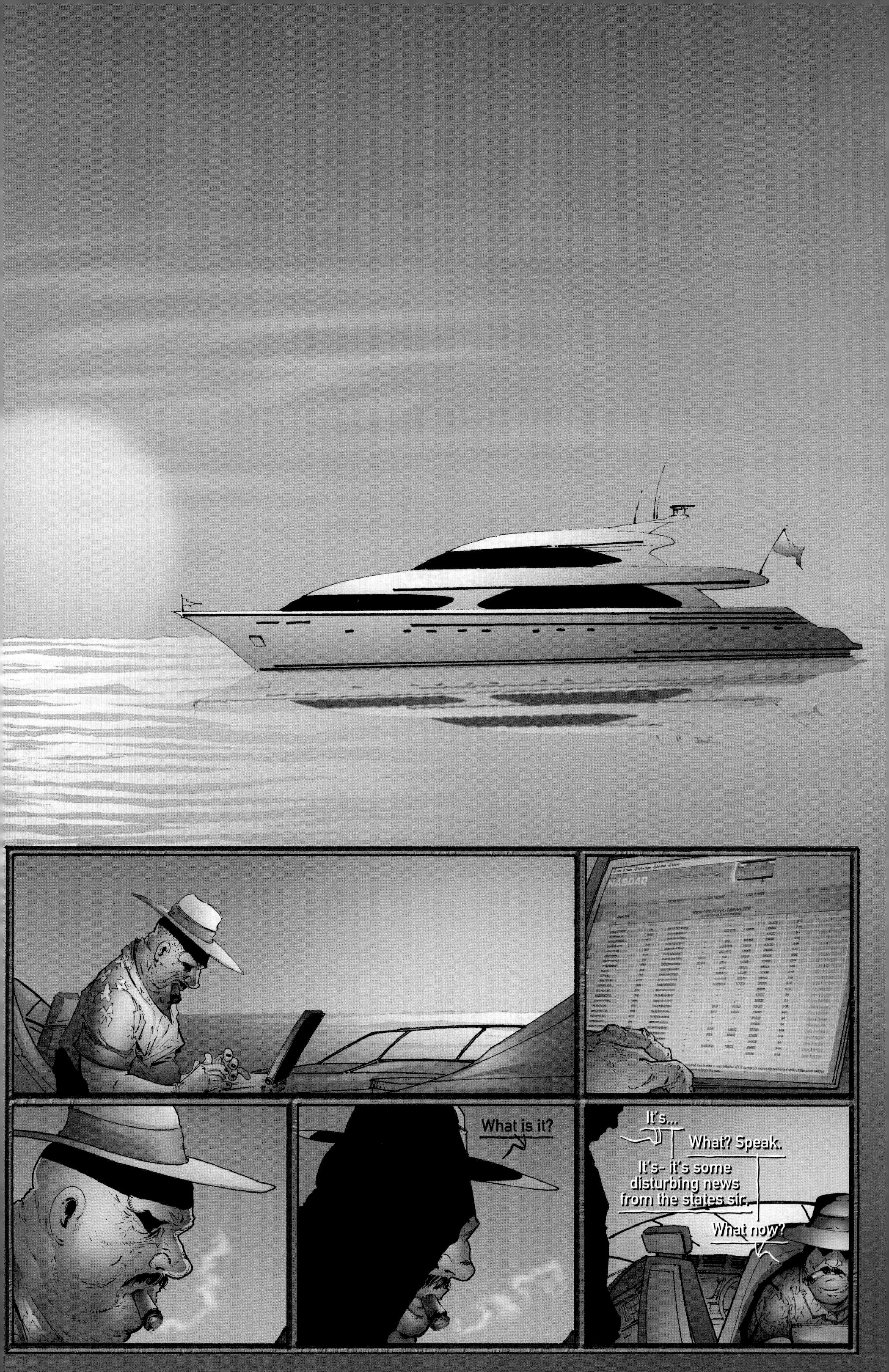
What is it?
It's...
What? Speak.
It's- it's some disturbing news from the states sir.
What now?

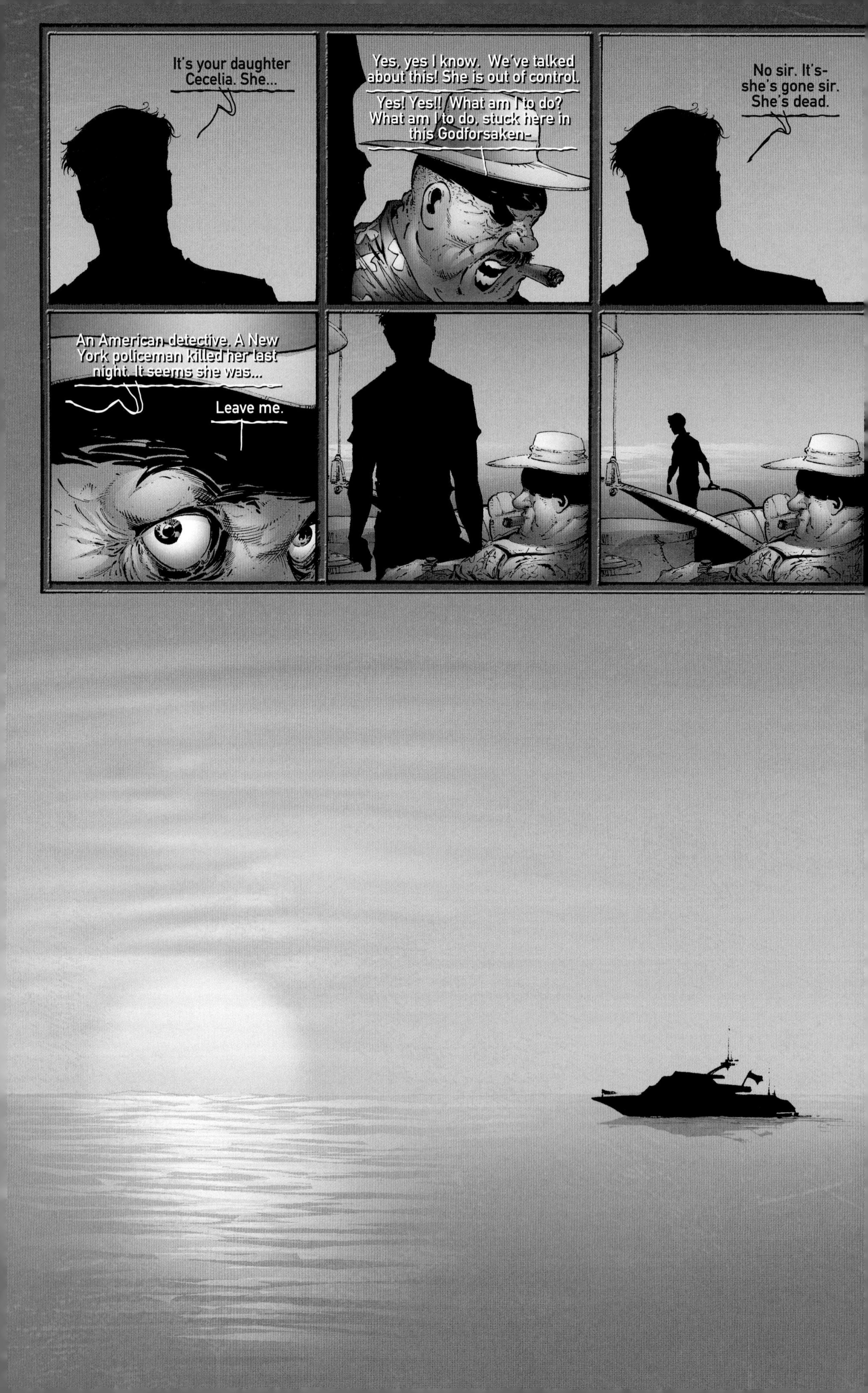
It's your daughter Cecelia. She...
Yes, yes I know. We've talked about this! She is out of control.
Yes! Yes!! What am I to do? What am I to do, stuck here in this Godforsaken-
No sir. It's- she's gone sir. She's dead.
An American detective. A New York policeman killed her last night. It seems she was...
Leave me.

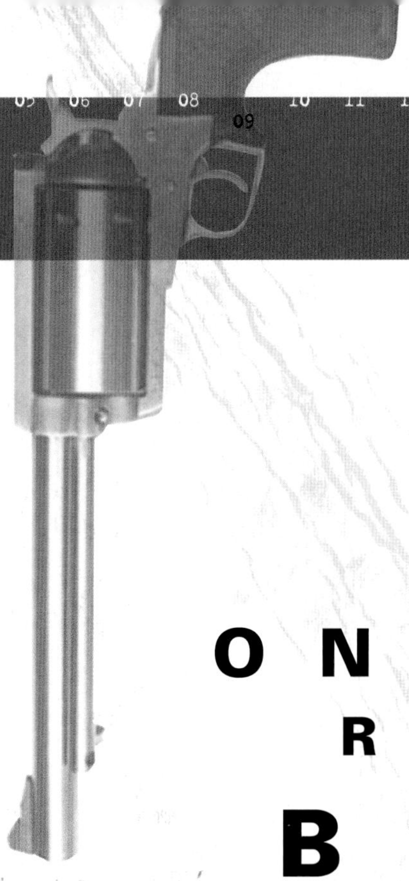

ONE REALLY BAD DAY

SAM AND TWITCH

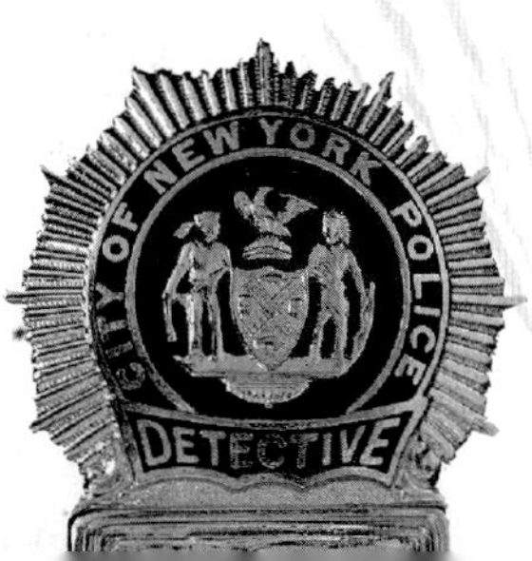
CITY OF NEW YORK POLICE
DETECTIVE

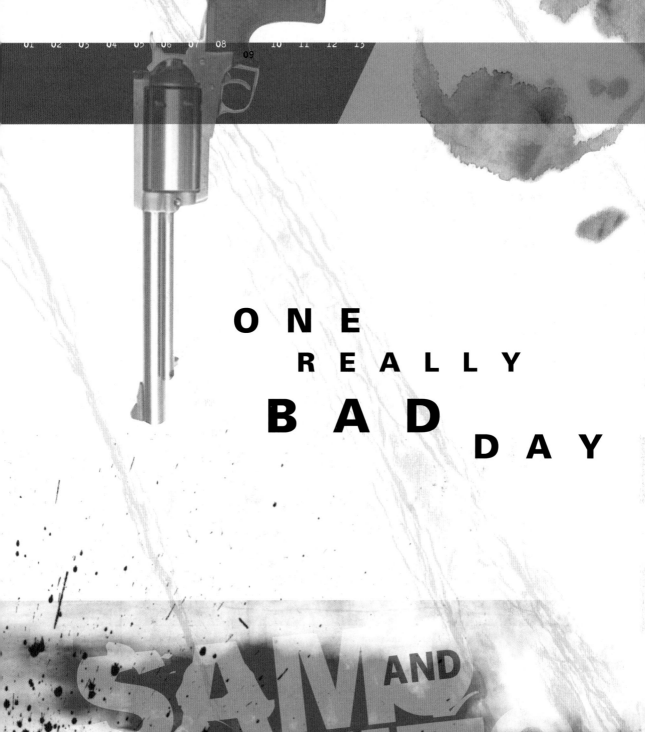

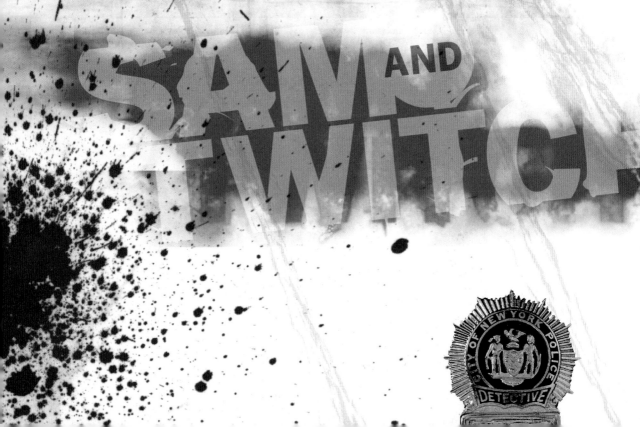

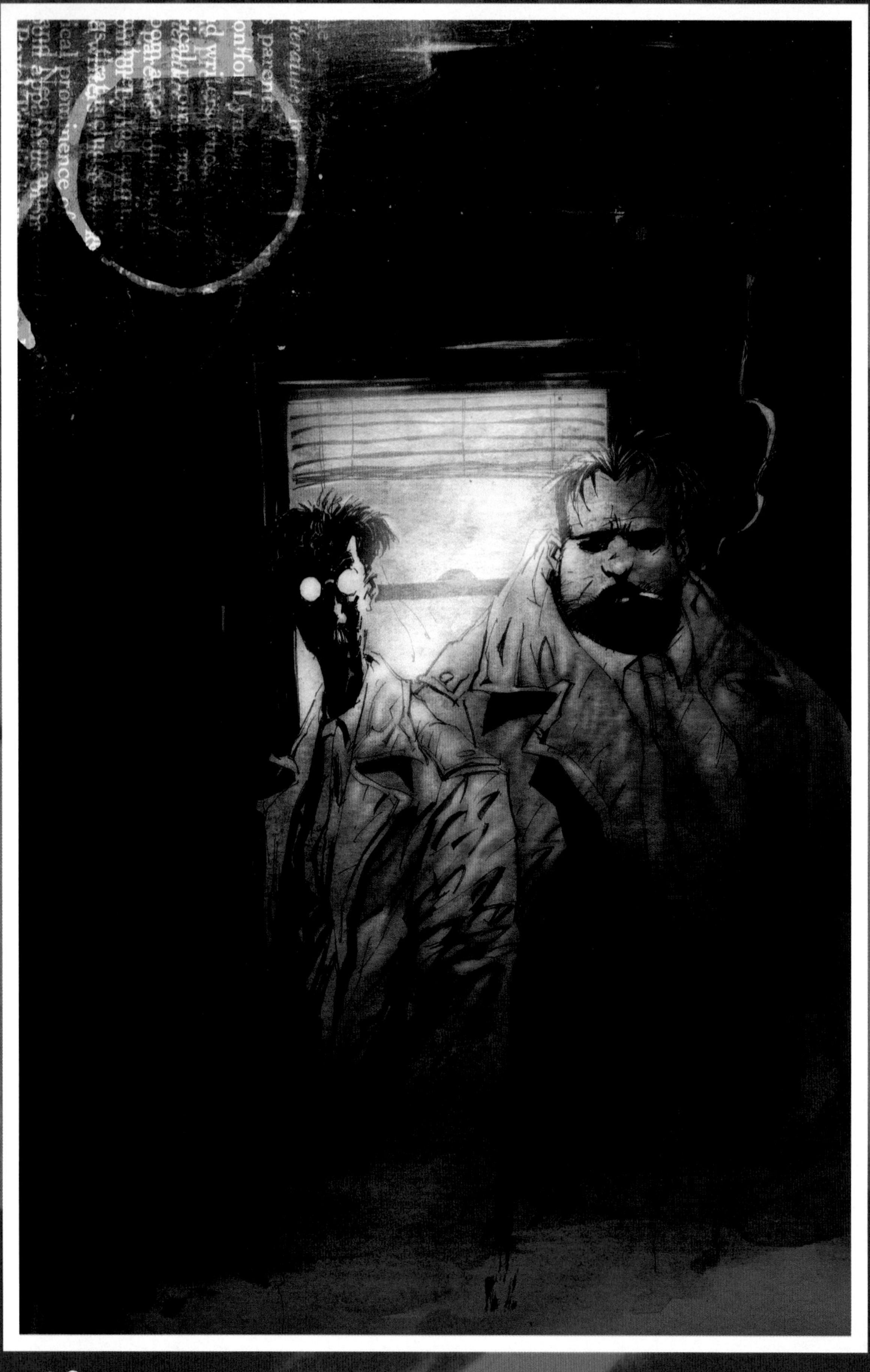

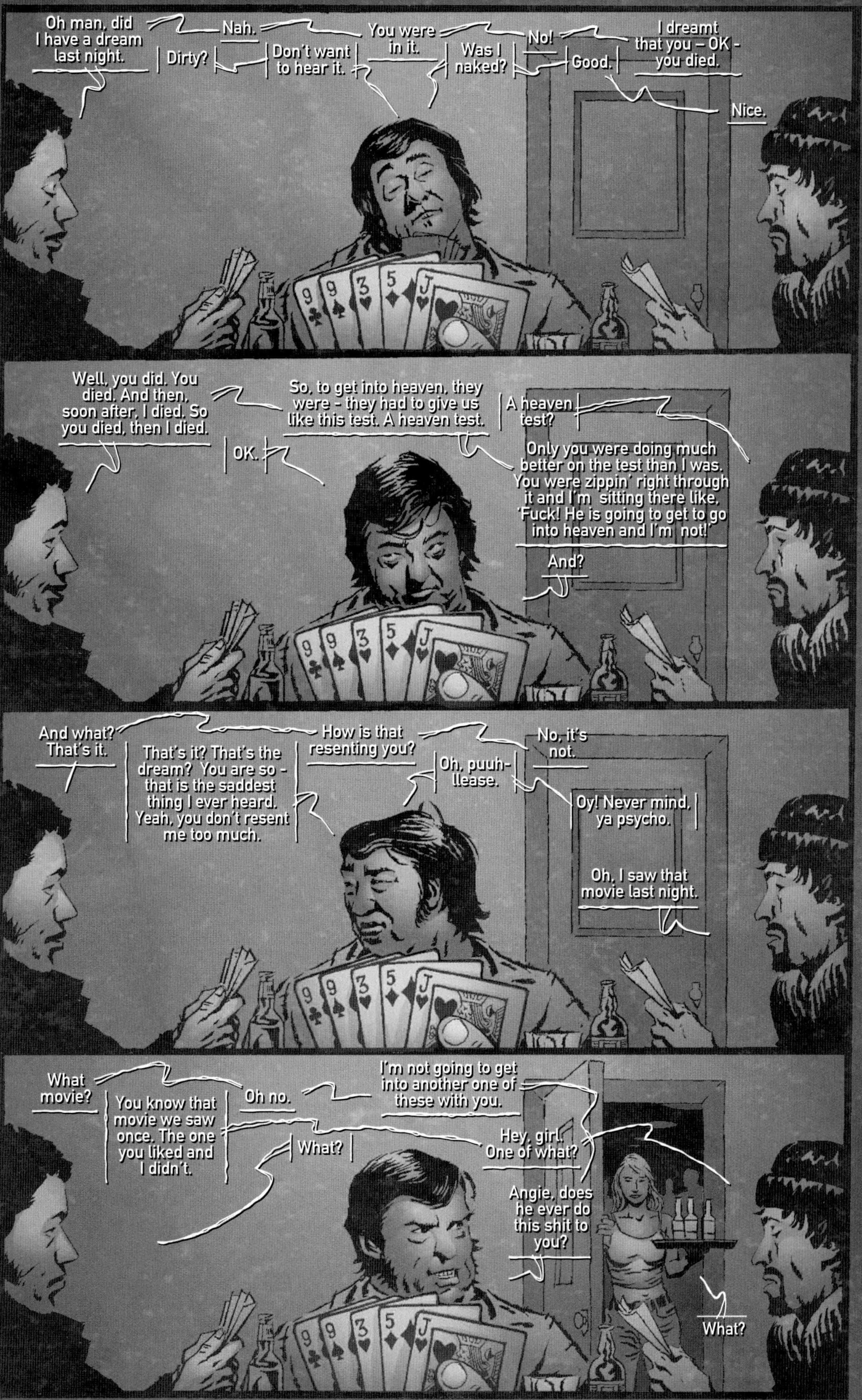
Oh man, did I have a dream last night.
Nah.
Dirty?
You were in it.
Don't want to hear it.
Was I naked?
No!
Good.
I dreamt that you – OK - you died.
Nice.
Well, you did. You died. And then, soon after, I died. So you died, then I died.
OK.
So, to get into heaven, they were - they had to give us like this test. A heaven test.
A heaven test?
Only you were doing much better on the test than I was. You were zippin' right through it and I'm sitting there like, 'Fuck! He is going to get to go into heaven and I'm not!'
And?
And what? That's it.
That's it? That's the dream? You are so - that is the saddest thing I ever heard. Yeah, you don't resent me too much.
How is that resenting you?
Oh, puuh-llease.
No, it's not.
Oy! Never mind, ya psycho.
Oh, I saw that movie last night.
What movie?
You know that movie we saw once. The one you liked and I didn't.
Oh no.
I'm not going to get into another one of these with you.
What?
Hey, girl. One of what?
Angie, does he ever do this shit to you?
What?

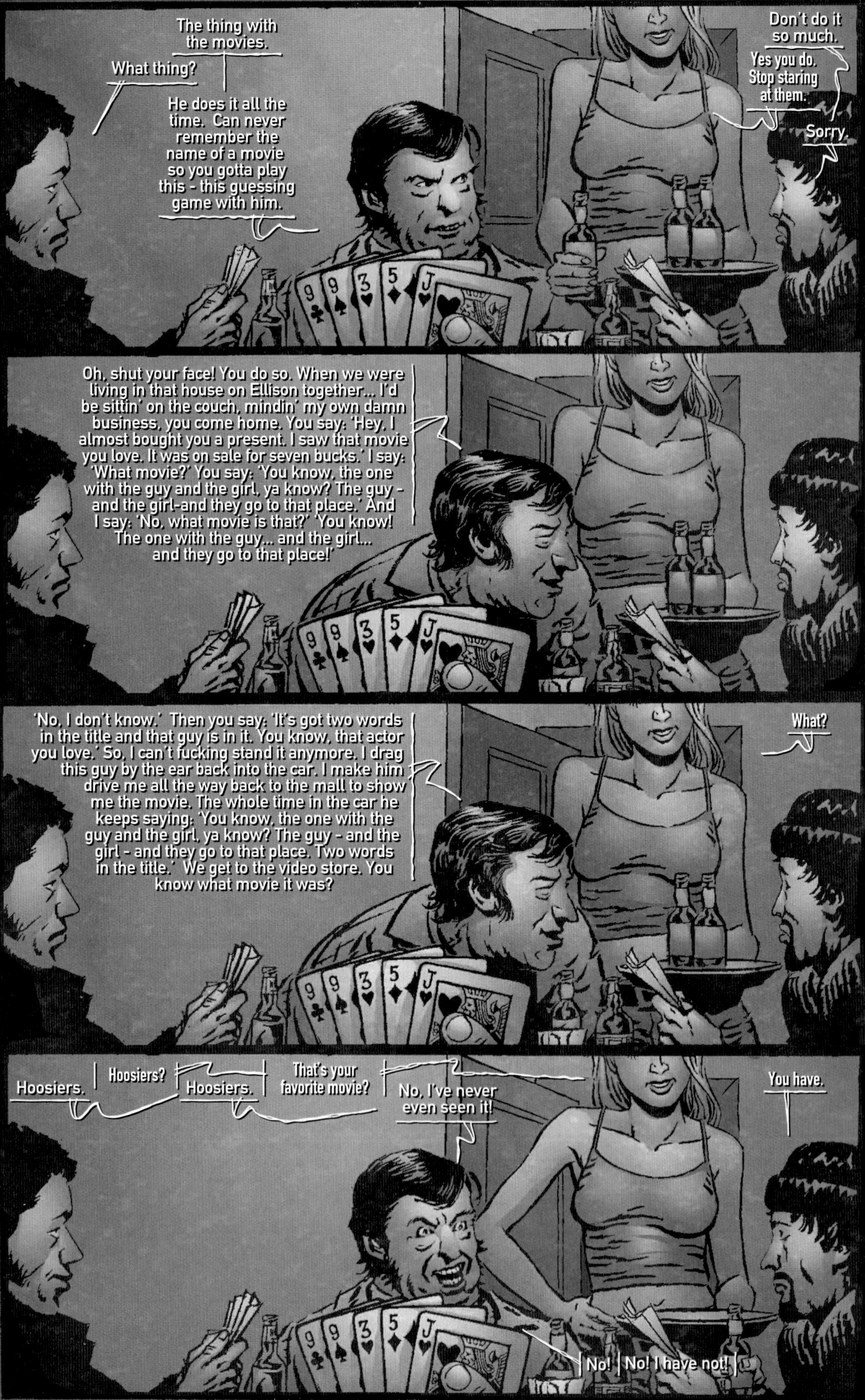
What thing?
The thing with the movies.
He does it all the time. Can never remember the name of a movie so you gotta play this - this guessing game with him.
Don't do it so much.
Yes you do. Stop staring at them.
Sorry.
Oh, shut your face! You do so. When we were living in that house on Ellison together... I'd be sittin' on the couch, mindin' my own damn business, you come home. You say: 'Hey, I almost bought you a present. I saw that movie you love. It was on sale for seven bucks.' I say: 'What movie?' You say: 'You know, the one with the guy and the girl, ya know? The guy - and the girl-and they go to that place.' And I say: 'No, what movie is that?' 'You know! The one with the guy... and the girl... and they go to that place!'
'No, I don't know.' Then you say: 'It's got two words in the title and that guy is in it. You know, that actor you love.' So, I can't fucking stand it anymore. I drag this guy by the ear back into the car. I make him drive me all the way back to the mall to show me the movie. The whole time in the car he keeps saying: 'You know, the one with the guy and the girl, ya know? The guy - and the girl - and they go to that place. Two words in the title.' We get to the video store. You know what movie it was?
What?
Hoosiers.
Hoosiers?
Hoosiers.
That's your favorite movie?
No, I've never even seen it!
You have.
No!
No! I have not!

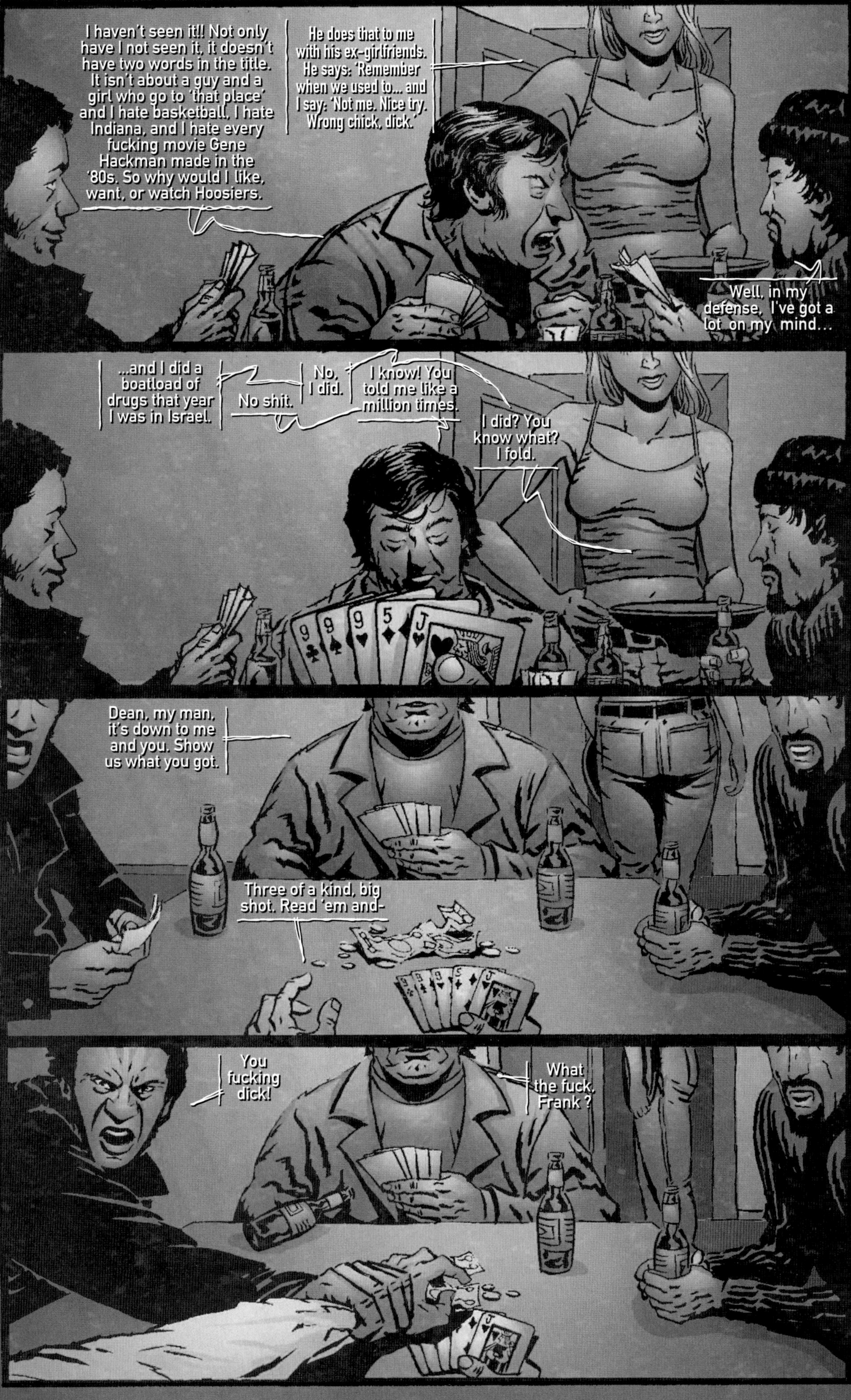
I haven't seen it!! Not only have I not seen it, it doesn't have two words in the title. It isn't about a guy and a girl who go to 'that place' and I hate basketball, I hate Indiana, and I hate every fucking movie Gene Hackman made in the '80s. So why would I like, want, or watch Hoosiers.
He does that to me with his ex-girlfriends. He says: 'Remember when we used to... and I say: 'Not me. Nice try. Wrong chick, dick.'
Well, in my defense, I've got a lot on my mind...
...and I did a boatload of drugs that year I was in Israel.
No shit.
No, I did.
I know! You told me like a million times.
I did? You know what? I fold.
Dean, my man, it's down to me and you. Show us what you got.
Three of a kind, big shot. Read 'em and-
You fucking dick!
What the fuck, Frank ?

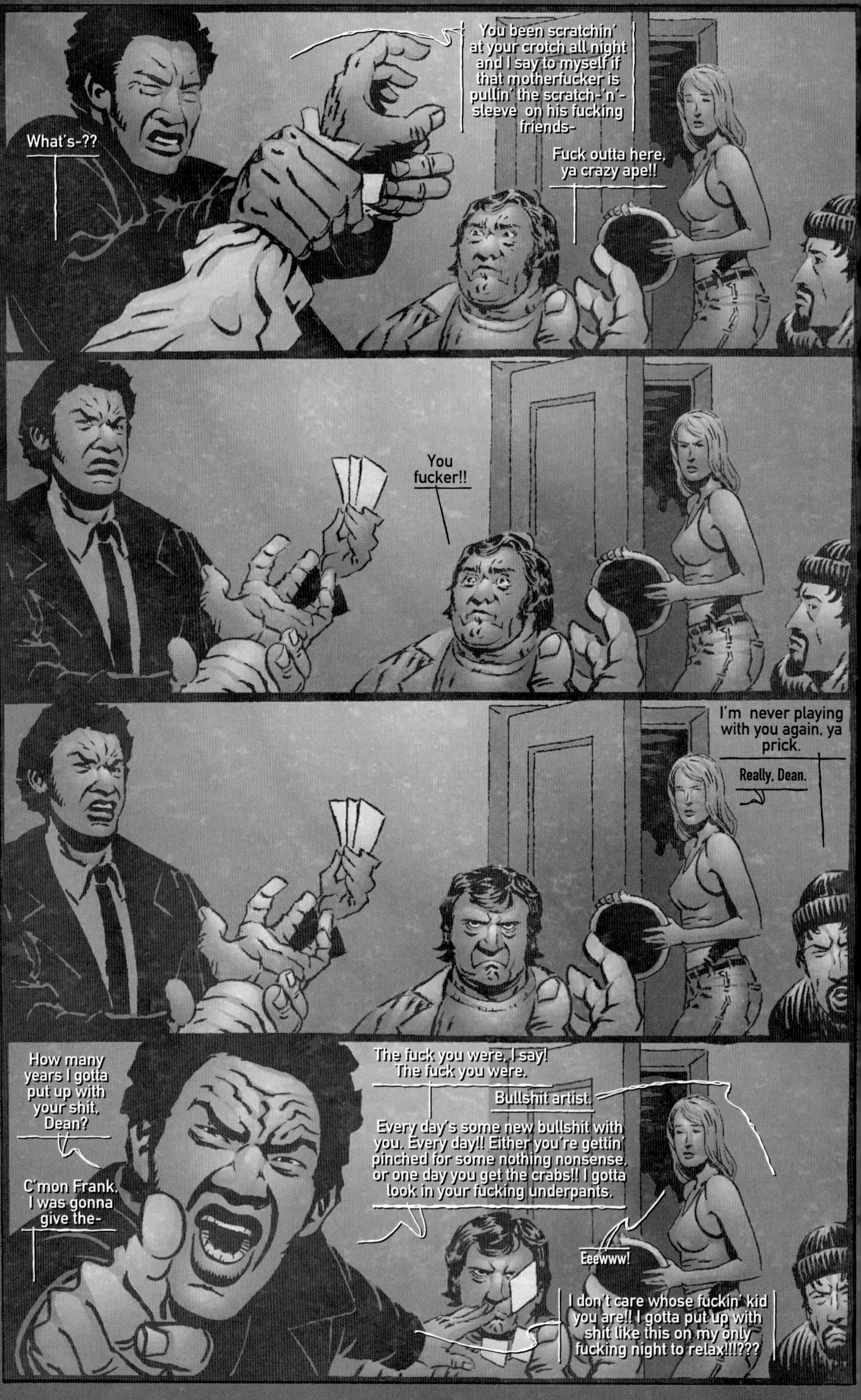
What's-??
You been scratchin' at your crotch all night and I say to myself if that motherfucker is pullin' the scratch-'n'-sleeve on his fucking friends-
Fuck outta here, ya crazy ape!!
You fucker!!
I'm never playing with you again, ya prick.
Really, Dean.
How many years I gotta put up with your shit, Dean?
C'mon Frank. I was gonna give the-
The fuck you were, I say! The fuck you were.
Bullshit artist.
Every day's some new bullshit with you. Every day!! Either you're gettin' pinched for some nothing nonsense, or one day you get the crabs!! I gotta look in your fucking underpants.
Eeewww!
I don't care whose fuckin' kid you are!! I gotta put up with shit like this on my only fucking night to relax!!!???

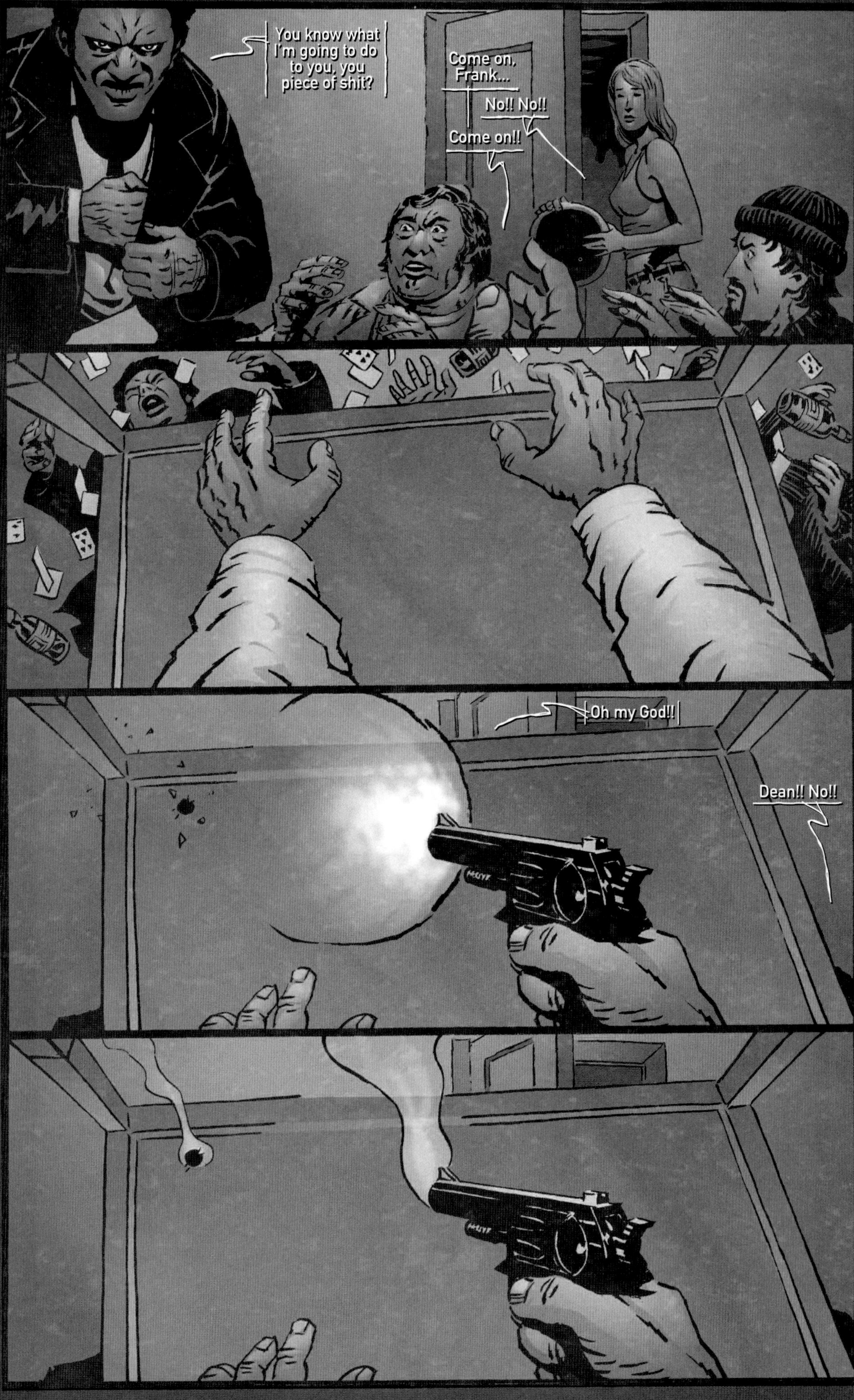

You know what I'm going to do to you, you piece of shit?
Come on, Frank...
No!! No!!
Come on!!
Oh my God!!
Dean!! No!!

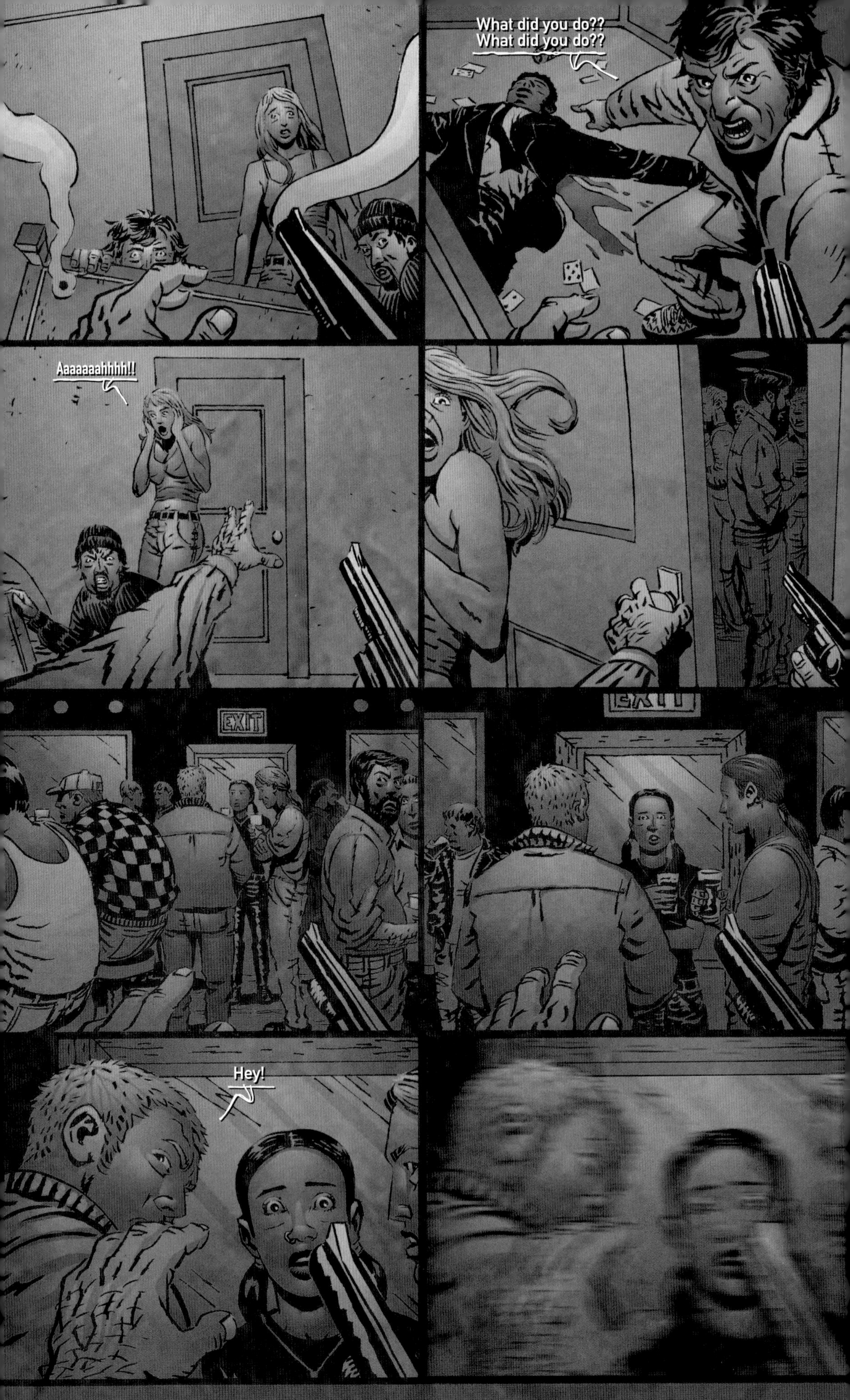
What did you do??
What did you do??
Aaaaaaahhhh!!
EXIT
Hey!

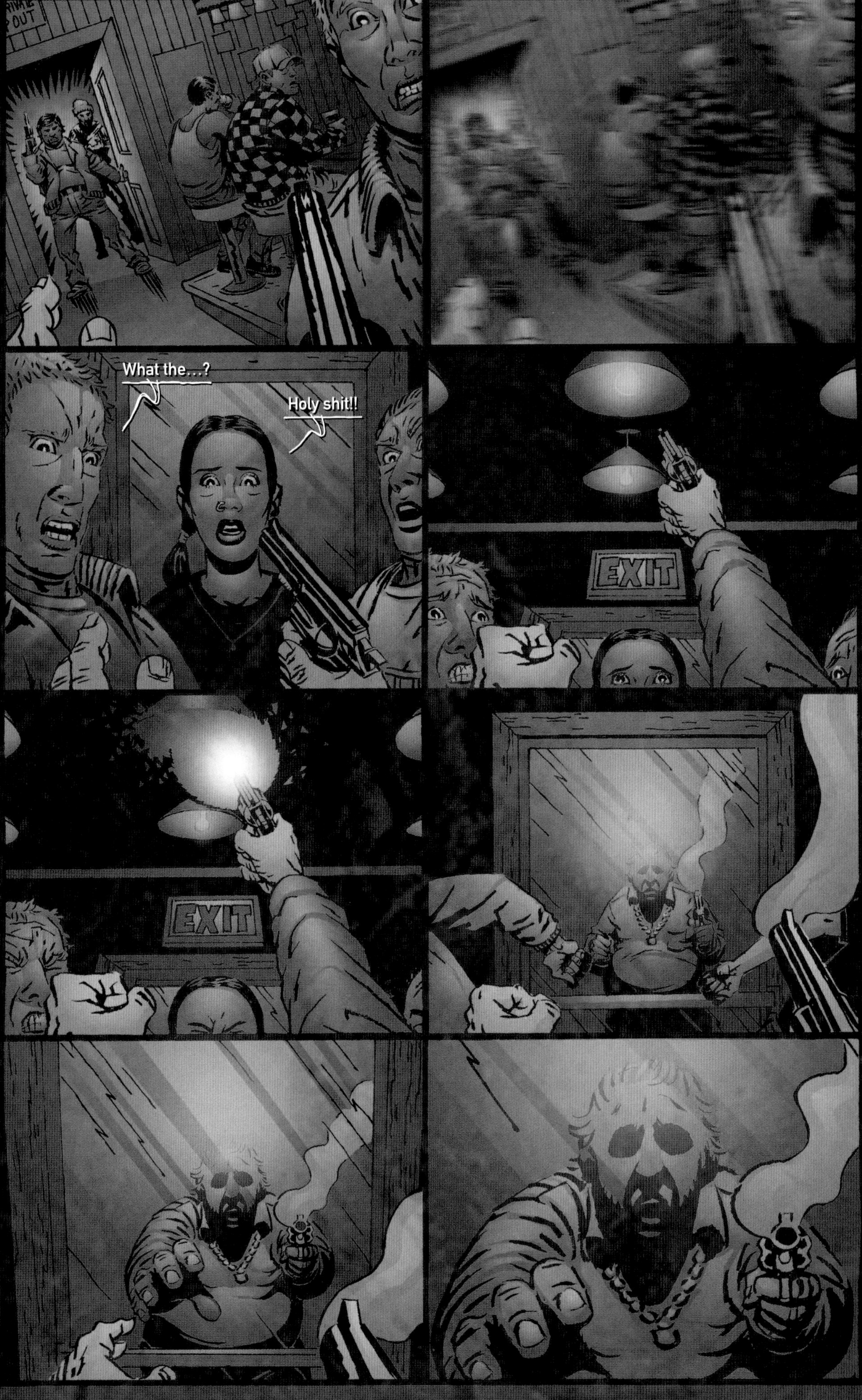
What the…?
Holy shit!!

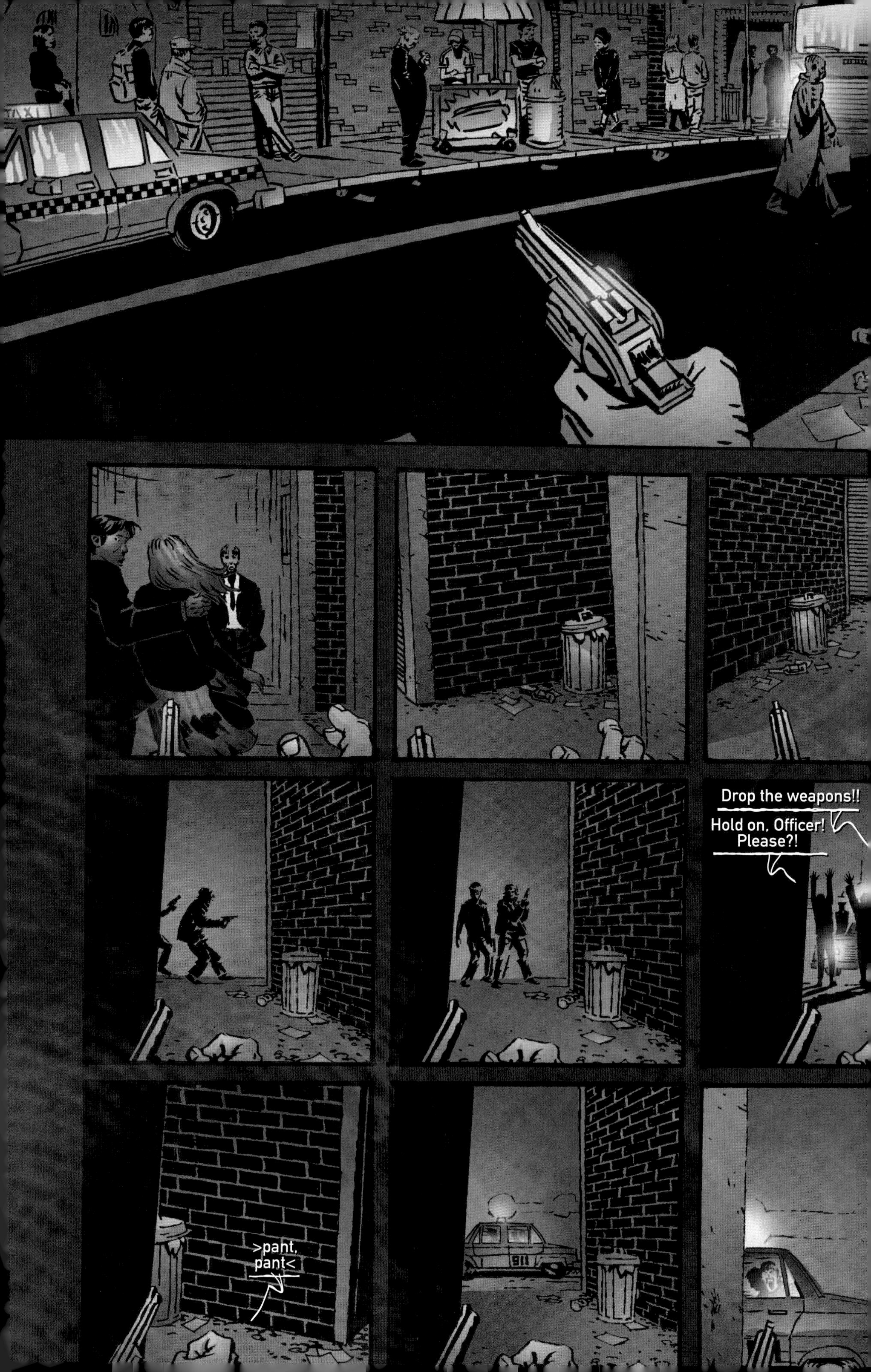
Drop the weapons!!
Hold on, Officer! Please?!
>pant, pant<

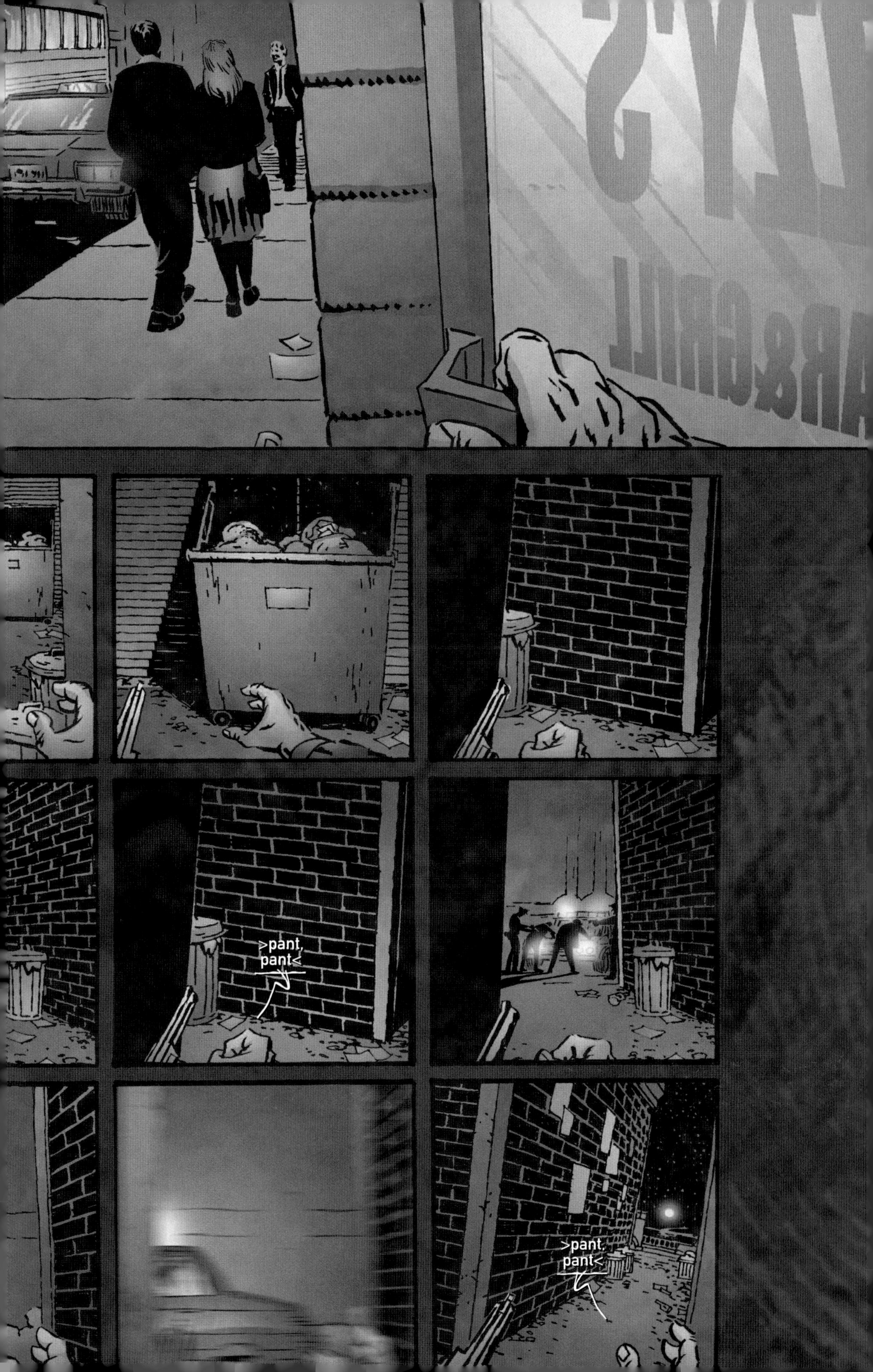
>pant, pant<
>pant, pant<

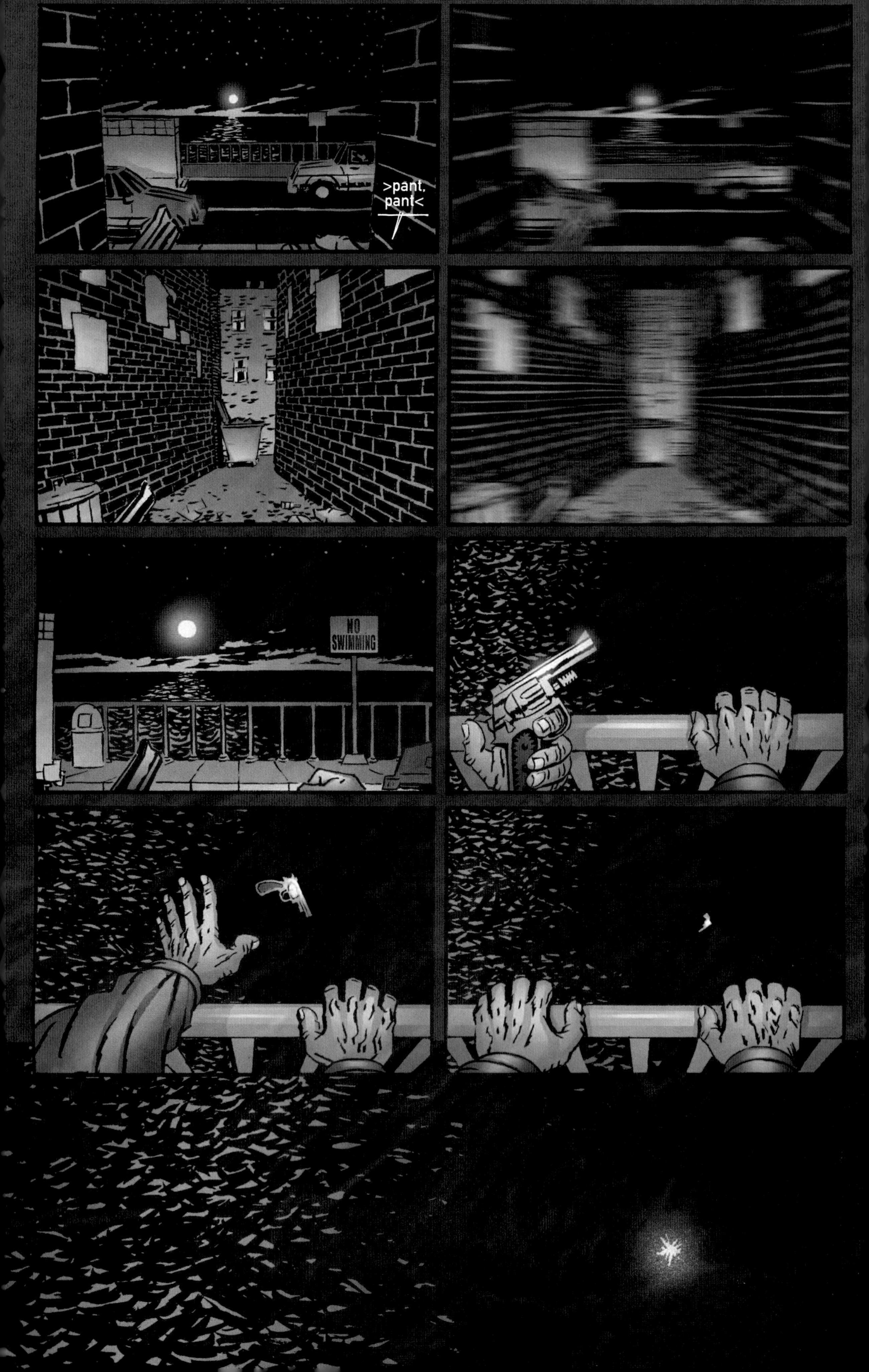
>pant, pant<
NO SWIMMING

So, what is she like in real life?

What?

Your wife. Tell me about her.

Now?

Yeah.

While I'm...?

Oh yeah.

Goddamn. You're a piece of work.

3B

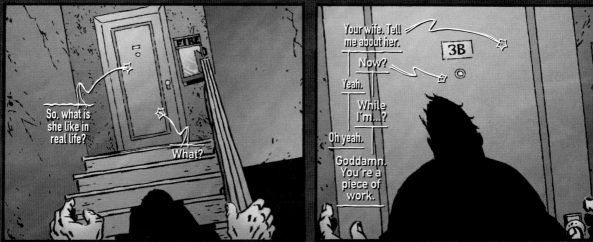

Tell me about her... oh...

Nothin' to tell. She ain't... uhgn... you. She's - she's Skanky Spice. Nothin' to her.

Skanky Spice? Don't tell me you just made a Spice Girls reference. That is so '96.

3B

Well, tellin' someone somethin' is so 'a certain year.' is so '93. And let me tell you something else. A Spice Girl reference is just as good as a Milli Vanilli. Some pop culture riffs are timeless.

Don't get semantic with a girl who is holding it in her hand.

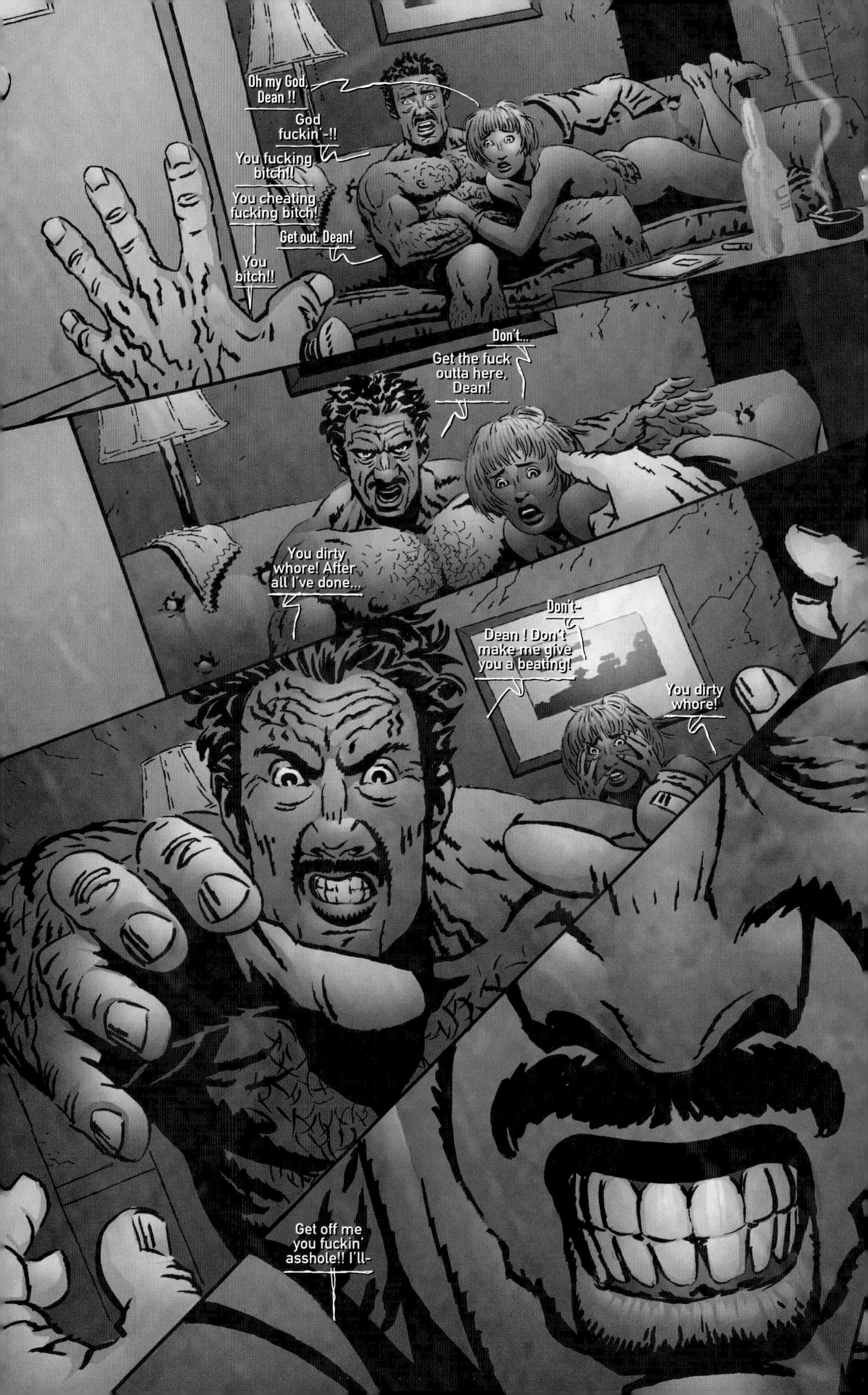
Oh my God, Dean !!
God fuckin'-!!
You fucking bitch!!
You cheating fucking bitch!
Get out, Dean!
You bitch!!
Don't...
Get the fuck outta here, Dean!
You dirty whore! After all I've done...
Don't-
Dean ! Don't make me give you a beating!
You dirty whore!
Get off me you fuckin' asshole!! I'll-

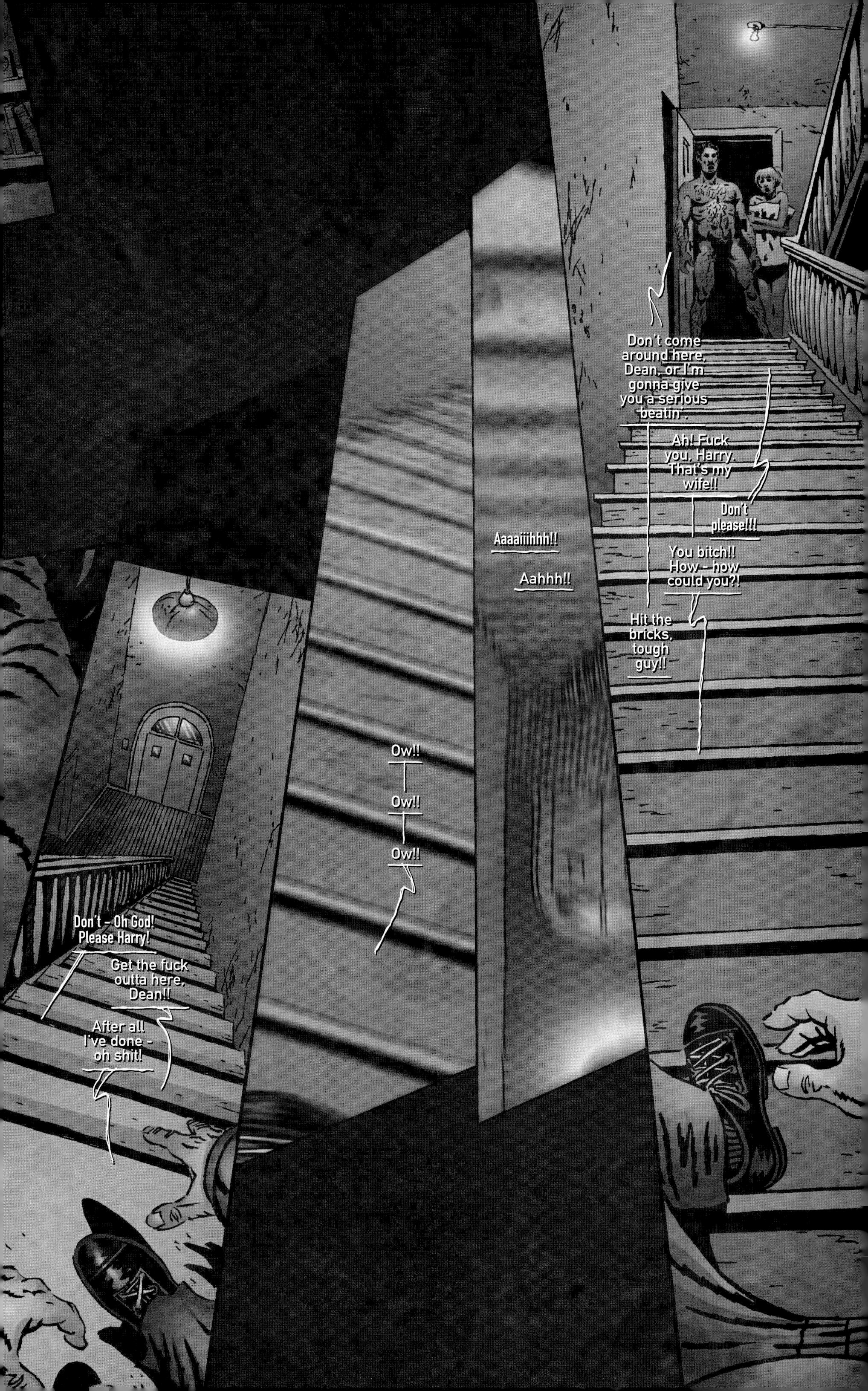
Don't come around here, Dean, or I'm gonna give you a serious beatin'.
Ah! Fuck you, Harry. That's my wife!!
Don't please!!!
You bitch!! How - how could you?!
Hit the bricks, tough guy!!
Don't - Oh God! Please Harry!
Get the fuck outta here, Dean!!
After all I've done - oh shit!
Ow!!
Ow!!
Ow!!
Aaaaiiihhh!!
Aahhh!!

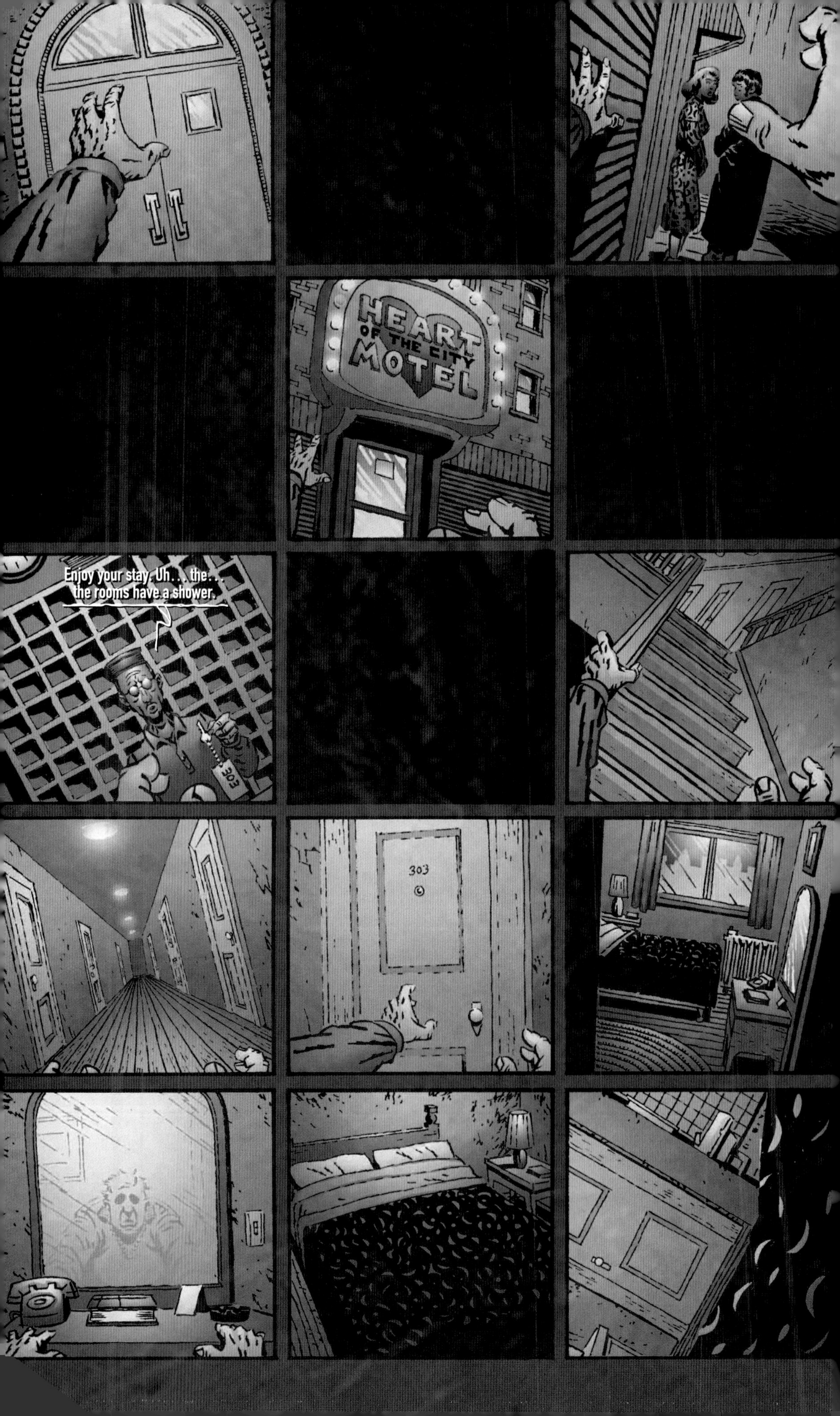
HEART OF THE CITY MOTEL
Enjoy your stay. Uh... the... the rooms have a shower.
303
303

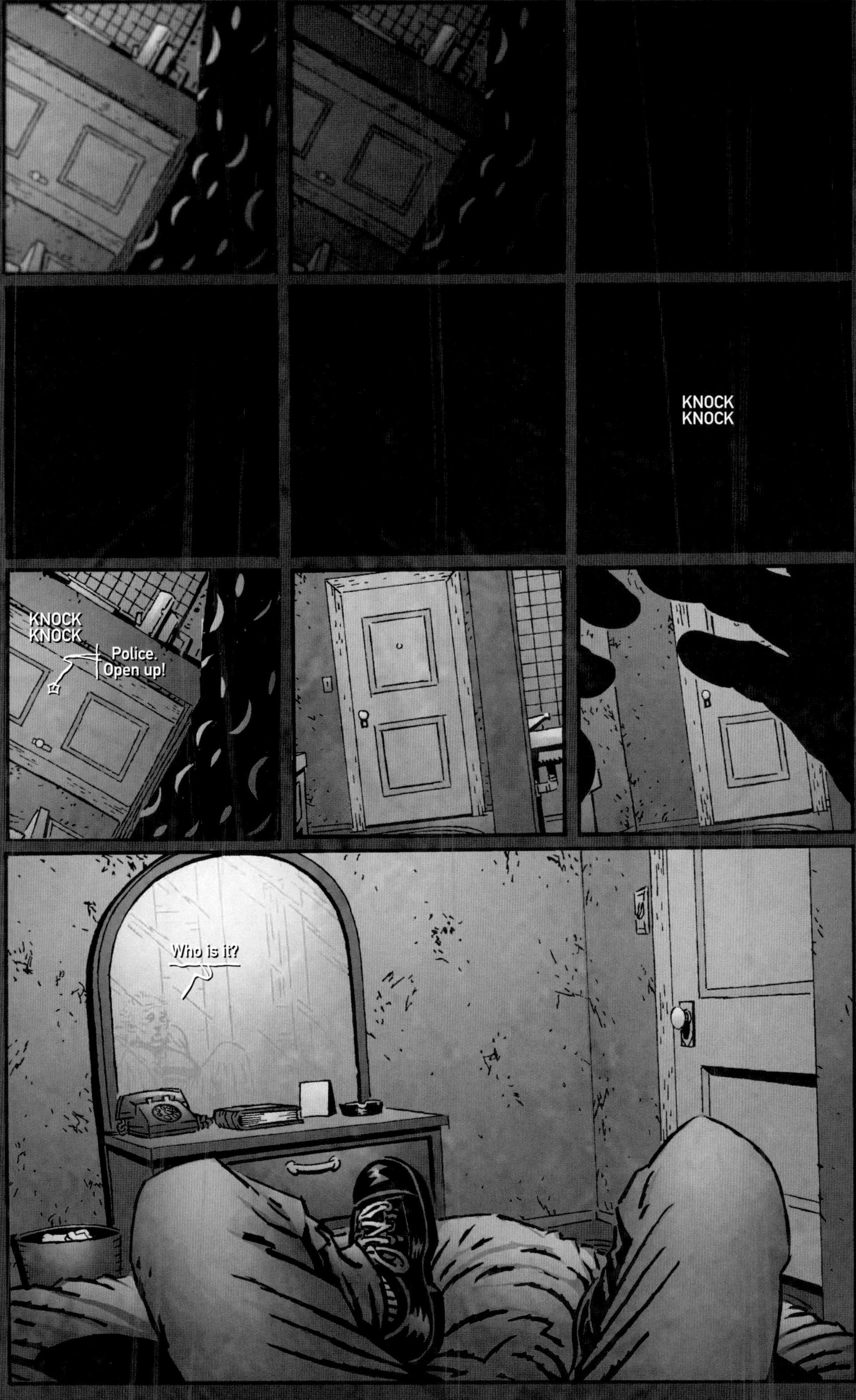
KNOCK
KNOCK
KNOCK
KNOCK
Police. Open up!
Who is it?

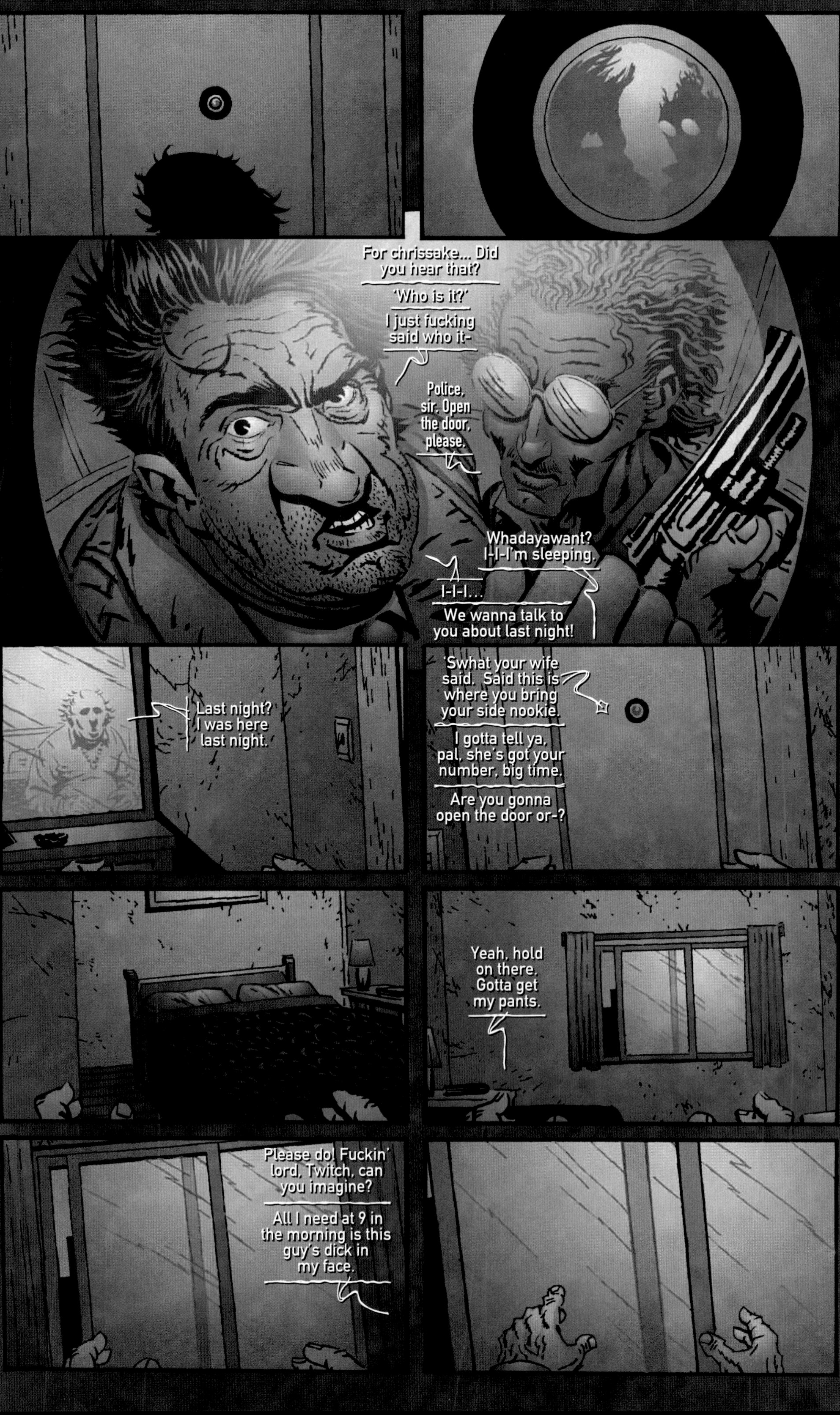
For chrissake... Did you hear that?
'Who is it?'
I just fucking said who it-
Police, sir. Open the door, please.
Whadayawant? I-I-I'm sleeping.
I-I-I...
We wanna talk to you about last night!
Last night? I was here last night.
'Swhat your wife said. Said this is where you bring your side nookie.
I gotta tell ya, pal, she's got your number, big time.
Are you gonna open the door or-?
Yeah, hold on there. Gotta get my pants.
Please do! Fuckin' lord, Twitch, can you imagine?
All I need at 9 in the morning is this guy's dick in my face.

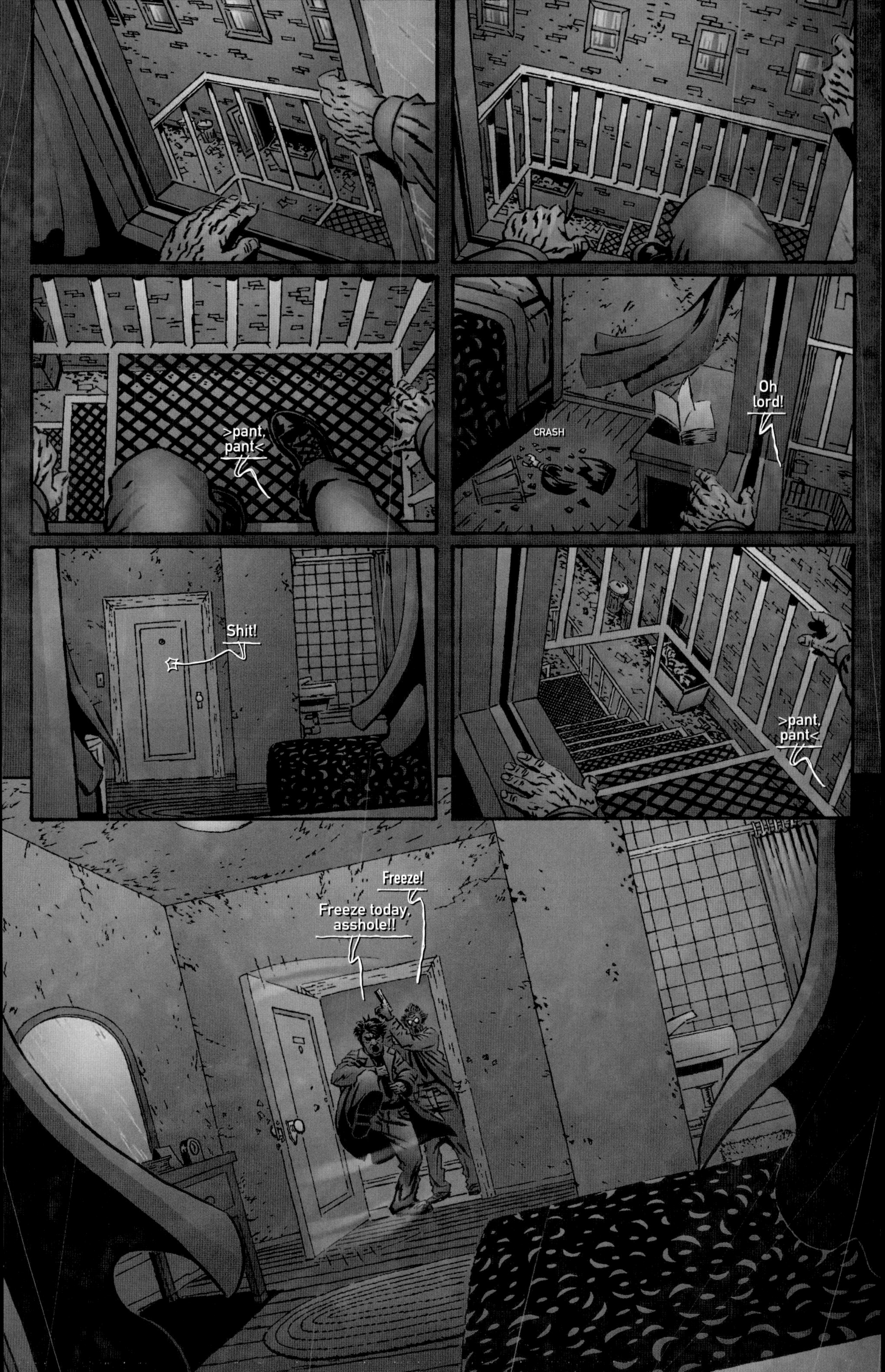

>pant, pant<
CRASH
Oh lord!
Shit!
>pant, pant<
Freeze!
Freeze today, asshole!!

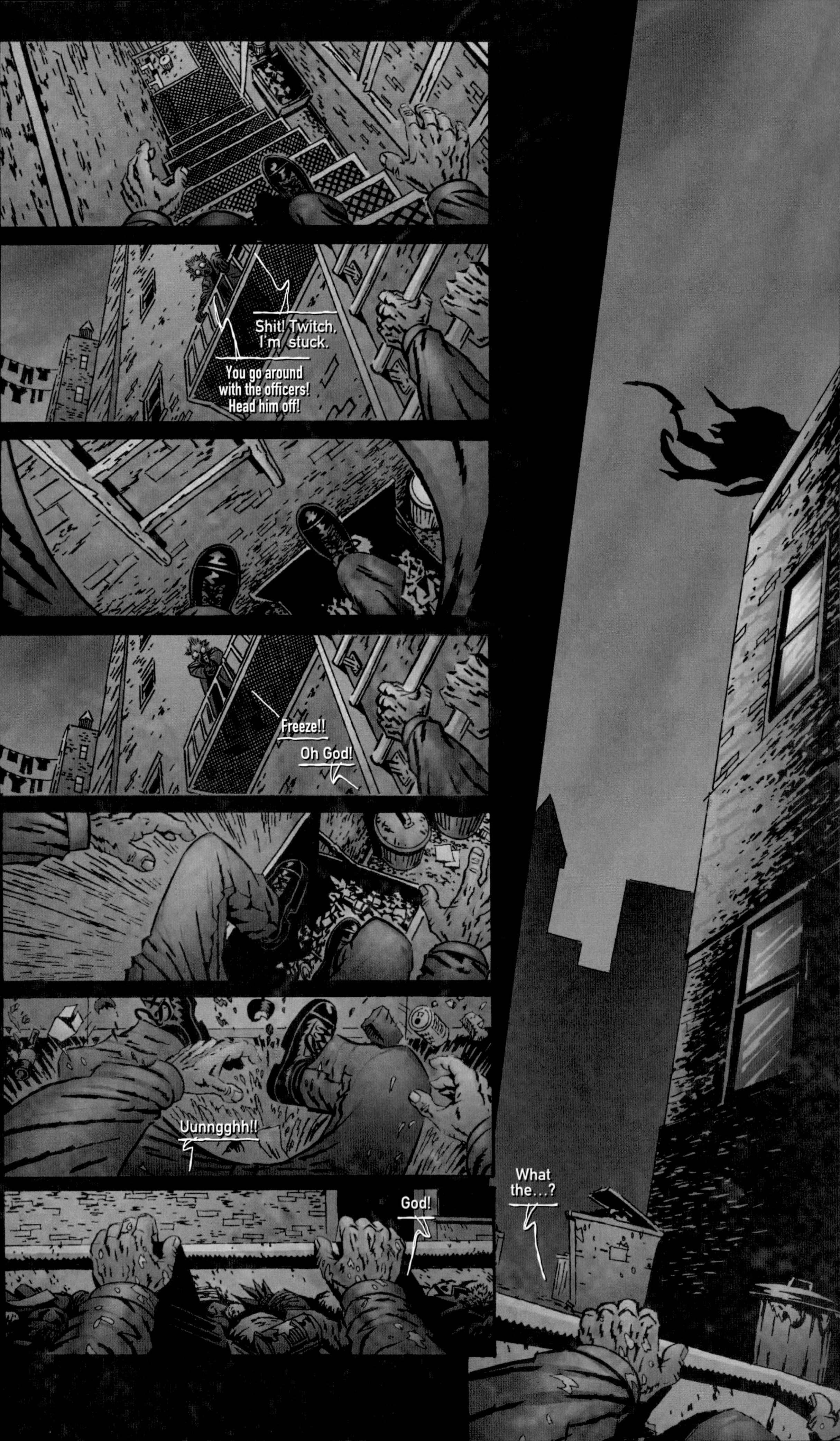

Shit! Twitch, I'm stuck.
You go around with the officers! Head him off!
Freeze!!
Oh God!
Uunngghh!!
God!
What the...?

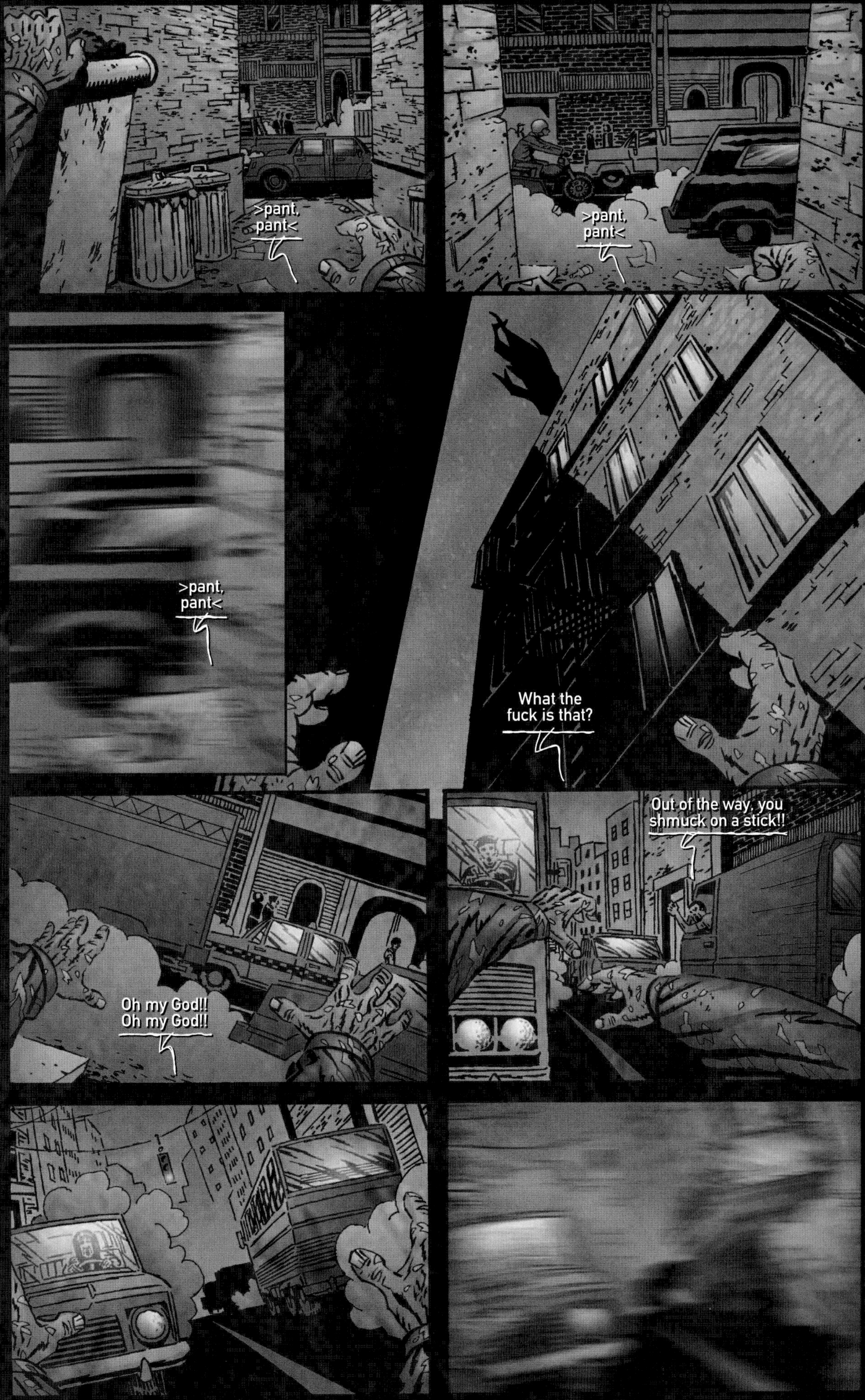

>pant, pant<
>pant, pant<
>pant, pant<
What the fuck is that?
Oh my God!! Oh my God!!
Out of the way, you shmuck on a stick!!

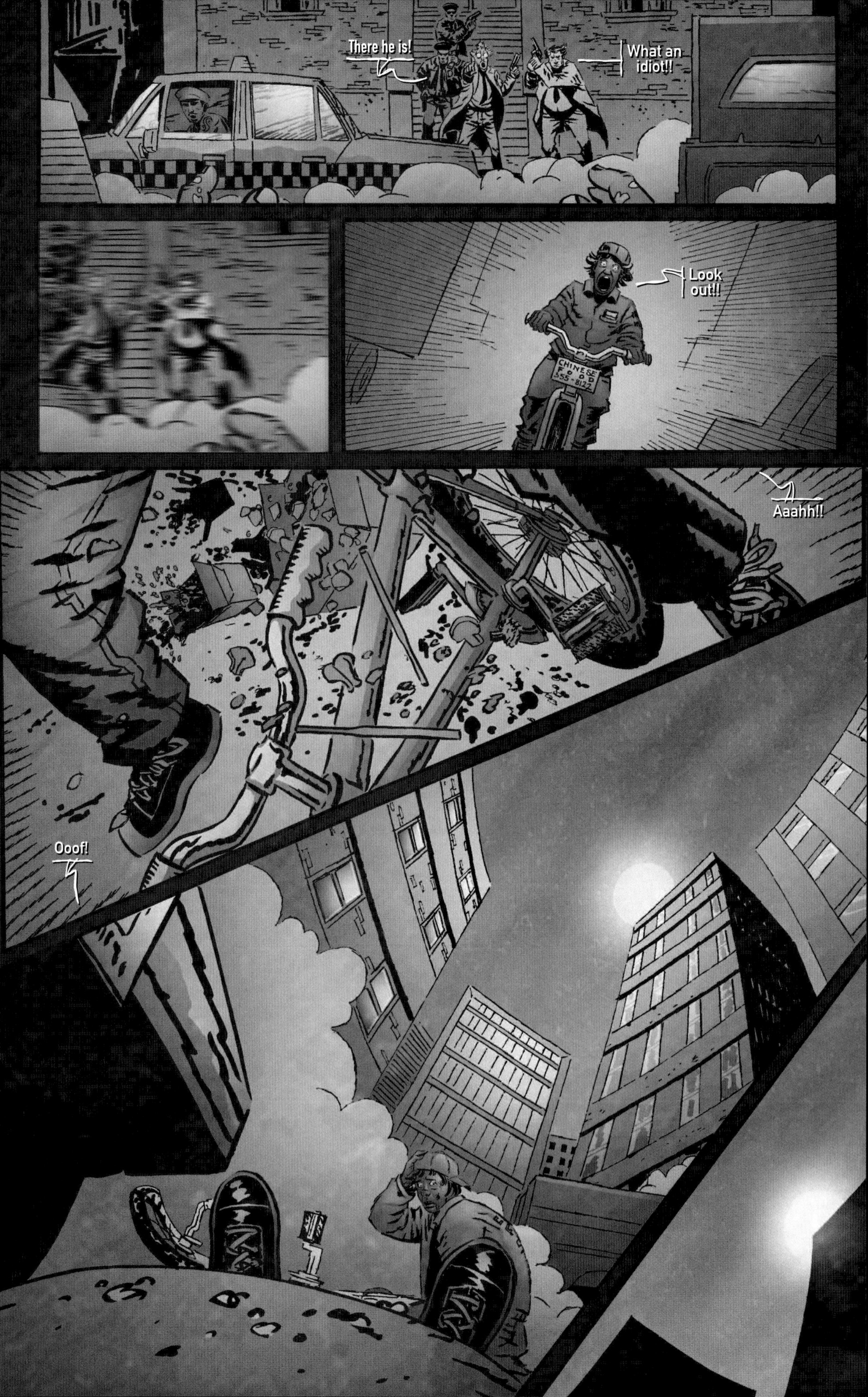
There he is!
What an idiot!!
Look out!!
Aaahh!!
Ooof!
CHINESE FOOD 555-8122

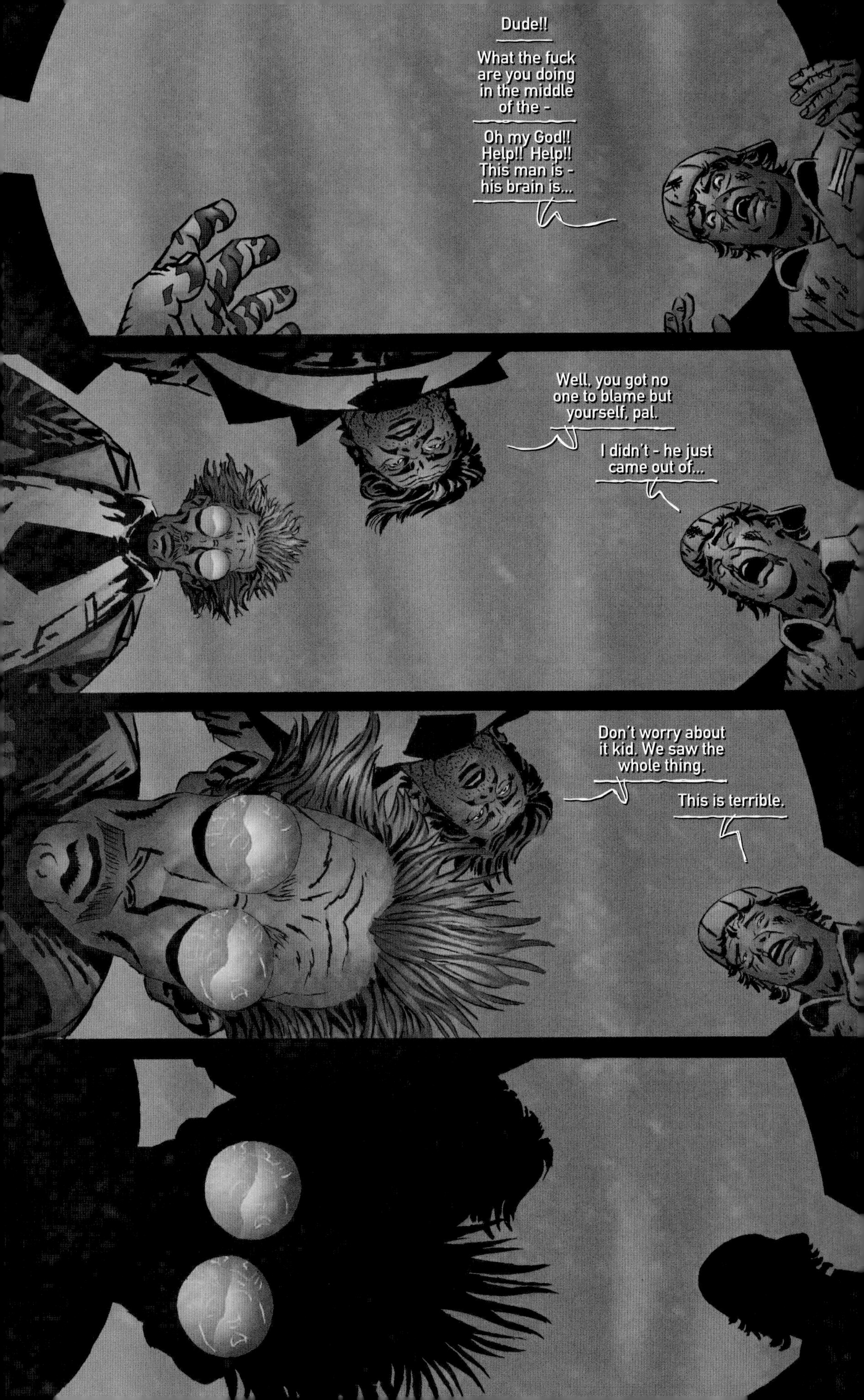
Dude!!
What the fuck are you doing in the middle of the -
Oh my God!! Help!! Help!! This man is - his brain is...
Well, you got no one to blame but yourself, pal.
I didn't - he just came out of...
Don't worry about it kid. We saw the whole thing.
This is terrible.

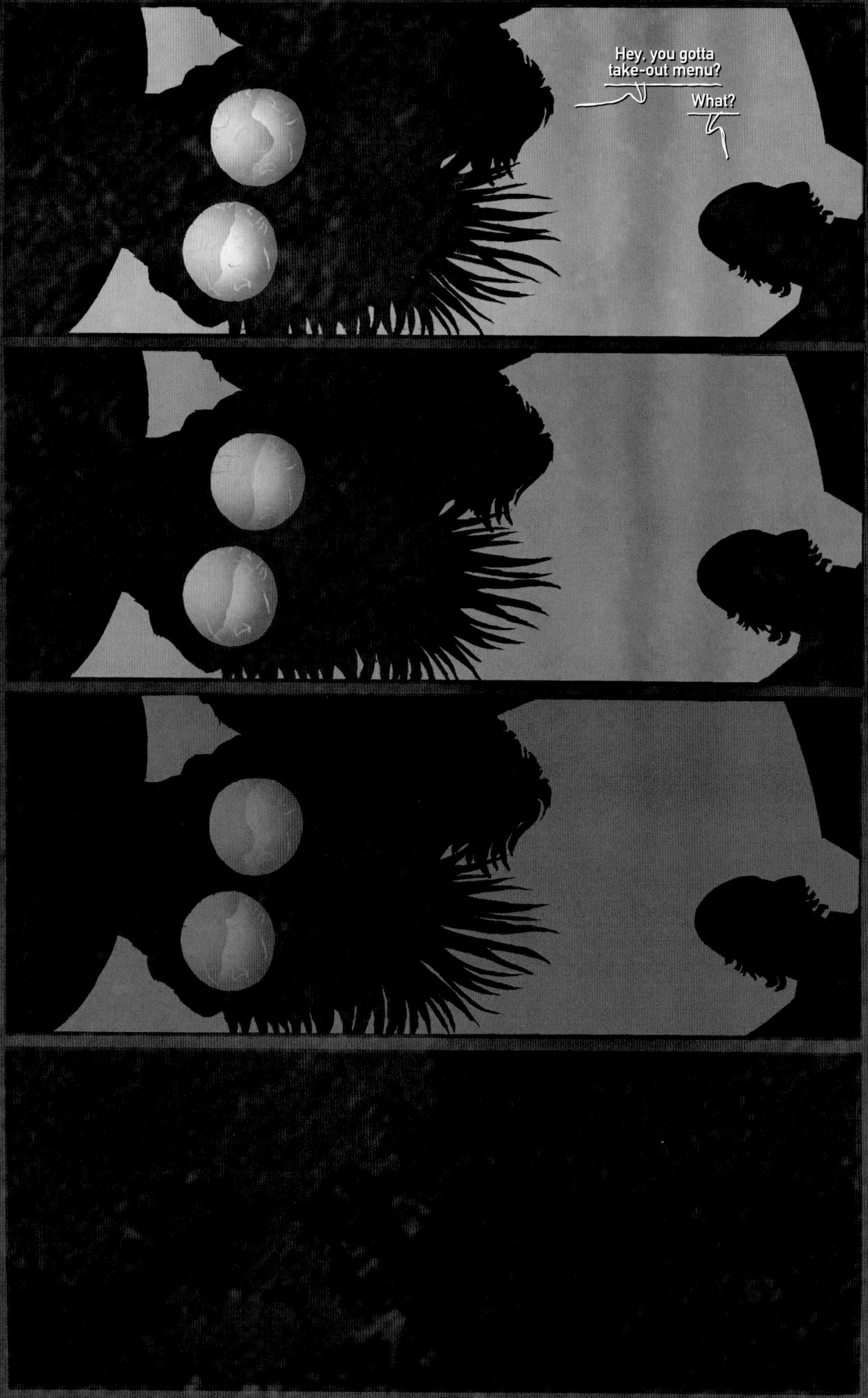
Hey, you gotta take-out menu?
What?

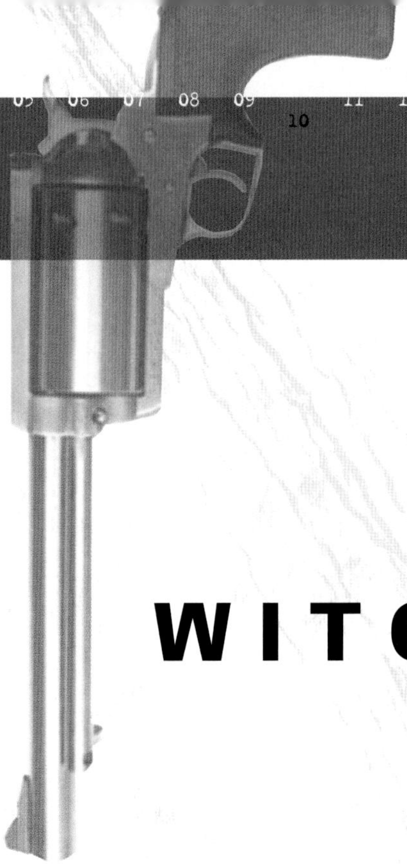

WITCHCRAFT

PART 1

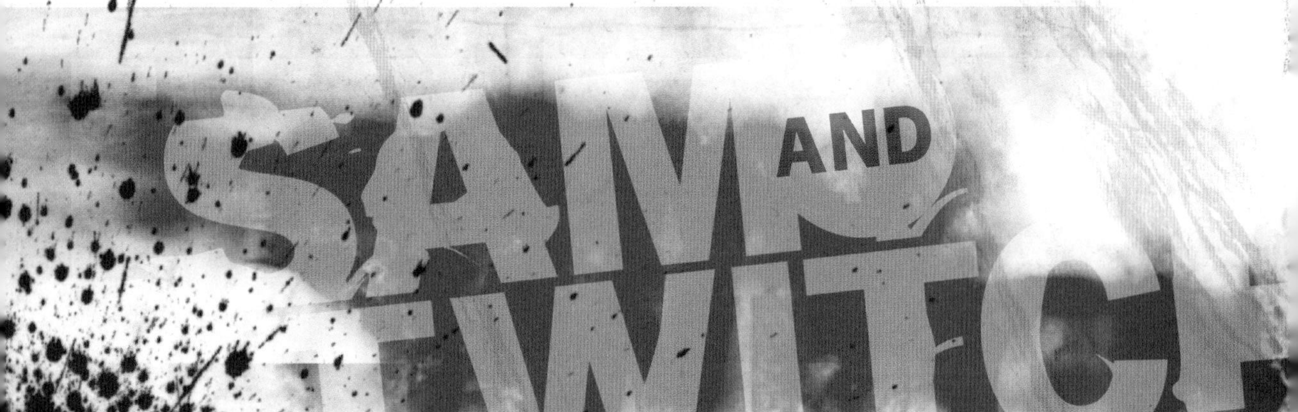
SAM AND TWITCH

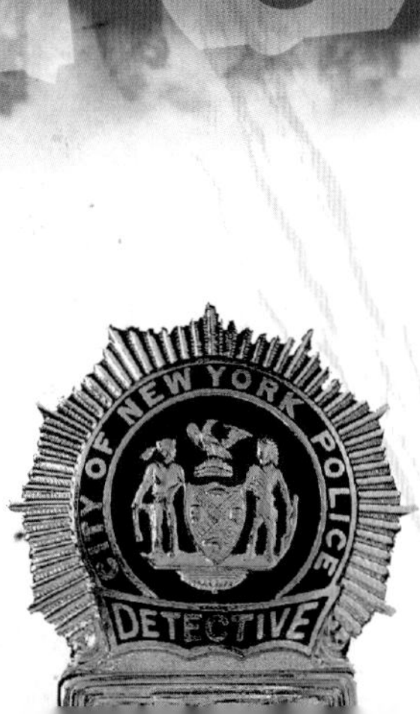
CITY OF NEW YORK POLICE
DETECTIVE

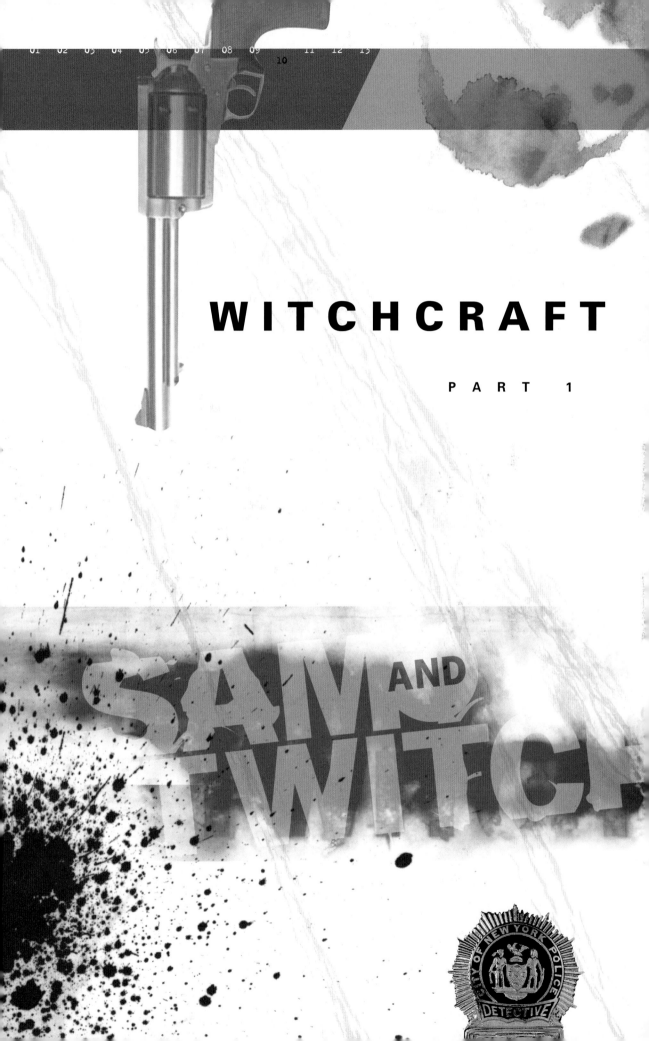

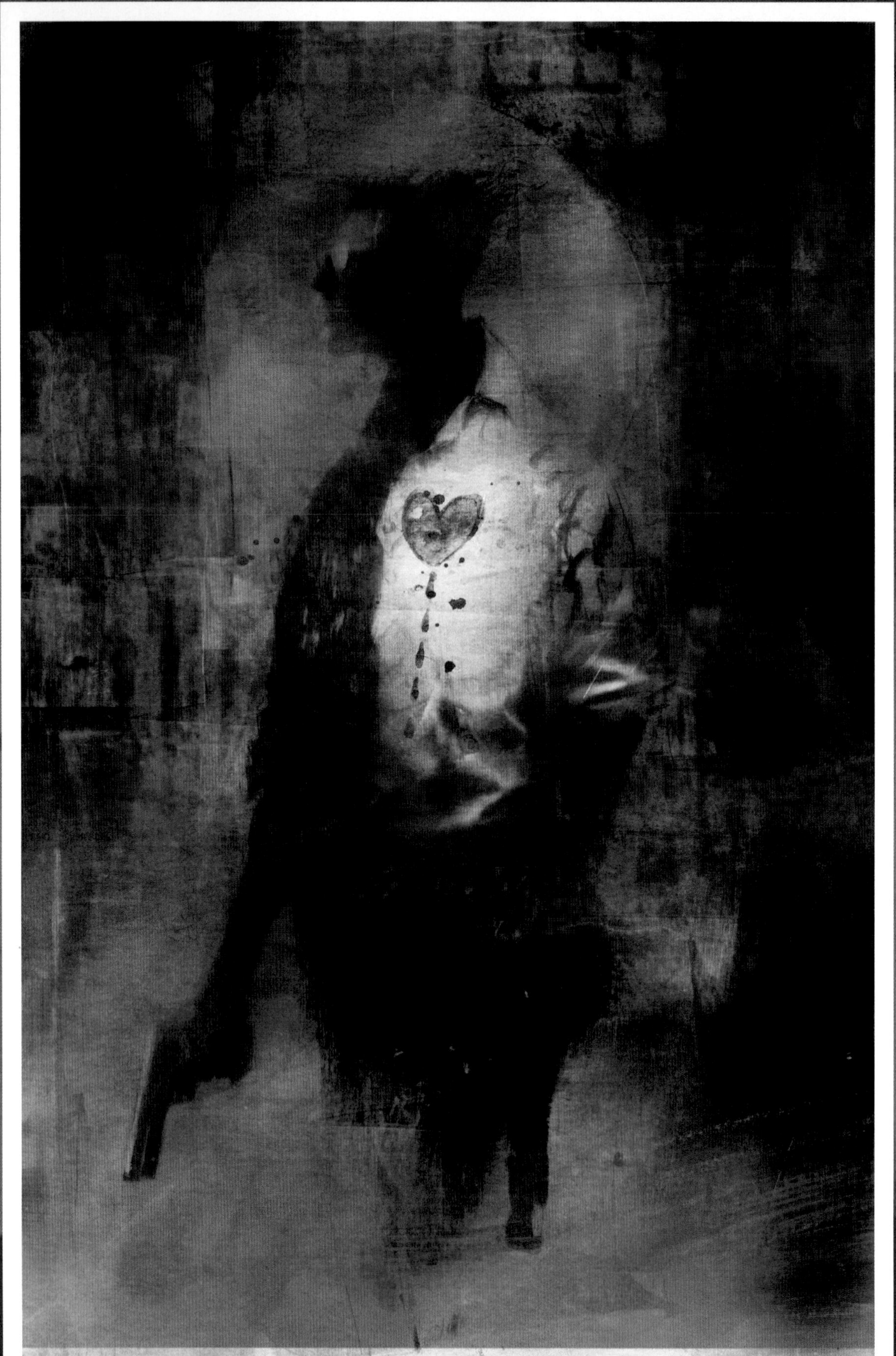

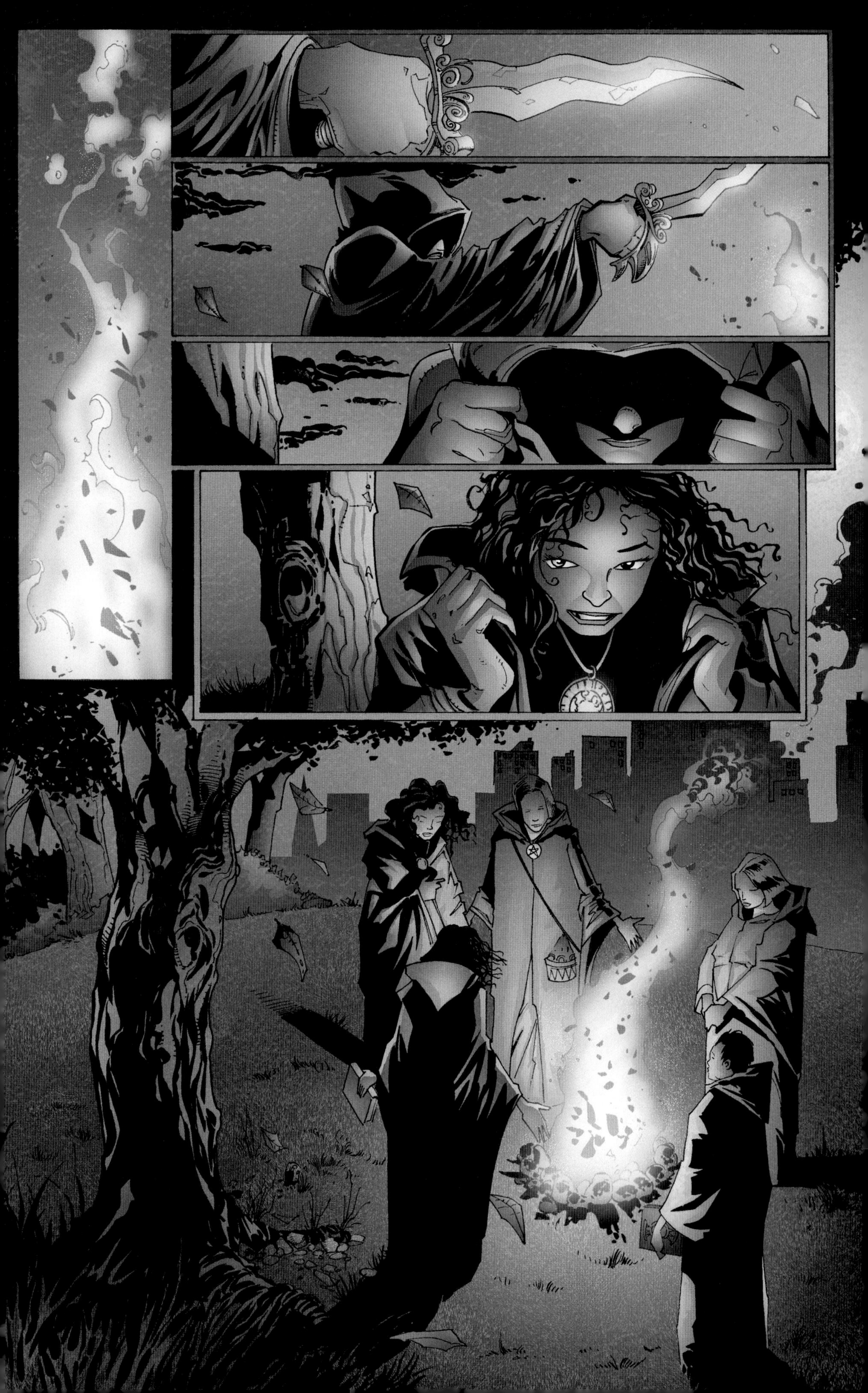

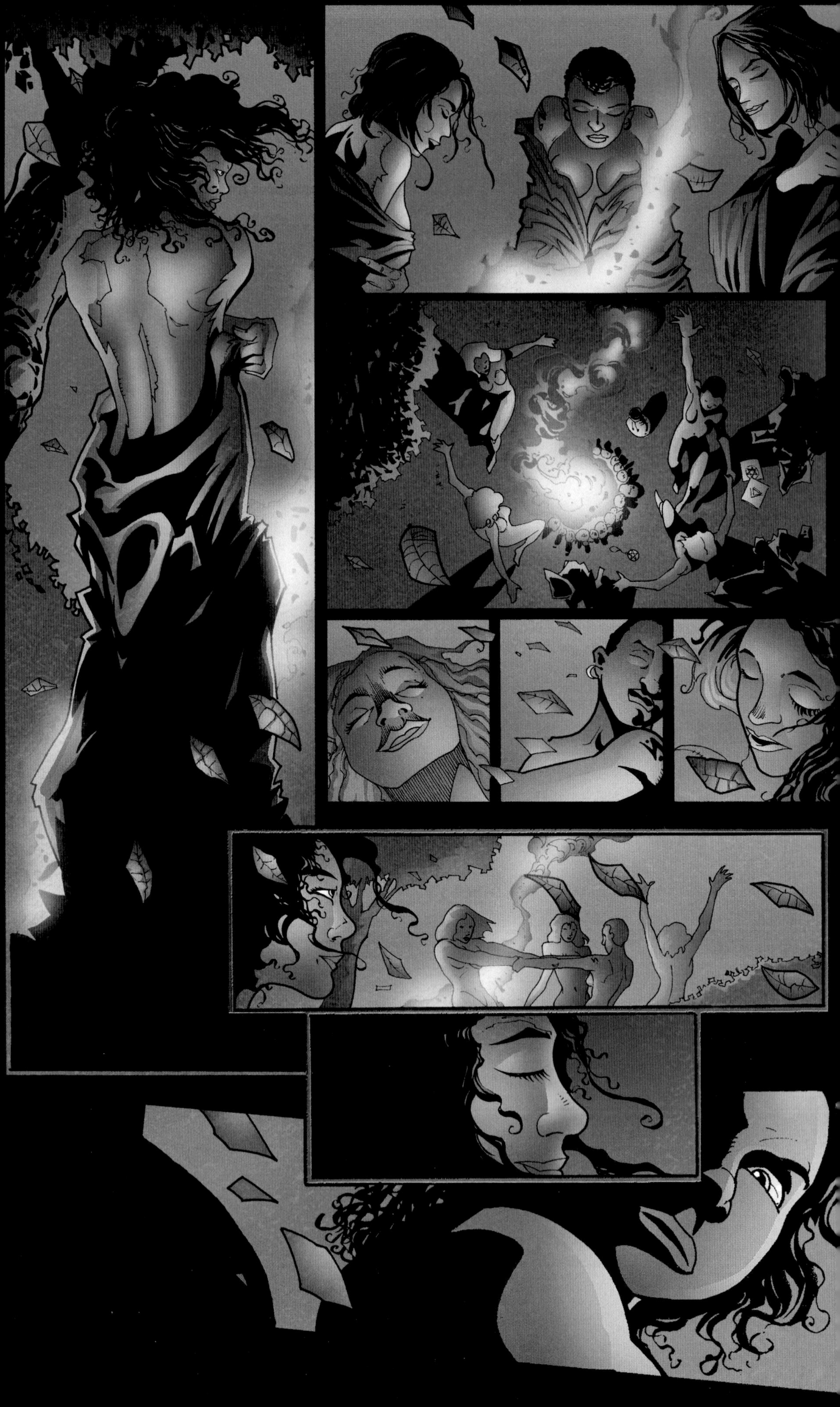

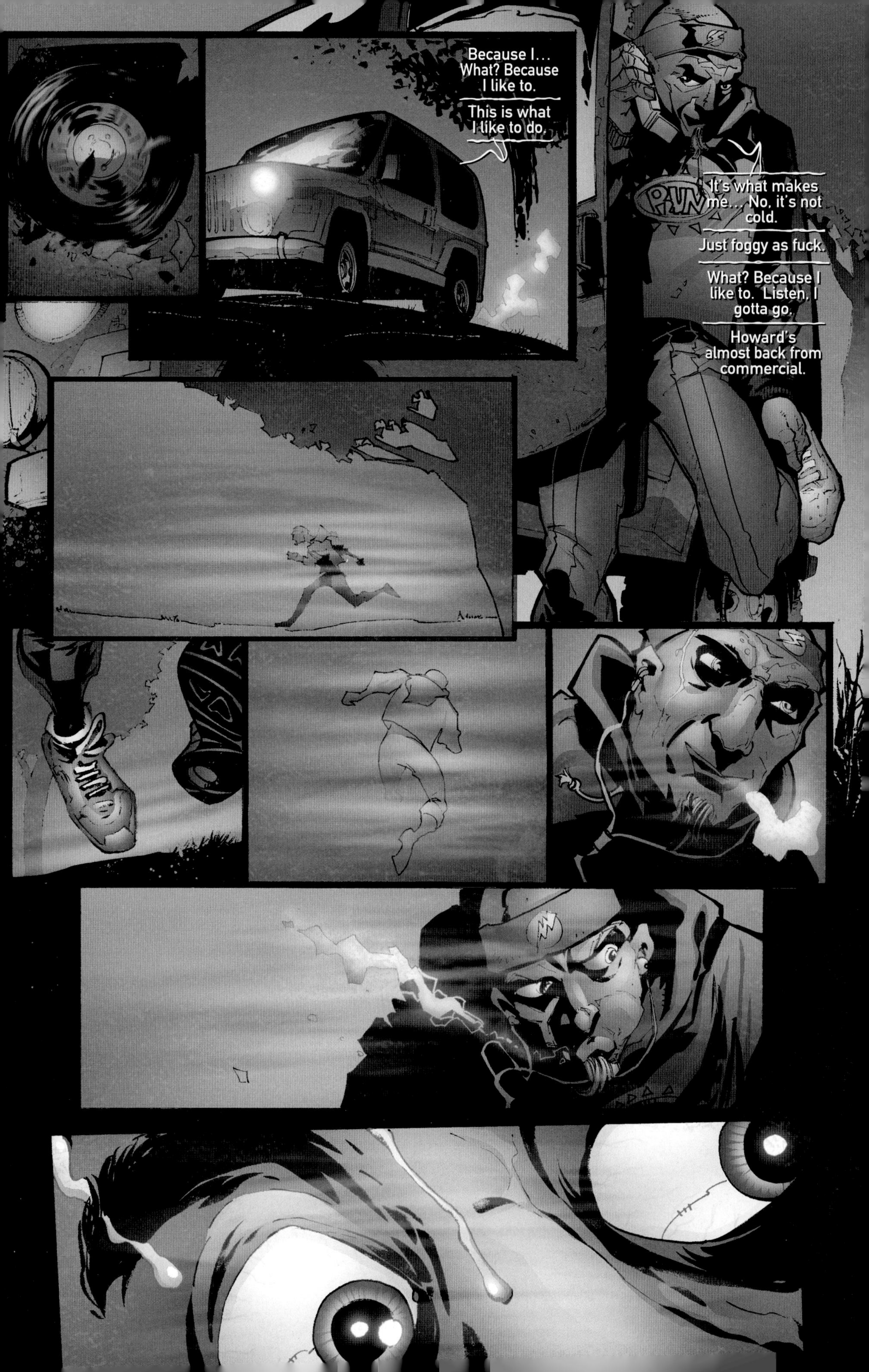
Because I… What? Because I like to.
This is what I like to do.
It's what makes me… No, it's not cold.
Just foggy as fuck.
What? Because I like to. Listen, I gotta go.
Howard's almost back from commercial.

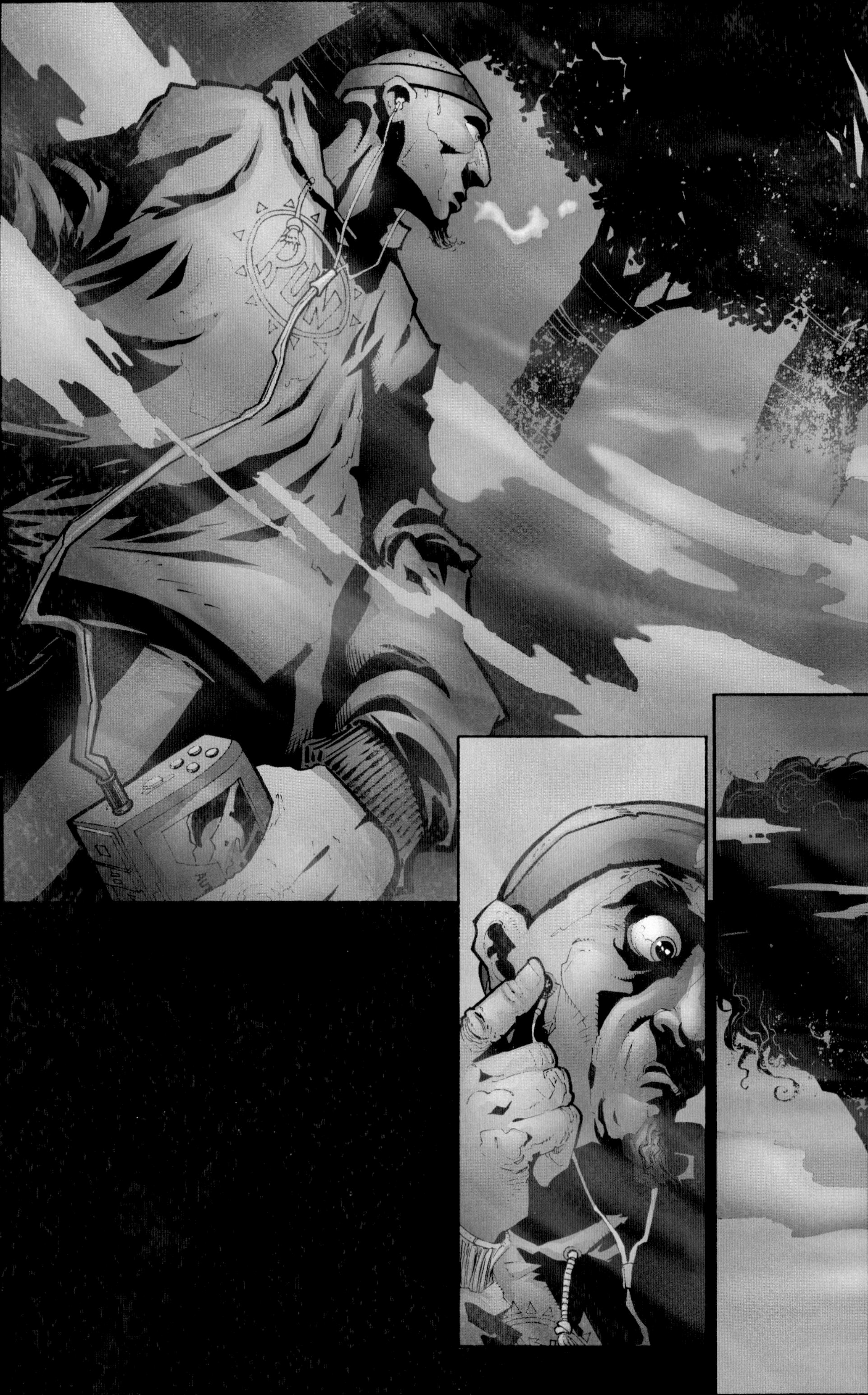

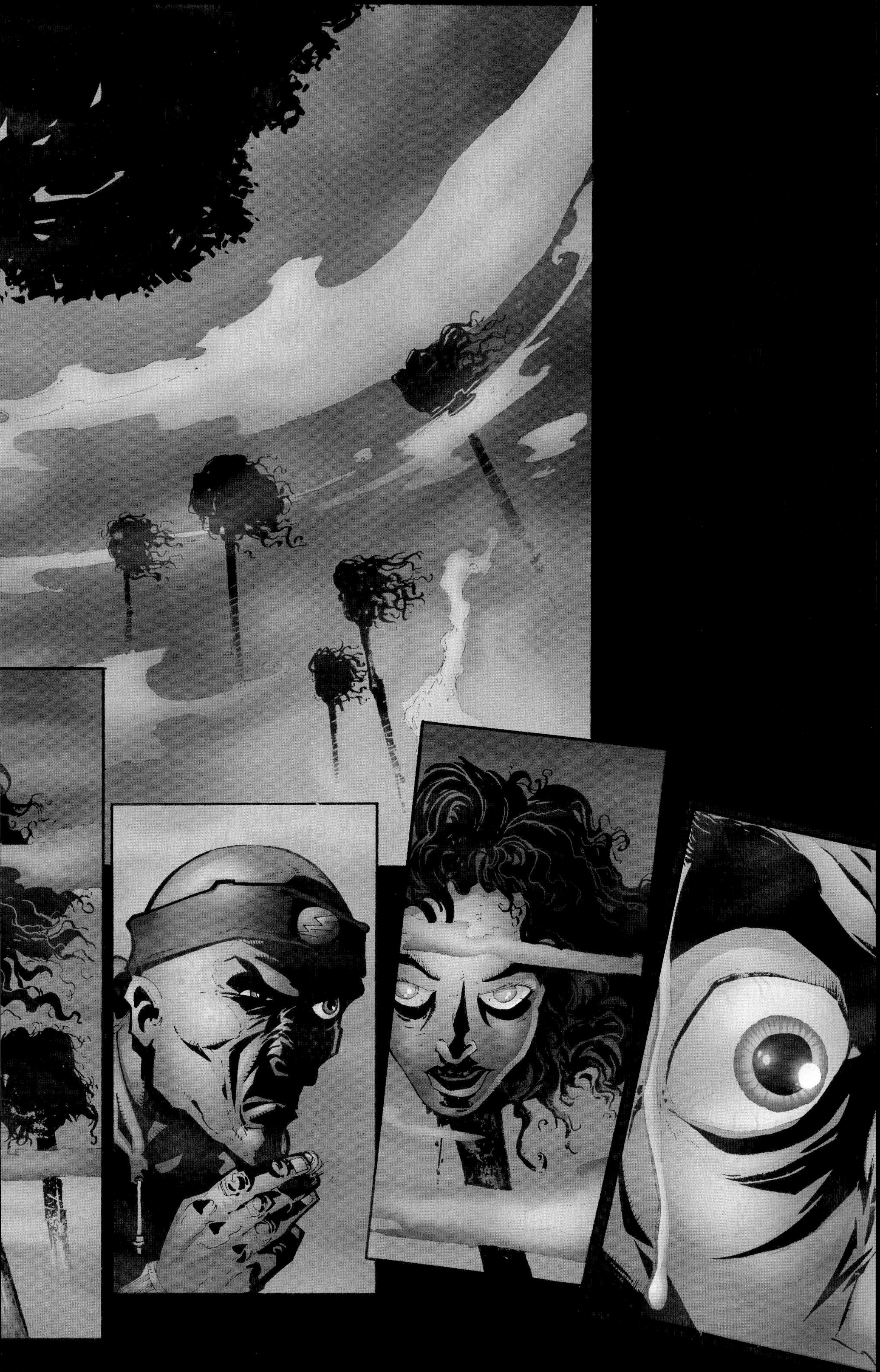

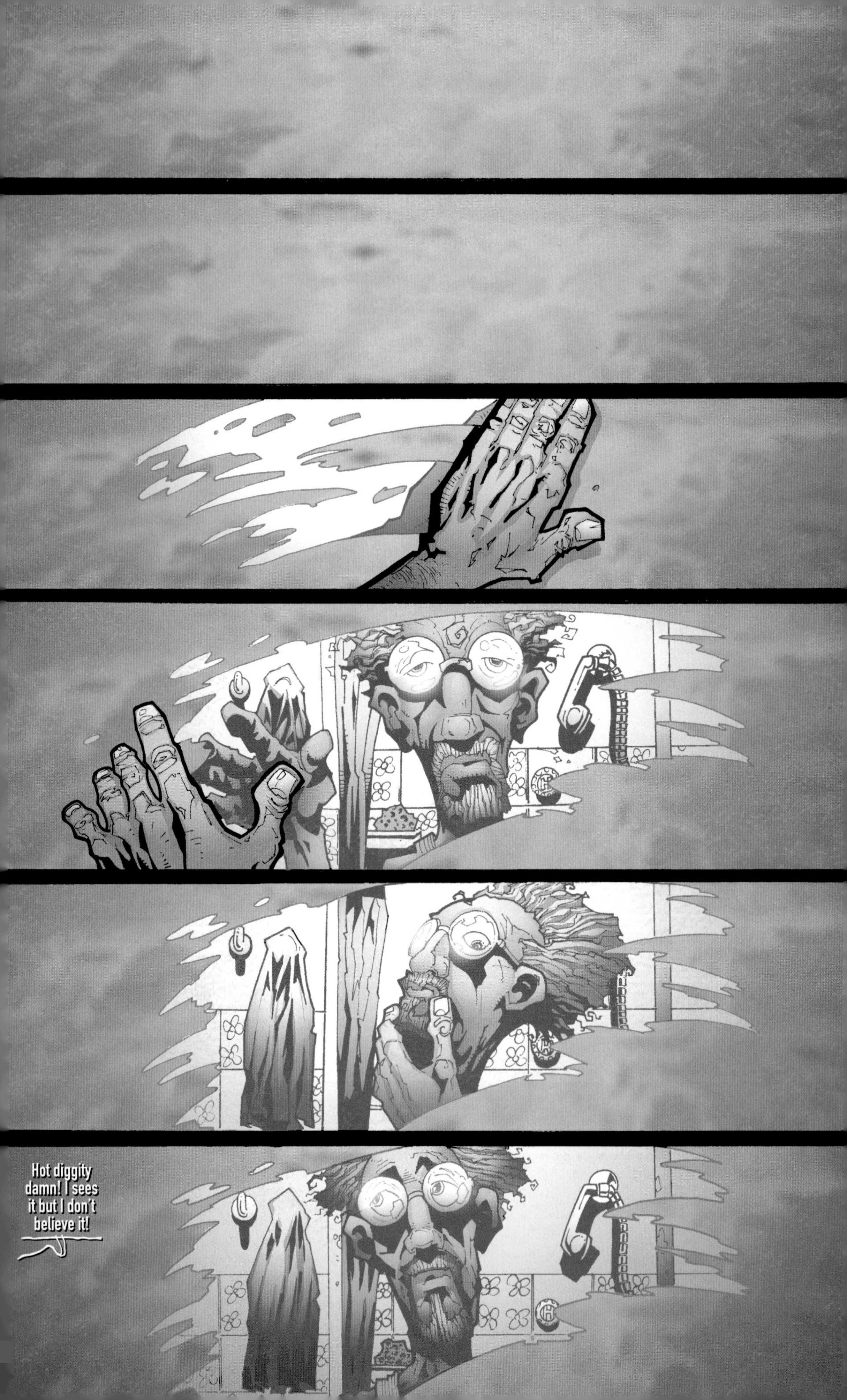
Hot diggity damn! I sees it but I don't believe it!

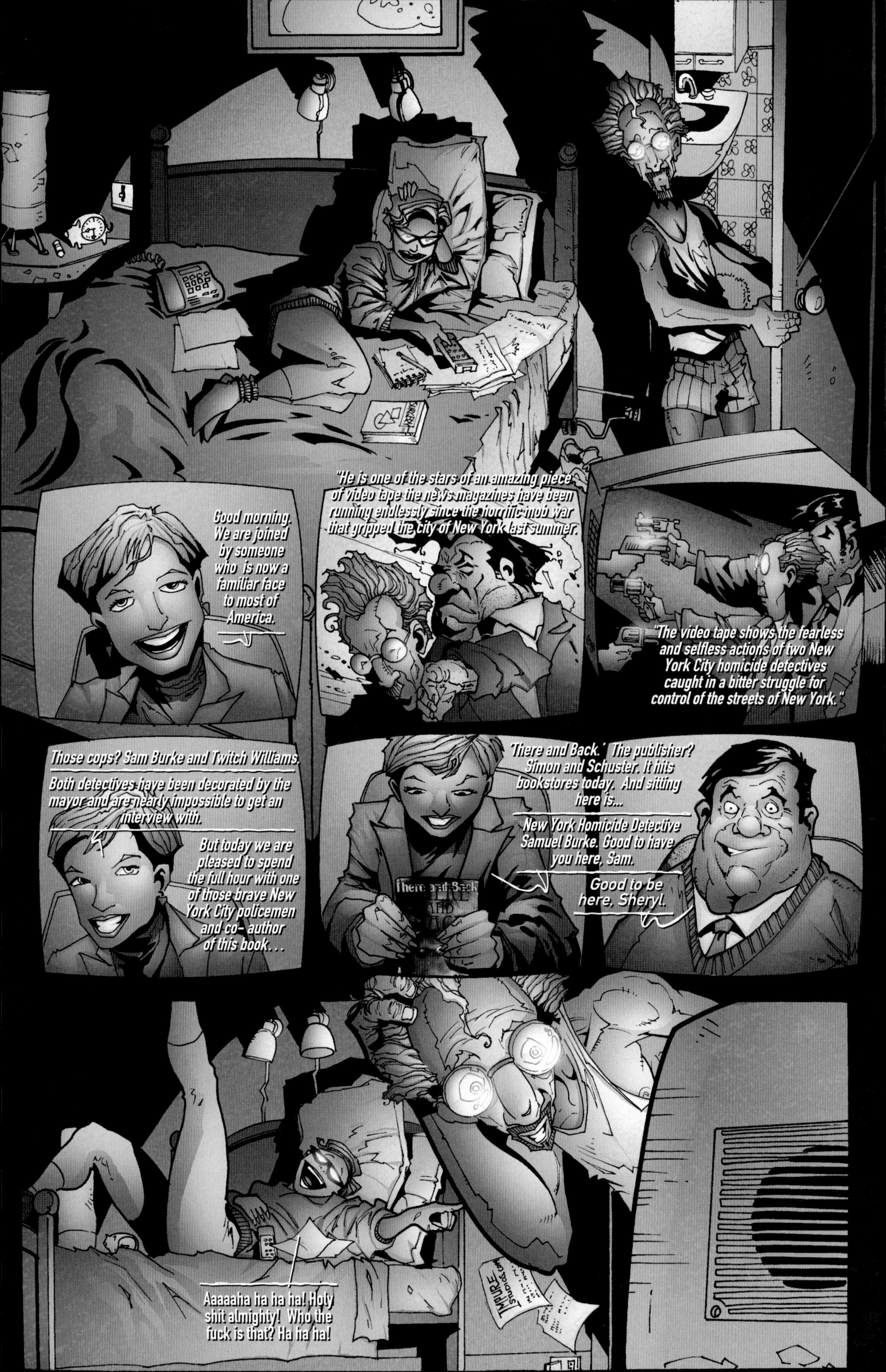
Good morning. We are joined by someone who is now a familiar face to most of America.
"He is one of the stars of an amazing piece of video tape the news magazines have been running endlessly since the horrific mob war that gripped the city of New York last summer.
"The video tape shows the fearless and selfless actions of two New York City homicide detectives caught in a bitter struggle for control of the streets of New York."
Those cops? Sam Burke and Twitch Williams.
Both detectives have been decorated by the mayor and are nearly impossible to get an interview with.
But today we are pleased to spend the full hour with one of those brave New York City policemen and co- author of this book...
'There and Back.' The publisher? Simon and Schuster. It hits bookstores today. And sitting here is...
New York Homicide Detective Samuel Burke. Good to have you here, Sam.
Good to be here, Sheryl.
Aaaaaha ha ha ha! Holy shit almighty! Who the fuck is that? Ha ha ha!

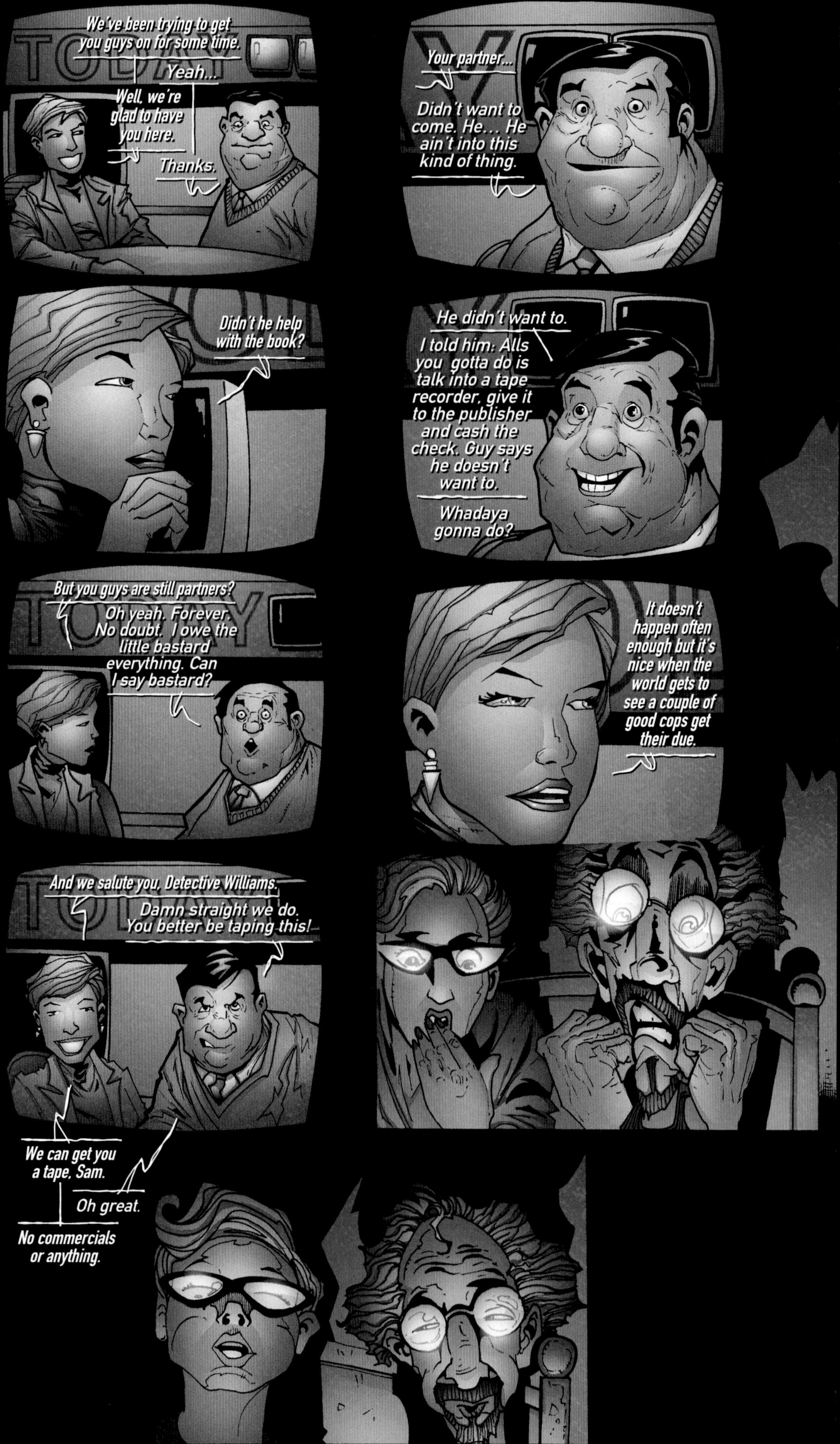
We've been trying to get you guys on for some time.
Yeah...
Well, we're glad to have you here.
Thanks.
Your partner...
Didn't want to come. He... He ain't into this kind of thing.
Didn't he help with the book?
He didn't want to.
I told him: Alls you gotta do is talk into a tape recorder, give it to the publisher and cash the check. Guy says he doesn't want to.
Whadaya gonna do?
But you guys are still partners?
Oh yeah. Forever. No doubt. I owe the little bastard everything. Can I say bastard?
It doesn't happen often enough but it's nice when the world gets to see a couple of good cops get their due.
And we salute you, Detective Williams.
Damn straight we do. You better be taping this!
We can get you a tape, Sam.
Oh great.
No commercials or anything.

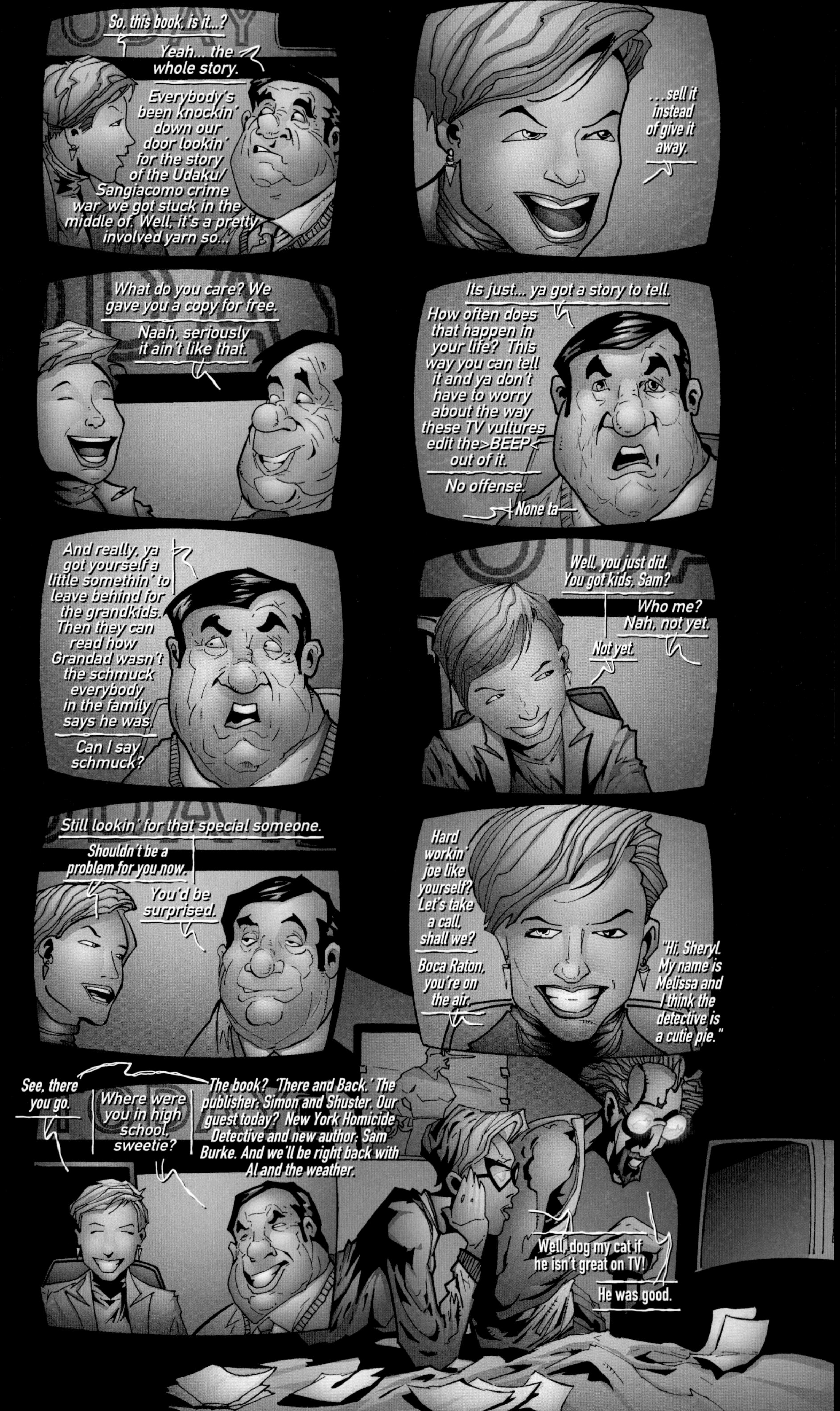

So, this book, is it...?
Yeah... the whole story.
Everybody's been knockin' down our door lookin' for the story of the Udaku/ Sangiacomo crime war we got stuck in the middle of. Well, it's a pretty involved yarn so...
...sell it instead of give it away.
What do you care? We gave you a copy for free.
Naah, seriously it ain't like that.
Its just... ya got a story to tell.
How often does that happen in your life? This way you can tell it and ya don't have to worry about the way these TV vultures edit the>BEEP< out of it.
No offense.
None ta—
And really, ya got yourself a little somethin' to leave behind for the grandkids. Then they can read how Grandad wasn't the schmuck everybody in the family says he was.
Can I say schmuck?
Well, you just did. You got kids, Sam?
Who me? Nah, not yet.
Not yet.
Still lookin' for that special someone.
Shouldn't be a problem for you now.
You'd be surprised.
Hard workin' joe like yourself? Let's take a call, shall we?
Boca Raton, you're on the air.
"Hi, Sheryl. My name is Melissa and I think the detective is a cutie pie."
See, there you go.
Where were you in high school, sweetie?
The book? 'There and Back.' The publisher: Simon and Shuster. Our guest today? New York Homicide Detective and new author: Sam Burke. And we'll be right back with Al and the weather.
Well, dog my cat if he isn't great on TV!
He was good.

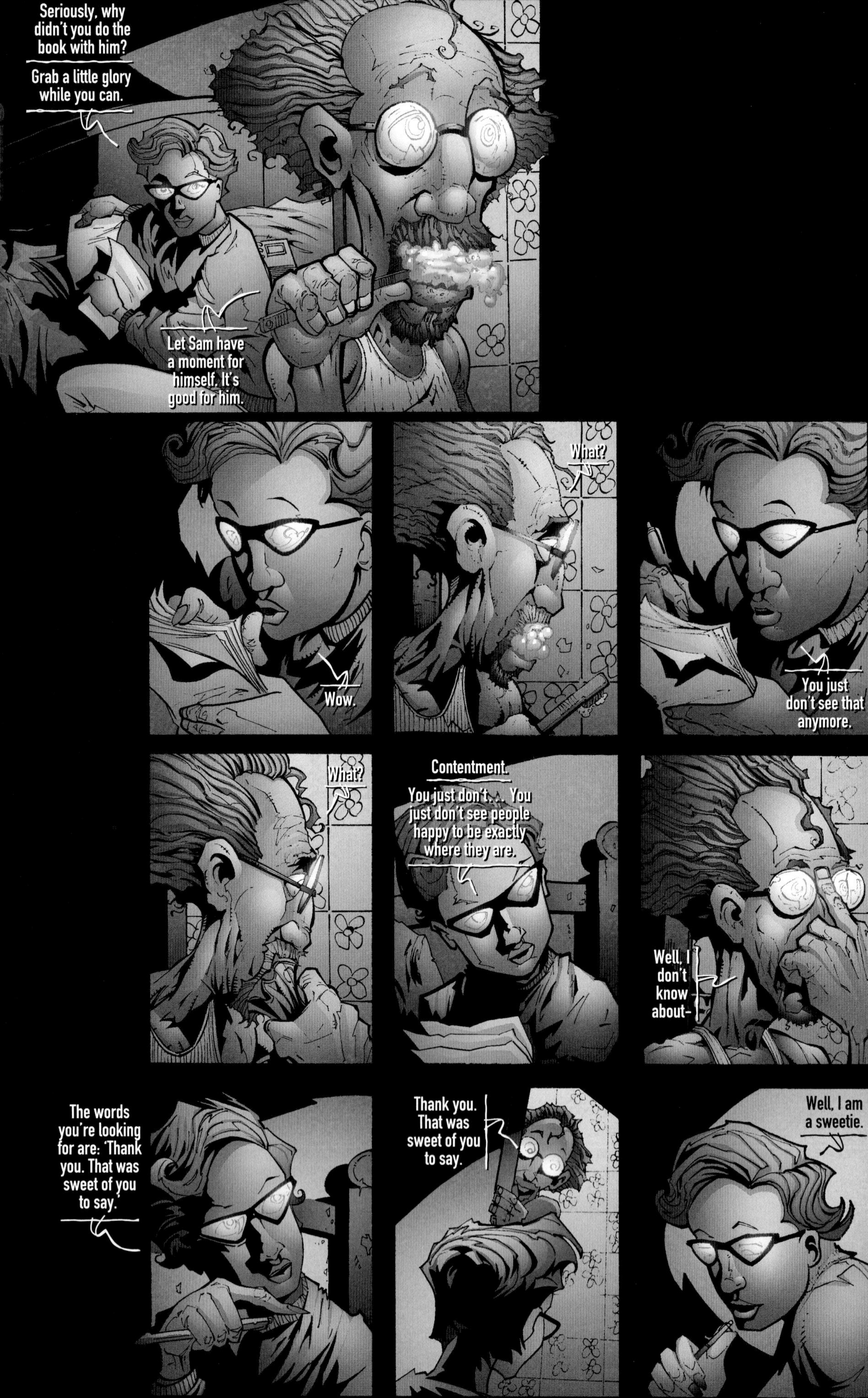
Seriously, why didn't you do the book with him?
Grab a little glory while you can.
Let Sam have a moment for himself. It's good for him.
Wow.
What?
You just don't see that anymore.
What?
Contentment.
You just don't... You just don't see people happy to be exactly where they are.
Well, I don't know about-
The words you're looking for are: 'Thank you. That was sweet of you to say.'
Thank you. That was sweet of you to say.
Well, I am a sweetie.

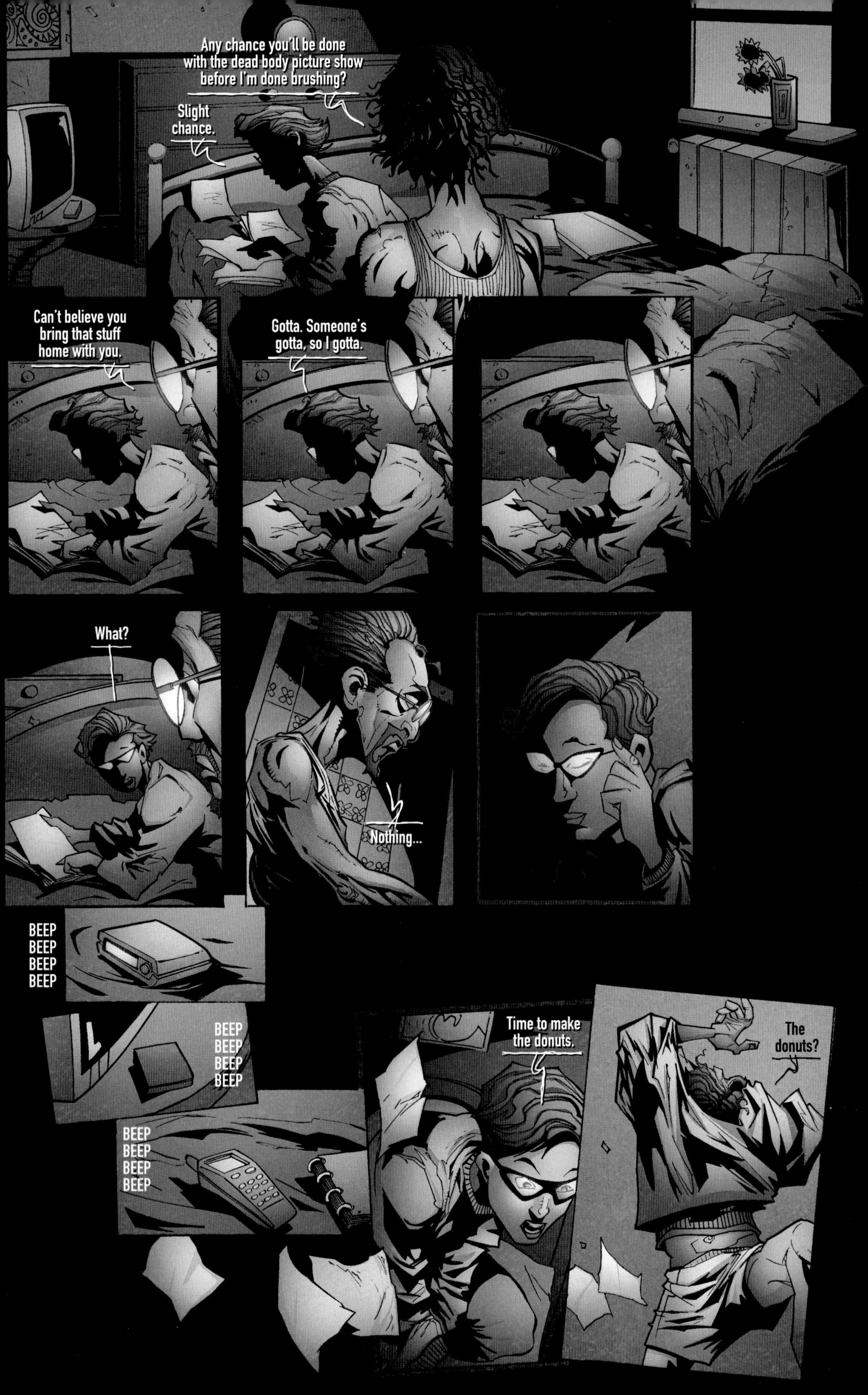
Any chance you'll be done with the dead body picture show before I'm done brushing?
Slight chance.
Can't believe you bring that stuff home with you.
Gotta. Someone's gotta, so I gotta.
What?
Nothing...
BEEP BEEP BEEP BEEP
BEEP BEEP BEEP BEEP
BEEP BEEP BEEP BEEP
Time to make the donuts.
The donuts?

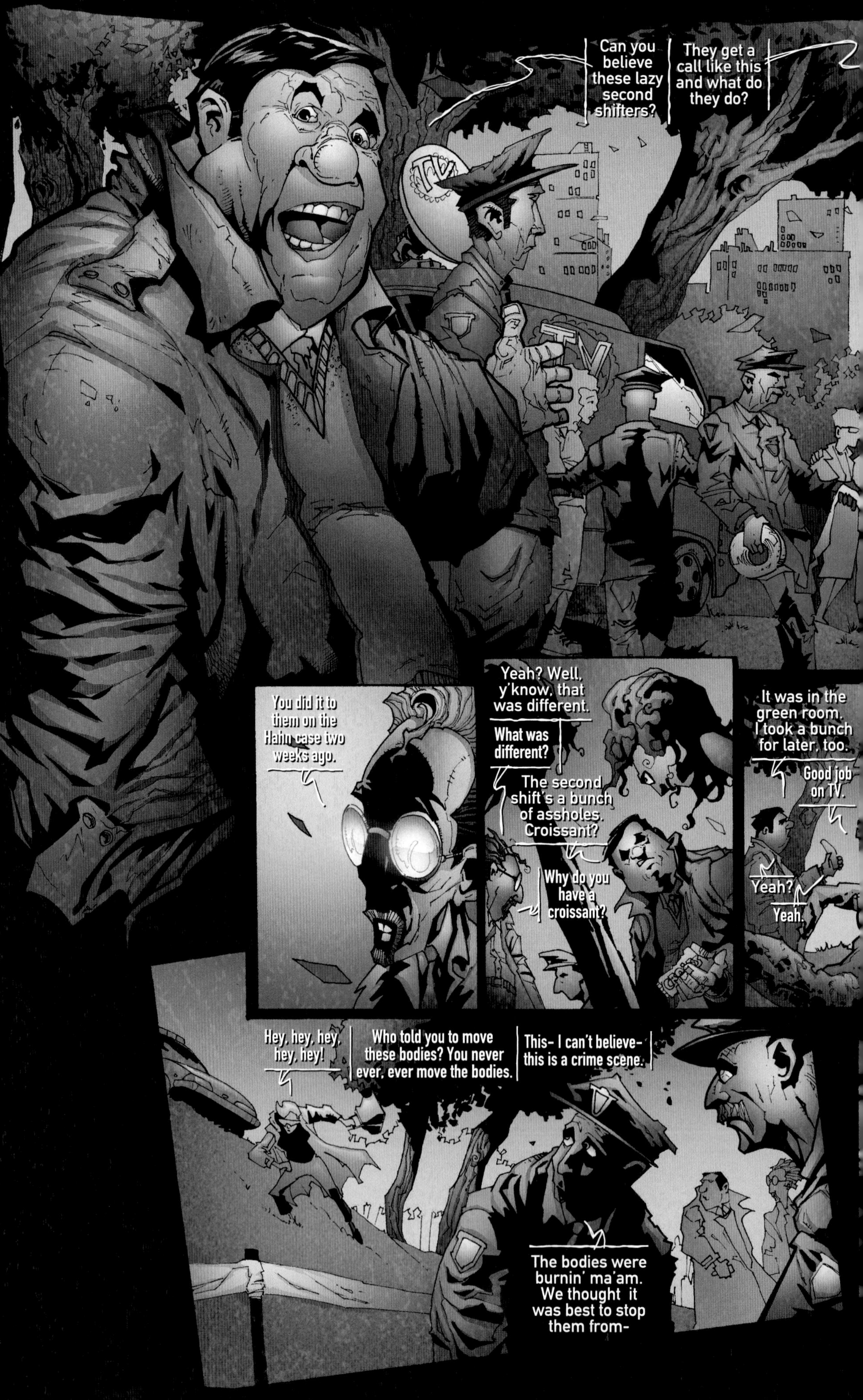
Can you believe these lazy second shifters?
They get a call like this and what do they do?
You did it to them on the Hahn case two weeks ago.
Yeah? Well, y'know, that was different.
What was different?
The second shift's a bunch of assholes. Croissant?
Why do you have a croissant?
It was in the green room. I took a bunch for later, too.
Good job on TV.
Yeah?
Yeah.
Hey, hey, hey, hey, hey!
Who told you to move these bodies? You never ever, ever move the bodies.
This- I can't believe- this is a crime scene.
The bodies were burnin' ma'am. We thought it was best to stop them from-

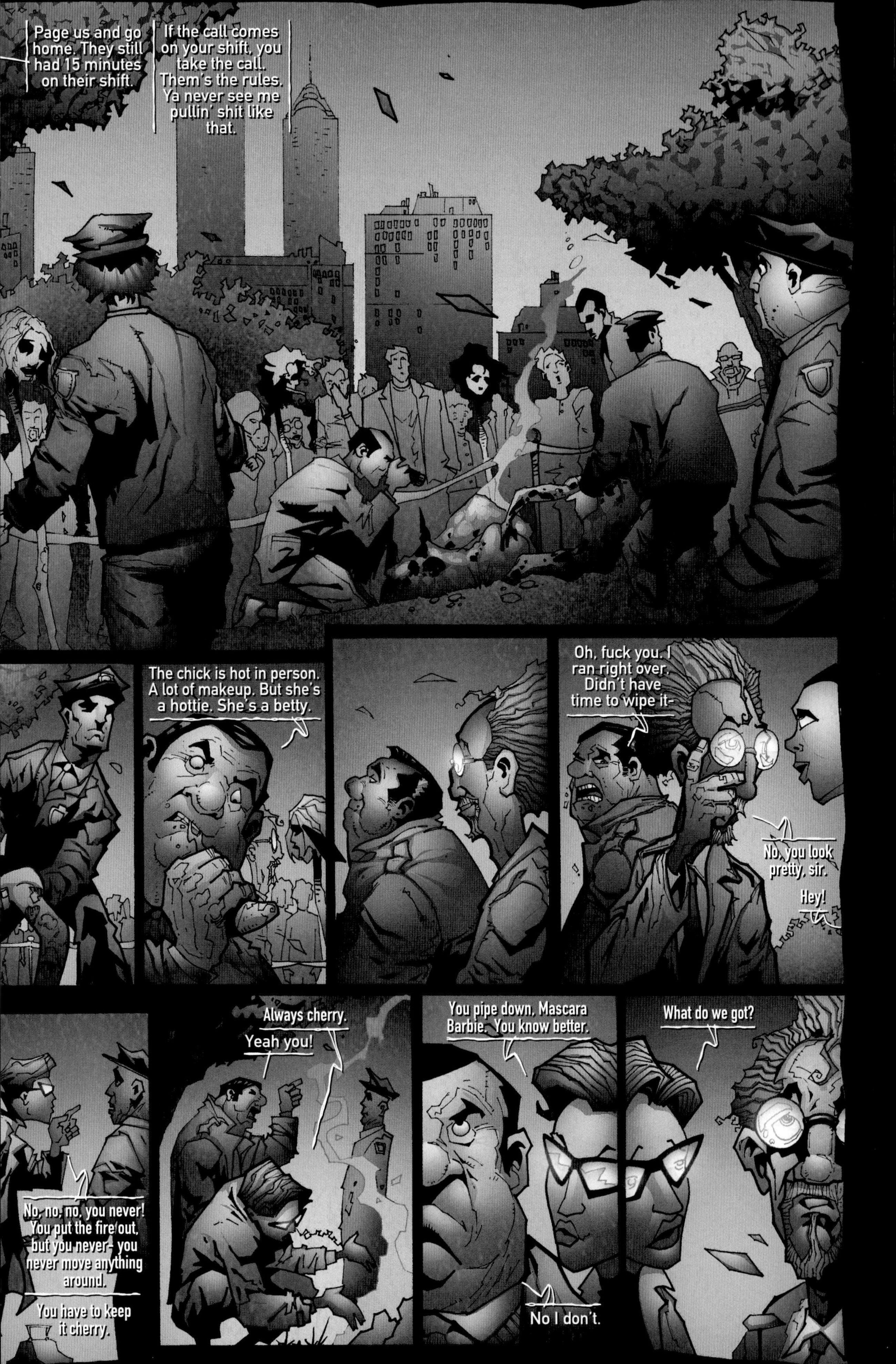

Page us and go home. They still had 15 minutes on their shift.
If the call comes on your shift, you take the call. Them's the rules. Ya never see me pullin' shit like that.
The chick is hot in person. A lot of makeup. But she's a hottie. She's a betty.
Oh, fuck you. I ran right over. Didn't have time to wipe it-
No, you look pretty, sir.
Hey!
No, no, no, you never! You put the fire out, but you never- you never move anything around.
You have to keep it cherry.
Always cherry.
Yeah you!
You pipe down, Mascara Barbie. You know better.
No I don't.
What do we got?

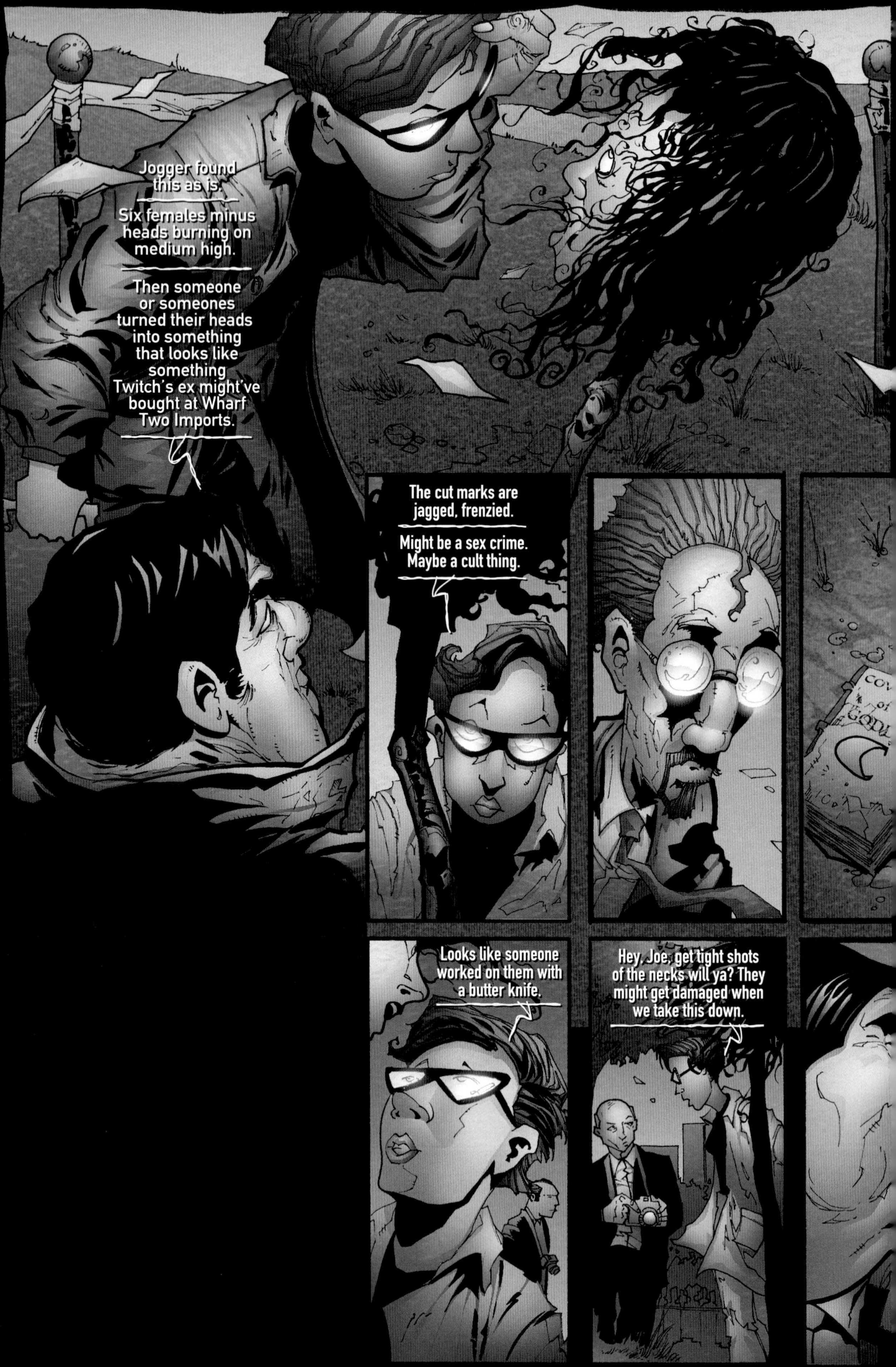
Jogger found this as is.
Six females minus heads burning on medium high.
Then someone or someones turned their heads into something that looks like something Twitch's ex might've bought at Wharf Two Imports.
The cut marks are jagged, frenzied.
Might be a sex crime. Maybe a cult thing.
Looks like someone worked on them with a butter knife.
Hey, Joe, get tight shots of the necks will ya? They might get damaged when we take this down.

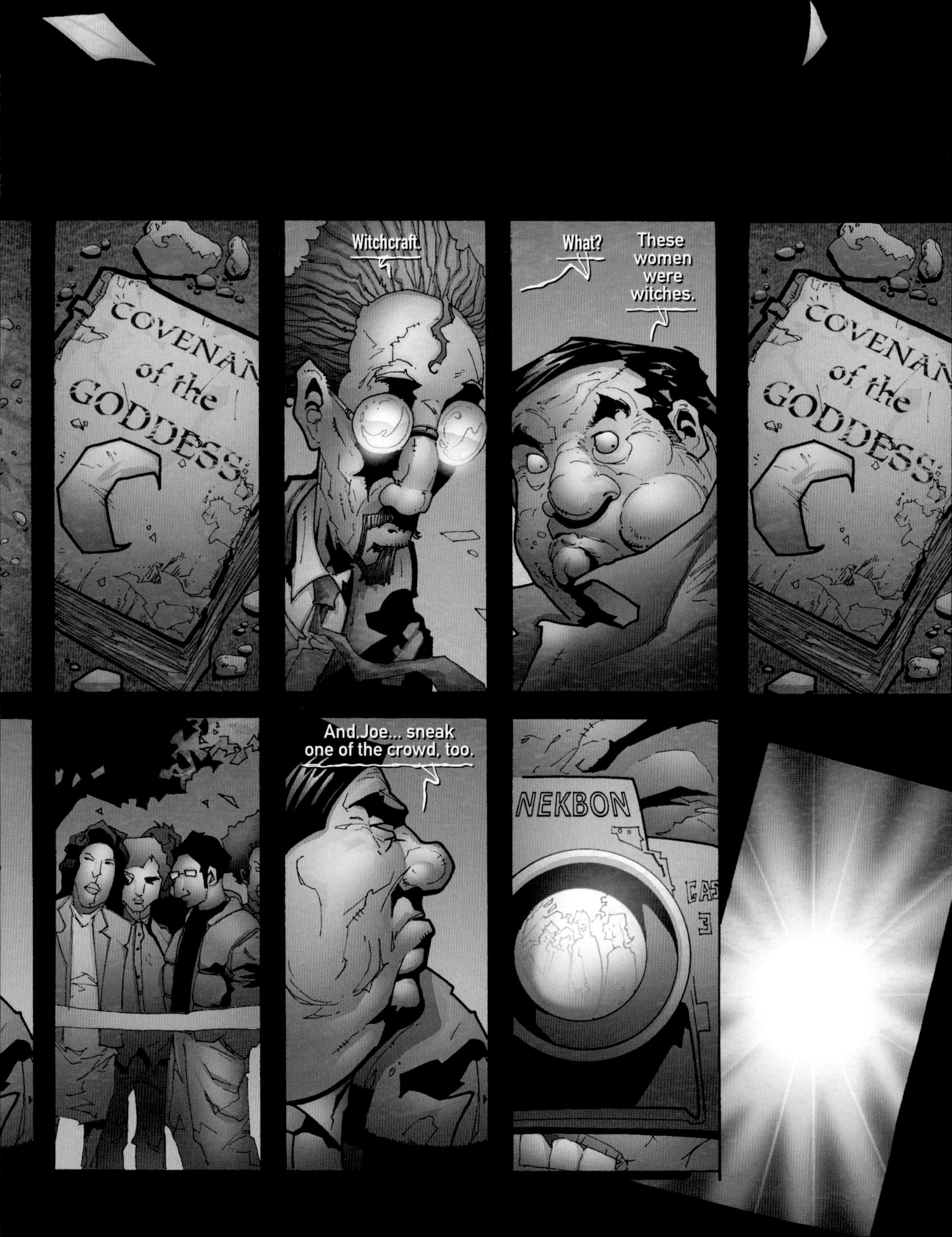
COVENANT of the GODDESS
Witchcraft.
What?
These women were witches.
COVENAN of the GODDESS
And, Joe... sneak one of the crowd, too.
NEKBON

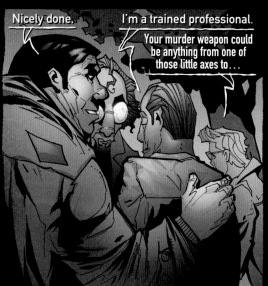

Nicely done.

I'm a trained professional. Your murder weapon could be anything from one of those little axes to...

To one of these?

That- that is a very ornate weapon. We should be able to trace it.

Definitely.

Yes.

"It's not a weapon..."

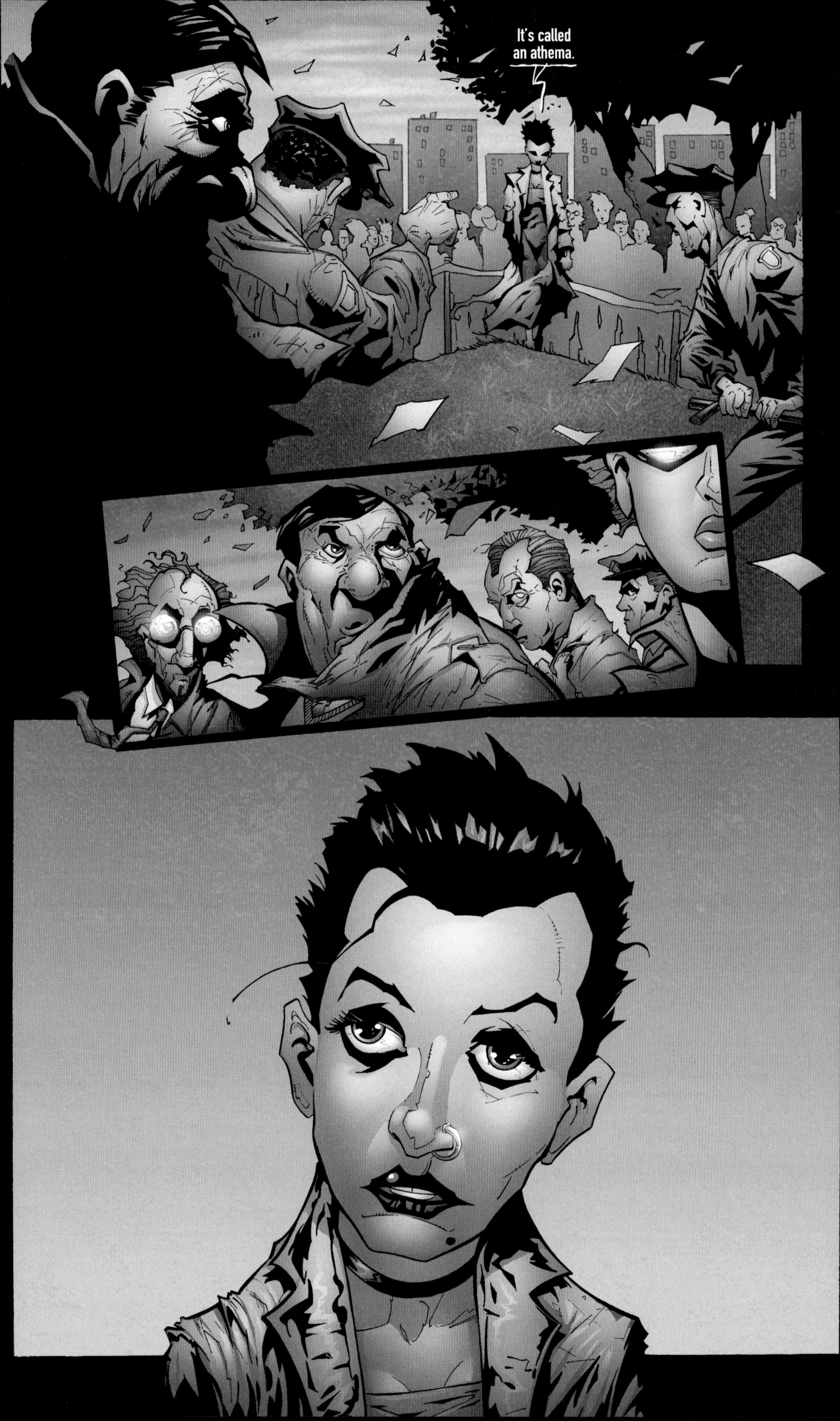
It's called an athema.

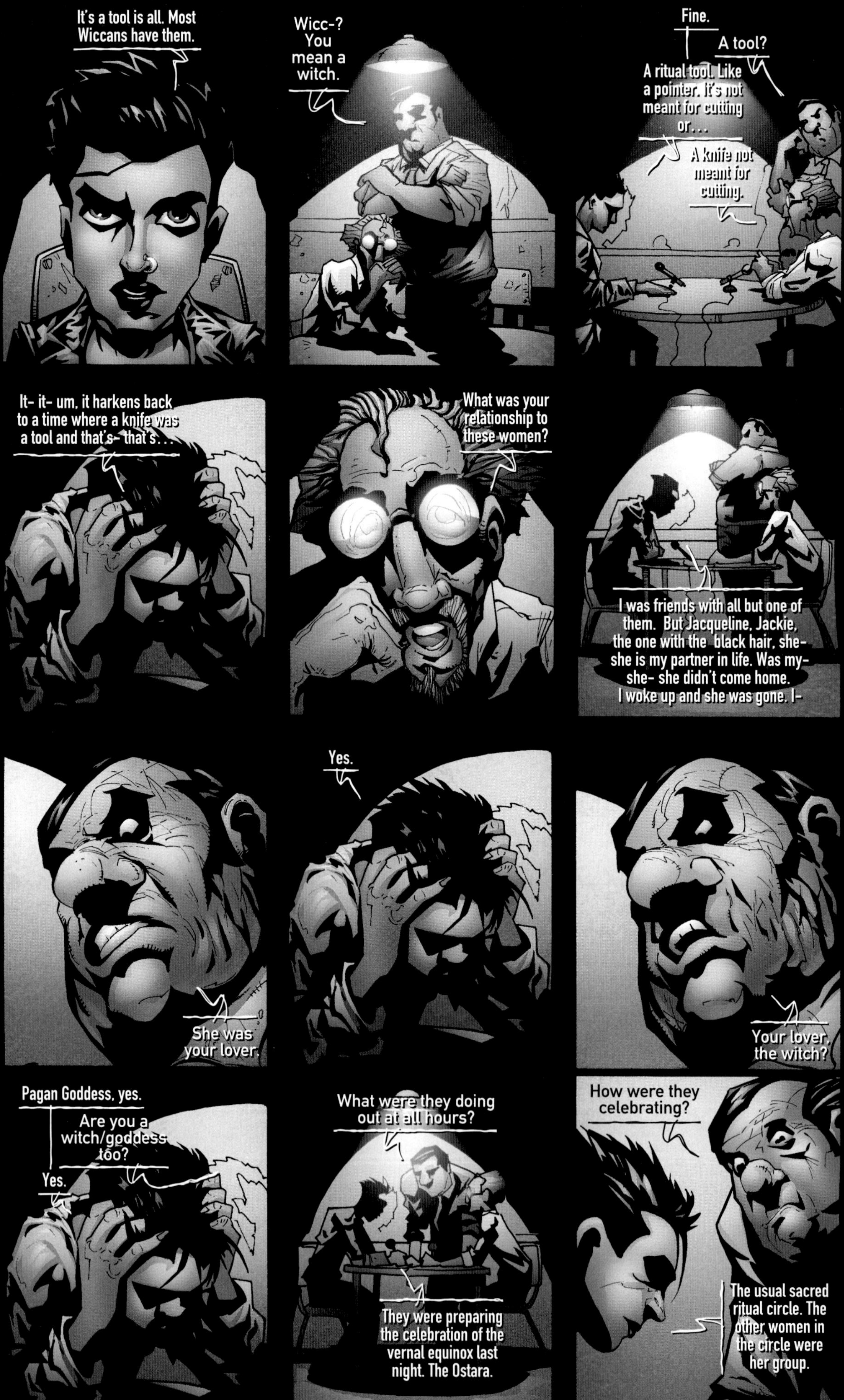
It's a tool is all. Most Wiccans have them.
Wicc-? You mean a witch.
Fine.
A tool?
A ritual tool. Like a pointer. It's not meant for cutting or...
A knife not meant for cutting.
It- it- um, it harkens back to a time where a knife was a tool and that's- that's...
What was your relationship to these women?
I was friends with all but one of them. But Jacqueline, Jackie, the one with the black hair, she- she is my partner in life. Was my- she- she didn't come home. I woke up and she was gone. I-
She was your lover.
Yes.
Your lover, the witch?
Pagan Goddess, yes.
Are you a witch/goddess too?
Yes.
What were they doing out at all hours?
They were preparing the celebration of the vernal equinox last night. The Ostara.
How were they celebrating?
The usual sacred ritual circle. The other women in the circle were her group.

They were doing this in the middle of the park?

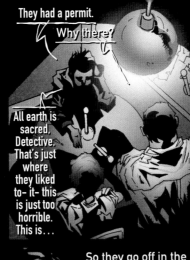

They had a permit.

Why there?

All earth is sacred, Detective. That's just where they liked to- it- this is just too horrible. This is...

I'm sorry to have to ask you these questions now, but it's important for us to-

I understand.

So they go off in the middle of the night and what are they doing; roasting marshmallows or...?

Oh, Goddess, please- please try to be respectful. He is-

Well, I just don't understand.

They went to celebrate. They- they celebrate and practice their magic.

Their magic? Uh huh.

What kind of- black magic or..?

It's- no. It's nothing like that. It's pagan. It's our belief system. It's a religion, OK?

Hey, you're the one that said magic.

It's not what you think. It's- it's-

What is it?

Can't you- I can't even think straight. Jackie she's- oh...

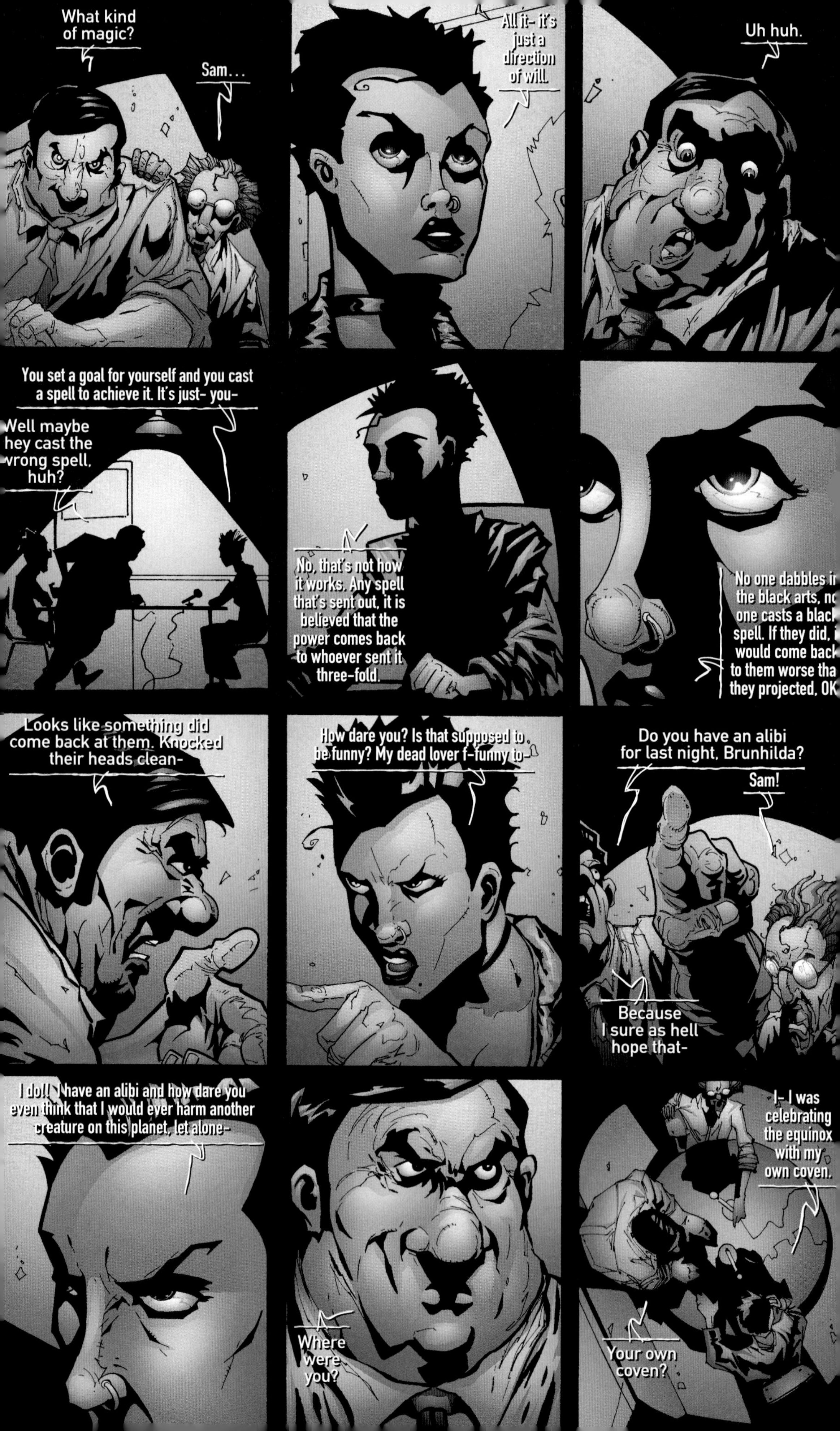
What kind of magic?
Sam...
All it- it's just a direction of will.
Uh huh.
You set a goal for yourself and you cast a spell to achieve it. It's just- you-
Well maybe hey cast the vrong spell, huh?
No, that's not how it works. Any spell that's sent out, it is believed that the power comes back to whoever sent it three-fold.
No one dabbles in the black arts, no one casts a black spell. If they did, it would come back to them worse than they projected, OK
Looks like something did come back at them. Knocked their heads clean-
How dare you? Is that supposed to be funny? My dead lover f-funny to-
Do you have an alibi for last night, Brunhilda?
Sam!
Because I sure as hell hope that-
I do!! I have an alibi and how dare you even think that I would ever harm another creature on this planet, let alone-
Where were you?
I- I was celebrating the equinox with my own coven.
Your own coven?

Yes, yes. We were in the basement of Clementine's on Bleeker. I- I- I can give you the name of everyone that was with me and for how long.

Good. But after?

The phone numbers-

After. I went home with Jennifer who shares- who rooms with us on the Upper West Side.

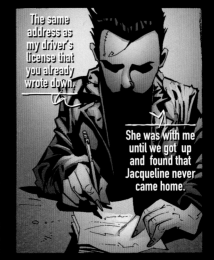

The same address as my driver's license that you already wrote down.

She was with me until we got up and found that Jacqueline never came home.

Why don't you share a coven with Jaqueline? You're so close...

The groups are very personal things. Our groups have different agendas and it just works out better.

Agendas? It's nothing sinister I assure you.

It's- it's just- it's- for you it's like a prayer. It's very intimate.

But you were with this Jennifer-broad instead of with your Jackie-broad?

Oh, God! You asked me for an alibi and I gave you one!!

We're very- we'll check on these alibis.

Yes.

I'm sorry about my partner. These murders are heinous. It must be horrible for you.

I just- who would- how? You see, we- we don't believe in hurting anything. Anything at all. Anything.

We worship the harmony with the Earth and all of life. Who would want to kill someone like that? Who?

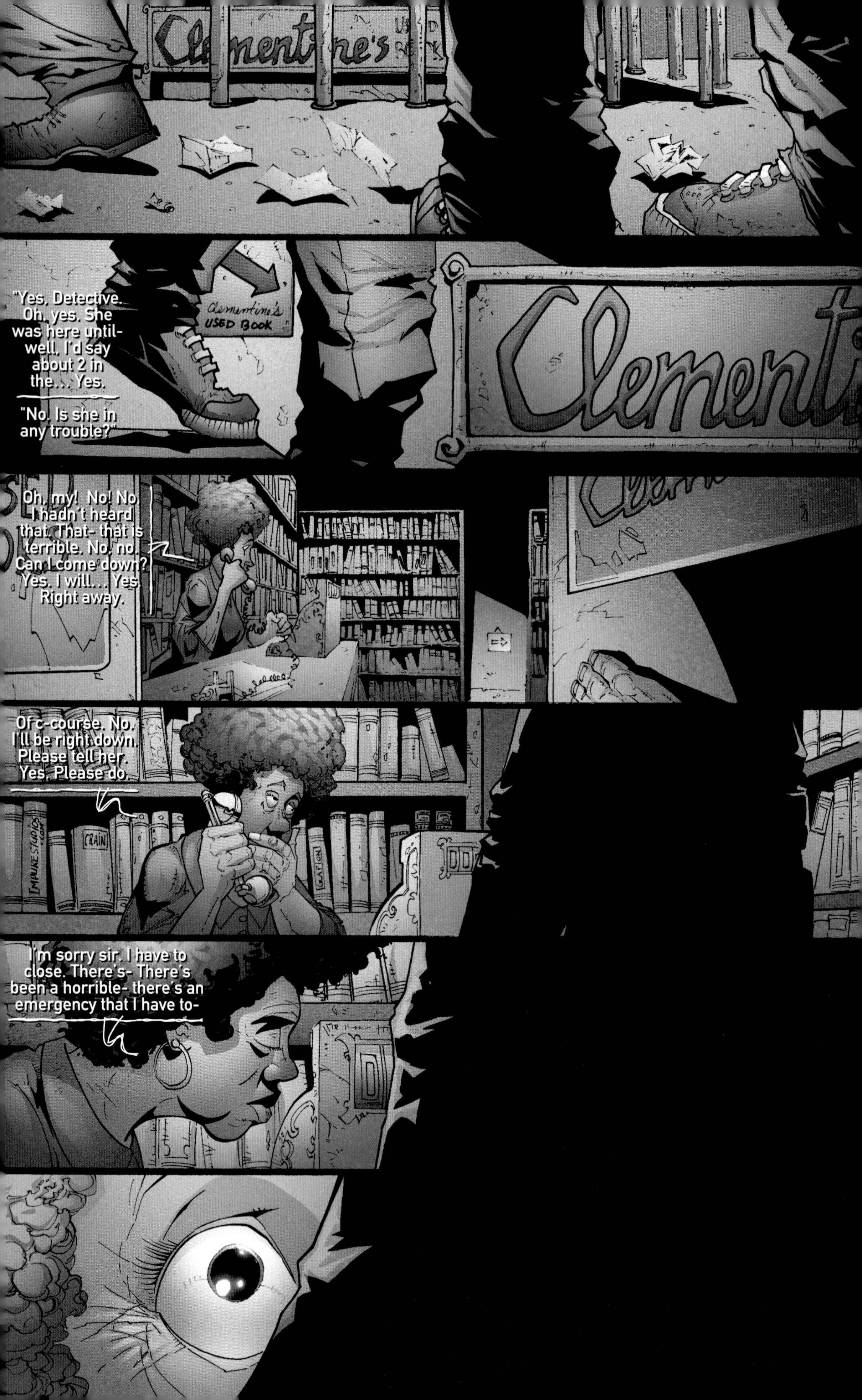
Clementine's
Used Book
Clementine's Used Book
"Yes, Detective. Oh, yes. She was here until- well, I'd say about 2 in the... Yes.
"No. Is she in any trouble?"
Oh, my! No! No. I hadn't heard that. That- that is terrible. No, no. Can I come down? Yes. I will... Yes. Right away.
Of c-course. No. I'll be right down. Please tell her. Yes. Please do.
I'm sorry sir. I have to close. There's- There's been a horrible- there's an emergency that I have to-

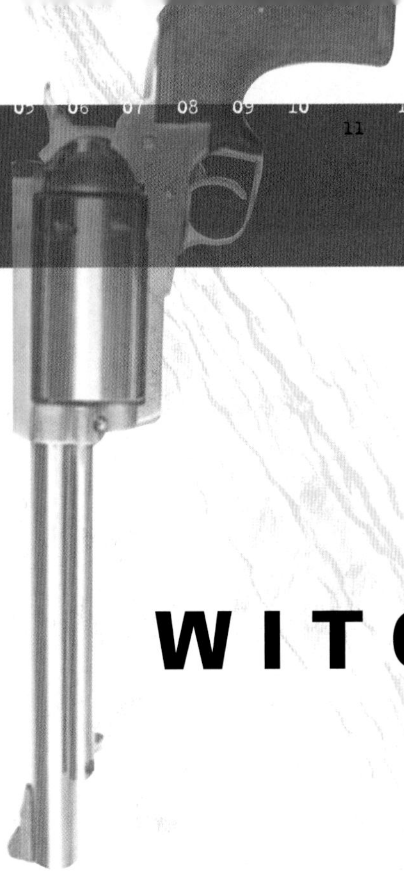

WITCHCRAFT

PART 2

SAM AND TWITCH

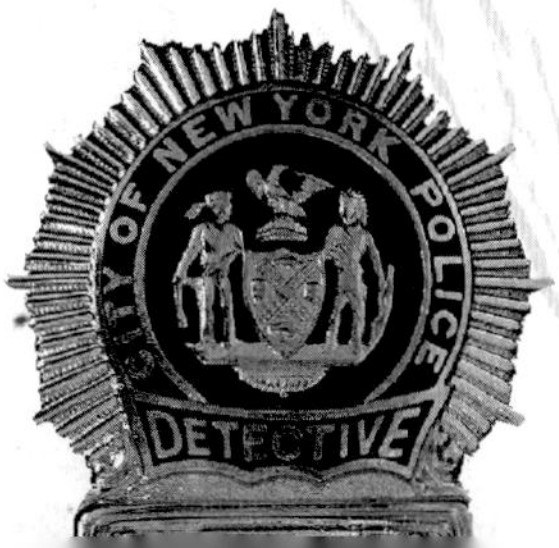
CITY OF NEW YORK POLICE
DETECTIVE

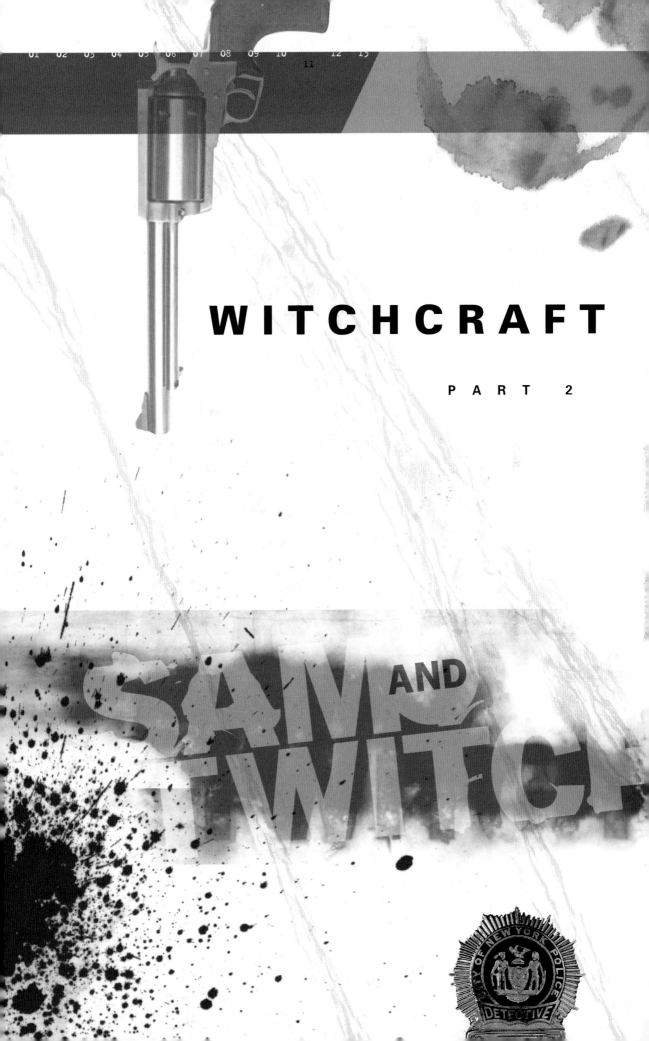

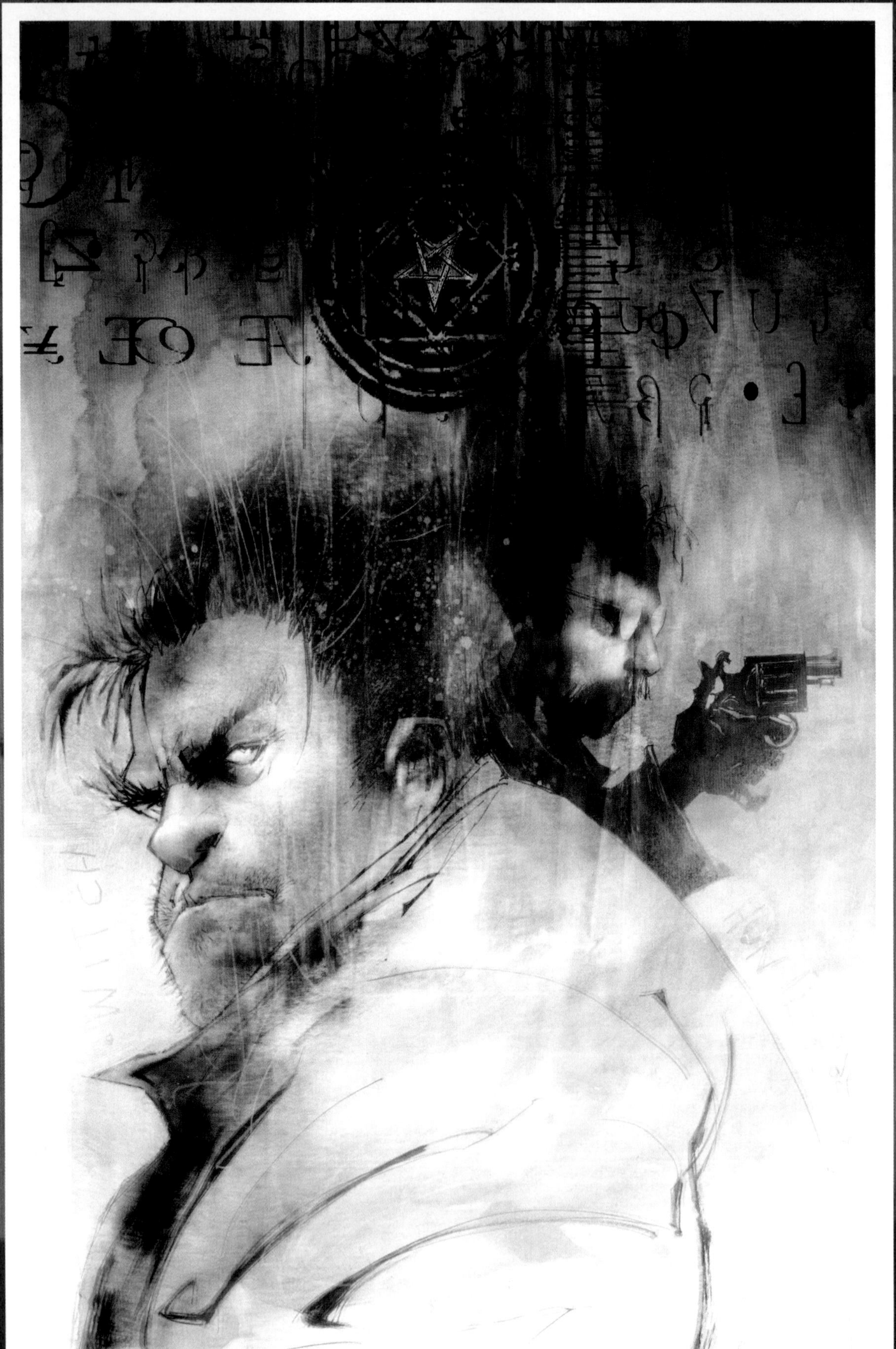

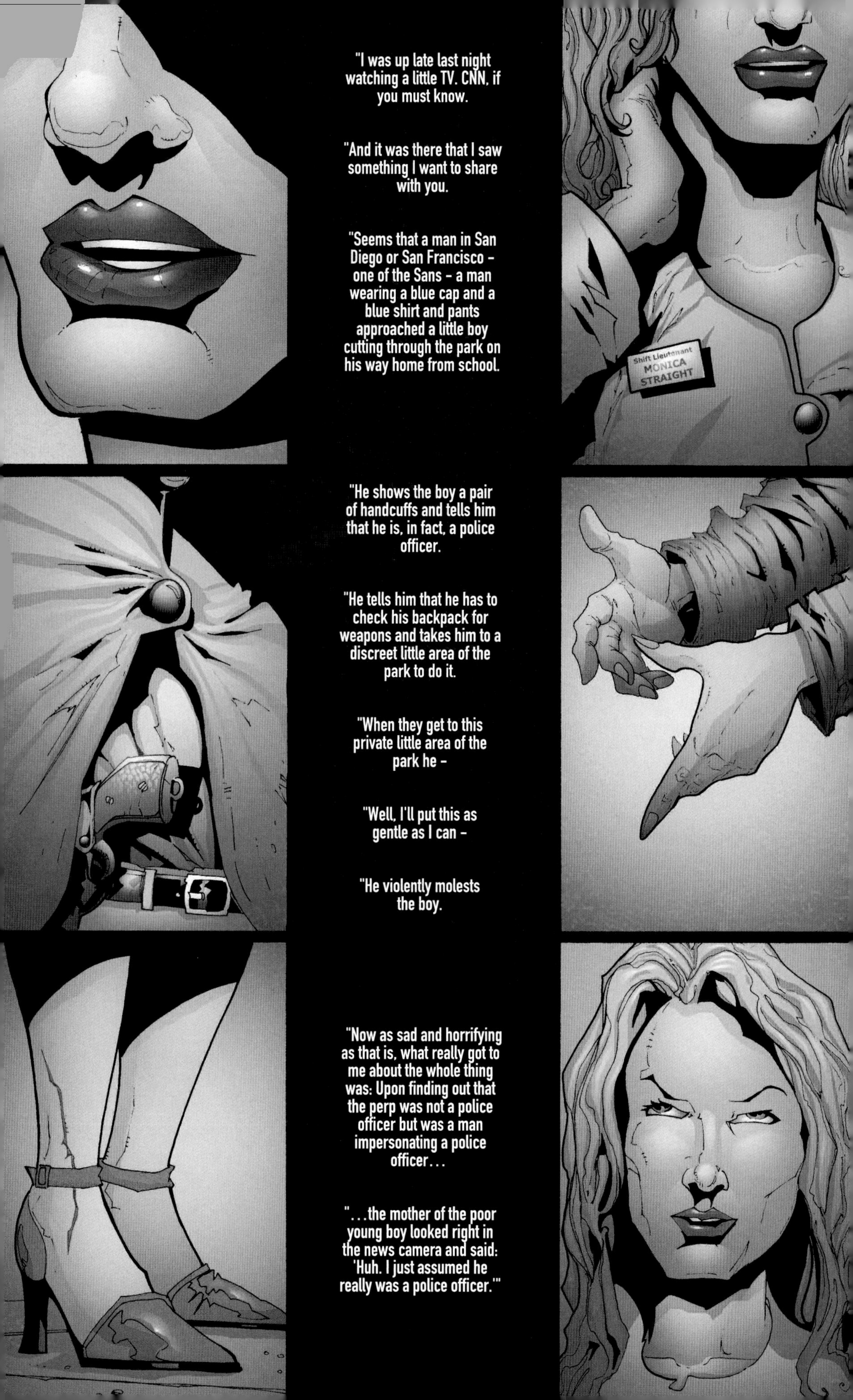
"I was up late last night watching a little TV. CNN, if you must know.
"And it was there that I saw something I want to share with you.
"Seems that a man in San Diego or San Francisco – one of the Sans – a man wearing a blue cap and a blue shirt and pants approached a little boy cutting through the park on his way home from school.
Shift Lieutenant MONICA STRAIGHT
"He shows the boy a pair of handcuffs and tells him that he is, in fact, a police officer.
"He tells him that he has to check his backpack for weapons and takes him to a discreet little area of the park to do it.
"When they get to this private little area of the park he –
"Well, I'll put this as gentle as I can –
"He violently molests the boy.
"Now as sad and horrifying as that is, what really got to me about the whole thing was: Upon finding out that the perp was not a police officer but was a man impersonating a police officer...
"...the mother of the poor young boy looked right in the news camera and said: 'Huh. I just assumed he really was a police officer.'"

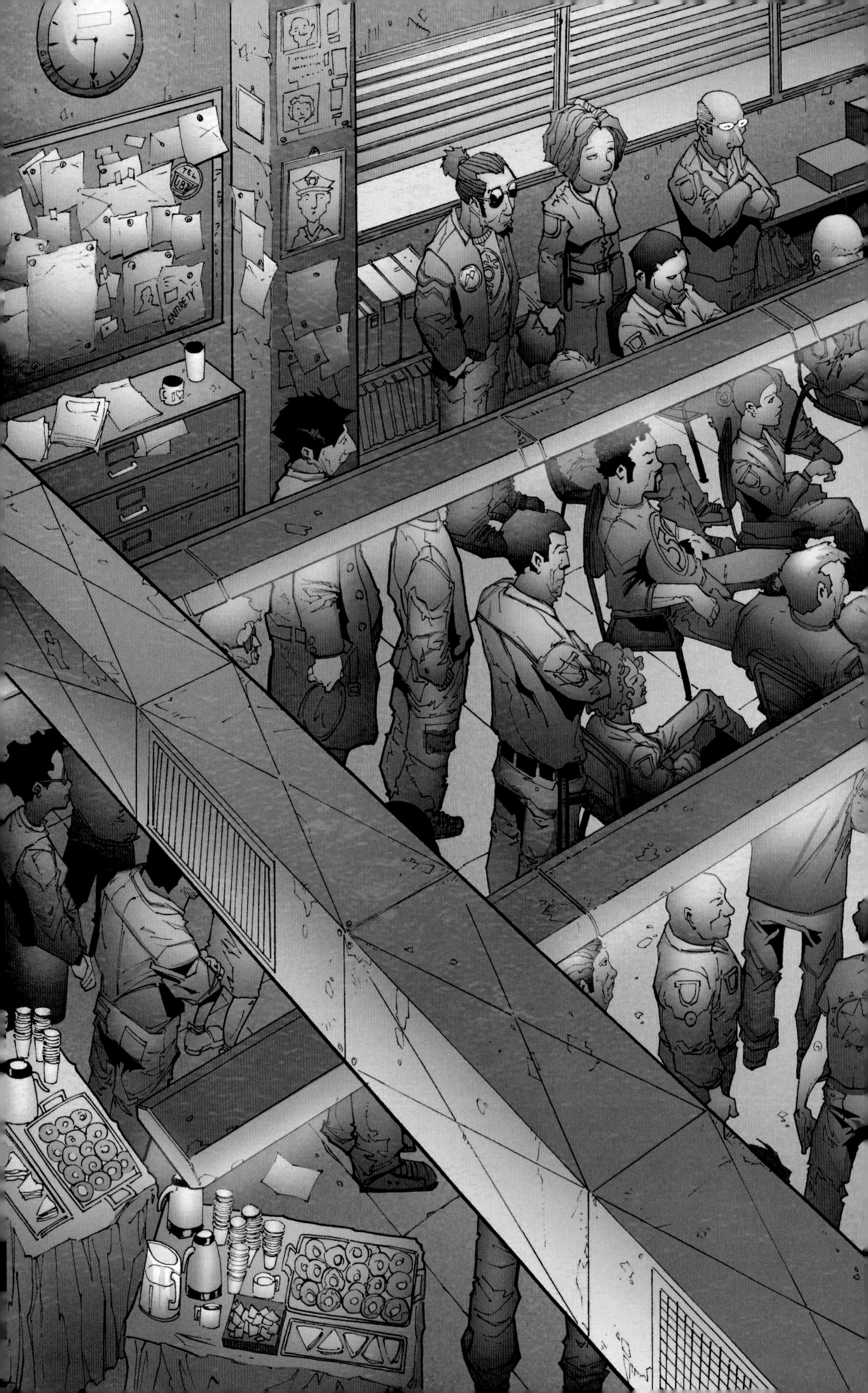

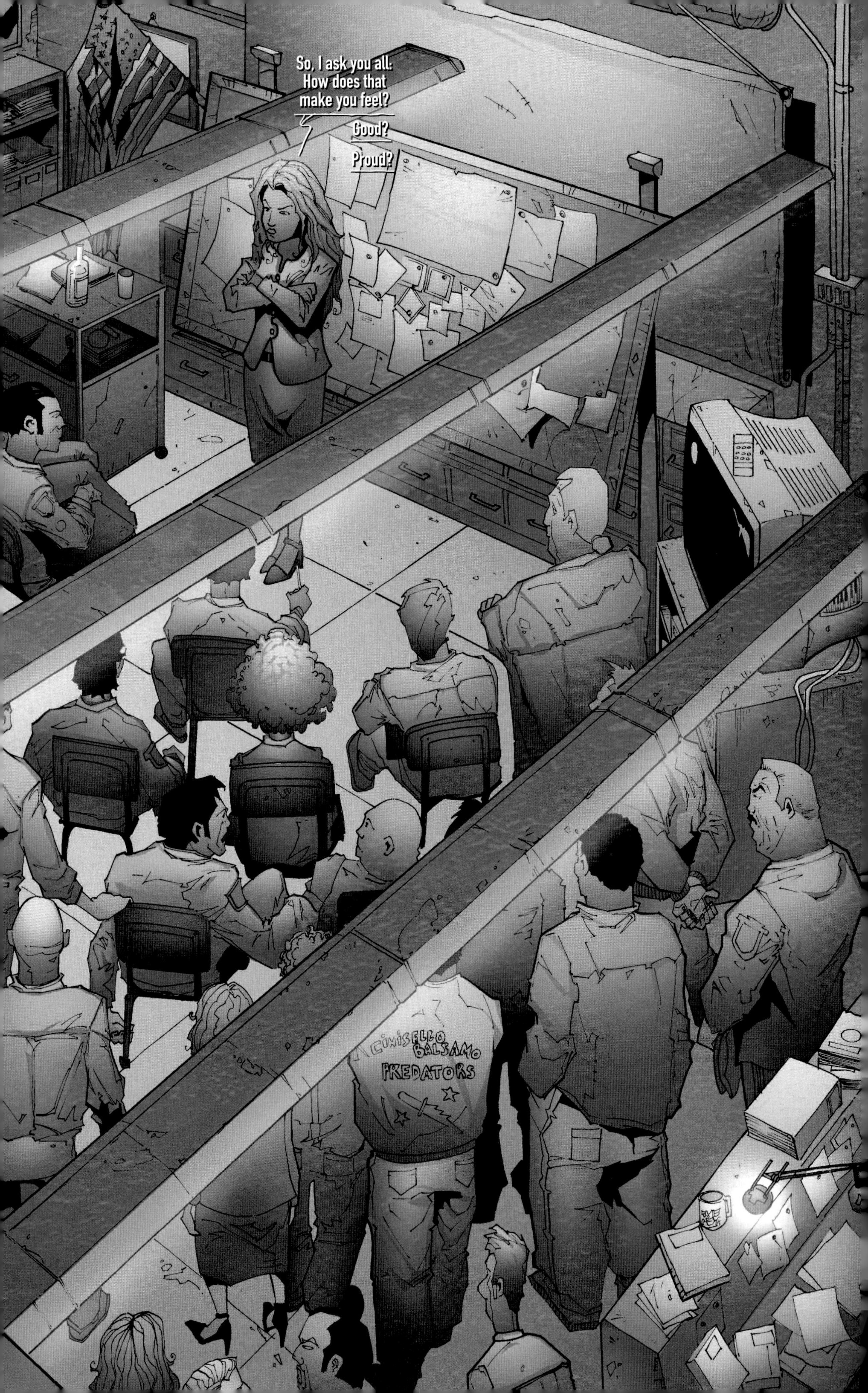
So, I ask you all: How does that make you feel?
Good?
Proud?
CINISELLO BALSAMO
PREDATORS

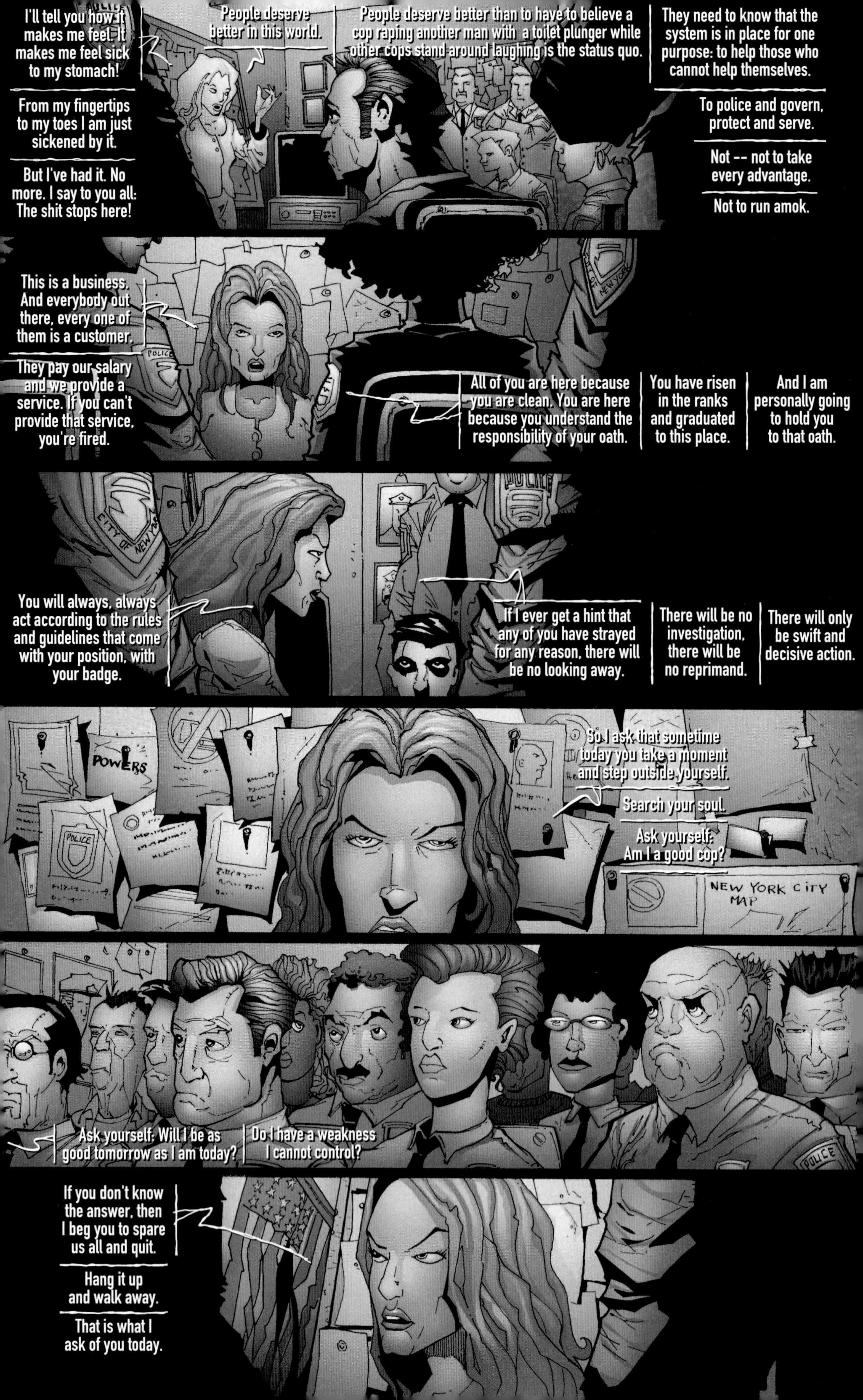
I'll tell you how it makes me feel. It makes me feel sick to my stomach!
From my fingertips to my toes I am just sickened by it.
But I've had it. No more. I say to you all: The shit stops here!
People deserve better in this world.
People deserve better than to have to believe a cop raping another man with a toilet plunger while other cops stand around laughing is the status quo.
They need to know that the system is in place for one purpose: to help those who cannot help themselves.
To police and govern, protect and serve.
Not -- not to take every advantage.
Not to run amok.
This is a business. And everybody out there, every one of them is a customer.
They pay our salary and we provide a service. If you can't provide that service, you're fired.
All of you are here because you are clean. You are here because you understand the responsibility of your oath.
You have risen in the ranks and graduated to this place.
And I am personally going to hold you to that oath.
You will always, always act according to the rules and guidelines that come with your position, with your badge.
If I ever get a hint that any of you have strayed for any reason, there will be no looking away.
There will be no investigation, there will be no reprimand.
There will only be swift and decisive action.
POWERS
POLICE
So I ask that sometime today you take a moment and step outside yourself.
Search your soul.
Ask yourself: Am I a good cop?
NEW YORK CITY MAP
Ask yourself: Will I be as good tomorrow as I am today?
Do I have a weakness I cannot control?
If you don't know the answer, then I beg you to spare us all and quit.
Hang it up and walk away.
That is what I ask of you today.

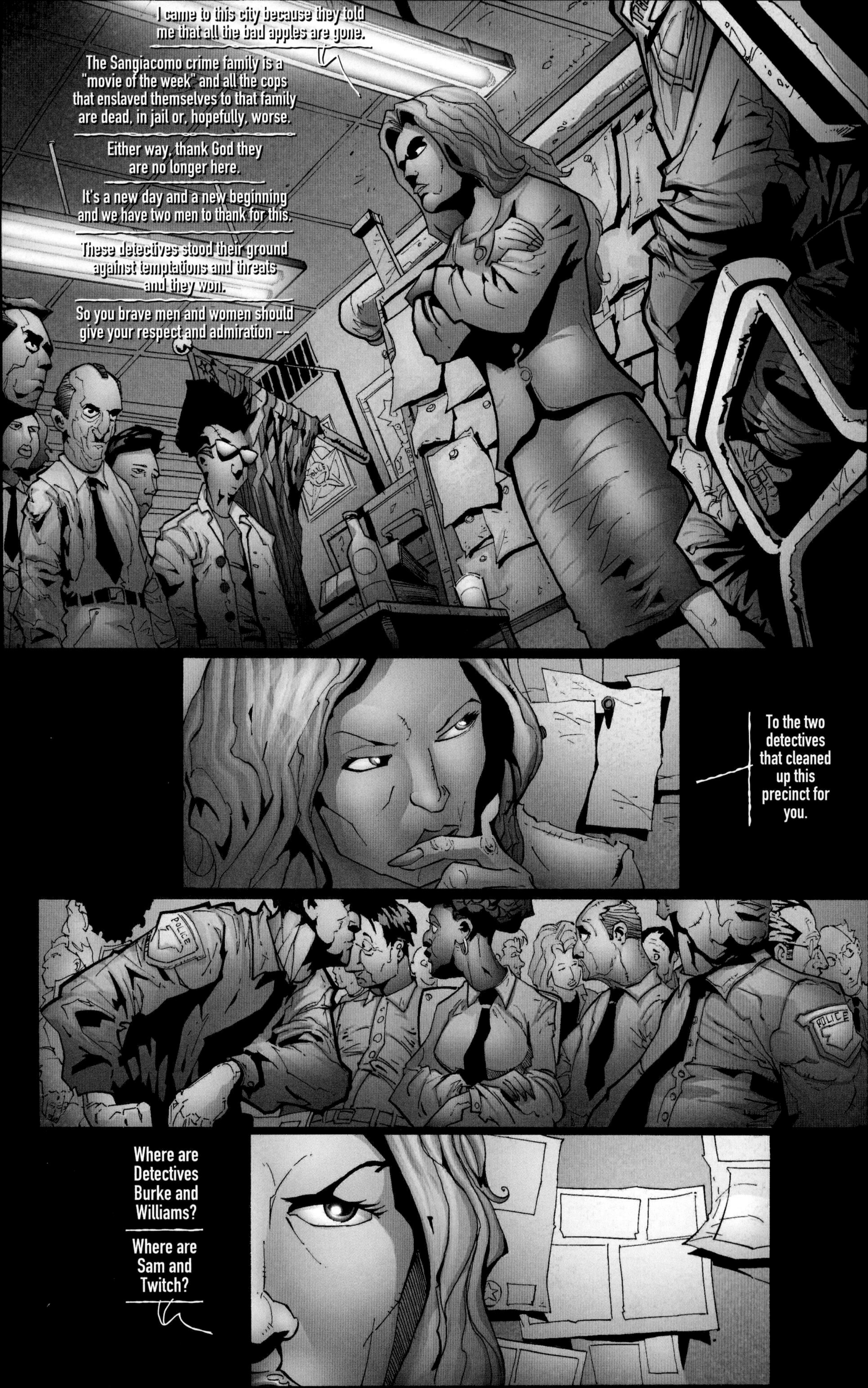
I came to this city because they told me that all the bad apples are gone.
The Sangiacomo crime family is a "movie of the week" and all the cops that enslaved themselves to that family are dead, in jail or, hopefully, worse.
Either way, thank God they are no longer here.
It's a new day and a new beginning and we have two men to thank for this.
These detectives stood their ground against temptations and threats and they won.
So you brave men and women should give your respect and admiration --
To the two detectives that cleaned up this precinct for you.
Where are Detectives Burke and Williams?
Where are Sam and Twitch?

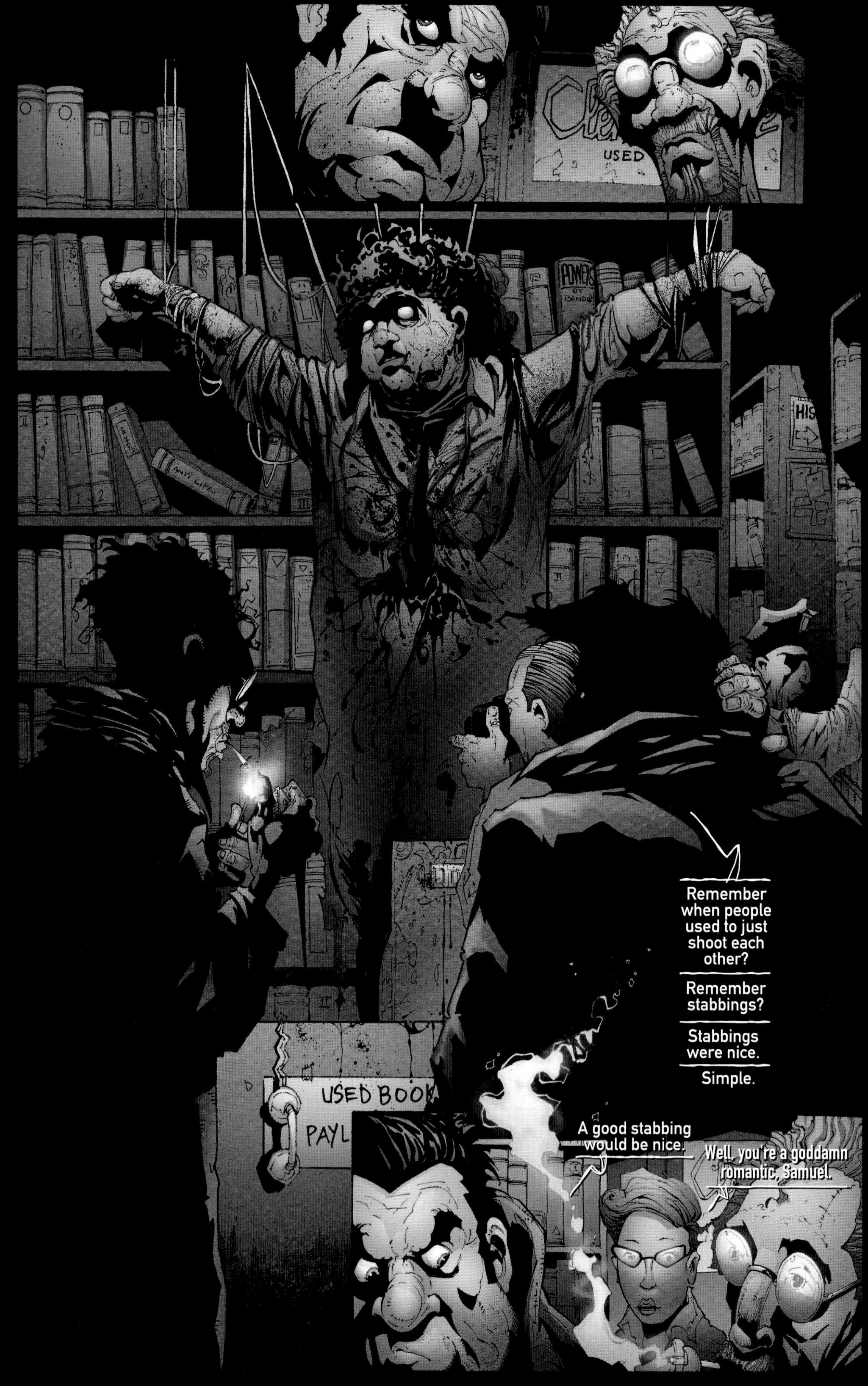

USED
POWERS BY BENDIS
ANTI LIFE
USED BOOK
PAYL
Remember when people used to just shoot each other?
Remember stabbings?
Stabbings were nice.
Simple.
A good stabbing would be nice.
Well, you're a goddamn romantic, Samuel.

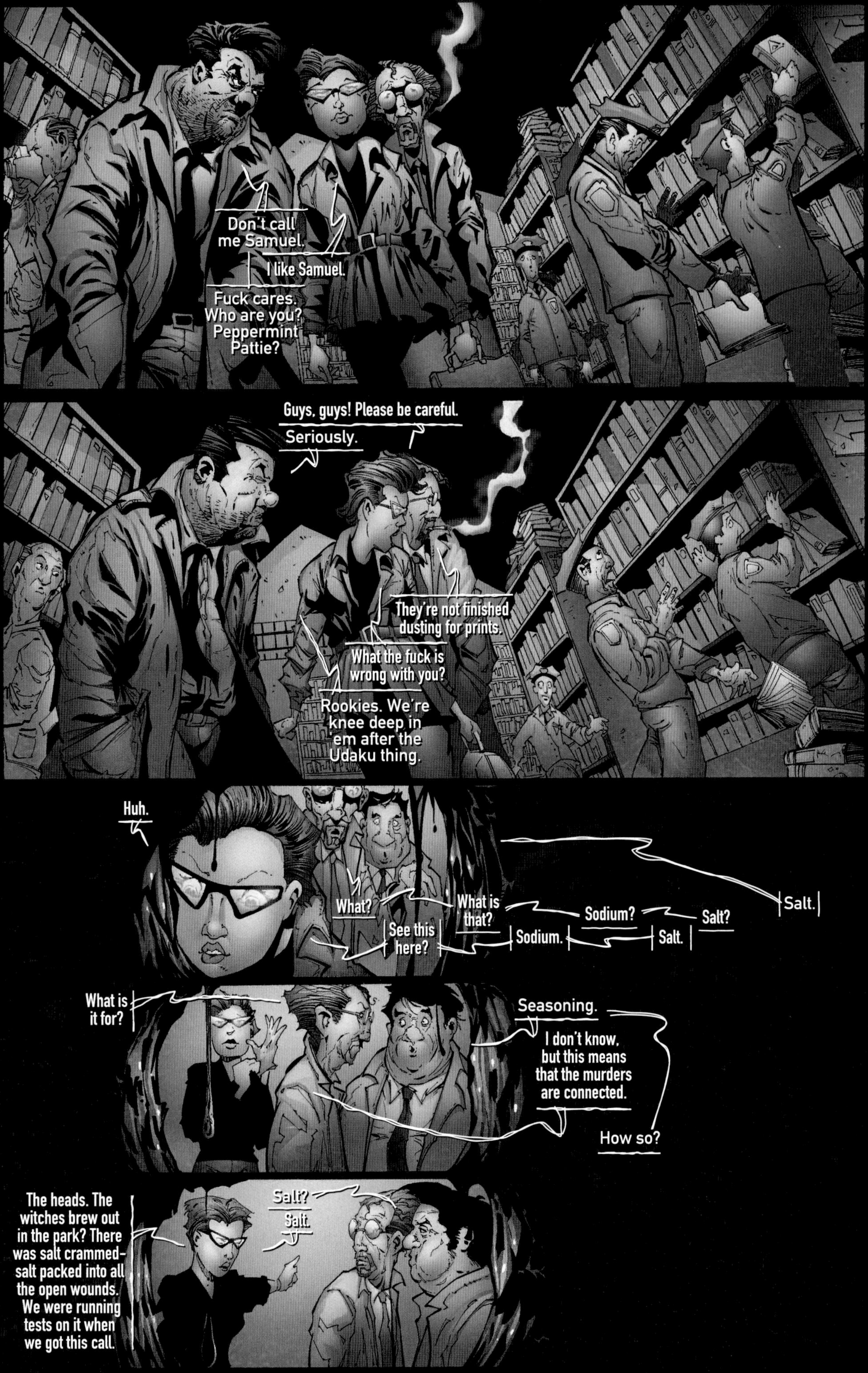

Don't call me Samuel.
I like Samuel.
Fuck cares. Who are you? Peppermint Pattie?
Guys, guys! Please be careful.
Seriously.
They're not finished dusting for prints.
What the fuck is wrong with you?
Rookies. We're knee deep in 'em after the Udaku thing.
Huh.
What?
See this here?
What is that?
Sodium.
Sodium?
Salt.
Salt?
Salt.
What is it for?
Seasoning.
I don't know, but this means that the murders are connected.
How so?
The heads. The witches brew out in the park? There was salt crammed- salt packed into all the open wounds. We were running tests on it when we got this call.
Salt?
Salt.

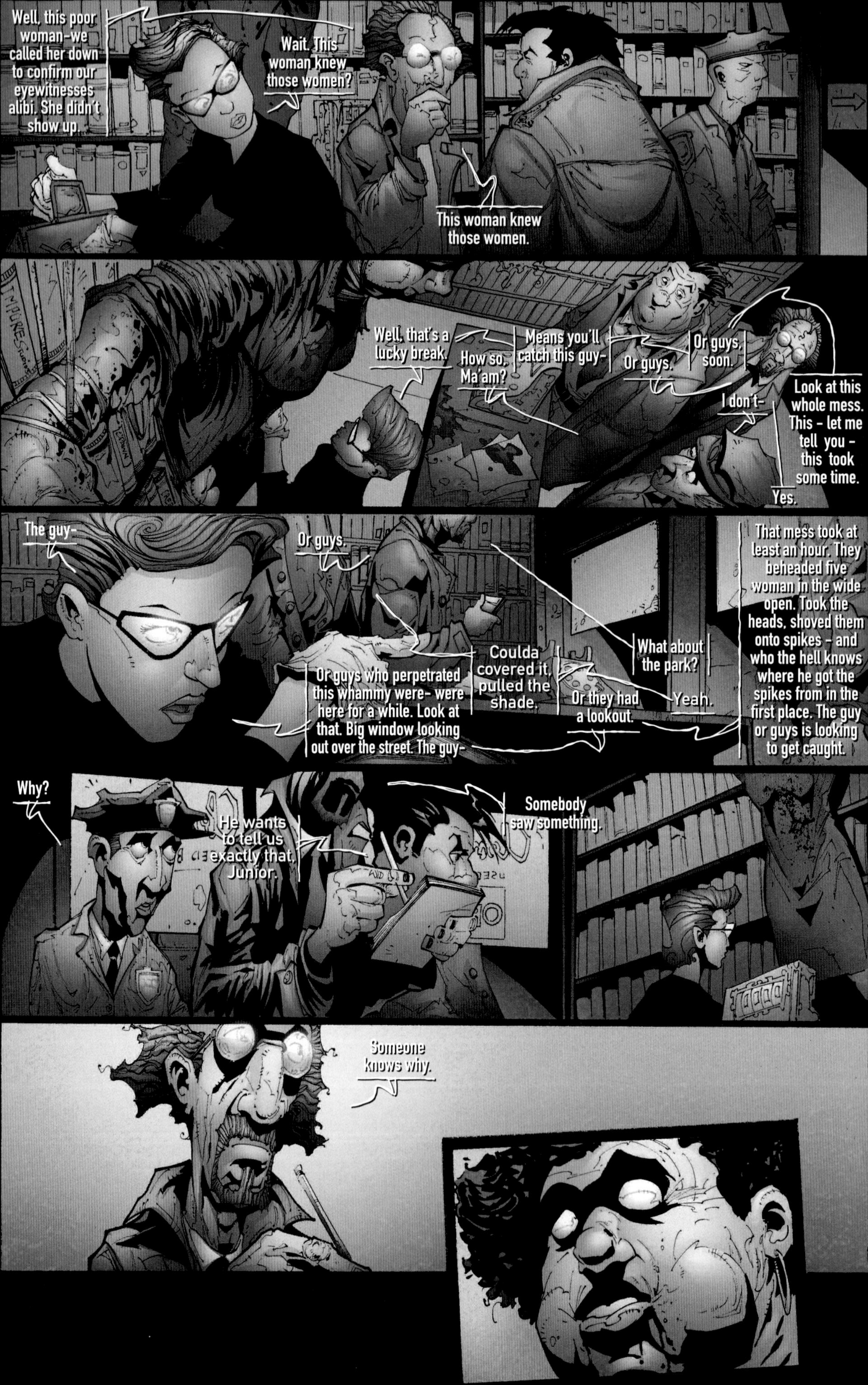
Well, this poor woman-we called her down to confirm our eyewitnesses alibi. She didn't show up.
Wait. This woman knew those women?
This woman knew those women.
Well, that's a lucky break.
How so, Ma'am?
Means you'll catch this guy-
Or guys.
Or guys, soon.
I don't-
Look at this whole mess. This - let me tell you - this took some time.
Yes.
The guy-
Or guys.
Or guys who perpetrated this whammy were- were here for a while. Look at that. Big window looking out over the street. The guy-
Coulda covered it, pulled the shade.
Or they had a lookout.
What about the park?
Yeah.
That mess took at least an hour. They beheaded five woman in the wide open. Took the heads, shoved them onto spikes - and who the hell knows where he got the spikes from in the first place. The guy or guys is looking to get caught.
Why?
He wants to tell us exactly that, Junior.
Somebody saw something.
Someone knows why.

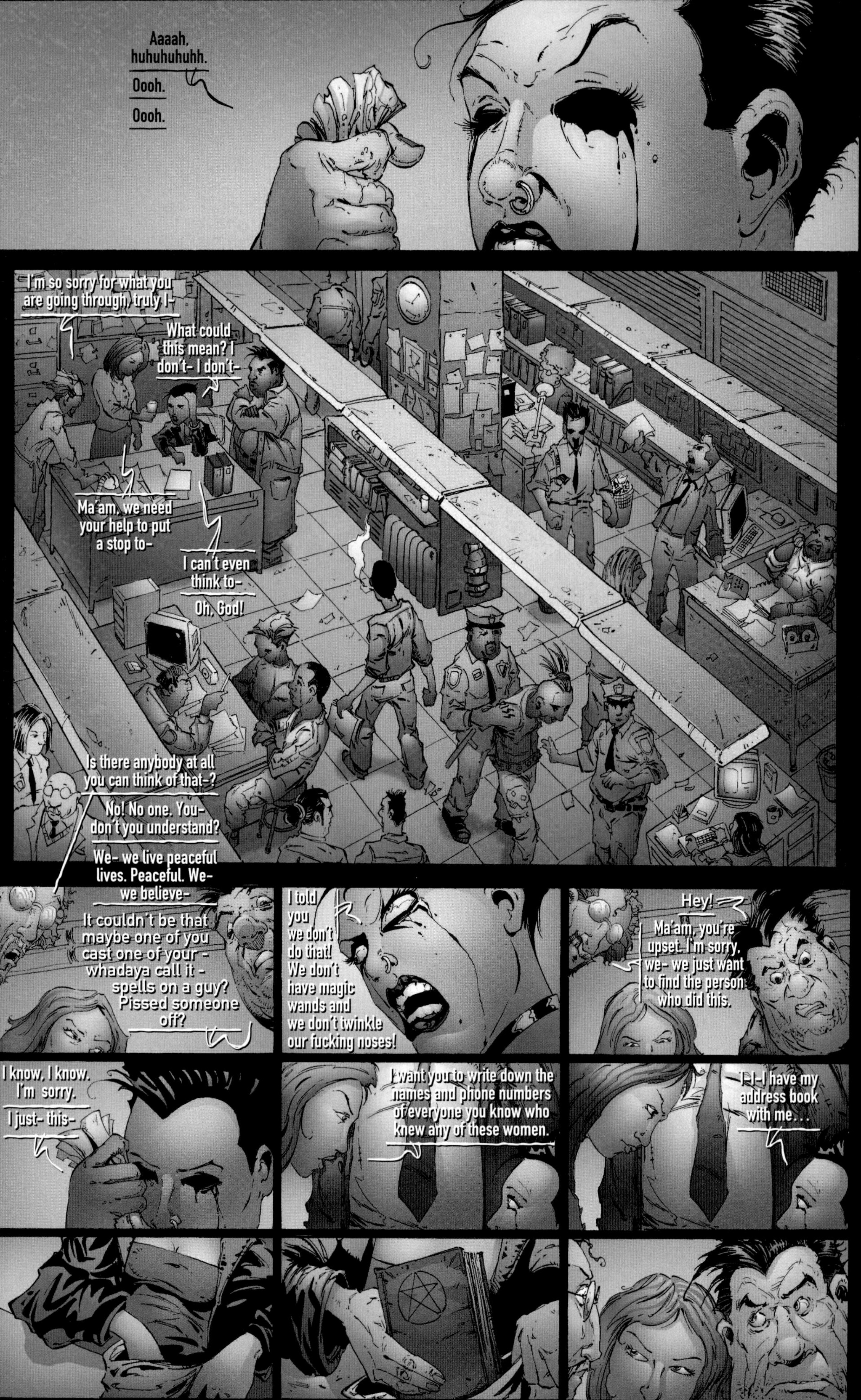
Aaaah, huhuhuhuhh.
Oooh.
Oooh.
I'm so sorry for what you are going through, truly I-
What could this mean? I don't- I don't-
Ma'am, we need your help to put a stop to-
I can't even think to-
Oh, God!
Is there anybody at all you can think of that-?
No! No one. You- don't you understand?
We- we live peaceful lives. Peaceful. We- we believe-
It couldn't be that maybe one of you cast one of your - whadaya call it - spells on a guy? Pissed someone off?
I told you we don't do that! We don't have magic wands and we don't twinkle our fucking noses!
Hey!
Ma'am, you're upset. I'm sorry, we- we just want to find the person who did this.
I know, I know. I'm sorry.
I just- this-
I want you to write down the names and phone numbers of everyone you know who knew any of these women.
I-I-I have my address book with me...

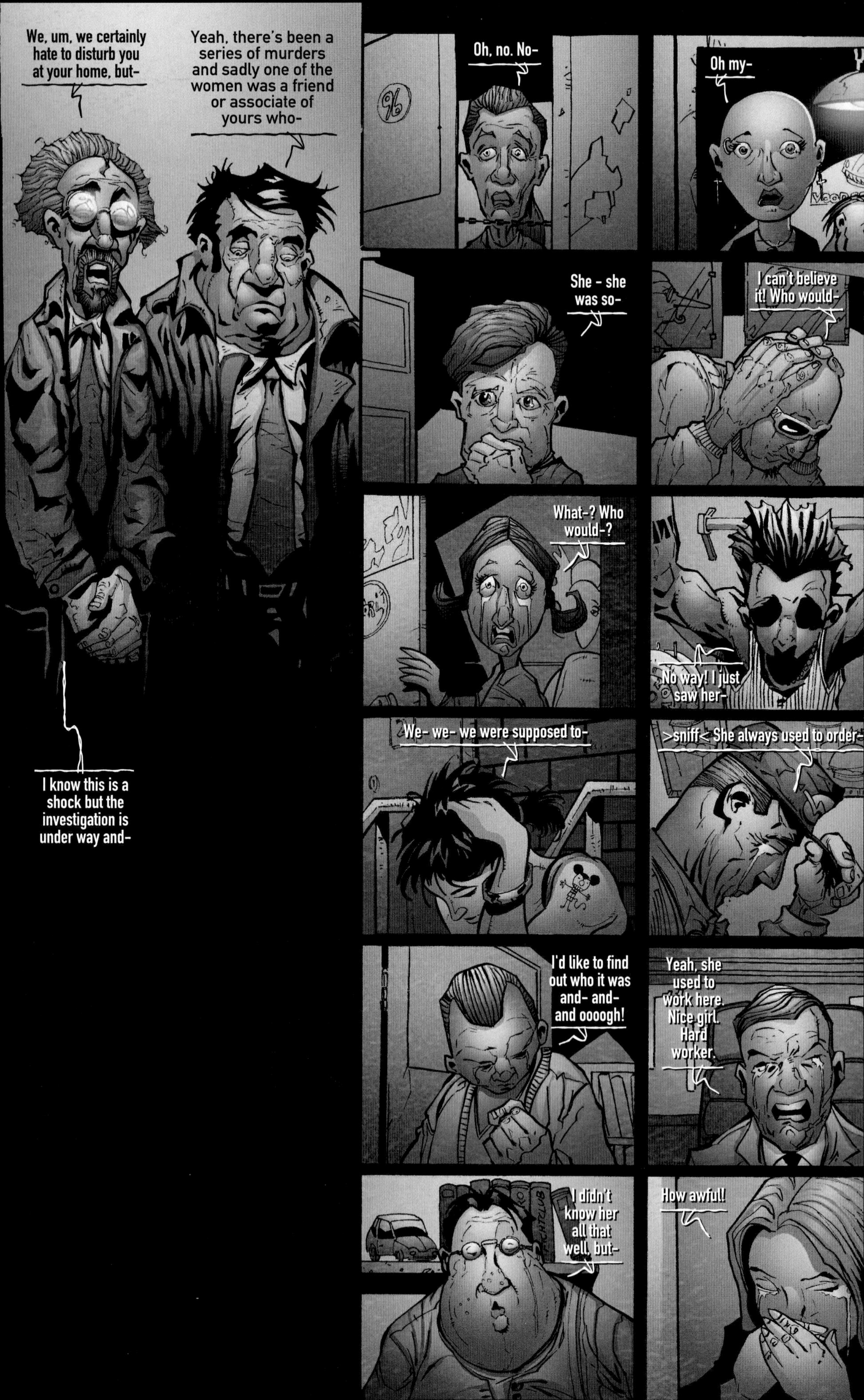

We, um, we certainly hate to disturb you at your home, but-
Yeah, there's been a series of murders and sadly one of the women was a friend or associate of yours who-
I know this is a shock but the investigation is under way and-
Oh, no. No-
Oh my-
She - she was so-
I can't believe it! Who would-
What-? Who would-?
No way! I just saw her-
We- we- we were supposed to-
>sniff< She always used to order-
I'd like to find out who it was and- and- and oooogh!
Yeah, she used to work here. Nice girl. Hard worker.
I didn't know her all that well, but-
How awful!

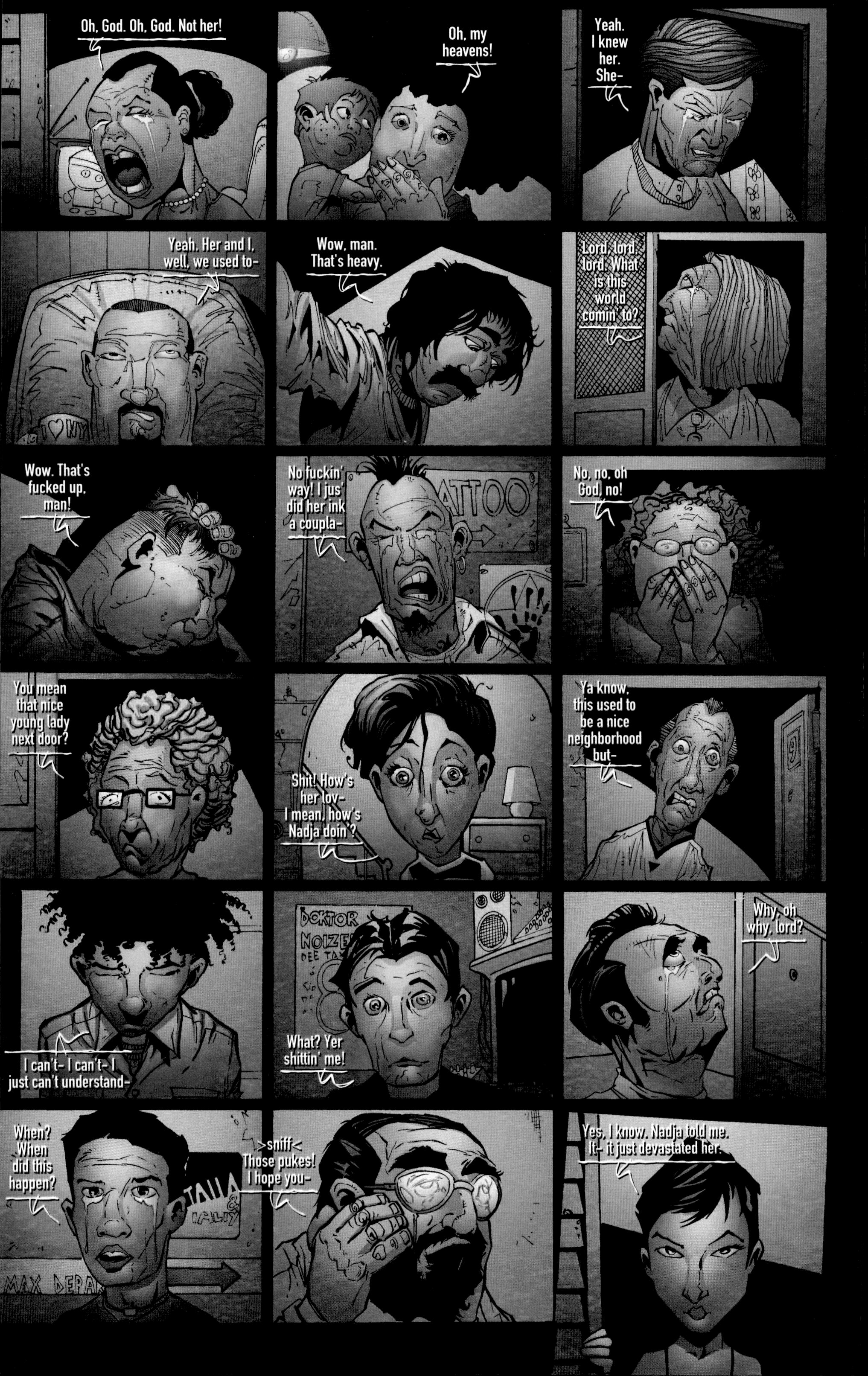
Oh, God. Oh, God. Not her!
Oh, my heavens!
Yeah. I knew her. She-
Yeah. Her and I, well, we used to-
Wow, man. That's heavy.
Lord, lord, lord. What is this world comin' to?
Wow. That's fucked up, man!
No fuckin' way! I jus' did her ink a coupla-
ATTOO
No, no, oh God, no!
You mean that nice young lady next door?
Shit! How's her lov- I mean, how's Nadja doin'?
Ya know, this used to be a nice neighborhood but-
I can't- I can't- I just can't understand-
DOKTOR NOIZE
What? Yer shittin' me!
Why, oh why, lord?
When? When did this happen?
>sniff< Those pukes! I hope you-
Yes, I know. Nadja told me. It- it just devastated her.

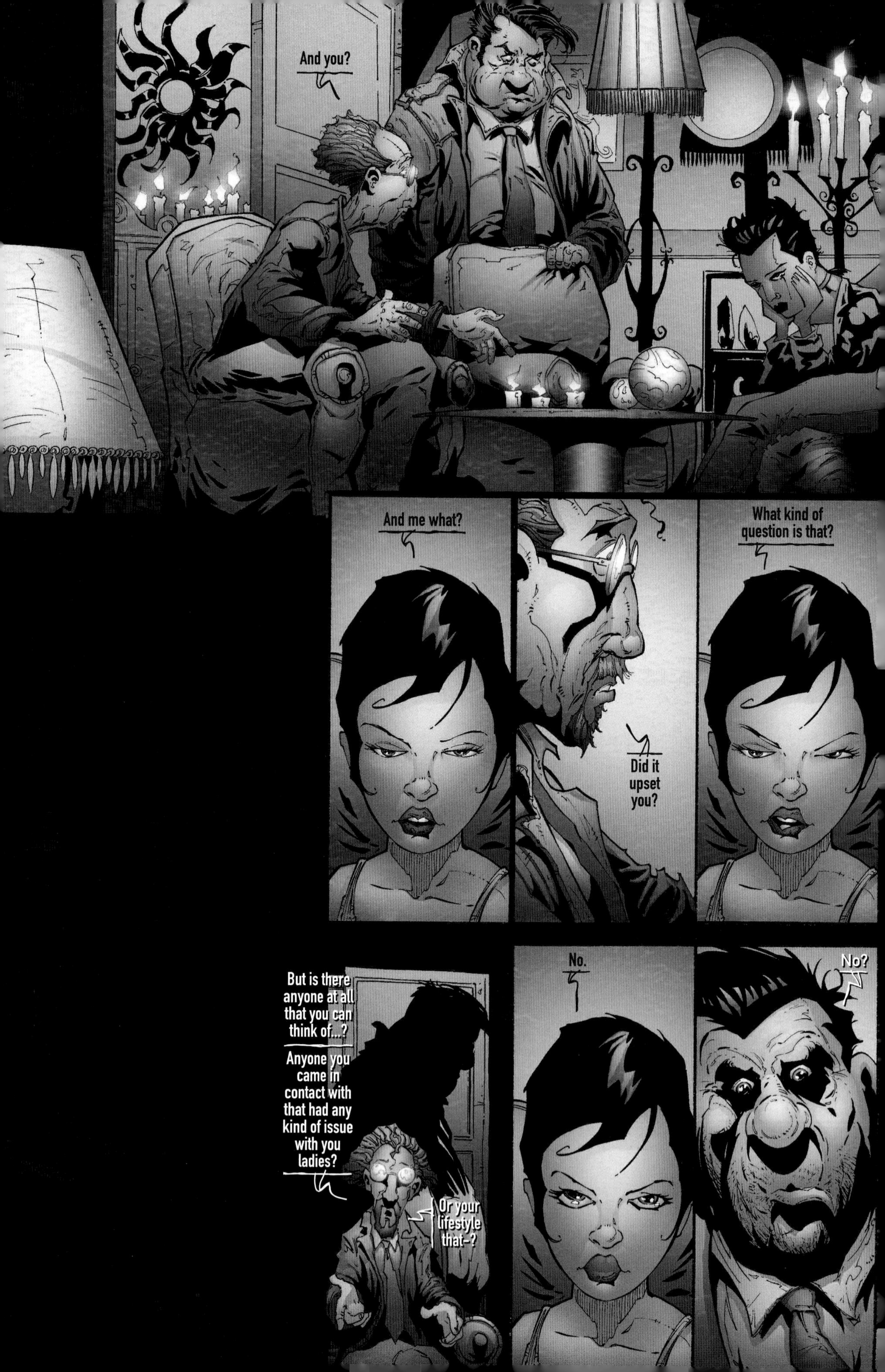
And you?
And me what?
Did it upset you?
What kind of question is that?
But is there anyone at all that you can think of...?
Anyone you came in contact with that had any kind of issue with you ladies?
Or your lifestyle that–?
No.
No?

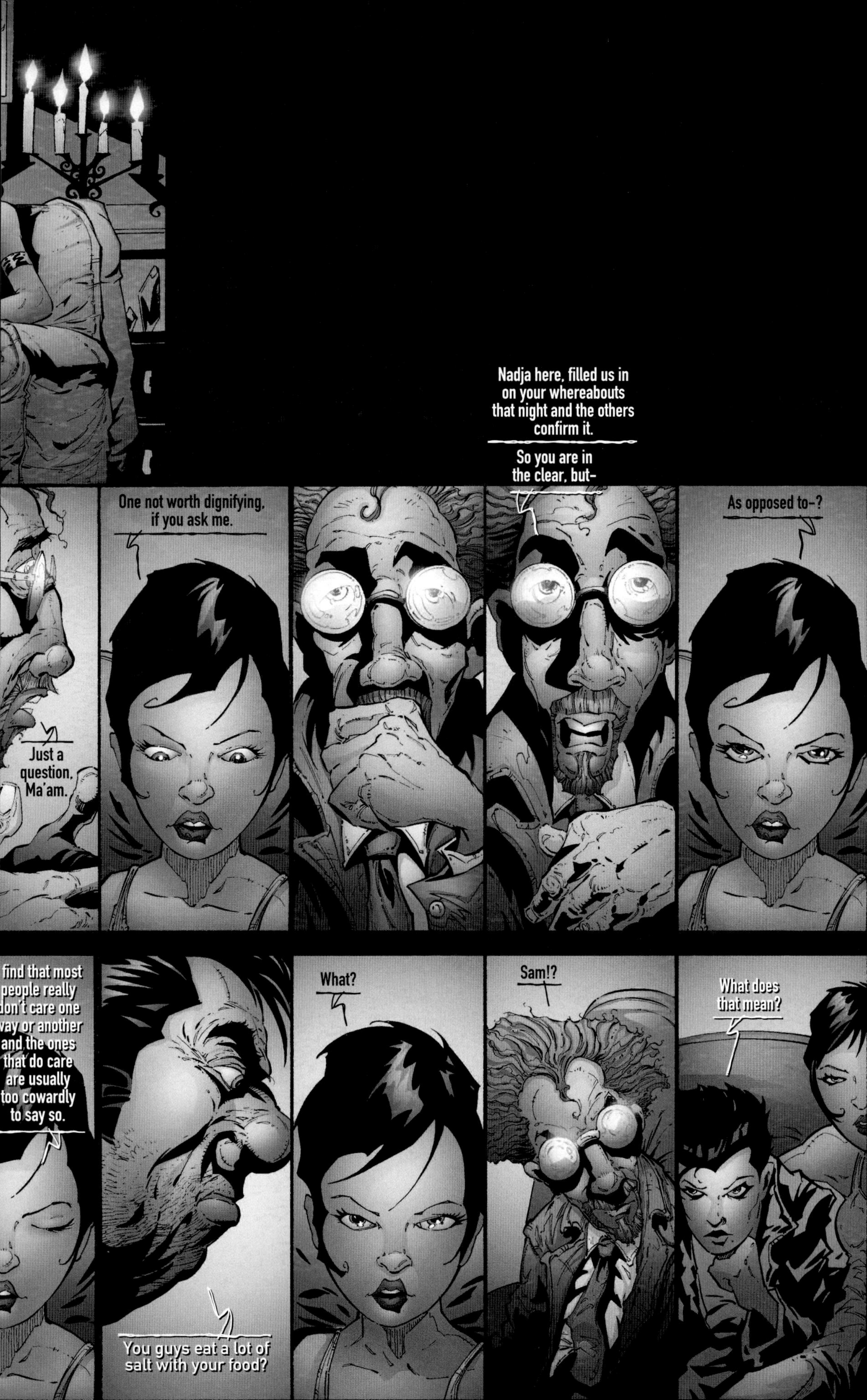

Nadja here, filled us in on your whereabouts that night and the others confirm it.
So you are in the clear, but-
Just a question, Ma'am.
One not worth dignifying, if you ask me.
As opposed to-?
find that most people really don't care one way or another and the ones that do care are usually too cowardly to say so.
You guys eat a lot of salt with your food?
What?
Sam!?
What does that mean?

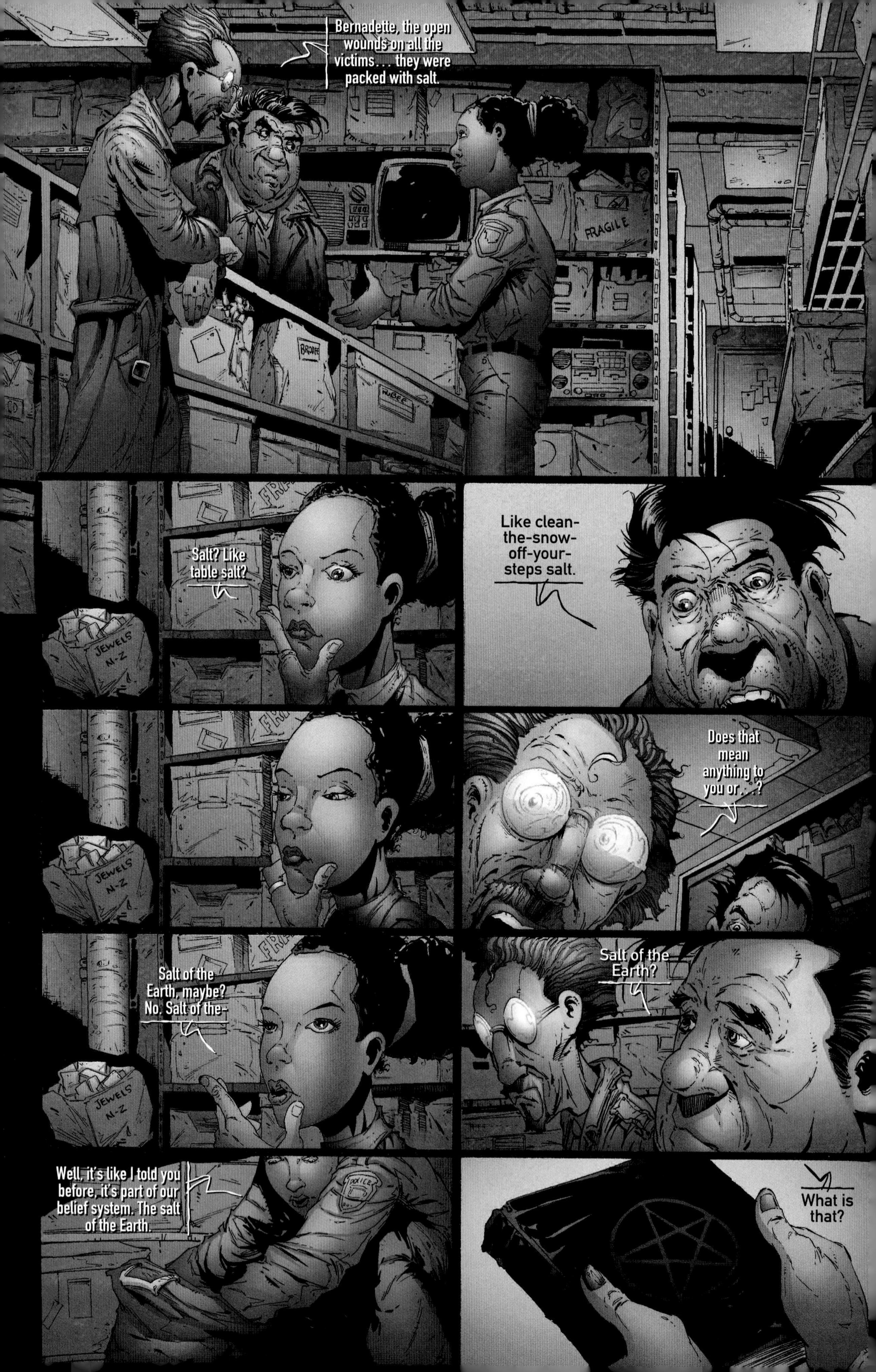
Bernadette, the open wounds on all the victims. . . they were packed with salt.
BRODIE
FRAGILE
Salt? Like table salt?
JEWELS N-Z
Like clean-the-snow-off-your-steps salt.
Does that mean anything to you or. . .?
Salt of the Earth, maybe? No. Salt of the-
Salt of the Earth?
Well, it's like I told you before, it's part of our belief system. The salt of the Earth.
What is that?

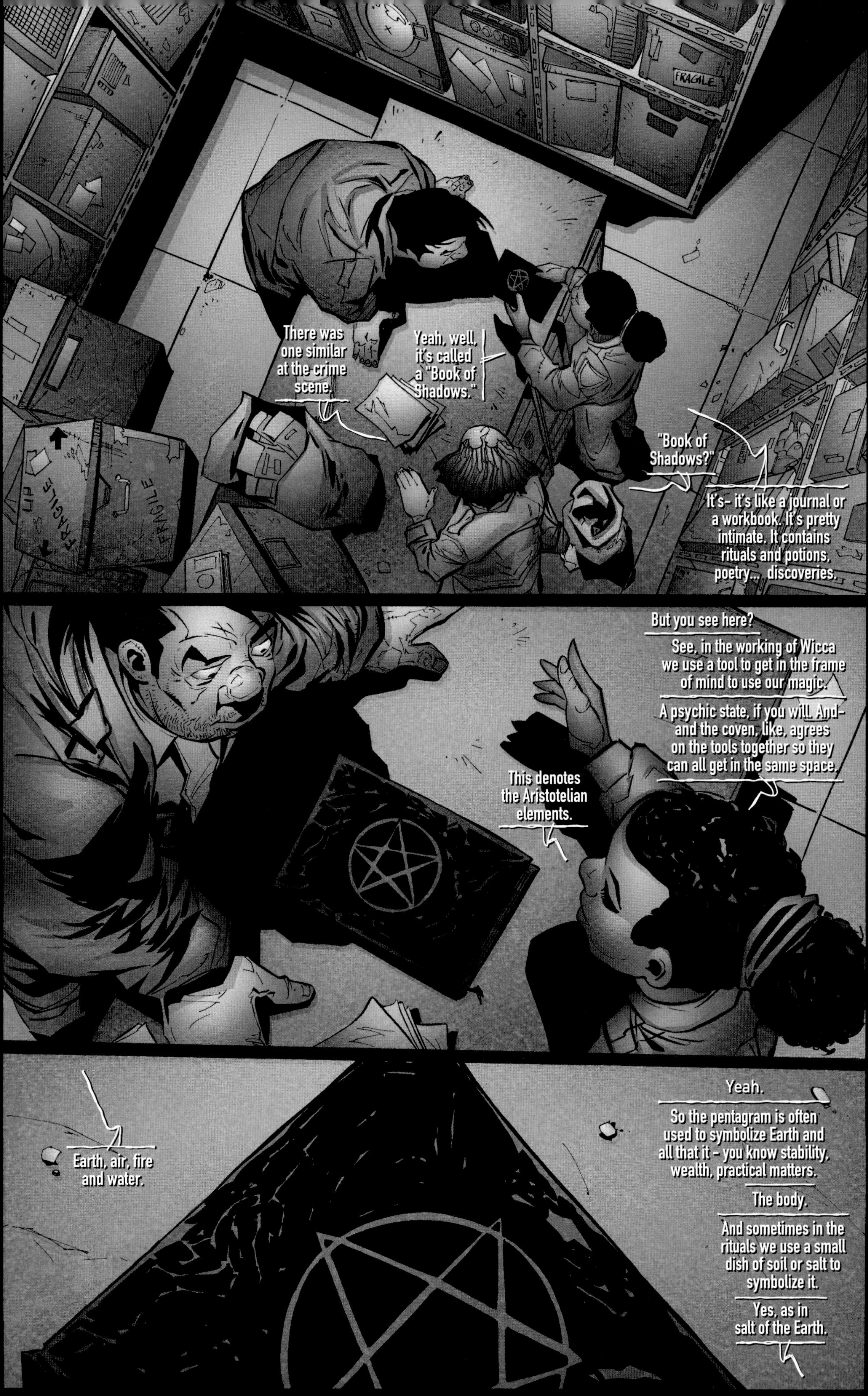
There was one similar at the crime scene.
Yeah, well, it's called a "Book of Shadows."
"Book of Shadows?"
It's- it's like a journal or a workbook. It's pretty intimate. It contains rituals and potions, poetry... discoveries.
But you see here?
See, in the working of Wicca we use a tool to get in the frame of mind to use our magic.
A psychic state, if you will. And- and the coven, like, agrees on the tools together so they can all get in the same space.
This denotes the Aristotelian elements.
Earth, air, fire and water.
Yeah.
So the pentagram is often used to symbolize Earth and all that it - you know stability, wealth, practical matters.
The body.
And sometimes in the rituals we use a small dish of soil or salt to symbolize it.
Yes, as in salt of the Earth.

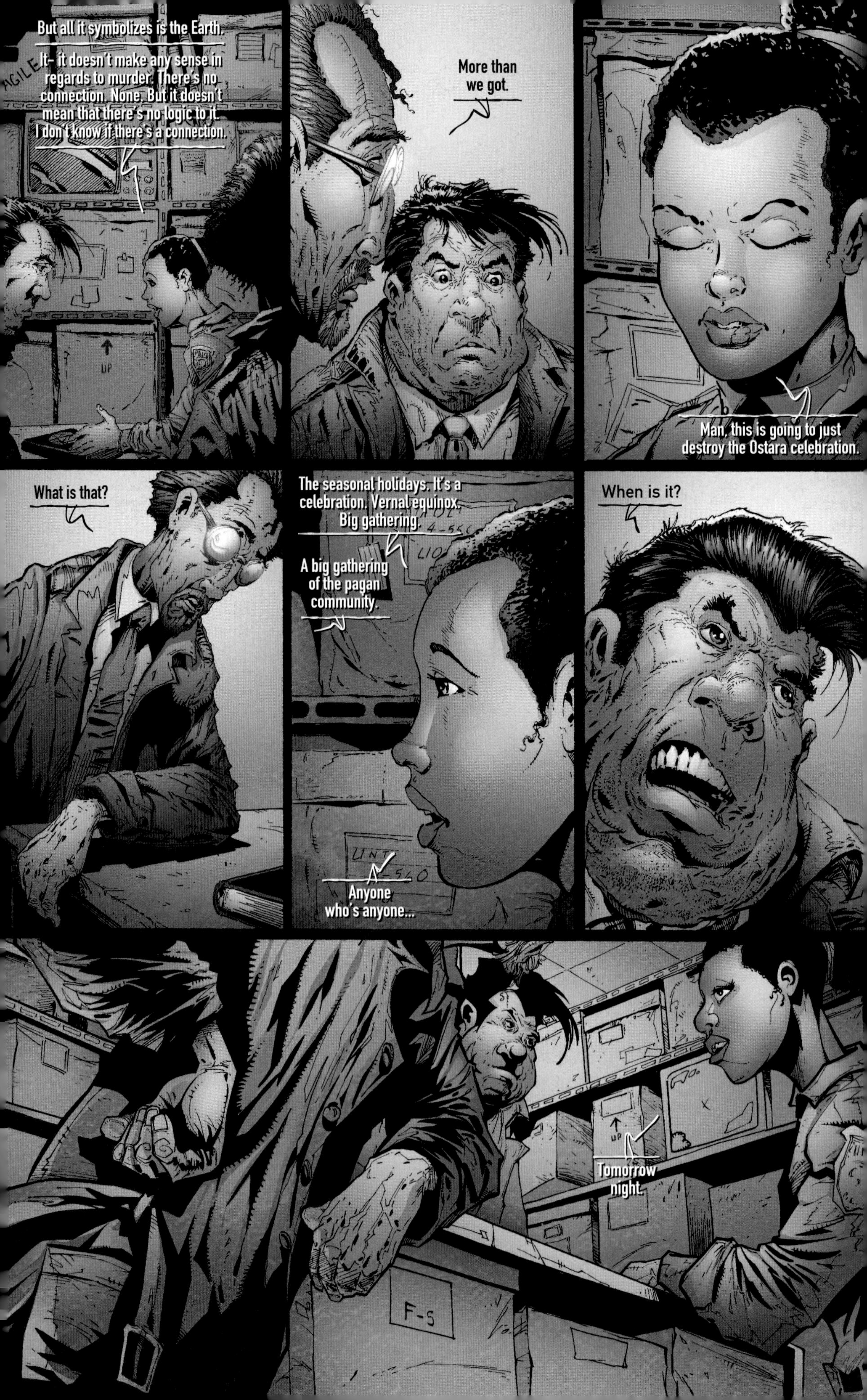
But all it symbolizes is the Earth.
It- it doesn't make any sense in regards to murder. There's no connection. None. But it doesn't mean that there's no logic to it. I don't know if there's a connection.
More than we got.
Man, this is going to just destroy the Ostara celebration.
What is that?
The seasonal holidays. It's a celebration. Vernal equinox. Big gathering.
A big gathering of the pagan community.
Anyone who's anyone...
When is it?
Tomorrow night.

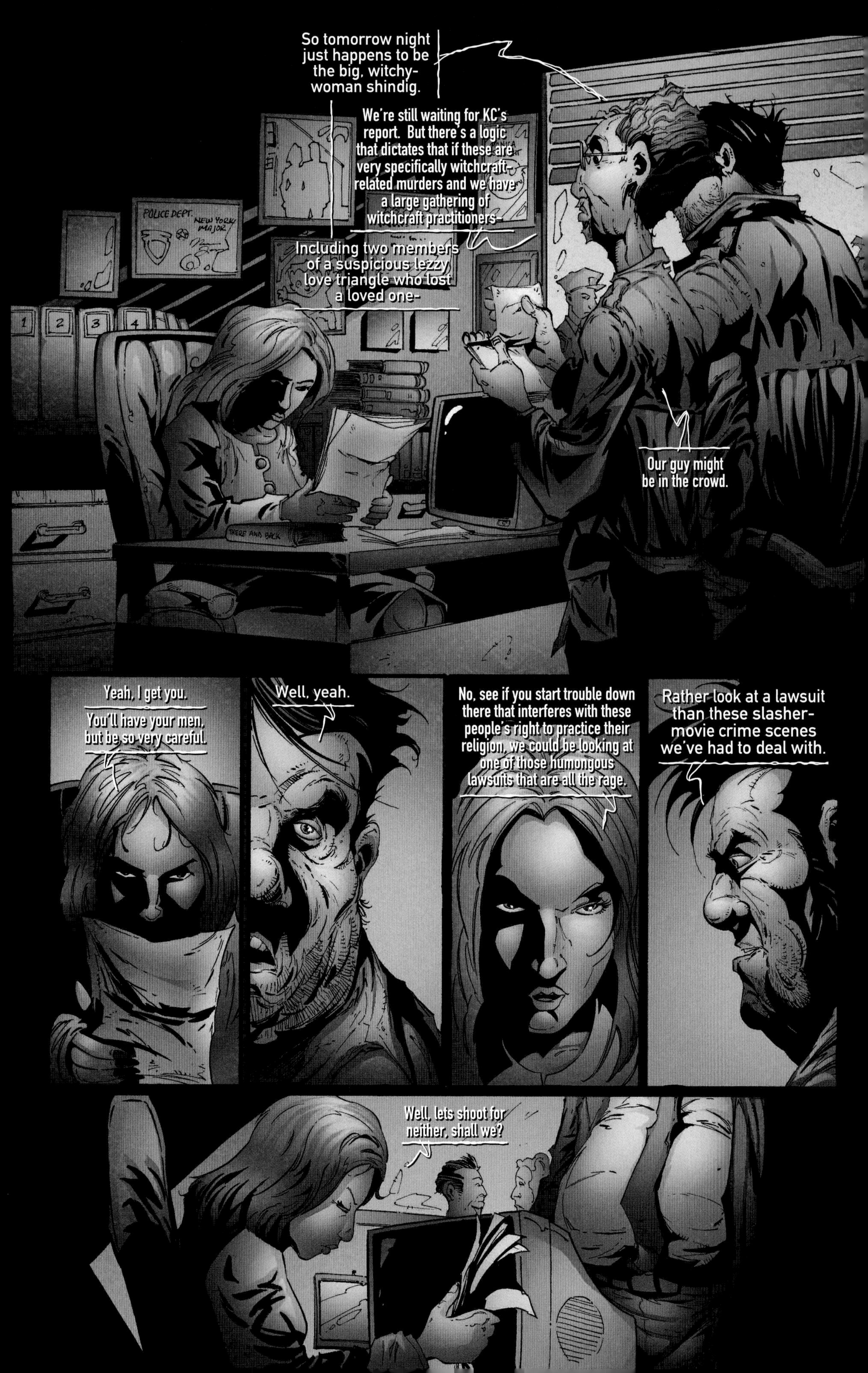
So tomorrow night just happens to be the big, witchy-woman shindig.
We're still waiting for KC's report. But there's a logic that dictates that if these are very specifically witchcraft-related murders and we have a large gathering of witchcraft practitioners-
Including two members of a suspicious lezzy love triangle who lost a loved one-
Our guy might be in the crowd.
POLICE DEPT.
NEW YORK MAJOR
THERE AND BACK
Yeah, I get you.
You'll have your men, but be so very careful.
Well, yeah.
No, see if you start trouble down there that interferes with these people's right to practice their religion, we could be looking at one of those humongous lawsuits that are all the rage.
Rather look at a lawsuit than these slasher-movie crime scenes we've had to deal with.
Well, lets shoot for neither, shall we?

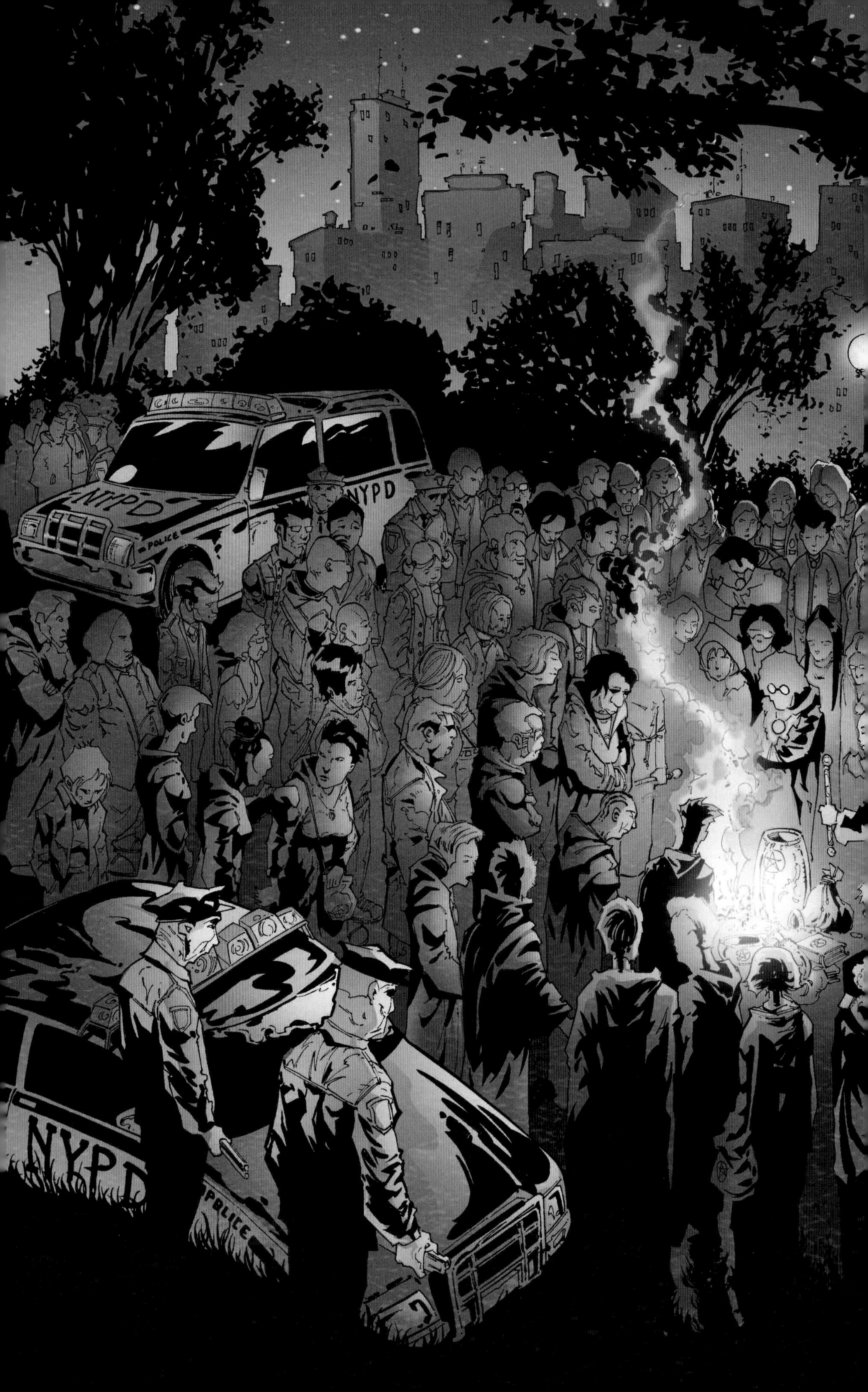
NYPD
POLICE
NYPD
NYPD
POLICE

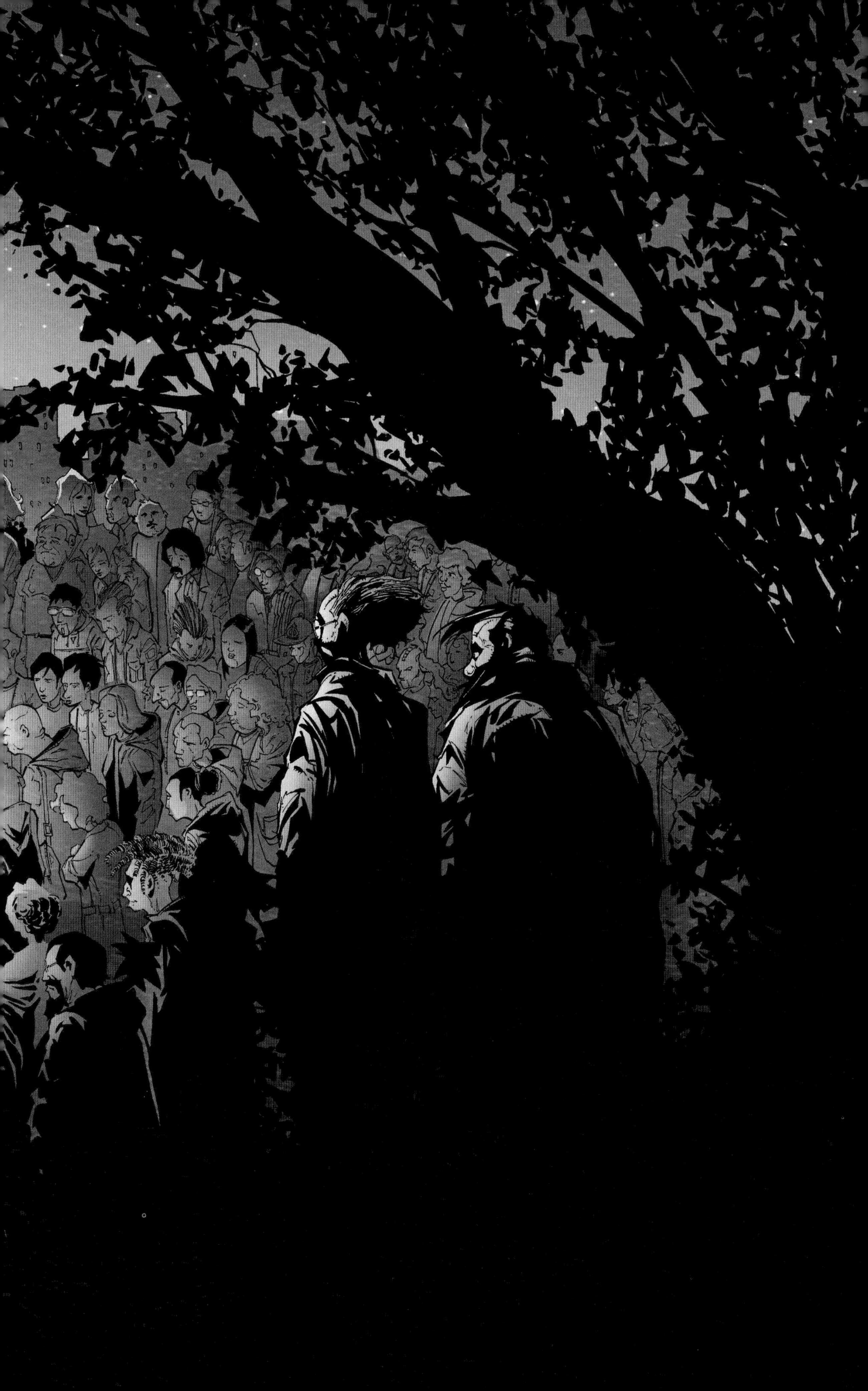

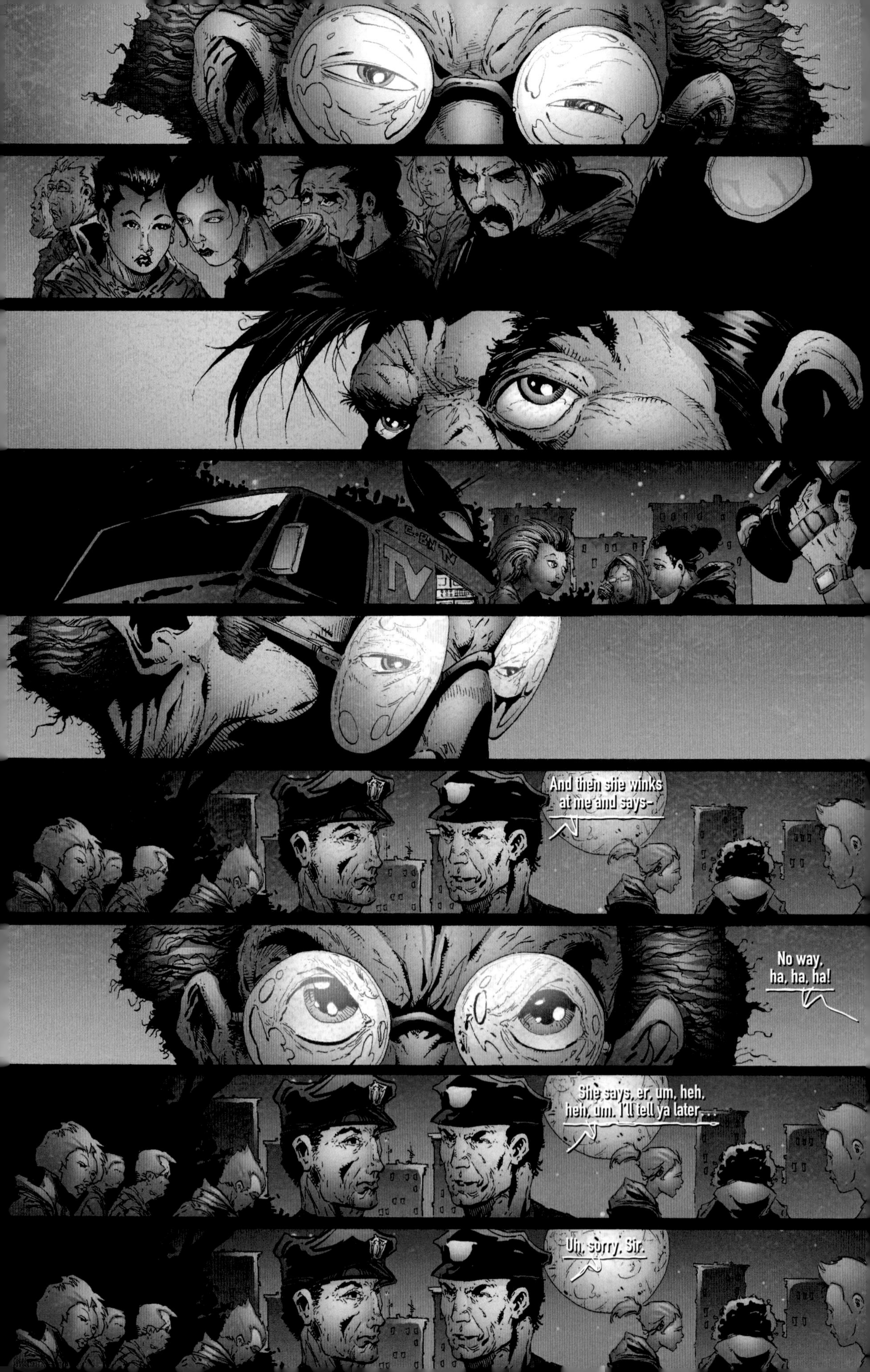
And then she winks at me and says–
No way, ha, ha, ha!
She says, er, um, heh, heh, um. I'll tell ya later. . .
Uh, sorry. Sir.

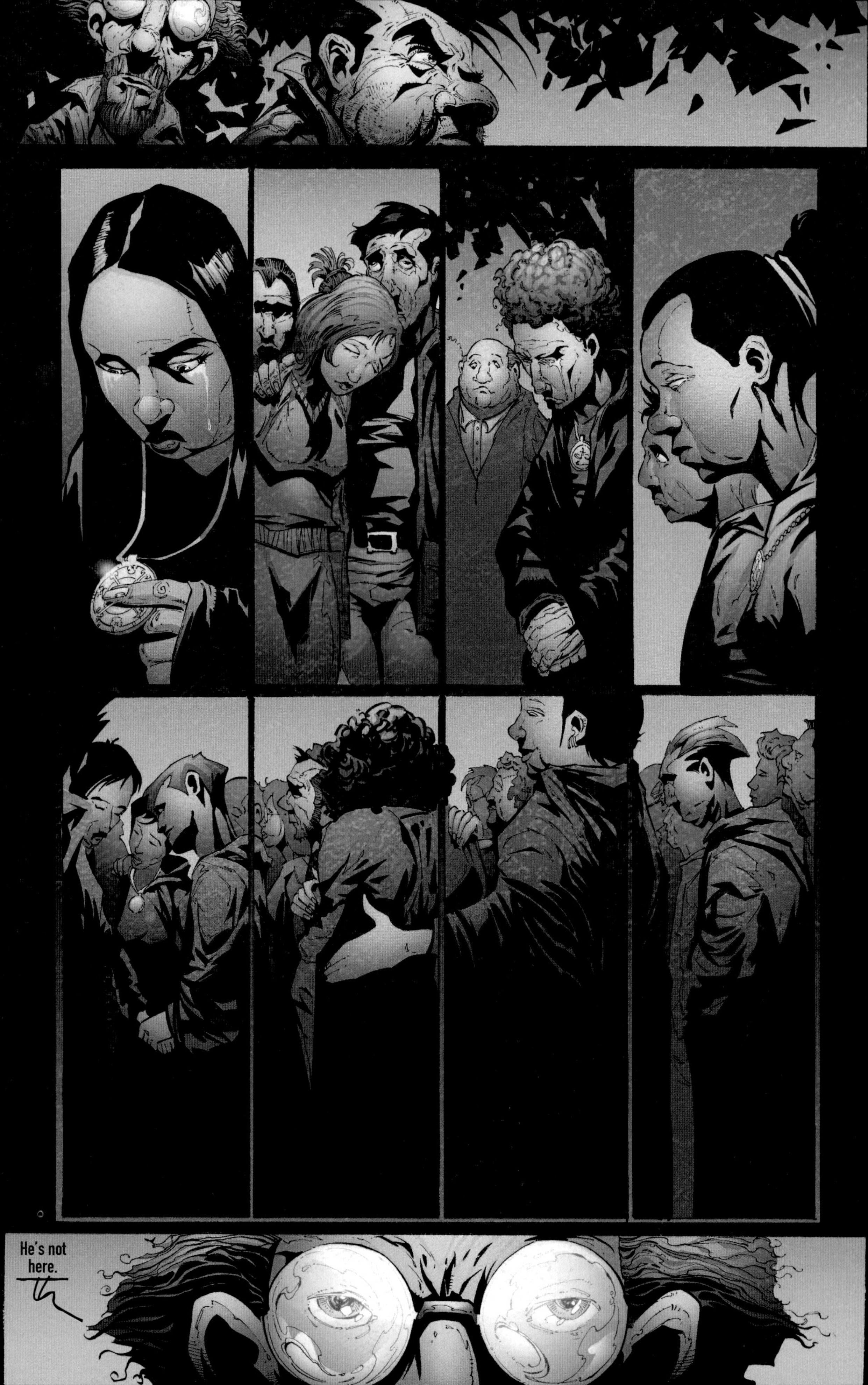
He's not here.

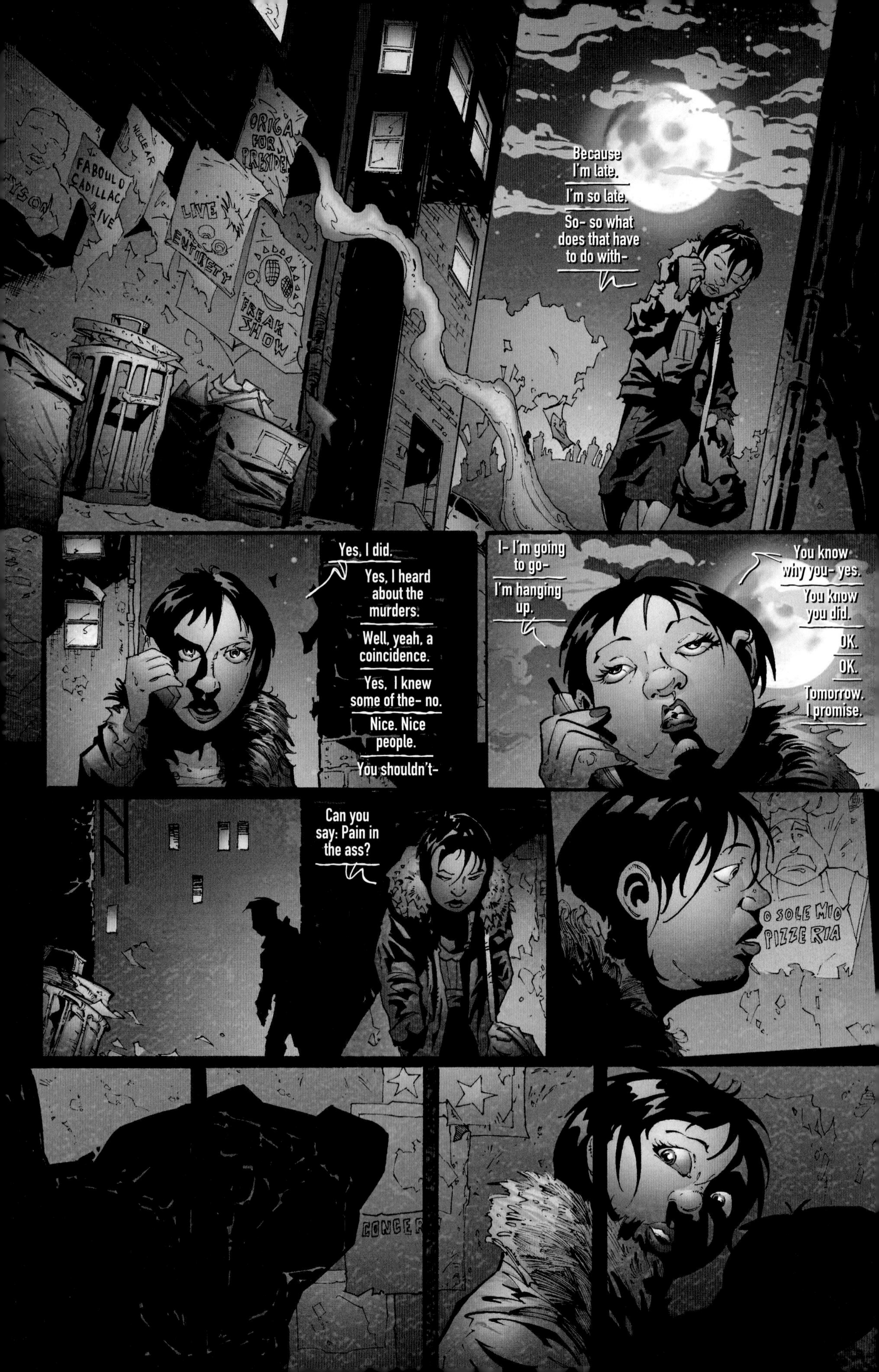

ORIGA FOR PRESIDEN
FABOULO CADILLAC LIVE
TYSON
NUCLEAR
LIVE ENTIRETY
FREAK SHOW
Because I'm late.
I'm so late.
So- so what does that have to do with-
Yes, I did.
Yes, I heard about the murders.
Well, yeah, a coincidence.
Yes, I knew some of the- no.
Nice. Nice people.
You shouldn't-
I- I'm going to go-
I'm hanging up.
You know why you- yes.
You know you did.
OK.
OK.
Tomorrow. I promise.
Can you say: Pain in the ass?
O SOLE MIO PIZZERIA
CONCER

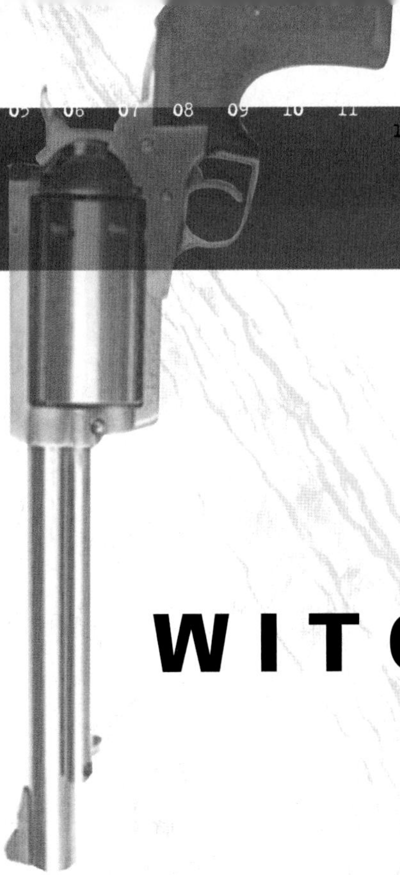

WITCHCRAFT

PART 3

SAM AND TWITCH

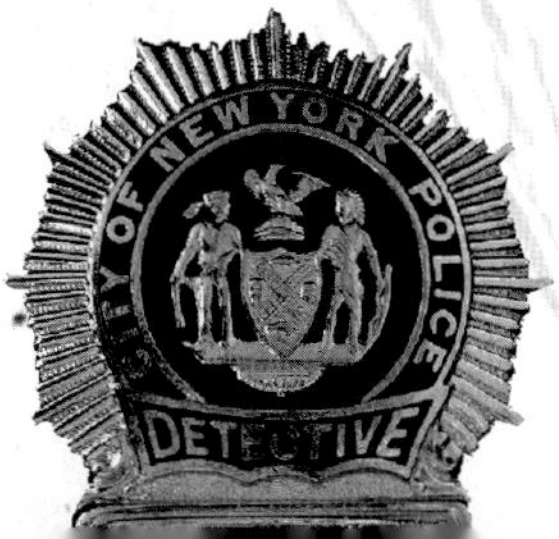
CITY OF NEW YORK POLICE
DETECTIVE

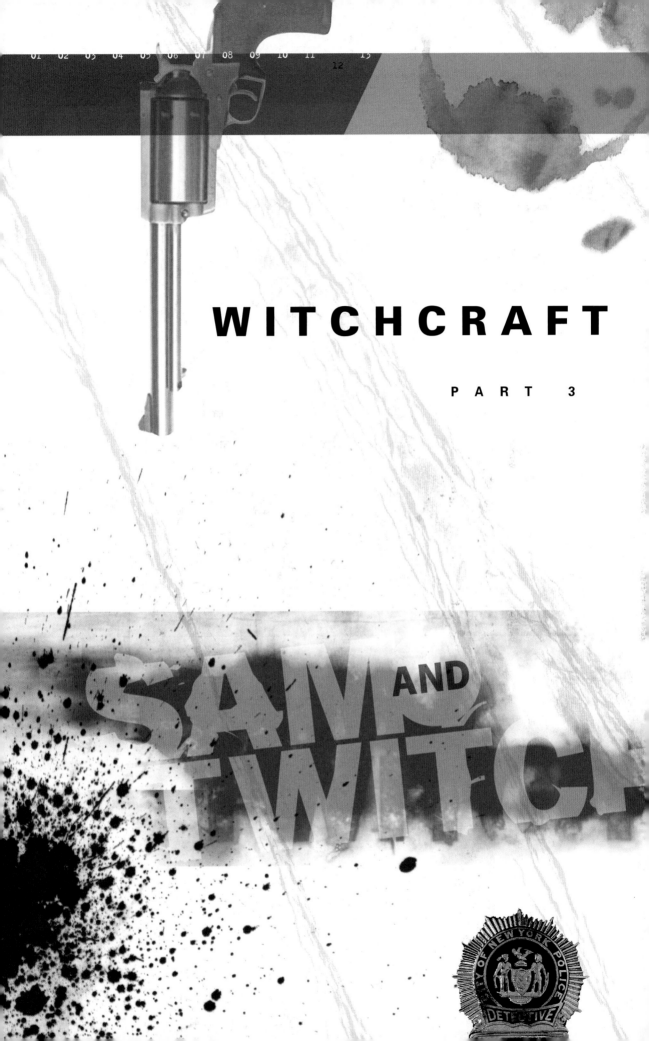

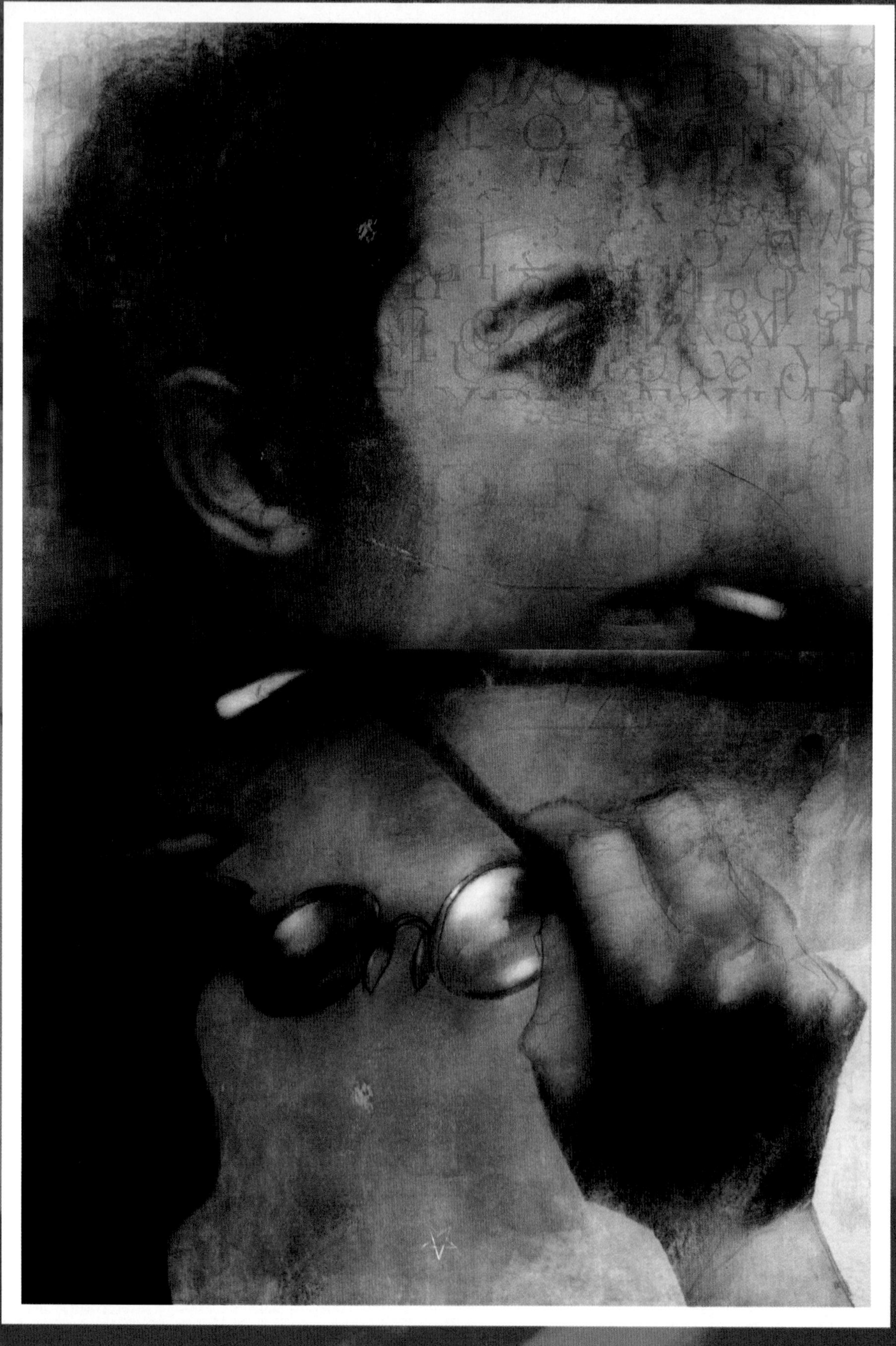

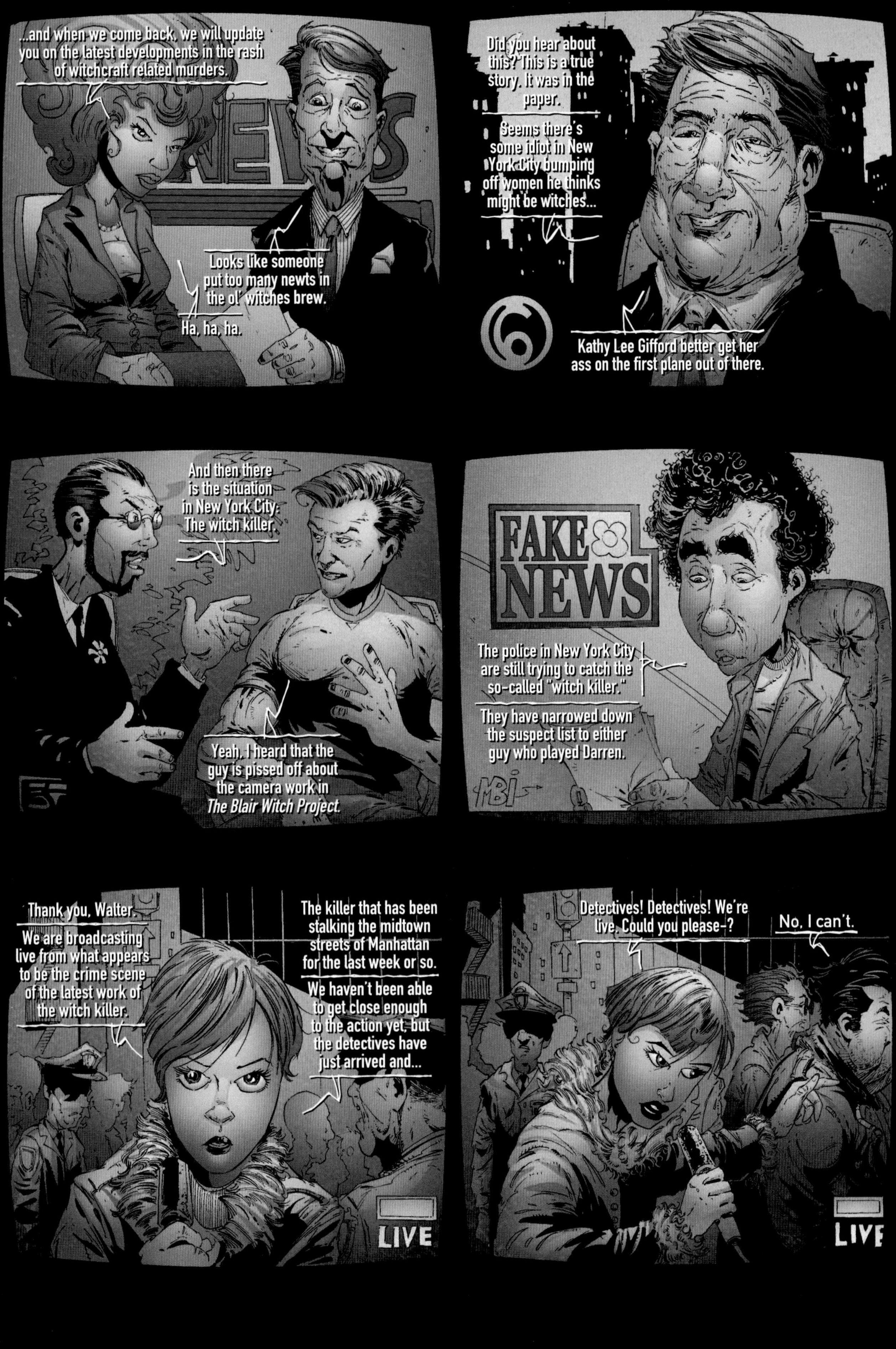

...and when we come back, we will update you on the latest developments in the rash of witchcraft related murders.
Looks like someone put too many newts in the ol' witches brew.
Ha, ha, ha.
Did you hear about this? This is a true story. It was in the paper.
Seems there's some idiot in New York City bumping off women he thinks might be witches...
Kathy Lee Gifford better get her ass on the first plane out of there.
And then there is the situation in New York City: The witch killer.
Yeah, I heard that the guy is pissed off about the camera work in *The Blair Witch Project.*
FAKE NEWS
The police in New York City are still trying to catch the so-called "witch killer."
They have narrowed down the suspect list to either guy who played Darren.
Thank you, Walter.
We are broadcasting live from what appears to be the crime scene of the latest work of the witch killer.
The killer that has been stalking the midtown streets of Manhattan for the last week or so.
We haven't been able to get close enough to the action yet, but the detectives have just arrived and...
LIVE
Detectives! Detectives! We're live. Could you please–?
No, I can't.
LIVE

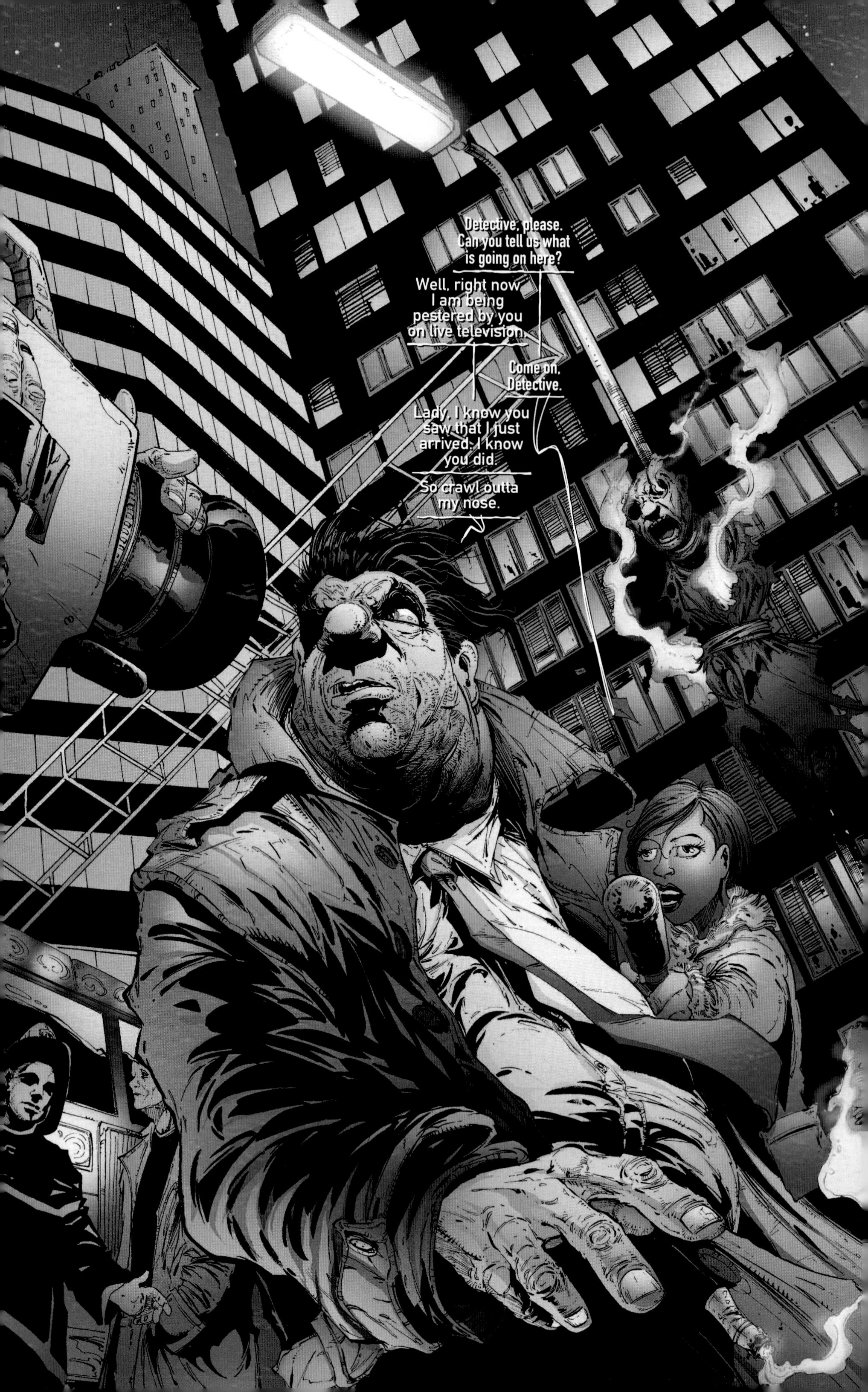
Detective, please. Can you tell us what is going on here?
Well, right now I am being pestered by you on live television.
Come on, Detective.
Lady, I know you saw that I just arrived. I know you did.
So crawl outta my nose.

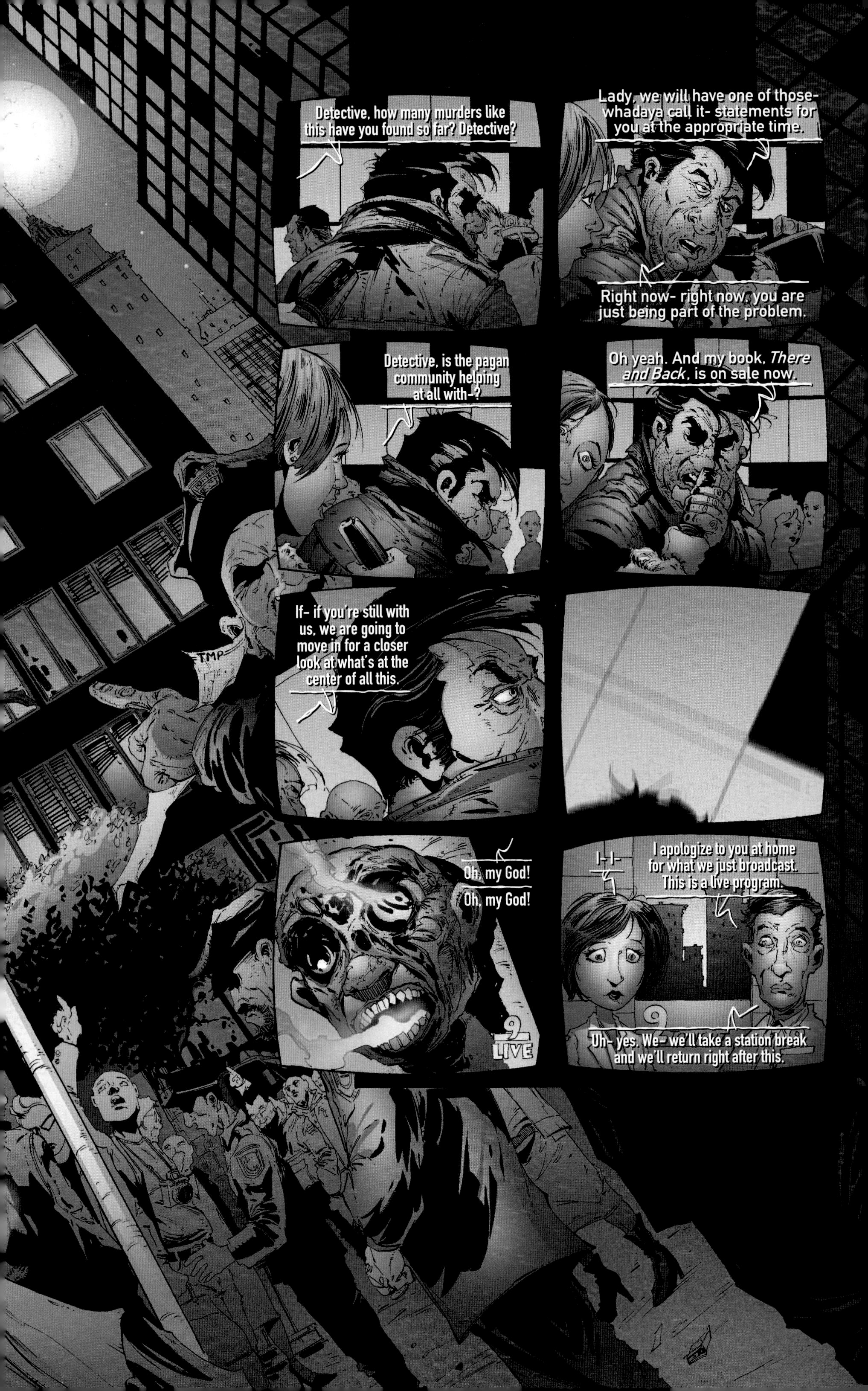

Detective, how many murders like this have you found so far? Detective?
Lady, we will have one of those- whadaya call it- statements for you at the appropriate time.
Right now- right now, you are just being part of the problem.
Detective, is the pagan community helping at all with-?
Oh yeah. And my book, *There and Back*, is on sale now.
If- if you're still with us, we are going to move in for a closer look at what's at the center of all this.
Oh, my God!
Oh, my God!
9 LIVE
I- I-
I apologize to you at home for what we just broadcast. This is a live program.
Uh- yes. We- we'll take a station break and we'll return right after this.

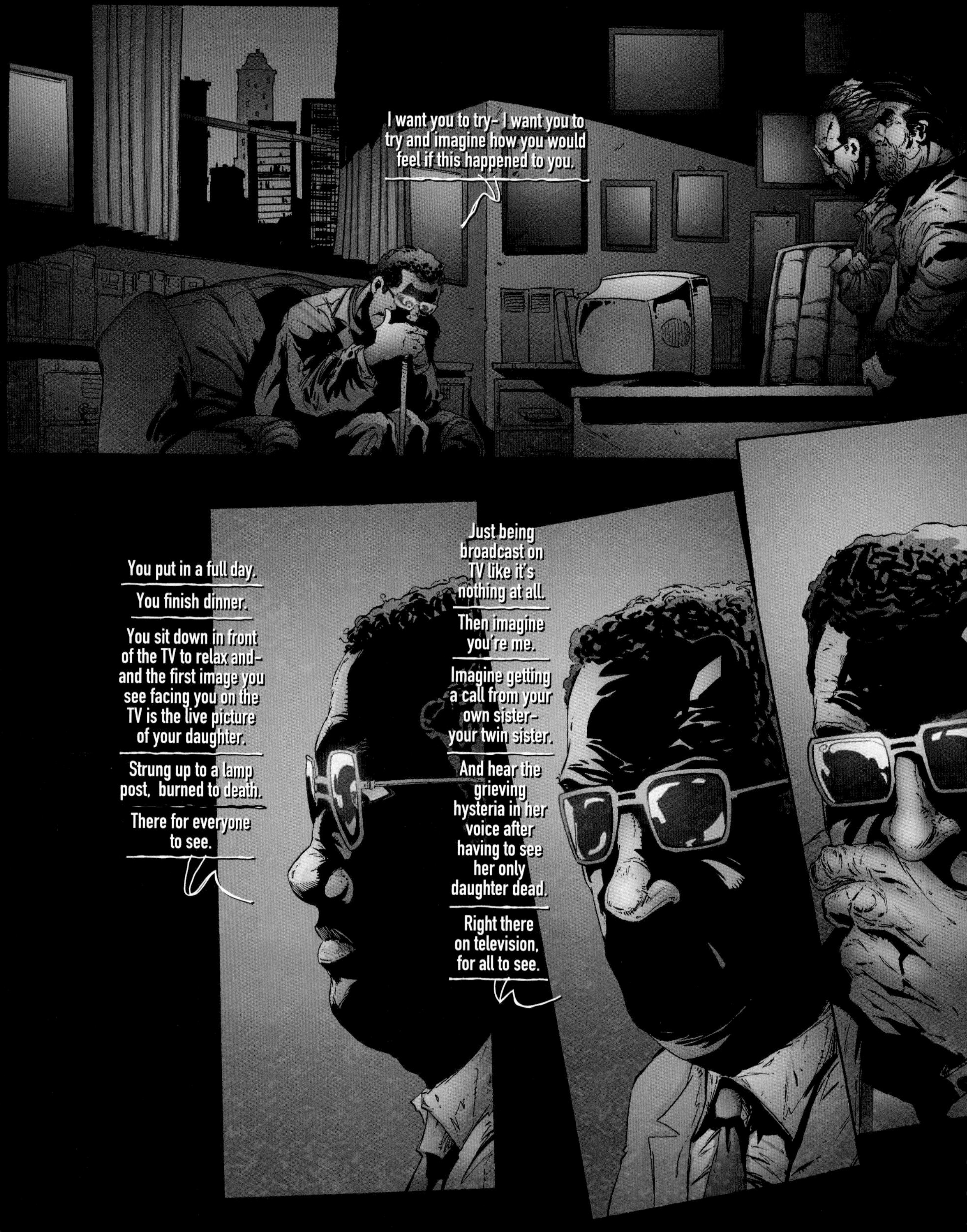
I want you to try- I want you to try and imagine how you would feel if this happened to you.
You put in a full day.
You finish dinner.
You sit down in front of the TV to relax and- and the first image you see facing you on the TV is the live picture of your daughter.
Strung up to a lamp post, burned to death.
There for everyone to see.
Just being broadcast on TV like it's nothing at all.
Then imagine you're me.
Imagine getting a call from your own sister- your twin sister.
And hear the grieving hysteria in her voice after having to see her only daughter dead.
Right there on television, for all to see.

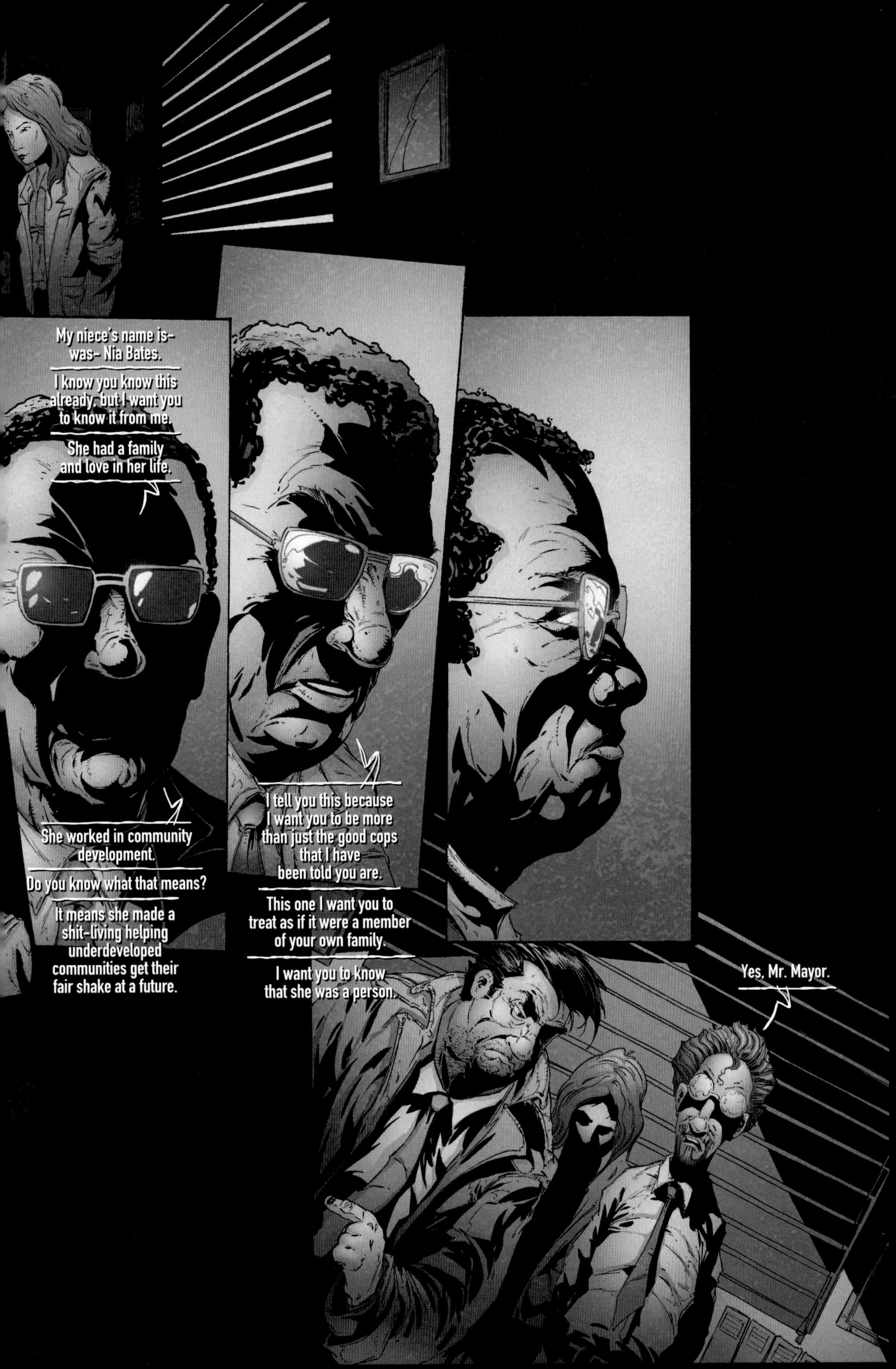
My niece's name is- was- Nia Bates.
I know you know this already, but I want you to know it from me.
She had a family and love in her life.
She worked in community development.
Do you know what that means?
It means she made a shit-living helping underdeveloped communities get their fair shake at a future.
I tell you this because I want you to be more than just the good cops that I have been told you are.
This one I want you to treat as if it were a member of your own family.
I want you to know that she was a person.
Yes, Mr. Mayor.

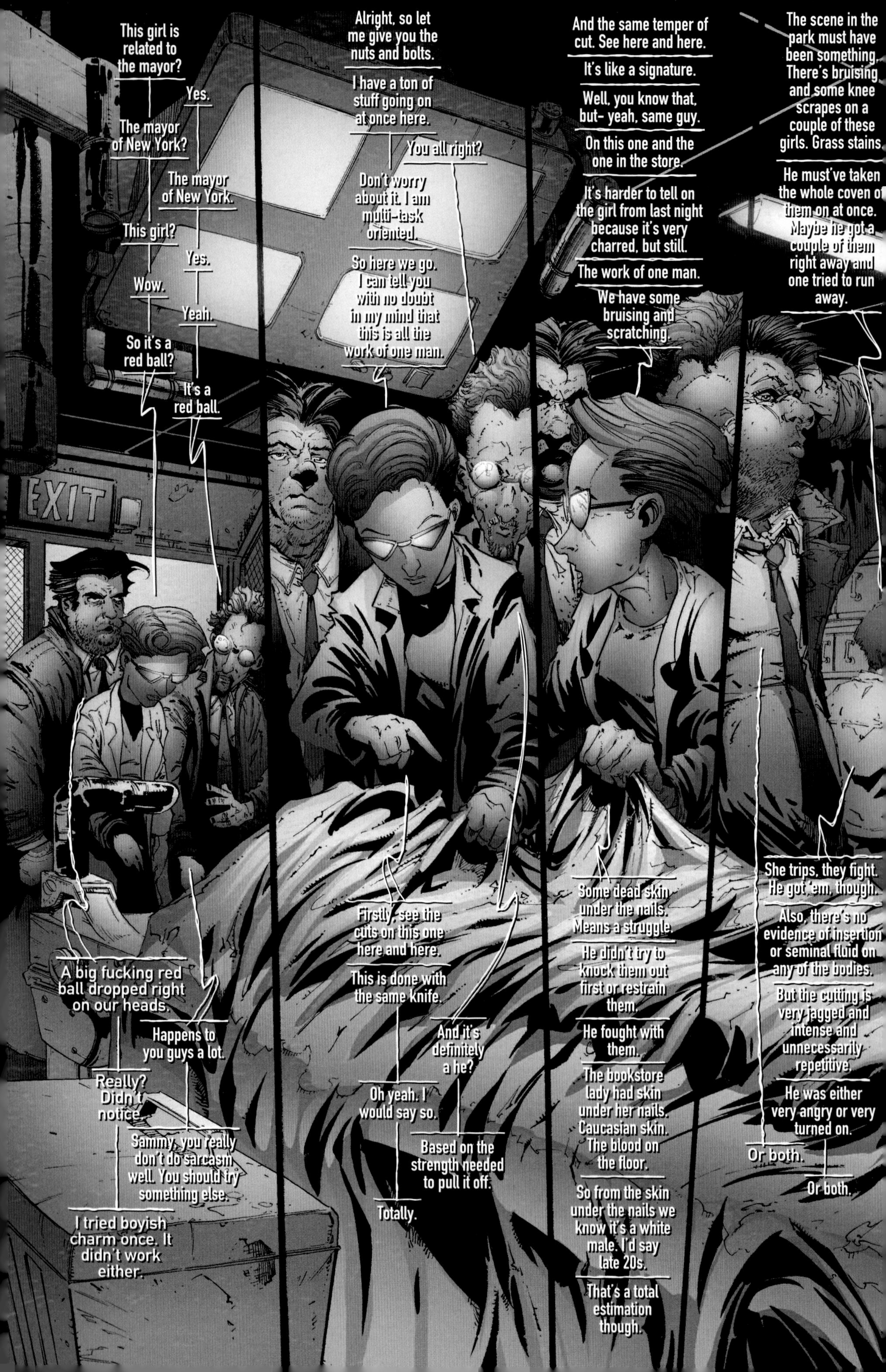
This girl is related to the mayor?
Yes.
The mayor of New York?
The mayor of New York.
This girl?
Yes.
Wow.
Yeah.
So it's a red ball?
It's a red ball.
A big fucking red ball dropped right on our heads.
Happens to you guys a lot.
Really? Didn't notice.
Sammy, you really don't do sarcasm well. You should try something else.
I tried boyish charm once. It didn't work either.
Alright, so let me give you the nuts and bolts.
I have a ton of stuff going on at once here.
You all right?
Don't worry about it. I am multi-task oriented.
So here we go. I can tell you with no doubt in my mind that this is all the work of one man.
Firstly, see the cuts on this one here and here.
This is done with the same knife.
And it's definitely a he?
Oh yeah. I would say so.
Based on the strength needed to pull it off.
Totally.
And the same temper of cut. See here and here.
It's like a signature.
Well, you know that, but- yeah, same guy.
On this one and the one in the store.
It's harder to tell on the girl from last night because it's very charred, but still.
The work of one man.
We have some bruising and scratching.
Some dead skin under the nails. Means a struggle.
He didn't try to knock them out first or restrain them.
He fought with them.
The bookstore lady had skin under her nails. Caucasian skin. The blood on the floor.
So from the skin under the nails we know it's a white male. I'd say late 20s.
That's a total estimation though.
The scene in the park must have been something. There's bruising and some knee scrapes on a couple of these girls. Grass stains.
He must've taken the whole coven of them on at once. Maybe he got a couple of them right away and one tried to run away.
She trips, they fight. He got 'em, though.
Also, there's no evidence of insertion or seminal fluid on any of the bodies.
But the cutting is very jagged and intense and unnecessarily repetitive.
He was either very angry or very turned on.
Or both.
Or both.

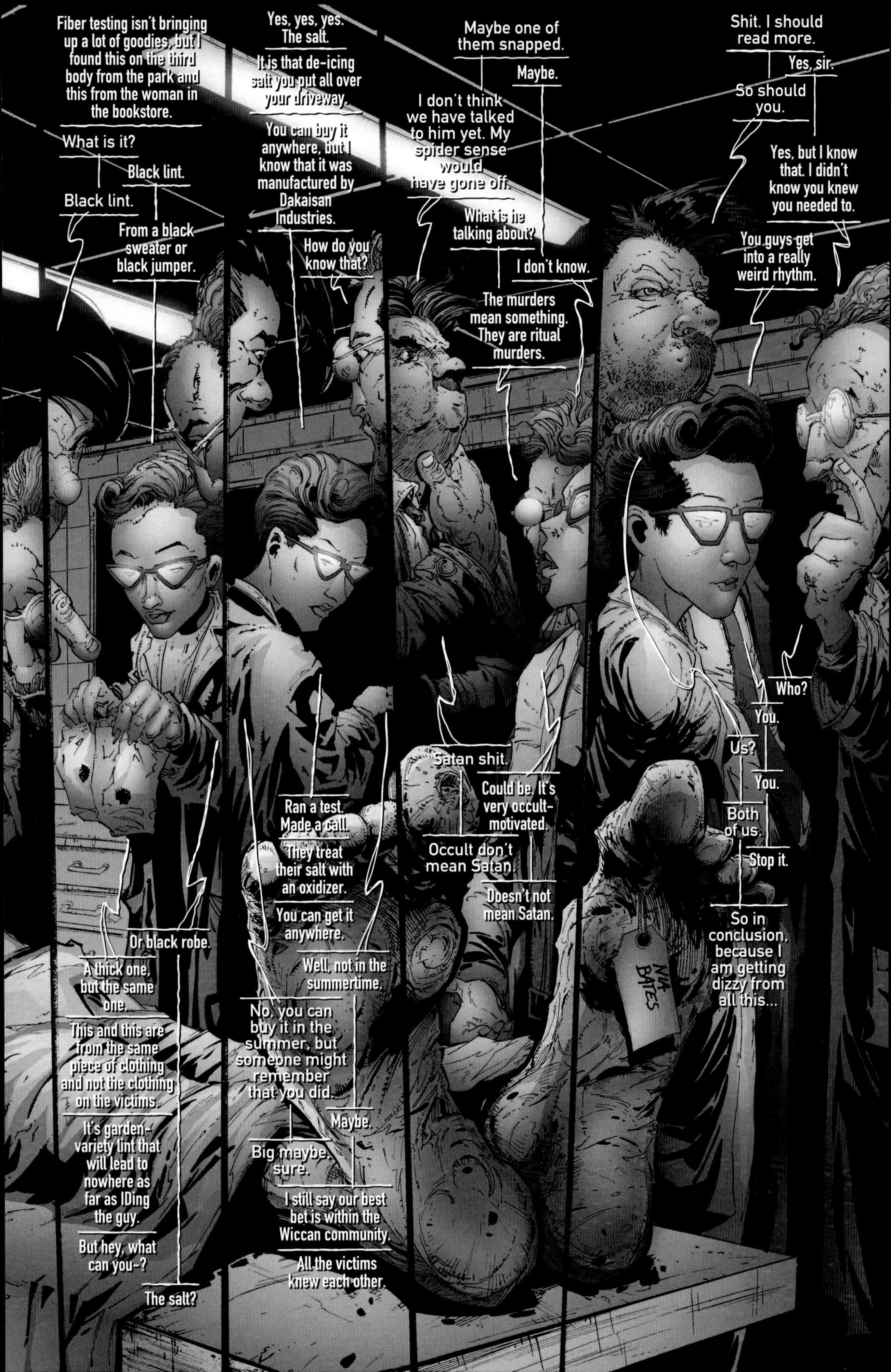

Fiber testing isn't bringing up a lot of goodies, but I found this on the third body from the park and this from the woman in the bookstore.
What is it?
Black lint.
Black lint.
From a black sweater or black jumper.
Or black robe.
A thick one, but the same one.
This and this are from the same piece of clothing and not the clothing on the victims.
It's garden-variety lint that will lead to nowhere as far as IDing the guy.
But hey, what can you-?
The salt?
Yes, yes, yes. The salt.
It is that de-icing salt you put all over your driveway.
You can buy it anywhere, but I know that it was manufactured by Dakaisan Industries.
How do you know that?
Ran a test. Made a call.
They treat their salt with an oxidizer.
You can get it anywhere.
Well, not in the summertime.
No, you can buy it in the summer, but someone might remember that you did.
Maybe.
Big maybe, sure.
I still say our best bet is within the Wiccan community.
All the victims knew each other.
Maybe one of them snapped.
Maybe.
I don't think we have talked to him yet. My spider sense would have gone off.
What is he talking about?
I don't know.
The murders mean something. They are ritual murders.
Satan shit.
Could be. It's very occult-motivated.
Occult don't mean Satan.
Doesn't not mean Satan.
Shit. I should read more.
Yes, sir.
So should you.
Yes, but I know that. I didn't know you knew you needed to.
You guys get into a really weird rhythm.
Who?
You.
Us?
You.
Both of us.
Stop it.
So in conclusion, because I am getting dizzy from all this...
NIA BATES

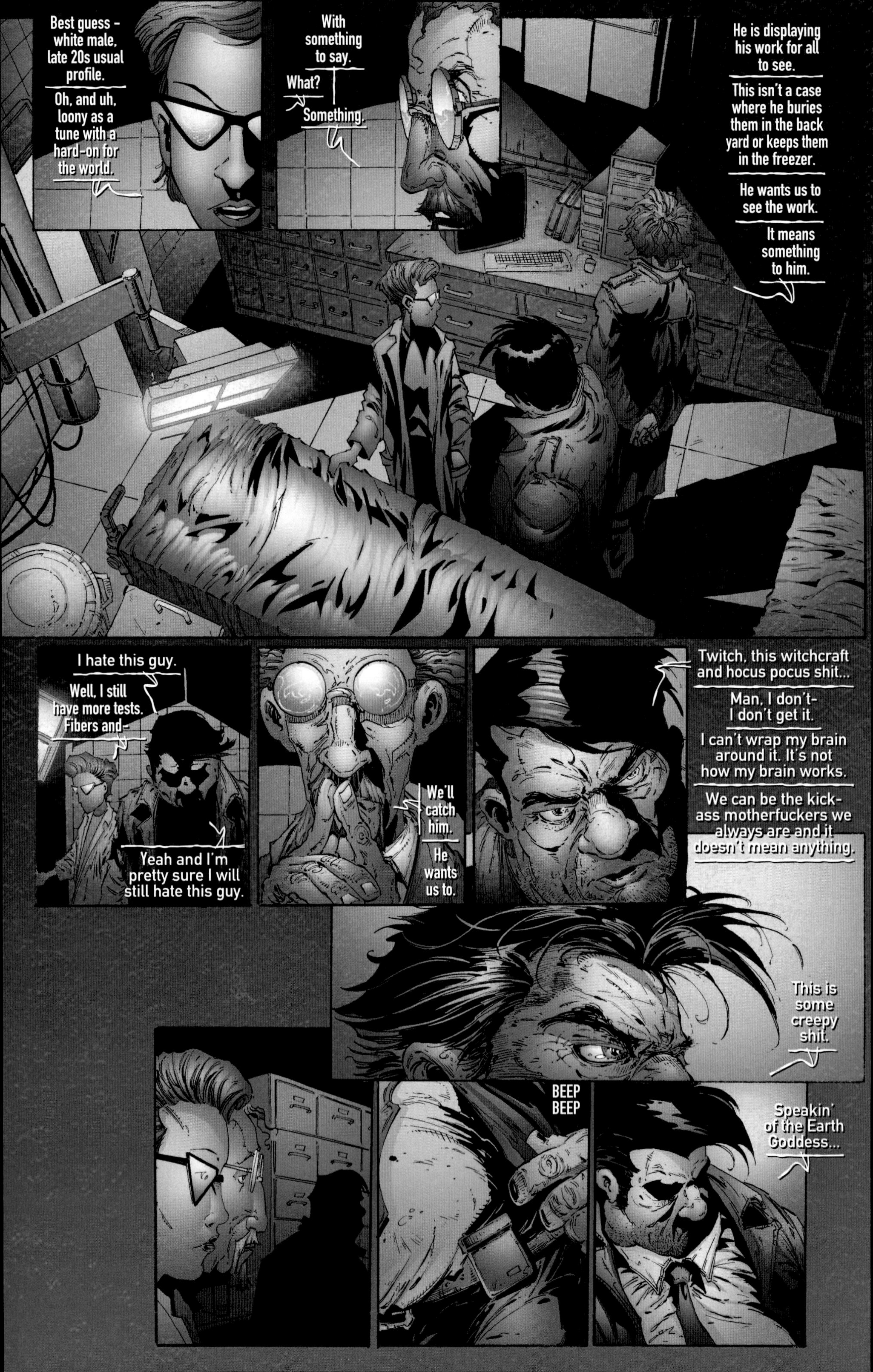

Best guess - white male, late 20s usual profile.
Oh, and uh, loony as a tune with a hard-on for the world.
With something to say.
What?
Something.
He is displaying his work for all to see.
This isn't a case where he buries them in the back yard or keeps them in the freezer.
He wants us to see the work.
It means something to him.
I hate this guy.
Well, I still have more tests. Fibers and-
Yeah and I'm pretty sure I will still hate this guy.
We'll catch him.
He wants us to.
Twitch, this witchcraft and hocus pocus shit...
Man, I don't- I don't get it.
I can't wrap my brain around it. It's not how my brain works.
We can be the kick-ass motherfuckers we always are and it doesn't mean anything.
This is some creepy shit.
BEEP BEEP
Speakin' of the Earth Goddess...

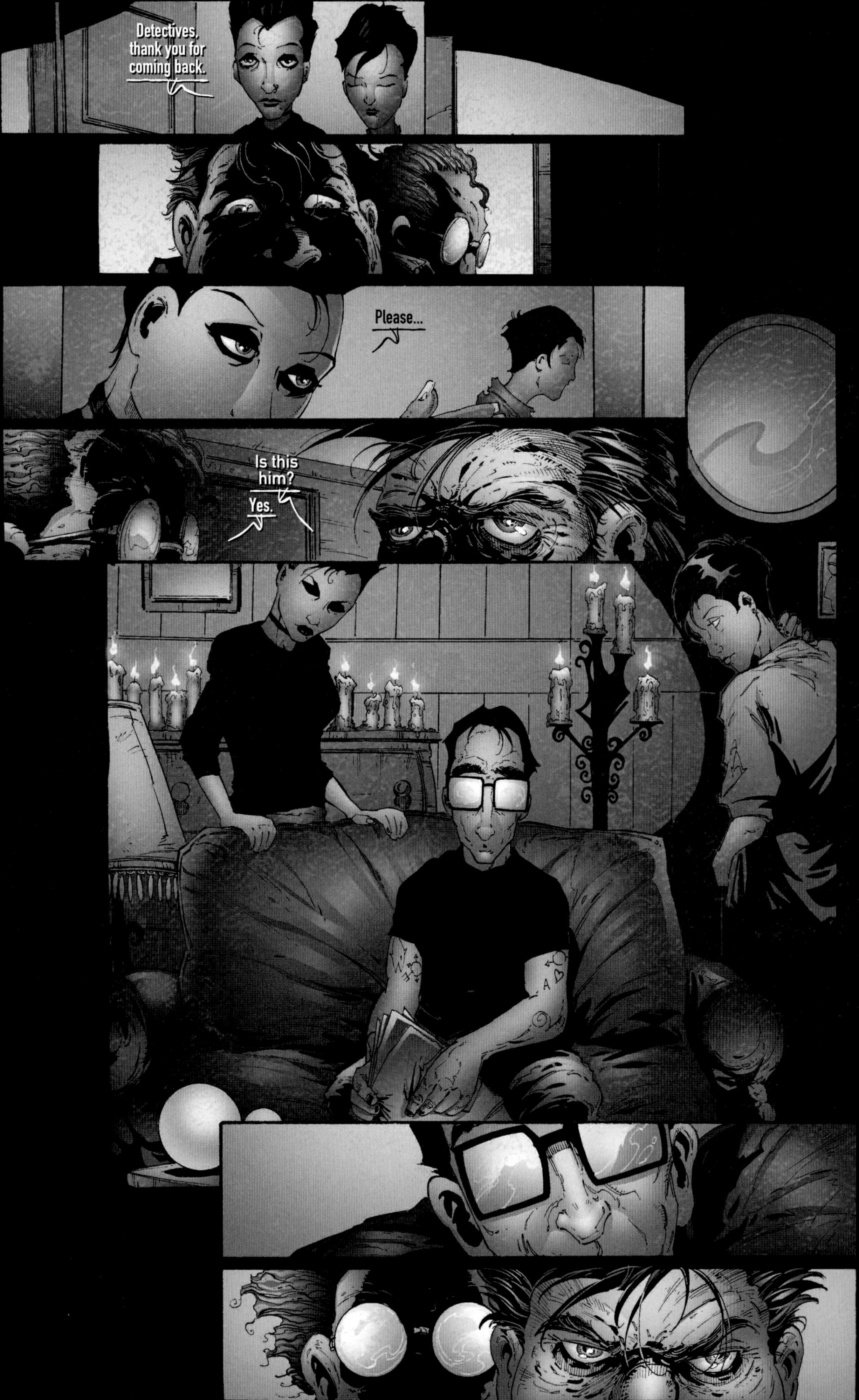
Detectives, thank you for coming back.
Please...
Is this him?
Yes.

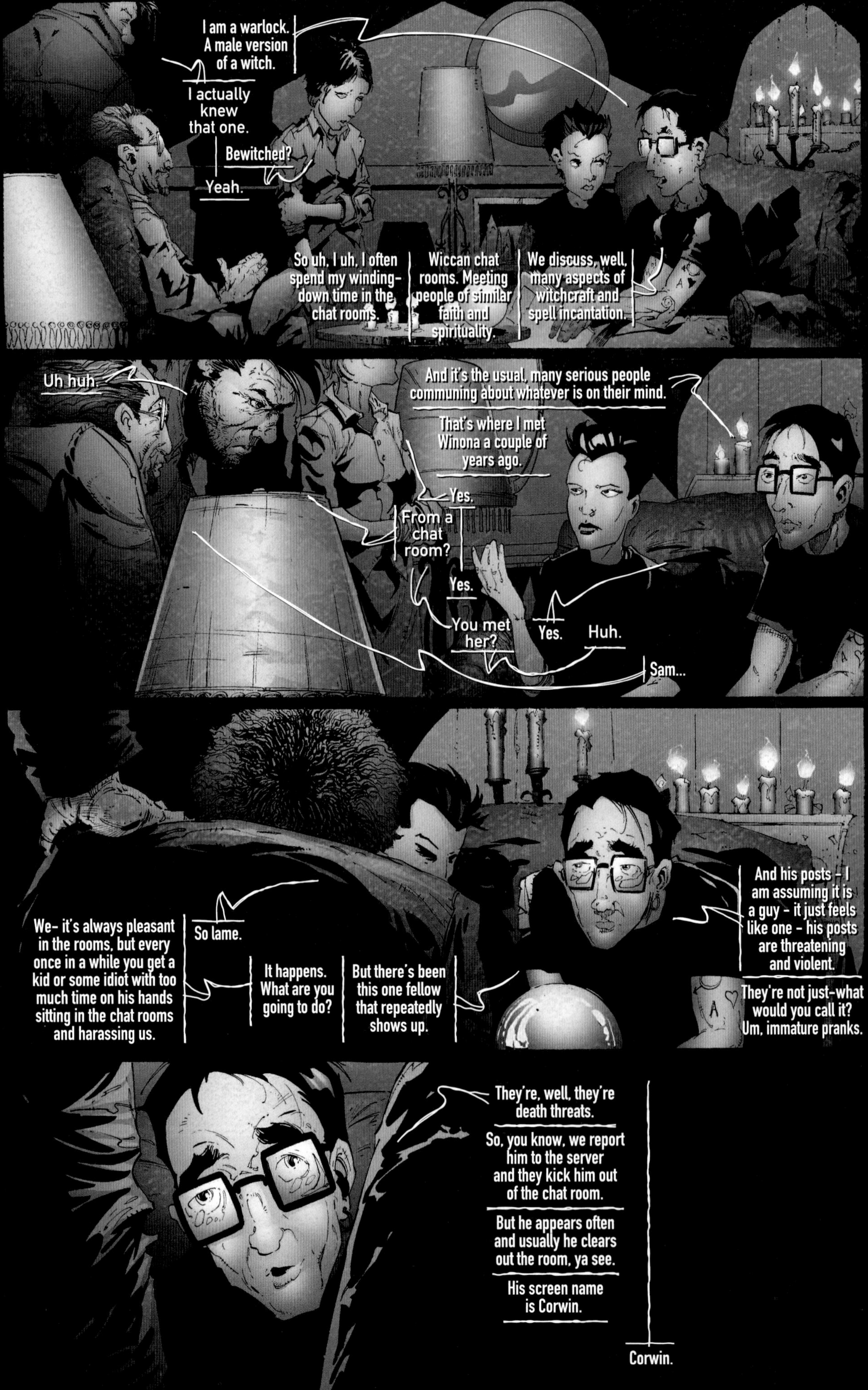
I am a warlock. A male version of a witch.
I actually knew that one.
Bewitched?
Yeah.
So uh, I uh, I often spend my winding-down time in the chat rooms.
Wiccan chat rooms. Meeting people of similar faith and spirituality.
We discuss, well, many aspects of witchcraft and spell incantation.
Uh huh.
And it's the usual, many serious people communing about whatever is on their mind.
That's where I met Winona a couple of years ago.
Yes.
From a chat room?
Yes.
You met her?
Yes.
Huh.
Sam...
We- it's always pleasant in the rooms, but every once in a while you get a kid or some idiot with too much time on his hands sitting in the chat rooms and harassing us.
So lame.
It happens. What are you going to do?
But there's been this one fellow that repeatedly shows up.
And his posts - I am assuming it is a guy - it just feels like one - his posts are threatening and violent.
They're not just-what would you call it? Um, immature pranks.
They're, well, they're death threats.
So, you know, we report him to the server and they kick him out of the chat room.
But he appears often and usually he clears out the room, ya see.
His screen name is Corwin.
Corwin.

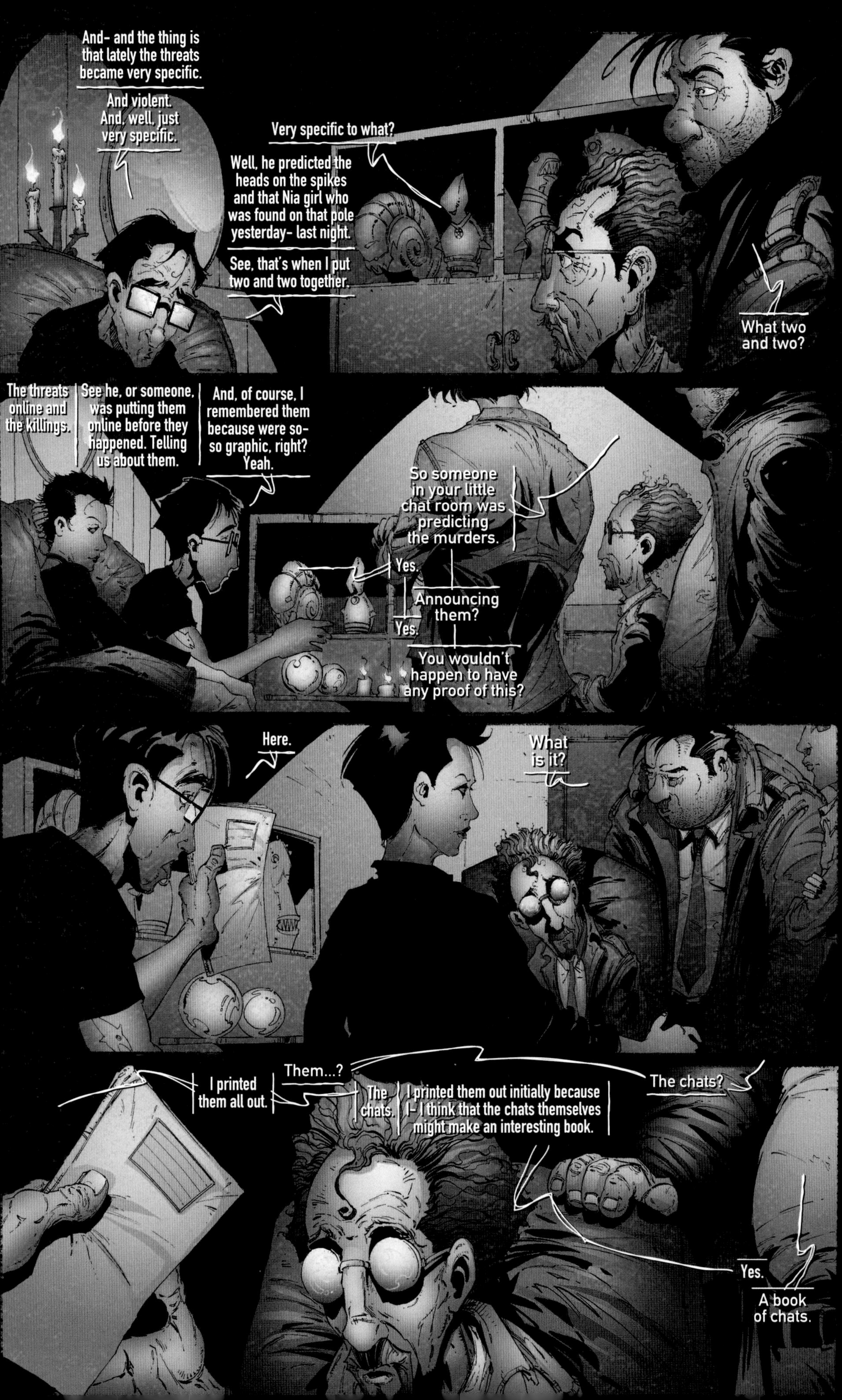

And- and the thing is that lately the threats became very specific.
And violent. And, well, just very specific.
Very specific to what?
Well, he predicted the heads on the spikes and that Nia girl who was found on that pole yesterday- last night.
See, that's when I put two and two together.
What two and two?
The threats online and the killings.
See he, or someone, was putting them online before they happened. Telling us about them.
And, of course, I remembered them because were so- so graphic, right? Yeah.
So someone in your little chat room was predicting the murders.
Yes.
Announcing them?
Yes.
You wouldn't happen to have any proof of this?
Here.
What is it?
I printed them all out.
Them...?
The chats.
I printed them out initially because I- I think that the chats themselves might make an interesting book.
The chats?
Yes.
A book of chats.

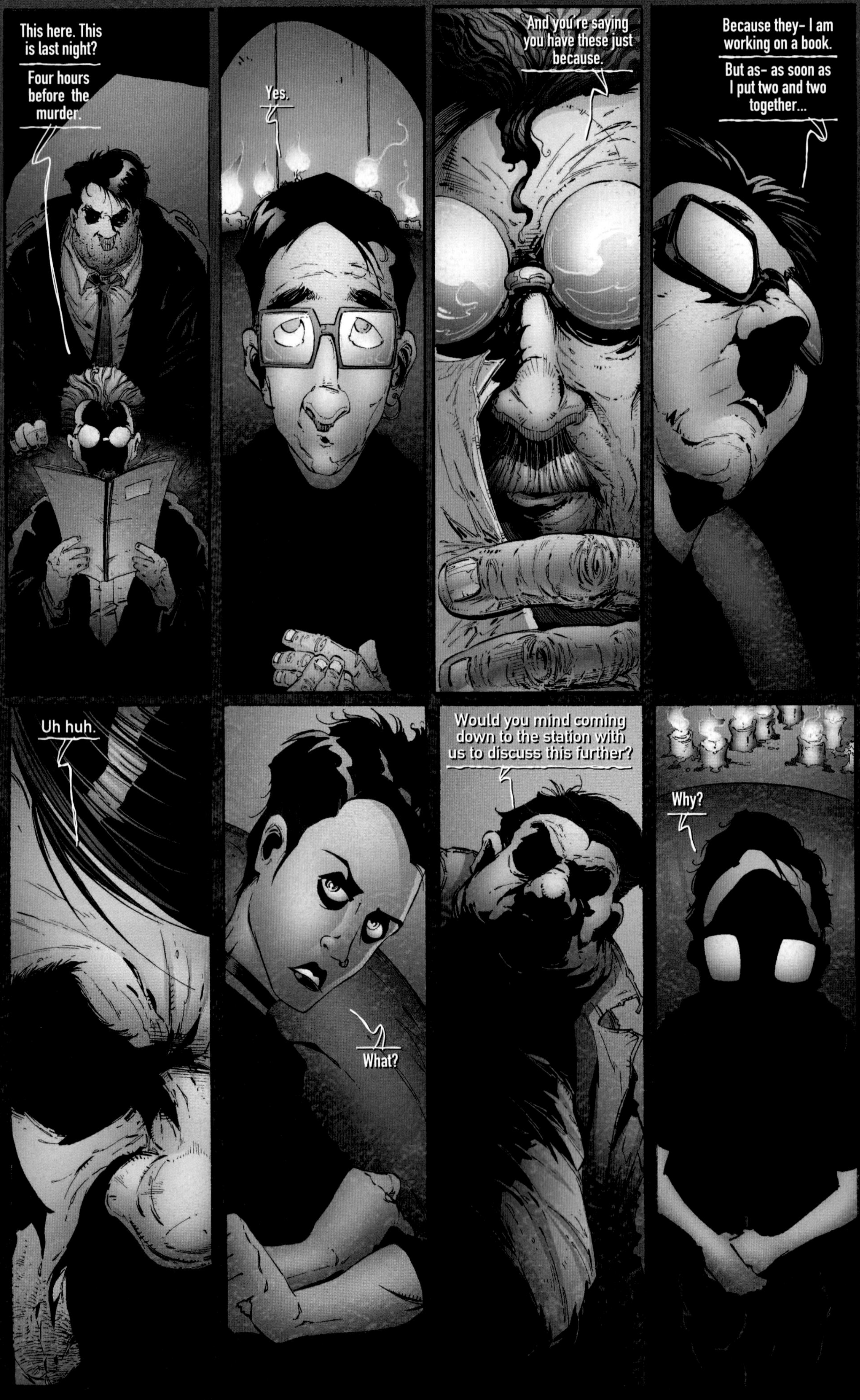
This here. This is last night?
Four hours before the murder.
Yes.
And you're saying you have these just because.
Because they- I am working on a book.
But as- as soon as I put two and two together...
Uh huh.
What?
Would you mind coming down to the station with us to discuss this further?
Why?

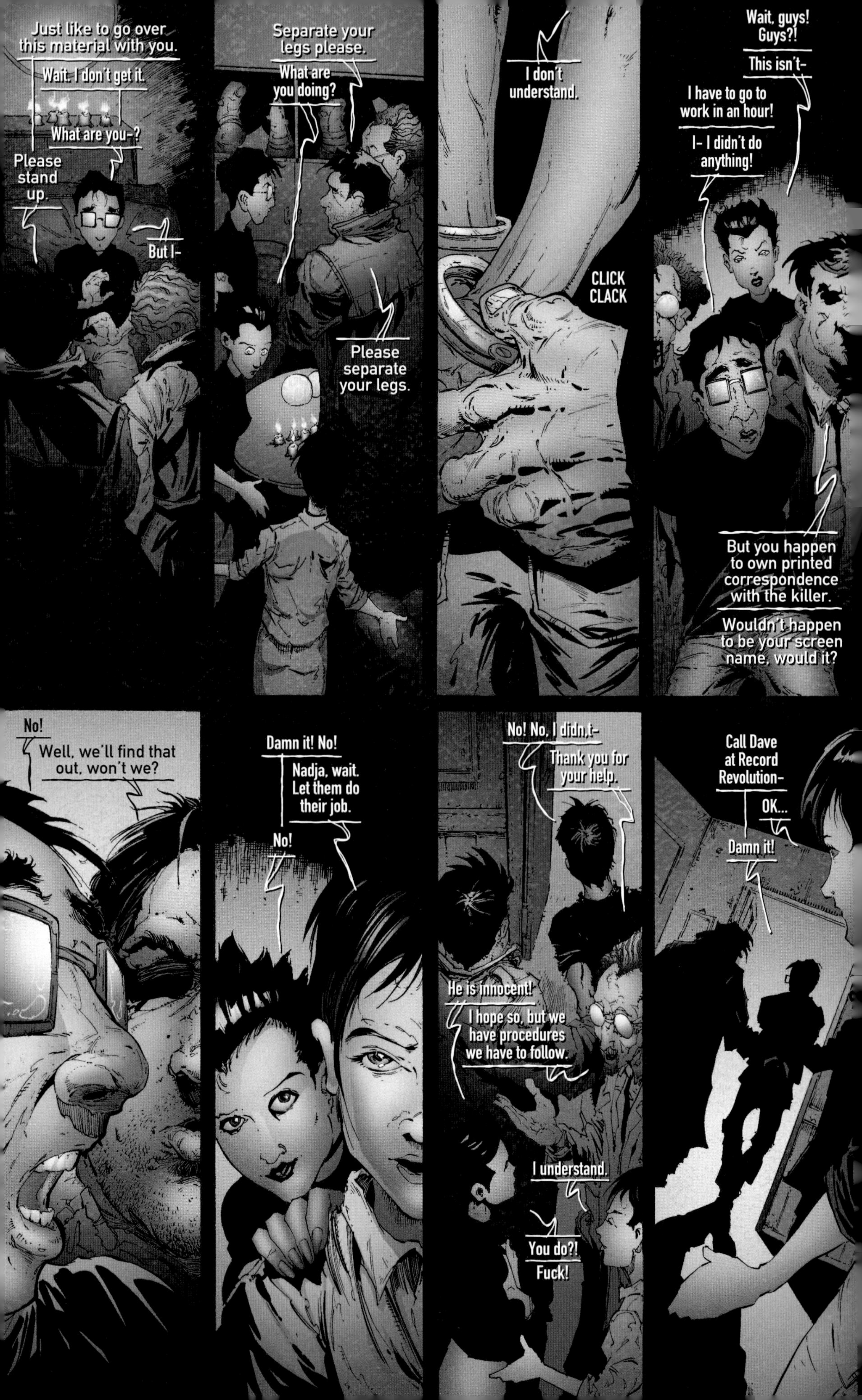
Just like to go over this material with you.
Wait. I don't get it.
What are you-?
Please stand up.
But I-
Separate your legs please.
What are you doing?
Please separate your legs.
I don't understand.
CLICK CLACK
Wait, guys! Guys?!
This isn't-
I have to go to work in an hour!
I- I didn't do anything!
But you happen to own printed correspondence with the killer.
Wouldn't happen to be your screen name, would it?
No!
Well, we'll find that out, won't we?
Damn it! No!
Nadja, wait. Let them do their job.
No!
No! No, I didn,t-
Thank you for your help.
He is innocent!
I hope so, but we have procedures we have to follow.
I understand.
You do?!
Fuck!
Call Dave at Record Revolution-
OK...
Damn it!

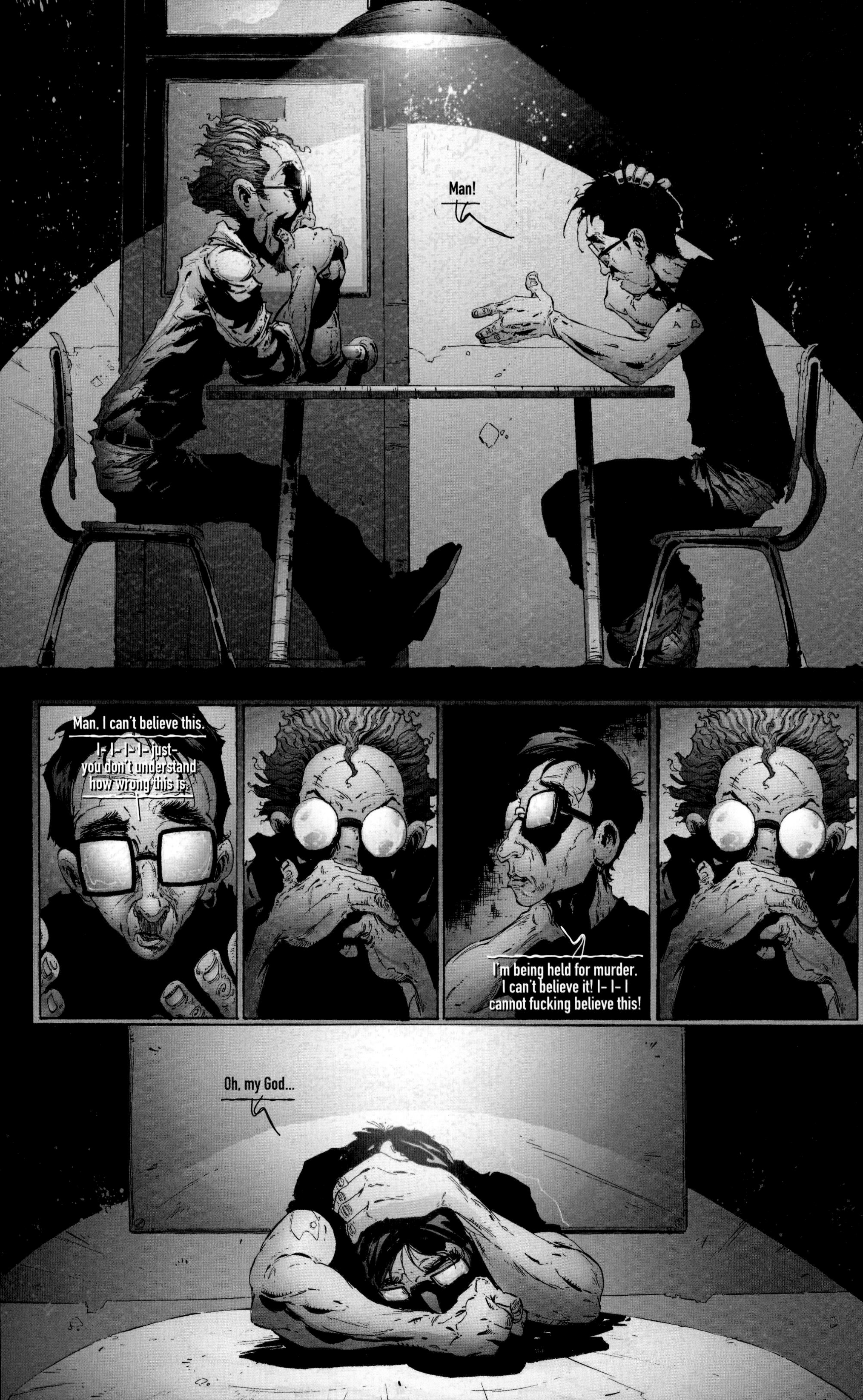

Man!
Man. I can't believe this.
I- I- I- I- just- you don't understand how wrong this is.
I'm being held for murder. I can't believe it! I- I- I cannot fucking believe this!
Oh, my God...

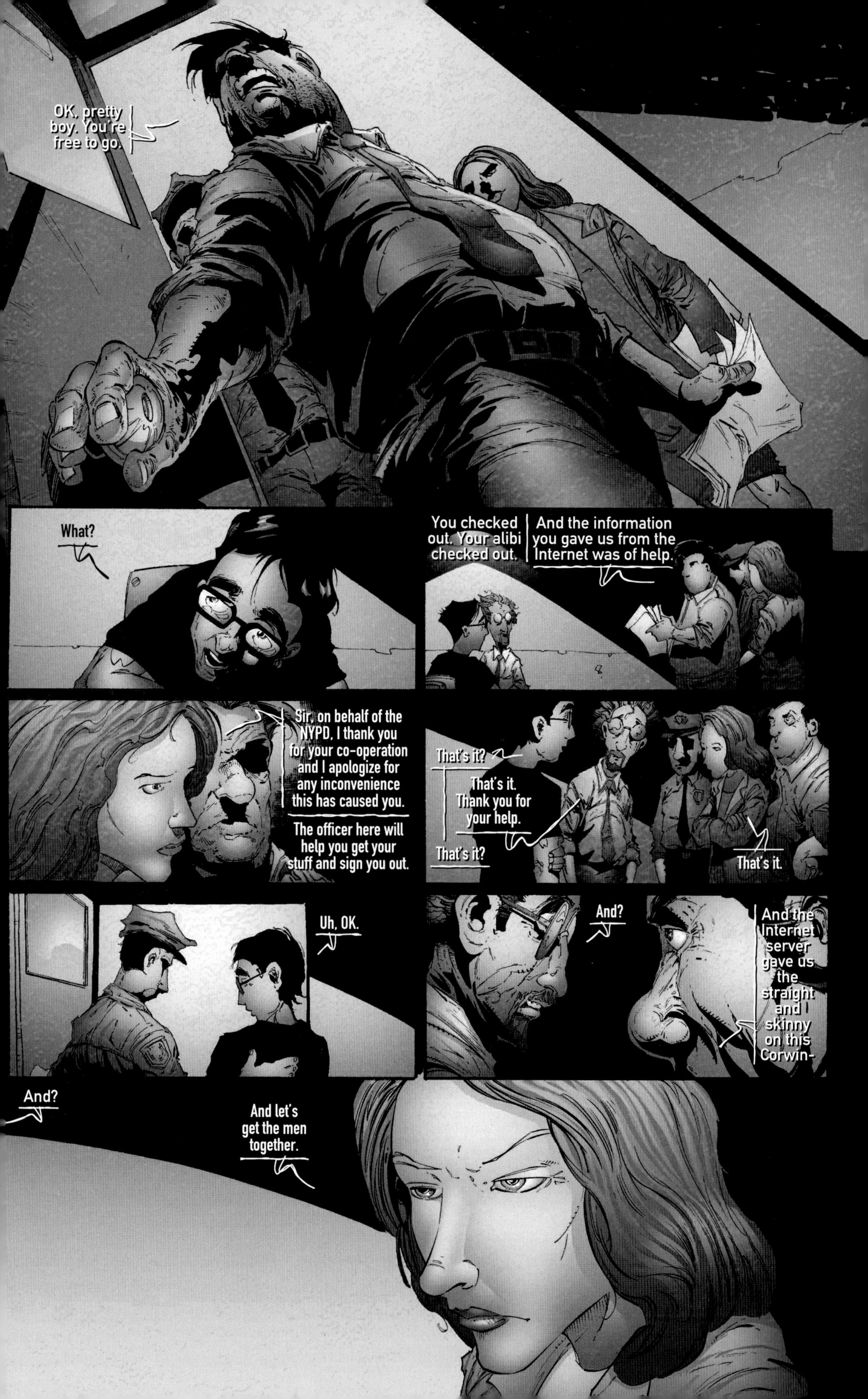
OK, pretty boy. You're free to go.
What?
You checked out. Your alibi checked out.
And the information you gave us from the Internet was of help.
Sir, on behalf of the NYPD, I thank you for your co-operation and I apologize for any inconvenience this has caused you.
The officer here will help you get your stuff and sign you out.
That's it?
That's it. Thank you for your help.
That's it?
That's it.
Uh, OK.
And?
And the Internet server gave us the straight and skinny on this Corwin-
And?
And let's get the men together.

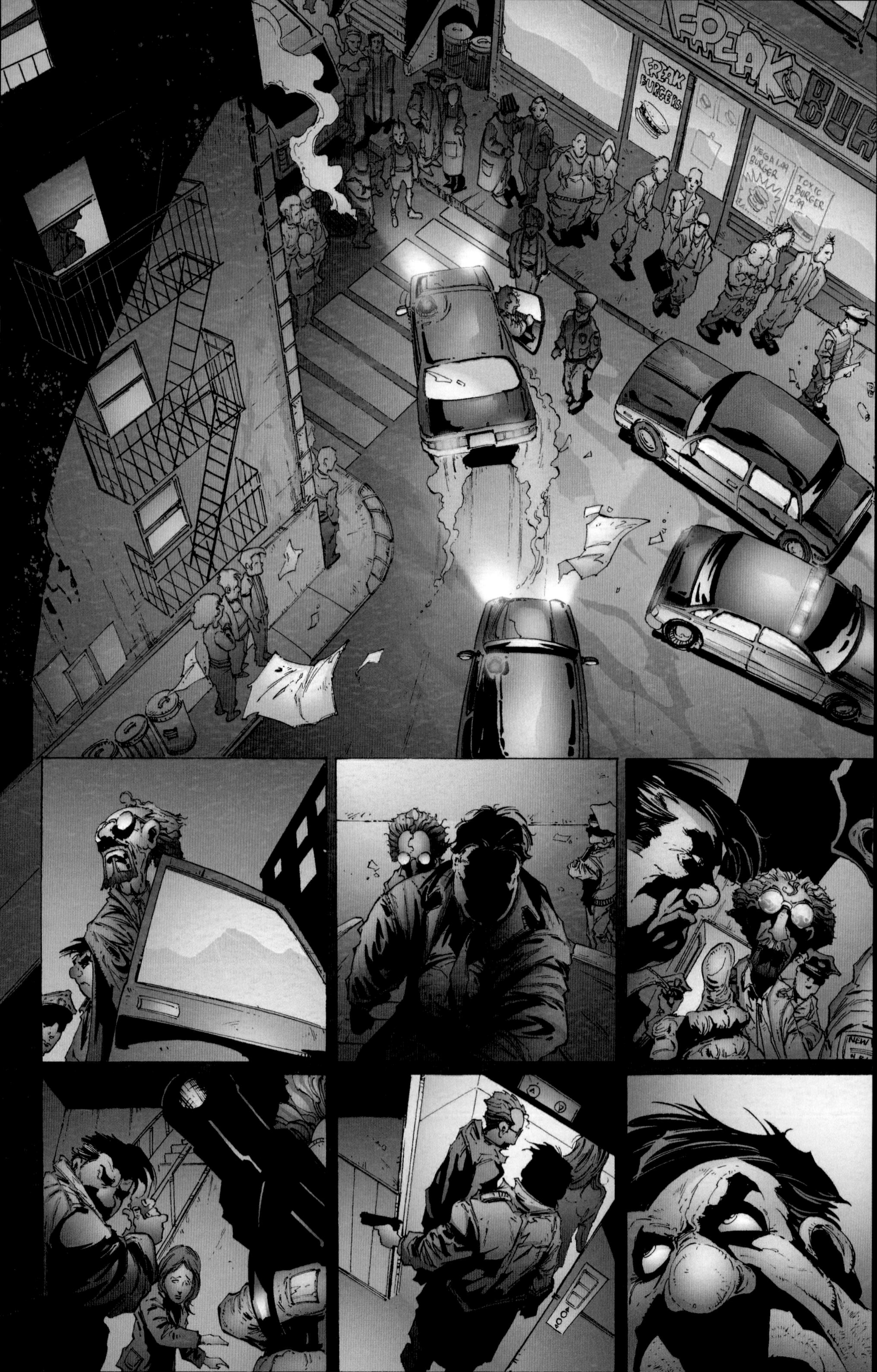
FREAK
FREAK BURGERS
VEGA 1.99 BURGER
TOXIC BURGER 2.99

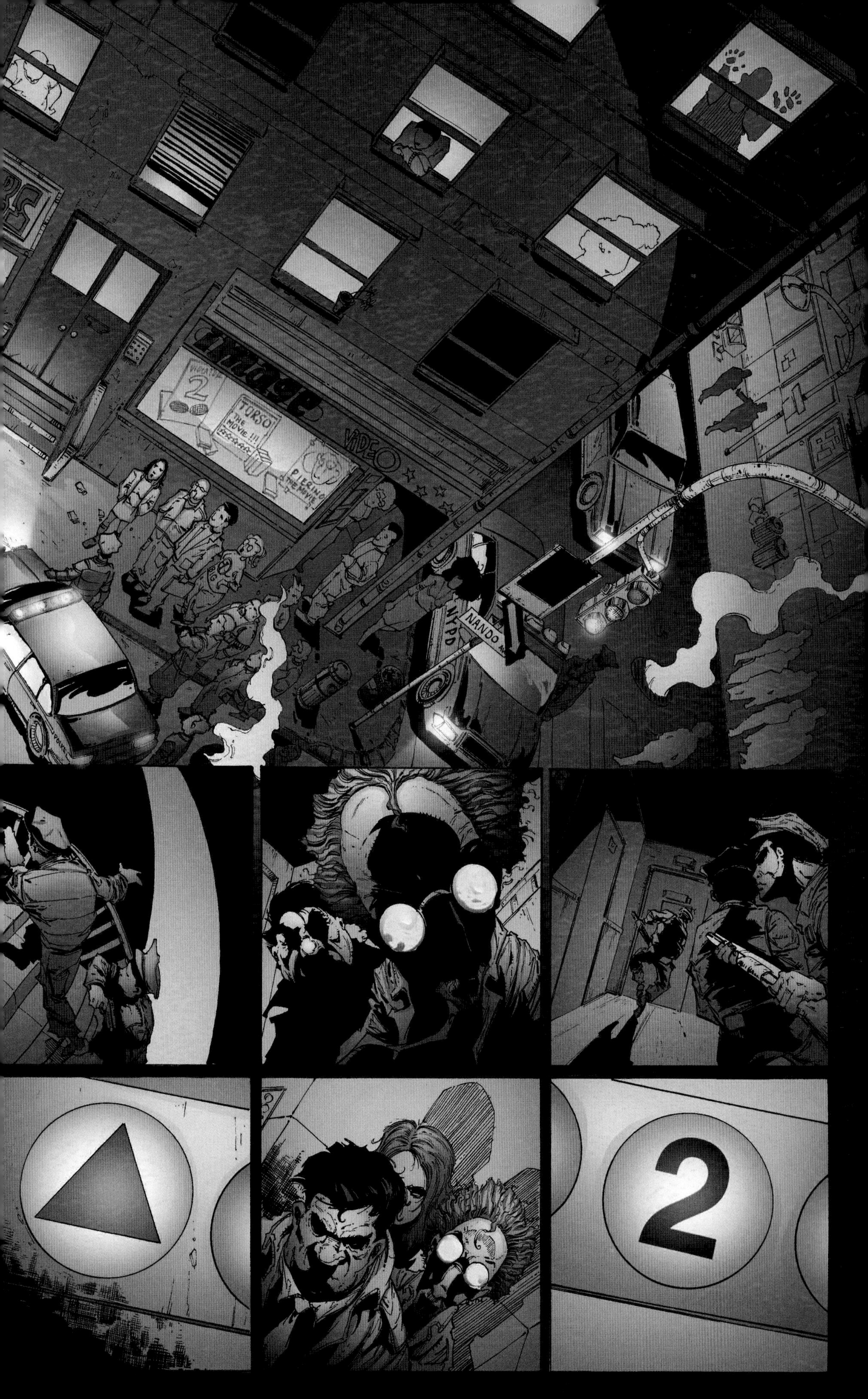
TORSO
THE MOVIE !!!
VIDEO
NYPD
2

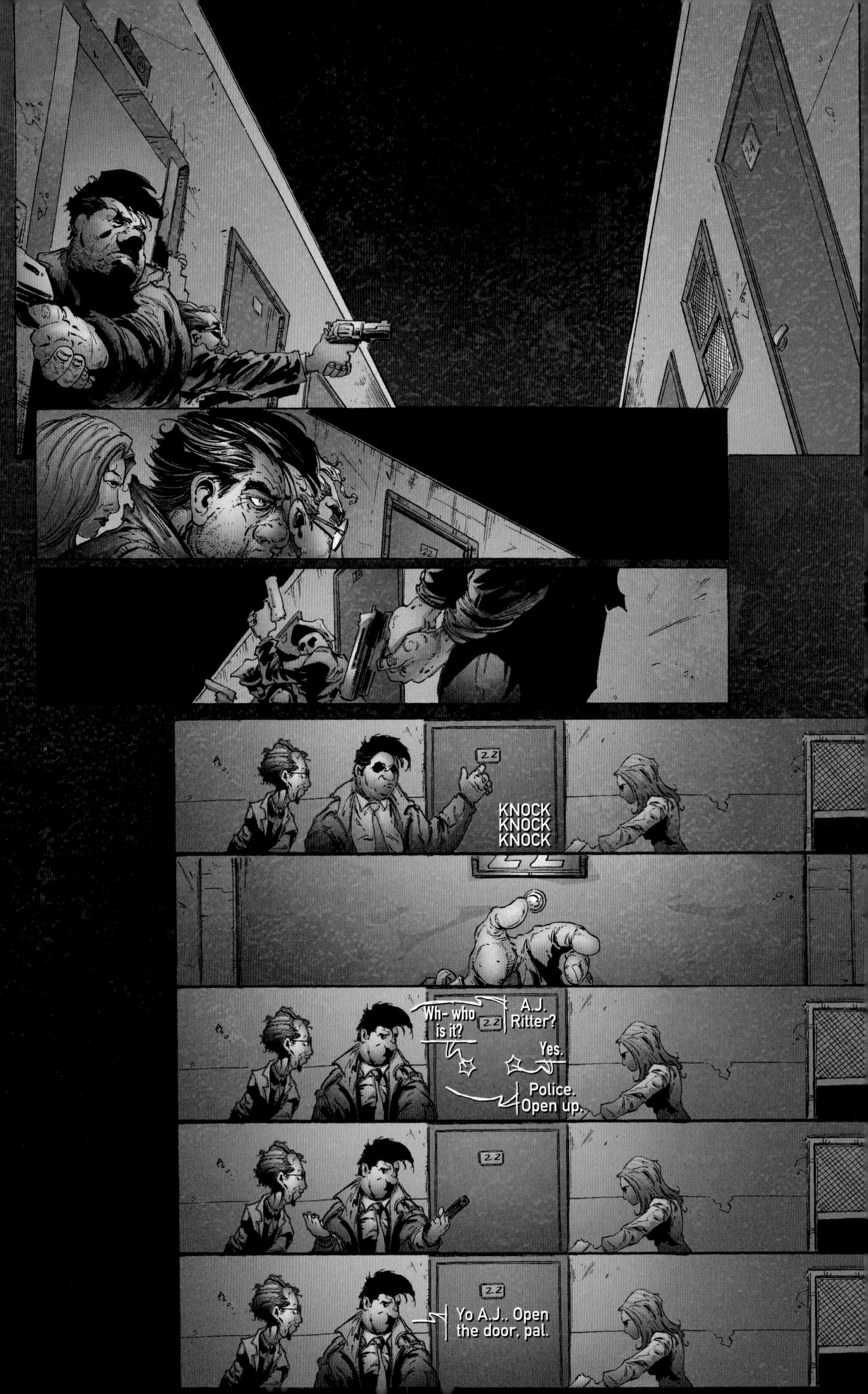
KNOCK
KNOCK
KNOCK
Wh- who is it?
A.J. Ritter?
Yes.
Police. Open up.
Yo A.J.. Open the door, pal.

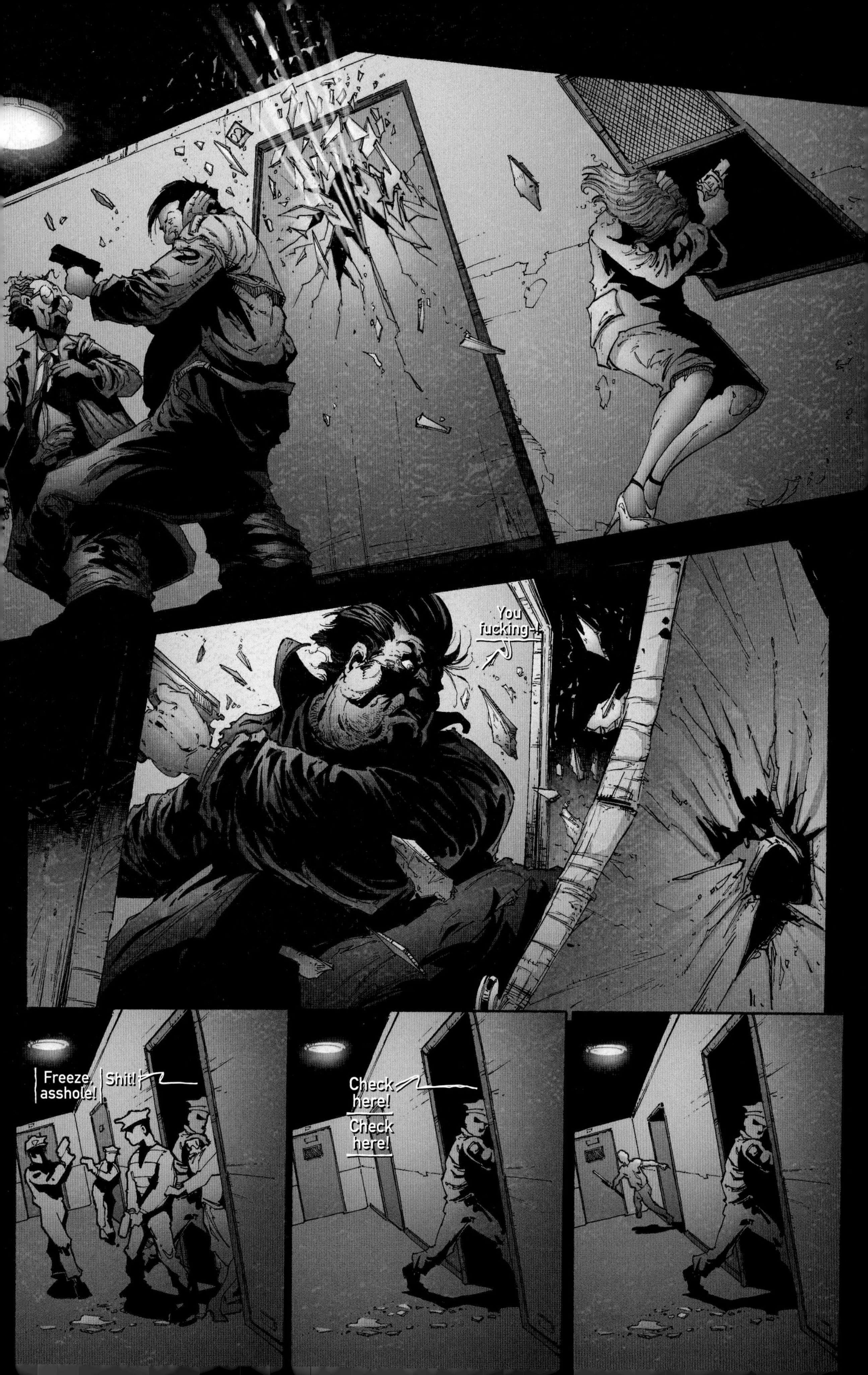
You fucking--!
Freeze, asshole!
Shit!
Check here!
Check here!

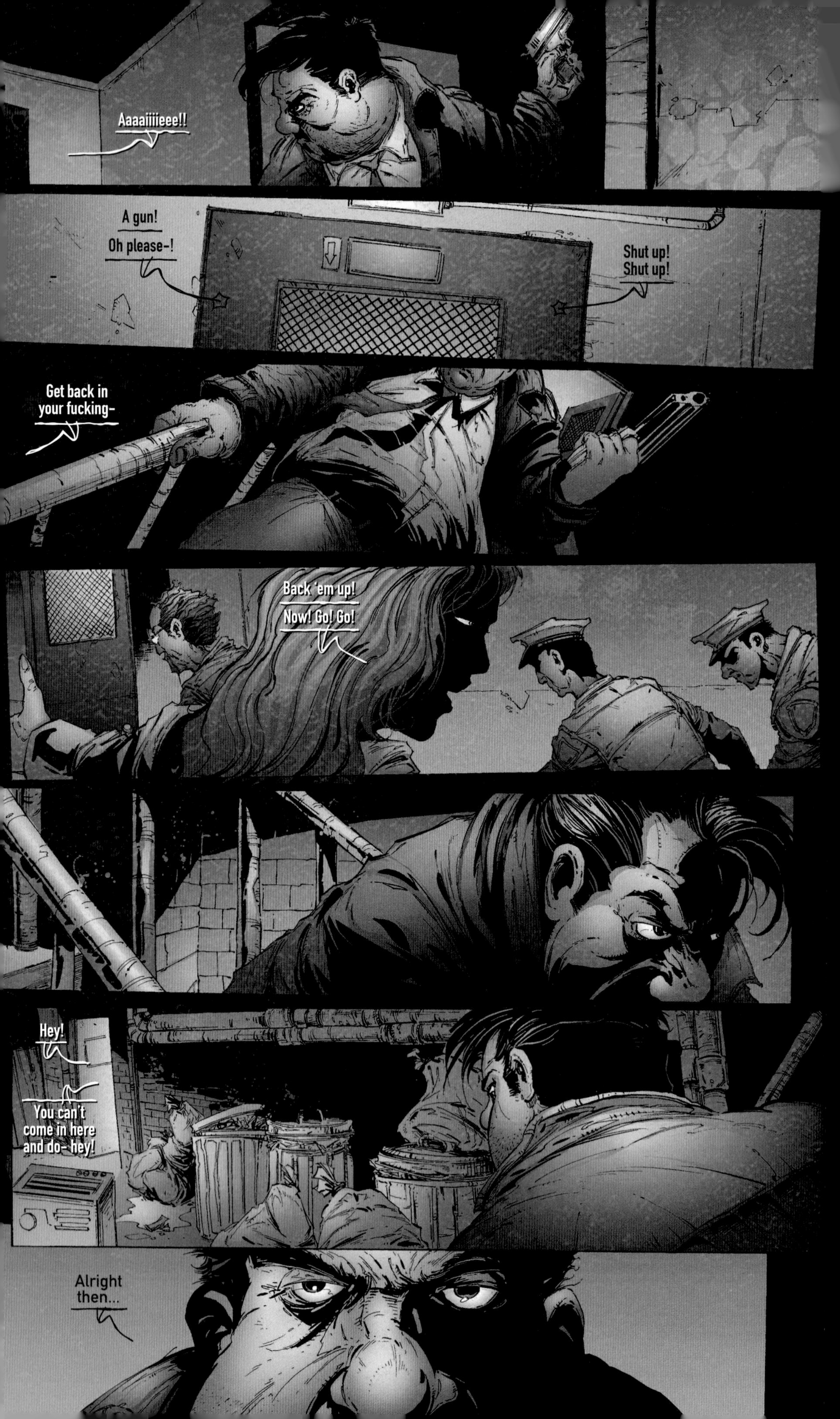
Aaaaiiiieee!!
A gun!
Oh please-!
Shut up!
Shut up!
Get back in your fucking-
Back 'em up!
Now! Go! Go!
Hey!
You can't come in here and do- hey!
Alright then...

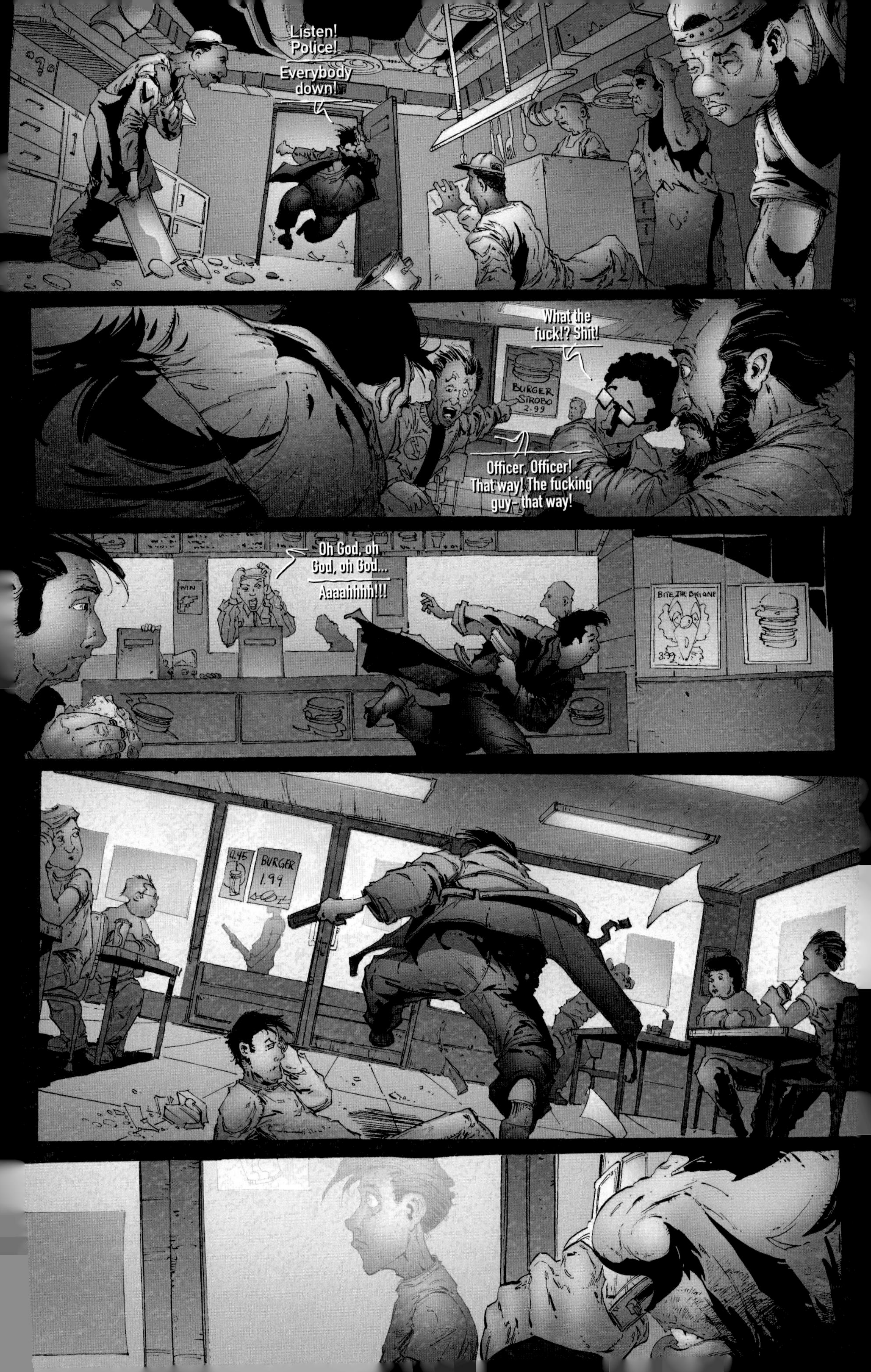
Listen! Police!
Everybody down!
What the fuck!? Shit!
BURGER STROBO 2.99
Officer, Officer! That way! The fucking guy– that way!
Oh God, oh God, oh God...
Aaaahhhh!!!
WIN
BITE THE BIG ONE
3.99
0.45
BURGER 1.99

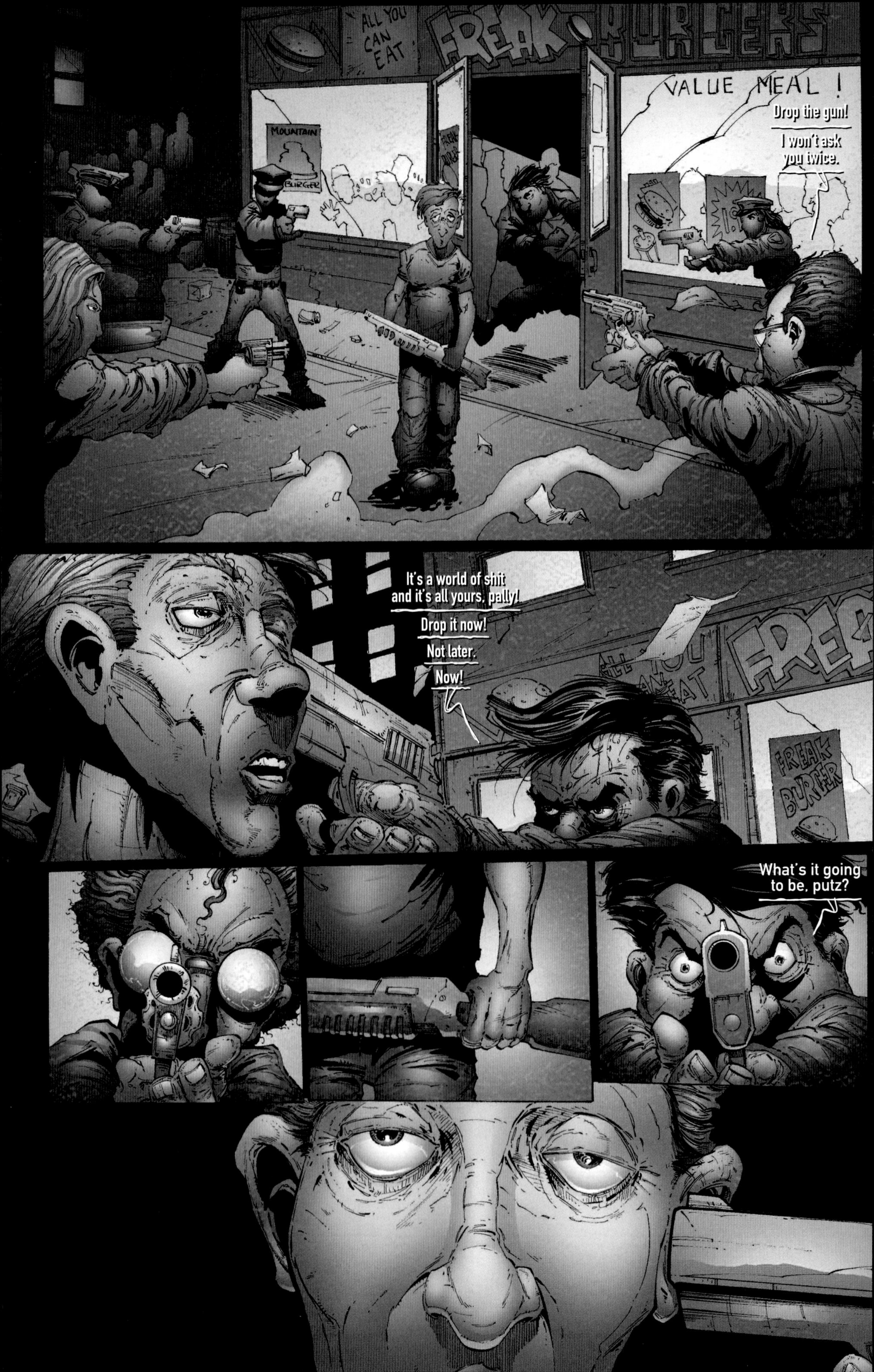

ALL YOU CAN EAT
FREAK BURGERS
VALUE MEAL !
MOUNTAIN BURGER
Drop the gun!
I won't ask you twice.
It's a world of shit and it's all yours, pally!
Drop it now!
Not later.
Now!
FREAK BURGER
What's it going to be, putz?

WITCHCRAFT

PART 4

SAM AND TWITCH

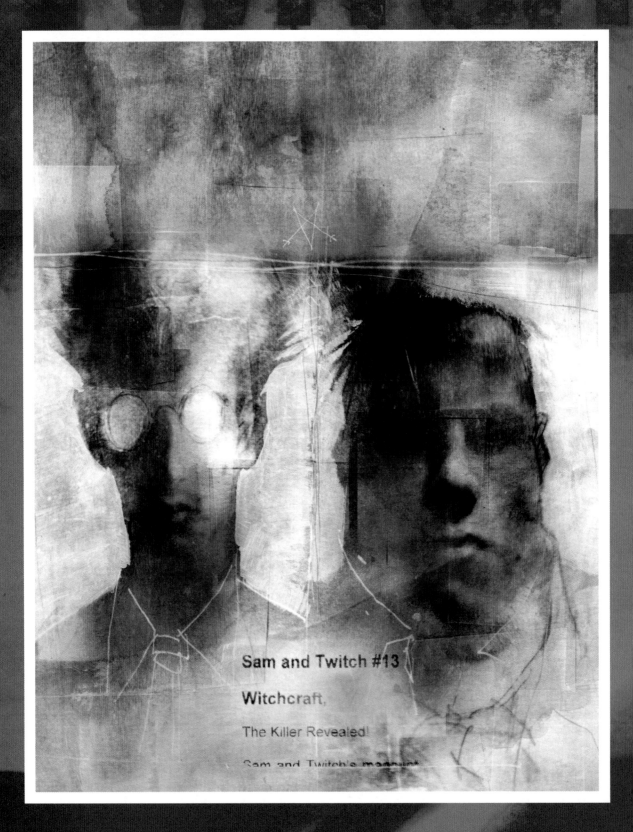

Sam and Twitch #13

Witchcraft,

The Killer Revealed!

Sam and Twitch's memoir

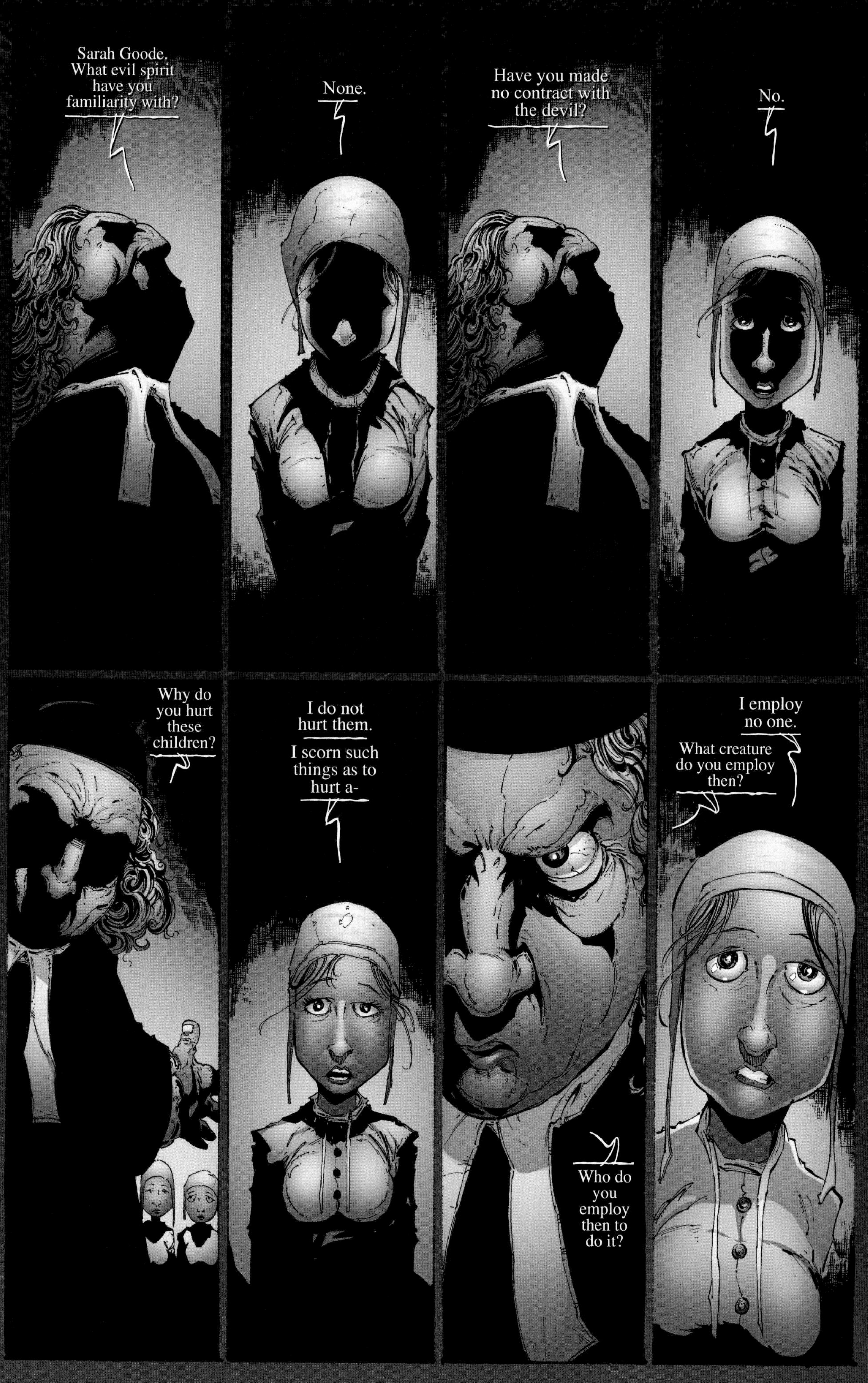
Sarah Goode. What evil spirit have you familiarity with?
None.
Have you made no contract with the devil?
No.
Why do you hurt these children?
I do not hurt them.
I scorn such things as to hurt a-
Who do you employ then to do it?
What creature do you employ then?
I employ no one.

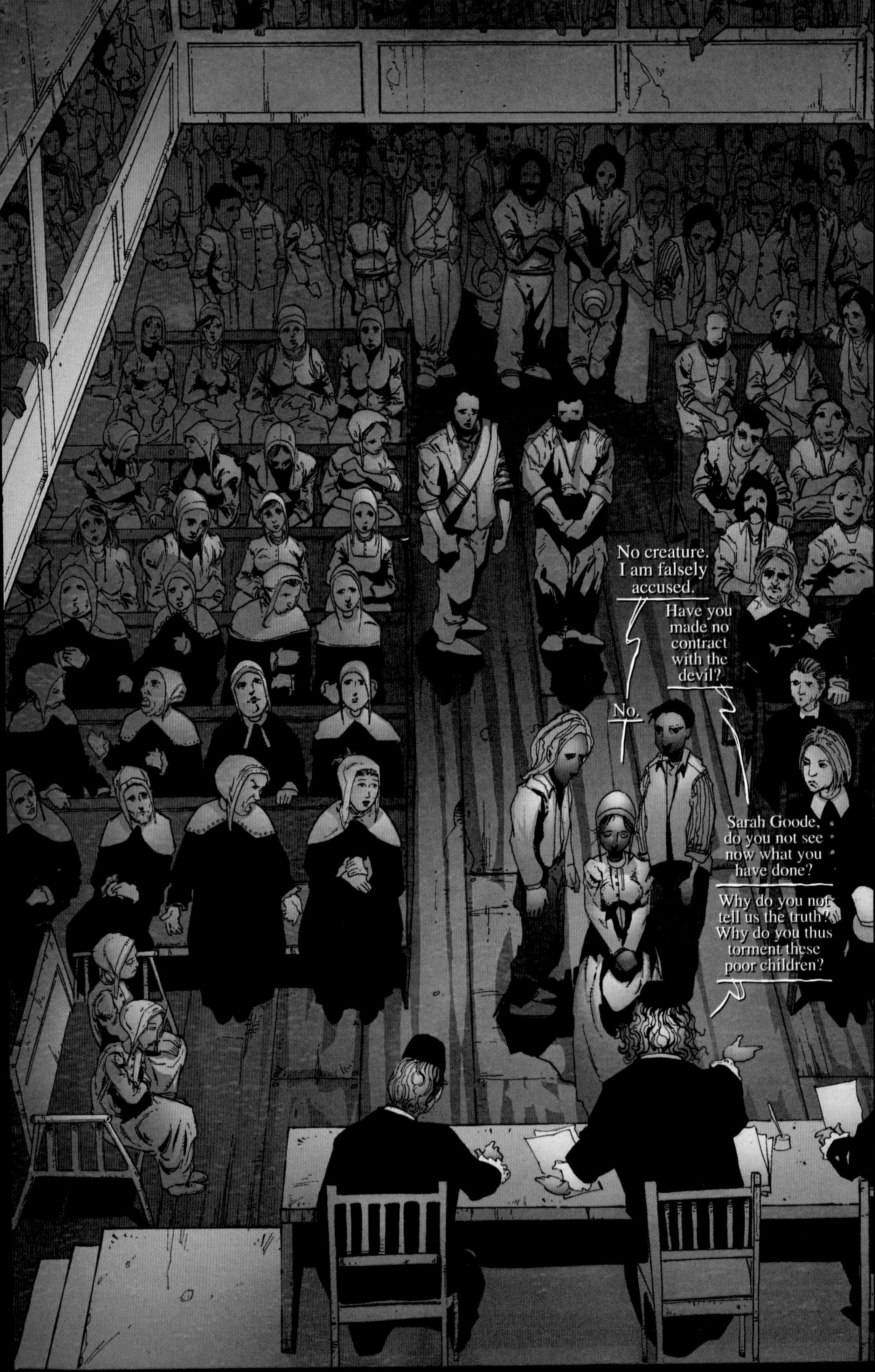
No creature. I am falsely accused.
Have you made no contract with the devil?
No.
Sarah Goode, do you not see now what you have done?
Why do you not tell us the truth? Why do you thus torment these poor children?

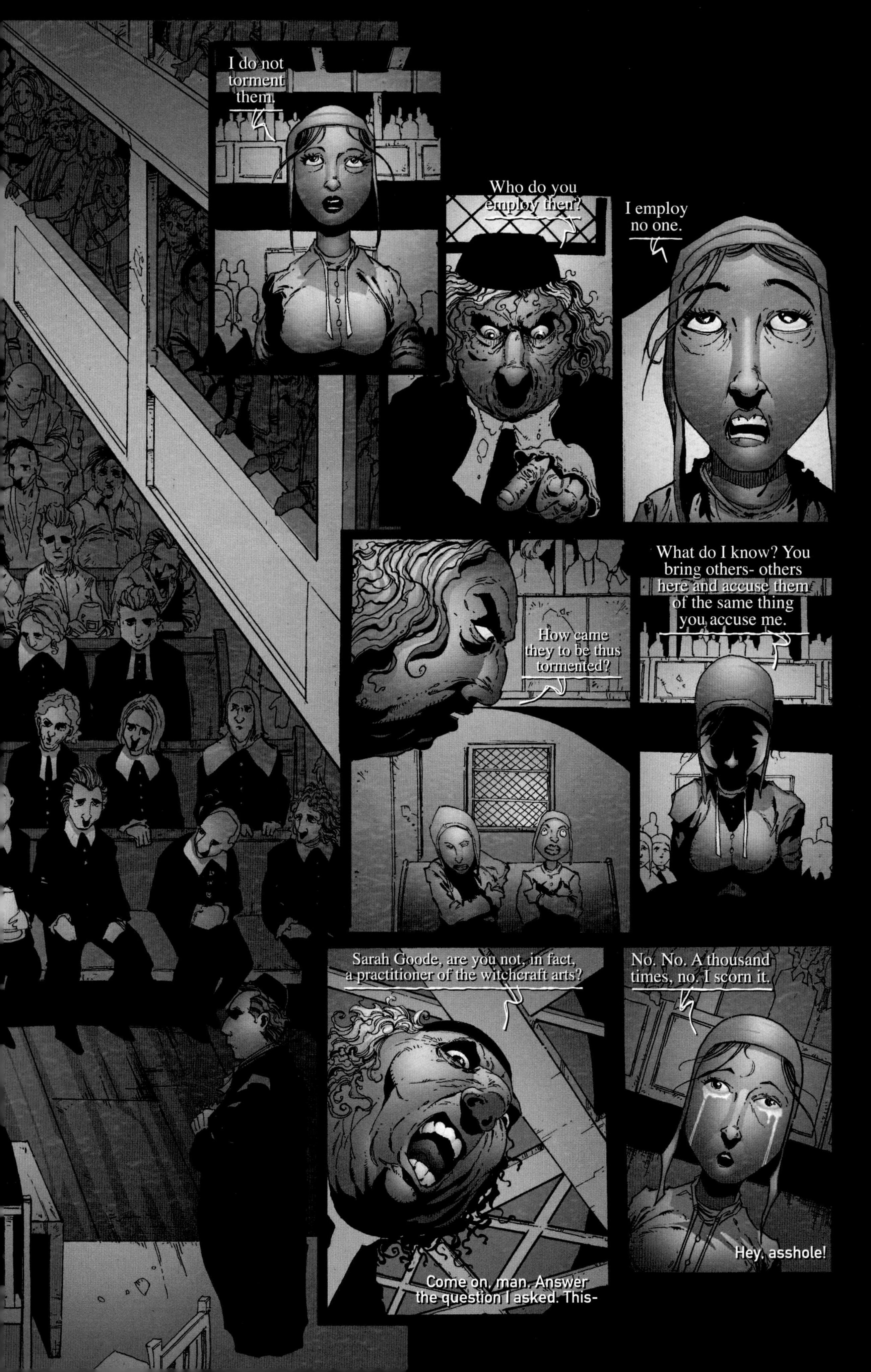
I do not torment them.
Who do you employ then?
I employ no one.
How came they to be thus tormented?
What do I know? You bring others- others here and accuse them of the same thing you accuse me.
Sarah Goode, are you not, in fact, a practitioner of the witchcraft arts?
No. No. A thousand times, no. I scorn it.
Come on, man. Answer the question I asked. This-
Hey, asshole!

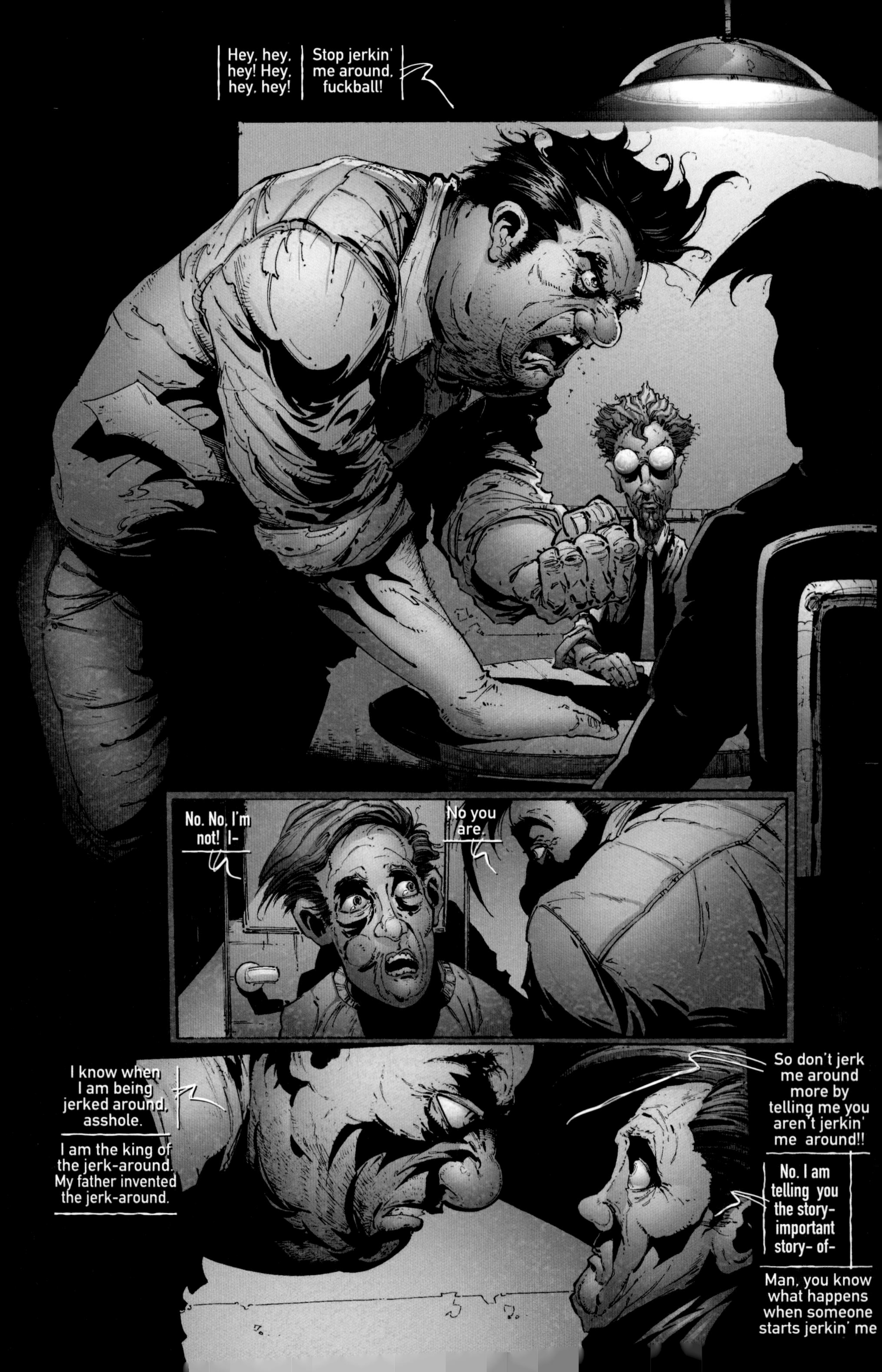
Hey, hey, hey! Hey, hey, hey!
Stop jerkin' me around, fuckball!
No. No, I'm not! I-
No you are.
I know when I am being jerked around, asshole.
I am the king of the jerk-around. My father invented the jerk-around.
So don't jerk me around more by telling me you aren't jerkin' me around!!
No. I am telling you the story-important story- of-
Man, you know what happens when someone starts jerkin' me

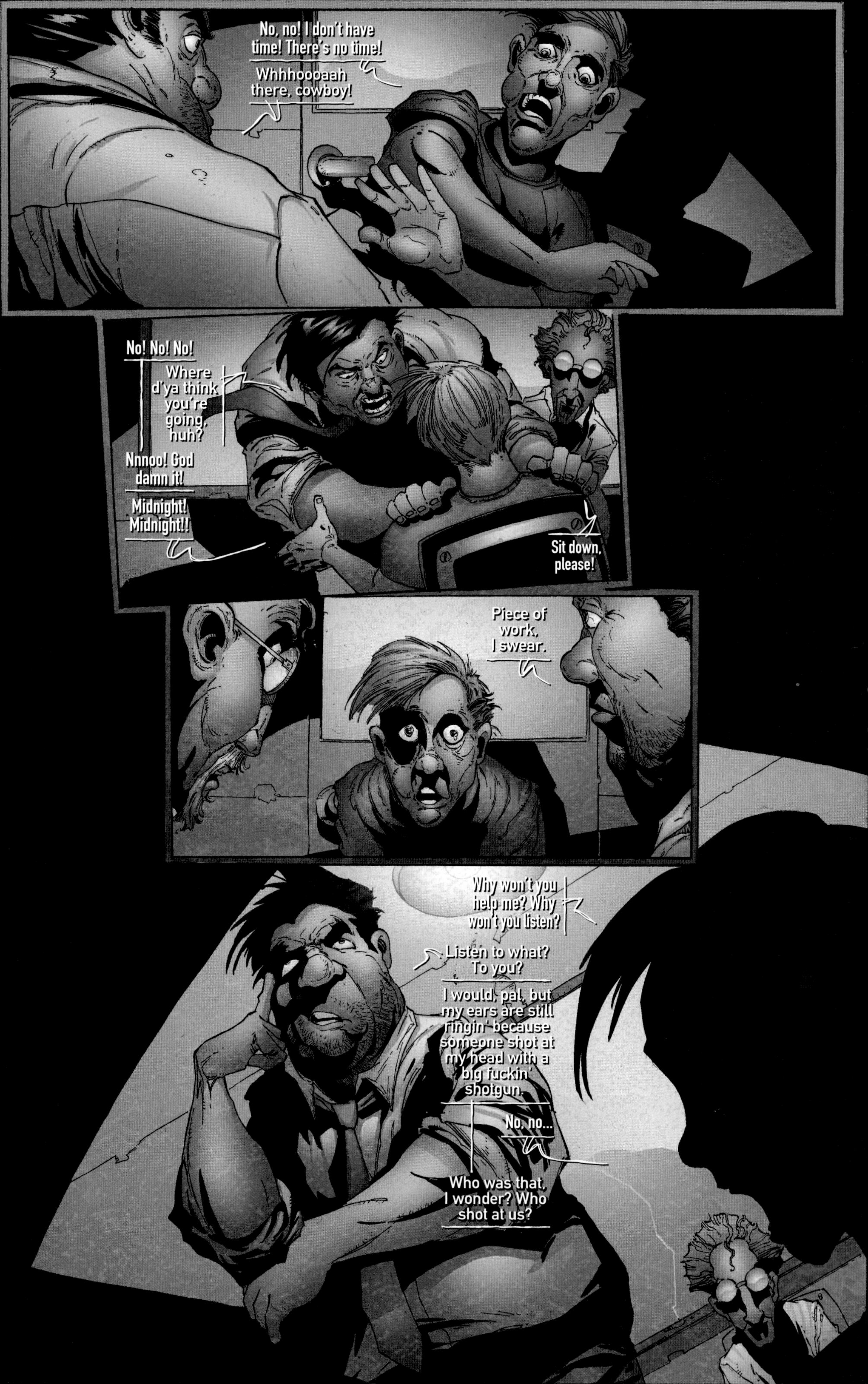
No, no! I don't have time! There's no time!
Whhhooooaah there, cowboy!
No! No! No!
Where d'ya think you're going, huh?
Nnnoo! God damn it!
Midnight! Midnight!!
Sit down, please!
Piece of work, I swear.
Why won't you help me? Why won't you listen?
Listen to what? To you?
I would, pal, but my ears are still ringin' because someone shot at my head with a big fuckin' shotgun.
No, no...
Who was that, I wonder? Who shot at us?

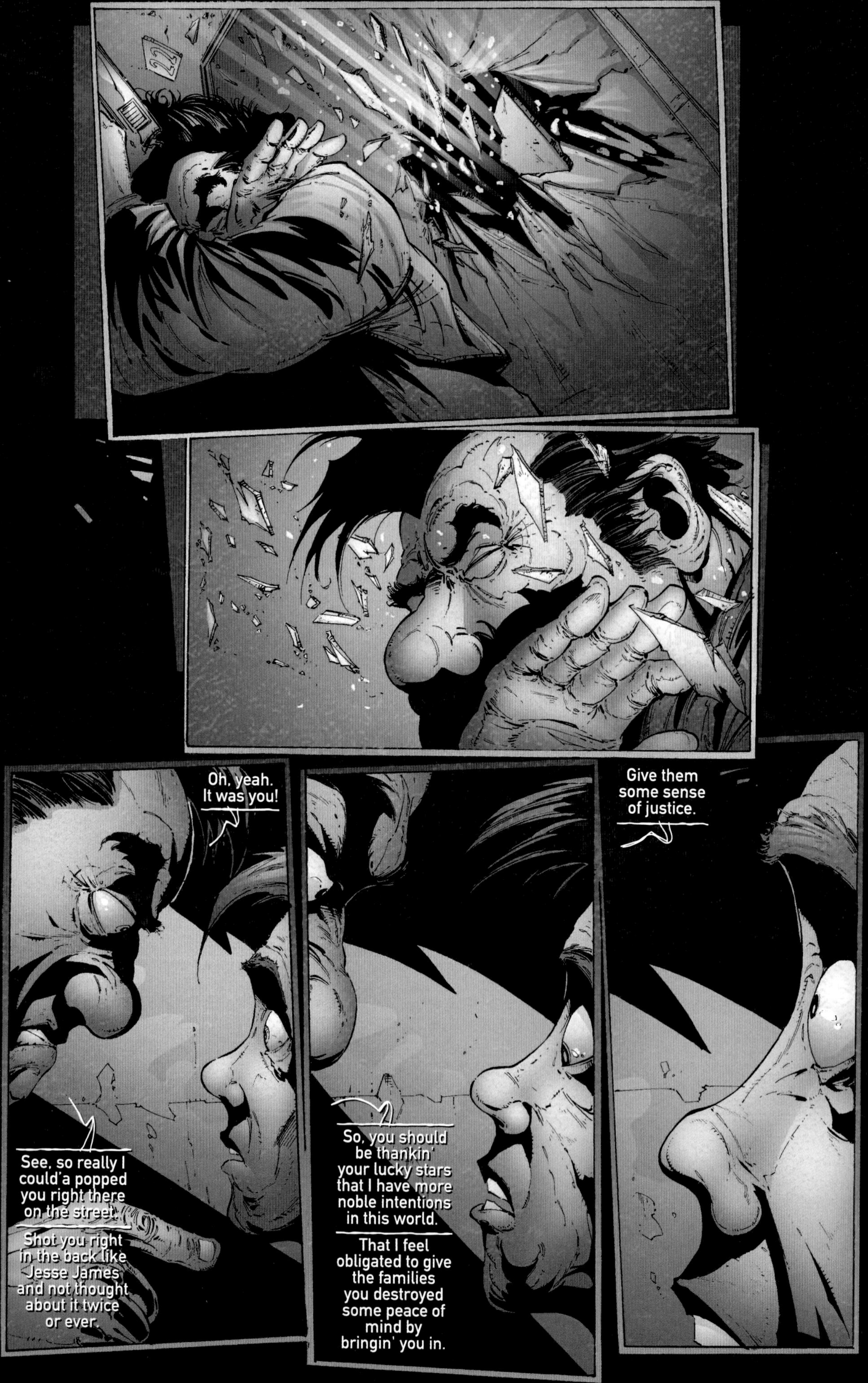
Oh, yeah. It was you!
See, so really I could'a popped you right there on the street.
Shot you right in the back like Jesse James and not thought about it twice or ever.
So, you should be thankin' your lucky stars that I have more noble intentions in this world.
That I feel obligated to give the families you destroyed some peace of mind by bringin' you in.
Give them some sense of justice.

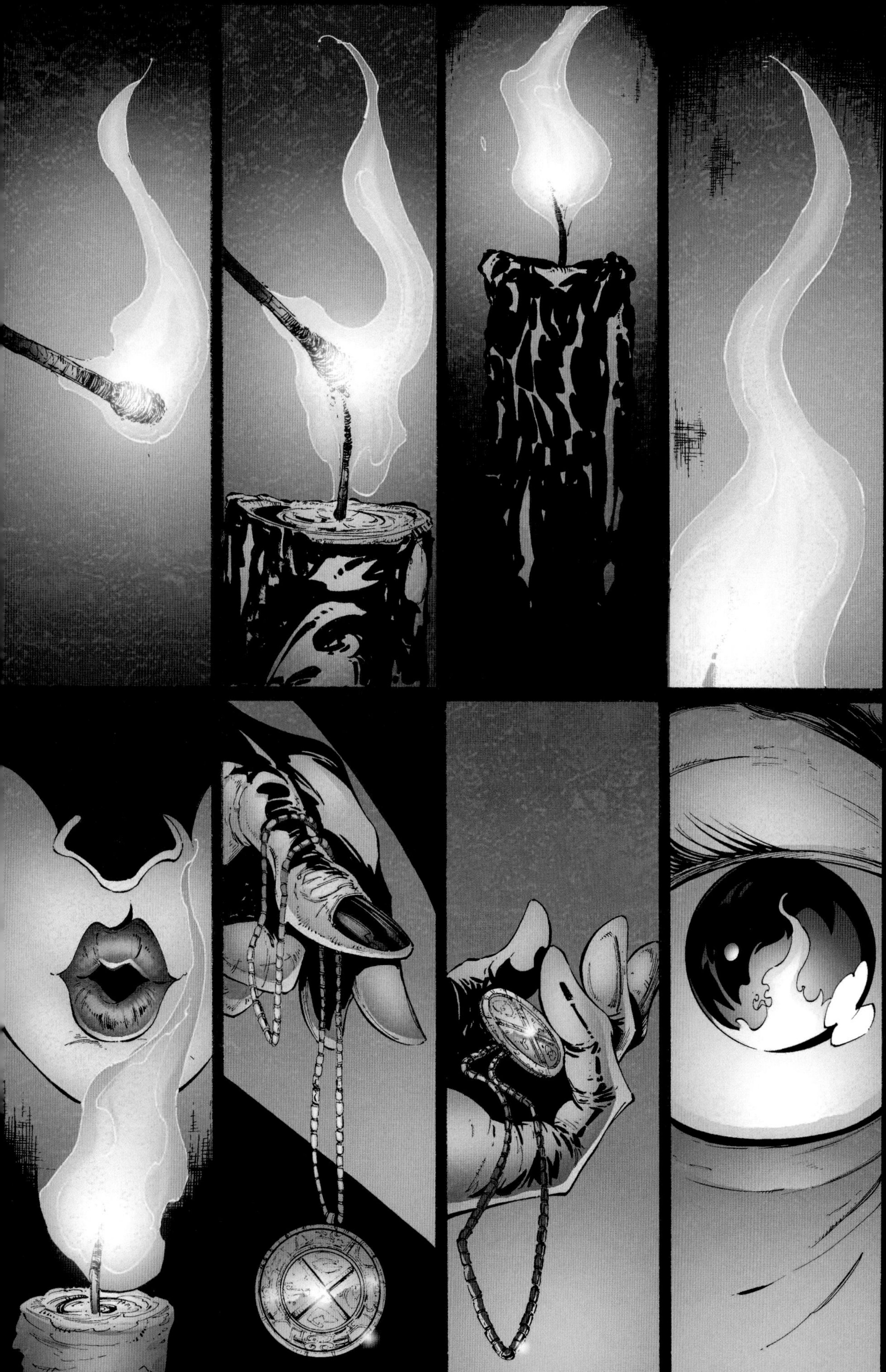

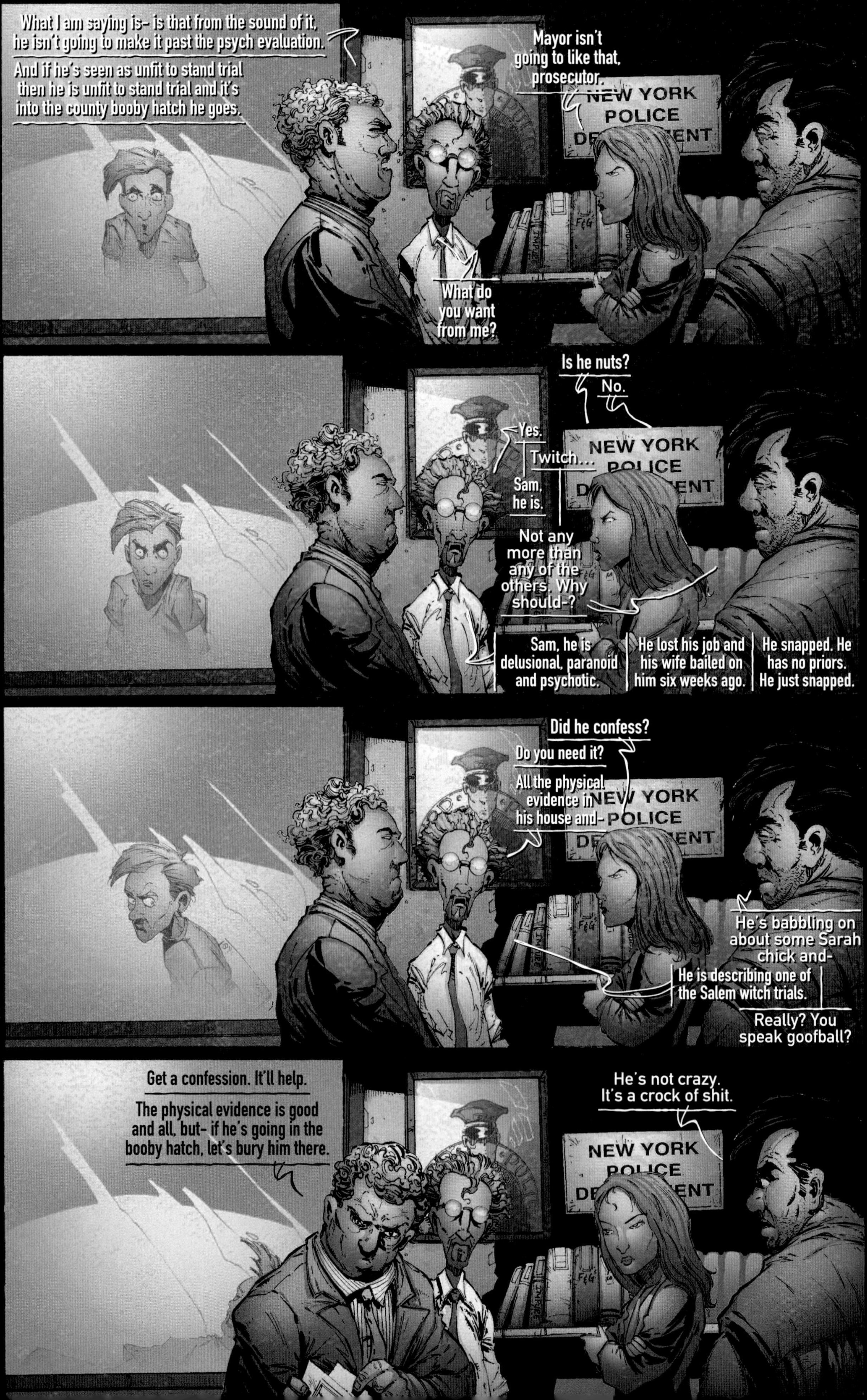
What I am saying is- is that from the sound of it, he isn't going to make it past the psych evaluation.
And if he's seen as unfit to stand trial then he is unfit to stand trial and it's into the county booby hatch he goes.
Mayor isn't going to like that, prosecutor.
NEW YORK POLICE DEPARTMENT
What do you want from me?
Is he nuts?
No.
Yes.
Twitch...
Sam, he is.
Not any more than any of the others. Why should-?
Sam, he is delusional, paranoid and psychotic.
He lost his job and his wife bailed on him six weeks ago.
He snapped. He has no priors. He just snapped.
Did he confess?
Do you need it?
All the physical evidence in his house and-
He's babbling on about some Sarah chick and-
He is describing one of the Salem witch trials.
Really? You speak goofball?
Get a confession. It'll help.
The physical evidence is good and all, but- if he's going in the booby hatch, let's bury him there.
He's not crazy. It's a crock of shit.

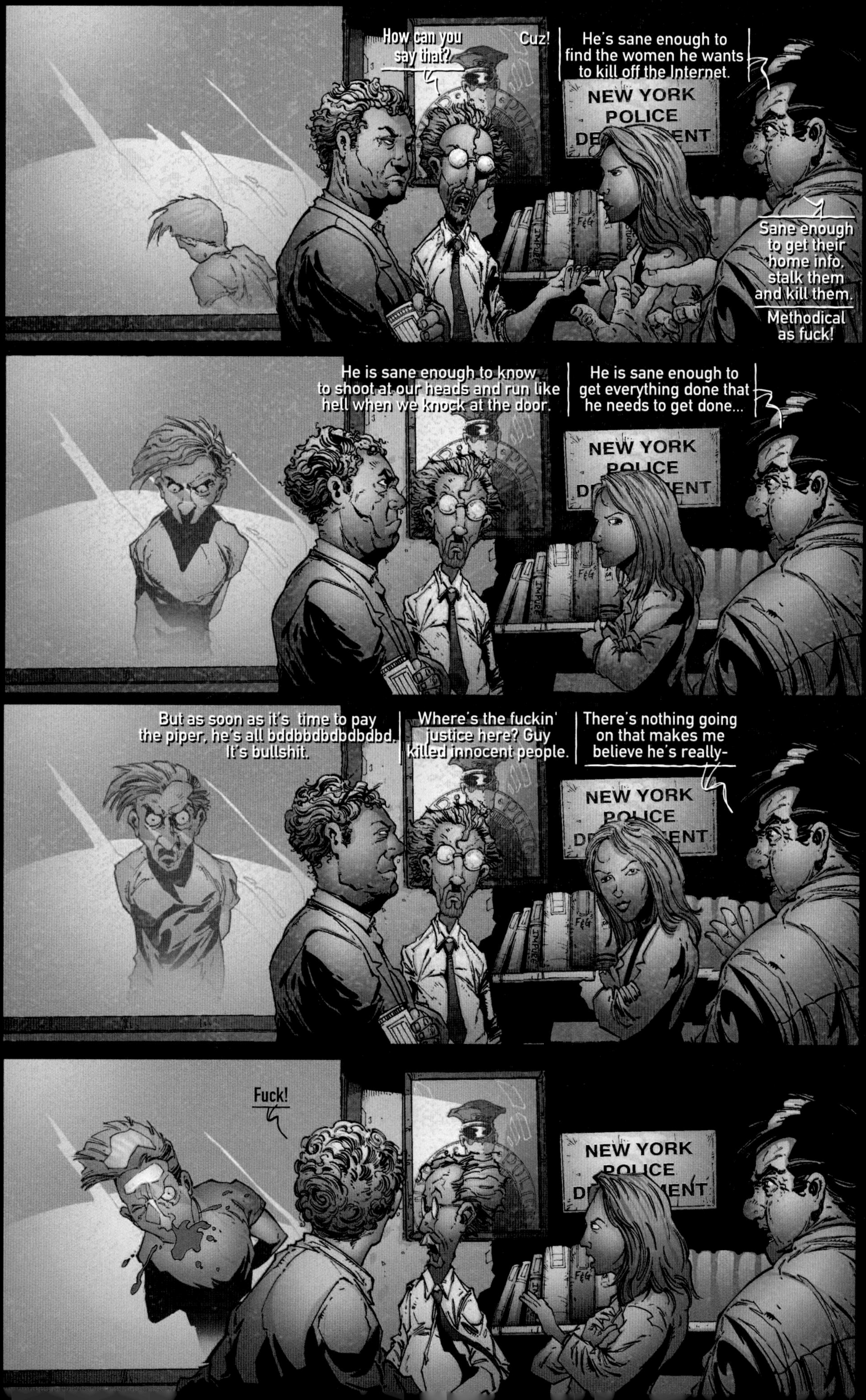
How can you say that?
Cuz!
He's sane enough to find the women he wants to kill off the Internet.
NEW YORK POLICE DEPARTMENT
Sane enough to get their home info, stalk them and kill them.
Methodical as fuck!
He is sane enough to know to shoot at our heads and run like hell when we knock at the door.
He is sane enough to get everything done that he needs to get done...
But as soon as it's time to pay the piper, he's all bddbbdbdbdbdbd. It's bullshit.
Where's the fuckin' justice here? Guy killed innocent people.
There's nothing going on that makes me believe he's really-
Fuck!

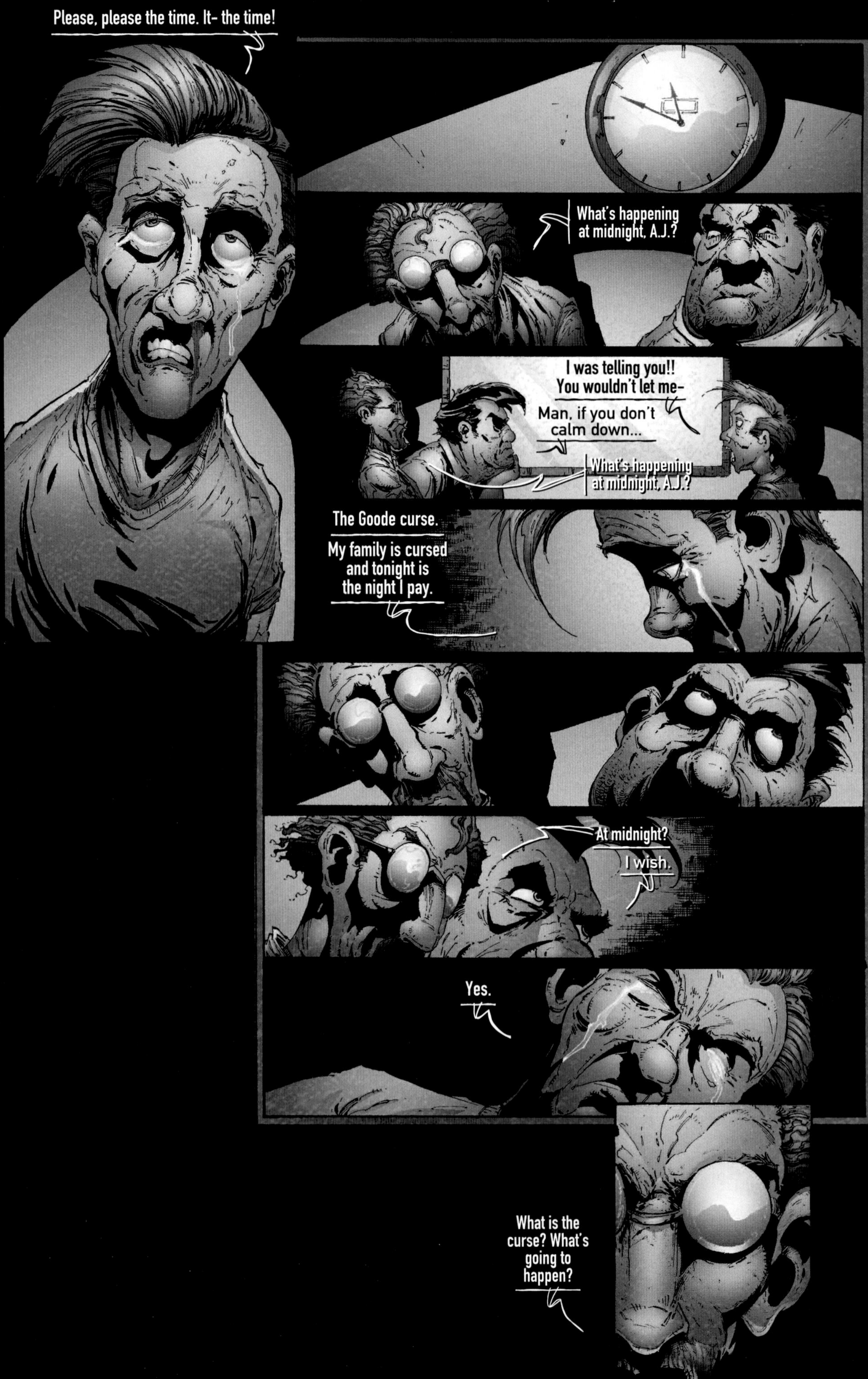

Please, please the time. It- the time!
What's happening at midnight, A.J.?
I was telling you!! You wouldn't let me-
Man, if you don't calm down...
What's happening at midnight, A.J.?
The Goode curse.
My family is cursed and tonight is the night I pay.
At midnight?
I wish.
Yes.
What is the curse? What's going to happen?

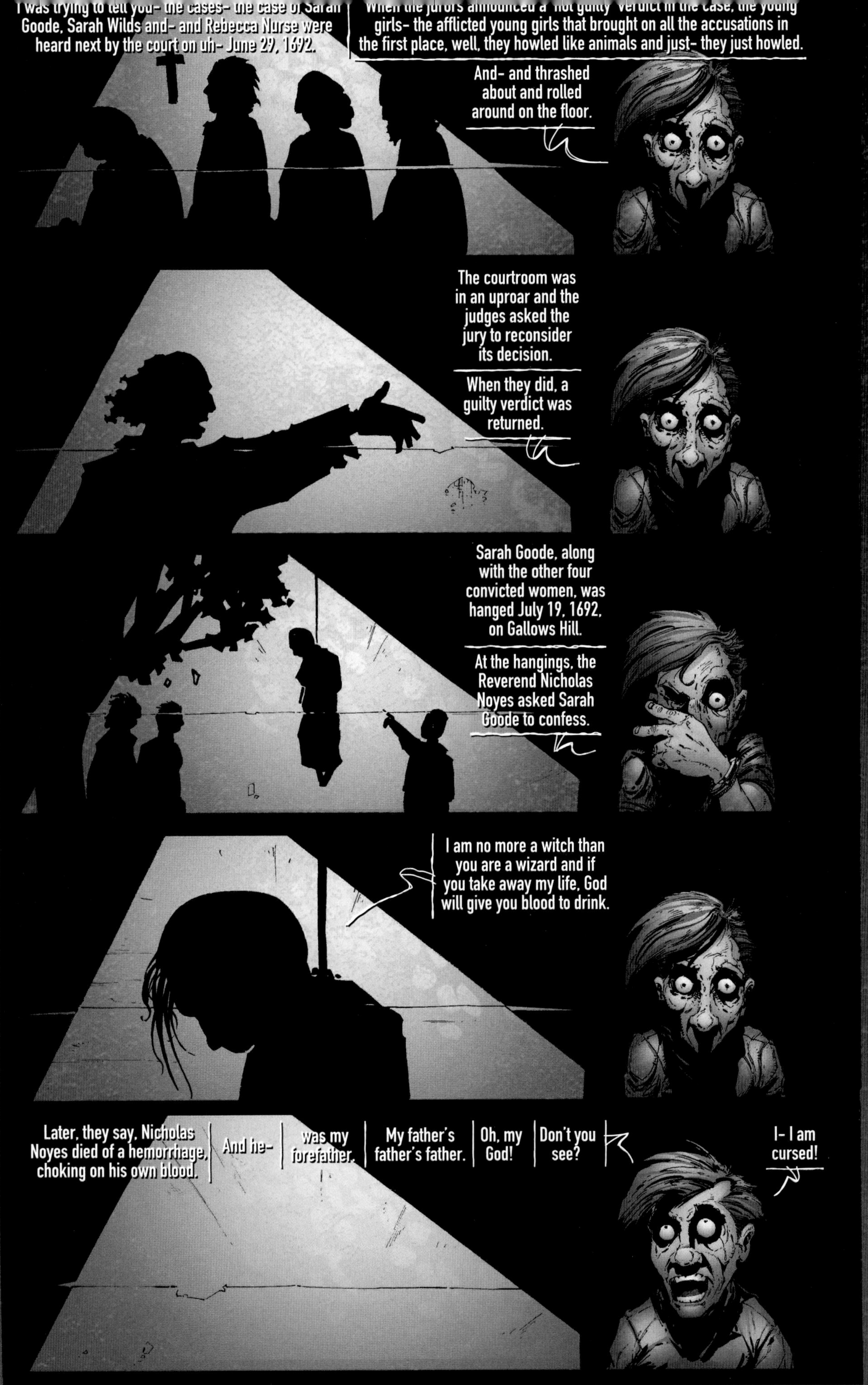
I was trying to tell you- the cases- the case of Sarah Goode, Sarah Wilds and- and Rebecca Nurse were heard next by the court on uh- June 29, 1692.
When the jurors announced a "not guilty" verdict in the case, the young girls- the afflicted young girls that brought on all the accusations in the first place, well, they howled like animals and just- they just howled.
And- and thrashed about and rolled around on the floor.
The courtroom was in an uproar and the judges asked the jury to reconsider its decision.
When they did, a guilty verdict was returned.
Sarah Goode, along with the other four convicted women, was hanged July 19, 1692, on Gallows Hill.
At the hangings, the Reverend Nicholas Noyes asked Sarah Goode to confess.
I am no more a witch than you are a wizard and if you take away my life, God will give you blood to drink.
Later, they say, Nicholas Noyes died of a hemorrhage, choking on his own blood.
And he-
was my forefather.
My father's father's father.
Oh, my God!
Don't you see?
I- I am cursed!

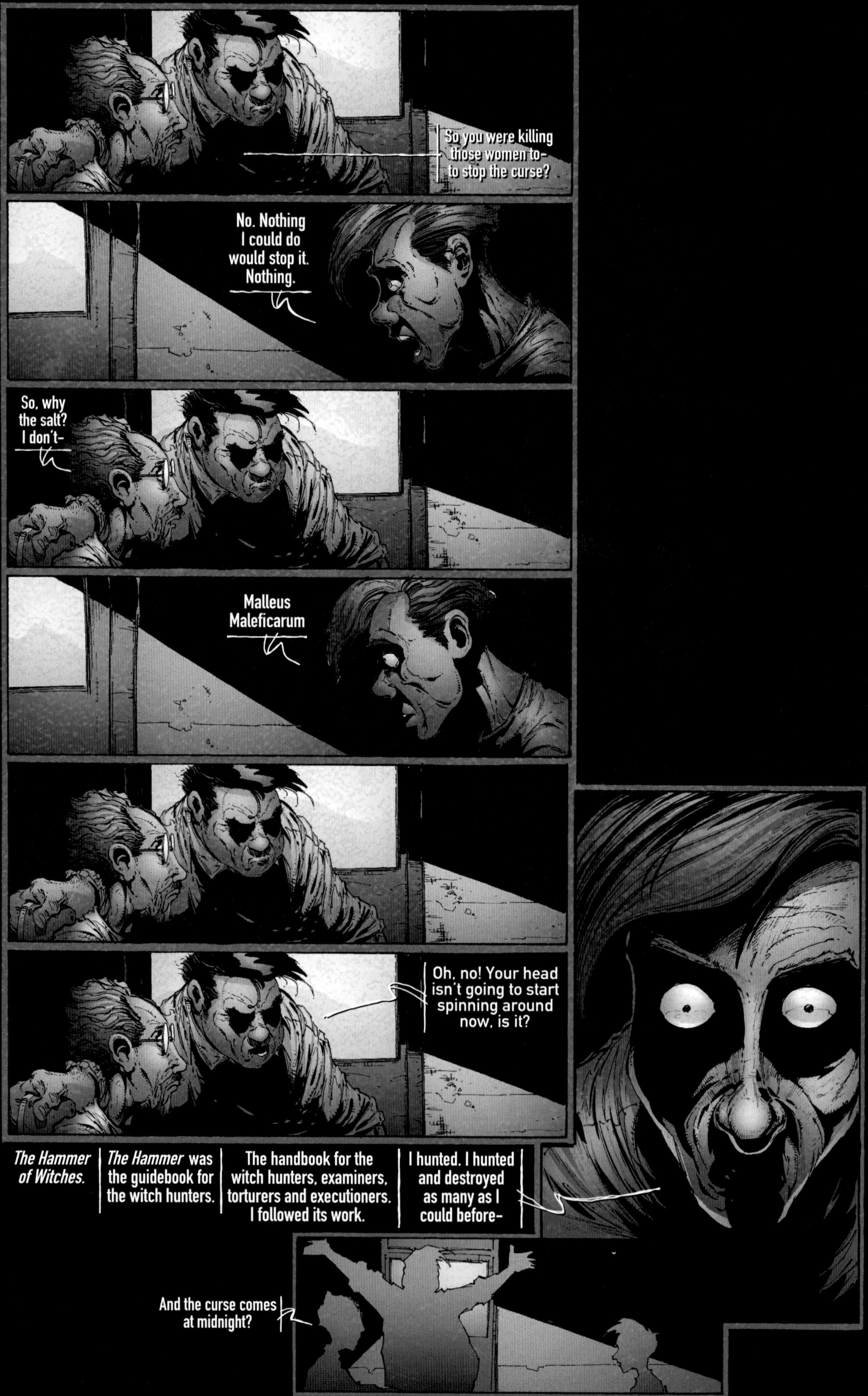
So you were killing those women to-to stop the curse?
No. Nothing I could do would stop it. Nothing.
So, why the salt? I don't-
Malleus Maleficarum
Oh, no! Your head isn't going to start spinning around now, is it?
The Hammer of Witches.
The Hammer was the guidebook for the witch hunters.
The handbook for the witch hunters, examiners, torturers and executioners. I followed its work.
I hunted. I hunted and destroyed as many as I could before-
And the curse comes at midnight?

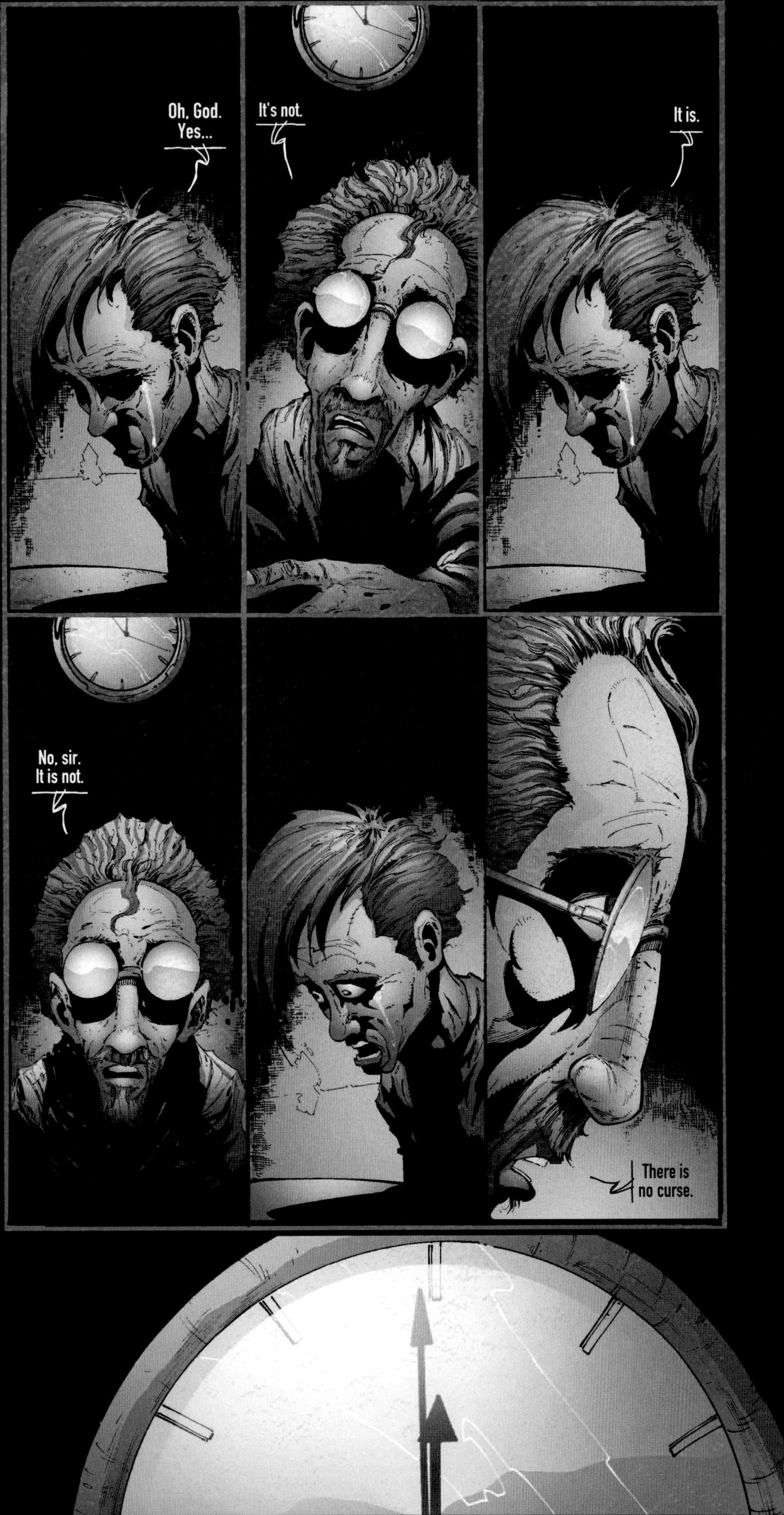
Oh, God. Yes...
It's not.
It is.
No, sir. It is not.
There is no curse.

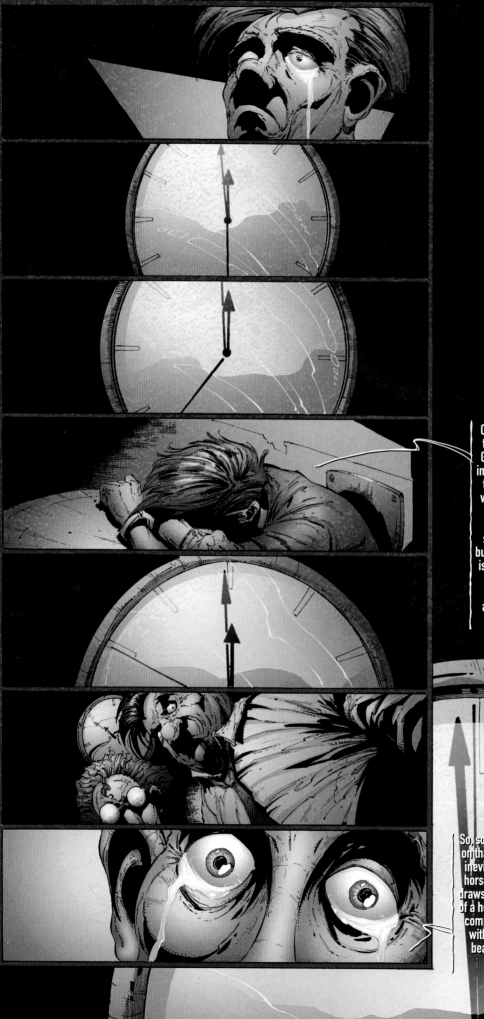

Ohmy, ohmy,ohmy, for by the power of devils, with God's permission, mental images long retained in the treasury of such images which is the memory, are drawn out, not from the understanding in which such images are stored, but from the memory which is the repository of mental images, and is situated at the back of the head, and are presented to the imaginative faculty.

So, so strongly are they impressed on that faculty that a man has an inevitable impulse to imagine a horse or a beast when the devil draws from the memory an image of a horse or a beast; and so he is compelled to think that he sees with his external eyes such a beast when there is actually no such beast to see.

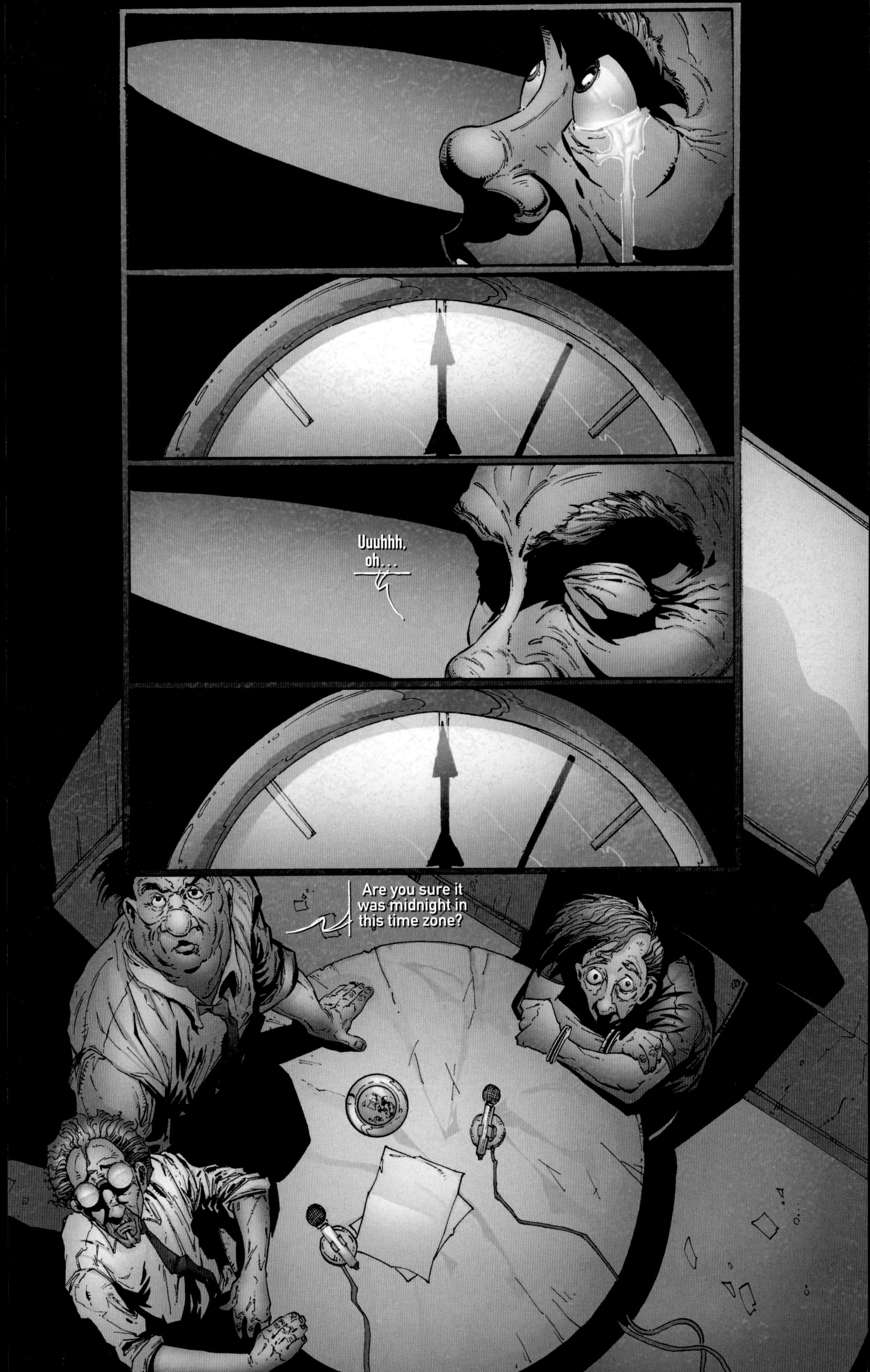
Uuuhhh, oh...
Are you sure it was midnight in this time zone?

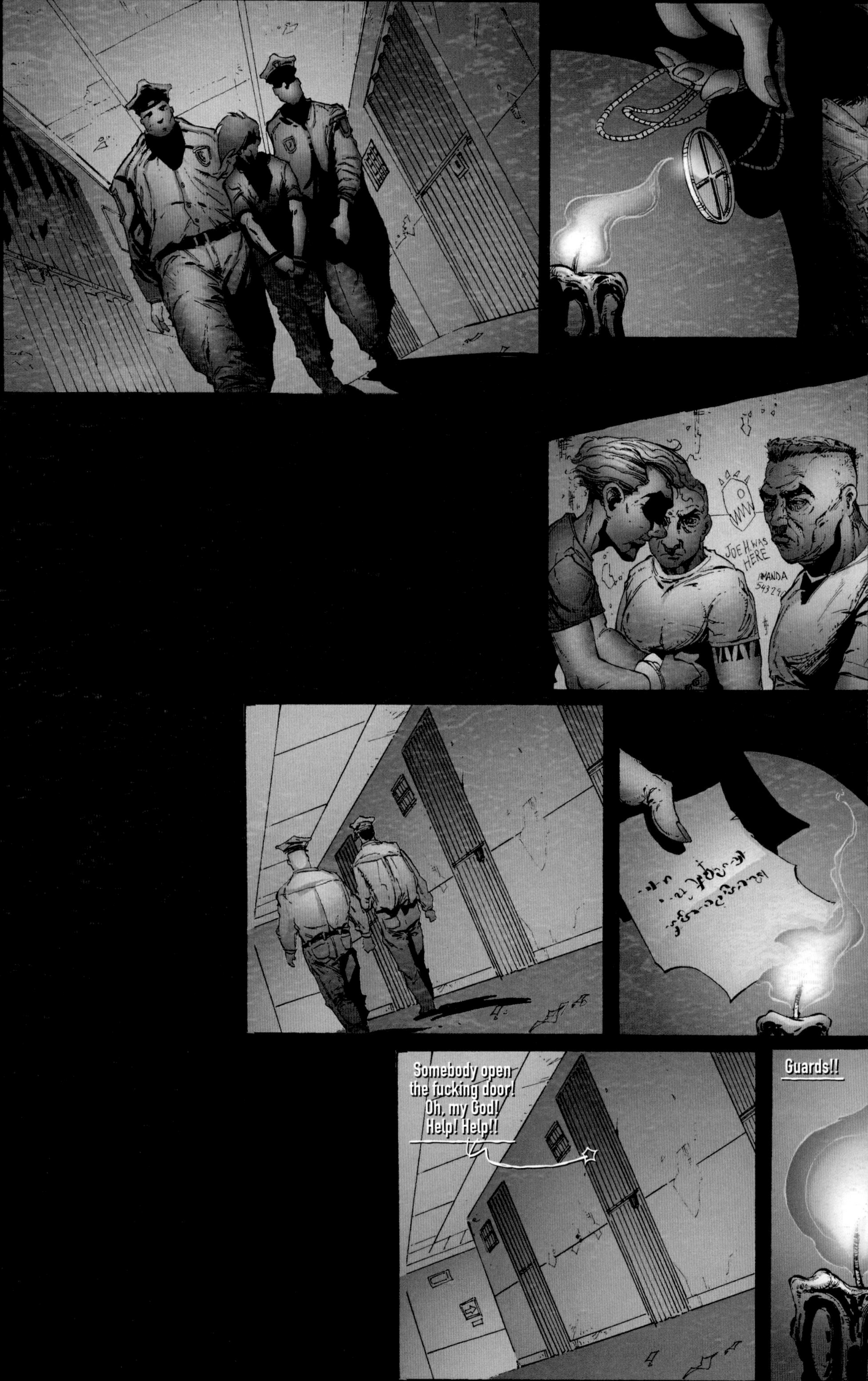
JOE H. WAS HERE
AMANDA
Somebody open the fucking door! Oh, my God! Help! Help!!
Guards!!

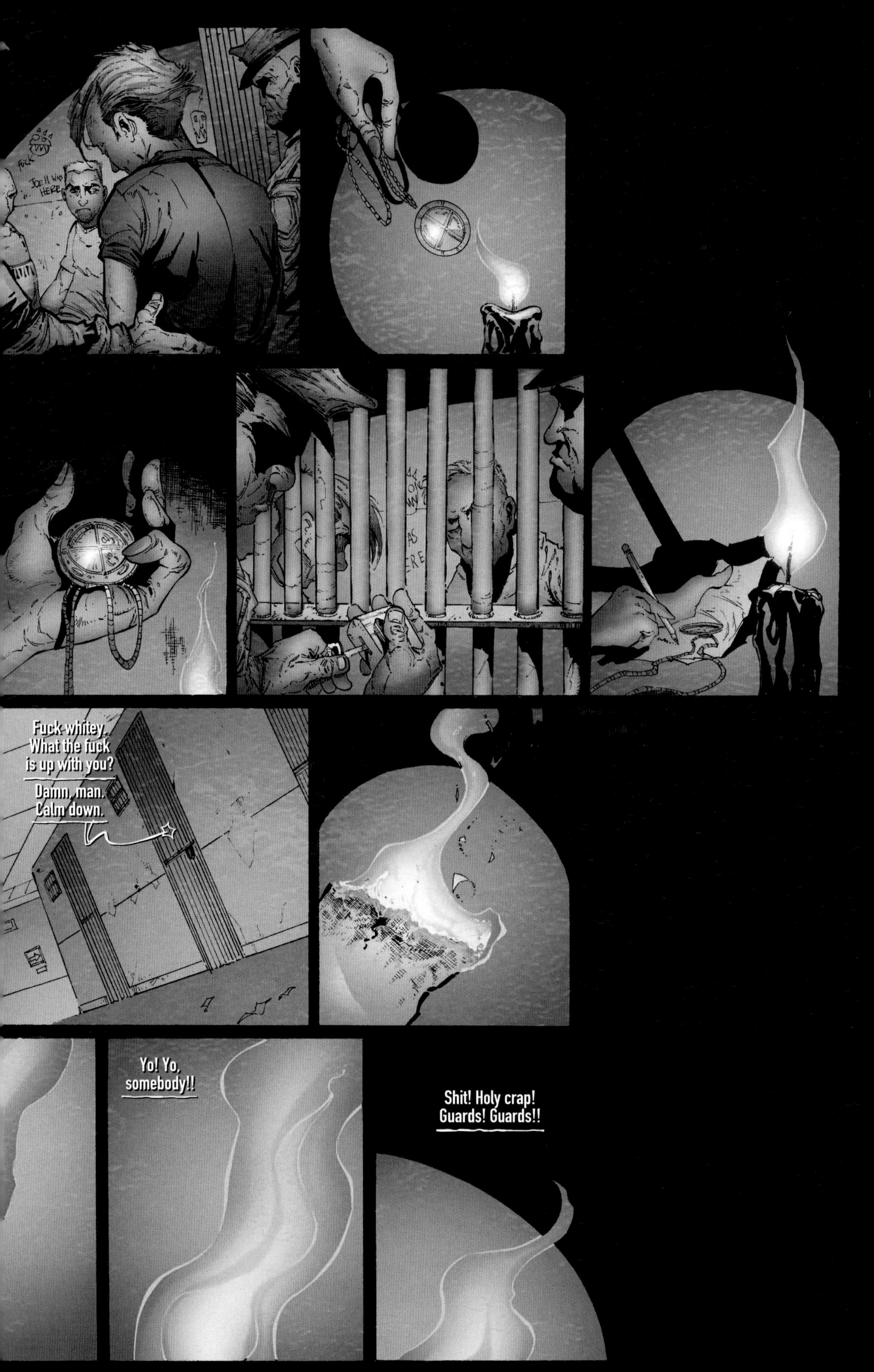
Fuck whitey. What the fuck is up with you?
Damn, man. Calm down.
Yo! Yo, somebody!!
Shit! Holy crap! Guards! Guards!!

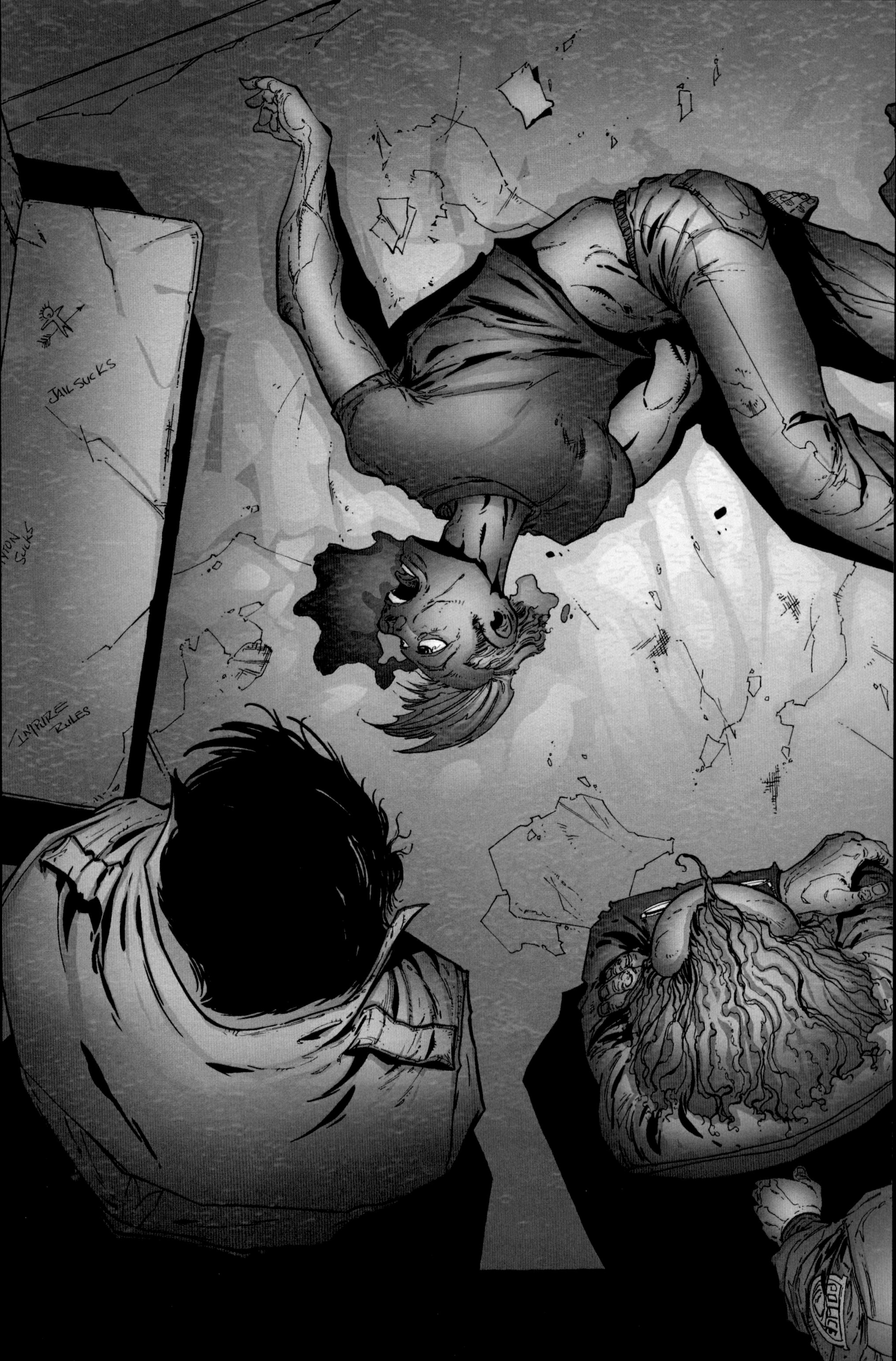
JAIL SUCKS

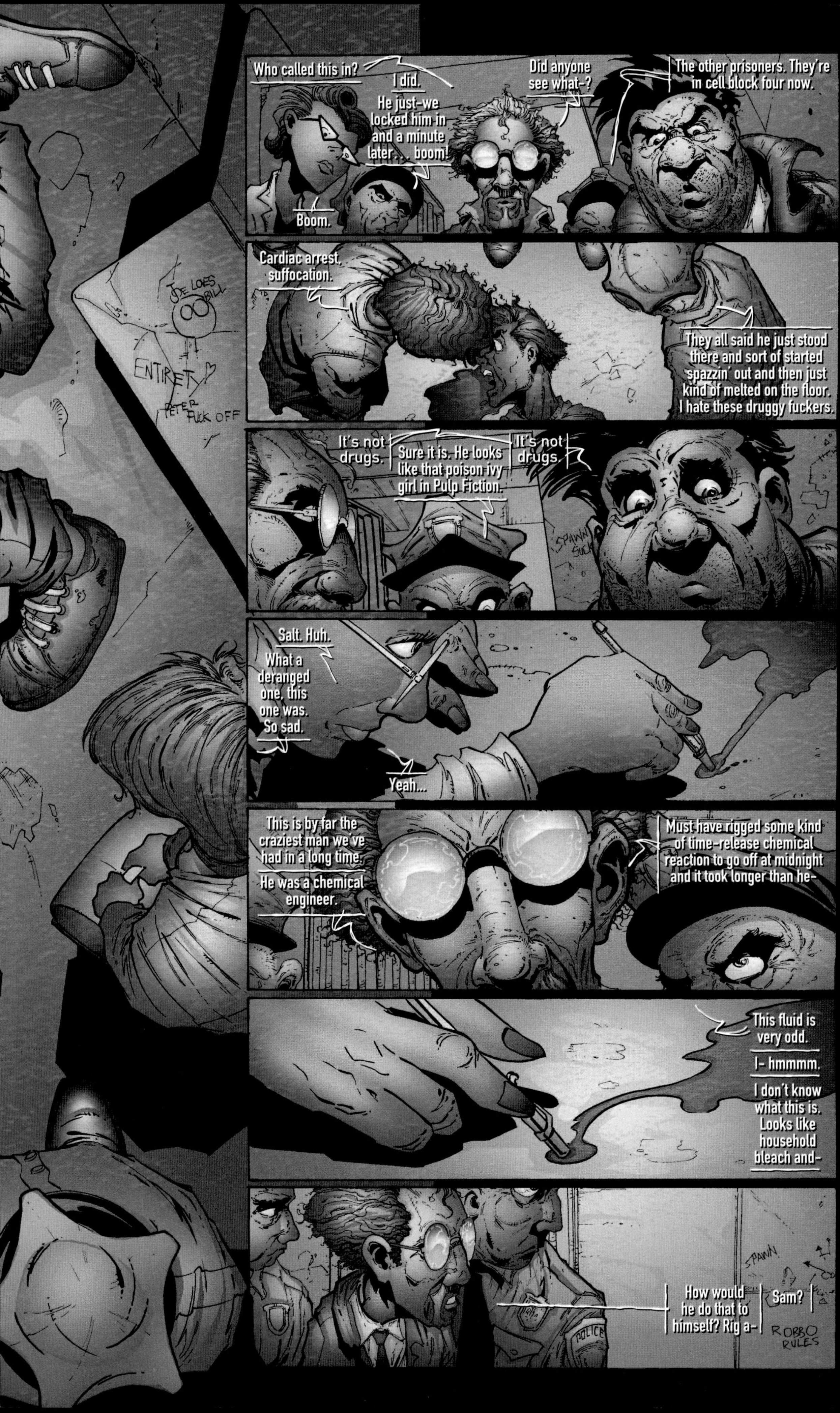
Who called this in?
I did.
He just-we locked him in and a minute later. . . boom!
Boom.
Did anyone see what-?
The other prisoners. They're in cell block four now.
JOE LOVES BILL
ENTIRETY
PETER FUCK OFF
Cardiac arrest, suffocation.
They all said he just stood there and sort of started spazzin' out and then just kind of melted on the floor. I hate these druggy fuckers.
It's not drugs.
Sure it is. He looks like that poison ivy girl in Pulp Fiction.
It's not drugs.
Salt. Huh.
What a deranged one, this one was. So sad.
Yeah...
This is by far the craziest man we've had in a long time.
He was a chemical engineer.
Must have rigged some kind of time-release chemical reaction to go off at midnight and it took longer than he-
This fluid is very odd.
I- hmmmm.
I don't know what this is. Looks like household bleach and-
How would he do that to himself? Rig a-
Sam?
ROBBO RULES

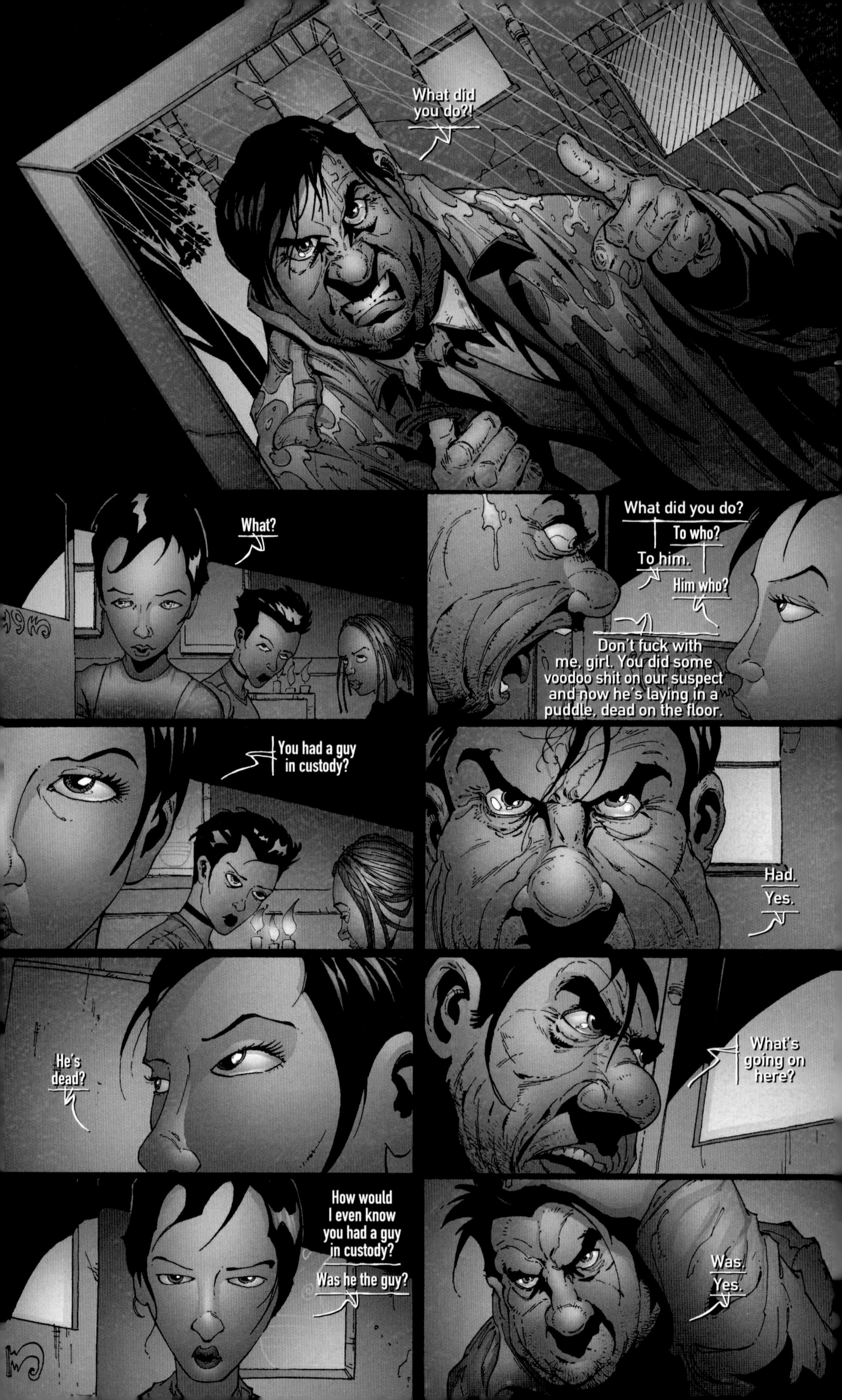
What did you do?!
What?
What did you do?
To who?
To him.
Him who?
Don't fuck with me, girl. You did some voodoo shit on our suspect and now he's laying in a puddle, dead on the floor.
You had a guy in custody?
Had.
Yes.
He's dead?
What's going on here?
How would I even know you had a guy in custody?
Was he the guy?
Was.
Yes.

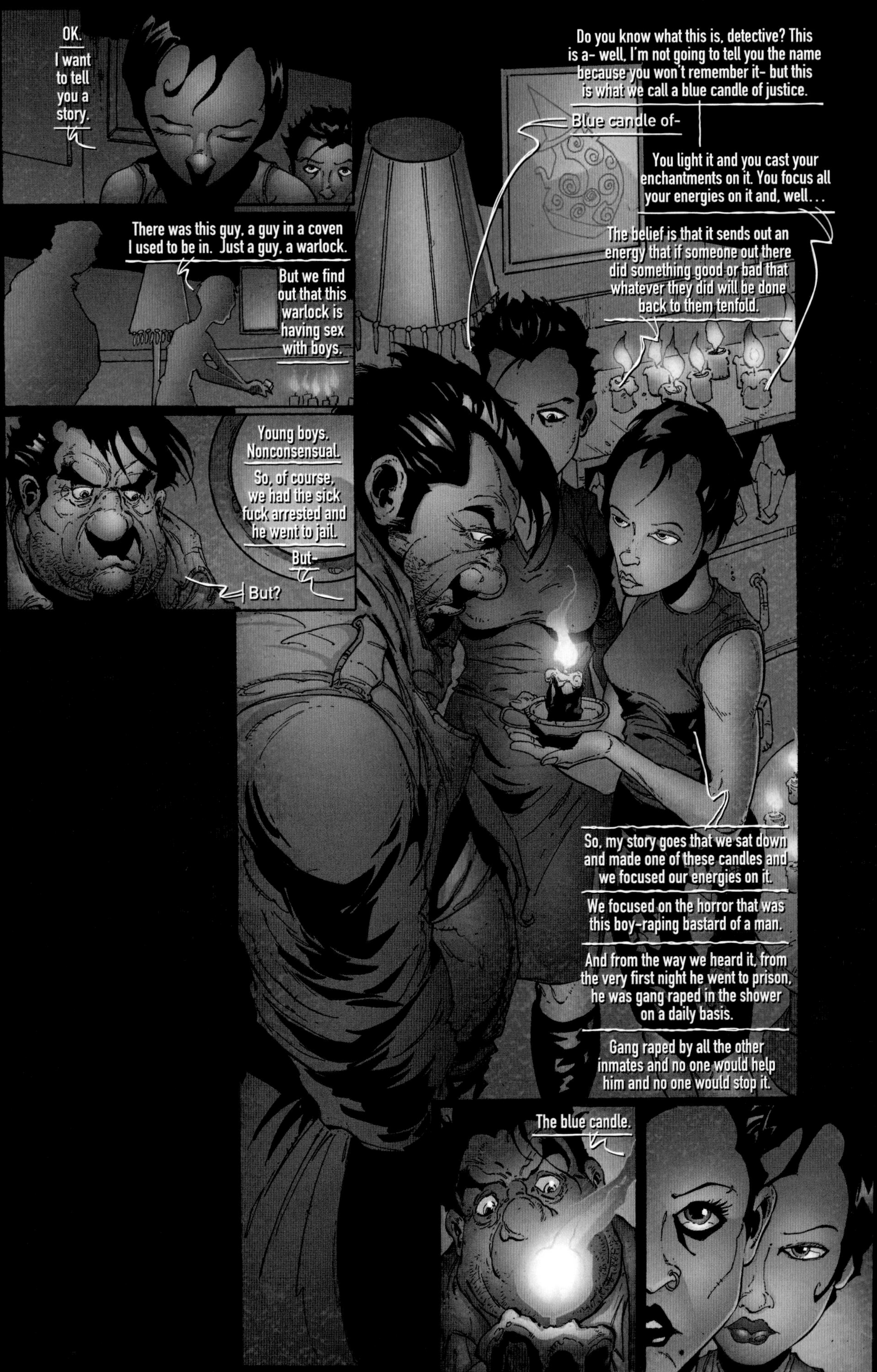
OK.
I want to tell you a story.
There was this guy, a guy in a coven I used to be in. Just a guy, a warlock.
But we find out that this warlock is having sex with boys.
Young boys. Nonconsensual.
So, of course, we had the sick fuck arrested and he went to jail.
But-
But?
Do you know what this is, detective? This is a- well, I'm not going to tell you the name because you won't remember it- but this is what we call a blue candle of justice.
Blue candle of-
You light it and you cast your enchantments on it. You focus all your energies on it and, well. . .
The belief is that it sends out an energy that if someone out there did something good or bad that whatever they did will be done back to them tenfold.
So, my story goes that we sat down and made one of these candles and we focused our energies on it.
We focused on the horror that was this boy-raping bastard of a man.
And from the way we heard it, from the very first night he went to prison, he was gang raped in the shower on a daily basis.
Gang raped by all the other inmates and no one would help him and no one would stop it.
The blue candle.

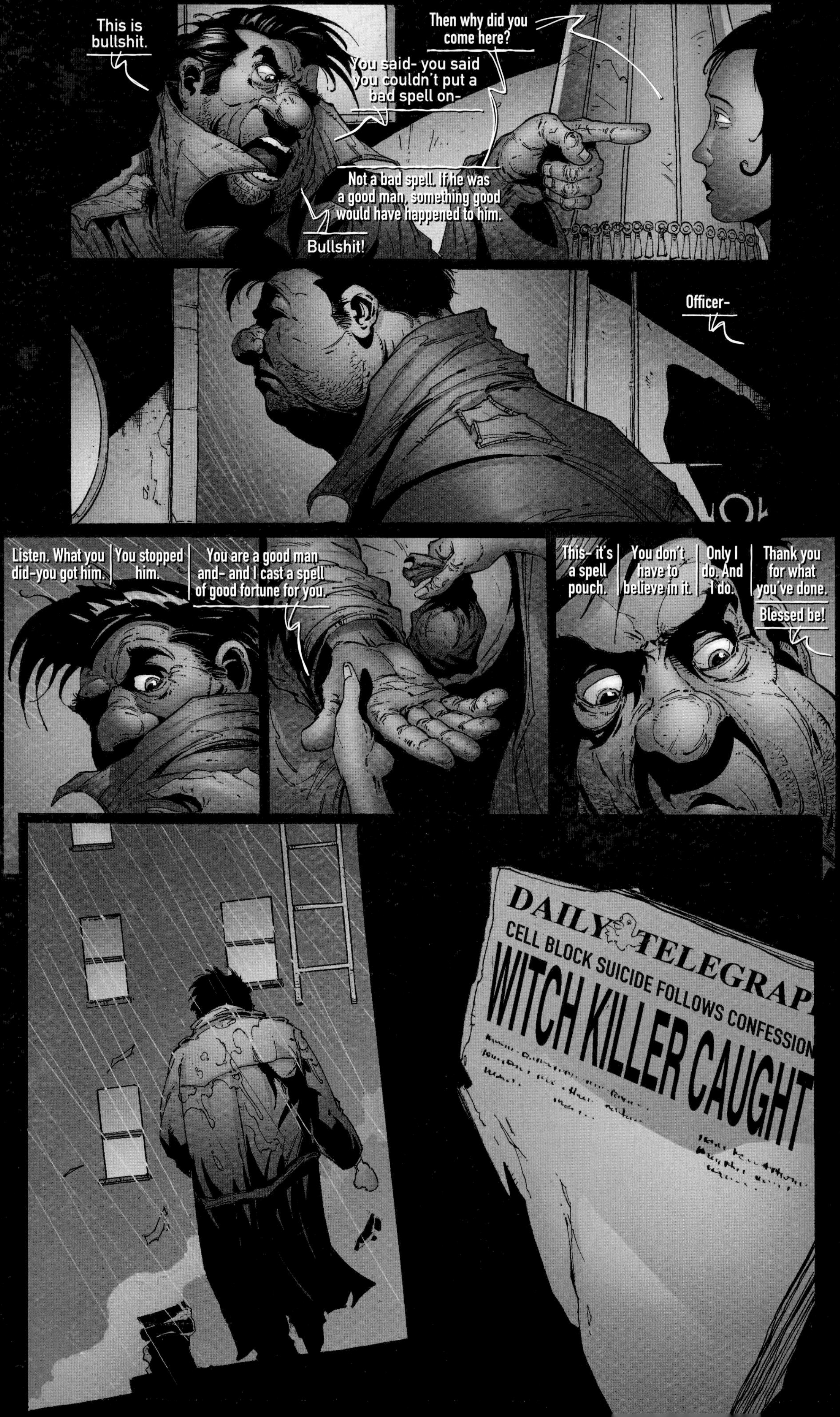
This is bullshit.
Then why did you come here?
You said- you said you couldn't put a bad spell on-
Not a bad spell. If he was a good man, something good would have happened to him.
Bullshit!
Officer-
Listen. What you did-you got him.
You stopped him.
You are a good man and- and I cast a spell of good fortune for you.
This- it's a spell pouch.
You don't have to believe in it.
Only I do. And I do.
Thank you for what you've done.
Blessed be!
DAILY TELEGRAP
CELL BLOCK SUICIDE FOLLOWS CONFESSION
WITCH KILLER CAUGHT

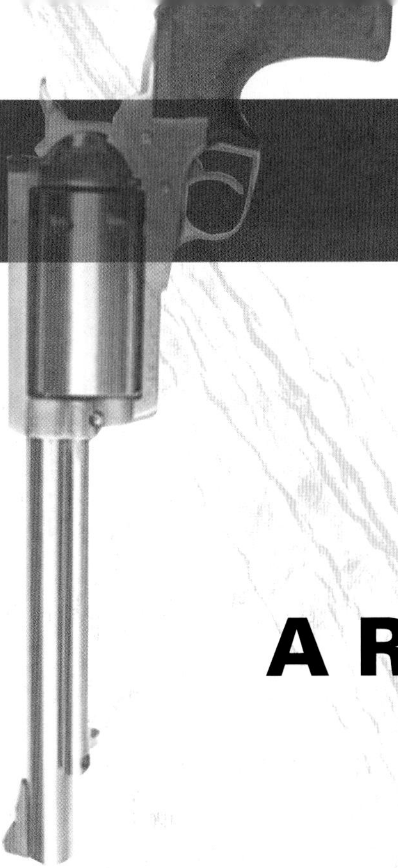

ART
GALLERY

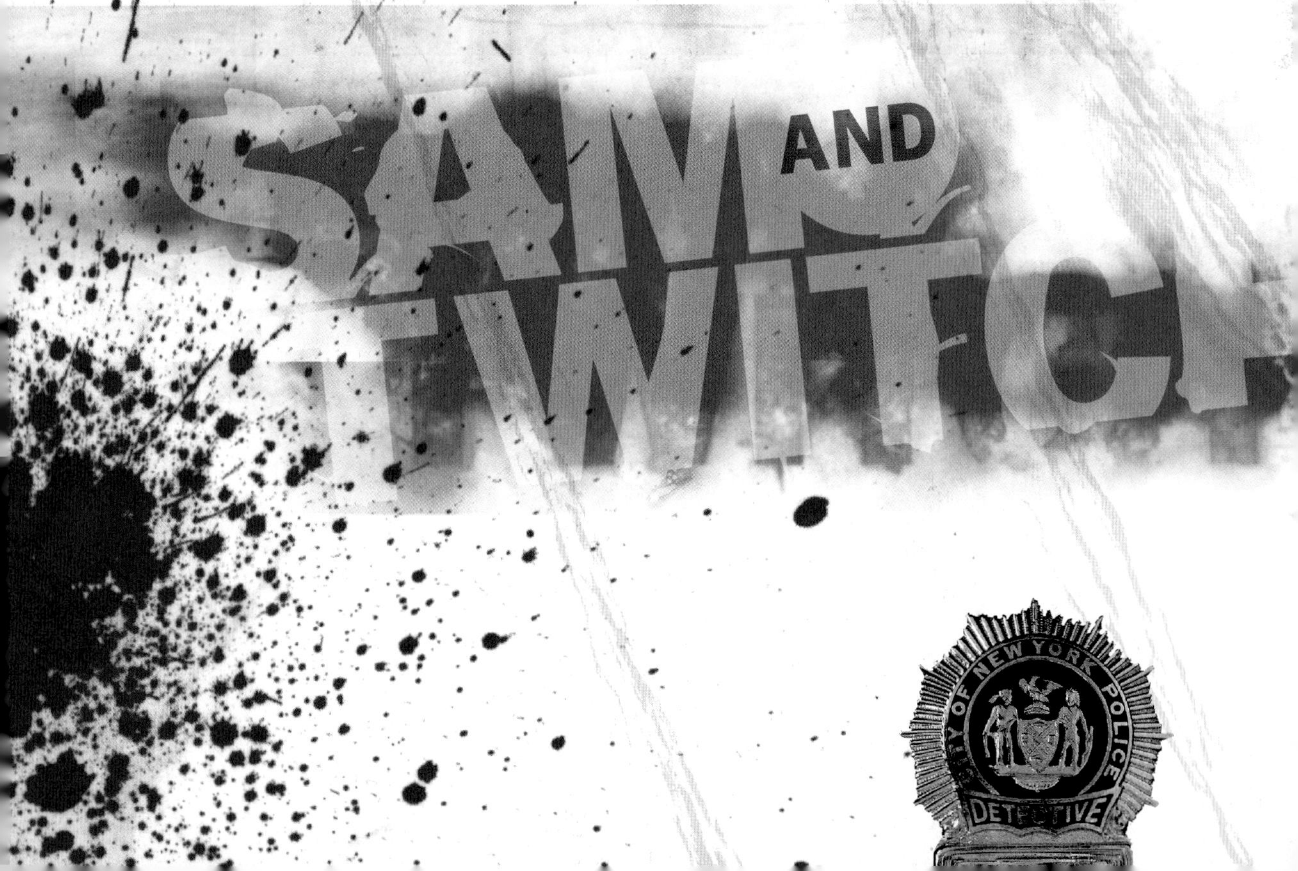
SAM
AND
NEW YORK POLICE
DETECTIVE

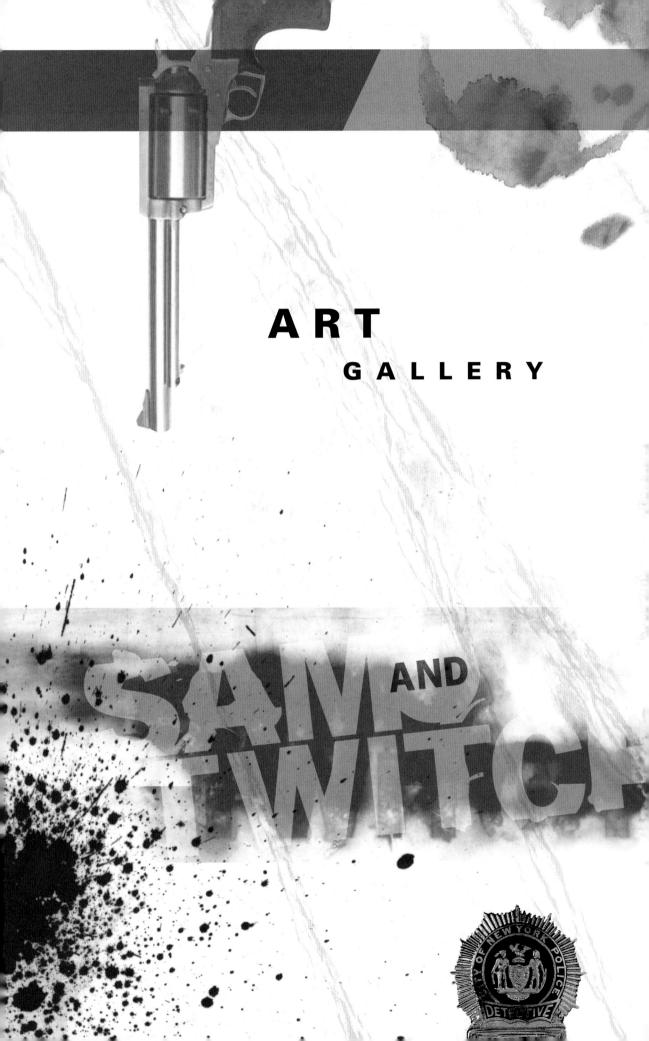

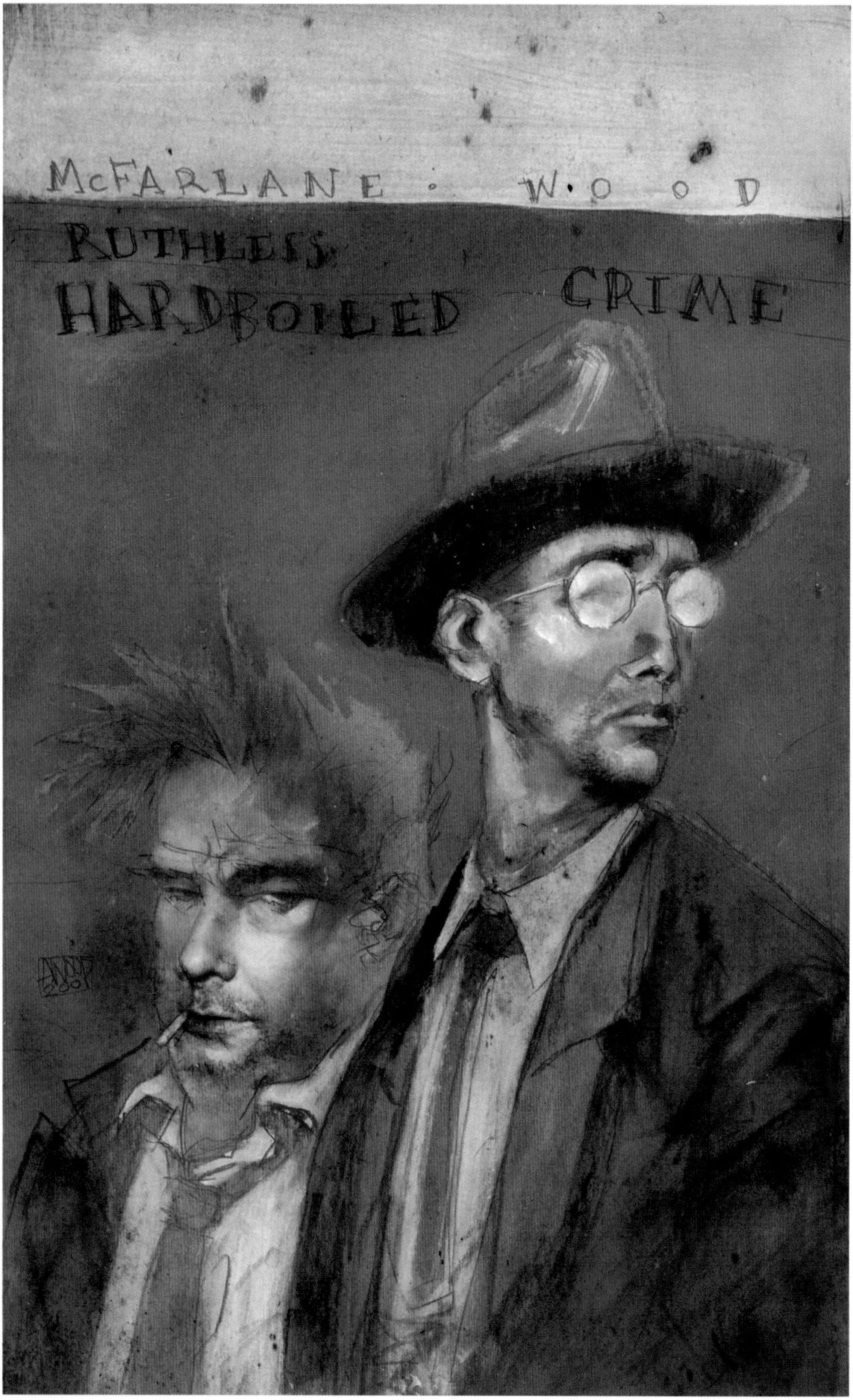
McFARLANE · WOOD
RUTHLESS
HARDBOILED CRIME

C Cover, unused, Ashley Wood

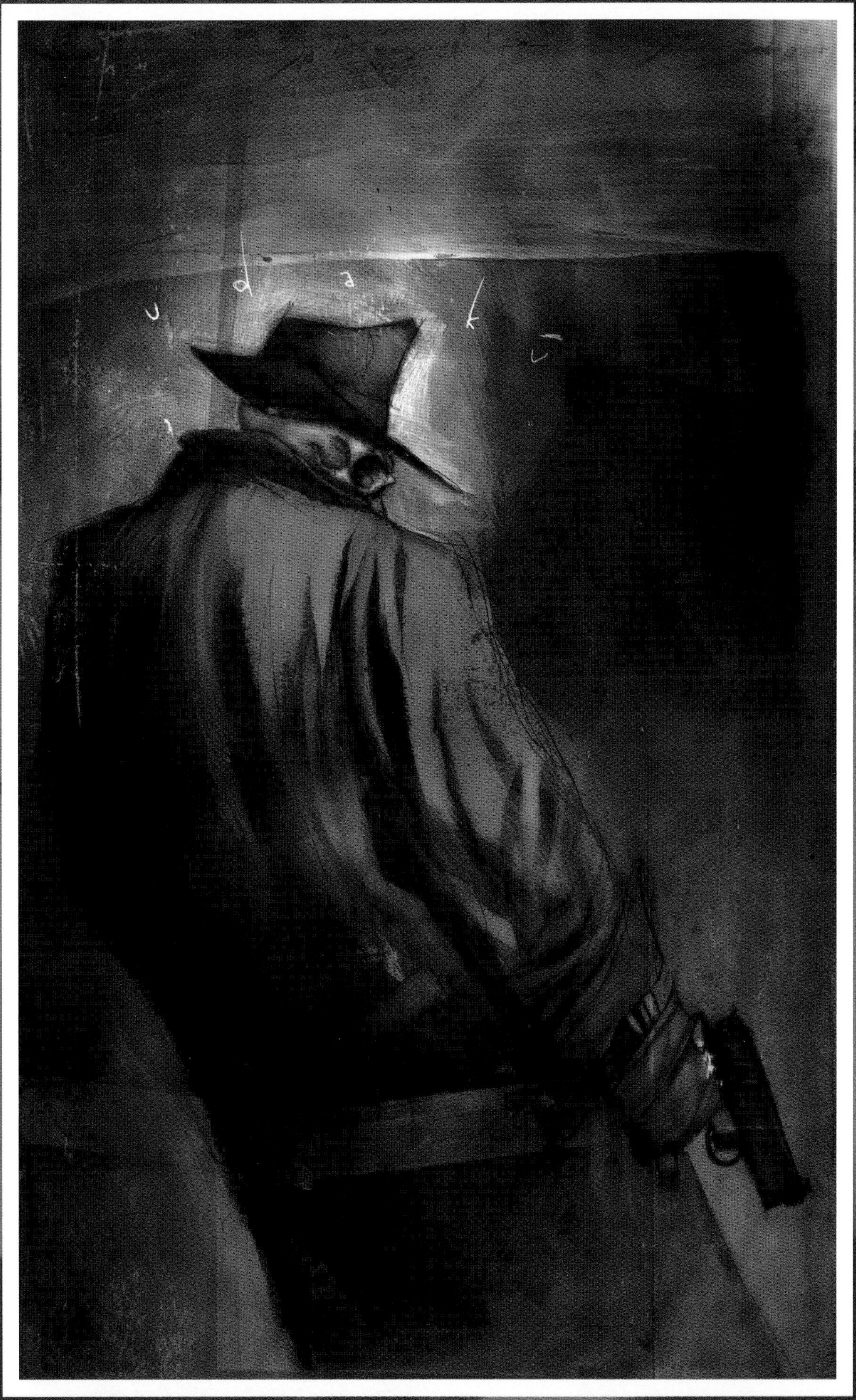

Cover, unused, Ashley Wood

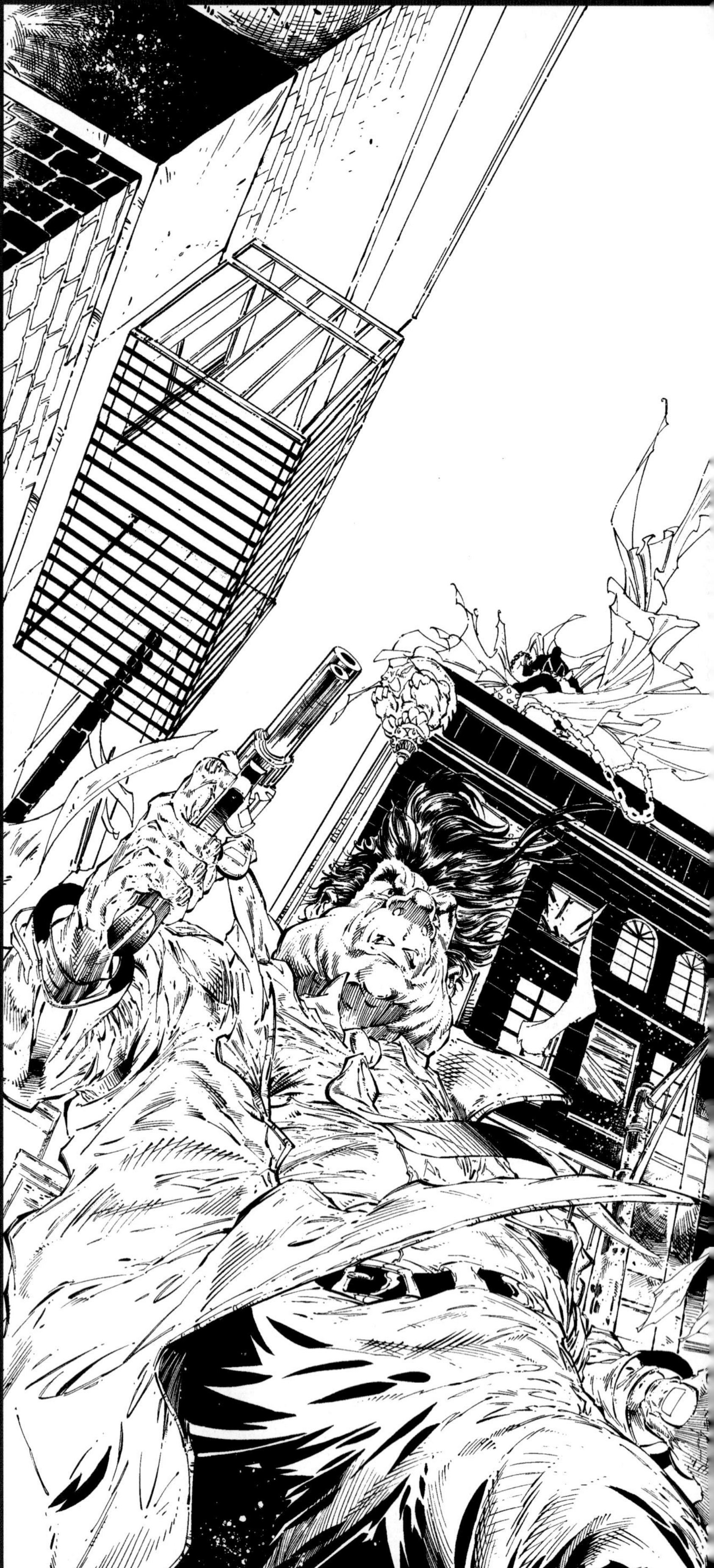

Issue

01 pages 04-05, ink

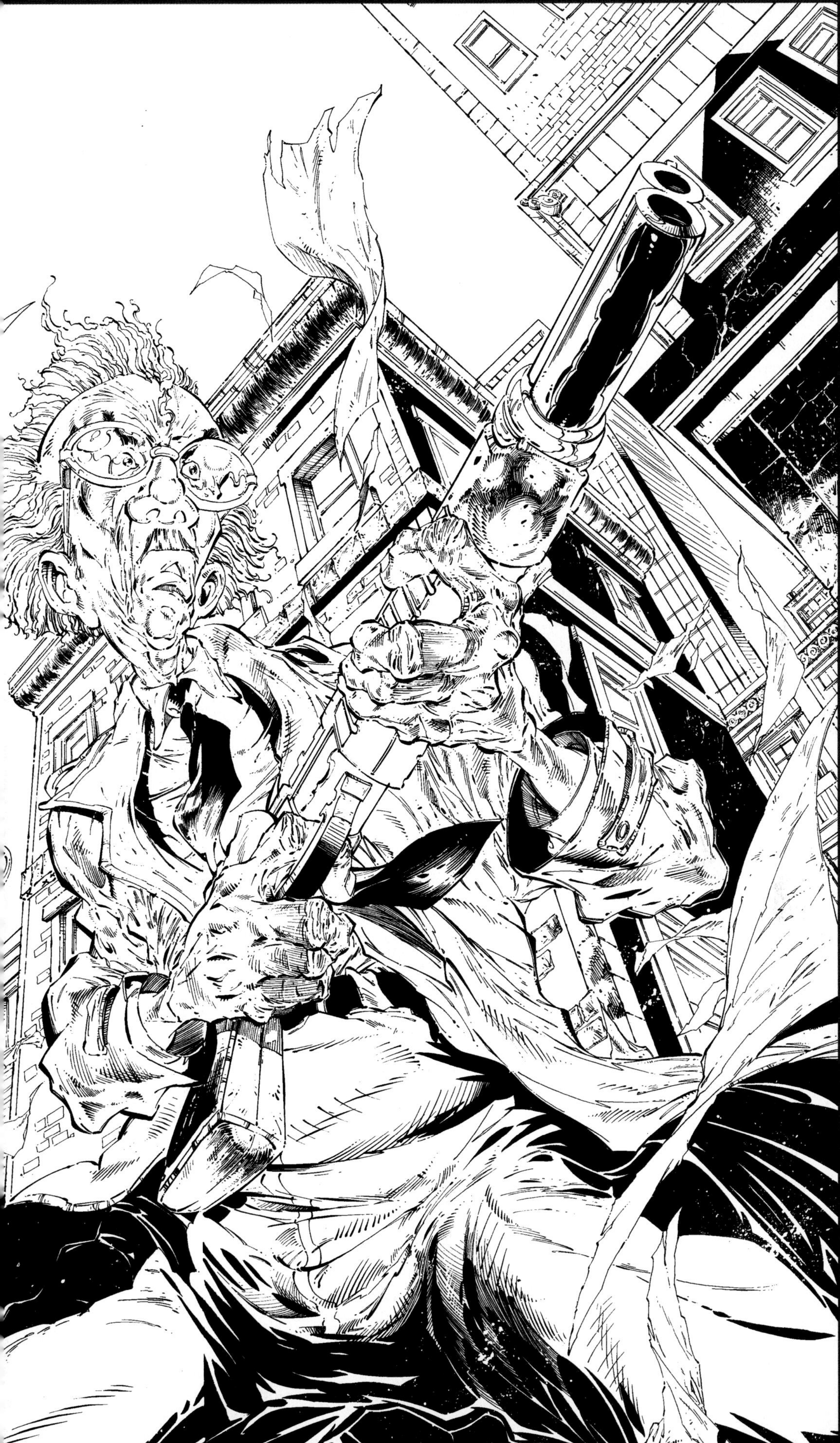

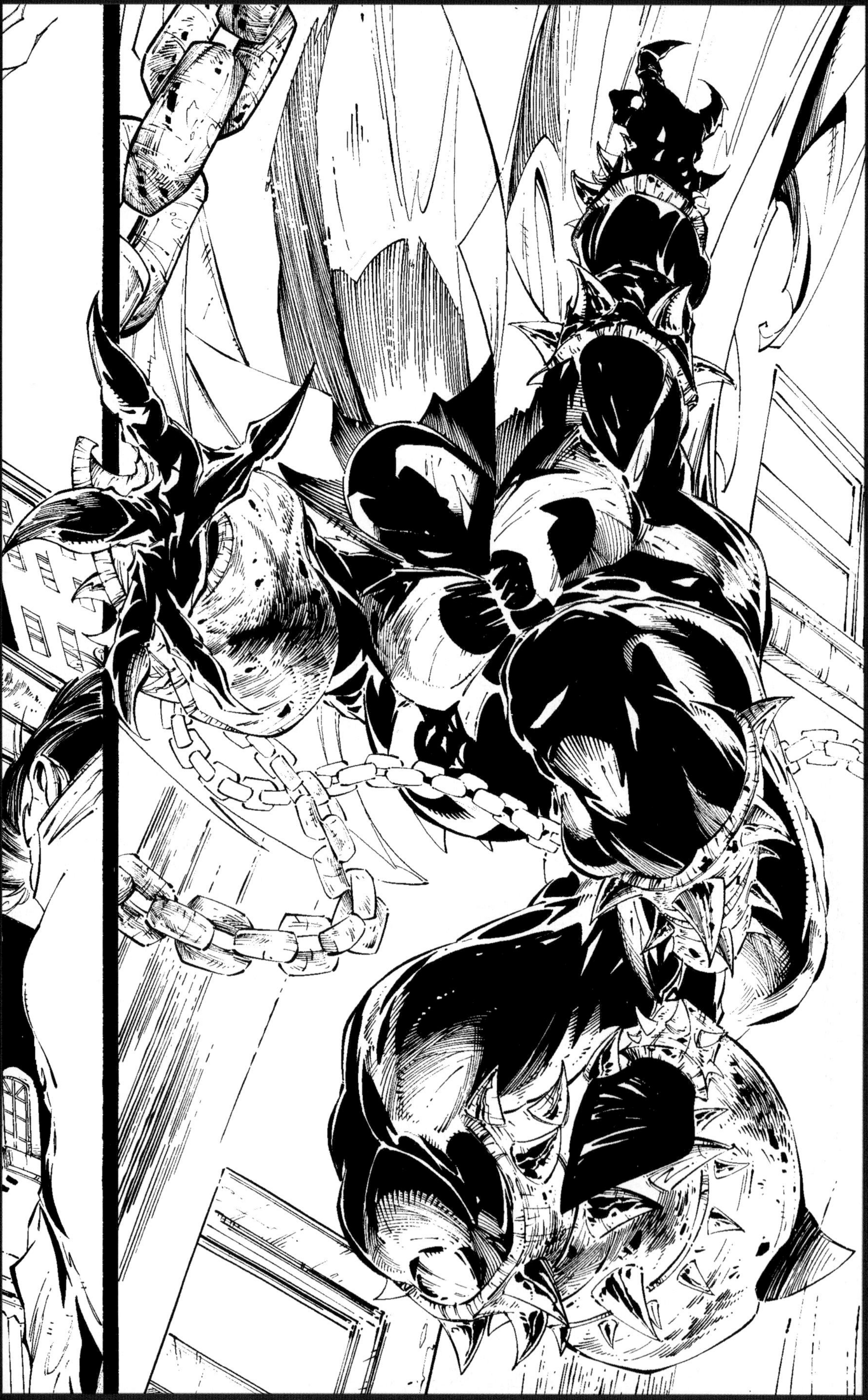

Issue
04 page 12, ink, (detail)

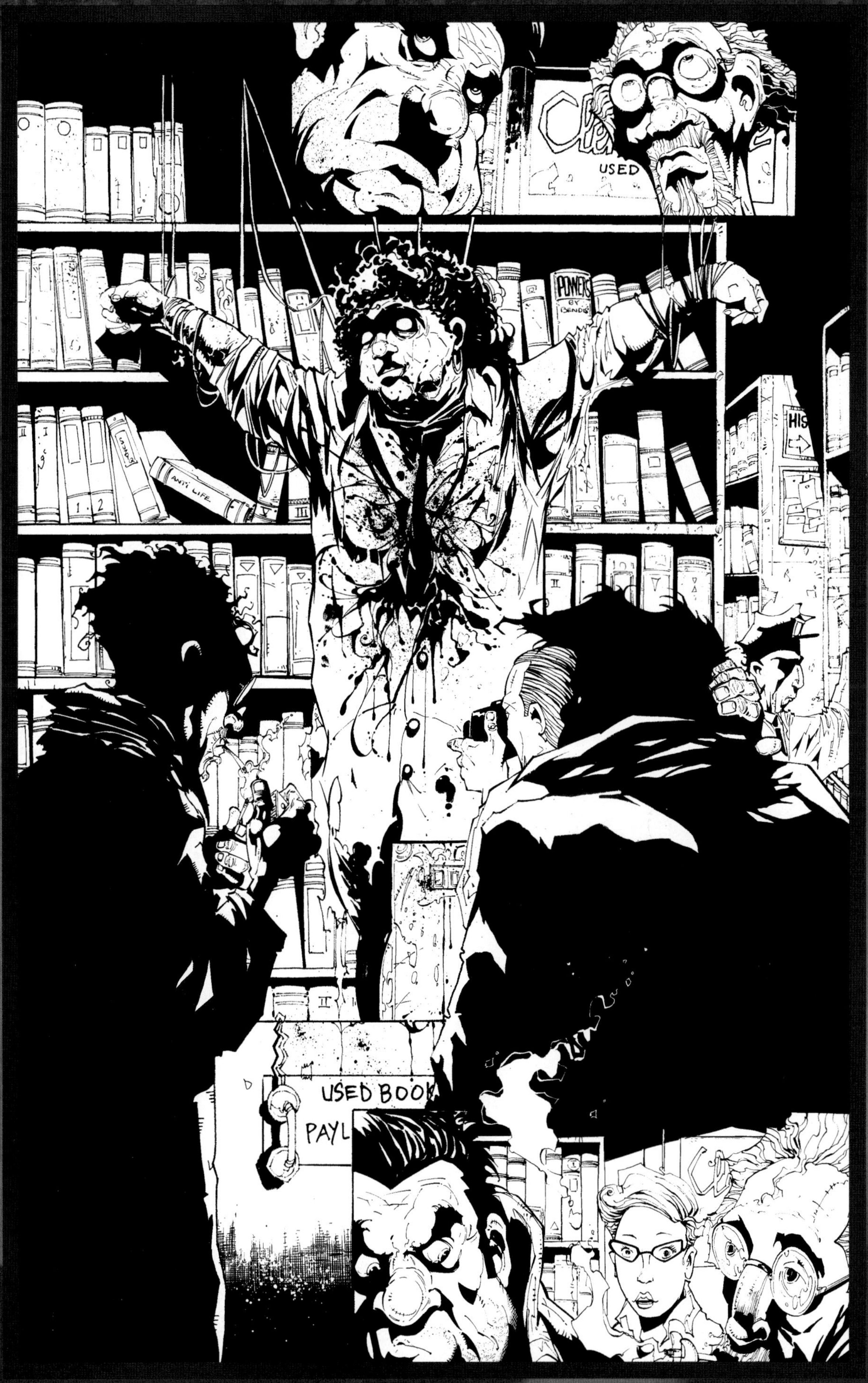
USED
POWERS
BY
ANTI LIFE
USED BOOK

Issue 11

page 06, ink

HELLO EVERYONE!

First of all, let me thank you on behalf of the entire *Sam & Twitch* crew for supporting our brand new comic. As much as I excel in the high art of bitching and whining about every facet of my everyday life, I can honestly say that as far as this book is concerned, I have nothing to bitch and whine about. In fact, this is so unusual for me that I don't know what to do with myself. But that bit of therapy aside, I welcome you.

I can't help but feel that some of you, not all of you, may have just read your first comic that didn't have a super hero or some sort of fantastical element in it. I remember that feeling from my younger days, and all I can say is I am thrilled for you. I remember picking up any number of comics in the mid-eighties that were just "good stories." I think I may have been tricked into getting them because some of my favorite creators' names were on the covers and I just had to have them, but I remember the feeling of having read "a story," just a good old-fashioned, interesting story. Obviously, it put a thrill into me that changed my life. In fact, if I hadn't read any of those damn good comics, I would still be working at McDonald's where life was simple and I just didn't know it. Sigh! Oh, Ronald, those were the days.

Now, if this book did anything similar for you, if it showed you the possibilities that comics have beyond whatever the current hype is in the teeny-tiny comic industry, I hope you take this feeling and run with it. I am totally jazzed for you as you find your way to some of the other new McFarlane titles and to some of the other great comic books on the rack. In fact, there really are more good books being put out than ever before. I know the comic industry will pull together before some of these comics get lost in the cracks.

To the fans of my bi-monthly *Jinx* crime comics and my *Jinx*, *Goldfish*, and *Torso* graphic novels, all published by Image, here is the monthly crime comic you have all whined to me about doing. So shut up!!! It's here. And this is how it came to be…

I guess it was a little over a year ago. I was slappin' down some India ink with one hand and typing like a fiend with the other when the phone rang:

"Hello, eh! Is this Brian Michael Bendis, creator of the crime graphic novel *Goldfish* from Image comics?"

"Why, yes it is," I beamed.

"Well, this is Todd McFarlane."

So I hung up.

"Who was that?" my smashing wife tore herself away from the TNT reruns of *ER* to ask.

"That was David Mack, critically acclaimed creator of *Kabuki*, fucking with me."

"You know, honey, I know David. You don't have to refer to him as that 'critically acclaimed creator of *Kabuki*' every time."

"Yes I do. He makes me."

"He does?"

"He also makes me mention him in comic book editorials that have nothing to do with him."

The phone rings again.

"Hello, eh! Is this Brian Michael Bendis, creator of the crime graphic novel *Goldfish* from Image comics?"

"Why, yes it is," I beamed.

Then I suddenly realized, "Shit! It was Todd McFarlane."

See, I had been brought to the cozy home of Image by Jim Valentino and Larry Marder and often wondered what the hell the other Image founders, whom I had never met, thought of this. I had visions of Todd McFarlane looking through the Previews catalogue and seeing my comics and wondering what the fuck I was doing at Image when he worked so hard to help establish the little lowercase "i." Turns out that for once, my deep-rooted paranoia, which makes Chris Carter look like Woody from Cheers, was unfounded. He wasn't calling to smack me back into the back of the catalogue from whence I came. Todd was all about The Bendis. He had come across my books on a fluke and he dug them. (And if that thought makes you want to go and buy them or order them from the Diamond Star system, well, go with that feeling.)

Todd digs the hard-boiled, character-driven urban horror and thought that maybe I should take the reigns of a monthly *Sam & Twitch* comic—you know, like the

one you're holding. I told him that I thought *Sam & Twitch* should be a space opera á la *Battlestar Galactica*, but Mr. Multi-Media-Empire, Number-One-Comic-In-America-For-Seven-Years thinks he knows better, so *Sam & Twitch* is a hard-boiled, character-driven urban-horror comic. He tossed me the keys to this comic, told me never to tell anyone about our phone conversation, and let me do my thing.

In the next issue, we will take a little behind-the-scenes look at the making of this issue. At that time, I will discuss the contributions of the amazing Angel Medina and all the other people responsible for this comic.

Brian Michael Bendis
Lakewood, Ohio
July 12, 1999

Originally published in *Sam and Twitch* #1, 1999.

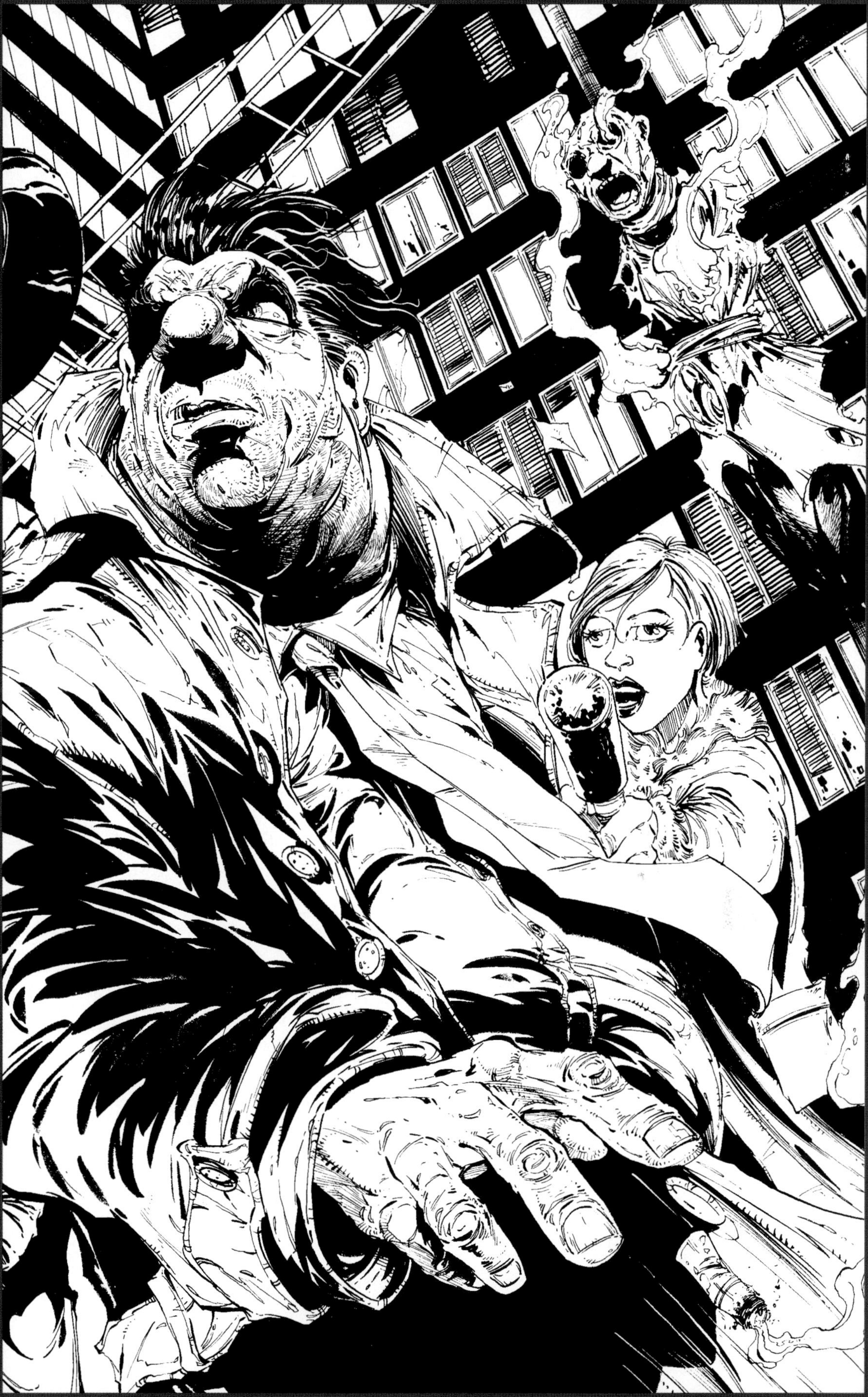

Issue
page 02, ink, (detail) 12

Here's a sample of a layout from *Sam and Twitch* issue 1, page 10.

PAGE 10

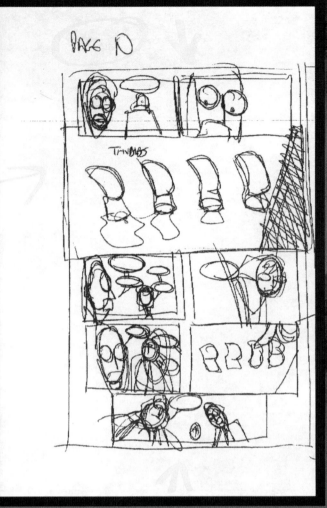

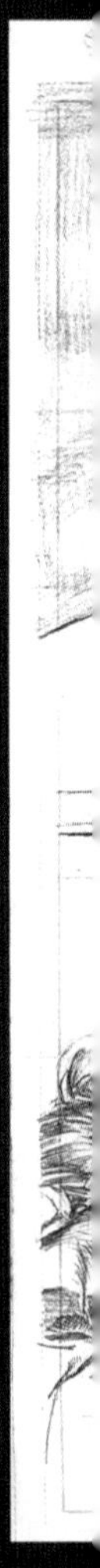

BRACE YOURSELF... THIS IS PRETTY SILLY.

BEHIND THE SCENES: THE MAKING OF *SAM AND TWITCH*

By: Brian Michael Bendis

While we all sat patiently aboard the McFarlane Enterprises Space Station that hovers in synchronized orbit around the planet earth, I waited for your letters of praise and admiration so we could put together the letter column for the next issue. Then, I decided to take up this page with a sneak peak at how these little shenanigans are put together. And if you thought that was a run-on sentence, just you wait.

Well, first it starts with me. Me, me, me, me, me!! A lot of people ask: "Where do you come up with your ideas?" (And by a lot of people, I mean my therapist.) Most of my ideas come from a variety of hard-core porn chat rooms on the world wide web, but the ideas I get for comic book stories can come from anywhere.

My past crime comic work, like *Goldfish* and *Jinx* (on sale now in a handsome trade paperback edition from Image Comics... Oh, you knew that was coming), was a pure mixture of characters I created and fell in love with, and a little good old-fashioned research. My latest work, *TORSO*, a book based on a true story, was all based on research. But for *Sam and Twitch*, the ideas came a little differently...

A couple of years ago, my wife turned to me in bed and said: "Get out!" No, I'm kidding. She said: "Boy, do I love the show *Homicide*."
I said: "I know. We have watched it together every Friday night for the last three years."
"You know what a great episode of *Homicide* would be?"
"What?"
"The detectives come on the crime scene and they find four severed thumbs."
"Yeah...?"
"But they all have the same fingerprint!!!"
"And...?"
"And what?"
"And then what happens? They find the thumbs all with the same fingerprint, and then what happens?"
"How should I know?? Who am I? David E. Kelley?"

Well, after recovering emotionally from getting a glimpse into the disturbing world that is my life partner's imagination, I jotted down the image and sat on it. Sometimes it's that simple. Somebody suggests an image so simple and powerful, it can inspire what will end up being 200 pages of comic book. I won't give away how I solved the problem of the thumbs; it'll come soon enough in the issues to follow, but there I was: concocting a crime story I was pretty happy with and surprised by.

Then Todd McFarlane started calling my house and harassing me. At first he wouldn't say anything; he would just hang up as soon as I picked up. Sometimes I could hear him breathing, trying to get the courage to speak. One time I heard his wife, Wanda, in the background, yelling for him to get off the phone and take his kids to baseball practice.

Eventually we started talking about *Sam and Twitch*. He wanted a crime comic that had a certain feel to it. He asked whether I could take the characters Sam and Twitch, create that feel, and maybe slap together a book for him. Luckily, I grasped the characters pretty fast. I knew the key to the book's success was to do the opposite of what people expected. To me, the opposite was to drop any semblance of a Laurel and Hardy routine. They had to be full and fleshed-out human beings, contradictory and human. Two guys so interesting that they could hold all of our attentions for as long as Todd let me write and as long as the comic industry would last.

So, I had a plot and I had damn good characters. Now all we needed was an artist. We started sifting through a gallery of guys we thought had what it took to pull off a comic that was dark, cinematic, and was an actual story, not just strung-together pin-up art. To everyone's surprise, *KISS Psycho Circus* artist Angel Medina said he had been waiting for this book his whole life; to the point that this book was so important to him, he was gonna knock us on our asses if we gave him a shot at drawing it. He even said he would not only draw it for free, but he would pay us! Well, we had found our artist!!! I explained that it was going to be the polar opposite of KISS in style and content. All he said was: "Bring it on. They do wear makeup, right?"

Then came Ashley Wood. I had only seen a little of his early work and was on the fence about how he would work for this book. (And I only say that because I know it will throw him into a tailspin of neurosis for a good five years.) Beau Smith showed me a drawing that eventually became the first issue's cover, and it knocked my socks off.

I said: "Damn! Ashley may be the most talented woman in comics!!"
Beau said: "Shee-it!! That ain't no dang-blamed woman! That there is one of them Australians. Down under, they like to name their kids all funny and stuff."

Man, woman – who really knows for sure? I just thought Ashley's stuff was right on the money. We had the beginnings of a killer team.

And the finished pencil version of the same page.

Aaaand the finished ink version of the same page.

Our inker is the only member of the crew I don't know personally, which saddens me because I really have no way to pointlessly make fun of him in this editorial. However, as you can see from his intricate work on this issue, he is everything Todd promised and more.

HERE'S THE PROCESS.

I write the script. Full script. Some writers still write in the Marvel way: a plot outline for the artist to pick over and figure out how to tell the story. Then the writer takes the pencils and writes dialogue around them. I couldn't do that if someone paid me, and someone is paying me.

I write the full script, and because I have been writing and drawing my own stuff for so many years, I also hand in a layout rough. A layout rough helps me communicate the pacing of the scene and the design of the page without stepping on the obviously creative toes of the artist. Both things I take pretty seriously, or it could be that I'm megalomaniacal and think I know better than everybody else. Only history will decide!!

Either way, the trick is to draw them as crudely as possible. That way Angel's powerful talent won't be stifled in any way.

After the pages are all done, I take the time to let the letterer know where the balloons should go. You would be surprised how a little thing like bad word balloon placement can kill a punch line. That is, it would if we actually had balloons in this book. At this time I take one more swipe at the dialogue and give it a little tweak. Most of the time I end up chopping lines out after I see that Angel has already expertly communicated in pictures what I was going to say. That's also when you know you have a great penciler.

Then comes Todd Broeker and company. Lil' Todd, as he is known around the space station, is a true artist in his own right, and man did I luck out. He has a huge hard-on for crime fiction and it shows in his work. He is the cinematographer of the comic. His fingerprint is on every pixel. In the early stages of the

book's production, Todd came to me with no less than six versions of how we could approach the color style of this book. I was stunned.

It was very hard to pick a style; one was just as good as the other. So we lined up all the Todd McFarlane licensed action figures in a row and let them vote. *Movie Maniacs Series 2* liked the first version, but *The Beatles, Ozzy,* and the *X-Files* guys liked the one we ended up with.

Then there is our editor, Melanie. She is the real behind-the-scenes, behind-the-scenes, behind-the-scenes person. She is so behind-the-scenes that she wrote this editorial and signed my name to it because I have been missing for three weeks on some party tear in Mexico City with actor-comedienne Andy Dick. But let me tell you something: no one works harder than Melanie. Just spelling mistakes alone on this book take up four whole working days a week. Well, I hope you enjoyed this little behind-the-scenes look as much as Brian would have liked to have written it if he were available.

Originally published in *Sam and Twitch* #2, 1999.

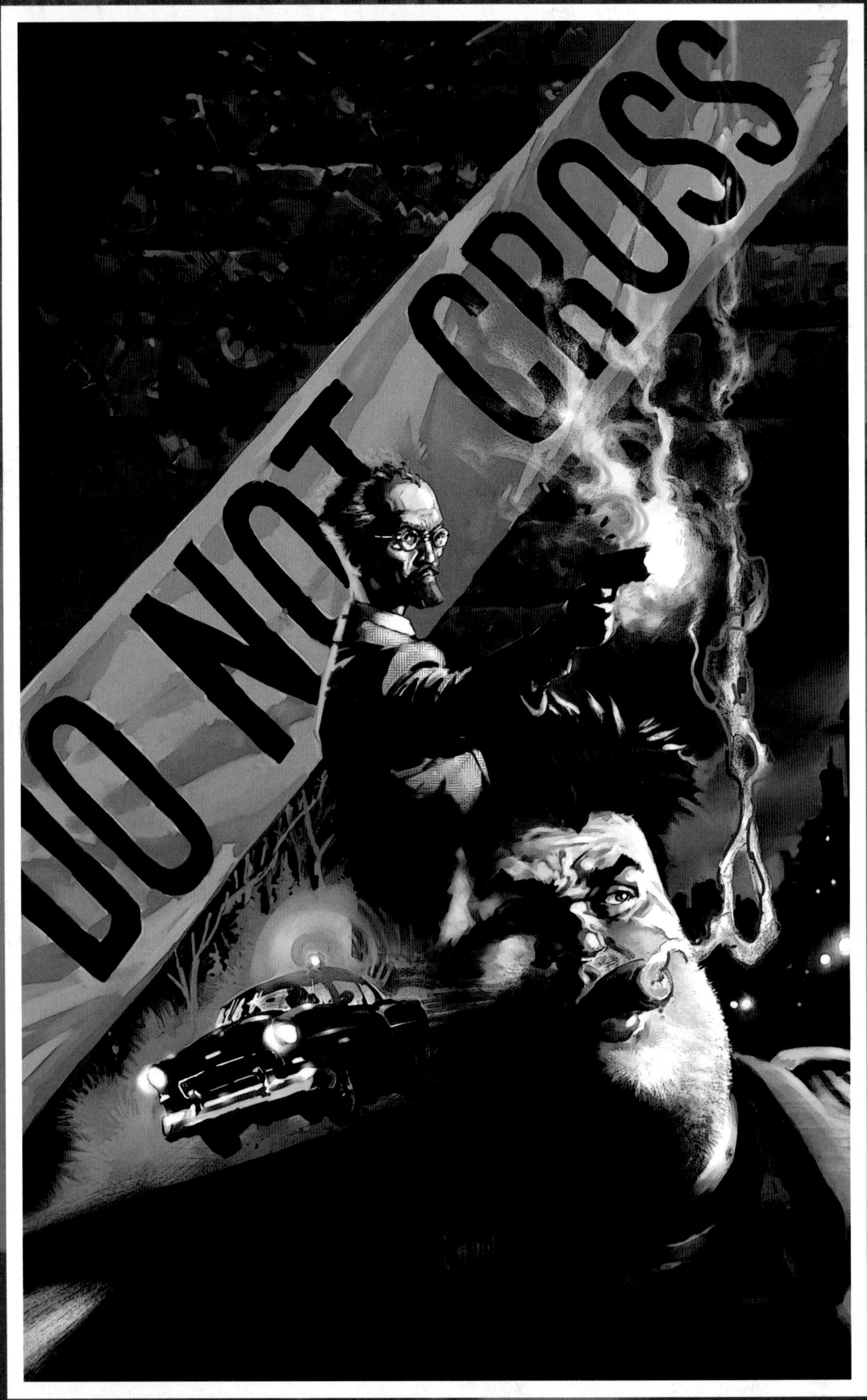
DO NOT CROSS

C Cover, trade paperback collection, Greg Capullo